AMONG THE GENTILES

THE ANCHOR YALE BIBLE REFERENCE LIBRARY is a project of international and interfaith scope in which Protestant, Catholic, and Jewish scholars from many countries contribute individual volumes. The project is not sponsored by any ecclesiastical organization and is not intended to reflect any particular theological doctrine.

The series is committed to producing volumes in the tradition established half a century ago by the founders of the Anchor Bible, William Foxwell Albright and David Noel Freedman. It aims to present the best contemporary scholarship in a way that is accessible not only to scholars but also to the educated nonspecialist. It is committed to work of sound philological and historical scholarship, supplemented by insight from modern methods, such as sociological and literary criticism.

John J. Collins
GENERAL EDITOR

THE ANCHOR YALE BIBLE REFERENCE LIBRARY

AMONG THE GENTILES

*Greco-Roman Religion
and Christianity*

LUKE TIMOTHY JOHNSON

Yale University Press

New Haven & London

The Anchor Yale logo is a trademark of Yale University.

Printed in the United States of America

Library of Congress Control Number: 2009928180

ISBN 978-0-300-14208-2 (hardcover : alk. paper)

A catalogue record for this book is available from the British Library.

This paper meets the requirements of ANSI/NISO Z39.48-1992 (Permanence of Paper).

10   9   8   7   6   5   4   3   2   1

To Joy
My Darling Girl

CONTENTS

Contents

PREFACE

The question of Christianity's relation to the other religions of the world is more pertinent and difficult today than ever before. It is more pertinent because we live in a global village that makes virtual neighbors of people in lands far away, and in which people living in our neighborhoods have religious commitments foreign to most Christians. It is more difficult because pluralism presses on us in a way that makes avoidance impossible, and because Christians are ill equipped to engage those adhering to religions other than their own.

Christianity's historical failure to appreciate or to actively engage Judaism is notorious. Less understood is Christianity's even more shoddy record with respect to "pagan" religions. Christians have inherited a virtually unanimous theological tradition that thinks of paganism in terms of demonic possession, and of Christian missions as a rescue operation that saves pagans from inherently evil practices.

At least in part, such perceptions are shaped by the same texts that have formed Christian attitudes toward Jews. Christianity's failure to adequately come to grips with its first pagan neighbors inhibits any positive effort to engage present-day adherents of world religions.

Except in its very last paragraphs, this book does not deal with theology. It is, rather, a study of religion. It undertakes a fresh inquiry into early Christianity and Greco-Roman religion. Rather than viewing "Christianity" and "paganism" as monolithic entities, I allow the sources to reveal unexpected complexities. At the level of sensibility or temperament, I argue, Christians were religious pretty much in the ways that Gentiles were religious.

I think that my argument may have some pertinence both to internal Christian ecumenism and to a chastened understanding of Christian mission. The heart of the book, however, is a close and (I hope) careful comparison between the ways of being religious among Gentiles and in Christianity. This is an exercise in religious studies; let readers draw theological inferences as they will.

The main surprise for some readers will be the way that some of my judgments concerning New Testament writings depart from scholarly consensus. In particular, I consider all the letters ascribed to Paul to have been authorized by him during the span of his ministry, even though the actual "writing" of them undoubtedly involved others. I do not, therefore, consider the three letters to Paul's delegates (1 Timothy, 2 Timothy, Titus) as evidence for second-century Christianity but for first-century Christianity. Similarly, I hold a minority position when I date Hebrews and James to a period roughly contemporaneous to Paul. These judgments are not arbitrary but are based in long study.

The first effort at constructing the book's argument took the form of a lecture called "*Threskeia*: Greco-Roman Religion and Earliest Christianity" that I delivered as a Phi Beta Kappa Visiting Scholar at Wake Forest University and Stetson University in 1997, to the Biblical and Archaeological Society of Greater Atlanta in 2000, and at Notre Dame University in 2003. I expanded the argument to three lectures that I delivered as the Caldwell Lectures at Louisville Presbyterian Theological Seminary in 2004, and as the Currie Lectures at Austin Presbyterian Theological Seminary in 2006. I deeply appreciate the hospitality shown toward me and these ideas on each occasion. I am particularly grateful to the Catholic Biblical Association of America, which provided the sabbatical support in 2007–2008 that enabled the completion of the study. The research libraries at Notre Dame and Emory Universities were rich in useful resources. Richard Manly Adams Jr. provided invaluable technical assistance in making the manuscript ready for publication. I owe special thanks to my friends: Mary Jo Weaver, a fine historian who first pushed me to recognize the fourth form of religiosity; Barry Jay Seltser, whose cheerful and quick response to chapters as they were written was both chastening and encouraging; and Steve Kraftchick, without whose high tolerance for nonsense my mental life would be diminished. And as always, I owe thanks most of all to my dear Joy, who supports with gracious love my every undertaking, however obscure.

AMONG THE GENTILES

BEYOND ATTACK AND APOLOGY: A NEW LOOK AT AN OLD DEBATE

Is there any kinship between paganism and Christianity? This is an old question. It is also a good question, and one that has never been answered satisfactorily. The second-century apologist Tertullian famously asked, "What indeed has Athens to do with Jerusalem?"[1] He meant to separate Christianity from Greek philosophy. Not all Christian thinkers agreed, and in a variety of ways Christianity eventually embraced and was enriched by a long engagement with Greek philosophers.

But if by "Athens" the questioner meant Greek and Roman religion, then all Christians agreed—and still tend to agree with Tertullian—that there is no connection at all. On one side is truth and on the other side is error, pure and simple. But as another famous epigrammatist reminded us, "the truth is rarely pure and seldom simple."[2] Perhaps the disjunction is too severe. And perhaps the characteristic way in which the question has been put has kept us from seeing connections and continuities that, while not simple, are nonetheless true.

ANCIENT ATTACK AND APOLOGY

From the very beginning, Christians emphasized the distance between themselves and practitioners of pagan religion. To hear them tell it, becoming Christian was something entirely new—there was no connection between Christianity and the Gentile religion practiced by their neighbors (and by themselves before their conversion). They identified themselves with the ancient texts of Israel rather than with the myths of the pagan gods. This is not to suggest that securing a place within the world of Torah was easy or uncontested. The New Testament offers abundant evidence of arguments between these followers of Jesus and Jews who did not recognize him as the Messiah. The earliest Christian compositions can be regarded, in fact, as a massive effort to reinterpret Torah in light of the distinctive Christian experiences and convictions connected with Jesus.[3] And part of this process of identity formation was a sustained polemic against the Jews who failed to see in Jesus either a Lord or a Messiah.[4]

Because of the long history of Christian anti-Semitism that fed on such vituperation, and above all because of the experience of the Holocaust, Christians and Jews alike are now highly sensitive to such slanderous language, and sometimes respond with moral outrage.[5] Here is a case where historical knowledge helps. It reminds contemporary readers that there is a great distance between a tiny cult trying to find its way in the world in competition with the more ancient and impressive rival, and an imperial church that had (and was willing to use) the power to extirpate its ancient foe. It reminds us as well that New Testament language against Jews by no means exceeds the bounds of ancient rhetorical conventions, which were liberal in the use of abuse between rival schools and sects.[6]

What contemporary readers, both Christian and Jewish, seldom notice is how much more sustained and savage the polemic of the New Testament is with respect to the Gentile world than with respect to Judaism. And the favorite target was Gentile religion. In this regard, the writers of the New Testament aligned themselves completely on the side of Judaism, which had already developed forms of polemics against pagan religion that were at least the equal of the fierce Gentile anti-Semitism directed against the Jews. The prophets of ancient Israel had long mocked the polytheism of their neighboring Gentiles, attacking their worship as idolatry.[7] And this tradition was continued in the fierce antagonism Jews showed toward the worship of the majority population in the Hellenistic Diaspora. In a stroke of translation that would prove to have enormous consequences, the Septuagint (LXX, ca. 250 BCE) rendered the Hebrew of Psalm 96:5, "The gods of the nations are idols," as "The gods of the nations are demons [*daimonia*]" (LXX Ps 95:5), thereby placing all pagan religion neatly into the realm of the demonic. The author of *Wisdom of Solomon* has this to say about the religious practices of his Gentile neighbors (probably in Egypt):

> It was not enough for them to err about the knowledge of God, but they live in great strife due to ignorance, and they call such great evils peace. For whether they kill their children in their initiations, or celebrate secret mysteries, or hold frenzied revels with strange customs, they no longer keep either their lives or their marriages pure, but they treacherously kill one another, or grieve one another by adultery, and all is a raging riot of blood and murder,

theft and deceit, corruption, faithlessness, tumult, perjury, confusion over what is good, forgetfulness of favors, pollution of souls, sex perversion, disorder in marriage, adultery, and debauchery. For the worship of idols not to be named is the beginning and cause and end of every evil. For their worshippers either rave in exaltation or prophesy lies, or live unrighteously, or readily commit perjury.[8]

The same animus toward Gentile religion pervades the writings of the New Testament. The very authors who attacked the Jews for their failure to follow Jesus, after all, were capable of making positive statements about the Jewish religious tradition and even about Jews. "Salvation," says Jesus in John's Gospel, is "from the Jews" (John 4:22). Paul boasts of his Jewish pedigree (Phil 3:4–6; 2 Cor 11:21; Gal 1:13–14) and says of his brethren, his kinsmen by race, "They are Israelites, and to them belong the sonship, the glory, the covenants, the giving of the law, the worship, and the promises; to them belong the patriarchs, and of their race, according to the flesh, is the Christ, who is God over all, blessed for ever. Amen" (Rom 9:3–5). Of the Jewish law, Paul declares that it is "holy, and the commandment is holy and just and good" (7:12), and that it is "spiritual" (7:14). Paul takes his stand on the Jewish conviction that "God is One" (3:30). Paul and other Christian writers find it astonishing that their fellow Jews do not follow them in their commitment to Jesus as the Messiah, but they do not challenge the truthfulness of the Jewish God, of the texts that reveal him, or of the moral precepts and practices that give him honor.

In contrast, only one New Testament passage pays explicit tribute to genuine religious impulses among Gentiles. The Acts of the Apostles places Paul on Mars Hill in Athens, where he declares, "Men of Athens, I perceive that in every way you are very religious [*deisidaimonesterous*]. For as I passed along, and observed the objects of your worship, I found also an altar with this inscription, 'To an Unknown God'" (Acts 17:22–23). But Paul's acknowledgement (rhetorically a *captatio benevolentiae*) simply serves as the basis for a correction of the Gentiles' explicit beliefs: "We ought not to think of the deity as like gold, or silver, or stone, a representation by the art and imagination of man" (17:29).[9]

The Paul of the letters, though, writing to mixed congregations of Gentiles and Jews, is far more outspoken in his rejection of Greco-Roman culture. Although scholars today can detect multiple ways in which Paul's correspondence is shaped by ancient rhetoric and moral philosophy,[10] he explicitly distances himself from both. He declares that his preaching to the Corinthians is not in elevated speech or wisdom but is the proclamation of the crucified Messiah (1 Cor 2:1–2). In response to critics, he recognizes that his own speech is negligible (2 Cor 10:10). He rejects human wisdom (*sophia*) for the wisdom revealed by God through the cross (1 Cor 1:18–2:5) and speaks rather of "God's wisdom" hidden in mystery as set in opposition to the "wisdom of this age" that refuses to acknowledge Christ (2:6–8). He warns the Colossians, "See to it that no one makes you a prey by philosophy and empty deceit, according to human tradition, according to the elemental spirits of the universe and not according to Christ" (Col 2:8).

Paul's negative view of Greco-Roman religion is even more pronounced. In his earliest extant letter, he tells the Thessalonians that they had turned "from idols to serve the living and true God" (1 Thess 1:9), that they should not act in the passion of lust "like the heathen who do not know God" (4:5), and that they should not grieve their dead like those "who have no hope" (4:13). Similarly, Paul tells his Gentile readers in the churches throughout Galatia, "Formerly, when you did not know God, you were in bondage to beings that by nature are not gods . . . weak and elemental spirits" (Gal 4:8–9). When warning them against "the works of the flesh" (5:20–21), he lists *eidōlolatria* ("idolatry") as a vice, placing it in his list after "fornication, impurity, and licentiousness" and before "sorcery" (or "magic": *pharmakeia*).[11] Writing to the Ephesians, Paul depicts the readers' Gentile past as one of "following the prince of the power of the air, the spirit that is now at work in the sons of disobedience," which involved them in unruly passions and desires (Eph 2:2–3); they were like people who had "no hope and without God in the world" (2:12).

In his letter to the Romans, Paul sketches, in contrast to the good news that reveals God's righteousness, a portrait of the unrighteousness that brings forth God's wrath, and he takes as his prime evidence the practice of pagan religion (Rom 1:18–32). He here totally adopts the Hellenistic Jewish view of Gentile religion. He declares that idolatry is the result of a fundamental refusal to acknowledge the true God (1:19–20), that the worship of images derives from a darkening of the mind consequent to the big lie, and that such false worship leads to the distortion of natural sexual relations and every sort of foul practice: "Since they did not see fit to acknowledge God, God gave them up to a base mind and to improper conduct" (1:28). Present-day readers of this passage tend to focus on its depiction of human depravity and forget that Paul connects every kind of vice to the religious practices of his readers' neighbors in Rome.

In his first letter to the Corinthians, Paul shows the same deep disdain for anything specifically Gentile in character. He rebukes his readers for failing to discipline a member of the community who lives in a kind of sexual immorality (*porneia*) "of a sort not heard of even among Gentiles" (1 Cor 5:1). Shortly thereafter, he takes up an issue that vexed members of his mixed Jewish-Gentile community, namely, whether purchasing and eating meats that had previously been offered in sacrifice at a pagan shrine is allowable, and, for the socially better connected among Gentile believers, whether participation in a meal at such a shrine dedicated to a pagan God is legitimate.[12] Paul walks a delicate line between two groups: there are "the strong," who, like him, know that "an idol has no real existence" (8:4) and that "although there may be so-called gods in heaven or on earth—as indeed there are many gods and many lords—yet for us there is one God, the Father, from whom are all things and for whom are all things, and one Lord Jesus Christ, through whom are all things and through whom we exist" (8:5–6); and there are "the weak," who do not have this knowledge and who may be encouraged, when seeing one of the strong eating such food or sitting in such a place, to act against their own conscience by sharing in such practices (8:7–13).

Paul knows that idols are not real gods, but he regards idolatry itself as having a real and negative power. The influence of the translation, "the gods of the nations are demons," in LXX Psalm 95:5, appears forcefully in Paul's dire warning to those who would presume on their own strength and take part in pagan sacral meals: "What do I imply then? That food offered to idols is anything, or that an idol is anything? No, I imply that what pagans sacrifice they offer to demons and not to God. I do not want you to be partners with demons. You cannot drink the cup of the Lord and the cup of demons. You cannot partake of the table of the Lord and the table of demons" (1 Cor 10:19–21). Paul regards such arrogance as opposing the true God: "Shall we provoke the Lord to jealousy? Are we stronger than he?" (10:22).

Even though Paul does not want his churches to "go out of the world" in order to avoid the immoral of this world, including the idolaters (1 Cor 5:9), and although he clearly envisages the *ekklēsia* of Christ to be accessible to outsiders, he nevertheless worries that certain community religious practices, especially those involving spiritual utterances, might be regarded by interested outsiders as a variation of Greco-Roman religion. The fear of such misapprehension may have something to do with his demand that women be veiled when praying or prophesying (11:2–16).[13] Paul's preference for the rational discourse that he calls prophecy, moreover, rather than the ecstatic babble that is *glōssolalia*, has much to do with the fact that it can challenge outsiders and convince them of the presence of the true God, rather than lead them to exclaim, *hoti mainesthe* ("these people are raving ecstatically")—as they could in response to cultic prophets among Greeks and Romans (14:20–25).[14]

By no means is Paul alone among the earliest Christian writers in his desire to distinguish the movement's religious practices from those of the Gentiles.

The First Letter of Peter sounds much like Paul when it tells its readers drawn from a Gentile background, "As obedient children, do not be conformed to the passions of your former ignorance" (1 Pet 1:14), and when it contrasts the behavior expected of them to that of their former associates: "Let the time that is past suffice for doing what the Gentiles like to do, living in licentiousness, passions, drunkenness, revels, carousing, and lawless idolatry. They are surprised that you do not now join them in the same wild profligacy, and they abuse you; but they will give an account to him who is ready to judge the living and the dead" (4:3–5). Matthew's Gospel has Jesus warn his disciples in the Sermon on the Mount, "And in praying, do not heap up empty phrases as the Gentiles do; for they think that they will be heard for their many words. Do not be like them, for your Father knows what you need before you ask him" (Matt 6:7–8).

As I have already noted, the Acts of the Apostles portrays Paul as appealing to the "religious instinct" (*deisidaimonia*) of the Athenians who constructed an altar to an unknown God. Acts also portrays a number of "righteous Gentiles" who are described as such not because of their dedication to pagan religion but because they are open to the truth as it is found in Judaism and the Gospel: the centurion Cornelius (Acts 10:1–5; compare with the centurion of the Gospel, Luke 7:2–4); the proconsul Sergius Publius (Acts 13:7, 12); the Philippian jailer (16:25–34), the proconsul Gallio (18:12–14); and Publius, the chief man on the island of Malta (28:7–10). But the naïve pagans in Lystra who confuse Barnabas with Zeus and Paul with Hermes and seek to worship them, are, like the philosophers on Mars Hill, rebuked and corrected by Paul's proclamation: "Men, why are you doing this? We also are men, of like nature with you, and bring you good news, that you should turn from these vain things to a living God who made the heaven and the earth and the sea and all that is in them" (14:8–18).

For the most part, Acts shares the perceptions of Paul and Peter with respect to Gentile religion. In fact, the progress of the Gospel from Jerusalem to Rome is marked by a series of turf battles between the apostles and representatives of Hellenistic religious practices, resulting in a literal expansion of "God's kingdom" throughout the empire, as Paul triumphs over the powers of magic (Acts 13:8–11; 19:18–19), over the divinatory powers of pagan prophecy (16:16–20), and even over the powerful interests involved in the cult of Artemis in Ephesus (19:23–41). These triumphs are portrayed by the author as the conquest of Satan's "counter-Kingdom" and as the revealing of the demonic forces at work in pagan religion.[15]

Christian apologists after the time of the New Testament continued the same lines of attack.[16] Although they occasionally (and increasingly) found a positive role for Greek poets and philosophers and agreed on the special status to be accorded the Sybil as a unique prophetic voice,[17] they were uniform in their rejection of all things religious in the Gentile world.

Yet there is a decided ambivalence in their evaluation, which may find its antecedent in Paul's discussion of food offered to idols in 1 Cor 8–10. On one side, we see Christian apologists confidently asserting the nonreality of the pagan gods, the worship of whom is simply vain.[18] The idols are the work of human hands, the fabrications of poets, or even the result of financial and political machinations.[19] Many of the apologists adopt a form of Euhemerism, claiming that the so-called gods were simply humans who were elevated by other humans to a divine status after death.[20] This strong-minded position regards the worship of the gods as a form of absurdity matching the silliness of the myths themselves.[21] Such comments extend Paul's bold statement, "An idol has no real existence" (8:4).

An even larger set of statements by these same apologists, however, continues Paul's own ambivalence toward pagan religious practices: idols may not be real, but something is at work in those shrines and meals, and that something is demonic power: "What pagans sacrifice they offer to demons and not to God" (1 Cor 10:20). In his response to Celsus, in fact, Origen quotes Paul on just this point: idolatry involves its worshippers in the realm of the demonic.[22] Origen follows Tatian in identifying Zeus himself as a demon,[23] and the identification of idols with demons is frequent.[24] Augustine speaks for the entire prior tradition when he declares that "Gods they are not, but malignant spirits,"[25] as does Minucius Felix when he says that Christians avoid contact with idols in order to avoid contact with demons.[26]

Christians were not alone in speaking about demons and the power of demons. The category was widely deployed in antiquity for a variety of divine and semidivine activities.[27] As Origen notes, "It is not we alone who speak of wicked demons, but almost all who acknowledge the existence of demons."[28] What did distinguish Christian discourse was its tendency to associate every manifestation of Greco-Roman religion with the demonic as well as its reduction of demonic activity to the maleficent. The connection between pagan religion and immorality that was noted already in the Jewish composition *Wisdom of Solomon* continues throughout the Christian apologetic literature. An easy target is the immorality of the gods as depicted in the myths. Not only are the gods depicted as doing wicked things; hearing myths about these gods stirs the listeners to base emotions and even incites them to evil deeds.[29] The most immediate manifestation of this evil influence is the practice of pagan religion itself. The Christian apologists miss no opportunity to characterize the festivals in honor of demons as displays of immoral behavior of the most shameful sort.[30] The

Mysteries are particularly reprehensible: their clandestine character and vows of secrecy serve as a cover for lewd and licentious behavior.[31] Clement of Alexandria goes into considerable detail in an effort to expose the sexual libertinism that he insists hides beneath the solemn flummery of the Mysteries.[32]

The apologists also reveal, however, a genuine level of anxiety concerning pagan religion. If demons are at work in idolatry, then something real and more than human is happening in pagan worship that must be taken into account. It will not do simply to say, "It is not real," for there is evidence for powerful phenomena that must be taken into consideration. It is in connection with this anxiety that we find the language about the "deceptions of demons" manifested in Greco-Roman religion. By speaking of demons and their deceptions, Christians are at once able to acknowledge the undeniable fact of powerful activity and yet ascribe it to malevolent forces that are lesser beings than the true God but who seek to captivate and destroy humans through such religious phenomena.[33]

Justin and Augustine speak of the myths concerning the gods as themselves the product of deceptive demons who seek to captivate and destroy humans through such fabrications concerning the divine.[34] Tatian and Justin, in turn, identify as demonic in origin the revelations that people receive from the gods through dreams.[35] Tertullian and Origen say that the healings performed at pagan shrines are doubly deceptive: the demons both cause the illness and take it away.[36] Augustine maintains that demons are at work when people undergo physical transformations (*metamorphoses*)[37] and adduces the moral precepts given through the Mysteries as further evidence of demonic deception.[38] Above all, prophetic revelation or divination is a sign of demonic power and deception.[39] All these complaints actually testify to the presence of something at work in pagan religion that even they could not deny but could only reframe as the work of lesser and malicious powers antagonistic to the true God and the good news.

It was a short step to extend the logic to categorize as demonic any powers inimical to Christianity. If the demons belong to a "counter-kingdom" ruled by Satan, then it makes sense to associate demons with the imperial powers that resisted the good news, especially since the practices of Greco-Roman religion were so inextricably involved with the state and society. It was therefore a small step to explicitly attribute the persecution of Christians by the state to the influence of demons.[40] And the logic can be extended even further, to include those who threaten the church from within. In 1 Timothy, Paul speaks of false teachers within the Ephesian church in this way: "Now the Spirit expressly says that in later times some will depart from the faith by giving heed to deceitful spirits and doctrines of demons" (1 Tim 4:1).[41] Justin Martyr does not therefore hesitate to associate Simon Magus and other heretics with demons.[42]

The language of demonization continued to flourish within Christianity as a mechanism for rejecting influences that were perceived to be not only wrong or wicked, but also capable of seducing others because of their "deceptive power." When the newly baptized "renounced Satan," they also renounced "all your worship," which Cyril of Jerusalem explicates this way: "Augury, divination, watching for omens, wearing amulets, writing on leaves, sorcery and other such practices are the worship of the devil. These, then, you must avoid, because if after renouncing the devil and making your act of adhesion to Christ you succumb to them, you will find Satan a harsher master in temptation."[43]

Thus, every form of religious practice that was innovative or borrowed from other than authorized sources could quickly be ascribed to demonic possession in the practitioner. Every form of heresy could be denominated as demonic. The false prophet Muhammad was obviously demonic. And Christian missions to every land on earth were motivated and driven by the conviction that poor pagan babies were captive to demons and needed rescue through the preaching of the gospel. From such a perspective, there was no possible link between Christianity and paganism, in the past or in the present. The pagan world was and is in darkness. The Gospel was and is the exclusive source of light in the world. It therefore was not and is not possible to recognize any light among Gentiles with respect to their religious practices and sensibilities.

THE MIXING OF ELEMENTS

Such a sharp division between Christianity and paganism was artificial, to be sure. Justin Martyr acknowledged that Christian doctrines brought to fuller expression precedents found among Gentile poets and philosophers, that Christian baptism had its analogies in pagan lustrations, and that the "mystic rites" of Mithras with respect to bread and water were a demonic imitation of the Eucharist.[44] Origen's charge that demons were at work in pagan shrines and prophecy was in response to Celsus' claim that the wonders worked by Christians were due to the power of demons.[45] In the *Octavius*, the pagan philosopher Caecilius claims that Christian beliefs are simply reshaped versions of pagan religious fantasy: "All such figments of unhealthy belief, and vain sources of comfort, with which deceiving poets have trifled in the sweetness of their verse, have been disgracefully remoulded by you, believing undoubtingly on your god."[46]

More forcefully, the Manichaean teacher Faustus, in his dispute with Augustine, argues that both Jews and Christians represent subsets of Gentile religion, whereas the Manichaeans represent a genuine alternative view of reality: "The sacrifices you change into love-feasts, the idols into martyrs, to whom you pray as they do their idols. You appease the shades of the departed with wine and food. You keep the same holidays as the Gentiles; for example, the calends and the solstices."[47] Faustus' claim is notable not only for the way in which it anticipates a number of the charges to be made in later internal Christian debates—he was claiming, remember, that the Manichaeans were true followers of Jesus because they regarded as authoritative only the words that came from him and not the interpretations of the Gospels—but also for his insight that both Judaism and Christianity had some real resemblances to Gentile religion.

By the time Faustus and Augustine debated (ca. 397 CE), it appeared that both Judaism and paganism were religions of the past—although in Augustine's youth (360–363) the emperor Julian had for a short time managed the restoration to the empire of pagan worship—while Christianity and Manichaeism seemed the obvious competitors as world religions. When Manichaeism faded, and Christianity seemed, especially to its Western European adherents, to be the obviously true religion, seamlessly linked to Israel through the biblical story, connections between Christianity and Gentile religion were easily forgotten, and the dichotomy of the apologists—God on one side, demons on the other—was received as sober truth rather than defensive polemic.

The situation began to change with the Italian Renaissance of the fifteenth century, when the translation of ancient Greek texts began to alter the perception of both the past and the present. The key figures here are Marsilius Ficinus (1433–1499) and Giovanni Pico della Mirandola (1463–1494), who in turn influenced the northern humanist John Reuchlin (1455–1522). Ficinus was the translator not only of Plato but also of Hermes Trismegistos, Iamblichus, and the Enneads of Plotinus. In all these authors, he found the language of the Greek Mysteries, and he considered the entire Platonic tradition to be one deeply consonant not only with the realm of the Mysteries but also with Christianity. He was a priest and wrote works such as *De Religione Christiana* (1474) and *Theologica Platonica* (1477) in order to draw atheists and skeptics to the Christian faith. He drew little or no distinction among the ritual, figurative, and theurgic dimensions of the language of the Mysteries and sought a synthesis between Christianity and Greek thought, arguing, for example, that Paul and Plato meant the same thing when they spoke of love. Pico della Mirandola also saw a deep consonance between Greek philosophy and the Bible and argued that the Hebrews had Mysteries as much as the pagans did. His work sought to establish and illuminate the secret affinity between pagan and biblical revelation, on the conviction that the respective texts spoke of the same mysterious reality. John Reuchlin, in turn, saw even further connections between Christianity and neo-Pythagorean number symbolism and Jewish Kabbalah. The language of the

Greek Mysteries, in short, was welcomed by the Italian humanists as a way of broadening and deepening the philosophical truth of Christianity.[48]

In the northern Europe of the Reformation, in contrast, the pagan Mysteries were once more the focus of attack and defense, this time within a divided Christianity. In one sense, the terms of controversy were set by Luther himself, who insisted on measuring the sacramental claims of the church against the witness of scripture alone.[49] Luther's theological opposition between the authentic Christianity found in scripture and the corrupt Christianity found in the later church was quickly translated by Matthias Flacius Illyricus (1520–1575) and his companions, the Centuriators of Magdeburg, into a historical account of Christianity (century by century) that emphasized a simple proposition, namely, that the pure Christianity of the New Testament was corrupted by the papal Antichrist.[50]

The Protestant attack was quickly answered by Cardinal Cesare Baronius. He directed 12 folio volumes against the Centuriators of Magdeburg, seeking to show that "as it was now, so was it always."[51] The exchange was closed, and also given a new shape, by the Protestant apologist Isaac Casaubon (1559–1614), who brought the beginnings of scientific historiography to the debate and used a significant degree of learning in antiquity to make his argument against Baronius that "a principio non ita fuit" ("from the beginning, it was not so"). Isaac Casaubon contrasted the simplicity of the Gospels to the developments that were introduced later, which, and here is the critical point, bore strong resemblance to pagan prayers and sacrifices and religious usages.[52]

A less learned and more visceral sort of criticism was initiated by British Deists such as Conyers Middleton, whose *Letter from Rome* (1729) attacked Roman Catholic ritual, "showing," as the subtitle states it, "an exact conformity between popery and paganism." Middleton stands near the start of a long tradition of polemic that Jonathan Z. Smith characterizes as "Pagano-Papism."[53] From the eighteenth century to the present, a series of popular writers—often widely read but rarely scientifically precise—repeated the same argument, namely, that pure Christianity had been corrupted by Catholicism, that is, by pagan Mystery religions.[54] Notable both for the sweep of its charges and for its influence on popular anti-Catholic polemic down to the present is Alexander Hislop's *The Two Babylons: Papal Worship Revealed to Be the Worship of Nimrod and His Wife*, which appeared first as a pamphlet in 1853 and has enjoyed an astonishing life in print.[55] For writers like these, it was obvious that in Catholic Christianity the "simple love of God and trust in Jesus was lost," because of the influence of Greek religion.[56]

The passion driving this polemical tradition was not unlike that inspiring the quest for the historical Jesus, which likewise first arose among British Deists of the eighteenth century and was then most vigorously pursued by the German inheritors of their Enlightenment perspective.[57] The search was never disinterestedly historical and was always at least implicitly theological. Just as the reformers had rejected a Catholic Christianity on the basis of scripture alone, these Enlightenment scholars sought a Jesus on the basis of reason alone. If Luther, however unintentionally, set up an opposition between scripture and church, the questers worked within an opposition between scripture and reason, on the premise that creedal faith, grounded in the teaching of Paul, himself a captive of Greek philosophy and Mystery religion, was already a corruption of the pure and natural religion that Jesus must have taught.[58] However elusive that unadorned Jesus proved to be, it is unquestionably the case that the quest was itself an important impetus to the development of more refined historiographical methods in the study of ancient Christianity.[59]

In the same way, the question of the relation between earliest Christianity and Greco-Roman religion clearly needed more science and less polemic. Beginning with the first serious effort to provide a critical assessment of the sources for the Mystery religions by Christian August Lobeck in 1829, scholars through the nineteenth and twentieth centuries made use of the steadily growing body of real knowledge provided by literary and archaeological evidence.[60] By no means did scholars using such sources agree in their conclusions. For every Loisy or Reitzenstein who saw Christianity as fundamentally shaped by the Mysteries, there was a Clemen or Angus who delicately distinguished what was "essential" in Christianity from the undoubted presence of Mystery sensibility.[61] The middle and moderate position was classically stated in the Hibbert Lectures of 1891 by Edwin Hatch.[62] Hatch argued that both Jesus and Paul were thoroughly Jewish and "poetic" in their religion and that elements of Greek rhetoric, thought, and religion grew within Christianity between the second and fourth century, a view that was repeated with considerable decisiveness by Arthur Darby Nock in 1928.[63]

But if there is no trace of Greco-Roman religion to be found in Jesus, can the same really be said of Paul? Did the transition from Jewish to Greek not begin when Paul transformed the message of Jesus into a Mystery religion?[64] Once more, the opinions are divided. Some scholars assert emphatically that Paul made Christianity into a mystery.[65] Others are more cautious, willing to find traces of Greco-Roman religion among Paul's congregants,[66] but insisting that Paul himself is more defined by Jewish concepts. A variation of this position is found in the "History of Religions School": like Jesus, the primitive Christianity of Palestine was thoroughly Jewish, but it was in the Diaspora (specifically Antioch) that Hellenistic Christians created the "Christ Cult" under the influence of the Mysteries, and this was the Christianity into which Paul was baptized and whose sacramental character he subsequently interpreted theologically.[67]

Albert Schweitzer, in contrast, centered his interpretation of Paul on the emphatic rejection of any version of a Mystery hypothesis and the attempt to explain all of Paul's language on the basis of Jewish eschatology.[68] For scholars wishing to protect the distinctiveness of Christianity against the charge of pagan influence, Judaism played a key but also—as J. Z. Smith perceptively notes—a deeply ambiguous role: "Judaism has served a double (or, a duplicitous) function. On one hand, it has provided apologetic scholars with an insulation for early Christianity, guarding it against 'influence' from its environment. On the other hand, it has been presented by the very same scholars as an object to be transcended by early Christianity."[69]

THE NEED FOR A NEW APPROACH

It is clear that the earlier conversation about Christianity and Greco-Roman religion, despite its genuine contributions to learning, was hampered in a number of ways. Most of the difficulties stemmed from the basic fact that all the discussants were, in one fashion or another, Christian. This meant that they all had a theological stake in the outcome of the argument.[70] But neither polemic nor apologetics advance understanding. Neither demonizing the Mysteries nor using them as a cudgel against a corrupt Catholicism serves the cause of knowledge.[71]

The Christian allegiances of the disputants also meant that the discussion tended to be shaped by specifically Christian concerns and commitments in at least four important ways. First, the internal Christian debate over the sacraments tended to focus attention on the Mysteries more than on other aspects of Greco-Roman (or Christian) religious practice. Second, the debate gave inordinate attention to the presence and meaning of certain words (such as *mystērion*) in certain contexts. To some extent, the argument was linguistic because the available sources were literary, but to some extent as well, the internal Christian tradition of theological disputation (such as the debate over the eucharist and transubstantiation) was at work.

Third, just as "Christianity" was conceived in unitary terms—as one easily identified reality, however internally divided—so was there a tendency to think of "paganism" as well as "Judaism" in a similarly unitary fashion. Little attention was paid to the internal complexities of Greco-Roman religion, still less to the complexities of first-century Judaism, and less still to the variety of ways of being Christian in the time before Constantine. Fourth, the discussion was carried out primarily in terms of "influence" or "dependence," as though that were the most important or even the most interesting question to be pursued, which, to be sure, it was for those fighting for "authentic Christianity." In short, since the Christian religion defined what the discussants assumed to be authentic religion, the debate was cast in essentially Christian terms.

In addition to theological bias, certain forms of academic bias limited the discussion. Just as the lack of a perspective distinctive to "religious studies" resulted in Christianity's supplying the categories of analysis and appreciation, so did the interests of discrete academic pursuits limit what could be seen and how it was viewed. For the greater part of this period, the discipline of history was interested primarily in the deeds of great men or the development of great ideas; the common practices of the common people, the experiences and convictions of women, children, and slaves, or the mundane matters of social arrangement seemed of little interest. For the greater part of this period, furthermore, the literature of the early empire seemed scarcely worth attention among those calling themselves classicists and philosophers. For classicists, Greek studies after Plato offered little charm and Latin studies after Virgil even less. For philosophers, likewise, the period of the early empire, with its popular sages like Seneca and Epictetus, was merely a dull interlude between Plato and Plotinus, when the great metaphysical symphony was resumed once more. The limited vision of what counted in history, literature, and philosophy meant that those most capable of subtle and professional analysis of religious sources paid least attention to them, so that the discussion of Greco-Roman religion and Christianity was left to passionate amateurs whose main interest was scoring points for their version of authentic Christianity.

Virtually all of these limitations have fallen away in recent decades. New ways of seeing, and, as a consequence, new things seen, have enabled new ways of thinking and speaking about ancient religion and Christianity's place within the religious life of the first-century Mediterranean world. Those changes, and the way they enable the sort of questions I want to pursue in this book, are the subject of the next chapter.

2

BEGINNING A NEW CONVERSATION

The long conversation that I have described concerning Greco-Roman religion and Christianity—if such a rancorous debate can be dignified by that term—was distorted, as we have seen, by passion and prejudice. Christians simply reduced paganism to "the other," either as a way of asserting Christianity's own privileged status or as an explanation for the corruption of original and authentic faith. The way to a new conversation has been opened, in turn, by a combination of new perspectives and new knowledge, which together make it possible to observe the ways in which Christians and pagans resemble each other as well as the ways in which they differ.

NEW PERSPECTIVES

New perspectives have come about in part through a change of tone and the addition of voices to the conversation. The earlier debate took place exclusively among Christians and their cultured despisers who were also Christian, and the point was less of mutual understanding than it was of vanquishing a foe. Among most Christians today, in contrast, a spirit of ecumenical cooperation has replaced that of polemic, and a desire to learn from each other has replaced the rhetoric of attack. The change in tone is by no means universal. Many Christians still demonize non-Christian religions, and some Protestants and Catholics continue the game of mutual recrimination. But among the Christians likely to take up our subject, the tone of voice has changed dramatically.

An even greater change has occurred because new voices have joined the conversation. The contributions of feminist scholars have dramatically altered such traditional disciplines as history, shifting everyone's sense of what matters in the study of the past. Attention to women's lives leads to a sense of history that is larger than recitals of war and great events, one that encompasses the world of the everyday and the domestic and enduring cultural patterns, in all of which ancient religion was involved.[1] The presence of voices other than those of Christians has also changed perspectives. Jewish scholars have complicated and enriched the conversation both by resisting the easy (supersessionist) reductions of Judaism by Christian theologians and by exposing the astonishing diversity of Jewish life—and its connections with paganism—in late antiquity.[2] And although representatives of ancient Gentile religion are not personally available for study, living participants in nonmonotheistic and nontheistic religious traditions—not only from the "great" world religions but as well from the often still vibrant local cults of Africa, Asia, and the Americas— have at once advanced their own claims to be taken seriously and have placed Christianity in a new and more interesting context. Now, "the nations" are present at the table in a way they could not be since the imperial victory of Christianity, and this provides the possibility for fairer comparison and contrast among religious traditions.[3]

New perspectives follow as well from the new academic setting for the study of religion. Especially in the United States, the last 40 years have seen a dramatic displacement of Christian schools of theology by university departments of religious studies as the center for serious conversation about religion. Schools of theology have had as their main goal the formation of Christian ministers, and theology (quite rightly) is taught as intricately linked to the convictions and practices of the life of faith. It is within the context of the university, however, that religious studies has truly come into its own, for in this setting it is not the life of the church that is primarily in view but rigorous scholarship; and the framework for studying religion is not Christian theology, but instead all the disciplines available in the setting of the university: the traditional fields of classics and literature and philosophy, yes, but also the social sciences, such as anthropology, psychology, and sociology, have vigorously joined in the study of human religious behavior.[4] Here, religion is far less likely to be studied in terms of authentic and inauthentic, of true or false, or "natural" and "revealed," than in terms of broadly attested human behavior that is placed on the same basic level as economics and politics and is analyzed in much the same manner. Scholars in the university might inquire into the "essence" or "nature" of religion, but they are likely to find more fascinating and illuminating the description, analysis, and comparison of the manifold manifestations of religion across diverse human cultures.[5]

Changes in intellectual fashion within universities also affect the study of religion. It is still occasionally possible to find academics engaged in the phenomenological study of religion or in the comparative study of religion—as I try to do in this book.[6] But the rise of a variety of ideological criticisms (liberationist, feminist, postcolonialist) has sharpened the hermeneutics of suspicion with regard to religious language and behavior that was already obvious in the enlightenment critique, which from the start sought to reduce religious claims of transcendence to the level of "what happens in Europe every day."[7] Like their predecessors, ideological critics regard religious behavior in terms of the manipulation of human power and study religious literature with an eye mainly to whose interest the rhetoric serves. Like social scientific approaches to religion, but to a still greater degree, they privilege the etic (the perspective and categories of the observer) over the emic (the perspective and language of the participant). Although such approaches have undoubtedly opened up new perspectives and generated new knowledge,[8] it is difficult to think that religious language and practice has adequately been understood as a human phenomenon simply because it has been revealed as politically interested.

Nevertheless, the university context has for the most part been good for the study of religion, and the distinctive ways in which religious studies has been able to approach the subject holds the promise of a more fruitful way of thinking about paganism and Christianity than did the old context of a divided church and the perspectives of theology. Scholars now generally understand religion as a constructive human activity in which experiences and convictions concerning ultimate power both depend on and reshape people's social structures and symbolic worlds, enabling a way of life based on and seeking to express through a variety of practices those experiences and convictions.[9] We can begin to work our way into this new perspective by considering each part of that sentence in more detail, showing in the process how new ways of looking can enable new ways of seeing.

I begin with the assertion that religions involve experiences and convictions concerning ultimate power, noting that the statement is broad enough to include virtually everything that calls itself religious, as well as some human activities that may not be so designated but in fact may be. Joachim Wach has supplied a careful and useful definition of that slippery category, "religious experience," calling it a response to what is perceived as ultimate power, involving the whole person, characterized by a peculiar intensity, and issuing in appropriate action.[10] I have added to Wach's description only the term "power," which Van der Leeuw has, correctly I think, located at the heart of religious activity.[11] Each phrase deserves further, though necessarily brief, parsing.

The first element is that of response. To the person having the experience, it is not something self-generated but is evoked by a reality greater and more powerful than the physical or psychic self.[12] The power to which one responds is not one that can be controlled but one that exercises control. It does not belong to the ordinary run of things but appears as extraordinary and compelling.[13] The response, furthermore, involves the whole person. It is not merely a matter of ideas (the mind), nor is it merely a matter of volition (the will) or simply a matter of feeling (the emotions), although each of these is in various ways somatically implicated in the response.[14] The body in question, furthermore, can be communal as well as individual: religious experience is not necessarily a private affair.[15] The second element is "peculiar intensity," which points to the sense of realness, energy, and urgency in the experience. Such urgency is not necessarily a matter of violent or externally visible reaction and can be entirely peaceful and quiet: one thinks of Elijah's "still small voice" in contrast to Sinai's spectacular kratophany. The intensity of the experience, however, makes it qualitatively distinct and existentially demanding. Other experiences do not compare.[16]

The most significant elements in Wach's description may be the phrases "perceived to be" and "issuing in appropriate action." The first phrase points to the inevitably hermeneutical character of all religious response. It is deeply subjective or, perhaps better, intersubjective. The ultimate power to which one responds is not the same for everyone; it is a matter of "being perceived" as ultimate. Notice how this small phrase opens the way to a more neutral analysis of religious phenomena. The issue is not whose ultimate is truly ultimate; the issue is the way a response to something as ultimate gives rise to certain behaviors. Religious experience therefore always involves an element of interpretation, not simply after the event but in the experiencing itself. Perception itself is a function of the social-symbolic construction of reality.[17] I can "see" something powerful as the work of the Holy Spirit only because my symbolic world contains a Holy Spirit that allows such sight. Another might "see" the same power in quite a different fashion. Religious experiences rely on a symbolic shape to reality, but they can also reshape the symbolic world. New things, after all, do happen, and they sometimes happen with sufficient force to require a complete reconstruction of a fractured symbolic universe.

For the present study, Wach's final phrase is most significant: "issuing in appropriate action" connects religious experiences with the religious practice and the organization of life around ultimate power that we term religion. Power tends to organize existence; ultimate power tends to organize all of existence. Once more, we observe how studiously nonjudgmental the term "appropriate" is in Wach's description: he means "appropriate to the nature of the power to which one responds." Moses and Siddhartha located the power to which they responded quite differently, and the organization of life that followed from each experience was also distinct, but what is significant is that in each case the organization followed appropriately from that experience of power. This is important precisely because it is from the organization of life—the way time and space is divided between sacred and profane, for example, or the way certain practices purport to mediate a share in the ultimate power[18]—that we are able to make guesses concerning the location and character of the power that organizes it. To be religious is not simply to think certain things but above all to act in certain ways, and these actions tend to fall into distinct patterns.

To take the "organization of life around (what is perceived as) ultimate power" as a shorthand working definition of a religion, then, means as well to have a flexible way of analyzing human behavior across a broad range of cultures. In looking at a religion, ancient or modern, we do not need to have immediate access to the "founding experience" or the "ultimate power," but can learn some things about them from the way in which life has been organized, especially in the allocation of time and space and in the logic of community practices. We can, in other words, work from the organization of life to experiences and convictions. But it is often not necessary even to raise the question of founding experiences and convictions, since the organization of life itself adequately represents the way in which power is deployed throughout the system.[19]

In fact, religious behavior need not regard itself as "religion" in order to be analyzed as such. The rise of National Socialism under the leadership of Adolf Hitler in twentieth-century Germany had obvious pseudoreligious traits. Less blatantly, twentieth-century Communism—especially in the Soviet Union and China—had distinct religious dimensions, even while its official ideology espoused atheism and formally rejected religion as the opiate of the people.[20] In the twenty-first-century Western world, patterns of addiction among individuals can easily be described in terms of Wach's description: the addictive substance serves as that which functionally "is perceived to be ultimate" and organizes time and space around itself with ruthless efficiency.[21] Contemporary group activity involving collegiate or professional sports—one thinks of the World Cup competition in soccer—lends itself to religious analysis: the patterns of activity especially among certain fans can only be called religious in their "peculiar intensity" and their perceived "ultimacy" for those involved.[22]

Glossolalia, or "speaking in tongues," provides a good illustration of the richer and more useful analysis that religious studies can provide. The New Testament touches on the phenomenon in three places: in the longer ending of Mark, "new tongues" are one of the powers given to Jesus' witnesses (Mark

16:17). At Pentecost, Luke describes those filled with the Holy Spirit as speaking in "other tongues" (Acts 2:4). And Paul devotes considerable attention to "tongues" as a gift of the Holy Spirit in 1 Cor 12–14. Within the discourse of Christian theology, only three questions were addressed concerning tongues, with no real resolution reached on any of them. First, the nature of the phenomenon: did people speak in real foreign languages or did they babble? No resolution was possible because the textual evidence could be read either way, and contemporary emic evidence (provided by tongue speakers) was unreliable.[23] Second, the origin of the phenomenon: was it directly inspired by the Holy Spirit and therefore inexplicable in human terms, or was it a manifestation of psychopathology?[24] Third, the worth of the phenomenon: was it the "sign of believers" that marked genuine Christianity (as claimed by Pentecostal traditions), or was it an unfortunate "enthusiasm" that led to heresy and schism (as its critics claimed)?[25] Because the conversation about this one religious phenomenon was reduced to claim and counterclaim, little headway could be made on actually understanding the religious significance of glossolalia.

Religious studies, in contrast, is able to bring a variety of cross-cultural, social-scientific, and literary perspectives to bear on the same phenomenon, not in order to ask "is this good or bad," or "is it from God or the psyche," or "should we do it or not," but simply in the quest for understanding glossolalia as a human religious activity. Linguists observing contemporary expressions of glossolalia, for example, have been unable to verify a single instance of the folkloric claim that tongues are languages that others translate in the assembly, and can show, to the contrary, that glossolalia is a form of "language-like" ordered babbling that is mimetic in nature—tongue speakers learn and imitate the phonic patterns of their leaders.[26] Psychologists, similarly, are able to state that glossolalia is not a sign of psychopathology, but is, especially in its initial expressions, often positively correlated with psychological dissociation and feelings of emotional liberation.[27] Sociologists studying contemporary Pentecostal groups are able to identify the way in which glossolalists strongly identify with leaders and can therefore sometimes join sectarian factions within a community.[28] Finally, anthropologists are able to show how, in communities in which spirit possession is part of the symbolic world, the claim to ecstatic experience can subvert official structures of authority and even establish competing centers of influence.[29]

These insights, in turn, can be brought to bear on examples of ecstatic utterance in diverse religious traditions, whether in the shamanism found among several aboriginal populations, or the ecstatic forms of prophecy found among the "sons of the prophets" in ancient Israel, or the mantic shouts of the priests of Cybele, or the utterances of the Pythian Oracle at Delphi.[30] The point of such comparison is not to reduce one expression to another, or to deny the validity of one or all of them, but rather, by means of correlation and comparison, to come to a better grasp of what glossolalia is and how it acts. Such study sedulously avoids either a supernaturalistic or naturalistic reduction. It does not seek to explain by means of appeal to God or to some subconscious (and therefore not fully human) impulse. It simply seeks to understand the phenomenon itself more fully and, in the process, to come also to a better understanding of why Paul, while regarding it as a gift of the Holy Spirit, nevertheless saw it as a problematic aspect of community life, requiring careful governance.[31]

NEW KNOWLEDGE

Changed theoretical perspectives have both encouraged and profited from an unparalleled flood of new knowledge about the ancient Mediterranean world that researchers have made available over the past century. Much of this new knowledge has been stimulated by archaeological discoveries. The dramatic discoveries in the Middle East—above all, the uncovering of the Jewish community and library at Wadi Qumran (beginning in 1947) and of the Gnostic library at Nag-Hammadi in 1945—had the effect of reshaping the understanding of first-century Judaism and of early Christianity.[32] Less generally publicized— because less directly related to the question of Christian uniqueness—but of equal importance are the astonishing archaeological discoveries carried out over the past two centuries across the entire sweep of the ancient empire, that give us new knowledge about Greco-Roman religion. From the border city of Dura-Europos in present-day Syria all the way to the seaside city of Bath in present-day England,[33] archaeological digs have revealed an unprecedented volume of real knowledge of the past. Sites include Palestinian cities of obvious interest to Christian origins, such as the city of Sepphoris in Galilee—a place where elements of Greek culture abound, only a few miles from Jesus' boyhood home of Nazareth—and Caesarea Maritime, which Herod made into a great Hellenistic port and where, according to Acts 24:7, Paul was imprisoned for two years.[34] They include as well cities in ancient Asia Minor, such as Sardis and Ephesus; cities in Achaia, such as Corinth; and in Italy, the amazingly well-preserved evidence of everyday life in the buried cities of Pompeii and Herculaneum.[35]

Out of such archaeological excavations have come not only countless cultural artifacts—from the most elaborate mosaics to the most modest lamps, from carved sarcophagi to stunning statues—but also the remains of buildings and city plans, so that the imagination of the setting and of some of the accoutrements of ancient life is abetted by the mnemonics of material evidence. A single overwhelming realization comes over anyone who has surveyed this evidence, and that is how impossible it would have been for either Jew or Christian to completely avoid contact with Greco-Roman religion, so public were its temples and shrines, so pervasive were its markers and emblems, so common were the depictions of its myths.

In addition to all these material remains—the stones and statues, temples and houses—archaeologists have also made available thousands of inscriptions that inform us not only about the doings of kings and rulers but also about how ordinary people ate and drank and bathed together in public. Long before the discoveries at Qumran and Nag-Hammadi, archaeologists uncovered thousands of papyri at Oxyrhynchus in Egypt, scraps of writing that sometimes contained religious texts—including variants of Gospel sayings—but that also testify to everyday domestic, commercial, educational, and political activity in the imperial province of Egypt.[36]

Four examples illustrate the way archaeological discoveries have had a significant impact on the subject of religion in the ancient Mediterranean world. Among the most spectacular discoveries were those made by Yale and French archaeologists between 1928 and 1937 at Dura-Europos, a Hellenistic city founded ca. 300 BCE, taken from the Parthians by the Romans early in the third century CE, and destroyed by the Parthians in 256 CE. As its history suggests, the city's location on a plateau facing the Euphrates River made it of strategic importance for competing empires. Between 1931 and 1933, archaeologists uncovered three buildings situated along the wall of the city facing west that were remarkably similar in architecture—they all were basically Roman houses—and function, since each was a place of worship. Near to each other were a Christian house church and a Jewish synagogue, while further down the street was a Mithraeum. Each meeting place, moreover, was richly decorated with frescoes.[37] The decorations in the synagogue were most startling, because they were the most dramatic instance yet discovered of the use of pictorial images in a place of Jewish worship, and even more because, under close examination, the depictions of Moses as leader of the people portrayed him in iconographic terms as a mystagogue.[38] Dura-Europos provides a sense not only of the way in which Judaism and Christianity developed together in the context of Greco-Roman practice, but also of the way in which Judaism could portray itself in terms of a Greco-Roman mystery.

Excavations at Sardis have shown how grand and elaborate the Jewish synagogue was in that city, providing a visual demonstration of the disparity in size and prestige between Judaism and nascent Christianity.[39] The many Jewish inscriptions (some in Hebrew but most in Greek) found there and at other sites have also proven instructive, indicating, first, the way in which wealthy Jews adopted the Greco-Roman practices of public display through inscriptions,[40] and, second, showing how Jewish women held important positions in the synagogue, some even bearing the designation "head of synagogue" (*archisynagō-gos*).[41] When wealthy Jewish women could be benefactors of the Jewish community and therefore hold such an official position, they occupied a place roughly equivalent to that held by Gentile women who served as priestesses in the imperial cult throughout Asia Minor.[42] The inscriptions tend to support the family resemblance among synagogues, house churches, and other Greco-Roman associations, and they suggest as well that the popular view that Jewish women would automatically have found Christianity appealing because of its more egalitarian ethos needs to be reexamined in light of such evidence.[43]

A vast number of inscriptions from Asia Minor have also shed more light on emperor worship itself. They reveal that the religious honor paid to the emperor and the imperial family was not a cult imposed by Roman megalomaniacs on resistant provinces, but was instead a popular expression of civic boosterism, with cities of a region competing with each other for the privilege of housing the cultus. Ephesus, for example, took great pride—revealed in its coinage—in being "Twice Neokoros," the keeper of the temple of the great goddess Artemis and keeper of the cult of the emperor.[44] The same inscriptions show how deeply enmeshed religious associations—those dedicated to emperor worship and others— were in the networks of society, so that membership and official status in such cults reflected social standing within the larger society.[45] The abundance of such inscriptions also suggests how hazardous it might be—simply at the level of social exclusion—for certain groups to reject membership or participation in the activities of such cults.

Finally, both monumental inscriptions and papyri have revealed a form of correspondence carried out between sovereigns and the delegates assigned to represent them in provinces or territories (see Dio Cassius, *Roman History*, 53.15.4). Sometimes called "royal correspondence" and sometimes *mandata principis* (instructions of the ruler) letters,[46] they contain two kinds of content that at first do not seem to fit logically together and make sense only when the function of the delegate as the ruler's personal representative is kept in mind. On one side, the letters provide specific instructions (mandates) concerning what the sovereign wishes would be accomplished. When these were posted or inscribed or read aloud, they authorized the activity of the delegate. But on the other side, some examples of these letters contain moral exhortation concerning the character of the delegate.[47] These exhortations thus also provided the populace with a sense of the moral standards that the sovereign expected in the delegate and therefore a standard to which they could hold the delegate accountable.[48] The same combination of elements appears in Paul's First Letter to Timothy and his Letter to Titus.[49] Because the elements were found in Hellenistic correspondence for several hundred years before Paul, there is no reason to see his "Pastoral Letters" as an inner-Christian development due to the passage of time and the growth of institution.[50] These letters can be accounted for on the basis of a common practice of correspondence among those in analogous social relationships.

Archaeology, in short, has provided a fresh set of facts on the ground that both enables and requires the reexamination of ancient literary evidence. In the case of the discoveries at Qumran, the extensive writings of this sectarian group stimulated a renewed reading of all ancient Jewish literature and led to new theories about diversity in first-century Judaism. In the case of the discoveries at Nag-Hammadi, the collection of Coptic compositions called the "Gnostic Library" similarly led to a fresh reading of both canonical and apocryphal Christian literature and led to the development of new positions concerning the historical Jesus and diversity in the early Christian movement. In the same fashion, the acquisition of new knowledge about the Greco-Roman world through archaeology has encouraged a reconsideration of literature previously available to scholars but now read with new interest and the potential for new insight.[51]

Scholars of religion read Greek and Roman novels,[52] for example, with a new appreciation for what they can tell us about religious attitudes and practices. Books X–XI of Apuleius' *Metamorphoses* (*The Golden Ass*) has long been appreciated as our most important source for the experience of initiation into a Mystery cult.[53] But once the notion of "religion" is extended to encompass more than "Mysteries," the novel becomes a source for equally important aspects of ancient religiosity: it provides a sharp portrayal of the practice of magic, for example (III.21–28), and contains a vivid portrait of the wandering prophets of the goddess Cybele (VIII.24–27). Other novels are being examined not for their plot and characterization, but for the way they depict social realities and religious sensibilities. H. J. Cadbury once remarked that Chariton of Aphrodisias' novel, *Chaereas and Callirhoe*, contained more similarities to the idiom and ideas of the *Acts of the Apostles* than did any other ancient text.[54] Cadbury's insight has invited more systematic comparison among the canonical Acts and Hellenistic novels and even more among Christian Apocryphal Acts of the Apostles and ancient Romances.[55]

Other literature is read with new interest in light of archaeology. Herodotus' *History* has long been admired as a rich if not always reliable source for religious exoterica, but he also provides information of a religious character even when that is not necessarily his intention, as when he shows how pivotal the oracle at Delphi was for the political life of Greece.[56] Similarly, Pliny the Elder's *Historia Naturalis*, Strabo's *Geography*, and especially Pausanius' *Description of Greece* find new pertinence for the study of Greco-Roman religion to the extent that they can be correlated with (or corrected by) new knowledge derived from archaeology.[57]

A fine example of the manner in which new archaeological knowledge and new theoretical perspectives on religion throw light on extant literature is the rhetorician Aelius Aristides, whose *Sacred Tales* provides vivid firsthand witness to the religious sensibilities connected (at least in his case) to the quest for healing from the god Asclepius that was offered at shrines located in Epidaurus and Pergamum.[58] Archaeology has revealed the complexity and size of these ancient sites dedicated to healing as well as the many inscriptions that attest to the healings that took place through medical regimens and the interventions of the god.[59] Aristides' *Sacred Tales* provides students of religion with genuine emic discourse corresponding to the *realia* exposed through excavation, offering evidence of a sickly man's passionate devotion to the healing powers of the god.[60] If religion is the organization of life around the perception of ultimate power, then Aelius Aristides is an invaluable witness to Greco-Roman religion.

Scholars have also begun to pay more serious attention to the moral philosophers of the early empire, especially since what Martha Nussbaum calls their "therapy of desire" fits within a framework that is, in many respects, distinctly religious.[61] The religious character of the traditions associated with Pythagoras and Epicurus, which originated before the period under study but continued to exist and exert influence, is patent. The several *Lives* of Pythagoras trace his origin to the gods, and Epicurus was worshipped by his follower Colotes even during his lifetime.[62] Disciples of each sage memorized their sayings as a guide to purification or as a prophylactic against fear,[63] and committed themselves to forms of friendship so intense that they required a life together in community. In the case of the Pythagoreans, the common life included shared meals and shared possessions and a period of probation for the assessing of candidates.[64] Philostratus' *Life of Apollonius of Tyana* and Heraclitus' *Letters* both bear witness to the conviction that such philosophers participated in and revealed to other humans something of the divine.[65]

Philosophers in the Cynic-Stoic tradition were more circumspect in their language and more individualistic in their outlook than were the Epicureans and Pythagoreans. But in figures such as Dio Chrysostom, Seneca, Marcus

Aurelius, and, above all, in that "grand old man," the exiled slave Epictetus, we find philosophy as the commitment to a way of life, indeed as a vocation to live a life worthy of God in service to other humans.[66] Commitment to philosophy demanded more than the wearing of a beard and a long cloak, certainly more than the knowledge of logic, cosmology, and ethics. It required a genuine conversion of life, a rejection of vice and the cultivation of virtue, a turning from sickness to health.[67] Even the satirist Lucian of Samosata, whose favorite targets included the faux philosophers who failed to live up to such expressed ideals—his portrayals of daytime public virtue followed by nighttime private vice have a startlingly contemporary tone—testifies in his admiring treatment of the noble philosophers Demonax and Nigrinus how much he himself shared those same ideals.[68]

Reading Greco-Roman moralists in light of new categories provided by religious studies is a splendid example of how the convergence of new evidence, changing theory, and the rereading of old evidence has opened up new possibilities for understanding Greco-Roman culture and its ways of being religious. The result is to make pagan religion far more complicated. Similar study over the past decades has also served to make first-century Judaism and nascent Christianity more complex than they were formerly thought to be. The conversation concerning the way or ways in which the religion of Greeks and Romans, Jews, and Christians intersected or interacted can no longer be reduced to a single factor (like the Mysteries) or a single dynamic (such as dependence), nor can it proceed on the assumption that interactions took place among three monolithic, highly defined, and distinct entities.

CHALLENGING OLD RECONSTRUCTIONS

Take, for example, the theory of early Christian development elaborated by the History of Religions School and found most fully expressed in the work of Wilhelm Bousset and Rudolf Bultmann.[69] It was based on a premise that Hellenistic and Jewish cultures could be separated into distinct geographical spheres. Judaism in Palestine was therefore untouched by Greco-Roman culture except as a force to be resisted. Only in the Diaspora could Jews like Philo seriously engage Hellenistic ways, and the intensity of Philo's engagement with Greek culture was regarded as exceptional.[70]

On the basis of this assumption, earliest Christianity in Palestine (Jewish Christianity) must be defined entirely by "Jewish" (that is, rabbinic and apocalyptic)—rather than "Greek"—categories. In Palestine, consequently, Jesus could not have been called "Lord" (*kyrios*) since that designation would be available only where Hellenistic cults operated.[71] The Christology of the Jewish community in Palestine must therefore have fitted traditional messianic expectations and been centered on the apocalyptic expectation of Jesus' return.[72] The designation of Jesus as Lord (*kyrios*) must have arisen in the Diaspora, where Christians would for the first time have encountered Greco-Roman Mystery religions, such as that devoted to Serapis, in which the god was designated as *kyrios*.[73]

It is in the Diaspora, then, that the "Jesus Movement" became a "Christ cult," under the direct influence of Greco-Roman Mysteries. Specifically, the dramatic transition took place when the missionaries mentioned in Acts 6:1–7 came to Antioch to proclaim Jesus for the first time directly to the Greeks (Acts 11:19–21).[74] Since Paul became a Christian in this Hellenistic environment (Acts 9:1–9), it was further inferred from his discourse about baptism and meals that he inherited this Hellenistic form of Christianity, with his theology of righteousness by faith standing in uneasy tension with the "sacramental" character of a Christianity already transformed into something of a Mystery cult.[75] Christianity therefore developed in three discrete stages: Palestinian, Hellenistic, and Pauline.

There were problems with this influential hypothesis from the start. It was based on faulty assumptions concerning the evidence in the New Testament sources: scholars were overly optimistic that the Gospels and the first part of Acts faithfully reported specifically Palestinian perspectives, and they disregarded epistolary writers arguably as early as Paul (James and the author of the Letter to the Hebrews).[76] More tellingly, the linguistic facts that formed the basis of the argument were other than the scholars thought. There was no need for Greek-speaking Jews to have contact with a Mystery cult to designate Jesus as *kyrios*. The Greek translation of the Hebrew scripture known as the Septuagint (LXX) had already translated the name Yahweh as *kyrios*. Those convinced that Jesus was powerfully alive and sharing in God's reign would need no contact with a Mystery to connect the title *kyrios* with Jesus; they had only to read the LXX version of Psalm 110:1: "The Lord (*ho kyrios*) said to my lord (*kyriō*), sit at my right hand until I make your enemies a footstool for my feet."[77]

Even more embarrassing was evidence for the fact that Jewish, Aramaic-speaking Christians had already designated Jesus as "Lord," through the prayer *marana tha* ("Come, Lord"). Paul quotes this prayer in his letter to the Greek-speaking believers in the church at Corinth (ca. 54 CE), in the full expectation that they would recognize this Aramaic prayer as well as its implications—that

Jesus is the risen one capable of returning in power (1 Cor 16:22). But since Aramaic was not normally spoken in the Greek diaspora but was a local dialect of Hebrew found in Palestine, it follows that the prayer quoted by Paul was a piece of the tradition that was transmitted from the Palestinian church to him and that he in turn had shared it with the Corinthians.[78] Again, there is no need to invoke a Greco-Roman Mystery cult to explain the usage.

Despite these obvious flaws, the argument enjoyed considerable favor and influence, because it appeared to provide a way of making sense of the available data. The biggest blow to the reconstruction came from the acquisition of new knowledge concerning the relations of Judaism and Hellenism in the first century, knowledge suggesting that the neat alignment of geography and culture was far too simple. The same archaeological impetus that is reshaping the understanding of Greco-Roman religion and revealing its unsuspected complexity has also impelled the reconsideration of first-century Judaism and made clearer not only that it was equally complex, but that it was also equally a sharer in Hellenistic culture. The pioneering work of scholars like Saul Liebermann showed that the categories separating Palestinian and Diaspora Judaism were artificial, and the impressive compilation of this knowledge by Martin Hengel has won near universal recognition among scholars.[79]

Monumental and literary evidence alike shows that Judaism had been negotiating its identity with Hellenism in Palestine as well as in the Diaspora since the conquests of Alexander the Great (d. 323 BCE), so that by the time the New Testament compositions were written, Jews had been in contact with and in various ways had adapted and assimilated to the dominant culture for a period longer than the entire history of the United States. Jews in Palestine, furthermore, had dealings with Roman administrators and soldiers for well over a hundred years.[80] The Greek language, and with it Greek rhetorical, political, and philosophical ideals, had touched Jewish life in profound ways. The quintessential expression of Jewish lore, the Talmud, is composed in Aramaic yet is studded with Greek loan words, a number of the midrashic *middoth* (rules for interpretation) find antecedent in Greek rhetoric, and the form of the sayings of the Rabbis resemble the Greek *chreia*.[81] Palestine was the home not only of great rabbinic scholars but also of Greek-speaking rhetoricians and philosophers.[82]

The most obvious example of early Jewish engagement with Greek culture is the translation of the Hebrew scriptures called the Septuagint (LXX), carried out some 250 years before the birth of Jesus.[83] According to the legend of the miraculous translation—according to which all 70 of the translators, working separately, produced identical versions—the work was carried out under the sponsorship of Ptolemy II Philadelphus (285–247 BCE) as an act of beneficence for Jews in the Diaspora, who no longer spoke their ancestral language.[84] But the translators were Jewish scholars from Palestine, whom the king brought to Egypt to accomplish the task. The translators, in other words, were Palestinian Jews who knew Greek as well as they knew Hebrew and were therefore capable of carrying out this delicate and sacred task. That such a translation was required is testimony to the thoroughly Hellenized condition of the (perhaps) millions of Jews living, mostly by choice and preference, outside Palestine[85]—a larger number than those dwelling in Palestine—but testifies as well to the thorough devotion they had to the scriptures of their people.

The Septuagint, in turn, became the basis of an extensive apologetic literature composed by Jews who sought to explain themselves in the terms of Greco-Roman culture and, in the process, became still more Hellenized. Philo of Alexandria and the author of the Wisdom of Solomon were intensely devoted to the one God of Israel and were equally loyal to their own people. Indeed, they had nothing but contempt for the idolatry of their pagan neighbors.[86] Yet, even in the compositions that defended their God and their customs against Gentile slanders, they reveal their profoundly Hellenistic sensibilities. Jews like Ezekiel the Tragedian and Pseudo-Phocylides even employed distinctive Hellenistic literary forms with such sophistication and subtlety that the Jewish authorship of their work is not easily apparent.[87] The heroic takes of resistance to Greek culture and religion, related by the books of the Maccabees, are written in Greek and reveal the influence of Hellenistic historiography and (in the case of 4 Maccabees) popular moral philosophy.[88] Even the profoundly conservative wisdom of the Palestinian Jewish sage Ben Sira, composed in Hebrew, was translated by the sage's grandson into Greek, for a Diaspora Judaism hungry for Jewish wisdom from the homeland but unable to read it in the original language (Sirach, prologue).

The synagogue paintings at Dura-Europos demonstrate that Philo was by no means the only Jew who could think of Israel's religion at least metaphorically in terms of the Eleusinian Mysteries, or who could conceive of Moses as both a philosopher and as a mystagogue who initiated adepts into the Mysteries contained in God's law.[89] In fact, a pseudonymous Jewish work in honor of Abraham and Moses—and perhaps ascribing to them something very much like divine honor—was penned under the name of Orpheus, the traditional patron of the Greek Mysteries.[90]

The most paradoxical example of Hellenistic influence in Palestinian Judaism is perhaps the Qumran community. No Jewish group was more deeply
dedicated to the Hebrew text of scripture and to the use of classical Hebrew in
its modes of scriptural interpretation and in its composition of new sectarian
literature.[91] Nor was any Jewish group more emphatic in its rejection not only
of the despised Gentiles, but also of any Jews who associated in the slightest
manner with Gentiles.[92] No Jewish sect could, on the surface, appear more
straightforwardly anti-Hellenistic. Yet, Qumran's system of probation and excommunication, and its way of life organized around an absolute community of
possessions, appears to owe more to Greek utopian models than to any precedent found in Torah.[93] When Josephus describes Moses as a philosopher
(*Against Apion* 2.168, 281), when he aligns the Jewish sects in Palestine with
Greek philosophical traditions (*Jewish War* 2.119–166), and when in particular
he compares the Essenes to the Pythagoreans (*Jewish War* 2.119–161, *Antiquities*
15.371), he does not do violence to the reality, but testifies to the complex ways
in which Jewish and Greek cultures interacted.

Hellenistic Judaism in the first century, both within and outside Palestine,
is of exceptional importance to any analysis of the relations between Greco-
Roman religion and early Christianity, in two ways. First, it serves as a reminder
of how complex and subtle were the modes of cultural and religious cross-
fertilization in the period of the early empire. Even for this most highly defined
and resistant tradition, there was a variety of ways in which the dominant
Hellenistic culture was negotiated, so that for some Jews, totally loyal to their
heritage, it was perfectly natural to think of their own religion as a form of
philosophy and as the best of Mysteries.

Second, it cautions us against using Judaism as an alternative to "Greco-
Roman" when examining the possible connections between paganism and
Christianity. Insisting that Christianity derives from Judaism does not by itself
answer the question of how Greco-Roman religious sensibilities may have been
among the elements of the symbolic world that Christians recatalyzed in light
of their own experience.

I have suggested that new perspectives and new knowledge have combined
to create the possibility of examining the question of Christianity and Greco-
Roman religion with fresh eyes. Even these introductory comments indicate,
however, that the examination has not become easier: the more we have learned
about Greco-Roman, Jewish, and early Christian traditions, the more internally
complex each appears, and the relations among them seem correspondingly
complex. It is not at all clear whether any way of organizing the data is useful.

The next stage of my argument presses that question, by showing in greater detail some of the range of religious responses within Greco-Roman culture, before proposing that a typology of ways of being religious might be the most neutral and helpful approach not only to paganism but to ancient Judaism and Christianity as well.[94]

3

A Preliminary Profile of Greco-Roman Religion

The more we learn about the ancient Mediterranean world, the more complex and sprawling the topic of Greco-Roman religion appears.[1] This preliminary profile attempts to provide some sense of the range of religious experiences, convictions, and practices in the early Roman Empire.[2] I make no effort to distinguish, for example, what is originally Greek and what is natively Roman in this religious world, or to develop stages of religion that unfold in evolutionary sequence or in response to spiritual crises.[3] Rather, I focus on the variety of religious phenomena observable across the empire and throughout the period when Christianity emerged.[4] I begin with the aspects of religion that are most visible and obvious, hoping that my broad generalizations will gain some depth and nuance from subsequent chapters. Even this preliminary discussion makes no pretense of comprehensiveness. My selection of topics and the way I discuss them is very much determined by the sort of conversation I want to develop between Greco-Roman religion and Christianity.

GENERAL FEATURES

I begin with a fairly safe set of observations about Greco-Roman *thrēskeia* or *religio* in the centuries immediately before and during Christianity's development. First, it was *pervasive*, touching peoples' lives in multiple ways that even the most pious of present-day Christians—unless they were Roman Catholics of a certain age—would find astonishing.[5] Signs of divine presence met a person on every side. Corresponding gestures of respect and gratitude to the *indigitamenta*—the gods who were associated or even identified with every place and activity—accompanied every daily activity: planting and harvesting, preparing meals, practicing crafts and trades, embarking on journeys, entering houses or shrines or battle.[6] The promise of votive offerings to such gods and short prayers such as "if God wills it"—found in Judaism only where influenced by Hellenistic piety—were often on the lips.[7] Religion for Greeks and Romans was not something done only with a part of one's time, space, and attention. It demanded attention in virtually every time and space, because every time and space was potentially an opening to a divine presence and power.

Greco-Roman religion was, therefore, not simply personal and private but had a genuinely *public* character. Understandings of religion as essentially individualistic and personal are Western and recent—as are the notions of privacy and individualism themselves. Greeks and Romans lived lives that were public in every sense of the word.[8] To be isolated and alone was for them the worst of fates, and full humanity was always a matter of "being with" others, whether family, friends, fellow citizens, or personal slaves.[9] Religion was correspondingly woven into the social fabric from top to bottom, rather than, as so often in contemporary Christian and post-Christian countries, relegated to interior dispositions and an occasional and relatively anonymous Sunday worship service.

Public time and public space alike were religiously organized. The calendars determined by priestly study were posted publicly to alert the populace concerning which days of a month were *Fasti*, and therefore available for markets and for public assemblies, and which were *Nefasti*, dedicated to the festival of a god and therefore sacred in character (making them dangerous for secular activities).[10] A given month was punctuated by the festivals that created pauses in profane activity and enabled communion among gods and humans through rest, ritual, and public feasting.[11] Temples and shrines were omnipresent and served multiple functions: they were sanctuaries for the pursued and prosecuted, and they served as repositories of wealth and administrative archives.[12] The gold of Athens was placed at Athena's feet in the Parthenon, and the shrine of Apollo at Delphi financed wars against the Persians.[13] As places where public sacrifices were performed, temples could also serve as the source of meat for households.[14] The link between the domestic and the civic can be shown by the piety that attached itself to the family hearth—the fire was never extinguished—and that connected to the cult of the Vestal Virgins, who oversaw the sacred and indistinguishable flame that protected the entire Roman *oikoumenē*.[15]

Holidays and festivals were, like periodic athletic contests, celebrations of and with the gods. Patron deities were invoked not only at the meals of religious associations (*thiasoi*) explicitly devoted to their cults, but were also greeted enthusiastically at the common meals of *collegia* and trade associations, funerary societies, and philosophical schools, whose drinking parties (*symposia*) under the aegis of Dionysius (Bacchus) inspired the table talk, both solemn and silly, that was recorded across the more than 500 years separating Plato and Plutarch, and that in many ways was the real gift of such gathering and drinking.[16] It was also in the name of the gods that such groups collected funds from members and held them in common for the support and mutual benefit of members.[17]

Because religion was public, it was also necessarily political in character. Matters of religion were also matters of state. Membership in colleges of priests came about through election or selection by political bodies and officers, and the priestly works of determining sacred days, organizing the *leitourgia* of the great festivals, carrying out sacrifices, and, above all, ensuring through the *auspices* that circumstances were favorable for the initiation of any great venture, such as going to war, were matters of critical importance for the political order.[18] The selection of whom held such offices was therefore also a matter of political concern, and serving as Augur or Pontifex was a significant item in the *cursus honorum*. Such positions were eagerly sought and gladly administered, for they placed men (and, in the case of the Vestals, women) so elected into positions of enormous prestige and real power.[19] The same was true in the provinces as in the city: holding priestly offices both effected and expressed political power.[20]

The proper regulation of religion was considered essential for the stability and safety of the state—and this conviction was as strong during both the Republic and the Principate. Although Rome was generally hospitable to new cults, if for any reason a practice was regarded as inimical to the established order, it could be suppressed, not only for the good of the state but also, since they went together, for the health of religion. The eastern cult image (a black stone) of the Great Mother was welcomed because the Sybil declared that her presence would secure Rome's safety.[21] The cult of Dionysius, in contrast, was repressed because it was perceived as threatening traditional order.[22] Plutarch's most serious charge against the Epicureans was that their denial of the gods (that is, the denial of the presence and power of the gods to ensure the populace's well-being) was expressed by a deliberate withdrawal from active participation in the life of the *polis*.[23] The Epicureans saw this as a legitimate search for a quiet life.[24] Plutarch, and with him the rest of the philosophical tradition, saw such withdrawal as a threat to the security of the civilized order.[25] The charge of atheism made against both Jews and Christians, likewise, was connected to the charge of *amixia* (failure to mingle, or participate), which was tantamount to *misanthrōpia* (hatred of humanity).[26]

The public-political character of Greco-Roman religion can be misunderstood in three ways if approached from the perspective of a developed Christianity. First, the entire system of festivals and auguries and sacrifices might be dismissed as relatively otiose because they are not discussed extensively in our extant religious literature. The opposite, however, is the case: what extant literary and archaeological evidence points us to is the realm of that which need not be discussed because it belongs to the realm of "what goes without saying" because it is so customary, so deeply entrenched in the culture. The inscriptional evidence pertinent to religious associations makes clear how socially enmeshed and interconnected were priestly and political offices.[27]

Second, one could assume that the public and political character of religion made it an "official" rather than a popular religion, an activity reserved for the elite rather than the masses. But although it is true that elements of class entered into matters like priestly elections, it is also the case that the round of festivals and sacrifices were "popular" precisely in the sense of inviting the participation of the populace as a whole.[28] The evidence does not suggest any sense of alienation from public religion, probably because, from the start, it was so consistently in line with domestic piety and so constantly reinforced a social cohesion that transcended lines of class and wealth. This may be the place to mention that neither was there a sharp line drawn on the basis of gender. While many religious responsibilities were assigned to males, there is abundant evidence for the activity of females in cultic settings, both in Greece and Rome. The full extent of their activity is, to be sure, obscured by the androcentric bias of the sources.[29] Third, it is important not to assume a dichotomy between formal religion and religious sincerity. The offering of incense to the image of an emperor was no less personal or meaningful for the Romans than voting in an election in which one's own candidate cannot win for those living in a democratic society.[30]

I have spoken of Greco-Roman religion during the late Republic and early Principate as pervasive, public, and political. It was also pious and pragmatic. The public religion of the people was an expression of *pietas*—the filial disposition of reverence and respect for one's ancestors (the *lares* both of the hearth and of the *oikoumenē*), for the laws, and for those who administered the laws in the city-state—and was intimately, indeed inextricably, linked to reverence and respect toward the gods.[31] Greco-Roman religion in this period was also practical more than it was theoretical. It was not a matter of theology but of properly negotiating the relationship among humans and gods, and in such negotiations, pragmatism was all-important.[32] If the proper conditions for sacrifice were not met, the sacrifice was postponed or repeated until performed correctly.[33] If the name of a god governing some place or activity was not known, then "whatever god might be here" was invoked.[34] Religion was very much a matter of what worked in the everyday world inhabited by gods and humans.

The feature of Greco-Roman religion that enabled both a remarkable diversity of expression and an impressive social cohesion is that it was polytheistic, the religious system of all ancient peoples except the Jews and (in a more ambiguous fashion) the Christians.[35] Polytheism conceives of the divine *dynamis/virtus* ("power") as personal but also as diffused through an elaborate extended family of gods, whose respective influence was exercised over the diverse domains of natural and human life. Much in the manner that Mediterranean culture ran on a complex system of patronage and honor that enabled intercourse between the lower and higher elements of society, so did the gods provide benefits to those who honored them.[36] Thus, there was a multiplication of minor deities (*indigimenta*) who controlled every sort of human activity (waking, sleeping, eating, planting, sailing); thus also, the intensely practical character of piety—the point was to honor the god who actually exercises power in a particular realm; thus, finally, the capacity of polytheism to provide social cohesion—it corresponds precisely to Greco-Roman social arrangements and dynamics, extending to the gods the same combination of hierarchical structure yet interdependent activity found among humans.

The realm of the gods did not simply mirror the world of humans. The membrane separating the human and the divine was permeable, with traffic moving in both directions. Nowhere is this more consistently or impressively displayed than in Ovid's *Metamorphoses*, a Latin rendering of shared Greco-Roman myths that portrays gods and humans in a constant change and exchange of forms.[37] The gods can make themselves immediately present in human form, as when Zeus and Hermes visit the aged Phrygian couple Baucis and Philemon.[38] Humans can also enter into the extended divine family through extraordinary wisdom or valor, transformed like the prototypical hero Herakles into a "son of god" through ascension or apotheosis.[39]

Polytheism is, in this sense, a generous and capacious religious system. There is always room for another member of the extended divine family. The early Christian proclamation of Jesus as a son of god in power through resurrection from the dead (Rom 1:4) would not have sounded nearly so strange to Gentiles as it did to Jews. For Gentiles, however, the designation would also not have carried with it any claim to uniqueness. They could (and did) question, furthermore, whether a human who died the way Jesus did—abandoned by followers, wracked with fear—could be considered worthy of a place among the immortals.[40]

If humans could in principle and sometimes in practice—as often occurred with emperors and even imperial favorites[41]—be elevated to the status of the divine, so could the gods worshipped by other peoples be included in the imperial pantheon. Rome adopted and extended the practice of religious syncretism initiated by the Hellenistic empire.[42] Syncretism involved the recognition of gods who operated under different names but with similar functions, as well as the adoption of foreign deities in subordinate positions. The most obvious case is the Roman adoption of virtually the entire Greek Olympic family (Zeus=Jupiter, Hera=Juno, Hermes=Mercury, etc.), but the same instinct enabled more complex adaptations and accommodations. It was, in fact, part of Rome's political genius to allow conquered peoples not only to continue to worship their native gods but also to join in the worship of the gods who truly ran the world.[43]

Polytheism's intrinsic permeability and expansiveness made the emperor cult not only intelligible but logical. If divinity is revealed through effective presence and power, then those who exercise imperial rule over the entire *oik-oumenē* are truly *theoi phenomenoi* ("visible gods").[44] Rome itself was relatively slow to accede to the worship of living rulers, but under the influence of the Greek provinces, where obeisance to rulers had begun already in the time of Alexander,[45] the Principate gradually overcame its republican scruples—the Consul was elected by the Senate, but the *Princeps* exercised rule dynastically— and adopted the practice, which in Asian provinces eventually included the entire imperial family.

It is polytheism that enables the complex interconnections of sacred time and space within the life of the people. Because there are many gods, there are also many temples and shrines, each with its statue symbolizing the divine presence, each with its altar where the sacrifice of animals serves to honor the deity and provide *koinōnia* ("fellowship") for the worshippers who share in the meat of the sacrifice.[46] And since every household also had its *lares* and *penates*, similarly recognized and honored by portions of grain and fruit that formed the individual family's food,[47] the entire *oikoumenē* was bound together by a cuisine of sacrifice that simultaneously bound humans to the gods and humans to each other. Because there are many gods, likewise, time itself was divided into days that were *fasti* or *nefasti*, depending on the obligation to sacrifice and celebrate in honor of some deity or another.[48]

Polytheism as a religious system had both positive and negative aspects. Positively, it maximized the diversity of divine presence—any spot or time could become sacred through encounter with a god or even through the sacrifice to a god—while also diffusing the burden of theodicy throughout the entire system. One god or goddess may take offense and bear a grudge against a human, but just as in human patronage, there is always another god or goddess to whom one can turn for help.[49] The very anthropomorphism that made the gods so available to humans, an extension of society's own system of patronage and honor, however, had the negative aspect of revealing the gods to be as petty, corruptible, and even immoral as humans themselves. The myths that the Romans took over from Hesiod, Homer, and the Tragedians exposed the Olympian gods in particular as driven by unseemly passions.

Some thoughtful Gentiles tended to view the Olympians much as the British do the equally fractious and embarrassing royal family—helpful and even necessary as societal glue but not much use for actual governance. Connected to this perception were two responses that in many ways were interconnected. Some sober-minded moralists like Cornutus, Heraclitus, and Plutarch strove to save the ancient traditions of the Greeks and a morally responsible piety by rendering the sometimes scandalous stories of the Olympian gods as allegories containing profound moral and spiritual truths. The development of allegorical interpretation enabled young people to read and learn from the classic texts that shaped their world, while understanding that what they were really about was not lust and adultery and rage, but the desire for wisdom and virtue.[50] Both Jews and Christians would, in turn, learn from such hermeneutical precedents and turn the same interpretive techniques to their own deeply problematic scriptures.[51]

A second response was to imagine a stronger, more unitary, and directing divine power superior to the many gods on display in the world. When viewed positively, such a governing power could be construed as providence (pronoia).[52] Some writers were confident that such divine providence worked for the reward of the good and the punishment of the wicked, giving polytheism a level of moral discourse that was otherwise only a minor element.[53] The language used in discussions of providence, sometimes associated with the personal name of Zeus or Dios, comes remarkably close to a functional and in some cases even a reflective monotheism (or, in some cases, pantheism).[54] Defenders of providence faced the same challenges as did the defenders of God's justice within monotheistic systems, namely, the evidence to the contrary suggesting that the evil go unpunished and that the good do not prosper.[55] When the writer's outlook was more grim, or the circumstances more dire, the limits imposed on gods and humans alike could be designated as moira ("Limit") or heimarmenē ("Fate"), an inexorable and relentless boundary against which there could be no appeal.[56] If circumstances were particularly capricious, the controlling divine force could also be personified as Tyche or Fortuna ("Chance" or "Fortune").[57]

Both allegorical interpretation and the search for an ordering principle superior to the anthropomorphic gods, however, remained within the framework and depended on the normative status of polytheism. They did not represent a rejection but rather a refinement of the religious system that pervaded Greco-Roman culture and gave it definition. That system, in all its manifestations, was about negotiating the divine *dynamis* in a manner beneficial to humans and to the social order.

SPECIFIC RELIGIOUS PHENOMENA

The assumption that the divine *dynamis* was accessible to humans for their benefit was operative not only in the ordinary round of domestic and civic observance but also in manifestations of piety that sometimes demanded great effort and the dislocation of everyday life. Five examples are of particular pertinence to a comparison with early Christianity: prophecy, healing, initiation into Mysteries, pilgrimages, and magic.

PROPHECY

Prophecy is sometimes thought to be a distinctive feature of "biblical" religion, but it is widely attested in other traditions and is a conspicuous feature of Greco-Roman religion.[58] The fundamental element in prophecy is communication from gods to humans, which may but need not (and often does not) involve prediction of the future. In this root sense, prophecy and revelation are closely aligned. In Greco-Roman religion, prophecy took several forms. Most common and routine were the various kinds of divination that accompanied the initiation of important actions, from sacrifices to war. This sort of technical prophecy (or augury) studied celestial and animal phenomena in order to determine divine favor of a specific undertaking.[59] Such auspices were the work of priests appointed to the task and were taken with great seriousness.[60] For example, if an animal brought to sacrifice did not signify its agreement to being slaughtered by shaking its head up and down when sprinkled with water, then the sacrifice must be postponed.[61] If the study of sacrificial entrails yielded evidence that was not positive, human plans must be deferred.[62] Similarly, meteorological events were taken as signs and portents indicating divine pleasure or displeasure at a plan of action.[63]

More highly esteemed by some—including Plato—were forms of prophecy called *mantic* (from *mania*=frenzy, madness), which was understood as the physical possession of the human psyche by the divine *pneuma* to create an altered and heightened state called *enthusiasmos*, which enabled the possessed to see and speak beyond normal human capacity.[64] The orgiastic ravings of the goddess Cybele's eunuch priests as described by Apuleius may be an example of such mantic prophecy—in their case apparently generated by rituals of dance and self-flagellation.[65] Much quieter and routine were the oracles delivered by the god Apollo at Delphi, where a woman seated on a tripod above a declivity in the earth, from which arose vapors, enunciated strange messages that required decipherment by the shrine's professional *prophētai*.[66]

Also associated with the god Apollo were the Sibyls—the most famous of whom spoke from a cave in Cumae—whose declarations were written in the *Sibylline Books*.[67] Her pronouncements were taken with great seriousness: the introduction of the cult of the Great Mother (*Magna Mater*=*Cybele*) from Asia into Rome came about because of a crisis in the war with Carthage and in response to a prophecy in her books, confirmed by the oracle at Delphi.[68] The connection of this form of prophecy with Apollo was confirmed by the placement of the *Sibylline Books* in the Temple of Apollo on the Palatine in 12 BCE.[69]

In his work, *On the Obsolescence of Oracles* (early second century CE), Plutarch—himself a priest of Apollo at Delphi—reports a conversation with friends in which deep puzzlement and dismay are expressed because Delphi no longer seems to speak oracles.[70] The dialogue offers a variety of scientific and theological explanations for the cessation of oracles. But the sense of dismay at the stoppage testifies to the premise that Plutarch shared with the less sophisticated, namely, that in one way or another the divine *pneuma* could seize hold of humans and use them to communicate truths not otherwise available to them. Greece's early history could be told, and, in fact, was told by Herodotus, at least partly in terms of the seriousness with which the Delphic oracles were taken in matters both private and public.[71] Here is an example of life organized around what is perceived as transcendent power: people traveled to the shrine, heard the divine message, and then lived their lives in response to what they heard, sometimes even engaging in war in obedience to what they considered the god was telling them. This is serious revelatory religion.

HEALING

The divine *dynamis* could also break through in acts of healing. There are occasional stories of curative or exorcistic powers worked by an emperor like Vespasian or a philosopher like Apollonius of Tyana as demonstrations of power operative in *theioi andres* ("divine men").[72] Of more religious importance, however, were the shrines of healing (*asclepeia*) dedicated to the god Asclepius, which combined the arts of medicine with the worship of the god; especially through divine visitations during sleep in the temple precincts (incubation), suppliants were led to physical restoration.[73] The cult began in Greece, and sanctuaries were found at Epidaurus, Cos, and Pergamum. The extant inscrip-

tions from Epidaurus (dating from the fourth century BCE) bear eloquent testimony to a religious sensibility that regarded the entire elaborate process of
medical and divine therapy as the work of the god in response to the faith of
those who came with broken limbs and lives.[74] Followers returned to their
homes, leaving behind in the sanctuary votive offerings in the form of casts of
healed limbs and organs, as well as testimonies—in the form of vivid vignettes—
to the wonders worked by the god. In response to a severe plague in their city
(in 293 BCE), the Romans vowed in 292 to construct a temple to Asclepius
after consulting the Sibylline Books. An embassy was sent to Epidaurus, and
according to custom for such new foundings, a huge sacred snake was brought
to Rome; when it swam to the Tiber Island, the omen indicated that the new
Asclepium should be built on that spot. The temple was erected in 291 BCE,
and its presence was credited with stopping the plague.[75]

MYSTERIES

The topic of "Mystery religions," as we have seen, dominated earlier discussions of Greco-Roman religion (see Chapter 1).[76] The Mysteries are indeed of
importance, but not more so than the other aspects of Gentile religion I am
describing. Five clarifications are helpful from the start: (1) the Mysteries are
not distinct "religions" in the modern sense that they provided alternatives to
the overarching Greco-Roman religious world; rather, they fitted perfectly
within that world, being distinguished mainly by the requirement of initiation
for participation in the cult; (2) they were not "secret" in the sense that they
were clandestine, but only in the sense that the details of initiation were restricted to the initiated; (3) they were not recent innovations; some Mysteries
(like that of Eleusis and that dedicated to Dionysius) were features of Greek religion from antiquity; (4) a claim associated with at least some Mysteries is
comfort concerning the afterlife for those initiated;[77] (5) the popularity of the
Mysteries has much to do with a love of association and a desire for status enhancement through multiple initiations.[78]

Part of the fascination of the Mysteries is their elusiveness. We know remarkably little about them. The practice of the *disciplina arcana*—maintaining secrecy about what was revealed through initiation—was so strict that it became
proverbial for keeping silence.[79] Information about the Mysteries that comes
from Christian critics needs to be carefully assessed for bias.[80] Our fullest information concerns the ancient rituals at Eleusis devoted to the goddess Demeter,
which celebrated the pattern of the death and renewal of the earth.[81] The Eleusinian Mysteries remained resolutely and exclusively local in character, and
their prestige was so great that even emperors traveled to the sacred place in

order to be among the initiates.[82] But even in the case of Eleusis, the precise elements of the ritual and myth remain obscure, although they were enacted in the presence of thousands.[83]

Mysteries progressively became part of Roman religion at least partly as a function of syncretism; gods originally native to Egypt and Syria were brought more fully—and not always without struggle—within the religious life of the empire. Now cults devoted to Cybele and Attis, Isis and Osiris (Serapis), and Mithras find a larger space within the expansive world of Greco-Roman poly-theism. As stated earlier, Cybele was formally invited to Rome under the title of Magna Mater in 204 BCE. Adjacent temples dedicated to Isis and Serapis were constructed in Rome around 43 BCE.[84] The Persian cult of Mithras arrived in Rome in the late first century BCE and expanded rapidly through the empire.[85]

Our best source for the religious sensibility connected to the Mysteries comes from Apuleius' picaresque novel, *Metamorphoses*.[86] It tells how the dabbling in magic of a young man named Lucius caused the goddess Tyche ("Fortune" or "Chance") to change him into an ass. Wearing the form of that animal, Lucius passes from one stage of alienation and degradation to another, ending up as a participant in a sexual sideshow. But one night on the beach at Cenchrae (the port for the city of Corinth), he has a vision of the goddess Isis.[87] She reveals herself to him as queen of the gods and supreme authority, capable of restoring him to his humanity in exchange for his devotion.[88] Lucius is promptly initiated into her Mystery,[89] finding in it participation in divine power, the restoration of his human form, and a hope for immortality. More than that, he gains greater success in his career as a lawyer. The novel makes clear that initiations into the Mysteries were multiple, for after a period of time, Lucius was initiated as well into the cult of Osiris, the consort of Isis.[90]

PILGRIMAGE

Implicit in the practices just described is the theme of religious pilgrimage, although it is not made thematic in the sources.[91] In polytheism, the divine power is distributed and most often local. The gods of one household could not simply be exchanged with those of another household; they needed to be honored at one's own hearth and table. One could pray to Minerva (that is, Athena) anywhere as patroness of crafts, but to offer her sacrifice one had to go to her temple on the Aventine hill. One could presumably seek guidance from Apollo anywhere, but to receive an oracle from Apollo, it was necessary to make the difficult trek to Delphi. Similarly, the healing power of the god Asclepius was exercised in a specific fashion in the temples dedicated to him in specific places. In order to be initiated into the cult of Demeter in Eleusis, one was required to travel to Athens, gather below the Acropolis in the *Eleusinion,* and then move with a great throng of people in solemn procession to Eleusis itself. The willingness to disrupt one's life to go to the place of power reveals both religion's ability to "organize life around itself" and how Greco-Roman religion in all these manifestations truly was about access to a divine power that could benefit humans in specific ways.

It is important to note that these modes of accessibility to divine power were not, either in theory or practice, mutually exclusive. Devotion to Asclepius or Apollo was by no means incompatible with initiation into the Mystery of Isis and Osiris. There is evidence not only for multiple initiations within cults but for pious people seeking initiation in multiple Mysteries.[92] Participation in Mysteries, furthermore, in no manner blocked full participation in the ordinary round of civic feasts and festivals in honor of the gods nor did it relieve devotees of the obligation of honoring the *lares* and *penates* of their own household. The point in all Greco-Roman religion was not correct doctrine and certainly not exclusive devotion. The point was the experience of power, and in that respect, Greco-Roman polytheism was a generous, cooperative, and noncompetitive religious system.

MAGIC

Precisely because access to transcendent power for human benefit was the point of Greco-Roman religion, it is necessary to at least acknowledge here the difficult issue of magic. Discussions of magic in the ancient as well as the contemporary world are complicated because of the social dynamics involved.[93] The charge of magic often serves a majority tradition to marginalize and discredit a tradition that, when viewed from within, considers itself as authentically "religious" as the regnant tradition. In antiquity, the charge of being a magician (*magos*) was frequently combined with that of being a charlatan (*goēs*) and is found in the polemic of opposing groups.[94] Nevertheless, magic was practiced in the Greco-Roman world, vigorously and often.[95] Its forms were various, but they all shared the use of powerful objects (such as amulets) and the casting of spells (using the names of gods).[96] There is some validity to the classic distinction between religion and magic as the difference between being acted on by divine powers and seeking to control divine powers (the difference between prayer and a spell). The more closely we examine all the forms of Greco-Roman religion, however, with its constant concern for access to power that benefits humans in the here and now, the hazier that distinction becomes.[97] In this sense, magic in the Greco-Roman world may be viewed as an extreme manifestation of a pervasive religious orientation.

WAYS OF BEING RELIGIOUS

If this catalog of religious phenomena in the Greco-Roman world could be extended almost indefinitely—and it could—the question grows more pressing: is there any meaningful way of organizing the data that threaten to overwhelm us? I have already suggested that analysis according to time periods or stages of development is not helpful: the mix of perceptions and practices is so complex that it is impossible to mark clearly defined epochs correlated to social or political factors, nor are there clear lines of internal development.[98] I have also stated that imposing categories drawn from Judaism or Christianity is inappropriate: we find no clash of theologies, no demands for exclusive loyalty, no competition for status as a uniquely true or uniquely effective manifestation of the divine.

In this book, I offer for consideration another way of giving some shape to and making some sense of the constant metamorphoses that make up Greco-Roman *thrēskeia*, namely, distinct ways of being religious. My focus is not only on the forms of religion but even more on the forms of religious sensibility. In my view, this approach not only clarifies aspects of Greco-Roman religion but makes possible a more meaningful set of comparisons to ancient Judaism and Christianity. These modes of religiosity involve distinct perceptions concerning divine power and corresponding responses to such perceptions. But before I sketch the four options that I have discerned (there may, indeed, be more), I must make one more preliminary point as vigorously as possible, namely, that despite the pervasively public character of Greco-Roman religion, by no means was everyone then, any more than people are now, equally religious. My four options comprise only those who are in some sense truly religious in their dispositions; not all ancient Greeks and Romans are included.

There was, in fact, a wide range of religious attitudes among the Gentiles speaking Greek and Latin. At one extreme were people whose concentration on religious practice was so intense, and whose credulity concerning the numinous was so marked, that they were considered by the more moderate to be superstitious. The term *deisidaimonia* can mean either "intensely religious" (in the good sense) or "superstitious" (in the bad sense).[99] The positive or negative nuance depended on the perspective of the speaker. Theophrastus provides a vivid depiction of the superstitious person: his "cowardice about divinity" drives him to a concern for purity and for religious initiations so exaggerated that today he would earn the clinical term "obsessive-compulsive."[100] Superstitious characters also populate Lucian of Samosata's satires: they are willing to believe any nonsense if it is sufficiently amazing.[101] Thoughtful observers like Plutarch considered superstition a vice rather than a virtue, because it was a religiosity driven by ignorance and fear.[102] He declares superstition to be worse than atheism, for if it is bad to deny the gods, it is even worse to think about them badly.

The credulous were the sort of people who were taken advantage of by those at the opposite extreme: the cynical manipulators of popular faith, who preyed upon the superstitious for their own fame and fortune. Lucian describes the philosophical charlatan Proteus Peregrinus, who used his public virtue as camouflage for private vice and was willing to do anything, even associate with despised Christians, in his quest for notoriety.[103] Peregrinus ends his life in a dramatic gesture of self-immolation before his followers, but Lucian regards it only as final evidence of his lust for vainglory.[104] Even more vivid is Lucian's satire of Alexander of Abonoteichus, a religious flim-flam artist who bilked the local populace of Paphlagonia by his invention of a new oracle cult—finding an egg in the mud, rigging a fake serpent out of a sock, taking advantage of dark rooms for effect.[105] The number of religious sideshow operators then, as now, probably corresponded to the number of those willing to be gulled.

Greco-Roman society also had critics of religion as it was commonly carried out. Some philosophers condemned the immorality found in religious myths (the "poets"), and others, most notably the Epicureans, based their whole manner of life on a rejection of the public round of religious ritual, which they regarded as superstitious, root and stem.[106] Not surprisingly, the satirist Lucian of Samosata portrays the Epicureans as distinctively immune to the religious frauds purveyed by charlatans.[107] He also depicts his ideal philosopher, Demonax, as a critic of traditional religious practices.[108] It is, to be sure, always difficult to assess satirists of religion, whether recent or ancient: are they, like Mark Twain, personally disappointed at religion, writing as angry lovers; or are they, like H. L. Mencken, simply disgusted at human folly, writing from a stance of intellectual superiority?

An even more devastating challenge to Greco-Roman religion may have been posed not by those who critiqued it but by those who simply ignored it. Inscriptions tell us a great deal about religious associations, and art informs us about sacrifices and festivals. But extant graffiti is also as coarsely and irreverently profane as that found on contemporary walls.[109] Comic dramatists from Aristophanes to Plautus wrote plays of considerable popular appeal that used religion, when they do, mostly as an incidental backdrop to profane (in every sense of the term) human activity.[110] And while many of the extant Greco-Roman novels—written between the first century BCE and fourth century CE— testify to the sort of pervasive religiosity described in this chapter (they are replete with visions, sacrifices, prayers, oracles, and even elements of magic,

such as necromancy), Petronius' *Satyrika* shows us characters seemingly devoid of any impulses beyond those having to do with pleasure and self-
preservation.[111]

When I turn in succeeding chapters to the "ways of being religious" in the
Greco-Roman world, then, I trust that readers will share my assumption that
the writers whom I isolate for analysis represent a tiny sample of the actual religious world of the ancient Mediterranean. They are special in three critical
ways. First, they are sufficiently passionate about the subject of religion to devote time and energy to engage it in their writing. Second, they are sufficiently
wealthy or well born to have enjoyed a certain level of education to enable
them to produce religious literature. Third, their works have, for whatever reasons, either survived through Christian transmission or have been recovered
through discovery, while many others—representing perhaps other varieties of
religious sensibility—remain unknown to us. With these cautions in mind,
then, I propose the four "ways" or "types" of religiosity that I consider well attested in the literature. They are distinguished by distinct perceptions concerning power and by corresponding responses to those perceptions.

THE WAY OF PARTICIPATION IN DIVINE BENEFITS

This type encompasses virtually all the religious perceptions and practices
I have described up to this point. Its emphasis is on the negotiation of divine
power in the present life, even when it has one eye on the future. The divine
dynamis is conceived as available to humans in the empirical world: revealing
through prophecy, healing through revelation, providing security and status
through Mysteries, enabling and providing for the daily successes of individuals,
households, cities, and empires. The role of sacrifice and prayer is to open the
channel for the flow of such power. Attention to the moral agency of the wor-
shipper may get some small attention, but in the extant sources it does not hold
a central place. If this type were asked what *salvation* meant, the instinctive response would be in terms of safety and success. The extreme version of this
type, as I have suggested, is found in the practice of magic. A splendid example
of this mode of religious sensibility is the rhetorician Aelius Aristides, whom I
will consider in the next chapter.

THE WAY OF MORAL TRANSFORMATION

The main examples of this type of religious sensibility are the moral philosophers. In Chapter 2, I explained how the categories of religious studies enable
us to see the religious character of the life found in some philosophical schools.
Among Pythagoreans—and, to a lesser degree, among Epicureans—we find

founders who have divine status ascribed to them, community of possessions, notions of purity, stages of admission and probation (as in the initiations of Mysteries), and the practice of mutual correction.[112] Even philosophers in the Cynic-Stoic tradition, though individualistic, often considered philosophy in terms of a way of life rather than a set of ideas and recognized certain marks of identity (long beard, robe, staff, leather purse, sandals, itinerancy) and social role (critic, gadfly, prophet, scout).[113] It is among philosophers that we find conversion in two senses: turning from vice to virtue, and turning from one school to another.[114] Therefore, it is also in philosophy that we find competition for adherents, as well as polemic directed against adherents of competing schools; if philosophers agreed on the goal, they disagreed on which school best achieved the goal.[115] In short, a great deal of what is regarded as true religion among many Christians is found among Greco-Roman philosophers.

My focus in this discussion is not on those religious forms but on a distinct religious sensibility. In moralists such as Dio of Prusa or Epictetus, we do not find a dismissal of popular piety of the sort ascribed to Demonax. But neither do we find any particular attention given to those manifestations of divine *dynamis* outside moral agency—the proportions are the opposite of those in Type A. They concentrate instead on the mandate implicit in being called by God to live a life worthy of God: their way is to imitate the divine agency in the world by the transformation of their life through moral effort, thus extending divine blessings to others. The divine power is present immanently through their own activity in the world. In this way of being religious, salvation (if the term should ever arise) is understood not in terms of participating in the benefits of security and success. Indeed, risk and adversity is frequently a part of the philosopher's countercultural stance.[116] Rather, salvation is understood in terms of the triumph of the human spirit—or, in Stoic terminology, of the divine *pneuma*—over ignorance and moral inertia. The philosophers' pattern of life was just as real and frequently more concentrated than that of those seeking oracles or healing; their piety was as real and often more intense—indeed, the philosophical life was a process of healing from vice.[117] But the arena of divine activity was, for them, moral transformation. To apply one of their favorite metaphors, theirs was an athletic form of religion.[118] In Chapter 5, I will analyze Epictetus as the best Greco-Roman example of this way of being religious.

THE WAY OF TRANSCENDING THE WORLD

The first two types are the easiest to locate, once contemporary categories of analysis enable us to see some philosophers as intensely religious even if they do not use specifically religious language. The third type is clear enough conceptually, but by its very nature is more difficult to pin down. It is especially hard to detect as a precise mode of religiosity before the rise of Christianity because it came to full flowering late. Its roots within Hellenism, however, are both deep and ancient.

It derives from the Orphic tradition (Orpheus is the ancient singer who gives access to the underworld) and from the tradition's permutations within the Pythagorean and Platonic worldviews, and it can be associated with certain aspects of the Mysteries as well. Orpheus was early aligned with the god Dionysius, whose myth tells of his dismemberment, the scattering of his body parts, and his reassembling—a myth that supports an unhappy start to existence and a perilous path to rescue.[119] This type can perhaps best be located by means of contrast to the first mode (Type A), which is fundamentally positive in its appreciation of the divine presence and power in the world, and to the second mode (Type B), which is basically positive concerning the power to change human behavior in a manner worthy of the divine. In this third way, the world and human existence are viewed more negatively, in terms of illusion and entrapment. The body is a tomb. Salvation is to be found not in the power made available through worldly systems, nor through moral endeavor, but by purification from the body and its worldly entanglements through a process revealed to elect people, leading to the eventual liberation of the soul, which alone is worth saving.[120] The human spirit is related through knowledge to a realm that transcends the empirical world of deception and corruption and seeks union with the realm that is the soul's true home. The earliest full expression of this sensibility within the Greco-Roman world—at least as is known to us and is extant— is the Hermetic literature, above all the tractate *Poimandres*, which is the subject of analysis in Chapter 6.

THE WAY OF STABILIZING THE WORLD

In some ways, this type is difficult to distinguish adequately from Type A, with which it has much in common. It could be regarded, in fact, as the "supply-side" of religiousness Type A (participation in divine benefits). I think here of all the keepers of shrines and temples (*neōkoroi*), all ministers and mystagogues of cults, all prophets who translated oracles and examined entrails and Sibylline utterances, all therapists who aided the god Asclepius in his healing work, all "liturgists" who organized and facilitated the festivals, all priests who carried out sacrifices, all Vestal Virgins whose presence and dedication ensured the permanence of the city. From one perspective, these are all "keepers of the flame" that enable the divine benefits to flow in all the religious phenomena identified as Type A.[121] From another perspective, while some such roles are inherited, others are chosen and elected and therefore draw certain kinds of people—or people with certain kinds of perceptions—to them. This, I am suggesting, is the religious sensibility of the emperor Augustus, who as *pontifex* reformed and restored traditional religion precisely to restore and stabilize the empire.[122] Such a religious sensibility is conscious of the political dimensions of religion in the fullest sense—that religion can be the glue or solvent of society—and chooses to cultivate religion's stabilizing functions through what can be termed, in a neutral rather than negative sense, priestcraft. This, I am suggesting, is the part of the many-sided Plutarch that is less concerned with moral development than with the continued success of the cult at Delphi, where he serves as priest of Apollo, the same part that led him to attack Epicureanism most vigorously because its atheism threatened the stability of the social order, which depended on the recognition and service of the gods.

These are the types of religiosity that I think can be found in the confusing welter of Greco-Roman religion and that enable meaningful comparison with Christianity in the first centuries of its development. In order to make such comparison more responsible, it is necessary to develop more fully the examples I have selected to represent each of the types: Aelius Aristides, Epictetus, *Poimandres*, and Plutarch.

4

RELIGION AS PARTICIPATION IN DIVINE
BENEFITS: AELIUS ARISTIDES

My preliminary profile of Greco-Roman religion provides a framework for the closer analysis of the four types of religiosity our sources suggest. I have suggested that these ways of being religious are distinguished on the basis of their perceptions concerning the divine *dynamis* (power): how access to it is attained and what its effects on humans are. The panoply of religious phenomena displayed in the previous chapter are all expressions of Religiousness A, participation in divine benefits: sacrifices and prayers, prophecy and healings, Mysteries and pilgrimages are not in competition but are complementary: the point of them all is making divine benefits available to humans. This mode of religiosity is optimistic about the empirical world as the arena of divine activity. It is intensely pragmatic about the benefits the gods offer: salvation involves security and success in this mortal life. If assurance concerning an afterlife can be offered by a Mystery, so much the better, but initiation into a cult is in any case worthwhile for the status elevation and social network it makes available.

No better representative of Religiousness A can be imagined than the second-century rhetorician Aelius Aristides (117–180 CE). He shows us how a powerful polytheistic piety could flourish throughout the period of Christianity's early development. Aelius Aristides was born around the time Ignatius of Antioch faced martyrdom, saw his rhetorical career develop in the same period that Justin Martyr was teaching, and died while Irenaeus was bishop of Lyons. He also shows that this way of being religious was found as much among the wealthy, well educated, and well traveled as it was among the poor, the ignorant, or the isolated: he was so wealthy that he never needed to take fees for his speaking, and he lived on a number of estates; his education was the best his era offered, including training both in rhetoric and philosophy; and despite his many illnesses, he traveled extensively in Egypt, Asia Minor, Greece, and Italy. Most of all, Aristides shows how the many forms of Greco-Roman religion could be embraced by a single individual with sincerity, enthusiasm, and even fervor.

AELIUS ARISTIDES AND THE SECOND SOPHISTIC

Aristides was a well-known public figure, part of a cultural phenomenon generally known as "the Second Sophistic."[1] As with virtually every other historical category, scholars debate the precise dimensions and character of the phenomenon that was first named in the early third century by Flavius Philostratus (170–205) in his *Lives of Sophists* (*Bioi Sophistōn* = VS), but certain aspects of the movement are clear.[2] For Philostratus, the term referred to the continuation of a rhetorical tradition that went back to classical Athens: while noteworthy rhetoricians like Gorgias entered into serious philosophical debate, there were other Athenian orators, notably, Aeschines (born in 389 BCE and the rival of Demosthenes), who specialized in easy rhetorical display and taught this skill to students. Philostratus considered the "Second Sophistic" to be the continuation during the time of the Roman *imperium* of the Greek tradition of epideictic rhetoric, with a specific emphasis on a public display of *ex tempore* fluency.

The term "Sophist" (*sophistēs*) was, even in ancient times, controverted.[3] For some who considered themselves philosophers, "Sophists" were not seekers of wisdom (*sophia*) but were charlatans who were willing to argue any side for a fee.[4] Indeed, even for some included among Philostratus' list of Sophists, notably, Dio of Prusa, *sophistēs* was a term of reproach to be used polemically against false teachers.[5] For Philostratus, however, and for many present-day scholars, the term applies to public intellectuals in the Greek-speaking cities of Greece and Asia Minor who kept alive the ancient ideal of *paideia* through their devotion to public speaking. They were proficient in epideictic oratory, to be sure, able to discourse with a moment's notice on matters great or small, and they gathered fees and awards for such public displays that served both to entertain and instruct. Such displays were more than a source of revenue; they were also competitive exercises that advanced the *philotimia* ("ambition"/"love of honor") of the rhetoricians.[6] In addition to declaiming at festivals and competitions, Sophists were educators. They drew students to themselves and shared with their disciples their vast knowledge of classical texts and of rhetorical technique. Sophists could also play a genuinely public role as mediators in disputes between cities or in representing cities to the emperor.

In his treatment of Aelius Aristides, Philostratus touches on the "poor health from boyhood" that the biographer understood to be a "palsy of the muscles," but emphasized that "he did not fail to work hard" (*VS*, 581) and focuses on the strengths and weaknesses of his oratory.[7] On the negative side, Philostratus notes that Aristides was not naturally talented in extempore eloquence, did not often address crowds—not being able to control his irritation at a crowd's failure to applaud—and did not travel as widely as other speakers (*VS*, 583). He acknowledges that some of Aristides' rhetorical efforts can be criticized, stating that in some passages the orator "driveled somewhat and has fallen into affectation" (*VS*, 585). On the positive side, Philostratus admits that even though Aristides did not come naturally to extempore discourse, he practiced it and could be effective at it (*VS*, 583). Most of all, though, he praises the orator's learning and diligence: "He strove after extreme accuracy, and turned his attention to the ancient writers" (*VS*, 582). Indeed, he is reported as telling the emperor that "I am one of those who do not vomit their speeches but try to make them perfect" (*VS*, 583). Philostratus praises "the man's erudition, force, and power of characterization, and it is by these that he ought to be estimated," and concludes, "Aristides was of all the sophists most deeply versed in his art, and his strength lay in the elaborate cogitation of a theme" (*VS*, 585). He also praises the rhetorician for his role in gaining imperial help in rebuilding the city of Smyrna when it had been destroyed by earthquake: "To say that Aristides founded Smyrna is no mere boastful eulogy but most just and true" (*VS*, 582).

In addition to Philostratus' *Lives*, a variety of inscriptions and literary works—in particular, the multifarious writings of Lucian of Samosata and the *Orations* of Dio of Prusa—testify to the activity and literary production of the Sophists.[8] A substantial number of Aelius Aristides' *Orations* have survived in a large number of manuscripts, testifying to the high esteem in which he was held as a model of excellence in rhetoric by later practitioners, both pagan and Christian. The English translation of his complete works includes 53 orations, six of them his *Sacred Tales*. An appendix to this edition, however, lists as lost some 40 orations that are mentioned by Aristides, as well as an additional 26 discourses mentioned by other ancient authors.[9] Aristides also mentions letters and two commentaries (one of them containing 300,000 lines of commentary on his dreams).[10] Despite his illnesses, the evidence suggests that he was a productive and respected public intellectual within the intensely competitive world of the Second Sophistic.

Aristides' extant orations provide ample support for the respect accorded him in antiquity, although one of his most admired qualities—the purity of his diction and the perfection of his cadences—cannot be as appreciated by us as it was by his linguistically competent contemporaries. His "Panathenaic Oration" (*Oration*, 1) is one among a glittering collection of orations in praise of cities (see 17–22) and regions (36) and is an exceptional display of sustained epideictic rhetoric. His three orations in response to Plato (2–4) are remarkable both for their close and critical reading of the philosopher and for their impassioned defense of the rhetorical art against the slanders of the great Athenian. His ability to declaim convincingly on either side of an issue is demonstrated in the "set-piece" orations devoted to ancient historical situations in the history of Greece (5–16). A sense of graceful spontaneity (undoubtedly the fruit of careful preparation) is communicated by his orations on the occasion of birthdays and funerals (30–32).

The orations composed in defense of his own practice as an orator (*Orations*, 28, 33, 34) reveal not only an expected level of *philotimia* with respect to himself but also an almost reverential sense of the importance of the art to which he had committed his skills. Indeed, he uses the language of the Mysteries when speaking of "initiation" into the art of oratory (34). Finally, a significant number of his orations are devoted (and dedicated to) the gods (37–46), revealing, even apart from the *Sacred Tales*, a distinct religious sensibility. Before considering that religious devotion more closely, it is helpful to provide a sketch of Aristides' life, as it can be reconstructed from the *Lives of the Sophists* and his own orations.

A SKETCH OF ARISTIDES' LIFE

Aelius Aristides was born in the town of Hadriani in Mysia in 117 CE.[11] His father was a priest of Zeus and a citizen of the city of Smyrna. The family gained Roman citizenship in 123. At Smyrna, Aristides was educated in grammar and rhetoric, and he studied philosophy in Athens. When he was 24 years old he took a tour of Egypt, visiting Alexandria and sailing up the Nile. He fell sick for the first time and sailed back to Smyrna. On this occasion he turned to the god Serapis as a savior from his illness (*Oration*, 45).

Illness would dominate most of the rest of his life. At age 26 he undertook an expedition to Rome but fell ill while still on his estate and then grew progressively worse on a wintertime journey that seemed interminable, forcing him finally to return by means of a horrific sea voyage to the warm springs outside Smyrna. It was during this period (December 143) that he received his first revelation from the healing god Asclepius, to whom he would dedicate the rest of his life and career. In 145 CE, when he was 28, he felt himself summoned by the god to stay at the Asclepium in Pergamum. He remained there for two full years with a group of fellow devotees who were also, to varying degrees, intellectuals. During this period, he experienced revelatory dreams and pursued the therapies recommended by the god. By no means were his studies neglected; during this period he wrote two of his orations in response to Plato (*Orations*, 2 and 4), an appreciation of his student Apellas (30), and a lengthy defense of the self-praise he had employed in an earlier speech (28).

At the age of 30 he began more active writing and lecturing, convinced that his rhetorical career was sponsored and directed by the god Asclepius: we can date several major discourses between 147 and 152 (*Orations*, 24, 32, 36, and 43). In 153, he was of strong enough health to travel frequently between his several estates, Smyrna, and Pergamum. During this time, his efforts were largely directed to resisting several efforts to assign him an official role in society. He engaged in legal maneuvers to reject his election as a high priest of Asia in 147, to serve as tax collector in Smyrna in 152, and to act as keeper of the peace in the province of Asia in 153. He was granted immunity from holding office and for the next 12 years (154–165) fully resumed his rhetorical career, lecturing in Greece (Athens and Corinth) and in Rome. He accepted students, although he refused to accept fees for his instruction (3.98–99). And despite developing a case of smallpox in 165 (at the age of 48), he continued to make public appearances and deliver orations through 176, his career reaching its apex with his speech that year (at the age of 59) before the emperor Marcus Aurelius in Smyrna. The next year (177), Smyrna was destroyed by earthquake, and Aristides was instrumental in securing imperial assistance for the restoration of the city (*Orations*, 18–21). These efforts appeared to end his active career, and he retired to his estate in Mysia, dying at the age of 63 in 180.

Even this outline of Aristides' life makes clear the critical role played by three factors: his recurrent and complex physical ailments, his consuming devotion to the god Asclepius, and his exalted sense of calling as an orator. Weighing these factors is difficult, and quite different evaluations can result. C. A. Behr, who has studied Aristides as closely as anyone, regards him as a deeply neurotic and vain person and his religious devotion as an aspect of his personality disorder. Behr refers to the orator's companions at the Asclepium at Pergamum as a "cultivated circle of neurasthenics" and to his dreams as "the psychopathology of 130 dreams"; Behr further suggests that an "unfortunate result of this period of [Aristides'] life was the notion that his literary career was due to Asclepius' grace," with the result that "his recovery was impeded." Behr calls Aristides' rejection of public service the manifestation of a personality "too insecure to commit himself to any obligation." After his spell of smallpox in 165, "his neurotic predispositions marred the rest of his life," and of the following 10 years Behr notes that Aristides "still made public appearances, but his physical complaints and his religious fixation resumed."[12]

Similar characterizations of Aristides as a "hypochondriac" and his religious behavior as "neurotic" are easy to find.[13] They can be countered, to be sure, by other evaluations that are more positive toward his religious experiences and convictions, and a more mature understanding of chronic illness—its complex causes and even more complex psychosomatic corollaries—ought at least to caution us against facilely applying the terms "neurotic" and "hypochondriac" to an ancient figure who seemed to have been afflicted by chronic physical distress.[14] It is also possible to ask whether Aristides' life of "sickness and salvation" might have helped rather than "impeded" his vocation as orator. Certainly, Philostratus considers Aristides' physical troubles as insignificant compared with his accomplishments and regards Aristides' art as more learned and profound because not dissipated in frequent public declamation. He refers to the *Sacred Tales* only in literary terms, never suggesting that Aristides was odd or unusual because of his religious convictions.[15]

It is not, however, the health or "authenticity" of Aristides' religion that is of interest to my investigation, but rather the way in which it reveals a distinct "way of being religious" in the Greco-Roman world, a way that I sketched in broad terms in the preliminary profile but now can examine in the astonishingly rich and revealing writings of one of antiquity's most educated and articulate speakers.

PARTICIPATION IN DIVINE BENEFITS

I begin with the evidence provided by Aristides' orations apart from the six that are distinguished as *The Sacred Tales,* not only to make the point that there was no gap between what the orator wrote for public consumption and what he composed for his personal reflection, but also because his orations exhibit so clearly the characteristics of what I have called Religiousness A. Virtually all the phenomena described in the previous chapter are attested to in his orations. His world is one of cities and gods in complex interaction (3.392); he speaks often of festivals (1.341) and of temples (29.4): in his *ekphrasis* of the city of Smyrna, he describes a visitor moving from temple to temple throughout the city (17.10–11; 18.6), and elsewhere he refers to the treasure that is stored in temples (3.106). He mentions "priests and prophets" in the same breath (3.12; 3.347; 36.1). Just as there are temples everywhere, so also are there gods everywhere (43.18) to whom humans give honor (1.338), not least by prayer (3.245; 24.17; 26.108–109; 30.1; 30.28); the Cynics are reviled because they do not believe in the gods (3.671–672), just as they do nothing to build the character of cities. He says, "They have never spoken, discovered, or written a fruitful word; they have never added adornment to national festivals, never honored the gods, never given advice to the cities, never consoled those in grief, never cared for decorum in their speech" (3.672).

Aristides pays particular attention to all of the manifestations of revelation or prophecy, including oracles (*Orations*, 1.399; 2.34–45; 2.46–49; 2.78; 2.82; 3.617; 28.103), especially those associated with the god Apollo (1.399; 2.86–88; 27.5; 28.14–15; 40.11) and above all those deriving from the shrine at Delphi (1.191; 3.311–324; 28.14–15, 28.81; 45.7), omens (29.12), and the practice of *haruspices* (2.165). Undoubtedly because of his personal experience, revelations of the gods through dreams are given special importance (45.7). He knows of, and has a personal interest in, the healing shrine at Epidaurus (2.83; 2.253; 38.21; 39.5). He speaks of the Mysteries with some frequency, paying particular respect to the most ancient rites at Eleusis (1.330; 1.334; 1.336–373; 23.25), where one is accorded, he says, "fairer hopes about death" (22.10). His own devotion to Asclepius he construes in terms of a Mystery (23.16), and oratory itself he considers a form of Mystery into which one is initiated (28.135; 32.7). He is perfectly at home in the context of emperor worship. He speaks of prayers to the gods for the emperor as well as prayers to the emperor (26.102); he says that the emperors "act under the guidance of the will of the gods" (20.1) and refers easily to "the gods and you" [emperors] (19. 6) and "divine rulers" (19.11), who share in divinity (27.35–37).

Aristides honors all the Greek gods and heroes in his orations: Poseidon (*Orations*, 3.276; 3.290; 17.16; 46.4), Hera (26.104–105), Hermes (28.103), Heracles (3.191–192 [with Pan]; 3.276 [with Poseidon]; 3.327; 34.59–60; 40.12; 38.26). He devotes orations to Athena (1.404; 26.104–105; 28.2; 37.2), Aphrodite (33.20), Dionysus (17.5–6; 24.52; 29.4; 29.30), and Orpheus (3.254), Athena (37), Heracles (40) and Dionysus (41). In Aristides' world, there is no competition among all these gods and goddesses; they are all to be honored, for they all seek the good of humans. They do this especially through acts of saving or healing (the verb *sōzein* carries both connotations): the gods in general and Heracles in particular are said to bring healing (2.62–65; 40.12).

Nevertheless, Aristides singles out three gods in particular for frequent and particular attention. He mentions Zeus often (*Orations*, 1.190; 1.322; 4.19; 18.1; 24.42; 26.104–105; 28.45–50; 28.109) as an individual god and devotes an entire oration (43) to him, but as in the works of other Greco-Roman authors, Zeus can also stand for the powers of the gods as a whole ("Zeus and you other gods"; 23.57). It is Zeus understood in this sense that is the subject of those few statements of Aristides that approach the theological. God, he declares, is the measure of all things (26.2) and creates everything (2.379; 3.100; 43.7–15). He gives power to humans and to the other gods (43.17). All things are to be attributed to Zeus (36.104): "Everything everywhere is filled with Zeus, and he is present everywhere at every deed" (43.256). Aristides is radiantly optimistic about the divine order. There is no evil among the gods, he declares, and all the acts of God are good (46.36). He sees "the providence of one of the gods" at work in everything (16.13; 16.22) and several times uses the phrase "some god has arranged all this" (see 7.10; 13.9). His sense of providence is personal and immediate, especially when "some god" is Asclepius, as we shall soon see.

The second god singled out by Aristides is Serapis. He refers to both Serapis and Asclepius as "savior gods" (*Orations*, 3.265–266; 27.39). We remember that when he became ill as a young man in Egypt, Aristides turned to Serapis for healing, and all of *Oration* 45 is dedicated to this "savior god." As in the case of Zeus, Aristides can ascribe to this single god attributes of "the divine" in the largest sense: "The deeds of Serapis are those by which the life of mankind is saved and administered" (45.16–17); "Thus he passes through every aspect of our lives and no place has been left untouched by this god" (45.19). Aristides' piety is given splendid expression in his statement concerning the benefits given by Serapis: "Let it be left to the Egyptian priests and writers to say and to know who, indeed, the god is and what is his nature. But our praise would be sufficient for the present if we should tell of the number and nature of the benefits he has shown to have given to mankind" (45.15). For Aristides generally, what mattered about the gods was that they were the source of benefits (1.311), and what made Serapis especially deserving of praise was that he brought Aristides safely to Smyrna (45.33).

Scholarly attention to Aristides' personal devotion to the healing god Asclepius is sometimes restricted to the *Sacred Tales*, but in fact the orator's extraordinary love for this god is expressed in many of his other orations as well (see, for example, *Orations*, 2.75; 19.6; 20.4; 21.19; 23.15; 23.16; 26.105; 27.2–3). Asclepius, he says, heals and thereby assists Zeus (43.27). Aristides speaks of Asclepius in terms of a Mystery (28.13), refers to his sacred games (30.25), connects him to prophecy through descent from Apollo (30.26; 42.4), and declares that the god possesses all power (42.5) and saves mankind (39.11; 39.14). Speaking of Pergamum, Aristides says, "the god came from Epidaurus and fell in love with this spot" (39.5; see also 23.15). Most striking is the way in which Aristides speaks of his own experience of the god Asclepius. In his response to Plato, "In Defense of Oratory," he declares, "Truly, just as the seers, initiated into the service of the gods who have given their name to their specialty, I have knowledge from the gods themselves. Through their aid, contrary to the likelihood of the circumstances,

I am alive, having escaped at different times through various kinds of consolation and advice on the part of the god" (2.67). In his speech "Concerning Concord," he says,

> And neither membership in a chorus, nor the companionship of a voyage, nor having the same teachers is so great a circumstance, as the gain and profit in having been fellow pilgrims at the Temple of Asclepius and having been initiated into the highest of rites under the fairest and most perfect Torch-Bearer and Mystagogue, and under him to whom every law of necessity yields. I myself am one of those who, under the god's protection, have lived not twice, but many, various lives, and who on this account regard their disease as profitable, and who in addition have won approval, in place of which I would not choose all the felicity of mankind. (*Oration*, 23.16)

In his "Oration Regarding Asclepius," Aristides again speaks of the many lives he has had because of the gift of this god: "Some say that they were resurrected when they were dead. . . . [W]e have received this benefit not only once, but it is not even easy to say how often" (*Oration*, 42.6). He is referring, it is clear, to the many recoveries from illness that he attributes to the god. Asclepius is, then, Aristides' patron (33.2), who gives him benefits (33.17; 42.5). He is, for Aristides, "the most gracious and generous of the gods" (39.5), who has elevated the orator to friendship with the emperor (42.14) and to whom the orator makes sacrifice and offers incense and daily orations (42.2). Indeed, the best gift that the god gave Aristides, the one that means the most to this orator most dedicated to his art, is the gift of oratory itself (42.12). Asclepius is his patron specifically with regard to oratory (28.156). The god proposes the subject of the orator's discourse (38.2) and even guides him in his speech (38.42). In sum, even without the *Sacred Tales*—to which Aristides makes reference in *Oration* 42.4—we would know a great deal about the intensity of the orator's love for the god Asclepius and the reasons for his devotion.

THE SACRED TALES

The six orations that make up Aristides' *Sacred Tales* (*ST*) provide rare access to a firsthand account of ancient religious experience.[16] They do not, however, make for easy reading. Present-day readers confront three distinct difficulties. The first is that the literary shape of the *Tales* is complex, shifting the reader from point to point in the author's life without much by way of guidance. The date of final composition is late in the orator's life (170–171), and the starting point seems to have been a diary that Aristides had composed some four years earlier, tracing his experience day by day from January 4 to February 15, 166 (*ST*, 1.5–57). From that point on, the author relates his memories of his experiences with the god without any chronological consistency. Lacking any clear narrative or thematic logic, readers can easily lose interest.[17]

The second difficulty is historical and cultural. The *Sacred Tales* assume the conditions of a world foreign to readers living in first-world conditions: a world in which severe weather was a threat more than an inconvenience, and in which, even for the wealthy, those traveling by sea were faced with the constant danger of storm and shipwreck, while those traveling by land were faced with the rigors of dangerous weather and unreliable lodging.[18] The *Tales* also suppose a world of sickness and healing at temples dedicated to the god Asclepius in places such as Epidaurus and Pergamum, where doctors could also be mystagogues and prescriptions revealed through dreams could compete or cooperate with those dictated by doctors. Both the range of symptoms and the variety of regimens can seem alien to readers who are familiar only with twenty-first-century medical practice.[19] Finally, the confidence that dreams, when properly interpreted, are genuinely revelatory is one shared widely in antiquity, giving rise to the science of oneirocriticism.[20]

The third difficulty is the extravagance of Aelius Aristides' language concerning every subject—his travels, his sicknesses, his regimens[21]—but above all concerning his own glory. He is not exceptional among ancients in his *philotimia*, but we do not often find in other ancient sources such naked expressions of what we would today consider vanity.[22] The same heightened, perhaps exaggerated, sensibility applies as well to his language about his religious experience. The evidence of his work supports the claim that Aristides was, indeed, exceptional in his talent, but his constant preoccupation with his exceptional excellence is culturally foreign to present-day readers.

Central to the *Sacred Tales* is the recounting of Aristides' dreams, which often included revelatory visions. He was once rebuked for not having written them down (2.1) but then makes clear that he had made notes of them all along (2.2); these notes were perhaps the basis of his extended commentaries on the dreams (no longer extant) and "The Book of Dreams" to which he makes reference (2.8). Short accounts of dreams run through the *Tales* (1.7; 1.9; 1.56; 3.3; 3.20; 3.21; 3.23; 3.25; 5.8; 5.11; 5.20), but of particular significance are those involving a divine vision (1.8; 1.76; 1.78; 4.56; 4.58–60; 5.22–24; 5.31; 5.44). The pattern seems to have begun with his first major illness, when he had a dream vision of Isis and Serapis (3.45–46) and attributed to them his safe arrival in Serapis, where he subsequently offered them sacrifice (3.49). On another occasion, he also had a dream vision involving Athena (2.41).

Most important were the experiences he had of his "savior god," Asclepius. His first dream vision of the god also occurred in the period of his first serious illness, leading him to cry out while still in his dream, "Great is Asclepius! The order is accomplished!" (2.7); subsequently, Asclepius appeared to him regularly (for example, 1.17; 1.66; 1.71; 2.13; 2.18 [as Apollo]). Particularly impressive is Aristides' description of one such vision: "For there was a seeming, as it were, to touch him and to perceive that he himself had come, and to be between sleep and waking, and to wish to look up and to be in anguish that he might depart too soon, and to strain the ears and to hear some things as in a dream, some as in a waking state. Hair stood straight, and there were tears with joy, and the pride of one's heart was inoffensive. And what man could describe these things in words? If any man has been initiated, he knows and understands" (2.32). Aristides took these visions with the greatest seriousness. He considered them to be prophetic in character (2.17; 5.16). Through the dreams, the god delivered oracles (4.5; 4.45) and gave commands (1.72; 4.108) that Aristides sought to obey (see 1.69; 3.40–41).

The contents of these dreams were various. In some, Aristides communed with great men of the past, including Plato and Alexander the Great (4.25; 4.48). In others, he received praise from the emperor, who expressed pleasure at Aristides being at once morally good and a good orator (1.49). In some, he composed hymns to the gods, above all Asclepius (3.4; 4.4), and even experienced a sense of identity with his god (4.51). He learned things about his illness (1.56) and received directly from Asclepius directions on how to treat it (2.26–27). In still other dreams, he gained ideas concerning oratorical themes (1.19; 1.35–37; 4.41; 5.16). Asclepius, in fact, took a direct hand in sponsoring and directing Aristides' career as a Sophist. In one dream vision, the god commands Aristides not to abandon oratory because of his illness (4.14) but rather to speak (4.29): "I thought I was giving an oratorical display and spoke among certain people, and in the midst of the speech with which I contended, I called on the god in this way, 'Lord Asclepius, if in fact I excel in oratory and excel much, grant me health and cause the envious to burst!' I happened to have seen these things in the dream, and when it was day, I took up some book and read it. In it I found what I had said" (4.69).

With respect both to his health and to his oratory, then, Asclepius was Aristides' "Lord": indeed, the two forms of "salvation" were inextricably mixed; the god, he declared, was the source both of obedience and of oratory (2.82), and in many ways, the best part of Aristides' experience was the way he enjoyed "communion in dreams" with the god (4.11; 4.25). He speaks of the "contentment and self-sufficiency" that came on him when he obeyed the god and how "there arose a feeling of comfort, and sometimes everything which pained me went completely away" (4.38).

In the *Sacred Tales*, there are really only two characters, Aristides and Asclepius. The doctors serve as foils who prescribe remedies (5.9) and perform procedures (2.47), make false predictions concerning Aristides' demise (2.39), fail to understand his illness (2.69), and express doubt concerning the god's prescriptions (2.34). The orator must decide whether to obey the god or the doctors (1.63), but since the god's advice is always better than that of the doctors or his friends (2.72–73), the doctors ultimately join Aristides' fretful friends (1.63) in yielding to the god (1.57) and serving as witnesses to the Asclepius' prescience and power (1.67; 2.20; 2.51). Aristides is grateful when relatives and acquaintances recover from their ailments (1.72; 1.78), but when the daughter of a foster sister falls ill and dies in the orator's absence, he declares, "This did not take place without some divine agency" (5.19–21), and when still another foster niece dies, he notes only that "some one of the gods guided me, whoever the god was" (5.27). It is not that Aristides is totally self-preoccupied; he does extend himself to help others (1.74–75; 1.78). But ultimately, it is what the god has done for him that sustains his interest.

How, then, does Aristides conceive of the benefits given by his patron god? What constitutes "salvation"? He naturally attributes the most obvious sort of rescues to Asclepius: it was the god who saved him from shipwreck (2.14) and the storm (4.36). Every form of ease in his symptoms is also ascribed to the directions of the god (for example, 3.14). After bathing in obedience to Asclepius' command, Aristides relates, "When I came out, all my skin had a rosy hue and there was a lightness throughout my body. There was also much shouting from those present and those coming up, shouting that celebrated phrase, 'Great is Asclepius!'" (2.21; see also 2.49). Aristides clearly did not, however, experience the sort of instantaneous "healing" that is the staple of the testimonies found at Epidaurus. His ailments recurred throughout his life, albeit with times of significant respite. The salvation wrought by Asclepius in the orator was not the cessation of troubles but the power to endure and even surmount them: "If someone should take these things into account and consider with how many and what sort of sufferings and with what necessary result for these he bore me to the sea and rivers and wells, and commanded me to contend with the winter, he will say that it is all truly beyond miracles, and he will see more clearly the power and the providence of the god, and will rejoice with me for the honor which I had, and would not be more grieved because of my sickness" (2.59).

Aristides' ability to endure, to overcome his symptoms, became the greatest proof of the god's power and providence. And the best gift of all was that

Asclepius enabled Aristides to continue his work as an orator, despite his physical afflictions. This was, in his eyes, an ongoing miracle. He remarks that the god's prescription to continue his oratory "was like an order to fly, the practice of oratory for one who could not breathe" (*ST*, 4.17), yet because he trusted the god, the strength to speak kept coming (4.22). On one occasion, in agony with a toothache, he began by the god's order to deliver his speech and found in the course of its delivery that the toothache had disappeared (4.30). He says, "The continual activity of the god is marvelous" (5.38).

The experience of this power was for Aristides like initiation into a Mystery (*ST*, 4.7–8), and it stirred in him all his ambition for the art of which he had despaired (4.47). He was living in effect a new life because of the god's intervention and continuing assistance: "Thus I had my life up to this time from the gods, and after this, I was given a new life from the gods, and, as it were, this kind of exchange occurred" (4.15). He was able to travel (4.8), join in debate (4.17–18; 5.40), and even engage in extempore speaking (5.41), all with the god's assistance (4.24). The point is made simply when he rejoices in the fact that he could declaim even from his bed (1.64). The greatest gift of Asclepius, his greatest healing, was to enable Aristides to pursue his art (5.36), and the orator's gratitude was expressed by attributing all that was good in his art to the god (2.11; 4.15). "Everything of mine," he says, "was a gift of the god" (4.53); "he saved me by means worth more than the act of being saved" (4.29). And again, "During all this time he was my savior and gave me one day after another, or rather, even now is my savior" (2.37). Writing in the autumn of 170, he states, "It also happened, during this time, that my physical condition was the most comfortable and at its brightest since I was first sick . . . and nothing of my accustomed oratorical practice was neglected, so that all congratulated me, both privately and publicly. In so far as even in this time I happened to fall ill for some days, the god cured me most miraculously and in his usual way" (5.48).

The *Sacred Tales*, then, are a kind of aretalogy in praise of the god,[23] a witness to the god's "power and providence," revealed not only in these words but also in all the powerful rhetoric of one of the greatest of the Sophists, through a witness who is, in the orator's view, all the more remarkable because the power of the god is demonstrated through the weakest of instruments, a sickly man whose every breath and word can come not through himself but through the power of the god to whom he has handed over his life.

Aelius Aristides may be exceptional in his learning and his eloquence, and he may be exceptional in the degree of his devotion—he embodies my definition of religion as the organization of life around an experience of perceived ultimate power—but he is not exceptional in his way of being religious.[24] He is, indeed, the perfect representative of Greco-Roman Religiousness A. He perceives the divine *dynamis* at work in the world and available to humans through a range of religious practices. The point of such accessibility to *dynamis*, furthermore, is participation in benefits from the gods. Salvation means success and security in the pursuits of this mortal life.

His way of being religious is given even sharper definition by means of contrast to the other types I have identified. Aristides reveals absolutely no pessimism concerning the empirical world nor any desire to escape from the world through a shedding of the body—despite his chronically ill condition. He does not show any interest, beyond the minimum demanded of any rhetorician in the Greco-Roman world, in religion as the stabilizer of the world. Indeed, he expends great efforts to avoid serving in the religious and civic offices offered to him (*ST*, 4.71–87).

Finally, in all of his extant speeches, I can count only the merest handful of places where he even touches on moral behavior (*Orations*, 2.201; 16.31; 24.48–-50; 29.7; 29.14).[25] In the *Sacred Tales*, his fullest statement concerning morality is self-congratulatory: he is not puffed up by his accomplishments (5.37). In another place, he hears the god say "that it was fitting that my mind be changed from its present condition," but he means by this, "having been changed, associate with the god, and by its association be superior to man's estate." And Aristides interprets the dream as pertaining "to oratory and divine communion" (4.52). We find in him virtually no trace of religion as moral transformation, such as we will find so splendidly displayed in the next chapter by Epictetus.

5

RELIGION AS MORAL TRANSFORMATION: EPICTETUS

The majority of those considering themselves religious in the Greco-Roman world no doubt exhibited the sort of religious sensibility demonstrated so well by Aelius Aristides, though probably with less fervor and certainly with less rhetorical polish. They thought of the divine *dynamis* as distributed throughout the empirical world and available through multiple practices, from prayer and sacrifice to divination and healing. The gods were the source of benefits in which their worshipers participated: the salvation they offered was mainly success and security in everyday life.

In this chapter, I consider the way of being religious that I have designated as Religiousness B: religion as moral transformation. This sensibility is no less optimistic than Religiousness A; the divine *dynamis* is similarly perceived as accessible and active on behalf of humans. In this type, however, the most important activity of the divine power is perceived as immanent within human moral endeavor, and "salvation" is less a matter of divine rescue from human failure and disaster than the ability of humans to endure such circumstances in a manner worthy of the gods.

Two questions immediately present themselves concerning the claim that this is a distinct form of religious sensibility. The first is whether we are really speaking about religion—am I not merely describing moral disposition? If religion is to mean anything specific, ought not it be restricted to divine myths and sacred rituals? Convincing proof depends on the examination of specific cases, but for now I remind the reader of my broad definition in Chapter 2, where I defined religion as a way of life organized around experiences and convictions concerning ultimate power. A "way of life" can be religious in character even if "the gods" are not explicitly invoked. As a happy *lagniappe*, however, the example I discuss not only employs religious language but does so with specific reference to moral endeavor. My definition arises from rather than imposes on the evidence.

The second question is whether we should simply call this "philosophical religion." Certainly, many whose main concern was moral instruction and formation were philosophers. But I hesitate to use the expression, because it suggests an intellectual refinement of popular religion, a reinterpretation of crude myths and rituals into intellectually acceptable form, a religion of ideas rather than of practices.[1] Such intellectual distancing, however, is not the dominant trait of Religiousness B as I understand it. In addition, as I suggested in Chapter 3, those bearing the label of "philosopher" in the Greco-Roman world displayed a variety of religious attitudes and practices.[2] Even within a single philosophical tradition, such as Stoicism, the religious disposition of individual philosophers could vary considerably. What is said about Epictetus in this chapter also could be said, in varying degrees, of his teacher, Musonius Rufus; his contemporary, Dio Chrysostom; and his later admirer, Marcus Aurelius.[3] But it would be difficult to make the case that Seneca the Younger, who shares virtually every other school tenet and moral preoccupation, had the same intensity of religious sensibility as Epictetus.[4]

No more than the piety of Aelius Aristides represents that of all second-century Sophists, then, does the distinctive piety of Epictetus represent all first-century philosophers. The value of each author is heuristic: they so clearly demonstrate distinctive ways of being religious that they provide a measure for less dramatic cases. Each author also defies the easy reduction of religious sensibility to social condition. Aelius Aristides enjoyed every social privilege and the best possible education yet had a religious sensibility that was indistinguishable in character from the masses who crowded festivals and shrines. Asclepius was his savior because the god enabled Aristides to practice oratory despite chronic illness. Epictetus was socially disadvantaged in every respect and shared with Aristides both a chronic physical disability and religious fervor, yet it is difficult, perhaps impossible, to imagine him joining the rhetorician at the Asclepium to seek healing. To discover why, it is necessary to examine the life and words of one of history's truly admirable human beings.

THE LIFE OF EPICTETUS

The few certain facts of the philosopher's life are drawn from a handful of inscriptions, testimonies by admiring ancient authors, and the *Discourses* taken down by his pupil, Flavius Arrian.[5] If the dates 50–120 CE are roughly accurate, then Epictetus was an exact contemporary of the biographer Plutarch and the historian Tacitus; he would have been a boy when Paul wrote Romans, a teen-ager when Paul was executed in Rome under Nero, and rounding into his favor-ite self-designation as "old man" when Ignatius of Antioch advanced from Syria to Rome as a prisoner of Christ.[6]

Epictetus was born in the city of Hierapolis in the province of Phrygia in Asia Minor, a territory well known for its religious fervor: it was the home of the enthusiastic cult of the mother-goddess Cybele and of the equally enthusiastic second-century Christian movement called Montanism. We know nothing of his father. His mother was a slave, and he himself was a slave for at least a time, owned by Epaphroditus, a freedman and secretary of the emperor Nero (*Discourses*, 1.26.12; 4.1.150). He was to some degree physically disabled, referring to himself as "lame" (*chōlos*; see 1.16.20; 3.20.5). Whether his disability was genetic or a result of a beating is not clear. The late second-century philosopher Celsus thought it resulted from abuse, and Origen agreed.[7] Probably in recognition of his natural mental abilities, Epictetus was allowed to study in Rome with "the Roman Socrates," Musonius Rufus, whose fragmentary writings testify to his reputation as a moral teacher who was both strict and humane.[8]

It is notoriously difficult with any author to move from life circumstances to moral preoccupations. How much did his physical disability matter to Epicte-tus? Enough, it seems, for him to characterize himself in one of his most elo-quent passages as "a lame old man like me" (*Discourses*, 1.16.20).[9] How severely was he marked by his background as a slave? The fact that the word "freedom" occurs over 130 times in his extant discourses, and that genuine freedom is con-sidered possible even in conditions of human servitude, may be suggestive. As for the influence of his teacher, it is unmistakable. Epictetus refers often to "Rufus" (see 1.1.2; 1.9.29; 3.6.10; 3.15.14) and says of his teacher that "he spoke in such a way that each of us as we sat there fancied someone had gone to Rufus and told him of our faults; so effective was his grasp of what men actually do, so vividly did he set before each man's eyes his particular weaknesses" (3.23.29).

The education Epictetus gained while sitting with others in Musonius Rufus' classroom could not compare to the wide-ranging education acquired by the rhetorician Aelius Aristides. The main fare was undoubtedly the reading of Chrysippus (ca. 280–206 BCE), the great systematizer of Stoic logic, physics, and (especially) ethics in over 705 works.[10] Epictetus makes reference to Homer, Plato, Xenophon, and the great tragedians, and he has a handbook acquain-tance with the teachings of rival philosophical schools. How much of this came from direct contact and how much was mediated by the reading of Chrysippus is impossible to determine. At some point, Epictetus assumed a role as philo-sophical teacher in his own right. He was sufficiently well known to have been included in the expulsion of philosophers from Rome by the emperor Domitian (89 or 92 CE). In exile, he established his own school in the city of Nicopolis in Epirus (opposite Actium), where he spent the remainder of his life teaching young men destined, for the most part, to take on roles in the civil order of the empire. He traveled only a bit (to Olympia and Athens) and lived with great personal simplicity, having in his room at Rome only a cot, a mat, and a single lamp, in addition to his *Lares* (shrine to the household gods). He apparently married only late in life to help raise a child who was threatened with exposure.

Although his life was confined in several ways, Epictetus' influence spread beyond his classroom. In the opening chapter of his *Meditations*, Marcus Aurelius (121–180) thanks his own teacher Rusticus for having introduced him to the *Discourses* of Epictetus (1.8) and quotes the philosopher several times (4.41; 11.37; 11.38; 11.39; 4.49.2–6). Lucian of Somasata (120–200) had his ideal philosopher Demonax joke about Epictetus' failure to marry until late in life (*Demonax*, 55) but expressed his own admiration for "that marvelous old man" in the *Ignorant Book Collector* (13). Together with his philosophical opponent Celsus, the Christian teacher Origen praises Epictetus' moral character (*Against Celsus*, 7.54) as well as the accessible character of his teaching: "It is easy indeed to observe that Plato is found only in the hands of those who profess to be literary men; while Epictetus is admired by persons of ordinary capacity, who have a desire to be benefited, and who perceive the improvement which may be derived from his writings" (6.2).

It was through the efforts of his student Flavius Arrian (ca. 86–146) that Epictetus' teachings continued after his death to live on in a world larger than his classroom; indeed, Arrian made the world Epictetus' classroom. Arrian was probably typical of Epictetus' students in that he went into imperial service, but untypical in that, besides serving as a governor of Cappadocia under Hadrian and repelling the Alan invasion in 134, he became a man of letters, producing such substantial historical accounts as the *Anabasis of Alexander* and the *Indica*. He made his teacher's words available to the larger world through two works. The *Encheiridion* (that is, "Handbook") is something of an epitome of Epictetus' teaching. It consists of 53 paragraphs of varying length and received such a welcome among Christian readers that it went through several adaptations.[11] The *Encheiridion* captures Epictetus' doctrines, but it does not contain his distinctive voice and personality. These are revealed vividly in Arrian's second production, the *Discourses* (*diatribai*), which originally consisted of eight books, only four of which are extant.

These (for the most part) short talks did not form the substance of Epictetus' students' work. As his constant references make clear, their curriculum of study undoubtedly focused on the writings of Chrysippus. The *Discourses* (or *Diatribes*), in all likelihood, represented something of a "daily homily" delivered by the master to the assembled students. They are neither systematic nor utterly random: their themes were probably set by the readings, by actual incidents, or by favorite themes (such as "providence"). In them, Epictetus appears as an unforgettable and eminently quotable teacher. The *Discourses* often take the form of fictive dialogues between the teacher and an imagined interlocutor (such as one of his students), in which the teacher uses a variety of glittering stylistic turns: apostrophe, rhetorical questions, quick retorts, vituperation, citation of classical writings, and lessons drawn from examples such as Heracles, Socrates, and Diogenes.[12] By no means are the diatribes free-form ramblings. Most of them work through an argument with considerable consistency and control.[13] So distinctive are these diatribes that two questions arise: is the literary form itself Epictetus' invention, and is it his voice that we hear or Arrian's?

There are enough other contemporary and near-contemporary writings that display the same rhetorical tropes—notably, the diatribes of Theon and the Christian letters of Paul and James—to support the conclusion that Epictetus was working with stock items and modes of argumentation.[14] The same observation reduces considerably the possibility of Epictetus' dependence on Christian writers or of Christians on him.[15] As for the second question, although it is theoretically conceivable that a writer of the Second Sophistic could have executed such a spectacular exercise in *prosōpopoiia* ("writing in character"),[16] Arrian declares in his letter of introduction to Lucius Gellius that he did not himself compose the *Discourses* but that "whatever I heard him say I used to write down, word for word, as best I could, endeavoring to preserve it as a memorial for my own future use, of his way of thinking and the frankness of his speech." Taking into account as well the marked difference between these talks and Arrian's published writings, it is probable that we truly do hear in these *Discourses* "the actual words of an extraordinarily gifted teacher upon scores, not to say hundreds of occasions, conversing with visitors, reproving, exhorting, encouraging his pupils."[17]

THE STOIC TEACHER

Epictetus was intensely loyal to the Stoicism he had learned from Musonius Rufus and was clearly capable of handling the technical issues that were stock in trade for the professional philosopher (see, for example, *Discourses*, 1.7; 1.17; 2.12; 2.25).[18] He was, indeed, a partisan of Stoic teaching, and he willingly engaged in the polemics typical of interschool rivalry. *Discourse* 2.20, for example, is completely dedicated to the rejection of what he considered the harmful teachings of the Academics and the Epicureans, and his criticisms recur in other places: the Academics are condemned for their skeptical suspension of judgment (1.5.9) and for the Sophistical arguments employed by Pyrrho (1.27.2); the Epicureans are scorned because their withdrawal from society and political involvement betrays the social character of humans (1.23.1–10) and is the consequence of corrupt judgment and behavior (3.7.19–28).[19]

Epictetus also embraces without question the optimistic Stoic view of nature and god, which in Stoic physics tend to merge.[20] Stoicism holds that the world is material but is at the same time the manifestation of divine rationality: the passive element of matter (*hylē*) and the active principle of god (*theos*) totally interpenetrate. At the level of empirical observation, these components appear as the four traditional elements that had formed the basis of pre-Socratic cosmological theories: earth, water, air, fire. Of these, earth and water are passive, while air and fire are active, forming the spirit (*pneuma*) that pervades and shapes all things. Spirit, in turn, is the vehicle of reason (*logos*) that governs— and is immanent within—the entire cosmos.

The Stoic universe is, in effect, a living being, and the best of all possible worlds, because it is the embodiment of reason. The cosmos, moreover, goes through cycles of regeneration, with each cycle ending in a great conflagration (*ekpyrōsis*) that gives birth, in turn, to another perfect world identical to the present one (see *Discourses*, 2.1.18; 3.13.4; 3.13.15). God (*theos*) is equated with the immanent principle of reason governing the world, and since the world is itself in some sense divine, it is providentially guided: all that is and that happens bears the signs of rational design. What makes human beings distinctive within the cosmos is the gift of rationality, in effect a participation in the divine nature, which enables humans to discern rightly the patterns of the world and follow them appropriately. In Stoicism, then, to act "according to nature" (*kata physin*) is implicitly to "follow god."

Such is the framework of physics within which Epictetus works, which he everywhere presupposes, and which he infuses with a distinctive piety. His main concern, however, is not with logic or physics but with ethics, with many of his discourses dealing with specific moral topics.[21] Imitating the traditional threefold distributions of subjects, in fact, he organizes the training of his young students around three areas of practice (*Discourses*, 3.2.1–2): the management of desires and aversions, never desiring the unattainable and never seeking to flee the unavoidable (control of passions); the management of choices, learning what is appropriate to do in life's circumstances and responsibilities (social duties); and control over one's assent, so that error and impulse are avoided. It is at this stage that epistemology and logic gain their point, helping one to

determine what is real and what is not; humans are easily seduced and fright-
ened by "appearances" and need practice in discerning (see, for example, *Discourse* 1.1, "On Things that are under our Control and not under our Control").
Human freedom consists precisely and exclusively in control over one's "moral
purpose."

The key element in his pedagogy is "practice" or "training" (*askēsis*; see *Discourses,* 2.9.13); philosophy is distorted when treated as a matter of learning
theory rather than as a matter of moral transformation.[22] He asks his students,
"Is it anything but cruel for me to leave you unreformed?" and reminds them of
the remarkable conversion (*metabolē*) of Polemo (3.1.10–14).[23] Epictetus argues
in 2.19 ("To Those who take up the Teachings of the Philosophers only to talk
about Them") that having opinions, even learned ones, is not what being a
Stoic is about; rather, it is the formation of a more authentic freedom that they
should seek (see 4.1). Many of Epictetus' talks challenge his students to close
the gap between book learning and true virtue. They say that progress should
be in virtue, but they persist in measuring it by the amount of Chrysippus they
have read (1.4.19). But an excessive study of argumentation can actually lead
away from the pursuit of virtue and toward vanity and enslavement (1.8.4–10).
Even greater vanity is learning philosophical opinions in order to impress others at banquets (1.26.9). Knowing Chrysippus, in truth, is valuable only insofar
as it helps them understand the law of nature and live according to it (1.17.13).
Since learning that does not lead to action is useless (1.29.35 and 55–57; 3.24.110),
the false philosopher can be recognized by the way in which his words are contradicted by his actions (2.9.13–21; 4.8.8–12).

Moral transformation is arduous work. It demands not simply understanding
but also training (*Discourses,* 1.12) and constant attentiveness (4.12). Why? Because moral transformation requires the change of habits: "What reinforce-
ment, then, is it possible to find with which to oppose habit? Why, the contrary
habit" (1.27.4). This is muscular philosophy, as much a matter of the body as of
the mind. Epictetus makes thorough use of the two great metaphors of ancient
moral philosophy: athletics and medicine. His students are like athletes preparing for the Olympics, and he is their coach (1.18.21–23); they are like sick people
and he is the physician (2.14.21):[24] "Men, the lecture hall of the philosopher is a
hospital; you ought not to walk out of it in pleasure, but in pain. For you are not
well when you come; one man has a dislocated shoulder, another an abscess,
another a fistula, another a headache. And am I to sit down and recite to you
dainty little notions and clever little mottoes, so that you will go out with words
of praise on your lips, one man carrying away his shoulder just as it was when
he came in, another his head in the same state, another his fistula, another his

abscess?" (3.23.30–32). Aelius Aristides sought healing from the savior god Asclepius at the temples dedicated to that god and regarded salvation as the ability
to sustain his career of epideictic oratory. Epictetus asks his students to seek
healing from their moral illness (their vices) in the hospital that is the philosophical schoolroom (*scholeia*), to engage in a process of conversion that required the continuous therapy of honest self-examination and mutual frankness
of speech. What we see here, however, is not religion versus philosophy but
rather two distinct modes of religious sensibility, as we discover when we examine Epictetus' remarkable use of religious language.[25]

RELIGION AS MORAL TRANSFORMATION

Consistent with his Stoic convictions, Epictetus considered honoring the gods
worshiped in Greco-Roman culture as among the public duties (*ta kathēkonta*)
required of citizenship in a "state made up of gods and men" (*Discourses*,
2.15.26; 3.24.12).[26] He has a shrine for his ancestral gods (*lares*; 1.18.15), appreci-
ates the logic involved in emperor worship (4.1.60),[27] and knows of the priesthood of Augustus (1.19.26). He speaks often of festivals (1.12.21), such as the
Saturnalia (1.25.8); temples (1.4.31), including those of Asclepius (2.12.17) in
which people sleep as they seek healing (2.16.17); altars (1.4.31);[28] and statues of
gods, such as Zeus and Athena (2.8.13–20; 2.29.26). He refers to such common
religious practices as sacrifices (1.4.32), including those carried out before sailing or planting (3.21.12); prayers (1.1.13) and hymns (1.16.16–21; 4.1.109); and
thanks directed to the gods (1.12.32; 1.16.6; 1.19.25).[29] He speaks knowledgably
about priests and prophets (2.20.27) and the various forms of prophecy (1.24.5),
including oracles (2.20.27)—especially that at Delphi (*Encheiridion*, 32)—and
the various forms of divination (*Discourses*, 1.17.18–19), including the examinations of entrails (3.7.12) and the observation of the movements of birds (3.1.37).
He is aware of the Mysteries at Eleusis (3.21.13) with its various ministers (3.21.15),
and he understands the significance of initiation into the Mysteries (4.1.106).
His *Discourses* refer as well to incantations (3.24.89) and omens (3.24.89), to
Fortune (4.4.40), the Fates (1.12.25), Hades (2.16.18; 3.13.15), the Furies and
Avengers (2.19.17), and evil demons (4.4.38). Epictetus shows some awareness of
Jews and their preoccupations (1.11.12–13; 1.22.4) and perhaps even knows about
Christians (2.9.20–22; 4.7.6). What is most remarkable about this catalog is that
with respect to none of these religious phenomena does the philosopher ex-
press either intellectual dismissal or moral disapproval.

The names he uses for the divine are similarly conventional. When speaking
emphatically, he uses "by Zeus" and "by the gods" interchangeably (*Discourses*,

1.7.126; 1.30.6).[30] Likewise, he refers often to "the gods" (for example, 1.1.7),[31] including Kore, Pluto, and Demeter (2.20.33); Hera (3.13.4); Pan and the Nymphs (3.23.11); Hermes (3.20.12); Apollo (3.1.16); and Athena and Asclepius (4.8.29). He can refer more broadly to the divine by speaking of "Zeus and the rest of the gods" (1.27.13; 1.16.7) or of "the divine" (*to theion*; 1.11.1). Far and away Zeus is his favorite designation for the divine power (1.1.10);[32] Zeus is "maker, father, guardian" (1.9.7); "rain-bringer, fruit-giver, father of men and gods" (1.19.12); "savior, rain-bringer, fruit-giver" (1.22.16); and the "god of fathers, god of kindred" (3.11.16). As often as he uses the name Zeus, he employs the designation "god" (*ho theos*; see 1.1.18).[33] Equivalent expressions are "the Giver" (4.4.47) and "Another" (*allos*), used especially in contexts suggesting God's oversight of human actions (1.1.32).[34] Epictetus combines the sense of the singular and the plural in his characterization of God when he states that Zeus communes with himself and is at peace with himself (3.13.7). Two usages that reflect Epictetus' Stoic convictions are his use of Providence (*pronoia*) as the expression of God's presence and power throughout all the cosmos—there is no evil in the universe (*Encheiridion*, 27; *Discourses*, 1.10.10)[35]—and his personification of Nature (*physis*; 1.6.20–22; 1.16.14), so that he can speak of "the will of nature" (1.17.17) or "the law of nature and of god" (1.29.19); he declares that "everything is filled with gods and divine powers (*daimonia*; 3.13.16).

Epictetus' distinctive religious preoccupations begin to emerge more clearly when we consider the way in which he characterizes God (*ho theos*), humans (*anthrōpoi*), and the relations between them. As we might expect, God is characterized in terms of intelligence, knowledge, and right reason (*Discourses*, 2.8.1–3); God is the ruler (2.17.23) who governs the universe (2.16.33; 4.7.7), overseeing all (3.11.16) as a witness (3.20.4). God's rule is exercised by his will (1.29.29; 2.17.22; 4.4.29; 4.7.20), which can hinder (2.1.26; 4.1.99) but is itself unhindered (4.1.83)—the sole exception, fascinatingly, is the human moral purpose: not even Zeus can dislodge a human from his moral purpose (3.3.10).

God is more than pure intelligence, though; he is also to be equated with goodness (*Discourses*, 2.8.1–3), a goodness that is expressed in a remarkable range of statements concerning his positive and personal relationship with regard to the cosmos and above all with humans: "the law of god is most good and most just" (1.29.13). God is not "father of men" (3.24.16) in a weak symbolic sense, but in the sense that he actually made humans (2.6.9; 2.8.19; 2.8.21; 4.1.108), as he made all things (4.7.6), and has made them to be happy (3.24.19). God cares for each person (1.27.12; 3.24.19). God is a giver of gifts (2.23.2–5),[36] who provides what we need to live with integrity (2.16.13–15). God has given humans a part of himself (1.17.27–28).[37] Epictetus says that other creatures are

God's work but that "They are not of primary importance, nor portions of divinity. But you are a being of primary importance; you are a fragment of god: you have within you a part of him" (2.8.11). God sets humans free (1.19.9), watches over them as a father (3.24.3), guides them (2.7.11; 3.21.12), provides them with signals of his will (1.29.29), gives them orders and directions (1.25.30) through his law (2.16.28; 4.3.12) and by assigning each one his place (*Encheiridion*, 22).

Humans, in turn, are characterized in extravagant terms. They are not inferior to the gods (*Discourses*, 1.12.26), are friends to the gods (2.17.29; 3.24.60; 4.3.9), like the gods (1.22.21), have fellowship with Zeus (2.19.27), and are equal to the gods (1.12.27): "You have a power (*dynamis*) equal (*isos*) to Zeus" (1.14.12). There is a kinship of gods and men (1.9.1; 1.9.22–26), whereby men are offspring of Zeus (1.13.4) and a brother has Zeus for a father (1.13.3). Epictetus says, "Our souls are so bound up with god, as being parts and portions of his being, does not god perceive their every motion as a motion of that which is his own and of one body with himself?" (1.14.69). Thus the designation "son of god" is rightly applied to Herakles (2.8.28), Sarpedon (1.27.8), Diogenes, and Heraclitus (*Encheiridion*, 15) and to all who live in authentic communion with the god whose being they share (*Discourses*, 1.9.6; 2.17.33): "Act according to nature [*kata physin*]. Whose? His in whom I am [*to ekeinou en hō eimi*]" (1.15.5). Yet it is possible not to live in this fashion: "Why, then, are you ignorant of your own kinship? Why do you not know the source from which you have sprung? Will you not bear in mind, whenever you eat, who you are that eat, and whom you are nourishing? Whenever you indulge in intercourse with women, who are you that do this? Whenever you mix in society, whenever you take physical exercise, whenever you converse, do you not know that you are nourishing god, exercising god? You are bearing god about with you, poor wretch, and know it not!" (2.8.11–13).

The task of human freedom is the proper alignment of the moral purpose with the god within. When Epictetus focuses on this side of things, his language about God tends to be less immanent. Humans are to "show piety towards the gods" (*Encheiridion*, 31) and to honor the divine (*Discourses*, 3.20.22). They are to give thanks to God (4.4.7; 4.4.18; 4.7.9; 4.5.36), to "remember god" (2.18.29; 4.4.47), and to call on God for help (2.18.29). This is done, however, through the exercise of mental and moral dispositions. Mentally, humans are to understand the dictate "know thyself" inscribed at Delphi (3.1.18; Frag. 1) in terms of their kinship with God and to understand the divine administration of the cosmos (2.10.3; 3.13.8) as God's providence. As friends of God, they are to be "of one mind" with God (2.19.26): "Now the philosophers say that the first thing we must learn is this: that there is a god, and that he provides for the universe, and that it is impossible for a man to conceal from Him not merely his actions, but even his purposes and thoughts. Next we must learn what the gods are like; for whatever their character is discovered to be, the man who is going to please and obey them must endeavor as best he can to resemble them. If the deity is faithful, he also must be faithful; if free, he also must be free; if beneficent, he also must be beneficent; if high-minded, he also must be high-minded; and so forth; therefore, in everything he says and does, he must act as an imitator of god" (2.14.11–13).

Humans are, therefore, to be intent on God (*Discourses*, 3.24.114), to look to God (2.16.42; 2.16.46; 2.19.29), and to follow God: "To follow the gods is man's end" (1.20.16; see 1.30.5). This involves making one's will as much as possible like the will of Zeus (4.1.89–90) as God works in the world, to yield to God what God has given (4.1.172), namely, everything (4.4.40). It is to render obedience to God (3.24.95; 3.24.110; 4.12.11–12; 3.1.37; 4.3.10) in every circumstance: to be happy because of God (3.24.63), to die like a god, and to bear disease like a god (2.8.28). Epictetus cries out to a student who sought to be "secure and unshaken" not only when awake but also when asleep and drunk and melancholy-mad: "Man you are a god, so great are the designs you cherish!" (2.17.33). Those who refuse to follow God in this manner by living in self-induced ignorance and vice "complain against" God (1.29.17; 2.12.12; 3.24.5) and "fight against god" (*theomachein*; 3.24.21; 3.24.24; 4.1.101). They have failed in their task of being "beautiful and pure in the sight of god" (2.18.19), of being "servants and followers of god" (4.7.20; 4.8.30) in the manner of Diogenes, who was a "Servant of Zeus" (3.24.65). They have missed the distinctive human vocation of bearing witness to God in the world (1.29.46–50; 3.24.112; 3.24.114).

That Epictetus merges moral transformation and religious piety is clear enough, but two final passages provide emphasis. The first occurs in *Encheiridion*, 32: Epictetus addresses one who seeks advice from a diviner. He does not question that divination can reveal circumstances, but he insists that whatever the circumstances, the philosopher already knows how to exercise his moral purpose: "For if the diviner forewarns you that the omens of sacrifice have been unfavorable, it is clear that death is portended, or the injury of some member of your body, or exile; yet reason requires that even at this risk you are to stand by your friend, and share the danger with your country. Wherefore, give heed to the greater diviner, the Pythian Apollo, who cast out of his temple the man who had not helped his friend when he was being murdered." And just as Aelius Aristides could speak of his healing therapies in terms of initiation into the Mysteries, so can Epictetus use the same language for a commitment to moral transformation. He compares students who come to the task of philosophy "without the help of the gods" and who simply learn opinions without putting them into practice to those "impious people" who "vulgarize the Mysteries" at Eleusis by parodying them without attention to what the sacred rites demand (3.21.13–14). "Nay, but a man ought to come [to philosophy] also with a sacrifice, and with prayers, and after a preliminary purification, and with his mind predisposed to the idea that he will be approaching holy rites, and holy rites of great antiquity. Only thus do the Mysteries become helpful [*ōphelima*], only thus do we arrive at the impression that all these things were established by men of old time for the purpose of education [*epi paideia*] and for amendment of our life [*epanorthōsei tou biou*]" (3.21.14–15).

THE PHILOSOPHER AS GOD'S MESSENGER

One of the best known of Epictetus' *Discourses* is "On the Calling of the Cynic" (3.22), a splendid example of a protreptic discourse urging students to the highest ideals of the philosophical life.[38] Because he was addressing students all too willing to take the easy path of merely verbal learning and thereby seek the status of being called philosophers, Epictetus focuses on the demands and hardships of this life. From his other discourses it is clear that he does not expect such a radical commitment from his students—or even totally from himself—but he sets before his students and himself the ideal as the standard by which their mutual progress is to be measured.

Becoming a Cynic, he insists, is a matter not of externals—of dress or style of speech—but of a lifelong commitment to virtue, to the transformation of the self. The true Cynic, indeed, must be called by God (*Discourses*, 3.22.2–8)[39] and must keep his own governing principle (*hēgemonikon*) pure (3.22.19–22). The Cynic does not serve the self but is, rather, sent as a scout (*kataskopos*) from God to humans, a witness who will speak the truth no matter what the cost (3.22.24–25). In fulfilling this function, the philosopher imitates Diogenes and Socrates. The first mode of witnessing is through speech: the one who sees clearly must speak clearly to others, and Epictetus provides a sample of a "Socratic speech" provided by the "messenger and scout" to the crowds (3.22.26–44).

Witness is not, however, simply a matter of speech. The Cynic must be able to offer his own life as an example from which others can learn (*Discourses*, 3.22.45–49). His life is like a moral Olympics, in which the athletic struggle to live according to reason is constant (3.22.50–52). To so present oneself to the world is a deeply dangerous proposition, so capable are humans of self-deception. It is necessary to know oneself and to be in accord with the deity (3.22.53–61).

Because it is so demanding, in turn, the calling of the Cynic is lonely and demands self-sufficiency. The Cynic does not have friends (3.22.62–66) or family (3.22.68–77). Instead, he takes on all of humanity as the family that he serves (3.22.77–82). This is, in truth, the best of all political involvements (3.22.83–85).

Epictetus acknowledges that such a witness requires certain natural endowments, such as a fit body that enables him to endure difficult circumstances with radiant health (*Discourses*, 3.22.86–89) and a wit and charm that enable his challenge to be heard as attractive rather than repulsive (3.22.90–92). These are, however, accidentals. The essence of such witness is the philosopher's purity of intention and constant application to the truth (3.22.94–96), which makes of him a general, a commander of other humans who is able to direct the lives of others without meddling (3.22.97–99) because he is concerned not with his own gain or reputation but solely with moral purpose (3.22.100–109).

Epictetus himself did not go about in the manner of the ideal Cynic, a wanderer without friends or family. He (eventually) married and adopted a child. And he strayed at his post in the classroom, teaching generations of young students. But his words were spread abroad, as was the example of his simple and sincere life, inspiring readers who come upon them thousands of years after his death to seek to adopt as he did the ideal of being a scout and messenger sent by Zeus to humans for their welfare. That this ideal was one he sought to live out is clear from the words he uses in several passages about himself. He frequently invokes the "Hymn of Cleanthes," whose words summarize a life of obedience to God: "Lead thou me on O Zeus and Destiny" (*Discourses*, 2.23.42).[40] His concluding words "On Providence" (1.16) are memorable:

> Are these the only works of providence in us? Nay, what language is adequate to praise them all or bring them home to our minds as they deserve? Why, if we had any sense, ought we be doing anything else, publicly and privately, than hymning and praising the Deity, and rehearsing His benefits? Ought we not, as we dig and plough and eat, to sing the hymn of praise to god? "Great is God, that he hath furnished us these instruments wherewith we shall till the earth. Great is God, that He hath given us hands, and power to swallow, and a belly, and power to grow unconsciously, and to breathe while asleep." This is what we ought to sing on every occasion, and above all to sing the greatest and divinest hymn, that God hath given us the faculty to comprehend these things and to follow the path of reason. What then? Since most of you have become blind, ought there not to be someone to fulfill this office for you, and in behalf of all sing the hymn of praise to god? Why, what else can

I, a lame old man, do but sing hymns to god? If, indeed, I were a nightingale, I should be singing as a nightingale; if a swan, as a swan. But as it is, I am a rational being, therefore, I must be singing hymns of praise to god. This is my task; I do it, and will not desert this post, so long as it may be given to me to fill it; I enjoin you to join me in the same song. (*Discourses*, 1.16.15–21)

Equally impressive are these (obviously personal) words in his discourse "On Those Who Leave School Because of Illness":

As for me, I would fain that death overtook me occupied with nothing but my own moral purpose, trying to make it tranquil, unhampered, unconstrained, free. This is what I wish to be engaged in when death finds me, so that I may be able to say to God, "Have I in any respect transgressed thy commands? Have I in any respect misused the resources that thou gavest me, or used my senses to no purpose, or my preconceptions? Have I ever found any fault with thee? Have I blamed thy governance at all? I fell sick, when it was thy will; so did other men, but I willingly. I became poor, it being thy will, but with joy. I have held no office, because thou did not will it, and I never set my heart upon office. Hast thou ever seen me for that reason greatly dejected? Have I not ever come before Thee with a radiant countenance, ready for any injunctions or orders that Thou mightest give? And now it is Thy will that I leave this festival; I go, I am full of gratitude to Thee that thou hast deemed me worthy to take part in this festival with Thee, and to see Thy works, and to understand thy governance." Be this my thought, this my writing, this my reading, when death comes upon me. (*Discourses*, 3.5.7–11)

Aelius Aristides and Epictetus have provided us with clear and strong impressions of the first two ways of being religious in the Greco-Roman world. They have, indeed, much in common. Both are optimistic concerning the presence and power of the divine within the empirical world and are confident that the divine *dynamis* is available to humans for their benefit. Both consider salvation as a matter of health and integrity in the present life. They differ mainly in the perceptions concerning the location of the divine *dynamis* and its mode of operation. For Religiousness A, the power is external to humans and touches them through forms of religious mediation. Religiousness B, as exemplified in Epictetus, neither denies nor scorns that form of power but is far more concerned with the divine *dynamis* as immanent within human activity and expressed through moral transformation.

Neither Aristides nor Epictetus, I suggest, would understand or appreciate a form of religiosity that sought salvation through escape from the world, out of the conviction that the divine *dynamis* was not to be found either in the cosmos or in human consciousness. Indeed, Epictetus gives voice to such a sensibility through one of his fictive interlocutors: "Epictetus, we can no longer endure to be imprisoned with this paltry body. . . . Are we not in a manner akin to god, and have we not come from Him? Suffer us to go back whence we came; suffer us at last to be freed from these fetters that are fastened to us and weight us down"; he answers, "Men, wait upon God. . . . Stay, nor be so unrational as to depart" (*Discourses*, 1.9.12–17). In the next chapter, we shall encounter such an "escape from the world" religiosity in full-blown form in the *Poimandres*.

6

RELIGION AS TRANSCENDING THE WORLD: *POIMANDRES*

The forms of religiosity represented respectively by Aelius Aristides and Epictetus are robustly positive toward the visible world as the arena for divine *dynamis* (power). The orator Aristides celebrated his participation in divine benefits through prophecy (oracles, dreams), sacrifices, and healing. While not disdaining such external manifestations of the divine, the philosopher Epictetus focused on the immanence of the divine *dynamis*, whose work was the moral transformation of humans. For both, the body—even when beset with illness as it was for both authors—was also evaluated positively: for Aristides, the power of Asclepius was most manifest in the god's intervention in sustaining the rhetorician's body through its manifold troubles; for Epictetus, his body was the instrument of moral reformation. Each saw his body as the instrument for bearing witness to the effective presence of the divine *dynamis* in the world.

Not all in the Greco-Roman world were so positive in their outlook toward the empirical world—above all the body. In this chapter, I consider the evidence for a third mode of religiosity that I call "the way of transcending the world," although it might with equal justice be designated as "the way of escape from the world." For this outlook, the body is a much more fundamental problem than in either Religiousness A or B, because a sharp distinction is drawn between what is material and what is immaterial: the realm of the divine is the realm of spirit (the immortal) rather than of matter (the mortal). Humans are construed in terms of an immortal spirit (the soul, *psychē*) that is trapped, or at least burdened, by a mortal body.

In contrast to the first two types of religious sensibility, for which embodied and mortal existence is simply a given, then, this third sort of religiosity regards human existence as at once tragic and exalted. It is tragic because something infinitely worthwhile that participates in the divine is trapped in the body and is in peril of being destroyed by the body's downward tropism. It is exalted because that most precious *psychē* does participate in the divine and can find its way back to its source in the realm of immortal spirit. The authentic self is to be identified not with the empirical body that acts in the world but with an inner spirit that seeks release from its material encasement. Salvation, in this perspective, is not understood in terms of security and success in worldly endeavors (as in Type A) or in terms of the transformation of habits from vice to virtue (as in Type B) but consists in the immortal soul's release from its mortal prison.

This more complex understanding of the human situation requires, in turn, a mythological underpinning distinct from the stories of the gods that did service for Religiousness A or even the philosophical reinterpretation of those tales that served the cause of moral transformation in Religiousness B. This third way of being religious pays considerable attention to the mythic accounts that answer the fundamental questions of cosmology (where did we come from), eschatology (where are we going), and ethics (what is the path back home). And since the authentic self's fundamental "problem" is its imprisonment in the body, the way toward liberation logically involves modes of purification from the body.

Poimandres, an anonymous revelatory composition—probably from the mid-second century—holds first position in a collection of writings called the Hermetic literature. It is the fullest and best representative of this way of being religious in the Greco-Roman world and, like Aristides and Epictetus, has been chosen precisely because of its exemplary character. Before examining *Poimandres,* however, it is helpful to trace some of the obscure roots of this religious sensibility, as well as the character of the Hermetic literature.

EARLY TRACES

We catch glimpses of this religious sensibility—or, more precisely, elements of this sensibility—in three phenomena, each of which presents distinct and difficult critical issues: Orphism, the Cult of Dionysius, and Pythagoreanism. Scholars are divided concerning the definition and dating of each of the phenomena and the possible interconnections among them. I touch on each here only to identify the problems and to isolate those elements in each that justify seeing it as a possible source for the sensibility we see so well formed in *Poimandres.*

1. Orphism draws its name from Orpheus, a pre-Homeric poet and lyre player who, according to legend, descended into the underworld to recover his wife, Eurydice, but lost her because he disobeyed the instruction of Persephone

not to look back; another myth concerning Orpheus had him torn to pieces either by women of Thrace or by female devotees of Dionysius.[1] Critical questions concern the degree to which "Orphism" represented a coherent view of life, much less an organized Mystery cult, and how much it may have influenced other, related, movements. The questions are difficult because of the extremely fragmentary and variegated character of the evidence—both archaeological and literary. No one today subscribes to the sort of "Pan-Orphism" that encompasses all the Mysteries, including Christianity.[2] Scholars tend rather to locate themselves between a strong synthetic view, which emphasizes points of continuity and argues for a distinct Orphic religion, and the opposing analytic tendency, which tends to deny any essential content to the term "Orphism."[3]

Without trying to solve problems over which generations of specialists have toiled,[4] it is possible to note some features that are commonly associated with Orphism and have some pertinence for the religious sensibility found in *Poimandres*: (1) the production of Orphic literature (such as the *Rhapsodies*) enabled the relatively few people who were literate access to an authoritative version of religious truth distinct from the ritual and speech of public civic performance; (2) the myths related in such literature claimed an antiquity greater than that of Homer and Hesiod and represented a darker representation of theogony; (3) Orphism had a concern for the future life, including teaching concerning rewards and punishments due souls; (4) speaking of the soul (*psychē*), it is the essential self that can pass, through metempsychosis, through multiple bodily forms, with an upward or downward movement; and (5) a primary religious concern is the purification of the soul through the observance of certain practices, such as vegetarianism.

2. Orphism has some connections to the cult of Dionysus, though these are difficult to determine precisely.[5] The worship of Dionysus is ancient and is best known as a form of a yearly public festival that was the occasion for the performance of dithyrambs and then drama (see Euripides' *Bacchai*).[6] The god Dionysus is associated with frenzy and ecstasy, a breaking of psychic and social roles, and is often seen in contrast to the supposedly more rational Apollo.[7] Also ancient is the development of a cult of Dionysus that was less public than the civic festivals and involved initiation. The communal drinking of wine—to the state of intoxication—was always a key element in the Dionysiac rites. Music, poetry, and dance also drew participants beyond the confines of normal social restraint to a sense of participation in a higher state.[8] Despite the presence of sexual symbolism, it is less clear how much sexual activity beyond ordinary constraints was involved in initiation, although the term *Bacchanalia* carried that popular connotation.[9]

Even within the context of polytheism, Dionysus is a protean figure, identified and merged with a variety of other deities, both in art and myth. Thus,
Dionysus can be brought into close conjunction with gods as disparate as
Hermes and Artemis.[10] Similarly, traditions concerning Dionysus intersect
those dealing with Orpheus. Both, for example, are said to have made journeys
to the underworld: Orpheus to seek his wife, Eurydice; Dionysus to bring back
his mother, Semele. Both are associated with stories of dismemberment. In the
story of Dionysus Zagreus, the other gods are jealous of this son of Zeus and
Demeter and arrange to have him torn to pieces; the goddess Pallas Athena
saves his heart and from it Zeus creates Dionysus. Orpheus, in turn, is said to
have been torn apart by the *Maenads* (female devotees of Dionysus) when he
paid homage to Apollo in preference over Dionysus.[11] In connection with these
tales, both Dionysus and Orpheus are associated with hopes for a blessed future
life.[12]

Both of them ancient and in large measure obscure, the Orphic and Dionysiac traditions suggest a "way of being religious" among Greeks and Romans
that sought something more than the benefits made available by the gods in
ordinary life, that saw something tragic in human limitations, that sought some
form of liberation from those limits through ecstasy or other forms of purification, and that offered "a walk on the sacred way" after death to those few whose
initiation gave them some sort of experiential foretaste, through knowledge, of
that future hope.[13]

3. In contrast to the mythic figures of Orpheus and Dionysus (one human,
one divine), Pythagoras is a genuinely historical figure (ca. 580–500 BCE)—
although followers assigned him a divine lineage—who was born in Greece,
traveled to Egypt, and founded a school in Crotona (present-day Italy, ca. 532).[14]
He is renowned as a mathematician whose theories (for example, "all is number") had a profound influence on Plato and others. It was the "way of life"
(*bios*) established by Pythagoras, however, that most influenced later political
thinking and showed traces of elements we have seen also in Orphism and the
cult of Dionysus.[15]

Building on the premise that "friends hold all things in common," Pythagoras established a community that was far more structured than the "schools"
that were to meet in the Academy or the Porch.[16] A genuine community of possessions enabled the maintenance of firm community boundaries both for admission and dismissal. Stages of initiation into full membership were not unlike
levels of initiation into the Mysteries, and like the Mysteries demanded the observance of silence.[17] The teachings of the master served not as topics for
examination but as revelatory pronouncements that guided practice in a truly

ascetical life, with rules for diet, sex, clothing, and things safe or unsafe to touch.[18]

The key tenet holding everything else together was the conviction that the essential self was the soul (*psychē*) and that this soul moved through successive existences (metempsychosis) either upward (away from entanglement with matter) or downward (into greater entanglement).[19] This tenet explains Pythagoras' reverence for all living beings who had souls—all living beings were, in this sense, "friends"—and the number of commands concerning the soul's purification.[20] The Pythagorean tradition does not invoke a myth of origins or of eventual future bliss, but the "religious" character of this philosophy is evident in two ways: it organizes all of life, and this organization depends on the apodictic instructions of a figure regarded as divine.

In the *Dialogues* of Plato (ca. 427–347 BCE), there are a number of passages that support the position that these traces of a religious sensibility were well known in classical Athens and that the version we find in *Poimandres* represents not a new and late creation so much as the fuller development of trends already present among some Greeks and Romans for centuries. In a passage that clearly alludes to the Pythagorean tradition, Plato has Socrates say, "I have heard a philosopher say that at this moment we are actually dead, and that the body [*sōma*] is our tomb [*sēma*]," before relating an elaborate set of metaphors about "the soul of the ignorant" and the importance of living temperately (*Gorgias*, 493C).[21] In *The Republic*, one of Socrates' interlocutors (Adeimantus) interjects into a discussion of justice the "strangest words about justice" that come from wandering priests and prophets who peddle "sacrifices and incantations [that] have accumulated a treasure of power from the gods" with the promise of expiating misdeeds (364B–D). These wandering ministers "produce a bushel of books of Musaeus and Orpheus" that they use in their rituals for remission of sins and "purifications for deeds of injustice" both for the living and the dead, to "deliver us from evils in that other world" (364E–365A).[22]

In a discussion on the nature of the soul in *Cratylus*, Plato has Socrates allude again to the position that the body is the tomb of the soul, "their notion being that the soul is buried in the present life." He ascribes the view to the "Orphic poets" who held that "the soul is undergoing punishment for something; they think it has the body as an enclosure to keep it safe, as a prison, and as the name itself denotes, the safe [*sōma*] for the soul, until the penalty is paid" (400C).[23] And in the *Laws*, Plato has the Athenian Stranger speak of tradition concerning people in the past who refused to perform animal sacrifices but who instead performed only "bloodless sacrifices" of meal and grain, a practice consistent with their having been forbidden "so much as to eat an ox": "from flesh they abstained as though it were unholy to eat it or to stain with blood the altars of the gods; instead of that, those of us men who then existed lived what is called as 'Orphic Life' [*orphikoi bioi*], keeping wholly to inanimate food, and contrariwise, abstaining wholly from things animate" (782C).[24]

That Plato is not unsympathetic to the Orphic-Pythagorean perspective is suggested by two passages in the *Phaedo*, a dialogue devoted to Socrates' last moments with his followers and subtitled "On the Soul." Explaining why suicide is forbidden, Socrates alludes to "a doctrine that is taught in secret about this matter, that we men are in a kind of prison, and must not set ourselves free or run away" (62B). More fully, he discourses on how the philosopher "would not devote himself to the body, but would so far as he was able, turn away from the body and concern himself with the soul" (64E), a course he subsequently elaborates: "And while we live, we shall, I think, be nearest knowledge when we avoid, so far as possible, intercourse and communion with the body, except what is absolutely necessary, and are not filled with its nature, and keep ourselves pure from it until God himself sets us free. And in this way, freeing ourselves from the foolishness of the body and being pure, we shall, I think, be with the pure and shall know of ourselves all that is pure—and that is, perhaps the truth. For it cannot be that the impure attain the pure" (67A–B).[25]

These traces of Orphic-Pythagorean perspectives in the great philosopher Plato not only confirm the antiquity of such traditions but also anticipate elements we meet again in the Hermetic literature: a view of the soul as superior to and entrapped by the body; a commitment to the "purification" of the soul through ascetical practices; the hope that this "essential self" has a future life; a grounding of such perceptions in revelatory books; a distinction between the path followed by the many and the knowledge given to the few; and the compatibility of this "way of life" with the love of wisdom, or "philosophy."

THE HERMETIC LITERATURE

The *Hermetica* is a complex collection of materials of Egyptian provenance associated with the revealer god Hermes—who was already by the third century BCE merged with the Egyptian god Thoth—which consists of "unlearned" writings of a theurgic character (largely dealing with magic and astrology) dating from the third century BCE and of "learned" writings of a revelatory character deriving from second- and third-century Alexandria.[26] It is the second kind of literature associated with the "Thrice-Greatest Hermes" (*Hermes Trismegistos*) that has primarily won the attention of scholars, and it is within this collection that we find *Poimandres*. Apart from some scattered testimonies in patristic and pagan writers, the material comes to us in three forms: (1) the *Corpus Hermeticum* itself, made up of 17 tracts written in Greek; (2) the Latin tractate *Asclepius*, which was once attributed to Apuleius; and (3) some 30 extracts from the sixth-century CE *Anthologium Graecum* of Stobaeus—including a lengthy segment of the tractate *Kore Kosmou* ("eye of the universe").[27]

The *Hermetica* take a number of literary forms. *Poimandres* is a first-person account of a revelation received from "the Mind of the Sovereignty" (*ho tēs authentias nous*) to an unnamed recipient. Other books include discourses—sometimes dialogues—directed to individuals, such as from Hermes to Asclepius and Tat (II, IV, XII, XIII, IV, *Asclepius*) and from Mind to Hermes (XI); letters from Asclepius to King Ammon (XVI, XVII); and general discourses ascribed to Hermes (III, VI, VII, VIII, IX, X, XVIII). The tractates share a pervasive religious mood, the motif of revelation, and a high level of abstraction—their language is rarely concrete or specific—which has the effect of making them seem to float in a timeless sphere.[28] Scholars have been able, nevertheless, to detect both Egyptian and Greek cultural influences.[29] In some tractates—including *Poimandres*—it is also possible to suggest a certain superficial level of acquaintance with the biblical creation story.[30] There is not, however, any reason to suppose contact with Christianity.[31] The *Hermetica* is a manifestation of genuinely Gentile religion.

Besides being generically diverse, the writings in the *Corpus Hermeticum* are impossible to fully harmonize in their outlook.[32] Scholars typically distinguish between tractates that are monistic (the divine is immanent; spirit pervades all) and those that are dualistic (the divine and world are distinguished; spirit and body are opposed), with the first group also considered more "optimistic" and the second more "pessimistic." Although this broad distinction has some merit—there are tractates that clearly represent extreme positions—it is more accurate to say that most of the tractates are to some extent "mixed" in their teaching, with elements both of monism and dualism.[33] In truth, the tractates differ most in what might be called their mythological elements (cosmogony and eschatology) and agree most in their exhortations (what humans are to do to be saved). The point can be demonstrated through a rapid comparison between monistic and dualistic tractates; such a review also helps provide a framework for a closer examination of *Poimandres*.

1. The monistic tractates tend to spend the most time developing cosmology, paying particular attention to the planets (III, IV, XI) that are connected to the influence of destiny or fate (*heimarmenē*; XII.1.5; XVI.16; *Asclepius*, 26 and 29). In various ways, these tractates declare that "all things are one" (*Asclepius*, 2a), that "god is the source of all" (XI.2.11–12), that "all things are full of god" (XI.1.6a),

and that evil is accidental (XIV.7). Nevertheless, these tractates also recognize a duality in humans (*Asclepius*, 7b). On one side, the soul is immortal (VIII.1a; *Asclepius*, 25) and immutable (XI.1.4a). The soul is filled with Mind and Mind with God (XI.1.4b): "The soul is in the body, Mind is in soul, God is in Mind" (XII.1.13b). The good and the real are not material (XIII.6). Mind, in turn, is of the very substance of God (XII.1.1) and participates in the good (*Asclepius*, 16a). Mind can overcome Destiny (XII.1.9; XVI.16).

On the other side is the body, which is material, mutable (XI.1.4a), and mortal (XIII.14). It is a source of disorder (VIII.3) that can subject the mind to itself (XII.1.11). Evil is inherent in the body (*Asclepius*, 22), is at the least a burden on the soul (*Asclepius*, 9), and can drive the soul astray (XVI.16), leading it downward away from its true home (XVI.8–9; *Asclepius*, 26). The soul is a traveler that can move upward or downward, away from its true place with the divine or away from it through successive existences (*Asclepius*, 12a). Salvation of the soul comes through knowledge (*gnōsis*; XIV.1) that is available only to the few (IX.1.4b; XIII.3; *Asclepius*, 10.16.22). Philosophy is knowledge of God (*Asclepius*, 12b), including the way for the soul to return to its fully divine condition (*Asclepius*, 11), and provides humans with a choice (XII.1.7).

The imperative embedded in these tractates is simply to leave the body (XIII.10), to quit the body in order to join the gods (XII.1.12), and to be restored to divinity (*Asclepius*, 11). Humans are, therefore, to regard the body as alien (*Asclepius*, 11a) and to avoid allowing their soul to be shut up in the body (XI.2.21a). They must scorn the body (*Asclepius*, 6a) and the body's desires (*Asclepius*, 11a) and put the body aside (*Asclepius*, 22). They are to experience the rebirth that comes through *gnōsis* (XIII.1), which demands of them that they "stop the working of [their] bodily senses, and then deity will be born in you" (XIII.7). They approach God by leaping clear of what is corporeal (XI.2.20b), which means avoiding flesh foods (*Asclepius*, 41b). They are to contemplate God in thought (XII.2.20b), because to worship God in this manner is to be free from evil (XII.2.23b).

2. When we turn to those tractates usually designated as dualistic and pessimistic, we find, perhaps surprisingly, some statements of a positive character, such as that God made all things (IV.1), God lacks nothing (VI.16), God supplies all things and is the cause of all things good (VI.1a), and even matter participates in good (VI.26). But these statements tend to get lost within negative evaluations of the world: "the world is a mass of evil, even as God is a mass of good" (VI.4a). Neither men nor "gods" are good; only God is good (II.14–16). Little actual cosmology appears in these tractates, however; their focus is on the human problem and how to solve it, rather than on an explanation of

causes. That problem is the divided character of humans, in which body and soul stand in opposition to each other (II.4a; II.86). God is the source of mind and truth (II.13), and the mind within humans is spirit, light, mind, truth, and good (II.12a–b). The pious soul is divine (X.19a), and the mind is divine (X.23). From the side of the soul, then, humans bear the image of God (IV.2). The spirit pertains to God or even is God (II.46).

Outside the realm of spirit, in contrast, and specifically in the realm of matter, all is evil (VI.2a). And since the body is made up of the four elements (II.11), they are filled with perturbation (VI.1a), and good cannot be found in perturbation (VI.2a). The material body has no room for the good, "hemmed in and gripped as such a body is by evil—by pains and griefs, desires and angry passions, delusions and foolish thoughts" (VI.3b). Insofar as a human being is matter, he is mortal, and man is evil insofar as he is mortal (X.12). The soul, then, is burdened by the body (II.9; X.8) and is imprisoned by the body (VII.1b). Indeed, as the physical body grows, so does evil grow (X.15b), and it is impossible in this world for things to be free of evil (VI.3a).

The soul is able to migrate either upward toward God or downward toward evil materiality (X.7–8). As the true essence of the human being comes from God, so can it return to God (X.24–25). What is required is "Mind" (*nous*) and the decision to live at the level of Mind, which means to live out the knowledge of one's true identity. Not all humans have "Mind" (IV.3); there are those without the knowledge (*gnōsis*; VI.6) that is the virtue of souls and is incorporeal (X.9–10). Those without such knowledge tend toward ignorance and vice (IV.3–5). But those who share in Mind have *gnōsis* (IV.4), the knowledge of God that is salvation (X.14).

There is a choice available to humans, then, to ascend to their true home or to descend into deeper alienation (IV.4). They can choose to be mortal or immortal (IV.6). They can begin to make progress toward God (IV.8–9). They do this by scorning the body (IV.5), hating the body (IV.6), suppressing the senses (X.6), and forsaking the familiar things of the senses even when they are needed (IV.9; VI.6). They seek a guide to the house of knowledge (VII.2a), understanding that freedom from the body is ascent to God (X.16), and that the knowledge of God is knowledge of the beautiful (VI.5). This turning from body to soul (Mind/Knowledge) is a kind of conversion. Readers are told that they can "find the bright light which is pure from darkness; there none are drunken, but all are sober, and they look up and see with the heart Him whose will is that with the heart alone should He be seen" (VII.2a). To do this, however, they must turn from the body: "First you must tear off this garment which you wear—this cloak of darkness, this web of ignorance, this prop of evil, this bond of corruption, this living death, this conscious corpse, this tomb you carry about with you, this robber in the house, this enemy who hates the things you seek after, and grudges you the things which you desire" (VII.2b).

POIMANDRES

The tractate draws its title from the name of the revealer, even though the precise meaning of that name remains obscure.[34] The phrase *ho tēs authentias nous* ("The Mind of the Sovereignty") follows the declaration "I am Poimandres" (2), in apposition and in effect providing an interpretation of the strange word.[35] Whatever the meaning of his name, Poimandres is clearly the revealer of the first God and is even equated with God (6), even though he speaks at times as though he was not (9 and 12) as he discloses saving *gnōsis* to the unnamed prophet. After the opening vision (1–3), Poimandres guides the prophet through a revelation consisting of a cosmogony (4–11), an anthropology (12–23), and an eschatology (24–26). The myth recital is periodically broken by dialogue between Poimandres and the prophet. Once having received the revelation, the prophet is commissioned to a career of preaching to others, a thumbnail sketch of which is provided (27–29). A hymn of thanksgiving closes the book (30–32).

The tractate deservedly heads up the *Corpus Hermeticum* because of its distinctive character: (1) it takes the form of a personal religious experience, involving both visions and auditions; (2) it provides a narrative framework for the relentlessly didactic tractates that follow, with a full cosmogony, anthropology, and eschatology; (3) it contains elements of specifically religious practice (preaching, conversion, prayer); and (4) it provides the basis for a community of the elect gathered by such an experience. In sum, *Poimandres* provides the mythic structure that helps make sense of the sometimes contradictory declarations found in the other hermetic tractates. If the consensus of scholars concerning *Poimandres'* second-century CE date is correct, then it presents us with a religious composition roughly contemporary with Aelius Aristides and Epictetus.[36]

The myth of origins must answer two questions of existential importance: the first is how a realm of pure light and goodness could have degenerated into a world of light-resistant matter; the second is how humans can at once be defined by the darkness of matter yet retain some element of light within them. The *Poimandres* myth solves these in typical fashion by interposing stages between the pure state of light and the fallen state of materiality. The myth thus recounts three not entirely compatible moments in the coming to be of the empirical world. In the first (4–6), darkness devolves from the light and becomes a wet and smoky substance from which emerge inarticulate cries; a responding word comes forth from the light and organizes the chaos into elements of fire and air, water and earth. In the second (7–8), a vision of the light itself discloses an infinity of powers, which organize themselves into a *kosmos*; here a brief role is played by the personified *boulē* ("will") of God. In the third, a Demiurge is produced from the Father, and his creative action brings about the celestial spheres that serve as the administrators of destiny (*heimarmenē*; 9–11a).

The origins of humanity are similarly complex. When material things had been separated out so that they were devoid of reason (10b), Mind the maker brought forth from this mindless material all the animals devoid of reason and then made an archetypal Human (*anthrōpos*) as a "being like to himself," "his own offspring," and "the likeness of the Father" (12), placing this archetypal Human over all mindless creatures. But now it gets complicated. The Human is given by each of the planetary spheres a share of their nature (13b) and then begins his tragic fall. Like Narcissus, he sees a reflection of himself in the mindless matter and wills to dwell there; and materiality, once it had the Human in its grasp, "wrapped him in her clasp, and they were mingled in one, for they were in love with one another" (14). At this point, Poimandres draws the critical anthropological lesson from the myth: "That is why man, unlike all other living creatures upon earth, is twofold. He is mortal by reason of his body; he is immortal by reason of the Man of eternal substance. He is immortal, and has all things in his power; yet he suffers the lot of a mortal, being subject to Destiny. He is exalted above the structure of the heavens; yet he is born a slave of Destiny; he is bisexual, as his Father is bisexual, and sleepless, as his Father is sleepless; yet he is mastered by carnal desire and oblivion" (15).

There follows a section dealing with the Seven First Men (16–17), which may have been of importance to the author, but whose significance is unclear, apart from serving to separate archetypal origins even further from present-day humans. The present human condition begins when "the bond which held all things together was loosed, by God's design" and humans were divided into two sexes. God commands them to increase and multiply but then adds, "Let the man who has mind in him recognize that he is immortal, and that the cause of death is carnal desire" (18). The seductive power of materiality, which drew Mind in the first place away from its place of origin and into entrapment, we are to understand, finds its most potent expression in the sexual desire between men and women.

Poimandres draws out the implications: "He who has recognized himself has entered into that Good which is above all being; but he who, being led astray by carnal desire, has set his affection on the body, continues wandering in the darkness of the sense-world, suffering the lot of death" (19). The reason why carnal people are lost is obvious: they have chosen to dwell in the primordial slime. But what does "recognize himself" mean? It means recognizing that one is from Light and Life and that knowing this, "you will go back into Life and Light" (21), a form of knowledge that comes to the holy and pure and good but not to all men (22). Such insight demands a life of asceticism: "Before they give up the body to the death that is proper to it, they loathe the bodily senses, knowing what manner of work the senses do. Nay, rather I myself, even Mind, will not suffer the workings of the body by which they are assailed to take effect; I will keep guard at the gates, and bar the entrance of the base and evil workings of the senses, cutting off all thought of them" (22). Such purification demands as well keeping away from those who live according to the demands of the senses (23).

Eschatology is the final part of the revelation. Poimandres explains how the material body will itself be changed after death, and the bodily senses will go back to their source in matter (24). Then "the human mounts upward through the structure of the heavens," and as the soul passes through the seven planetary zones, it progressively sheds the aspects of materiality that obscure the light: (1) sensual desire, (2) evil cunning, (3) deceitful lust, (4) domineering arrogance, (5) unholy daring and rash audacity, (6) strivings after wealth, and (7) falsehood that seeks to harm (25). The soul then ascends to the eighth sphere, where it joins the others already waiting there in singing hymns to the Father: "And being made like to those with whom he dwells, he hears the powers, who are above the substance of the eighth sphere, singing praise to God with a voice that is theirs alone. And thereafter, each in his turn, they mount upward to the Father; they give themselves to the powers, and becoming powers themselves, they enter into God. This is the good; this is the consummation, for those who have got *gnōsis*" (26a).

Having disclosed the threefold truth of from whence humans came, where they are going, and how they can get there, Poimandres commissions the prophet to make himself a guide to those who are worthy to receive the gift, "so that mankind may through you be saved by God" (26b). Being filled with power, "and having been taught the nature of all that is, and seen the supreme vision," the seer begins preaching to others "the beauty of piety and the knowledge of God" in terms that are classic for religious conversion: "Hearken ye folk, men born of earth, who have given yourselves up to drunkenness and sleep in your ignorance of God; awake to soberness, cease to be sodden with strong drink and lulled in sleep devoid of reason" (28).[37] And when some gather around him, he tells them, "Repent, ye who have journeyed with error, and joined company with ignorance; and rid yourself of darkness, and lay hold on light; partake of immortality, forsaking corruption" (29). Some rejected his call, but others "besought me that they might be taught" and the seer became "a guide to mankind, teaching them the doctrine, and how in what wise they might be saved" (29).[38]

The tractate concludes with the seer declaring that having "become god-inspired, I attained to the abode of truth," and composing a hymn of praise to God (31).[39] He then prays "that I may never fall away from that knowledge of Thee which matches with our being" and that he might "enlighten those of my race who are in ignorance, my brothers and thy sons" (32).

In *Poimandres*—to say nothing of the rest of the Hermetic literature—we have the perfect expression of Religiousness C: the divine *dynamis* is not found in the material processes of the world but only in the realm of immortal spirit and light. Salvation is rescuing the spark of light that has fallen into a bodily prison and returning it, through asceticism and death itself, to the realm from which it first came. It is triumph through escape. This perspective privileges the soul and despises the body. Its morality is one of purification, and its call is to the few among humans who can respond to its ascetical demands.

We can, at the end of this chapter, briefly review the three types of religious sensibility by imagining Aristides, Epictetus, and the author of *Poimandres* at a temple of Asclepius. Aristides would have enthusiastically sung a hymn of praise to his savior god for the healing of his body and would have gladly offered a sacrifice to his divine benefactor. Epictetus, in turn, could have participated in the ritual out of a sense of duty to the gods and would in no fashion have despised the act of worship, but he would have been far more concerned with the moral dispositions he brought to the bearing of his illness and would, indeed, have been tempted to make of Asclepius a type of the philosopher-physician who transformed the sickness of vice into the moral health of virtue.

The author of *Poimandres*, finally, would also have thought in terms of disease and health (see *Asclepius*, 22a) but much more radically: the disease was the body itself, and health was freeing the soul from the body's prison. He would, I think, have regarded Aristides' sacrifice as only another form of bodily imprisonment and would have thought Epictetus' internalization far from sufficiently radical (*Asclepius*, 37–38). He may have stood at a distance, offering silent prayer, seeking to keep his pure thoughts about the divine unaffected by the sound of songs and the smell of incense, convinced that "such gifts as these are unfit for him; for he is filled with all things that exist, and lacks nothing," and remembering the instruction, "Let us adore him rather with thanksgiving; for words of praise are the only offering that he accepts" (*Asclepius*, 41a).

7

RELIGION AS STABILIZING THE WORLD: PLUTARCH

The fourth way of being religious in the Greco-Roman world is in some ways the most difficult to assess, partly because of the deep-seated bias that many Christian scholars bring to it, partly because of the paucity of sources for a "sensibility"—people who follow this path do not necessarily express their religious impulses in literature—and partly because in many respects it is complementary to Religiousness A ("Participation in Divine Benefits"). I approach my characterization of this sensibility by considering the three difficulties in reverse order.

1. In my preliminary profile of Greco-Roman religion (see Chapter 3), I surveyed all the ways in which the divine *dynamis* was available, not only in the ordinary round of domestic and public observance (in festivals, sacrifices, meals, and prayers), but also in the specific manifestations of prophecy, healing, the Mysteries, and pilgrimage. Throngs of people participated in such religious practices. Among them were the many in the Greco-Roman world who made such practices possible, such access to the divine *dynamis* available. They are the ones who organized and funded the festivals, prepared and carried out the sacrifices, cleaned and guarded the temples, and provided expertise for divination and prophecy; they are the ones who staffed the shrines at Epidaurus and Pergamum, Delphi and Dodonna; they offered their services to the oversight of religious calendars and feasts; they served as Vestal Virgins and on the board of Pontiffs. In short, though fewer in number than those who sought benefit from power made available through the rituals, there were many whose concern was to support and organize those sources of power. They represent, in a sense, the "supply side" of Religiousness A.[1] They are not necessarily easy to see because they "hide in plain sight" within the ritual, or they work behind the scenes to make the ritual possible.

2. One reason why such highly visible and active enablers of religious ritual remain relatively hidden from present-day observers is that their religious identity so perfectly meshes with the public character of so much Greco-Roman observance. We do not find them writing revelatory literature urging people to turn from visible ritual, such as in the *Hermetica*, nor do we find them urging a moral expression of the divine presence, such as in Epictetus. We might, indeed, find them writing hymns and prayers to be performed in honor of the gods in the manner of Aristides, but lacking his distinctive personality, they would be less likely to attach their name to such efforts.[2] For the most part, then, we do not find the expression of this religious sensibility in the form of literature. Instead, we are required to construct what the sensibility must have been from the rich inscriptional evidence for the participation of individuals, associations, and rulers of every sort as the patrons of civic religion. Such archaeologically recovered inscriptions not only give us some of our best information concerning what actually happened in ritual; they also show how countless people expressed their piety by making ritual possible.

3. A final obstacle to appreciating this fourth type of religiosity is the deep-seated bias of some Christian theology toward all expressions of religion that are formal, public, institutional, and sacramental.[3] Insofar as certain forms of Christianity defined themselves in contrast to what was called Jewish legalism ("outward religion") in favor of the inwardness of faith, and insofar as these same forms have rejected such elements even within Christianity as a distortion of authentic faith,[4] it is difficult for scholars shaped by such traditions to grant that the form of Greco-Roman religiosity that finds expression precisely in cultic acts and ritual performance might be "sincere" or "authentic." The heartfelt devotion of the ailing Aristides, yes; the noble resignation of the crippled Epictetus, yes; the longing for escape from the body by the author of *Poimandres*, yes: all these can be readily appreciated as authentic in conviction and experience. But empathy does not extend to the man who seeks a seat in the College of Augurs, the mother who places her daughter in nomination for the Vestal Virgins, the wealthy patron who sponsors the Panathenaic festival, or the emperor who builds the *Ara Pacis*. Yet, the contrast between outer observance and interior disposition has never been a legitimate one. Not only is there as little likelihood of assessing the "sincerity" of a mystic as there is that of the patron of a festival; there is every reason to suppose that such patronage expresses a distinctive way of *being* religious. It is the task of this chapter, in fact, to attempt a sympathetic reading of the evidence.

The impulses of this sensibility are at once public and conservative: public in that it supports and enables many diverse forms of religious observance insofar as they express the identity of the city-state and empire; conservative in that it regards such observances as critical for the preservation of the city-state and empire. The first three forms of religious sensibility thought in terms of individual body, either as the arena of divine power (Type A and Type B) or as the prison from which the authentic self must be saved (Type C). The type we consider now thinks in terms of the social body and the way in which the divine *dynamis* is needed for its stability and success. The salvation not of the individual but of society is the point of religion. In the most positive sense of each term, we can even designate this "priestcraft as statecraft," for the two aspects are clearly related: cult in service of the city/empire, and the city/empire as the locus for divine beneficence. This form of religiousness accepts completely the ancient premise that religion is the glue of society, so that the regular, decent, and appropriate honor paid to all the gods can be regarded not only as the highest form of piety but also as the most noble and altruistic expression of citizenship.

In this chapter, I devote some attention to the way in which the public character of Greco-Roman religion combined piety and politics and then consider the ancient writer who comes closest to giving literary expression to this sensibility, Plutarch of Chaeronea. Plutarch, as we shall see, is far too complex a figure to be a simple representative of anything, but as a rough contemporary of the other religious figures we have analyzed, his voice is a necessary addition to the mix.

MAINTAINING THE CITY OF GODS AND MEN

The intricate interconnections of religion and politics can be traced to the origins of Greek religion. The worship of specific divine powers probably originated at the local level, among households and clans, and it probably seemed equally natural that the male leaders of such social groups were responsible for carrying out the rituals in honor of the local deities. In such fashion, the sacrificial community both expresses and is a model for the social grouping.[5] Those who exercise rule in the family and clan also lead in worship.

With the firm establishment of the Greek city-state, the cult continues to express the political reality. Just as many families and clans are represented in the city, so is there a family of gods that the city as such must worship.[6] And as the sense of the city as a distinct entity develops, so does there grow the need to ensure that all the gods of the city are honored. Necessarily, then, ritual tasks need to be articulated in the same manner that other social roles are. The city as a whole becomes the sacrificial community. But the political unity of the

Greek *polis* dissolves neither the plurality of the gods nor the relative autonomy of its free citizens. The notion of *leitourgia*, or public service, applied equally to the service of the state and of the gods[7]—they went together—and depended both on the pressure of social expectation (*noblesse oblige*) and the perception of citizens that the good of the *polis* could require extraordinary service, because the continuing prosperity of the citizen and the citizen's family or clan depended on the security of the *polis*.

The city's claim to exercise a monopoly on cults was, moreover, constantly countered by the capacity of religious experience to escape centralized control. As important as the Mysteries at Eleusis were to Athens, they stayed under the authority of two families, the Eumolpidari, who supplied the Hierophant, and the Kerykes, who supplied Torchbearers and Heralds.[8] Cult Associations, such as those connected with Dionysus, also found ritual expression and forms of social interaction outside the city-organized festivals. Some local cult centers, furthermore, took on significance larger than an individual city. Thus we see an Ionian Amphictyony gathered around the cult of Poseidon and, more significant still, the Pylean Amphictyony organized in the sixth century BCE around the Demeter sanctuary at Thermopolae and the shrine of Apollo at Delphi. Religious worship forged political alliance and a sense of Greek civilization that was larger than the family, clan, and even city.[9]

Both the inclusion of many gods within the worship of a city and the extension of the worship of specific gods outside the control of specific cities tended to enlarge the religious imagination of those who were citizens of cities in two ways: first, giving honor to all the gods (neglecting none of them) was of supreme importance, for all the gods were part of the same extended family that corresponded to the extended family that was the city; second, the worship of all the gods served the stability of the city and indeed of the world. Because "the world" worth inhabiting for the Greeks was increasingly the world of the *polis*, and since the survival and prosperity of the *polis* depended directly on the beneficence of the gods, religious devotion to the gods through the public cult, in the strictest sense of the term, was world maintenance. Those who made such worship possible had the right to consider themselves the best and most purely religious of all citizens, for they sought not only private benefit but the good of the whole.

During the Republic, Rome had a complex set of priesthoods that were similarly enmeshed in the political life of the city.[10] For Roman males who were patrician and wealthy, a life of service to the city was expected and also well rewarded. With skill and good fortune, a young man (even a "new man" like Cicero) could pass through the stages of the *cursus honorum* to ever more important magistracies: Quaestor, Aedile, Praetor, Consul.[11] Advancement in the political order could be helped considerably by membership in one of the priestly colleges: before taking on any of his other roles, Julius Caesar was elected to the College of Pontiffs.[12] With the exceptions to be noted later, all priests were patrician men, although over time some plebeians were included. Priests were chosen from within the already existing membership or were elected.[13]

The College of Pontiffs eventually numbered 16 and oversaw the widest range of Roman religious observances as well as giving advice to the Senate on religious decisions.[14] The College of Augurs also numbered 16. It discerned the approval or disapproval of the gods for political and military acts and also advised the Senate.[15] Similarly involved with prophecy, the *Quindecemviri* (15–16 members) had charge of the Sibylline Books and supervised foreign cults in the city.[16] There were also the *Fetiales*, consisting of 20 members, who were responsible for the religious aspects of Rome's dealings with outsiders, including treaties and the making of war.[17] Less sweeping responsibilities were exercised by other priesthoods. The *Fratres Arvales* (Arval Brotherhood, numbering 12) was an ancient pre-republican priesthood that had charge of the cult of Dea Dia,[18] and the *Potii and Pinarii* (members of two families) managed the cult of Hercules. The *Luperci* (two groups, number unknown) managed the festival called *Lupercalia*.[19] The Salian priests (24 in number) performed rituals throughout the city in March and October—the start and end of the war season. The *Septemviri Epulones* took over from the Pontiffs the organization of ritual feasts for the gods.[20]

In addition to these administrative boards of priests, whose decisions and advice often helped shape the political life of the city, there were a variety of individual priesthoods that were marked by exclusion from politics, such as the *Rex Sacrorum*, who was prohibited from a political career, and the *Flamens*, priests of specific named gods.[21] The most sacred was the *Flamen Dialis*, chosen by the head of the College of Pontiffs, the *Pontifex Maximus*. He was selected to a lifetime of service—with his wife—in the cult of Jupiter. He wore special clothes and was so surrounded by taboos that a senatorial career was virtually impossible.[22] Also appointed for life were the *Flamen Martialis* and the *Flamen Quirinales*, who performed similar cult observances in honor of Mars and Quirinus. The Minor *Flamines* (12) were drawn from the plebeians and managed the cult of individual deities. Female representation in this complex web of priesthoods was restricted (with the exception of the *Flaminica Dialis*—the wife of the priest of Jupiter) to the symbolic functions of Virgins. The six Vestal Virgins were chosen from patrician candidates between the ages of six and 10 and served a term of 30 years, after which they could return to normal life; they guarded the sacred hearth of Vesta and took part in other rituals.[23] A group of plebeian women were designated as Salian Virgins (number not known) and joined in worship with the Pontifex Maximus in an annual sacrifice.[24]

The impression given by all these forms of priesthood is threefold: first, many Romans could be involved (over 100 at this upper level) in the administration of the cults; second, the Roman love for organization is reflected in the "Colleges" that served both to run religion and critical aspects of the life of the city; third, the play of political power was real but diffused and interconnected, just as was the play of religious power. It is easy to understand how those who sought a consolidation of political power would seek also to control such priesthoods. Thus, Julius Caesar, who was elected to the College of Pontiffs in 74 BCE, and was made *Pontifex Maximus* in 63 BCE, also made himself the head of the College of Augurs on becoming dictator in 46 BCE.[25]

The political significance of the religious priesthoods is indicated as well by the way in which Caesar Augustus gathered all the important ones to himself as *imperator*.[26] In the *Res Gestae*, published when he was 76, Augustus highlights the contributions he made to the religious life of Rome.[27] He had served as Senator for 40 years but had also been *Pontifex Maximus*, head of the College of Augurs, a member of the *Quindecemviri* (Sibylline Books) and the Arval Brotherhood, and one of the *Titii Sodales* (identity unknown) and of the *Fetiales* (7). He had, in other words, combined in himself every important office of religious oversight. From those positions, he built and restored temples (19--20) in the city, on his own land (21), and throughout Asia (23); he was prayed for by the colleges of priests and the people, even having his name inserted into the hymn of the Salian Priests (9–10); he carried out sacrifices (11) and constructed the magnificent *Ara Pacis* (Altar of Peace); most impressive, with the *Quindecemviri*, he inaugurated in 17 BCE the Secular Games, which had the exact opposite religious significance than the same words would mean in present-day parlance. It is easy to regard Augustus' gathering of religious offices as a cynical manipulation of the state's power, and it is naturally impossible to assess his internal dispositions. But from the perspective of Religiousness D, it could also be regarded as a supreme act of piety through which the emperor helped secure the Roman world by maintaining devotion to all the traditional Roman gods.[28]

In fact, however, Augustus' concentration of religious authority in himself (through the traditional Colleges of Priests) could have had only minimal real effect on the religious life of the empire as a whole, which continued to flourish independently in all the complex ways that it had before.[29] There were multiple temples and cults and priesthoods in every city, all of them supported by local patronage—occasionally supplemented by emperors—and all of them with local deities to worship as well as those honored throughout the empire as a whole.[30] Each province of the empire, in turn, had its own rich ecology of religious practice and custom, offering multiple opportunities for citizens to exercise civic virtue and religious piety simultaneously through participation in local and regional priesthoods.[31] Far more important for the political cohesion of the empire than Augustus' assumption of multiple priesthoods was the development of the imperial cult. First the emperors and then the imperial families were embraced by religious associations across the entire empire, as close as Sparta and as far away as Gaul.[32]

THE MANY-SIDED PLUTARCH

Of the individuals we have considered, Plutarch is by far the most complex and, ultimately, influential. He was born into a wealthy and well-connected family in the town of Chaeronea in Boeotia (east central Greece) in 45/46 CE.[33] His father, Autobulus, was himself a biographer and philosopher.[34] Plutarch had two brothers, Lamprias and Timon.[35] Plutarch studied mathematics and philosophy in Athens in 66–67 under Ammonius of Lamptrae, a Platonist with a strong Aristotelian bent. He traveled extensively in Greece, Egypt, and Asia Minor, gathering a vast amount of learning wherever he went. He lectured publicly in Rome on Platonic Philosophy and enjoyed Roman citizenship. Indeed, he was granted the (largely honorific) title of Ex-Consul by the emperor Trajan. It is less likely that he was made governor of Greece by Hadrian, but he did take the role of chief magistrate in his hometown of Chaeronea and filled a number of other local magistracies. In 95, he was appointed priest for life at the ancient shrine of Apollo at Delphi. While holding that position, and becoming the father of four sons, he also taught philosophy in the school he had established in his home. He died around 120 CE. His nephew, Sextus, was a friend and an important influence on Marcus Aurelius.[36]

Plutarch enjoyed a long and distinguished career as a writer. Many of his works have been lost, but what remains is substantial and impressive.[37] The 65 lectures, dialogues, essays, and collections of anecdotes are gathered together under the general rubric of *Moralia*. His *Parallel Lives of Greeks and Romans* contains 50 biographies, 46 in the form of comparative matches (e.g., Demosthenes and Cicero, Alexander and Julius Caesar) and four standing alone. There is a material connection between the two bodies of writing, since Plutarch used some of the *Moralia* to stockpile the raw material used also in the *Lives*.[38]

Plutarch deserves attention on five basic counts: (1) his writings are literarily diverse and have had a great impact on Western culture, both as a source for Shakespearean drama and as a theorist of education;[39] (2) his works contain a simply astonishing amount of specific lore about antiquity that remains of first importance to students of Greek and Roman Culture;[40] (3) he is a significant figure in the development of Platonism, blending a devotion to Plato's vision of reality with a thoroughgoing use of Aristotelian logic and ethics;[41] (4) he is a persuasive and often charming moral teacher, whose dissection of vices and virtues remains of enduring value for their psychological insight;[42] (5) he is an astute student of religion, bringing a philosophical disposition to the traditional practices of Greco-Roman piety.

It is this last aspect that makes Plutarch of interest to my investigation of the ways of being religious in the Greco-Roman world. But where exactly does he fit within these discrete religious sensibilities? He does not fit comfortably within Religiousness A: although he was probably initiated into the Dionysian Mysteries (*Isis and Osiris*, 35) and was a priest of Apollo at Delphi, there is little evidence anywhere in his writings of the sort of personal devotion to a deity exhibited by Aristides. More significant, he never speaks of religious observance in terms of a personal participation in divine benefits. His is also clearly not the sort of sensibility we have seen in Religiousness C. Despite his affirmation of a Platonic vision of the soul and its afterlife, nothing in his writings suggests a desire to withdraw from the complexities of worldly life in the body or a detestation of social engagement.

Does Plutarch, then, fit within Religiousness B, the way of moral transformation, so wonderfully displayed by the philosopher Epictetus? One might be tempted to so categorize one of antiquity's great moralists, and there is no doubt that the author of *Progress in Virtue* considered such moral transformation important. What is striking in all of his moral treatises, however, is their lack of religious discourse: although he subscribes to the Platonic ideal of "imitating god" through the moral life,[43] he lacks altogether the conviction that the virtuous life is a form of witnessing to God or that the philosopher has the divine vocation of healing other humans through moral instruction. And if he lacks the religious self-preoccupation of an Aristides that expresses itself in a simultaneously anxious and blissful devotion centered on Asclepius, he equally lacks the deeply personal awareness of living within divine providence that we find in some of Epictetus' most moving passages. There is, in fact, very little of "self" in any sense that emerges from Plutarch's writings; for an author so prolific, we know remarkably little about his interior life. If Aristides and Epictetus are religiously "warm," then Plutarch is definitely "cool."

The process of elimination suggests that Plutarch does not fit easily in the other categories, but there are also positive reasons for picking him to represent Type D: religion as stabilizing the world. First, he is a full participant in the accepted social, political, and religious forms. Unlike Aristides, he accepts rather than refuses the responsibility of exercising civic magistracies. He not only serves as a priest of Apollo at Delphi but shows a remarkable level of commitment to the administration of the shrine, expending considerable effort (and unquestionably personal funds) to improve the site and return it to its former prestige.[44] He is an advocate for the cult over which he has been assigned supervision. Second, he is a student of religion as such, particularly in its social dimension; among the authors we have reviewed, he comes closest to a concern for the way religion affects the well-being of the social order rather than the benefit it brings to an individual.[45] Third, a substantial number of his religious compositions are based on specific aspects of cult; his "philosophical religion" is not one that replaces bodily gesture with ideas but rather seeks to think rightly about bodily gesture.

PIETY AND THE PRESERVATION OF CIVILIZATION

Because my treatment of Plutarch's often lengthy religious writings is necessarily brief, I begin this discussion with an overview that can help guide the reader through the subsequent discussion of specific texts. In good Aristotelian fashion, Plutarch locates the ideal of genuine religious virtue between the extremes of two religious vices. The virtue is "piety" (*eusebeia*), which involves both an appropriate employment of religious rituals and a philosophically appropriate way of thinking about the gods. The extreme on one side is "superstition" (*deisidaimonia*), which consists of an obsessive and fearful observance of religious rituals, and thinking wrongly (even wickedly) about the gods. The extreme on the other side is "atheism" (*atheotēs*), which dismisses the traditional gods with intellectual contempt and withdraws from participation in traditional cult.

SUPERSTITION

Of the two vices, Plutarch regards superstition as the worse. He takes up the subject explicitly in his relatively brief work, *On Superstition* (*peri deisidaimonias*), which takes the form of a straightforward lecture (Mor., 164E–171F).[46] He begins with a comparison and contrast between superstition and atheism. Both express "ignorance and blindness with regard to the gods," and both are the sort of error that have real consequences for life. Atheism is found mostly in "hardened characters" while superstition flourishes among "tender characters" (*On*

Superstition, 1). The atheist's rejection of the existence of the gods leads to a kind of indifference (*apatheia*); the superstitious person, in contrast, is driven from start to finish by fear;[47] while the atheist denies that the gods exist, the superstitious person thinks they exist and "are the cause of pain and injury." What is wrong here is that properly understood, the gods—or the providence that works through them—is beneficent and moral. Plutarch nicely summarizes: "Whence it follows that atheism is falsified reason, and superstition is an emotion (*pathos*) engendered by false reason" (2).

Superstitious fear is, in fact, the most impotent and helpless of all fears: "he who fears the gods fears all things, earth and sea, air and sky, darkness and light, sound and silence, and a dream" (3). Because such fear—we would say anxiety—is so pervasive and all-encompassing, it affects every aspect of the person's life, including religious observances themselves—the shrines to which people flee for sanctuary, the altars where slaves seek refuge, are the very things that terrify them the most (4). The superstitious person not only does harm to himself; by regarding the gods as the cause of his every calamity, he thinks wrongly about them: "For he puts the responsibility for his lot upon no man nor upon Fortune nor upon occasion nor upon himself, but lays the responsibility for everything upon God, and says that from that source a heaven-sent stream of mischief has come upon him with full force" (7).

In two passages, Plutarch describes the extreme observances superstition engenders. It is not simply a matter of carrying out ordinary ritual with an attitude of fear; new and bizarre practices are cultivated. The superstitious listen to "conjurers and imposters" who encourage "magical purifications," such as "smearing oneself with mud, wallowing in filth, immersions, casting oneself down with face to the ground, disgraceful besieging of the gods, and uncouth prostrations" (3). Plutarch also refers to "magic charms and spells, rushing about and beating of drums, impure purifications and dirty sanctifications, barbarous and outlandish penances and mortifications at the shrines" (12). The adjective "barbarous" (*barbaroi*) in this last description is revealing: a reason why superstitious fear is destructive is that it leads to practices that are not Greek—that is, not part of the civilized order, which for Plutarch is coextensive with the "city of gods and men."

That this is genuinely on his mind can be seen also in the first description I quoted, which is introduced by a quotation from Euripides, "Greeks from barbarians finding evil ways" (*The Trojan Women*, 764): the religious practices foisted on the superstitious threaten the integrity of Greek religion and therefore of Greek culture. Plutarch goes on to observe in the same passage that the superstitious, rather than singing to the gods in the manner taught by Greek tradition, "by distorting and sullying one's own tongue with strange names and barbarous phrases . . . disgrace and transgress the god-given ancestral dignity of our religion" (*On Superstition*, 3). And later, after providing several examples of how true Greek piety combines the supplication and honor of the gods together with robust and responsible action, even that of war, he gives a counterexample from a barbarian people: "But the Jews, because it was the Sabbath day, sat in their places immoveable, while the enemy were planting ladders against the walls and capturing the defenses, and they did not get up, but remained there, fast bound in the toils of superstition as in one great net" (8).[48]

The final social consequence of superstition is that it actually encourages atheism in others. Indeed, says Plutarch, the superstitious person "by preference would be an atheist, but is too weak to hold the opinion about the gods he wishes to hold" (*On Superstition*, 11). Instead, driven by fear of the gods, the superstitious person acts in such an offensive fashion as to give religion itself a bad name: "All these [superstitious activities] give occasion to some to say that it were better that there should be no gods at all than gods who accept with pleasure such forms of worship, and are so overbearing, so petty, and so easily offended" (12). Plutarch thinks it is as unholy (*anosion*) to have a mean opinion of the gods as to speak meanly about them (11) and says, "Hence it occurs to me to wonder at those who say that atheism is impiety [*asebeia*] and do not say the same thing about superstition" (10). In short, superstition is not simply an individual spiritual pathology; it has deleterious social consequences.

Superstition is a concern also in one of Plutarch's longest works on the topic of religion, *Isis and Osiris* (Mor., 351C–384C), dedicated to Clea, a woman who served with him as a priestess at Delphi, who had been consecrated by her mother and father to the holy rites of Isis (*Isis and Osiris*, 35).[49] The treatise contains a wealth of information about the specifics of the cult, but it is as an occasion for Plutarch's thought on true religion that I find it valuable for this study. In light of the connection between superstition and barbarism that he drew in *On Superstition*, we can understand why the cult of the Egyptian god Osiris (the consort of Isis) might have presented a particularly daunting difficulty for Plutarch. On one side, the cult had gained widespread acceptance in the Greco-Roman world, not least because of the identification, already in Herodotus, of Osiris with the Greek god Dionysus,[50] and the acceptance of him by the Romans under the title of Serapis, but also because of the popularity of the goddess Isis. On the other side, the myths associated with Osiris were convoluted, self-contradictory, and not morally attractive. Plutarch was required to tread carefully as he led his admired female colleague to a "philosophical" appreciation of the cult to which she had been dedicated.

He begins by asserting his two basic principles: first, all good things come from the gods, including knowledge of them (1); and second, seeking the truth about the gods is itself a longing for the divine (2). Plutarch does not, however, separate what we would call a "theological" path from the highly specific actions of the cult. Key to his argument, indeed, is a concentration on "the things done" (*ta drōmena*) in the cult more than on the myths associated with the actions. His strategy is simple. He seeks to assimilate the cult of Osiris to the native Greek cult of Dionysus;[51] he develops a theory of how cult actions are themselves revelatory; and he advocates the allegorical interpretation of the myths (as well as the ceremonies). The effect is to move this barbarian cult away from superstition and closer to the true piety of the Greeks.

First, like Herodotus, he asserts that Osiris is "identical with Dionysus" and argues this on the basis of similarity in ceremonies in the two cults:[52] the Bacchic procession, the wearing of the skins of animals, the shoutings, and the movements that are reminiscent of those in Bacchic frenzy (35). At the mythic level as well, what is said about Osiris reminds Plutarch of Dionysus, "the creative and fostering spirit" (40). And he further aligns ceremonies associated with Isis with those observed by the Greeks (69).

Second, Plutarch focuses Clea's attention not on the extravagant tales of Osiris but on the rituals. They are obscure, but Isis can reveal their wisdom to those who bear in their souls the sacred writings about the gods "clear of all superstition or pedantry" (3). He shows first how the observances of the Egyptian priests, who were themselves wise (9), were the source of wisdom. Properly understood, "nothing that is irrational or fabulous or prompted by superstition, as some believe, has ever been given a place in their rites, but in them are some things that have practical and moral values, and others that are not without their share in the refinements of history or natural science" (8). The ceremonies are one of the ways Osiris liberated the Egyptians from barbarism: he gave them agriculture, laws, and worship (13). Indeed, Plutarch asserts that Providence has arranged it so that "there have arisen among different peoples, in accordance with their customs, different honors and appellations [for gods]. Thus men make use of consecrated symbols, some employing symbols that are obscure, but others that are clearer, in guiding the intelligence toward things divine, though not without a certain hazard" (67).

What is the hazard? "That some go completely astray and become engulfed in superstition; and others, while they fly from superstition as from a quagmire, on the other hand fall, unwittingly as it were, over a precipice into atheism" (67). He repeatedly asserts that the role of the rituals is to teach morality for

those who understand them properly (20, 27, 37, 44). But how is proper understanding given? Hermeneutics is the third part of Plutarch's strategy.

He tells Clea, "you must not think that any of these tales actually happened in
the manner in which they are related" (11). He declares that as a guide in religious
Mysteries, we must adopt the "reasoning that comes from philosophy" (*logos ek
philosophias*) in considering "each one of the things that are said and done" (*le-
gomena kai drōmena*) (68). This means, in effect, the vigorous application of allegorical interpretation both to myths and rituals, a task that Plutarch pursues
vigorously throughout the treatise, turning the offenses and obscurities of a barbarous religion into profound moral lessons and natural science. He assures Clea,
"If, then, you listen to the stories about the gods in this way, accepting them from
those who interpret the story reverently and philosophically [*hosiōs kai philoso-
phōs*], and if you always perform and observe the established rites of worship, and
believe that no sacrifice that you can offer, no deed that you may do, will be more
likely to find favor with the gods than your belief in their true nature, you may
avoid superstition which is no less an evil than atheism" (11).

ATHEISM

One way in which atheism is superior to superstition is that it does not blame
the gods; when evil happens, the atheist looks to other causes (*On Superstition*,
7). But Plutarch nevertheless regards atheism as much a vice as its opposite:
atheism is a form of impiety (*asebeia*; 10), a bad judgment with regard to the
divine that leads to a sort of indifference (3). It is a sad lack of sight (5), a form of
blindness that prevents the sight of the gods and, as a result, leads to an incapacity to appreciate the good (6) and to a harsh mockery of religious ritual: "the
atheist on these occasions gives way to insane and sardonic laughter at such ceremonies, and remarks made to his cronies that people must cherish a vain and
silly conceit to think that these rites are performed in honor of the gods" (9).
Still, Plutarch thinks it worse to think badly about the gods than to deny them
and, as we saw above, actually blames superstition for atheism: "For thus it is that
some persons, in trying to escape superstition, rush into a rough and hardened
atheism, thus overleaping true religion which lies between" (*en mesō keimenēn
tēn eusebeian*) (14).

Egregious atheism in the Greco-Roman world was best exemplified by the
Epicureans. Plutarch's anti-Epicurean treatises provide him with the opportunity to expand these ideas further. His short essay "Is 'Live Unknown' a Wise
Precept" (Mor., 1128B–1133oE) takes up the Epicurean maxim *lathe biōsas*
and, in his usual polemic mode, shows the self-contradictions inherent in the

proposition.[53] Among these contradictions is the fact that the philosopher who coined the maxim did so in order to be famous (1). Plutarch also exploits the common perception of the Epicureans' tight community as an opportunity to escape detection of their vice. He declares that living privately is fine if one wants to engage in secret and shameful pleasures and contrasts this with his own ideal of life: "But take one who in natural philosophy extols God and justice and providence, in ethics law and society and participation in public affairs, and in political life the upright and not the utilitarian act, what need has he to live unknown?" (4). We notice the combination of religious piety, moral probity, and political engagement, all of which are, in Plutarch's view, rejected by atheists.

Plutarch wrote several other anti-Epicurean works that are lost, but the two substantial extant compositions, *Against Colotes* (Mor., 1107D–1127) and *A Pleasant Life Impossible* (Mor., 1086C–1107C), show that he continued to press the same themes with respect to the topic of atheism. *Against Colotes* is in the form of a lecture delivered by Plutarch and is far harsher in tone. *A Pleasant Life Impossible* is in the form of a dialogue that took place after his lecture, principally involving his students Aristodemus and Theon.

Once more, Plutarch defines atheism as a kind of indifference toward the gods. Although atheism eliminates superstitious fear, "it allows no joy and delight to come to us from the gods. . . . We expect nothing from them either good or evil" (*Pleasant Life*, 20). Plutarch also, however, charges the Epicureans with the most bizarre form of religious hypocrisy: they reject the gods of the city but construct a pseudo-religion around their own founder (*Pleasant Life*, 15, 18; *Colotes*, 17). An even greater hypocrisy is their willingness to enjoy the benefits of Greek civilization, without paying their dues (*Colotes*, 33). Plutarch directly connects the Epicurean refusal of public service—"shunning office and political activity and the friendship of kings" (*Pleasant Life*, 19)—with their denial of the gods, for the two are inextricably linked: "If oracles and divination and divine providence and the affection and love of parent for child and political activity and leadership and holding office are honorable and of good report, so surely those who say there is no need to save Greece, but rather eat and drink so as to gratify the belly without harming it, are bound to suffer in repute and to be regarded as bad men" (*Pleasant Life*, 19; see also *Colotes*, 2).

Plutarch charges that the Epicurean teaching that the names of the gods corresponded to nothing has real and grievous consequences: "When you tear from the gods the appellations attached to them and by that single act annihilate all sacrifices, mysteries, processions and festivals . . . these views affect matters of the highest and gravest import, and error in them involves reality, not a set of vocables or the conjunction of meanings or the accepted usage of words" (*Colotes*, 22). The "matters of gravest import" Plutarch has in mind are the ways in which religious ritual grounds the civilization of the Greek *polis*: "No praise accordingly can ever do justice to the men who dealt with these brutish feelings [of animals—i.e., barbarians] by establishing laws and with them states and governments and a system of legislation. But who are the men who nullify these things, overthrowing the state and utterly abolishing the laws? Is it not those who withdraw themselves and their disciples from participation in the state?" (31). For Plutarch, the worship of the gods is the essential element in the constitution of the state: "In your travels you may come upon cities without walls, writing, king, houses or property, doing without currency, having no notion of a theatre or gymnasium; but a city without holy places and gods, without any observance of prayers, oaths, oracles, sacrifices for blessings received or rites to avoid evils, no traveler has ever seen or will ever see. No, I think a city might rather be formed without the ground it stands on than a government, once you remove all religion from under it, get itself established or once established survive" (31). If superstition has as its social consequence a reversion to barbarism even within the structure of civilization, atheism has as its inevitable result the collapse of civilization itself.

PIETY

Perhaps something of Plutarch's own religious sensibility is revealed in his statement of delight in religious ritual: "No visit delights us more than a visit to a temple; no occasion than a holy day; no act or spectacle than what we see and what we do ourselves in matters that involve the gods, whether we celebrate a ritual or take part in a choral dance or attend a sacrifice or ceremony of initiation." Here, he states, true pleasure is to be found: "when it is a feast held on the occasion of some sacred rite or sacrifice, and when they believe that their thoughts come closest to God as they do him honour and reverence, it brings pleasure and sweetness of a far superior kind" (*Pleasant Life*, 21).

Plutarch's life as a priest and philosopher at the shrine of Apollo at Delphi enabled him to combine a dedication to the ritual dimension of religion together with an interpretation of it in light of the highest conceptions of the divine. Each of the religious compositions written from the context of Delphi (in addition to *Isis and Osiris*) shows this combination as well as a lingering desire to defend traditional religion against the atheistic challenge of Epicureanism. His dialogue *On the Delay of the Divine Vengeance* (Mor., 548B–568),[54] for example, takes place in the colonnade at the shrine; Plutarch engages three interlocutors in a discussion of the objections hurled against divine providence by a certain "Epicurus," who had left just before the conversation began and whose attack had apparently focused on the delay in the judgment of the wicked. Plutarch defends providence against the charge of delay and at the end of the dialogue presents a mythic account of future life in which people find their appropriate destiny.

His dialogue on *The E at Delphi* (Mor., 384D–394C) takes its start from one of the inscriptions that greeted visitors to the oracle, together with such otherwise well-known ones as "know thyself" and "nothing too much." The actual inscription was *EI* and was sufficiently mysterious to give rise to multiple possibilities, from the banal (the god used the fifth letter of the Greek alphabet to certify the number of sages or the importance of the number five in mathematics) to the sublime (the letters form the singular verb "thou art" and address the god as eternal). More important than any of the specific answers is Plutarch's conviction that "the god is no less a philosopher than a prophet" (2) and that even the minutiae of the shrine's ritual can yield profound meaning.

In his dialogue *The Oracles at Delphi No Longer Given in Verse* (Mor., 394D–409D), Plutarch places in the mouths of a group of Delphi habitués—some of them functioning as guides who explain the furnishings of the site (statues, inscriptions) to visitors (2)—a conversation concerning what appears to be a sign of decline in the shrine, which was, despite Plutarch's earnest efforts, not in its time of greatest glory. In Plutarch's time, more ordinary people sought straightforward guidance for their lives; in the old days, kings and rulers came on matters of great import. Correspondingly, oracles formerly were delivered in the form of hexameters, whereas in Plutarch's day they were spoken in simple prose. There is some urgency to the issue, caused by the presence of a mathematician named Boëthus, who was "changing his allegiance in the direction of Epicureanism" and was willing to mock the oracle as a purely human phenomenon (5). Plutarch saw this as militating against "confidence in the oracle, since people assume one of two things: either that the prophetic priestess does not come near the region in which is the godhead, or else that the spirit has been completely quenched and her powers have forsaken her" (17). His instinct is "not to show hostility towards the god, nor do away with his providence and divine powers together with his prophetic gift; but we must seek for explanations of such matters as seem to stand in the way, and not relinquish the reverent faith [*eusebeia*] of our fathers" (18). His discourse, then, is at once a defense of God's providence, the shrine's power, and true piety's capacity to avoid the extremes of atheism and superstition (30).

Plutarch faces a similar issue in the dialogue *The Obsolescence of Oracles* (Mor., 409E–438E), namely, the fact that so many oracles across Greece have ceased to function (5). Though less obviously, the shadow of atheism also falls across this topic: "Epicureans, because of their admirable nature-studies, have an arrogant contempt, as they themselves aver, for all such things as oracles" (45). And once more, Plutarch's argument, though convoluted, comes down to a defense of divine providence. He wants to avoid the conclusion that if a natural cause can be found, then there must be no divine cause (8). Therefore, he argues that just as in the case of poetry versus prose in which the god was seen to adapt to the human capacities of the prophetess, so in the case of fewer prophetic shrines the answer must be sought in divine accommodation: the relative depopulation of Greece in their day means that fewer oracles are required to meet the people's needs (8). Plutarch holds in his theory of inspiration as in other religious matters for two causes, human and divine (48). To assert only the human is to fall into atheism; to assert only the divine is to fall into superstition. Piety asserts both, and philosophy seeks how the two work together.

Like the other figures I have chosen to represent the ways of being religious in the Greco-Roman world, Plutarch is unusual. It is unlikely that other priests at Delphi wrote in defense of divine providence or attacked the Epicureans. Plutarch was a philosopher as well as a priest. Yet I think his writings support my decision to place him among all those anonymous priests and patrons of the cult that I described in the first part of this chapter, as displaying a distinctive mode of religiosity. His interest is less personal than it is social, even political. His appreciation for the cult is less what it can do for him than what it does for the city-state; his sense of the benefits given by religion is not controlled by the healing of the individual body but by the stabilization of the civilized world. The divine *dynamis* is found above all in the ways providence directs, through countless secondary causes, the complex world of gods and men.

How would Plutarch have viewed the other figures I have described, were he to encounter them? We can easily imagine that he would appreciate Aelius Aristides' robust affirmation of the Greek way of life within the Roman order— Plutarch also was pleased at the Roman peace (*Oracles at Delphi*, 28)—and would have taken delight in the manner in which Aristides wove together the destiny of the gods and of Athens in his *Panathenaic Oration*. He would, however, have been uneasy at Aristides' rejection of civic responsibilities. And the intense personal piety of Aristides would have worried Plutarch. The orator, after all, was one of those who "wallowed in the mud" and did other extravagant things in response to Asclepius' command. Plutarch could well have considered Aristides to walk uneasily on the border between authentic piety and superstition.

Although not a Stoic or even an admirer of Stoicism, Plutarch would have been willing to applaud Epictetus' embrace of the traditional religious practices as well as his attack on the Epicureans for weakening the state by their atheism. Himself a teacher of morals, he would have appreciated Epictetus' commitment to his students' progress in virtue. He would also, perhaps, have found Epictetus slightly too intense in his assertions about the kinship of gods and men, slightly too self-involved in his understanding of providence.

For the author of *Poimandres*, I think that Plutarch would have little sympathy. This might surprise us if we look only at religious ideas, for as a Platonist, Plutarch also could assert the value of the soul over the body and picture a future life for the soul. His antipathy, however, would be directed to the world-renouncing tendencies of those whose piety was Hermetic. Insofar as Hermetic ascetics despised all bodily forms, even that of public worship, they would be, in Plutarch's eyes, little better than the Epicureans, who also, from a perspective of a claimed higher knowledge, withdrew from participation in the civic cults and thereby enjoyed the fruits of civilization without paying the costs of actual engagement.

8

WAYS OF BEING JEWISH IN THE GRECO-ROMAN WORLD

My interest in this study is the comparison between the ways of being religious in the Greco-Roman world and the ways of being Christian between the first and fourth centuries. It is nevertheless both natural and necessary to devote some attention to Judaism in the same period of time, for at least three reasons. First, Christianity arose as a Jewish sect in the mid-first century and from the beginning interpreted itself with explicit reference to the symbolic world of Torah that it shared with Judaism; the things that made Judaism distinct within the Greco-Roman world are also the things that, to a lesser degree, made Christianity distinct.

Second, although Judaism could be viewed from one perspective as the cult of an extended family ("the Children of Israel") and from another perspective as a national religion,[1] it could (and was) also viewed by Jews and Gentiles alike as a Mystery cult and a philosophy among others in the Greco-Roman world. Judaism makes for an excellent point of comparison to the ways nascent Christianity could be perceived by others and the ways it perceived itself within the same context.

Third, across the first four centuries of the Common Era, Judaism's internal development took a turn exactly opposite to that of its intimate rival: as Christianity over time came to resemble more fully the broad range of Gentile religions, Judaism pulled back from its cultural entanglement with Hellenism and asserted its ancestral Hebrew traditions even more sharply.[2]

JUDAISM IN THE GRECO-ROMAN WORLD

By the time Christianity appeared, the majority of Jews had for hundreds of years lived outside Palestine in the Diaspora.[3] We know less about the Jews scattered through the territories east of the empire—descendents of those exiled due to Assyrian and then Babylonian conquest—except as can be inferred from the continuing production of literature in Aramaic among them.[4] About the Jews living in North Africa (Cyrene, Egypt), Syria, Asia Minor, Greece, and Italy, in contrast, we know considerably more, because of the extensive Jewish literature composed in Greek, the considerable inscriptional evidence, and observations made about the Jews by outsiders.[5]

For pagan observers who knew nothing about the roots of the *Ioudaioi* in Palestine—their astounding sanctuary in the city of Jerusalem, their ancient scriptures in the Hebrew language, their traditions of prophecy and kingship—the Jews would have appeared much like other cultic associations from the East that had made their way into the Greco-Roman world. Greeks and Romans had welcomed from Egypt the cults of Isis and Serapis, and from Phrygia the cult of the Great Mother, Cybele.[6] The association (*synagōgē*) of the Jews resembled in many respects those of other religions: they were financed by wealthy patrons, they had a similar organizational structure, and they had instruments for the assistance of members in need.[7] Their actual religious practices, however, marked them off as distinct among other cults. They did not, for example, meet to offer sacrifice or celebrate cultic meals in honor of their deity; their meetings were devoted to the reading and study of scriptures and the prayers and hymns that formed responses to those readings.[8] Similarly, the rules binding them to practices of purity in diet and association were not temporary and in service of making sacrifice, but were permanent and formed an all-pervasive way of life.[9]

With more contact with the Jewish associations, the pagan observer would become aware of other differences. Jews would welcome interested pagans to their assemblies but would not themselves attend any form of worship except their own. Indeed, they insisted that there was only one true God and that the temples and statues that drew the devotion of their neighbors were a form of false worship, of idols or demons.[10] They were conspicuous for their absence from the civic festivals through which the populace expressed its thanks to its patron deities and for their recognition of only one day as *nefastus*, namely, their Sabbath, which they dedicated to worship and rest from all other activities.[11]

The Jews' denial of all other gods but their own, together with the claim that their god was invisible and incapable of being represented by any material form—even at their magnificent temple in Jerusalem, which was one of the world's architectural marvels[12]—led easily to their being perceived as a species of superstition or atheism. Like the Epicureans, they were sometimes resented for their participation in the benefits of the city-state without paying their religious dues.[13] Rather than contribute to the *leitourgia* of the city-state, Jews paid a yearly temple tax to their faraway shrine in Palestine and thought of that arid country as the homeland to which they would, when able, make pilgrimage to the home of the "living God."[14] Indeed, so intense was their sense of identification with their ancestral land that Jews referred to non-Jews as "the nations" (or "gentiles"; *ta ethnē*), a designation that makes sense only from the perspective of a people that considers itself unique.[15]

It was precisely that combination in the Jews of their similarity to and difference from the Gentiles that led to a mixed response of attraction and repulsion among outsiders.[16] Some were attracted to the strong sense of identity held by the Jews, their demanding morality, and their "rational worship." Some Gentiles joined this exclusive cult, which demanded not only eschewing all other forms of worship but, for males, undergoing as well the physical ordeal of circumcision, and, for all converts, adopting the impressive array of ritual observances that marked this cult as a "people."[17] Other admiring Gentiles were not, for one reason or another, able to make such a total commitment, but as "God-Fearers" participated as they were able in the worship of the "the Lord," whom they confessed with their new associates to be "the One God."[18]

Other Gentiles were repulsed by the Jewish claims to uniqueness and superiority and above all by their presence in Greco-Roman culture as beneficiaries but not contributors.[19] Such resentment was exacerbated by the official privileges accorded the Jews by the empire. Rome was, to be sure, generous in its recognition of foreign cults,[20] but the legitimation of Judaism must be seen as extraordinary precisely because of its separatist impulses. Nevertheless, at least partly because "the Jewish nation" had become allies of Rome during the Maccabean revolt against Antiochus IV Epiphanes, and partly because it served Rome's purposes to keep the province of Palestine with its notoriously restive population as quiescent as possible, Judaism in the imperial dispersion enjoyed approval as well as protection for its adherents to practice the Sabbath observance, to convene internal courts, to avoid military service, and to pay temple taxes to Jerusalem.[21] Resentment found its outlet in local riots, especially in the infamously unstable population of Hellenistic Alexandria, and the production of anti-Jewish literature, which elaborated a variety of charges, all of which boiled down to the unforgivable offenses of *misanthrōpia* ("hatred of humanity") and *amixia* ("failure to mingle").[22] Jewish separation had legal protection but not universal popular approval.

Pagan perceptions of the Jews were understandably superficial and only partially accurate. Jewish life and identity in the first centuries of the Common Era were more complex and difficult than Gentile observers could imagine. Jews presented to outsiders a remarkably united front and did, in fact, share many identity markers.[23] The ways in which Jews distinguished themselves from each other during the same period were less obvious to outsiders but were as important as the things they held in common. In order to understand Judaism in this era more accurately, it is necessary to consider insider as well as outsider perceptions and the forms of Jewish life in Palestine as well as in the Diaspora.

A UNITED AND DIVIDED PEOPLE

The single greatest factor distinguishing Jews from Gentiles was monotheism. Jews considered "the Lord their God" not only as the supreme deity but also as the only legitimate claimant to the title of God.[24] This monotheism was a hard-won accomplishment within Israel and was as jealously guarded as the Jewish God was said to be jealous for honor to be ascribed to him alone.[25] It was not a matter merely of confession but of cult; Jews would not acknowledge through prayer or vow or sacrifice any power in the world except that exercised by the Lord, whom they regarded as the source and goal of all existing things.[26] All other so-called gods were considered by Jews to be idols, mere projections of human desire.[27]

Corresponding to the conviction that there was one God went the sense of being an elect people, chosen by the Lord of heaven and earth among all "the nations" as a place for his glory (*doxa*), that is, as a manifestation of the divine *dynamis* that the Lord alone exercises as creator of all that is.[28] The Lord's choice of the Jews was enacted by covenant (*berith*), the binding treaty that obligated the Lord to be faithful and compassionate toward this people and that obligated Jews to serve and obey only the Lord.[29] The requirements of covenantal obedience, in turn, were spelled out by the positive and negative laws (*mitzvoth*) that regulated the religious relations between God and people and the social relations among the people.

All of these convictions found expression in the set of sacred writings that most sharply distinguished Jews from Greeks and Romans. The term *Torah* meant first of all the five books of Moses, which could claim an antiquity greater even than Homer; then the looser collection called "the prophets" (*nebiim*); and finally a still less determinate set of compositions called simply "the writings" (*ketubim*).[30] Although the TaNaK was not yet during this period formally canonized, it was sufficiently coherent and widely read (and preached) to stand as the main shaping factor in the symbolic world called Judaism.[31] These compositions provided the identity-forming narrative of the people, from the remote ancestor Abraham, through the liberator and lawgiver Moses and the dynasty-establishing David, to the Exile and restoration: the story spoke of a people that often failed its God but of a God that never failed the people.

Torah also contained the full range of the *mitzvoth* required of the people, with no distinction drawn, at the level of obligation, between such moral commands as "love your neighbor as yourself" (Lev 19:18) and such ritual commands as "keep holy the Sabbath day" (Ex 20:8–11). The scope of the commandments was by no means merely individual: Torah regulated every social interaction from birth to death, providing guidance for practices of planting, commerce, and even war, with an eye always toward the "holiness"—the distinctive character—of this people dedicated to the Lord.[32] Since Torah revealed the will of the one who created the universe and gave form to every creature, pious Jews understood the commandments of Torah to represent as well the highest form of wisdom (*chokmah*), so that the observance and study of the commandments alike honored their God.[33]

There is no reason to suppose that Jews in general had higher rates of literacy than did the Gentiles, but the persistent and public exposition of the sacred writings in synagogue worship and study made the stories, commandments, and wisdom of Torah widely known among them. The translation of Torah into Greek in third-century BCE Alexandria (the Septuagint, LXX), together with the extensive literature generated by Jews based on that translation, as well as on the Hebrew version,[34] suggest that Torah both formed the basis of the symbolic world that drew Jews throughout the world together and was the arena for contention among them.

Some of the differences among Jews were the inevitable result of the same basic tradition developing over centuries in two distinct geographical, linguistic, and cultural settings. The differences should not be exaggerated. The evidence suggests that Jews in the Diaspora maintained close ties with the homeland and had great loyalty to it.[35] And the influence of Greek culture and Roman rule was as important in Palestine as it was in the Greco-Roman Diaspora.[36] The differences are a matter of degree or intensity and, above all, the way in which religious symbols were or were not connected with specific social and political institutions.

I have already stated that Jews in the Greco-Roman Diaspora experienced from outsiders a mixed response of attraction and repulsion. Such ambivalence matched the experience of Jews from within, for they, too, were pulled between the poles of attraction and separation with respect to the dominant culture. Assimilation expressed itself in degrees of accommodation: change of language, change of name, and acquisition of Greek *paideia* in addition to instruction in Torah.[37] The Septuagint translation of Torah facilitated assimilation by putting scripture in Greek terms and inviting interpretation from a Greek perspective.[38] It is no surprise to find Hellenized Jews using allegory to interpret the sometimes scandalous and often obscure scriptures in the same manner that their pagan contemporaries interpreted Homer and Hesiod and the myths of Isis and Osiris.[39] Reading scripture "philosophically" among Alexandrian Jews meant, as it did for Plutarch, avoiding a superstitious literalism.[40] Some apparently took assimilation to the extreme of abandoning ritual practices like circumcision, but our chief example of a Jewish allegorist, Philo of Alexandria, rejected such a radical spiritualization of the tradition.[41]

Jews in cities like Alexandria and Antioch also felt the pull of separation from the circumambient culture because of the imperative declared by the Lord to "be holy as I am holy" (Lev 19:2). We cannot know how many of the prescribed ritual laws meant to express the distinct character of the Lord's people were actually observed by Jews in the Greco-Roman Diaspora, but certain important observances (for example, circumcision, Sabbath, and certain dietary practices) were sufficiently obvious as to draw the attention of outsiders.[42] Other practices, such as making pilgrimage to Jerusalem for the great feasts and paying a yearly tax to the temple, also marked the Jews off from their neighbors, whose *leitourgia* was almost invariably local.

Jews in the Greco-Roman Diaspora could legitimately consider themselves "aliens and exiles," even if they or their grandparents had willingly chosen to live outside Palestine and they had no real desire to return.[43] They inevitably lived in the tension experienced by any distinctive minority population within a dominant culture. The apologetic literature that Diaspora Jews generated in response to anti-Semitic attacks perfectly expressed their ambivalence. On the surface, the stream of histories, pleas, encomia, and wisdom writings had the function of defending Jews against the charges made against them, especially that of *misanthrōpia*;[44] quite the contrary, Jews argued: their law and their lives demonstrated *philanthrōpia*, the highest form of love for humanity.[45] Such apologetic works also had the less obvious function of defining Jews to themselves in the language of outsiders. Paradoxically, the effort to make oneself intelligible—and acceptable—to others involves a subtle reshaping of identity according to the categories of the outsiders.[46] Thus, it was natural in that context for Jews to cast their tradition in terms of a Mystery religion or philosophy.[47]

The biggest advantage to Jews in the Greco-Roman Diaspora was that they were able to exercise their traditions freely without reference to the specific and local social structures and institutions of Palestine. They were irreducibly a minority and could never hope to change the *bruta facta* of Greek culture and Roman Empire; they were free, indeed, to regard both as fundamentally beneficial to them as well as to others.[48] The fact that Jews appeared to others and to a great extent acted like another Greco-Roman association—with, to be sure, some distinctive features—was entirely to the benefit of their religious flourishing. Jews in the Diaspora could engage Hellenistic culture positively without fear of compromising or even corrupting ancestral places and practices. The difference between Plutarch and Philo of Alexandria is that both read Plato, but only Philo also read Torah. His reading of Torah, however, could be as allegorical as Plutarch's reading of the Osiris myth, because the demands of piety were not defined by Palestinian conditions.

For Jews living in Palestine, in contrast, the tensions were all the more severe because of the link between religious symbols and specific social and political institutions. I leave aside here the long-standing internal rift between Jews and Samaritans—both committed to Torah but with rival temples and versions of their history[49]—and focus only on the tensions created by Greco-Roman culture in Palestine. The threat of an aggressive Hellenistic culture, with its attractive form of civilization, its syncretistic religious impulse—and intrusive Roman rule—and its willingness to exercise its unquestionable power either indirectly through Jewish puppets or directly through harsh prefects, was all the greater because the story of Jews on the land after the Exile was one of severe retrenchment and resistance to foreigners.[50]

Among fervent post-Exilic Jews, the rebuilt temple was more than a symbol; it was an actual structure whose purity needed to be maintained.[51] The expectation of a king in the line of David was not a spiritual fantasy but a political agenda based upon a historical precedent.[52] The agricultural and economic laws of Torah were not simply demonstrations of God's justice; they were intended to be the actual law of the land.[53] Indeed, just as the people were called to be holy, so also was the land to be holy (Lev 18:24–19:2; 20:23–26).

The Palestinian Jewish sources reveal not a united front of resistance but rather a broad range of responses: some Jews eagerly accepted both Greek ways and the Roman *imperium*, finding no absolute contradiction between their religious convictions and such cultural and political accommodations.[54] In the eyes of some others, however, assimilated Jews were no longer Jews at all—any stage of assimilation was a step too far. Differences among Jews in Palestine tended to become divisions based on ideological positions concerning the demands of holiness—as well as the social realities to which holiness was particularly attached. The Jewish sects described by Josephus in terms of philosophical schools were also, inevitably, divided on the basis of their political stances.[55] If we are to identify the sectarians at Qumran with at least one branch of those Josephus calls Essenes—as it seems we should—the discovery of their own compositions at Wadi Qumran in 1947 revealed them to be violently antagonistic not only toward the *Kittim* (the Gentiles) but also toward their fellow Jews whom they regarded as corrupted by contact with the Gentiles, above all the "wicked priests" in Jerusalem who had desecrated the temple, but also the moderate Pharisees who chose to live among the general populace.[56] The Essenes identified their own community as the living temple that purified the land and were willing to fight to the death in battle against Rome.[57]

The party of the Zealots, whose presence became visible during the Jewish war against Rome (67–70),[58] was even more extreme in its posture of political resistance, seeking to drive the Romans out and to establish a Jewish king. The Jewish historian Josephus, who was a Jewish general in the war against Rome but went over to the Roman side, regarded the Zealots as charlatans—that is, as false philosophers and deceivers[59]—but would undoubtedly (if we had any written sources from the Zealots) have been excoriated in turn by those who considered themselves the most "jealous" of all Jews for the rule of God. At the other political extreme was the party of the Sadducees, who associated themselves with the temple, whose membership was closely connected to the high-priestly families, and who sought accommodation with Hellenism and Roman rule.[60]

The Pharisees, who earlier had been politically involved but by the first century appeared primarily as a "school" devoted to the observance of ritual purity, developed a less violent response toward Greco-Roman realities.[61] Their devotion to Torah led them to form associations pledged to the strict observance of the laws, and they expressed contempt for the "sinners" who did not share their degree of commitment to purity,[62] but they neither fought against the Romans nor withdrew physically from society. Instead, they used the intricate midrashic abilities of the Scribes to determine how the ancient laws could be applied in a changed cultural context.[63] Because of their relative detachment from traditional symbols other than Torah (the land, the king, the temple) and because of their flexible interpretive approach, the Pharisees were able to survive the conflict with Rome and the destruction of the temple (70 CE)—when all those symbols were lost—as the dominant expression of Judaism, the chief rival to Christianity's claim to the heritage of Israel.[64]

The essential point toward which my exposition has been moving is this: it is impossible to understand Judaism between 200 BCE and 200 CE apart from Greco-Roman culture. The conclusion is most obvious with regard to the Diaspora, where the very claim to distinctiveness by Jews is clothed in the language and symbols of the Greek world. But it is equally unavoidable with respect to Palestinian Judaism, where the formation of Jewish sects stands as evidence of the need to negotiate Greek culture and Roman rule, as well as deep disagreement concerning the terms and limits of negotiation. The question that is of most interest to my study, however, is whether the ways of being religious that I have detected among Gentiles in the early empire find any expression among Jews as well.

WAYS OF BEING RELIGIOUS AS JEWS

To answer that question—or at least to approach an answer to it—means focusing on Jewish religious experiences and practices. This does not mean bracketing the "political" as though it were not pertinent. Indeed, one of the basic points of continuity between Jewish and Gentile religion is that it was never something simply private but always had public and political dimensions. But having acknowledged the role that the political dimension played in dividing Jews in the early empire, it is legitimate to shift focus to specific practices, to test whether aspects of similarity or dissimilarity between Jew and Gentile are more obvious.

We naturally expect some elements of continuity, for the number of religious practices available to humans is finite. We can also anticipate elements of discontinuity, for Jews truly were different and were perceived to be different than their Gentile neighbors. The most intriguing possibility is that Jews in this period were in some important ways religiously different also from Jews in earlier times precisely because of the need to define themselves within the context of Greco-Roman culture. Since my examination of Greco-Roman religion has yielded the categories of analysis, it is fair to approach the extant evidence for Judaism and ask to what extent those categories fit, especially in the turbulent period of the first two centuries of the Common Era.

RELIGION AS PARTICIPATION IN DIVINE BENEFITS

In Greco-Roman religion, as I showed in Chapter 3, this type of religiousness is characterized by its attention to the divine *dynamis* as it is manifested in the empirical world and is made accessible to humans through the practices of piety, with an emphasis on this-worldly benefits to the individuals who participate in such practices. It is expressed most publicly through the designation of days (*Fasti* and *Nefasti*) and through the festivals, sacrifices, prayers, and hymns in petition and praise directed to the many gods at multiple altars, shrines, and temples. Participation in divine benefits is expressed as well in the specific practices associated with prophecy and healing, the Mysteries and religious pilgrimage. Do we find this religious sensibility in the Judaism of the period?

We can begin by considering the relatively novel institution of the synagogue that appeared after the Exile throughout the Diaspora and Palestine—even in the precincts of the Jerusalem temple—and marks the Jews as distinctive in several ways.[65] The term refers first not to a sacred place but to the association of people, whether in a separate building also so designated or in a private dwelling.[66] From the outside, as I have suggested, such voluntary associations resembled those of pagans in worship of their many gods. For Jews, however, synagogue worship expressed devotion only to the one God of Israel. The optional names used for the gathering place—house of the assembly, house of prayer, or house of study—indicated, furthermore, that the worship of the synagogue did not involve any animal sacrifice but only the "spiritual sacrifice" shaped by the reading, study, and proclamation of Torah.[67] To the extent that synagogue worship was dedicated to "instruction in the laws," it tended to justify the claim of Jews that theirs was truly a philosophical religion. From the extant evidence, it is difficult to say how much participants in synagogue worship did so as a means of participating in divine benefits and how much as an act of obedience to divine precept.

Until its destruction in the war against Rome in 70 CE, the Jewish temple in Jerusalem, rebuilt by Herod the Great,[68] gathered to itself the practices that enable both a comparison and contrast to pagan temples and shrines. Other temple claimants within the tradition of Israel (the Samaritan shrine at Shechem and the Egyptian temple of the Jews at Leontopolis) had little prestige by comparison.[69] Due to the program of centralizing the Jewish cult that began with the Deuteronomic reform of the sixth century BCE, all the sacrificial activities that in paganism were distributed across hundreds if not thousands of temples were concentrated for Jews into one great sacrificial center devoted to the one God of the Jews.[70]

The *Letter of Aristeas* describes the majesty of the temple cult, involving hundreds of priests at a time and (at times of the great feasts) thousands of sacrificial animals.[71] The huge precincts of the temple provided space for great throngs of worshipers, prayer, religious instruction, and the monetary services common (and necessary) for temples in antiquity.[72] In addition to the Sabbath observance, furthermore, Torah prescribed for festivals in honor of the Lord by all the people.[73] These ancient feasts, rooted in agricultural cycles but given historical valence through the narratives of Torah, were occasions for pilgrimage to Jerusalem.[74] Josephus tells of the massive population of the city during the times of pilgrimage, when religious fervor and nationalistic fanaticism alike gained intensity from such numbers sharing the same sacred time and space.[75]

The Jerusalem temple, in short, concentrated in itself a remarkable amount of the religious practice that was in paganism distributed in many places assigned to many gods: the one temple made a mute but not unpersuasive argument for uniquely representing the religion of the one God. The place of the temple in popular Jewish imagination can be estimated by the response to its destruction in the war against Rome. As I have stated, the other sects of Judaism that had flourished before 70 disappeared after the war, including the Sadducees who were so intimately linked to the temple. But the temple survived in the religious imagination and the practice of Jews without significant interruption and without the inconvenience of killing animals.

The remnant form of Judaism after 70 (symbolized by the "Council at Yamnia") was shaped by the religious convictions and scribal practices of the Pharisees, whose commitment to purity and tithes could be carried out even in the absence of a physical sanctuary. Especially after the climactic and bloody collapse of Jewish expectations of independence in the Bar Kochba revolt (135 CE), these Pharisaic sensibilities spread through what was now primarily a diasporic religion, to form classical or Talmudic Judaism.[76] The *Talmud of the Land of Israel* and the *Babylonian Talmud*, however, each grew out of commentary on the foundational text of the *Mishnah*, a compilation of Jewish law that reached written form under Judah ha Nasi circa 200 CE; the *Mishnah* creates an imaginative universe in which the study of the laws of sacrifice prescribed for the temple in Jerusalem is equivalent, for the pious Jew, to making those sacrifices.[77]

In Greco-Roman religion, prophecy played a public and highly visible role through practices of divination (auspices, haruspices) and oracles. Although Jewish religion was prophetic from the first—Moses is the great prophet who reveals God's law—and the Jewish scriptures contained stories and sayings of prophets from Elijah to Malachi,[78] active and visible prophecy was not obviously a dominant feature of Judaism as we view it in our period. Divination is scarcely attested, and apart from the major exceptions of John the Baptist and Jesus, contemporary figures identified as prophets do not appear.[79] Set shrines for oracular consultation were now absent from the land.[80] Yet the prophetic impulse remained powerful in two ways.

First, the interpretation of prophecy from the past as the legitimation for aspirations of the present (and future) was a feature of break-off communities such as the Essenes and the Christians—each group interpreted the ancient prophecies with reference to themselves—and probably gave support as well to the variety of messianic figures that generated popular support in the turbulent years of the first and early second century.[81] Followers of revolutionaries and messiahs who promised an end to Roman rule and a restoration of *eretz Israel* as a land dedicated exclusively to the Lord can legitimately be classified as those whose religious sensibility is "participation in divine benefits" through enacted prophecy.[82]

Second, Jews during this same period exercised a more covert form of prophecy through the production of literature. In Palestine, Jews resistant to Roman rule and Hellenistic culture contemporized prophecy through a highly coded and allusive literature that has come to be called apocalyptic.[83] Beginning with the Book of Daniel, composed during the persecution of faithful Jews under Antiochus IV Epiphanes in the second century BCE, and continuing through the first century CE, pious Jews wrote in the name of ancient heroes messages of consolation to those experiencing oppression or marginalization because of Hellenistic culture and Roman rule.[84] Beneath its complex symbolism of numbers, animals, and cosmic beings, such literature carried a straightforward interpretation of history—the God of Israel, despite appearances, was in charge and would intervene on behalf of his people—and a simple religious message: hold fast until that intervention occurs.[85] Greek-speaking Jews employed another sort of pseudo-epigraphical prophecy, by expanding the *Sibylline Books* in a manner that retained the tone of "pagan" prophecy but also managed to communicate distinctively Jewish convictions and interpretation of history.[86]

As we saw in Chapter 3 and in the case study of Aelius Aristides, healing was a prominent element in Greco-Roman religion. The capacity to heal another from a physical ailment or to drive out a harmful demon revealed the one with this power as a *theios anēr*, deserving of honor as a revealer of the divine *dynamis*. And the multiple shrines dedicated to the healing god Asclepius drew thousands of the afflicted to their healing baths and dream interpretations. What is perhaps most surprising is the paucity of evidence for the practice of healing as a religious phenomenon in Judaism during the same period. There are scattered references to charismatic figures through whom healing and exorcism occurred,[87] to be sure, but what is lacking is the institutional commitment to the healing of physical afflictions in association with God. In contrast to the priests at the Asclepeia, for example, who would prescribe therapies intended to relieve symptoms, one of the functions of Jewish priests was to ensure the well-being (the holiness) of the community as a whole by quarantining certain forms of threatening disorder, such as leprosy.[88]

We can ask finally about the Mysteries, which were such a prominent feature of Greco-Roman religious practice and language. Answering the question about whether there is any trace of the Mysteries in the Judaism of the early empire is, however, exceptionally difficult and a matter of scholarly debate.[89]

The evidence comes primarily from the Diaspora, where Jewish exposure to Greco-Roman religion would have been most intense. Using the extensive "Mystery" language employed especially—but not exclusively—by Philo, and connecting such language to the iconographic evidence provided by the excavated third-century CE synagogue at Dura Europos, an argument has been made that there was a distinct "Hellenistic Judaism" whose language and practices—and religious perceptions—represented a Jewish form of Mystery religion.[90] This position is probably too extreme, but it is clear that even Jewish writers of the Diaspora who explicitly rejected the pagan Mysteries could and did use Mystery symbolism to speak of Judaism, and the fact that an Orphic composition can safely be attributed to a Jewish author suggests that the degree of assimilation to the dominant culture could in some cases be extreme.[91]

RELIGION AS MORAL TRANSFORMATION

The second form of religious sensibility in Greco-Roman religion also focused on the divine *dynamis* as active in the empirical world, but it placed its emphasis not on the display of that power outside human agency but on the way in which human agency can be transformed through it. Did the same sensibility appear among Jews of this era? In one sense, the conviction that the religious covenant with the Lord demanded the keeping of commandments, both ritual and moral, was common to Jews from antiquity, for the prohibition of adultery, murder, stealing, lying, and coveting were already to be found in the ancient "Ten Words" delivered to the people by Moses. Moral instruction, furthermore, is at the heart both of both the prophets and the proverbs.[92] Jews, in short, did not need to be instructed by Gentiles in morality or moral discourse; these were essential and inseparable elements of the covenant. A Jew could not be said to have fully observed Yom Kippur, for example, simply by carrying out the external procedures for sacrifice described in Leviticus 16. The response of repentance within the heart was necessary.[93] The first answer to the question, then, is "yes, this sensibility is everywhere there are Jews."

Another way of phrasing the question is to ask whether exposure to Greco-Roman religion and philosophy had a marked effect on the way in which this moral sensibility was expressed by Jews. The most obvious new thing within Judaism in the first century was the development of sects that Josephus not only designates as "schools" (*haireseis*) but then describes in terms familiar in Greek philosophy, in his recital of their convictions and practices. A reader familiar with Greek philosophical schools, furthermore, would recognize that Josephus shades his portrait of the Essenes in the direction of the Pythagoreans, the Pharisees of the Stoics, and the Sadducees of the Epicureans.[94]

The similarity between the Essenes and Pythagoreans is particularly striking: both had clear ranks within the community as well as stages of probation
and the possibility of excommunication; both practiced a strict sharing of possessions; both were dedicated to purity through diet and the avoidance of pol-
lutants, and both had convictions concerning future life.[95] The *Therapeutae*
described by Philo also shared some of these characteristics.[96] Less is known
about the organizational aspects of the Pharisaic *chaburah*, and still less about
the Sadducees.[97] Nevertheless, two firm assertions can be made about these
Jewish parties: first, they are unattested before Jewish contact with Hellenism
and therefore represent a new "way of being Jewish" in the Greco-Roman context;[98] second, evidence for the fierce polemic used by these Jewish groups
against their rivals locates them within the social world of Greco-Roman
philosophy.[99]

Jewish wisdom literature also felt the effect of contact with Hellenism. The
degree to which Qoheleth bears the marks of Epicureanism can be debated,
but there is no mistaking the influence of Platonism on Wisdom of Solomon.[100]
The Greek version of *The Testaments of the 12 Patriarchs* weaves wisdom and
apocalyptic themes into a narrative elaboration of the Joseph story but are most
striking for the way in which each testament elaborates a standard Greek virtue
or vice, employing the *topoi* already standard in Aristotle.[101] A similar meshing
of Jewish story and Greco-Roman moral discourse is 4 Maccabees, an encomium on the virtue of courage exemplified by the seven martyred brothers and
their mother.[102] The *Sentences of Pseudo-Phocylides*, in turn, not only borrows
the name of a renowned Greek writer but so camouflages the Jewish character
of its teaching in Greek form than it could (and did) pass for centuries as a
Gentile rather than Jewish composition.[103]

Most impressive, to be sure, are the extensive writings of Philo of Alexandria.[104] Philo, like Plutarch, is a sufficiently complex figure to elude simple
classification. I have already mentioned him twice in this chapter, and he will
appear again under other categories. One of the most significant aspects of his
work, however, is the way in which he interprets the biblical narrative and laws
in terms of Greek philosophy and, in particular, Greek moral discourse.[105]
Noteworthy here is the fact that he is not content simply to "save the text" from
its absurd or offensive character by providing, in the manner of the Stoic allego-
rizers of Homer, a transposition of the story, through allegory, into a moral lesson.[106] He is committed as well to demonstrating the profound moral character
of the Jewish laws and does so by expounding them as guides to the cultivation
of virtue—that is, to moral transformation.[107]

The comparison with Plutarch is not entirely fanciful. Philo anticipates the Greco-Roman philosopher-priest by shaping the biographies of biblical heroes into *exempla* of moral virtues. Abraham, Jacob, Isaac, and Joseph are *nomoi empsychoi*: even before Moses reveals the law on Mt. Sinai, they embody through their character the virtues that observance of the law will make explicit.[108] Moses, in turn, is rendered by Philo as priest and prophet, to be sure, but also as general and philosopher.[109] In the same manner, the titles of Philo's treatments of discrete aspects of the biblical story anticipate Plutarch's *Moralia* in their development of specific moral themes.[110] Finally, Philo saves his greatest praise for those Jews who so dedicate themselves to the law that they form themselves into philosophical communities.[111]

All of this extensive literary production, as well as the examples of organization into intentional communities, suggests that some Jews, while not in the least turning their backs on the traditional forms of observance, sought a way of honoring their God that involved moral transformation. They were not content with maintaining purity or even with keeping those remarkable commandments that molded Jews into a most moral people. They sought as well to shape a character in conformity with God's will at the level of internal dispositions and of the curing of the passions, and in pursuit of this goal, they employed the language and insights of Greco-Roman philosophy.

RELIGION AS TRANSCENDING THE WORLD

The third mode of religiosity in Greco-Roman religion, as we saw exemplified in *Poimandres*, had a profoundly dualistic view of reality and sought the divine *dynamis* not in the city of gods and men, nor in moral transformation, but in an escape from the body for the rescue of the true self found in the soul. We would not expect to find this way of being religious in Judaism. The one God creates all things and declares all things to be good (Gen 1:1–31). The human body, moreover, is unequivocally part of that goodness (Gen 2:21–25).[112] It may suffer pollution and impurity, but these are not ontological conditions; they can be removed through the appropriate rituals of cleansing.[113] Belief in the resurrection of the dead, furthermore, embraces a future life precisely for the bodies of the righteous. The conviction that the righteous dead are "in the hands of the Lord" and would share a future life first appears explicitly in the Book of Daniel, finds expression in apocalyptic literature, and becomes standard for the dominant form of Judaism after the fall of the temple.[114]

If the third type of religiosity demands a cosmic dualism—with the stress on "flight from the world"—then it is lacking in the Judaism of the period. But if this type also embraces the desire and striving for contact with the realm of the gods—with the stress on "transcending the world"—through visions and heavenly ascents, then there is substantial evidence for this way of being religious among Jews in the Greco-Roman world. In the Hellenistic Diaspora, Philo of Alexandria envisages Moses' encounter with God as such a visionary ascent and speaks of the state of mystic ecstasy in a manner that suggests he himself had experienced it.[115] The poem of Pseudo-Orpheus imagines the patriarch Abraham (or perhaps Moses) in the presence of the divine.[116] In Palestinian Judaism, several forms of mystical ascent are attested. At Qumran, the *Songs of Sabbath Sacrifice* suggest that community members participate in heavenly worship with the angels—here, the element of "participation in divine benefits" also emerges—and in apoca- lyptic writings, the motif of revelation to a visionary who has ascended into heaven is a staple.[117] If the tradition that extends *Merkabah Mysticism* all the way back to this period is correct, then heavenly ascents were believed to have been practiced even among the founding figures of classical Judaism.[118]

In contrast to the world-denying dualism that characterizes the Hermetic lit- erature and the search for personal immortality that marks the Orphic tradition, however, the traces of mysticism in Judaism affirm the majority views of a good creation and the resurrection of the bodies of the righteous. The extant litera- ture suggests not a rejection of the popular forms of religion practiced by other Jews but a deeply personal intensification of them through actual visionary ex- periences and through the composition of literature that recounts such experi- ences. Physical asceticism is not an all-pervasive regimen to purify the soul from the body, but only a temporary preparation for the rigors of the ascent.[119] The insistence within the *Merkabah* tradition that only the most observant and learned of teachers can risk such experiences is telling: Jewish mysticism does not reject outward forms but seeks the deeper reality within them.[120]

RELIGION AS STABILIZING THE WORLD

The fourth type of sensibility in Greco-Roman religion was political in the broadest sense. One aspect was the willingness to serve both the city-state and the gods by financially supporting and serving as priests in worship, while an- other aspect was an explicit concern for the ways in which religion provided the glue for society. We saw these elements combined in Plutarch, who enthusiasti- cally served as a priest of Apollo at Delphi and who in his writings connected genuine piety with a worship of the gods that was consonant with Greek cul- ture, in contrast to superstition and atheism, each of which threatened the sta- bility of the world of gods and men.

In Greco-Roman religion, we can see a smooth and logical progression from local to city and from city to empire, with no major adjustment required at any stage. Because all gods were to be worshiped in any case, the main concern was for a political order that would be secured by the appropriate attention to all the gods. And since divine power is nothing if not power displayed, then religious devotion to the monarch who displays supreme power makes sense. Discussion of this sensibility in Judaism is much more complicated because of ancient Israel's difficult path over many centuries from polytheism to monotheism; because of the precarious position of monarchy within this history; and, in Palestine, because of the ways in which Greek and then Roman political hegemony elicited diverse political and religious responses.

Both literary and archaeological evidence shows that the religion of ancient Israel—as distinct from "biblical religion"—began with a form of polytheism not totally unlike that of its ancient Near Eastern neighbors, with the singular devotion to Yahweh being a form of *henotheism* that asserts the superiority of one god over others but does not deny the existence of competing deities.[121] The evidence further suggests that the prescription for a single cultic center spelled out in Deuteronomy was achieved slowly and imperfectly. Before the Exile, there were many local cult centers devoted to Yahweh or to Baal or to some other Canaanite deity, so that the arrangement of priesthoods probably substantially resembled that in ancient Greece, with this important exception: the priests and prophets of Yahweh demanded the exclusion of the other deities and an exclusive loyalty to Yahweh, rather than the inclusive and all-encompassing piety found in Greece.[122]

The establishment of a monarchy in Israel helped unite a loose confederation of tribes into a nation like other nations. King David was quick to house the sacred ark of the covenant in his capital city (2 Sam 6:1–7:7), and his son Solomon built the first great temple in Jerusalem as a place for Yahweh to dwell (1 Kings 6:1–38; 7:1–66). The worship of the one god was symbolically linked to the rule of one king. Yet the very institution of monarchy was at first challenged by the Israelite prophets as a betrayal of complete commitment to the Lord (1 Samuel 8:1–22), and the prophets also challenged too great a religious reliance on the temple as the symbol of God's presence (Jer 7:1–34). The experience of the Exile, in fact, had the paradoxical effect of at once deepening the monotheism of faithful Jews—Yahweh is not only the "god of Israel" but Lord of all the earth and creator of all things—and weakening the link between Yahweh and the symbols of temple and king: the Lord of all the earth can be worshipped anywhere and in every circumstance.[123]

This history set the framework for the contentious responses within Palestinian Judaism to the threat of Hellenistic and Roman hegemony, with Jew pitted against Jew precisely on the issue of how necessarily the worship of the one God was linked to the institutions of land, king, or temple. As noted earlier in this chapter, the well-known sects of the Jews were divided along political as well as theological lines. On one side, Sadducees could embrace a relationship with the established priestly orders and join in the temple sessions of the Sanhedrin.[124] On the other side, the Essene withdrawal to the desert to form a pure people and spiritual temple is unintelligible except as a response to a perception that the people had been polluted by contact with foreigners and that the temple had been profaned by unworthy priests.[125] The appearance of messianic movements—and the Zealots' pitched battle to the death in the temple and at Masada[126]—makes sense only if allegiance to Yahweh is inseparable from a Jewish king and temple. In Palestine, "priestcraft as statecraft" was not a theoretical but a passionately practical issue; it had less to do with stabilizing the world as it is than with overturning an unjust order and making it righteous.

In the Diaspora, inscriptional evidence concerning the establishment and support of synagogues shows that male and female Jews who served as *archisynagōgoi* played the same role of financial patrons as did the priests and priestesses of pagan cults; their piety was expressed through institutional support and involvement.[127] In the Diaspora synagogue as well, Jews filled the lower ranks of service that corresponded to the *neōkoroi* of pagan shrines.[128] As with most of their pagan counterparts, however, these Jews remained silent concerning their piety, apart from the very few hints provided by the inscriptions.

For a sense of such piety among Diaspora Jews, Philo of Alexandria again offers the best evidence. I have noted the way in which Philo anticipates the *Bioi* and *Moralia* of Plutarch through his reading of Torah through the lens of Greek philosophy. He resembles Plutarch also by exemplifying within Judaism the same sort of religious sensibility: in both we find no trace of a self-interested religiosity, preoccupied with personal benefits or even personal perfection; instead, both reveal a concern for true piety as the basis for an authentic civilization. Plutarch was active in his patronage of the cult and the city through his service as a priest and magistrate. Philo defended his fellow Jews of Alexandria against the cruelty of a Roman prefect, and he took part in a delegation to the emperor Caligula to prevent the profaning of the temple in Jerusalem through the installation of the emperor's image. Especially in his compositions that set out to interpret the Jewish laws, furthermore, Philo makes an argument beyond the simple defense of Jews as philanthropic rather than misanthropic; he proposes that the law established by Moses actually forms the best *politeia* imaginable, since it conforms in every respect to the will of the creator God.[129] He presents in a far more elaborate fashion the bold claim of Artapanus that Moses taught Orpheus the rudiments of Greek culture:[130] Judaism not only has a place in the civilized order; when properly understood as *eusebeia* rather than as *deisidaimonia*, Judaism also provides the basis on which civilization can best be ordered.

Approaching Judaism from the perspective and using the categories of Greco-Roman religion has made two things clear: first, how different Judaism truly was in that world. Monotheism and the sense of divine election set this people apart distinctively, and the specifically Jewish rituals (Sabbath, circumcision, dietary laws) made that distinctiveness visible. Adherence to a single "jealous" God, moreover, ensured that there were limits to the ability of Jews to assimilate to Greco-Roman culture and still remain Jews. Second, this approach to Judaism makes clear how impressively even this most resistant of traditions was in fact affected by its long involvement (willing and unwilling) with Hellenistic culture. Jews not only wrote in Greek but also adopted forms of Greek historiography, rhetoric, poetry, and philosophy when seeking to express their distinctive identity, and by so doing, they made that identity just a little bit more Greek. And Jews who eschewed the use of Greek sometimes gave mute and unwitting testimony to the culture they rejected; the Essenes truly do resemble the Pythagoreans more than any form of Judaism that preceded them.

Perhaps the greatest benefit of this transitional exercise, however, has been to provide a point of comparison and contrast to Christianity in its engagement with Greco-Roman culture. We shall see that the ways Greco-Roman religion finds expression in Christianity is more profound and certainly longer lasting than in the case of Judaism.

9

THE APPEARANCE OF CHRISTIANITY IN THE GRECO-ROMAN WORLD

In the middle of the first century CE, a new religious movement made its appearance in the Greco-Roman world. Those first designated by others—and then designating themselves—as "Christians" sought and increasingly found a place in the Mediterranean world.[1] Christianity began as one among other Jewish sects. After the destruction of the Jerusalem temple in 70, in fact, the Messianists could be regarded as one of the two surviving claimants, with the Pharisees, to the heritage of Israel.[2] By the late second century CE, however, Christianity was predominantly if not exclusively a Gentile religion, and its path of interaction with Greco-Roman culture was sharply distinct from Formative Judaism's.

Judaism's encounter with Hellenism, as I suggested in the previous chapter, was preceded by a long if tumultuous history and by a sharp sense of self-definition in the years immediately preceding the rule of Alexander, providing it with an alternative to the seductive attractions of Greco-Roman culture. The long dalliance between Jews and Greek culture had a definite impact on the ways of being Jewish between 200 BCE and 200 CE. After that date, however, there can be found few traces of Hellenism in the Judaism that built itself up on the foundation of the *Mishnah*. The internal myth of "Normative Judaism" was so seamless, in fact, that the long period of Hellenistic influence could be dismissed as of little importance, found mainly among those who were deviant in their Judaism.[3] The fact that Philo and other Hellenistic Jewish authors found an honored place in subsequent Christian literature but virtually no mention in the Talmudic tradition is revealing.[4]

The course followed by Christianity is the exact opposite. It engages Hellenism not after a long period of internal development but from the moment of its inception. Although it has its roots in Judaism, those roots are both shallow and distributed across a diverse and divided first-century Judaism that was itself deeply marked by Greco-Roman culture. From the first, Christianity drew as directly and powerfully from Greco-Roman culture as it did from Jewish culture. The influence of Hellenism was all the more profound because of the instability inherent in a new religious movement; as I show in this chapter, the conditions under which Christianity first existed made inevitable its extensive entanglement with the Greek and Roman world. At the very point in the late second century when Judaism turned away from Hellenism and back to its ancestral traditions, moreover, Christianity continued to draw from and contribute to Greco-Roman culture, becoming ever more decisively a "Gentile religion."

It is perfectly appropriate to begin with the beginning, at the moment when this religious movement first appeared, not because that "moment of origins" represents a privileged moment with regard to the essence of the religion, but because the specific circumstances attending its birth also affect its growth and development.[5] The present chapter sketches the distinctive character of the Christian religion—as best we can determine it—in the first century. Before attempting that description, however, it is necessary to state my position on four disputed issues.

First, I consider the writings of the New Testament to be the earliest sources available for this analysis.[6] Dating of these compositions is difficult—and inevitably circular—but with some few exceptions, all the compositions that were canonized in the second-century disputes can safely be dated within the first 70 years after the death of Jesus.[7] And although the development of Christianity from its starting point to the fourth century is pertinent to this study, no benefit to this analysis is derived from a search for lines of development that might be discerned behind the New Testament compositions as they now stand.[8]

Second, I approach earliest (and subsequent) Christianity in precisely the same way as I did the Greco-Roman and Jewish materials as evidence for religious experiences, convictions, and dispositions. This means, on one hand, that I do not privilege Christianity by terming it "faith" in contrast to "religion"; and, on the other hand, I do not reduce Christian religiosity to some other dimension of life.[9] Instead, just as I treated the religious sensibility of Aelius Aristides, Epictetus, and Plutarch, so do I also empathically engage the evidence for specifically religious experience and behavior among early Christians.

Third, with most contemporary scholars, I see Christianity as beginning in diversity and reaching its most significant self-definition in the second rather than the first century.[10] In contrast to some contemporary theories, however,

I see early Christian diversity as relative rather than absolute—there were from the start genuine elements of commonality[11]—and regard the process of self-definition as involving religious convictions as much as political interest.

Fourth, I take development within the Christian religion as obvious but offer no evaluation of that development, regarding it as neither the course of natural and positive growth nor as a decline from primitive purity.[12] My interest, rather, is in describing the types of religiosity that can be discerned at each stage of development.

CHRISTIANITY'S FIRST EXPANSION

The *Acts of the Apostles* is the second part of a two-volume narrative composed around 85 CE and, with all its limitations, provides the best chance of locating the first appearance and spread of the movement associated with Jesus in terms of geography and chronology. Its portrayal of witnesses carrying the good news from city to city, from Jerusalem to Rome, in fulfillment of the prophecy of the resurrected Jesus (Acts 1:8) is clearly overneat and idealized. The author of Acts is not only selective in what he chooses to relate; he also shapes the account in a manner to express his own convictions, especially concerning the unity among the first missionaries and the continuity between Judaism and the church.[13] Nevertheless, when Acts is tested against our other earliest evidence—above all the letters of Paul—its account can be accepted as fundamentally historical in terms of its broad scope as well as accurate in some of its specific facts.[14] Indeed, it is impossible to construct a satisfying account of Paul's life and correspondence without the assistance of Acts.[15] It is a necessary if inadequate source for earliest Christian history.

When the evidence in Acts is considered together with that in the earliest epistolary literature, a number of historically responsible statements can be made about the earliest stage of the Christ cult within the Greco-Roman world. First, the movement spread with impressive speed: within 10 years of the death of Jesus, there were communities of believers in Judaea, Samaria, and Syria (Acts 1–11); in 15 years, communities could be found in Asia Minor (Acts 14); in 20 years, through Asia Minor and into Greece (Acts 16–18); and in 25 years, in the capital city of Rome (Acts 28:14)—with ambitions to spread the movement also to Spain.[16] Such rapidity of expansion is the more impressive when it is remembered that the evidence for the movement's spread concerns the existence of *ekklēsiai* (associations, gatherings, communities) and not simply the conversion of individuals.[17]

The rapid pace of expansion was not entirely due to enthusiastic reception of the message wherever it was brought. The earliest missionaries experienced harassment and persecution (primarily from fellow Jews and incidentally from Roman authorities), so that movement from one place to another was impelled as much by rejection as by acceptance.[18] Christianity's itinerant expansion began not after a long period of settled existence in Jerusalem but immediately and under less than ideal circumstances. Within two decades, the nascent movement was forced to negotiate geographical, cultural, linguistic, and demographic transitions.[19] The transitions had to be accomplished, moreover, under conditions not only of external duress but also of internal instability. The most prominent leaders of the cult were killed within the first 30 years.[20] The "mother church" of Jerusalem was impoverished and in need of assistance from other communities.[21] Even when it tried, it could not offer effective control over a movement that had spread over such a vast area at such a rapid pace.[22] Nor could coherence be accomplished through textual controls—there was as yet no collection of Christian writings, and Torah scrolls were not easily transported or deployed in circumstances of rapid expansion.[23]

All these factors help explain the diversity of expression and perspective in the earliest Christian writings. Christianity was, in the first generation, virtually something new everywhere it appeared, taking its shape from the experience and conviction of the local or itinerant founder, the conditions and response of those who joined the movement, and the combination of social circumstance and continuing experience of communities through time. The diversity of the New Testament writings, in short, is grounded in the diversity of Christianity itself in its first appearances across the Mediterranean world. The real surprise, once we grasp the historical circumstances of the first expansion, is not the degree of diversity we find in the literature, but the opposite, that there is any discernible unity at all.

RELIGIOUS EXPERIENCE AND CONFESSION

Further grounds for nascent Christianity's inherent instability as a religious movement can be found in its claims and convictions. One of the most striking aspects of the movement in its earliest appearance is the extraordinary claims it made for itself, claims that were all the more remarkable because they were so discrepant with the actual worldly circumstances of the smattering of small and persecuted communities scattered across the Mediterranean world.[24] The claims included a sense of mission to the entire world (Acts 1:8; Matt 28:19) and, indeed, an ascendancy over the world.[25] Christians play a pivotal role for the future of the world, reconciling it to God (2 Cor 5:19; Rom 11:15) and anticipating the liberation of all creation (Rom 8:20–22); the church, indeed, is the place where God's purpose for the world is being revealed.[26]

The Christian claims to cosmic significance were based on other claims concerning their present experience. What is important for the present analysis is not the physical or psychological aspects of that experience but its claimed effects, such as release from the cosmic forces that controlled human existence: believers were no longer subject to the "powers and principalities"; nor were they captive to systems of law that had been used by such "elements of the universe" to hold humans in bondage.[27] Indeed, they were free from the terrors of death that all such systems employed to subjugate humans.[28] A central term for the claimed experience was, therefore, salvation (*sōtēria*), which they thought of not as something that would happen to them but as something that had in a real sense already happened: they had been moved from a negative to a positive condition in their own lives.[29] The positive condition could be described in terms familiar to Greco-Roman philosophical traditions: Christians claimed freedom (*eleutheria*) and "free-speech" (*parrēsia*), or the kind of boldness that enabled witness even before hostile hearers.[30] It could also be described in terms of certain states in which they found themselves—such as a state of peace with God and humans and a state of joy that was compatible even with suffering—and in terms of dispositions, such as faith, hope, and love—dispositions that had specific behavioral manifestations.[31]

The earliest Christians claimed, in short, empowerment. Whether using terms like "authority" (*exousia*) or "energy" (*energeia*) or "power" (*dynamis*)—or their cognates—the New Testament compositions are shot through with claims associating believers with a power that manifested itself outwardly in various "signs and wonders," such as healings and prophecies, as well as in the preaching of the good news.[32] The power was present equally, however, in the process of personal transformation.[33] As striking as the frequency of these claims to possess or be possessed by power—and its effects—is the insistence that power is not something longed for or even to be striven for, but rather is a past and present reality. The states, dispositions, and transformations are experienced now rather than simply desired.[34] The power that brought about these capacities and changes, moreover, was not self-generated but came from another, as gift (*charis*): it came from the one to whom all power properly belonged, the one God of Israel,[35] who constantly renews creation. With remarkable consistency, the New Testament's language about power can be correlated to its language about "the Holy Spirit" (*to pneuma to hagion*),[36] a phrase that at once suggests the character of the power (it has to do with capacities of human freedom), its origin, and its ultimacy ("Holy"=from God). And since the power they were being given was God's own *dynamis*, Christians claimed to represent not novelty in a world dedicated to antiquity, but something utterly and definitively new: a new life, a new covenant, a new creation, a new humanity.[37]

Christian claims to have experienced the divine *dynamis* are not themselves unique in the first-century Mediterranean world: Aelius Aristides made claims of direct divine intervention for saving and healing, and Epictetus claimed the power of Zeus for moral transformation. The frequency, intensity, and immediacy of the claims in the New Testament writings are nevertheless stunning. Such emphasis on the religious experience of power is not, however, stabilizing, since both "experience" and "power" are peculiarly motile phenomena. But the factor that made this new cult least stable was the very figure around whom the movement was organized and who was claimed to be the medium through whom God poured out the Holy Spirit (Acts 2:32–33). This is above all because the movement was born, grew, and took on its distinctive shape not during Jesus' life or on the basis of his words or actions but after his death and on the basis of experiences and convictions concerning his resurrection.[38]

Jesus of Nazareth exercised what can appropriately be called a prophetic ministry in Galilee and Judaea. He summoned followers and taught them.[39] But on the basis of that activity Jesus cannot be called the founder of the movement that carried his name in the same way that Muhammad can legitimately be called the founder of Islam or Siddhartha the founder of Buddhism. His time of active ministry was at most three years in length and perhaps little more than a year.[40] He did not develop a system of law that contained a vision for society or that organized a community. His teaching was rather more indirect and allusive, more a matter of aphorism and parable than of legal dictate.[41] His characteristic activity of healing, moreover, was sporadic rather than systematic; he is better viewed as a wandering charismatic figure than as the officer of a cult center.[42] Whatever his own messianic intentions, his activity came to an abrupt and violent end when he was crucified under Roman authority under the *titulus* "King of the Jews."[43] As for his disciples, one betrayed him (Mark 14:10–11; 43–45), another denied him (14:66–72), and the rest fled when he was arrested (14:50–51). Whatever it had been during his life, the "Jesus movement" appeared decisively to end with his death.

The Christ cult began, however, when his followers claimed to have experienced Jesus more powerfully after his death than before, indeed, to have encountered him and received from him a commission to proclaim the good news to the nations. Because the claim about Jesus' resurrection is so central, it is important to define its meaning as closely as possible,[44] beginning with what it does not mean before attempting to state what it does. It does not mean that Jesus "lived on" among others in some vestigial "afterlife" constituted by the memory of his sayings and deeds or a sharing in his vision concerning God's rule.[45] Nor does it mean that he was resuscitated, returning after clinical death to his empirical existence—although the realism of some of the Gospel narratives could give that impression.[46] The earliest Christian conviction concerning the resurrection seems to have a dual character: it is both something that happened to Jesus and something that happens to his followers; it is an event of the past but just as much a continuing reality in the present. With regard to Jesus, he was exalted "to the right hand of the God." Unpacking the dense symbolism of Psalm 110:1, this language states that Jesus, after his death, entered into God's own life and power. With regard to his followers, the *dynamis* of the exalted Jesus is given to them through the Holy Spirit.[47] Paul states it succinctly: "the last Adam [Jesus] has become life-giving spirit" (*to pneuma to zōopoioun*; 1 Cor 15:45). Jesus becomes the most highly mobile of all cult centers. He is also an inherently unstable center for the nascent movement energized by that experience and conviction, as shown by a closer look at two of the titles ascribed to him.

The title "Lord" (*kyrios*) was probably the earliest used by the first believers to express their conviction that Jesus was exalted to a share in God's power (1 Cor 12:3; Rom 10:9).[48] Writing to the Philippian church, Paul declares that "God has greatly exalted him and has given him a name above every name, so that at the name of Jesus every knee should bend, above the heavens and upon the earth and in the depths, and every tongue should confess that Jesus Christ is Lord" (Phil 2:9–11). In the Greco-Roman world, this designation for the divine was common: we have noted how Aelius Aristides spoke of "Lord Serapis" and "Lord Asclepius."[49] It was, in fact, the connection of this title to Hellenistic cults that led to the theory that the Jesus movement only became the "Christ cult" when it went outside Palestine and encountered Greco-Roman religion.[50] The weakness of this hypothesis I noted earlier:[51] not only was Hellenism pervasive within Palestine, so that geographical expansion was not required for the use of this title, but more tellingly, the title "Lord" (*kyrios*) was used in the LXX to translate the proper name of Israel's God (Yahweh), as indicated by the verse that was widely used as a proof text for the resurrection: "The Lord (*kyrios*) said to my Lord (*kyrios*), Sit at my right hand until I make your enemies a footstool for your feet."[52] For religious practice (in cult, in prayer), the designation "Lord" was perfectly clear to both Jews and Gentiles: an executed human being was being proclaimed as divine. For religious understanding, to be sure, the title's ambiguity could cause concern. For Gentile converts, it would be easy to view Jesus as one among many gods so designated. For Jewish members, the use of the most holy name for the resurrected one meant declaring "two powers in heaven" and becoming, in the eyes of other Jews, polytheists.[53] The difficulty is wonderfully displayed by the careful language Paul uses in his first letter to the Corinthians: "We know that there is no idol in the world and no God but one. For even if there are many designated as gods either in heaven or on earth—as indeed there are many gods and many lords—for us there is one God, the Father, from whom are all things and toward whom we are, and there is one Lord, Jesus Christ, through whom are all things, and we are through him" (1 Cor 8:4–6).

The title "Messiah" or "Christ" (*Christos*) is if anything even more problematic when used for someone crucified by the Romans and then proclaimed as sharing God's power to give life.[54] On one hand, the title demands interpretation from within the symbolic world of Torah, for it has no significance in Greco-Roman culture. On the other hand, from the perspective of that worldview, Jesus is an unlikely bearer of the title. There were, to be sure, no specific job description for the Jewish Messiah; expectations were various.[55] But at the very least, a messiah was expected to make things better for Jews, and by any measure, Jesus failed at this. He did not establish a Jewish kingdom, restore the temple, or punish the enemies of the people. So, by any measure used by Jews, Jesus did not produce the "signs" of a messiah (1 Cor 1:22). Worse, because of the character of his life, he could be regarded as a false messiah, one of the charlatans who "seduced the people" and led them astray (Luke 23:14). The Gospels report him as reinterpreting Moses on his own authority (Matt 5:17–48), as flouting the laws concerning the Sabbath (Mark 2:22–28; Luke 13:10–17), and as associating with tax collectors and sinners (Luke 7:34–50; 15:1–2).

Worse still, the manner of his death—crucifixion—could be taken as confirmation that he was cursed by God: Deuteronomy 21:23 declared cursed anyone hanged upon a tree (see Gal 3:13). For believers to proclaim Jesus as "Christ crucified," therefore, was to present a "stumbling block" (*skandalon*) to fellow Jews, as well as something foolish (*mōria*) to fellow pagans,[56] even if to those inside the community this proclamation seemed "the power of God and the wisdom of God" (1 Cor 1:24). The cognitive dissonance created by the declaration concerning the crucified Jesus that "god has made him both Lord and Christ" (Acts 2:36) was part of the generative matrix for the composition of the New Testament and would continue to fuel theological disputes within Christianity for centuries. The earliest Christian experience and conviction, in sum, was itself deeply ambiguous and capable of being led in different directions.

SOCIAL SETTINGS

A final element contributing to the instability of earliest Christianity is its uncertain place within the social world. It began as an intentional community: for the most part, members were Christian not because of the accidents of birth but because of a choice to belong.[57] Intentional communities are inherently fragile and require the construction and maintenance of firm identity boundaries if they are to survive.[58] This task was especially difficult for the first generation of Christians because their community was not entirely grounded in either Greco-Roman or Jewish traditions, but existed uneasily among and between both, needing to define itself against each respectively even as it inevitably (and not always consciously) drew from them. Since converts joined the community as adults directly from Jewish and Gentile backgrounds and with already formed religious practices, the problems created were real and difficult. I have already mentioned how different understandings of "Lord" might arise because of differing religious backgrounds. Even more pressing—because it threatened *koinōnia* ("fellowship") itself—was the issue of Torah observance, specifically with regard to participating in pagan meals and with regard to Jews and Gentiles sharing the same table.[59]

Christians did not invent a new form of society in order to negotiate these tensions but adopted the most readily available model, that of the association (*ekklēsia*), used throughout the Greco-Roman world for a wide variety of social and religious groups, including Diaspora Jews (the synagogue). Christians did not at first have their own separate buildings but, like many of the Jewish and Greco-Roman associations, met in households.[60] Implicit in this practice is some form of patronage, since the head of a household would voluntarily make such provision for the community.[61] Such minimal forms of patronage suggest at least some degree of economic stratification, and there is some evidence that the Greco-Roman assumptions concerning patronage caused tension within communities.[62]

The exercise of authority in the earliest assemblies was less straightforward than in many Greco-Roman associations. First, founders of communities (like Paul) and itinerant leaders (like the "superapostles") could exercise authority over specific communities through their presence or letters.[63] Second, within local communities, there was no clear demarcation between the charismatic authority exercised through the "gifts of the spirit" and the routine administration effected by the sort of leadership standard for associations.[64] That there were such forms of local leadership even in Pauline churches is clear.[65] The evidence suggests that such leadership was organized based on the model of the

Diaspora synagogue, which itself shared many features with Greco-Roman associations.[66] It further seems likely that leaders were expected to carry out the same sort of routine obligations expected of their Jewish and Hellenistic counterparts: supporting the community financially, providing hospitality and travel provisions, overseeing charity for the needy, settling internal disputes.[67]

Two cultic activities of early assemblies would easily be recognized by members of Greco-Roman religious associations. The first was baptism, the ritual of initiation that marked entry into the community.[68] As an initiatory ritual, it was notable primarily for its simplicity and its singularity; in the Mysteries, initiations tended to be complex and multiple.[69] For Jewish believers, baptismal washing for males would represent an addition to the Jewish ritual of circumcision; for Gentile converts, baptism replaced circumcision (Col 2:11–12)—a circumstance that also could be the occasion for conflict.[70] The second cultic activity was the meal. Some version of "breaking bread in houses" (Acts 2:42, 46) that Paul calls the "Lord's Banquet" (*kyriakon deipnon*; 1 Cor 11:20) was celebrated in the gathered assembly, probably on the day of resurrection, the first day of the week (1 Cor 16:2; see Rev 1:10).[71] The rituals of initiation and meals were occasions for enacting the presence of the risen Lord in the assembly and for remembering the words and deeds of Jesus in the context of his continuing powerful presence.[72]

Other elements of worship resembled the practices of the Jewish synagogue. Although pagans prayed with vigor and frequency, the forms of prayer in the New Testament most resemble those found in Judaism, and several short prayer formulae even appear in Aramaic rather than in Greek.[73] Similarly, hymns were addressed to God and to Christ.[74] As in synagogues, practices of reading (Torah), preaching, and teaching also took place within the context of the assembly.[75] All these would have made the assemblies meeting in the name of Jesus appear closer to the synagogues from which at least some of the worshippers had come to join this new movement. The practice of ecstatic utterance within worship, whether in the form of glossolalia or prophecy, in contrast, would have seemed strange in the synagogue but at least conceivable as a practice within Greco-Roman cults.[76]

Greco-Roman associations and synagogues often maintained social interactions with other communities through personal communication and correspondence.[77] The same patterns of *koinōnia* can be observed among the earliest Christian assemblies. Leaders and communities alike sent delegates to other assemblies to represent them.[78] The epistolary literature of the New Testament emerges from the same impulse to maintain connections.[79] Finally, exchange of financial resources undoubtedly served to cement ties between local assemblies:

Paul's great collection effort had as its intention a greater degree of *koinōnia* among Jewish and Gentile churches and served to advance the notion of scattered communities constituting a single *ekklēsia*.[80]

No matter how extensive its expansion or impressive its networking, Christianity in its first decades remained a negligible speck within the vastness of the Roman political order. By the end of Paul's ministry, it was sufficiently visible and vulnerable for Nero to blame it for Rome's fire.[81] By the first decade of the second century, it was sufficiently active and popular to irritate a provincial governor, but Pliny the Younger's query to Trajan concerning the treatment of Christians assumed no greater importance than the establishment of a volunteer fire brigade.[82] During the entire period when the New Testament compositions were being written, the scattered communities had no real stake in the *oikoumenē*. Not surprisingly, views of the empire within those compositions tend to correspond to the particular experience—positive or negative—the community had of the empire.[83]

This all-too-rapid sketch of Christianity in its first manifestation has revealed a number of factors contributing to the instability of the nascent religious movement: its rapid expansion in circumstances of duress, its explosive claims to experience, its powerful yet ambiguous confession of a crucified man as Lord and Messiah, its social location as an intentional community drawing members from both Judaism and Hellenism, as well as its political insignificance and vulnerability.

WAYS OF BEING RELIGIOUS

I have already stated my agreement with the proposition that there was diversity in the earliest Christian movement. There are more than trivial differences, for example, between the compositions deriving from "Pauline" circles and the "Johannine School," and there are significant differences even within discrete compositions within those groupings.[84]

Differences among New Testament writings range from such surface elements as genre and forms of rhetoric to fundamental perspectives on critical issues. My interest in this study is not to catalog such differences but to ask the same question of earliest Christianity that I put to Greco-Roman religion and Judaism: is it possible to discern in this earliest period distinct "ways of being religious?"

My argument over the next two chapters is that two of the four distinct modes of religiosity I have detected in Greco-Roman religion—and, in a more complex configuration, also in Judaism—are found within the writings of the New Testament. Religiousness A (participation in divine benefits) is unmistakable, and Religiousness B (moral transformation) is also clearly present. There is, in contrast, only the slightest hint in the New Testament of Religiousness C (transcending/escaping the world) and no sign of Religiousness D (stabilizing the world). Subsequent chapters will trace the emergence of these further types as well as the continuation (and modulation) of the first two.

Before developing that argument, I must close this chapter as I opened it, with some cautionary comments. The reader should bear in mind first the peculiar complexity of the New Testament compositions. I mean by this not only the fascinating way in which Greco-Roman literary genres are fused and transformed,[85] but even more the way the central convictions of this movement bend everything around them: just as the one God and Torah made Hellenistic Judaism something distinct within the Greco-Roman world, so the New Testament's central concern with a crucified and raised Christ—in addition to its convictions concerning the one God and Torah—catalyzes Greco-Roman religious sensibilities. Next, the search for different types of religious sensibility must necessarily remain on the surface of what the New Testament compositions make available; no judgments can be made about the "religious type" of historical individuals or of groups. Indeed, we can be less certain about the sensibilities that gave rise to the texts than about the sort of sensibilities to which the texts would give rise.

It is important, furthermore, not to allow typology to become stereotyping. My interest is in differences of emphasis, the ways in which religious people diversely perceive the location of the divine *dynamis* and its purpose, not in placing people in closed compartments or opposing ideologies. To state that Aelius Aristides is an almost pure example of Religiousness A, for example, does not lead to the judgment that he never longed to die, that he had no concern for the state, or that he was lacking in moral virtue. To agree that Epictetus perfectly represents Religiousness B, similarly, does not imply that he failed to participate in the round of festivals and sacrifices or that he regarded piety as a completely private rather than public concern. The same applies to the distinction among types of religiosity in the New Testament. Finding Religiousness A among Paul's communities does not mean that those with that sensibility could not also be morally upright or socially engaged; determining that Paul and the author of the letter to the Hebrews represent Religiousness B does not in the least suggest that they denied or despised the outward manifestations of the divine power. Finally, I remind the reader that making distinctions is not the same as stating preferences; the point of this exercise is analysis rather than advocacy.

10

NEW TESTAMENT CHRISTIANITY AS PARTICIPATION IN DIVINE BENEFITS

Within a very short period of time, Gentiles joined the movement that had gathered around the crucified and raised Jewish Messiah Jesus, and within decades such Gentile converts formed a majority of its members.[1] Given this influx of Gentile members, and given the elements of instability described in the previous chapter, we would expect the Christian movement to be marked in some fashion by the Greco-Roman religious background of such converts. And since the greatest portion of religious Gentiles belonged to what I have described as Religiousness A, we should not be surprised to find traces of this form of religiosity in earliest Christianity.

I have defined Religiousness A in terms of "participation in divine benefits." This mode of religiosity perceives the divine *dynamis* as active in the empirical world and accessible through religious practice. The point of engaging such *dynamis* is the benefit that accrues to the participant: the answering of prayers for everyday success, the effectiveness of prophecy in guiding decisions, the experience of healing or other kinds of "salvation," the initiation into a cult that enhances one's place in the world and gives hope for future bliss. Gentiles of such sensibility would logically be attracted to a new cult that compensated for its lack of antiquity by its claims to powerful experiences of the divine.[2]

The major problem in analyzing Religiousness A in earliest Christianity is the indirect character of the evidence. We have no firsthand witness like Aelius Aristides to proclaim the benefits received through participation in the cult of the Messiah. Our access to this sensibility is primarily through Paul's letters and the Gospel narratives. Each form of witness needs careful handling. The value of Paul's letters is that they introduce us to the religious impulses of his readers just as he perceives them in the "real time" of his correspondence with a church. The drawback to this correspondence is that, since Paul is writing primarily to correct his readers, his perceptions provide only a partial picture. Part of my task in this chapter is to enter appreciatively into the experiences and convictions of the ordinary members of Paul's congregations. The value of the Gospel narratives—including Acts—is that they enthusiastically communicate the elements in the good news that fit within Religiousness A. The drawback to these narratives is that they are not simple aretalogies—they also are complex compositions shaped by the evangelists for pedagogical purposes, requiring us to assess their witness carefully.

THE ENTHUSIASTIC CORINTHIANS

Paul's readers in Corinth have often been analyzed in terms of a theological position, whether a "Gnosticism" that gave certain members an exaggerated sense of wisdom or a "realized eschatology" that emphasized the present experience of power to the neglect of the message of the cross.[3] It is perhaps just as plausible to see them as Gentile converts who enthusiastically embraced Paul's proclamation of the resurrection (1 Cor 15:4), the reception of the Holy Spirit (12:13), and all the ways in which "the kingdom of God consists in power [*dynamis*]" (4:19).[4] Paul reminded them, in fact, that "signs and wonders and powerful deeds [*semeia kai terata kai dynameis*]" had been worked among them (2 Cor 12:12). We can, indeed, see them as Gentile converts who embraced all this with the attitudes characteristic of Religiousness A: for them the point of the *dynamis* was participation in its benefits.

This perspective helps us understand the difficulty inherent in Paul's treatment of the practice of eating food that had been offered to idols (that is, Gentile gods). It is in this discussion that he reminds his readers, as I noted above, that although there are in heaven and on earth many called gods—and indeed there are many gods and lords—there was "for them" only one God and one Lord (1 Cor 8:5–6). He says this as a reminder to his readers that "not all have this knowledge" (8:7) that he takes for granted, namely, that "there is no idol on earth or god except one" (8:4). The subsequent passage shows clearly that although some of Paul's Gentile converts shared this knowledge—Jews would not have needed the reminder—and could be counted on as "strong," there were others who were "weak in conscience" (8:7). They may have known that idols were not real, but their knowledge was not sufficiently deep or entrenched to enable them to eat idol offerings as though they were "nothing."

The question that needs asking is why such Gentile believers would have put themselves in the position of eating food offered to idols or, even more dramatic, attending a meal with unbelievers where such food would be served as a matter of course (1 Cor 10:25–30). A partial answer can be found, to be sure, in the facts of Greco-Roman social life: if one were to have meat for a meal, it was difficult to get it apart from that made available at temples.[5] And if one were not to "go out of the world" (5:9), then eating with fellow Gentiles at the meals of their associations would be difficult to avoid—given the way in which networks were formed through such social contacts.[6] But we find the specific answer, I think, in the logic proper to Religiousness A: if allegiance to one lord brings benefits, then allegiance to many lords must bring more benefits; if participation in the ritual meal of one cult achieves a blessing, how much more blessing will come from participating in the meals of other cults.

The effectiveness of Paul's response is difficult to assess, for it comes from a completely different religious logic, namely, that of Jewish monotheism. Participation in cults other than those of the one God is not an added good but an apostasy that brings on punishment (1 Cor 10:1–13). Meals at pagan shrines involves eating not what is offered to gods but to demons, which means that those participating in the meal are in communion with demons (10:19–22). Although Paul sees a place for freedom with respect to eating idol food, so long as care is taken not to scandalize the weak (8:9–13; 10:23–30), he demands an absolute separation from such table fellowship and that in which "the cup of the Lord" is shared (10:20–21). It is not at all clear how powerful such arguments would be to those whose religious sensibility was shaped not by covenant with one God but by participation in benefits from as many gods as possible.

The logic of Religiousness A may also explain the practices that Paul condemns in the Corinthians' own cult meal, the *kyriakon deipnon* (1 Cor 11:20). What actually occurred at this meal is unknown. Paul charges the Corinthians with "going ahead with each one's meal" so that some get drunk and others go hungry (11:21). He considers this a despising of the assembly and of those who have nothing (11:22), and he reminds them of the tradition concerning the death of Jesus associated with this meal (11:23–26). He wants them to eat and drink "worthily of the Lord," which appears to mean discerning the body (of the community) rather than eating and drinking condemnation to themselves (11:27–29). It has plausibly been suggested that a Greco-Roman understanding of patronage lies behind this passage. Those who sponsor the meal would have eaten first and others later.[7] But specific religious assumptions may also be at work. The first is that the point of participating in a meal in honor of an exalted Lord is participating in the power of the Lord's presence rather than an opportunity for moral awareness. The second is that such participation is precisely for the benefit of the individual—asking about the possible benefit to the community as a whole demands another way of thinking. The third is that social roles in religious cults reinscribe the social distinctions of the larger society rather than obliterate them.[8]

The most impressive example of Religiousness A among the Corinthians appears in Paul's lengthy discussion of spiritual gifts (*charismata*) in 1 Cor 12–14. Paul and his readers share the perception that such gifts come from the Holy Spirit (1 Cor 12:4). In his listing of them, Paul includes "powerful deeds [*dynameis*]" and "gifts of healing [*charismata iamatōn*]" (12:28), but the focus of his discussion in chapter 14 is on the gifts reflecting the Corinthians' rich endowment "in all speech and in all knowledge" (1:5), namely, prophecy and speaking in tongues (12:30).

While all forms of prophecy were esteemed in Greco-Roman religion, there is no doubt that the form most attractive to Religiousness A would be *enthusiasmos*, in which human capacities are taken over by the *pneuma* of the god, and mysteries are expressed through unintelligible ravings requiring interpretation.[9] Here is a manifestation of divine *dynamis* even more impressive than Asclepius' directing of Aelius Aristides' orations, for the prophet is directly under the power of the god in an unmistakable manner, with the ordinary processes of human thinking and speech completely bypassed: it is the god who speaks. For Gentile converts to a new cult, what greater proof could there be that Jesus was indeed exalted as Lord than such a direct infusion of the Holy Spirit among humans (1 Cor 12:3)? The demonstration would be all the more impressive, given anxiety concerning the decline in traditional sites for such prophecy.[10] This new cult delivered what older traditions only remembered.

It is small wonder that some Corinthians considered speaking in tongues to be the most highly desirable gift of the spirit (1 Cor 14:22), since ecstatic speech simultaneously revealed the presence of the Lord and bestowed on the speaker the status of prophet.[11] While not denying the reality or validity of this gift, Paul tries to turn his readers' minds toward the question of the appropriateness of its expression. But by so doing he reveals—as we shall see in the next chapter—a religious sensibility different than that of at least some of his readers in the Corinthian congregation.

RITUAL IMPRINTING IN PHRYGIA

Further evidence for Religiousness A among Paul's readers is found in the two letters addressed to churches in the territory of Phrygia, Galatians and Colossians. Beyond the fact that Galatians is universally accepted as authentic while the Pauline authorship of Colossians is doubted by some, there are real differences between the letters. Paul was the founder of the churches in Galatia to whom he writes (Gal 1:11; 4:13–20), yet his apostolic authority appears to be questioned.[12] In his passionate yet rhetorically sophisticated argument, Paul makes heavy use of language drawn from Torah.[13] The church at Colossae has been founded by Epaphras,[14] one of Paul's associates, who at the time of composition is Paul's fellow prisoner (Col 4:3; Phlm 23). In this letter, neither the interpretation of Torah nor the question of Paul's authority is salient.[15] Instead, Paul's response is shaped by shared traditions (Col 1:5–7; 2:6–7), especially those connected to baptism and the identity of Christ.[16]

The situations addressed by the letters are, nevertheless, strikingly similar. In both cases, the ethnic and cultural background of the readers is Gentile rather than Jewish—they have turned to Christ directly from paganism.[17] Whether under the influence of outsiders or inside agitators, in both communities members are seeking a further initiation beyond baptism. In Galatia, some members are having themselves circumcised, and in Colossae, there is a desire for circumcision as well as for further visionary experiences.[18] In both situations, such ambition is connected to notions of perfection or maturity.[19] Finally, there is the suggestion that those who undergo further initiation are superior to those who have received only baptism in Christ.[20] Scholarship on these letters has tended to focus on the identity of Paul's "opponents," as though the issue was a difference in theology.[21] But the real question is religious: why would adult males seek to undergo a painful and even dangerous genital mutilation within a short time of an easy and painless initiation by water into the *ekklēsia* gathered around the Lord Jesus?

The answer is found in the combination of elements that point clearly to a religious sensibility of the Greco-Roman world that these Gentile converts carried with them into the messianic cult. They reasoned by analogy: if the cult of the Messiah was an association (*ekklēsia*) rather than a domestic cult or local cult shrine or civic liturgy, then it can be thought of as a Mystery—especially if it proclaimed as Lord a human being who had died and was raised. And if it was a Mystery, then initiations within it would naturally be multiple.[22] Further initiations (as into the cult of Moses) would require an ordeal (such as circumcision or physical asceticism), to be sure, but they would also provide lore not available to others (such as Torah) and an elevated status within the association.[23] Particularly in Phrygia, sexual mutilation would have been familiar as a sign of advanced status within a cult.[24] The quest for "perfection" through successive initiations is a splendid example of Religiousness A among Paul's readers.[25]

JESUS AS BRINGER OF BENEFITS

Just as in the case of Paul's letters, it is important to remember that our access to Religiousness A is limited by his personal perspective, so in the case of New Testament narratives, we must be aware of another sort of indirectness. The Gospels—including in this category the Acts of the Apostles as the second volume of Luke's Gospel—are not simply aretalogies, even though they all contain materials that would fit nicely into an aretalogy.[26] The Gospels all stand at a distance from what they report about Jesus: they are distant in time from the figure about whom they write, being composed some 40–60 years after Jesus' death.[27] They are distant also because what they tell about Jesus has been selected and shaped by the process of transmission in communities.[28] They are distant as well because of their perspective: they are all written from a position of belief in Jesus as the resurrected Lord, and that perspective affects the entire telling of the story.[29] Finally, they are distant because of the authorial purposes at work in the shaping of each Gospel narrative.[30]

Just as in Paul's letters we find a mixture of Religiousness A—found above all in Paul's readers—and Religiousness B (to be shown in the next chapter), so also in the Gospels do we find the inclusion of elements that could be argued to represent moral transformation (the teaching found especially in Matthew and Luke) or transcending the world (the apocalyptic sections of Mark and Matthew). Yet it is fair to state that the dominant strain of religiosity found in all four Gospels is the one I have dubbed Religiousness A, participation in divine benefits. This is clearer when we remember that the defining element in each sensibility is the understanding of divine *dynamis* and how it is available. In the Gospels, such *dynamis* is entirely connected to the figure of Jesus and is available through contact with him.

This reality is mitigated but not contradicted by the theme of suffering (both for Jesus and for his disciples) that pervades the Gospels, for, as we have seen in the case of Aelius Aristides, Religiousness A can accommodate suffering within its sense of the divine power at work in the empirical realm. It is enough here, I think, simply to enumerate those elements in the Gospels—beginning with the Synoptics—that communicate to the reader that in Jesus the divine *dynamis* has come among humans to their benefit. The obvious starting point is the account of Jesus' birth in Matthew and Luke.[31]

In Matthew, Jesus is conceived by a virgin through divine intervention—through the power of the Holy Spirit (Matt 1:18, 22–23)—and her husband has a dream in which the angel of the Lord instructs him in the matter (1:20–21). This is the first of several dreams that reveal to Joseph how to protect his family from harm (2:13, 19, 22). The supernatural character of the birth is certified by a heavenly portent, the star appearing to *magoi* from the east (2:1), with the portent being interpreted through scriptural prophecies by the college of priests and scribes in Jerusalem (2:3–5). The *magoi* honor the child as a king by prostration and the offering of precious gifts (2:11), and then, themselves warned in a dream, they return home (2:12). All of these dreams and portents serve to assert that Jesus is not only the Messiah (1:16) but the Son of God (1:23; 2:15), the Emmanuel who means, indeed, "God with us" (1:23).

Luke's infancy account has a similar range of supernatural elements.[32] Both John and Jesus are born through divine intervention (Luke 1:18–19; 2:31–36), and both have their births prophesied by direct revelation of an angel (1:11–20; 2:26–37). An angel also appears to shepherds to announce the birth of Jesus as Messiah and Lord (2:9–10), and a multitude of the heavenly host proclaims this birth as one that brings divine benefits: "Glory to God in the highest and on earth peace to those on whom his favor [*eudokia*] rests" (2:14). Jesus is recognized as God's Messiah by the prophetic figures Simeon and Anna (2:28–38). As a 12-year-old, Jesus astounds the teachers in the temple with his understanding and his answers (2:46–47), and when his worried parents find him, he claims that "it is necessary for me to be about my father's affairs" (2:49). As in Matthew's version, Jesus is emphatically portrayed as "Son of God" (2:35).

The account of Jesus' ministry in the Synoptic Gospels makes clear that the divine *dynamis* is active through him: his proclamation of the good news of the kingdom of God (Mark 1:15) is enacted by deeds that reveal the divine presence.[33] At his baptism, the heavens open and he is proclaimed by a voice from heaven as God's Son (1:9–11), and at his transfiguration, he appears in glory to his followers and is again identified by the heavenly voice as God's Son (9:2–8). Jesus calls disciples to follow him with a mere word of command (2:16–20; 2:14).[34] He manifests his contact with the divine by his powers of prophecy: he foretells with minute precision the circumstances of his death and of his resurrection (8:31; 9:31; 10:33) and predicts the persecution of his followers and the fall of the temple (13:2–13), which make his as yet unfulfilled prophecy concerning the end-time more convincing.[35] Jesus' powers as a thaumaturge also show his divine character. He exercises the divine *dynamis* with respect to the world: he calms a storm at sea (4:35–41) and walks to his disciples on the Sea of Galilee (6:45–52). He curses a fig tree and it withers (11:12–14, 20–21).

But his acts are not random demonstrations of power; they serve to benefit others. Thus, he turns a few loaves and fish into food for multitudes, feeding in one case more than 5,000 people (Mark 6:34–44) and in another case more than 4,000 (8:1–9). His exorcisms show his authority over demonic forces but also liberate humans from "unclean spirits" (1:21–28; 5:1–20; 7:24–30; 9:14–29).[36] He heals people with an astonishing array of sicknesses (1:29–34, 40–45; 2:1–12; 3:1–6; 5:21–34; 6:55–56; 7:31–37; 8:22–26; 10:46–52).[37] He even raises people from the dead (4:35–42).[38] The number and nature of these healings—carried out by an individual, instantaneously, at a word of command—is unparalleled in extant contemporary religious literature.[39] The benefits bestowed on those exorcised, healed, and raised from the dead are obvious: physical health and restoration to society. Their "salvation" is not a matter of eternal destiny but of present rescue and restoration.

The account of Jesus' passion and death in the Synoptic Gospels does not shy away from any of the facts that made his execution a *skandalon*, but by emphasizing that his death was that of an innocent man obedient to God's will (Mark 14:32–40), they interpret the hardest part of the Jesus story (from the perspective of Religiousness A) as ultimate evidence of his divine benefaction: his death is undergone willingly "for others" (10:45) in accordance with prophecy. At his last meal, he tells the disciples that "the Son of Man goes as it is written of him" (14:21) and gives them bread and wine interpreted as his body and blood "for many" (14:22–24). The scripture text of Zechariah 13:7 is cited by Jesus concerning his disciples' betrayal: "You will all fall away; for it is written, 'I will smite the shepherd and the sheep will be scattered.'" But, then, as in his earlier three predications of the passion, Jesus concludes with a triumphant prophecy of his resurrection: "But after I am raised up, I will go before you to Galilee" (14:27). The moment of Jesus' death is entirely clothed with the words of Torah. Not only does Jesus quote Psalm 22:1 (LXX 21:1), with its intimation of divine vindication,[40] but the narrative uses the very language of scripture to depict his death.[41]

The accounts of Jesus' resurrection, in turn, serve to validate the prophecies Jesus had made concerning his rising again (Matt 27:6; Mark 16:7; Luke 24:7, 25–27, 44–46) and to show how the resurrected Lord bestows his power on his followers. In Matthew, Jesus declares that "all power in heaven and on earth has been given to me" and commissions the 11 disciples to make disciples of all nations, promising, "I am with you always, until the end of the age" (Matt 27:18–20). In Mark's longer ending, Jesus declares that "these signs will accompany those who believe: in my name they will drive out demons, they will speak new languages. They will pick up serpents, and if they drink any deadly thing, it will not harm them. They will lay hands on the sick, and they will recover" (Mark 16:15–18). Jesus then ascends into heaven—but he continues to confirm the preaching of his followers through accompanying signs (16:19–20). In Luke, Jesus also ascends into heaven (24:51)—in Greco-Roman religion the supreme confirmation of divine status—after declaring to his disciples, "Behold, I am sending the promise of the Father upon you; but stay in the city until you are clothed with power [*dynamis*] from on high" (24:49).[42]

The link between Jesus as bringer of benefits and his followers as participants in divine benefits is made most clearly by the second volume of Luke's work, the Acts of the Apostles. It opens with the exalted Lord (Acts 1:9–11) receiving the Holy Spirit and then pouring it out (2:33) on his gathered followers in spectacular fashion: a strong wind and tongues of fire accompany their speaking in tongues (2:1–4) in a manner intelligible to Jews gathered from every part of the Diaspora for the Feast of Weeks (2:5–11). Peter's speech interprets the event in terms of the prophecy of Joel 3:1–5 that a prophetic spirit would be poured out on all flesh (Acts 2:17–21), a spirit that would manifest itself in "wonders and signs" (*terata kai sēmeia*; 2:19). Making sure that the link between the prophetic Jesus and these prophetic emissaries is not missed, Peter immediately speaks of Jesus' ministry as one of "powerful deeds and wonders and signs" (*dynameis kai terata kai sēmeia*; 2:22).

From the very beginning, then, Acts invites readers to view the narrative concerning the apostles as the continuation of the narrative about Jesus: just as Jesus brought benefits through his deeds, so do these emissaries filled with his own prophetic spirit both participate in and communicate the same benefits to humans. That the divine *dynamis* is expressed first of all in terms of prophecy is significant, for prophecy was regarded with singular reverence not only in Judaism but also in Greco-Roman religion. For Religiousness A, prophecy is a clear expression of divine power and presence. Jesus, the reader would have already learned, was so powerful a prophet that he was able to predict the circumstances of his own death with precision (Luke 9:22, 44–45; 18:31–33; see also 24:6–7). He also prophesied the destiny of his disciples (Luke 21:12–19) and the course of their mission to the ends of the earth (Acts 1:7–8), both of which prophesies will be demonstrated as accurate by the unfolding of Luke's narrative.

In his ministry, Jesus was already the prophet whom God raised up to visit the people (Luke 7:16). Now, with his resurrection and exaltation, he is even more the prophet like Moses whom God raised up (see Acts 3:22; 7:37) precisely to extend the divine *dynamis* not only to Jews but also to Gentiles (Luke 2:32; 3:6; Acts 2:38–39; 13:47) through those sharing his prophetic spirit. Luke shows this prophetic succession first by the use of literary characterization. Peter and John, Stephen and Philip, Barnabas and Paul, all are "filled with the Holy Spirit" (2:4; 4:8, 31; 6:3, 5; 7:55; 8:29, 39; 9:17; 13:9) and "work signs and wonders" (see 2:43; 4:16, 22, 30; 5:12; 6:8; 8:6, 13; 14:3; 15:12) as they proclaim the good news "with boldness" (*parrēsia*; 2:29; 4:13, 29, 31; 9:27–28; 13:46; 14:3; 18:26; 19:8; 26:26; 28:31).

Luke's second way of showing the continuity of the divine *dynamis* at work in Jesus and in his apostles is by describing their powerful deeds, which mirror those performed by Jesus. Thus, Peter and John heal a lame man at the gates of the temple (3:1–10), a deed that Peter asserts is not done "by our power [*dynamis*] or piety [*eusebeia*]" but by the power of the resurrected one (3:12–15). And the power at work in them, Luke makes clear, is even more vividly present than in Jesus' ministry: even the apostles' shadows falling on the ill and afflicted have the power to heal (5:15–16). Peter alone also heals (9:32–35) and raises someone from the dead (9:36–43). His prophetic power is so great that, when confronted with it, Ananias and Sapphira fall dead (5:1–11). Philip also performs many exorcisms (6:7), and Paul heals (19:11–12; 28:9), exorcises (19:13–17), and resuscitates (20:7–12). Both Peter and Paul wage successful war against the powers of magic that are sponsored by demons (8:18–25; 13:4–12; 19:18–20).[43]

Luke's third way of demonstrating the divine *dynamis* at work in the prophetic successors of Jesus is through the remarkable success of their mission despite all efforts to stop it. Yes, the Jerusalem apostles are scourged (Acts 5:40), Stephen and James are martyred (7:54–60; 12:2), and Paul suffers in synagogues (14:19); but the apostles are released by the Sanhedrin because the authorities fear becoming *theomachoi* by opposing a movement from God (4:21; 5:39–41), Peter is rescued from Herod's prison by an angel (12:3–17), and Paul and Barnabas are freed from jail by an earthquake (16:25–40).[44] Paul escapes from a storm at sea and shipwreck, having prophesied accurately in the midst of the catastrophe that all would be saved (27:33–34, 44). Paul is not harmed when bitten by a viper on Malta, leading the natives of that island to declare that "he is a god" (28:6).

This is not the first time that Gentiles have responded to the apostolic *dynamis* in a manner consistent with Religiousness A. When Peter visits the house of Cornelius, he must deflect the Gentile soldier's attempt to worship him (10:25), saying, "Get up, I myself am also a human being [*anthrōpos*]." Even more dramatically, when the Phrygian inhabitants of Lystra witness Paul and Barnabas healing a man who was lame from birth, they declare, "The Gods have come upon us in human form [*hoi theoi homoiōthentes anthrōpois katebēsan pros hēmas*]" and seek to offer sacrifice to Barnabas as Zeus and Paul as Hermes (14:11–12).[45] The apostles deflect such worship, declaring themselves to be "of the same nature as you, human beings [*homoiopatheis esmen humin anthrōpoi*]," and use the misunderstanding as a way of turning the Gentiles "from foolish things to the living God" (14:15). The "misunderstanding," however, is one that arises naturally from the way in which Luke has constructed his narrative, and although the distinction he has the apostles make is clearly an important one for him, it has been made necessary by his portrayal of the apostles as *theoi andrēs*.

Having made a positive case for reading the Synoptic Gospels and Acts as witnesses to Religiousness A in early Christianity, and before turning to the fourth Gospel, it may be helpful to consider possible objections to my analysis. It might be objected that I have too flattened the portrayal of Jesus in the Synoptics, focusing instead exclusively on thaumaturgic material. It is true that I have not addressed Jesus the speaker in parables or Jesus' ministry to the outcast. But I ask whether these strands in the Gospels in any fashion contradict the portrayal of Jesus as prophet and bringer of benefits and must answer that they clearly do not.

Another possible objection—one that I have already alluded to briefly—is that I have distorted the powerful theme of Jesus' suffering and the opposition he experienced from demons and humans, a theme that continues in Acts with the persecution of the apostles. In fact, however, the theme of suffering is entirely compatible with an emphasis on Jesus as bringer of benefits. That the divine savior should enter fully into the human condition of suffering in order to rescue those who experience suffering is ultimately an extraordinary claim to the efficacy of this specific bringer of benefits.

Another objection might be that the Gospels and Acts contain elements of the other religious sensibilities I have catalogued, above all Religiousness B—religion as moral transformation. After all, Jesus is a teacher who calls for repentance and provides moral instruction.[46] Acts portrays the first believers, moreover, in terms befitting philosophers as well as prophets: they boldly bear witness before human authorities and gather themselves into a community of possessions.[47] Such elements are undoubtedly present. The decisive element of Religiousness B, however, is missing, namely, the perception of the divine *dynamis* being immanently present precisely in order to effect a moral transformation. In the Gospels and Acts, the emphasis clearly is on participation in divine benefits brought about through contact with Jesus and his Holy Spirit. As for the two other types of religious sensibility in the Gentile world, there is no trace in these compositions of a flight from or transcending of the world—everything is about present power that benefits humans here and now—nor is there a trace of religion as stabilizing the world—if anything these compositions emphasize the destabilizing effects of this prophetic movement.[48]

THE MAN FROM HEAVEN

The special character of John among the Gospels has always drawn attention.[49] It is a simple matter to catalog the ways in which it differs from the Synoptics,[50] but accounting for its distinctiveness is more difficult. For many readers, John has seemed the most "Greek" of the Gospels. Focusing on the Gospel's abstract language and lengthy discourses, some historians attributed its Hellenistic feel to a late date: John was written when Christianity had come into contact with Greek philosophy in the Diaspora.[51] Other historians focused on the Gospel's dualism and revelatory monologues and located the origin of John's special character in an early form of Christian Gnosticism.[52] More recent research shows that there is no reason for dating John later or for locating it in the Diaspora: its knowledge of Palestinian lore is as good as that found in the Synoptics, and its dualistic symbolism is available in the contemporary Jewish community at Qumran.[53] Early Christian Gnosticism, in turn, has turned out to be something of a chimera.[54] These explanations have, then, failed to account for the character of the fourth Gospel as a whole. Given the fact that it is a composition of considerable poetic force and theological insight, it is unlikely that any explanation that relies on an aspect of cultural background would seem satisfying. Yet, attempts at such explanation are not unworthy, for they enable us to see things in the Gospel that we might otherwise overlook.

It is in just such a spirit of experimentation that I propose to read John from the perspective of Greco-Roman Religiousness A. I make no pretense of accounting for everything in John, only of seeing how much light is thrown on everything by taking with full seriousness that religious sensibility. And in light of the history of research on John, it is appropriate in this case to begin with objections to the analysis of the fourth Gospel as exhibiting Religiousness A before making the positive argument. The fourth Gospel in no way exhibits signs of Religiousness B: there is no element of moral transformation and indeed little moral instruction beyond the command to love. Equally, John has no element of Religiousness D: far from seeking to stabilize the world, it advocates instead a certain withdrawal from the world; its concern is not the larger political order but a small group of adherents. The choice lies between Religiousness A and C, and the determination rests on the character of Johannine dualism.

A case can be made that the fourth Gospel represents the sensibility of fleeing or transcending the world. As we shall see in Chapter 14, it was certainly read this way by second-century Christian Gnostics.[55] Not only is the Gospel laden with dualistic symbolism (light/darkness; flesh/spirit; truth/falsehood;

death/life),[56] its plot strongly resembles that in the revelatory literature associated with Religiousness C: Jesus is a heavenly revealer who comes from God and returns to God. He descends from the realm of light into the realm of darkness, and the darkness can neither grasp nor overcome the light. Jesus' lengthy, self-referential monologues similarly resemble those found in texts related to Religiousness C: Jesus' main revelation is that he is the revealer.[57] But only the few accept the light he brings into the world. They are rejected by the world just as he was hated by the world. But just as he goes to the Father—returning to the place from which he came—they will also follow him there.

In my analysis of Religiousness C in Greco-Roman religion, however, none of these elements, however intriguing they are singly and together, are probative. The distinguishing feature of Religiousness C, as with the other types, is the perception of the divine *dynamis* and its purpose. In the Orphic and Hermetic traditions, the divine *dynamis* is not to be found in the empirical world but in another realm. The physical body, indeed, is the problem. The authentic self, the soul, is trapped in materiality and can achieve salvation only by distancing itself from the flesh and ultimately returning to its source in the light. The dualism is clearly matter/spirit, and the split is within the human person.

John's Gospel simply does not share this cosmology, psychology, and eschatology. The world is loved by God; indeed, Jesus is sent as savior because of God's love of the world (3:16–17). The word that was facing God and was God "became flesh and dwelt among us" (1:14). There is a flesh/spirit dualism in John, but it is not a split within the human person. The "flesh" (*sarx*) in John stands for the human condition as such in all its frailty and incapacity, rather than for the material dimension of humans, and "spirit" (*pneuma*) points to the power of God rather than to the higher portion of the human person.[58] The divine visitor Jesus not only "becomes flesh" but exuberantly embraces material things in order to transform them; in one of the Gospel's more shocking statements, Jesus declares "unless you eat [*phagēte*] the flesh of the Son of Man and drink his blood, you do not have life within you" (6:53). In the Hermetic literature, furthermore, the point of revelation concerned the hearers: they were called to realize their true essence (they were already light) and to turn away from the entanglement of matter in order to liberate the light for its return home. In John's Gospel, in contrast, the revelatory discourses all concern Jesus' authority to reveal. Jesus' hearers were given "the power to become children of God," not through a realization of what they already were, but by "accepting him" and "believing in his name" (1:12). It is faith in Jesus rather than self-knowledge that defines those "born of God" (1:13). It is because they can participate in the benefits he brings (as branches of a vine; 15:1–10) that they can follow him to the Father.

While acknowledging the elements that could support categorizing the Gospel of John as Religiousness C, then, and while recognizing that his dualistic symbolism was undoubtedly appropriated by second-century Christian Gnostics, I now present the positive reasons why John, in this aspect very much like the Synoptics, should be regarded as an expression of Religiousness A in early Christianity. The prologue is the obvious starting point.

John does not, in the manner of Matthew and Luke, begin with an infancy account filled with portents of greatness; instead, he begins with the origin of the *logos* in the presence of God (1:1). By making the *logos* the agent of creation (1:3) and then become flesh (1:14), John establishes that the empirical world is indeed the place where the divine *dynamis* is active. The glory (*doxa*) of the one dwelling among them, furthermore, is perceptible to humans: "We saw his glory, the glory as of the Father's only son" (1:14). This *doxa* is to be understood, the subsequent narrative makes clear, in light of the Septuagint's language about Yahweh's effective presence among the people.[59] The point is made, in fact, by the final phrase in 1:14, "full of grace and truth" (*plērēs charitos kai alētheias*), which recalls the self-designation of Yahweh in Exodus 34:6: "The Lord, the Lord, a merciful and gracious God, slow to anger and rich in kindness and fidelity."[60] Jesus is not the revealer of a god other than the one who creates the world; rather, he reveals definitively the God whose presence is in all creation but who remains unseen (John 1:18). The point of all this is that, for John, the divine *dynamis* is not absent from the empirical world; rather, Jesus as God's enfleshed *logos* brings to explicit expression the presence of the *dynamis* that was implicit in creation.

A second aspect of John's prologue also supports seeing it as Religiousness A, namely, its emphasis on the human benefits derived from this bringer of God's glory. John's language suggests that those who accept Jesus as God's revealer become participants in the benefits he brings: they "see his glory," and he gives them "the power [*exousia*] to become children of God [*tekna theou*]" (1:12), that is, to share in some fashion in the presence and power of "the only Son, God" (*monogenēs theos*) who reveals the God whom no one has seen (1:18).[61] The point is made again in 1:16–17: "From his fullness [*plēroma*] we have all received, gift in place of gift [*charin anti charitos*]; for the law was given through Moses, grace and truth [*charis kai alētheia*] through Jesus Christ."[62]

Even more than the Synoptics, the narrative of the fourth Gospel presents Jesus in a manner instantly recognizable to Gentile readers as a *theios anēr*.[63] John the Baptist declares that the Spirit came upon Jesus and remained with him and identifies him as the Son of God (1:32–34). Jesus immediately shows himself to have the spirit of prophecy in a series of exchanges that involve people seeking to name him and ending with him calling them (1:35–49): he knows Nathaniel from a distance and names his character (1:47–49). The passage ends by Jesus evoking the story of Jacob's vision of a heavenly ladder (Gen 28:10–17), with Jesus as Son of Man identified as the place where heaven and earth meet: "You will see the sky opened and the angels of God ascending and descending on the Son of Man" (John 1:51). Jesus' prophetic power is displayed throughout the narrative in his ability to see into the hearts of others and to predict the future (2:24–25; 4:17–19, 44; 48–50; 6:15, 64, 70–71; 7:19, 34; 11:4; 12:7, 23; 13:3, 11, 21–27, 36–38), leading the Samaritan woman to declare, "Sir, I can see that you are a prophet" (4:19), and the people to say, "This is truly the prophet, the one who is to come into the world" (6:14). Jesus further establishes his prophetic credentials by his cleansing of the temple—it is "my father's house"—and announcing his ability to raise it in three days if it is destroyed, a boast that the narrator connects to Jesus' body as the temple (2:13–21).

John calls Jesus' thaumaturgic actions "signs" (2:1, 23; 4:54), for they form the evidence supporting the claim that Jesus is God's Son and that the divine *dynamis* (or "glory") is present among humans. Some of the signs simply demonstrate that he is the divine presence: his multiplication of the loaves leads the people to proclaim him prophet and to seek to make him king (6:1–15); his walking to the disciples across the sea in a high wind (6:16–21) enables him to calm his followers with the declaration, "It is I. Do not be afraid," a declaration that in the context of the Gospel as a whole demands being heard as a claim to divine status.[64] Other signs demonstrate both the divine *dynamis* and the benefits brought to others: Jesus provides pleasure to the company by the transformation of water to wine at a wedding (2:1–11);[65] heals an official's child who is close to death (4:46–54); enables a man paralyzed for 38 years to walk (5:1–9); gives sight to a man born blind (9:1–7); and raises his friend Lazarus from the dead (11:1–44). The miracles in John's Gospel are marked by a certain extravagance—the wine is far more than needed, Lazarus far more deceased than necessary—making clear that the deeds are not simply the tricks of a clever human being but the revelation of God's own presence and power ("glory").

The last part of John's narrative, extending from Jesus' final meal with his disciples to his resurrection appearances (13:1–20:31), has appropriately been called "The Book of Glory,"[66] for despite dealing with the scandal of Jesus' suffering and death, John convincingly portrays Jesus, even in these circumstances, as *theios anēr*. Jesus is fully aware that this is the time of his return to the Father (13:1); he knows of Judas' betrayal (13:11–30) and of Peter's denial

(13:36–38) before they happen. He comforts his followers with a lengthy final discourse (14:1–16:33) that promises a continuation of the divine *dynamis* among them through the Holy Spirit (15:26–27; 16:5–15) and declares his identity fully in a final prayer for his followers (17:1–26). He causes those arresting him to fall to the ground by his declaration, "I am" (18:5–8). He boldly resists the questions of the high priest (18:19–24) and engages the Roman prefect Pilate in just the sort of courageous dialogue of which philosophers dreamed (18:28–38; 19:9–11). When crucified, he gives his mother into the care of his beloved disciple (19:26–27). He dies in full awareness of having fulfilled the divine plan (19:28), and saying, "It is finished," he hands over his spirit.[67] He appears after his death to his followers—passing through locked doors—and commissions them by giving them the Holy Spirit he had promised (20:19–23). In the epilogue to the Gospel, Jesus performs another wondrous sign—the catch of 153 fishes—and clarifies the future destiny of the beloved disciple and Peter (21:1–23).

In this chapter, I have focused on strands of religious expression in earliest Christianity that can confidently be seen as representing Religiousness A: participation in divine benefits. Paul's Gentile readers in Corinth and Phrygia and the four evangelists perceive the divine *dynamis* as active in the world and in their community through the presence of the Lord Jesus, manifested in "signs and wonders" such as healing, visions, prophecy, and ecstatic utterances. The point of such powerful deeds was to provide them with participation in divine benefits both now and in the future.

It is no surprise that Gentiles would be drawn by such benefits—from the evidence in Paul and the Gospels, the divine *dynamis* seems to have been active in these communities, and in this savior, to an extraordinary degree. Nor is it a surprise that these same Gentiles would have carried over to the worship of this new Lord some of the assumptions of Greco-Roman Religiousness A: that worship of one Lord did not exclude participation in the worship of others; that ecstatic prophecy was the most desired of all gifts; that one initiation to a cult should be followed by others. Nor, given the increasingly Gentile character of Christianity, should we be surprised to find this mode of religiosity continuing into the next century and, indeed, through all of Christian history to the present day. But before pursuing that suggestion, I must turn to the other major form of religiosity in earliest Christianity: the way of moral transformation.

11

NEW TESTAMENT CHRISTIANITY AS MORAL TRANSFORMATION

My analysis of Epictetus in Chapter 5 made the point that Religiousness B ("the way of moral transformation") had much in common with Religiousness A ("participation in divine benefits"), for both sensibilities perceive the divine *dynamis* as active in the empirical world and accessible to humans. The essential mark of difference is that Religiousness B is more interested in the way that same *dynamis* can transform humans as moral agents. Thus, Epictetus did not scorn or reject the round of popular piety within the empire, did not in any passage deny the reality of the gods or the efficacy of the rituals. Epictetus and Aelius Aristides in fact share a wide range of religious language. But nowhere in Aristides do we see concern for moral change as a specifically religious endeavor, whereas precisely that concern dominates Epictetus' teaching.

We find precisely the same combination of factors in the authors I am treating in this chapter as representing Religiousness B in earliest Christianity. Paul, James, and the author of Hebrews all celebrate the power of the Lord manifested in the world. None of them scorns as unworthy popular forms of prayer and piety or the impressive displays of prophecy and healing experienced in early communities. But each of them, in the manner of Greco-Roman philosophers, seeks to locate the most important expression of the risen Lord's *dynamis* in the change of moral disposition and behavior among believers. On one side, their interest is marked by the way they explicitly connect moral categories, such as virtue and vice, to the faithful service of God. In their use of such language, we find constant reminders of Greco-Roman moral philosophers such as Dio Chrysostom and Epictetus. On the other side, they are far less focused on the individual than Greco-Roman moralists typically are; their moral concern is consistently directed to the formation of communities that were morally righteous.[1] Such focus undoubtedly owes something to the fact that each of these writers was addressing intentional communities, but it also reveals an important dimension of the Jewish roots of the movement: for the Israel of God, holiness is never merely a personal matter; it is a question of the people's integrity.

PAUL AS MORAL TEACHER

The apostle Paul perfectly represents Religiousness B in earliest Christianity.[2] He does not remove himself from participation in the divine benefits brought by the resurrected Christ in order to propagate a "higher" form of religion. He is, in fact, our most valuable witness concerning those benefits, not only among others, but preeminently in himself.[3] He is a personal witness to the resurrection and is called by the risen Lord to be an apostle (1 Cor 9:1; 15:8; Gal 1:11). He has experienced grace (1 Cor 15:10; Rom 1:5) and has the spirit (1 Cor 7:40). He speaks of himself in terms suggestive of a prophet like Isaiah or Jeremiah (Gal 1:15; 2 Cor 13:10).[4] He practices glossolalia more vigorously than his congregants (1 Cor 14:18). He has mystical experiences: he has ascended to the third heaven (2 Cor 12:1–5),[5] hears the voice of the Lord (2 Cor 12:9), and bears in his body the marks (*stigmata*) of Jesus (Gal 5:17). He preaches the word of God with power (1 Thess 1:5) and reminds his readers of the "signs and wonders and powerful deeds" that, despite his lack of worldly eloquence (2 Cor 10:10), accompanied his preaching (2 Cor 12:12). He agrees that the kingdom of God does not consist in words but in power (1 Cor 4:20).

Paul does not stint in his recognition of divine *dynamis* active among his readers. His own experience is not unique but is shared in varying degrees by all in the assemblies. They have all been baptized into the death and resurrection of Christ (Rom 6:1–11). When they eat the *kyriakon deipnon* ("Lord's Banquet"), they have participation (*koinōnia*; "fellowship") in the body and blood of the Lord (1 Cor 10:16–17). They have all "been made to drink" of the same Holy Spirit (12:13). Paul therefore acknowledges the rich and varied gifts of the Holy Spirit among the Corinthians (1:6–7): both women and men in that assembly pray ecstatically (11:3–16), speak in tongues, prophesy, receive revelations, and perform healings (12:27–30).

Nor is such participation in benefits totally a matter of spectacular spiritual outbursts. Paul asserts both for himself and for his readers that their being "in Christ" and Christ being "in them" through the power of the Holy Spirit means that their faithful endurance of suffering—whether through external persecution or through their own "weakness"—serves to manifest the divine *dynamis* even more impressively.[6] As he reports the risen Lord saying to him when Paul asked to be freed from the stake in his flesh, "My grace [*charis*—that is, "bene-fit"] is sufficient for you, for [my] power [*dynamis*] is brought to perfection [*teleitai*] in weakness" (2 Cor 12:9).[7] In short, as much as his readers or the four evangelists, Paul acknowledges and celebrates the extraordinary power let loose among humans by the exaltation of the crucified Messiah Jesus through which he became "life-giving spirit" (*to pneuma to zōopoioun*; 1 Cor 15:45).

Paul's distinctive sensibility, then, is not a matter of subtraction but addition. He consistently addresses his readers as moral agents as well as receivers of divine benefits. By morality, I do not mean simply a listing of behavioral norms—as we have seen, these can be found plentifully within Religiousness A.[8] I mean rather that Paul thinks morally and invites his readers to think that way as well. It is difficult to miss the frequency with which Paul uses cognitive terms either to introduce a topic or to rebuke his readers.[9] He seeks out the moral implications to his and their religious experience, based on the *cause* of such experience (the Holy Spirit coming from Jesus' death and exaltation as Lord) and on the *shape* of that cause (Jesus' human faith and love). Paul asks his readers to cultivate the *nous* (that is, the mind) as an instrument of moral discernment concerning their religious benefits. Thus, Paul says that believers did not receive "the spirit of the world" but "the spirit of God, so that we may understand the things freely given us [*charismata*] by God" (1 Cor 2:12). That Paul's preference for prophecy over tongues among the Corinthians is linked to the fact that prophecy uses the *nous* is not, I think, surprising, for it is the *nous* that enables the speaker to discern (*diakrinein*) the appropriateness of speaking in one circumstance or another.[10]

Paul uses the term *nous* in much the same way that Aristotle did in the *Nicomachean Ethics*: the *nous* is more than the source of thinking; it is closer to what we might call a "mind-set"—that is, it involves a construal of reality that forms the basis for the prudence (*phronēsis*) that guides specific decisions.[11] The *nous*, in other words, has a form or content that shapes the direction of choices. For Paul, the shape of the *nous* is given by the crucified and raised Messiah Jesus. In 1 Cor 2:16, after reminding his readers that they have a spirit from God that enables them to understand God's benefits (2:12), and asserting the unknowability of God's mind—"who has known the mind of the Lord?" (Isa 40:13)—Paul crisply asserts, "But we have the mind of Christ" (*nous Christou*).

The "mind of Christ" provides a framework for moral thinking, a construal of reality that helps determine specific choices. Paul wants it to become a central determinant in the Christian character. He tells the Romans, "Do not conform yourself to this age, but be transformed by the renewal of mind [*nous*], that you may discern [*dokimazein*] what is the will of God, what is good and pleasing and perfect" (Rom 12:2). This "mind" is thus portable and transposable and works through analogical reasoning. The "pattern of the messiah" (*nomos tou Christou*; Gal 6:2), displayed narratively in the character of Jesus,[12] is applied analogously to dispositions and decisions within the Christian community. The most explicit statement of Paul's principle is found in Philippians 2:1–11. Paul proposes the (vertical) self-emptying and obedience shown by Jesus toward God—not clinging to the status that was his by right (2:6–11)—as the sort of attitude his readers are to have (horizontally) toward each other in the community: each should look not only to his or her own interest, but also to that of others (2:4). The link between the goal and its exemplar is found in 2:5: "think [*phroneite*] this one thing [*hen*] among yourselves that is also in Christ Jesus [*ho kai en Christō Iēsou*]."[13]

How Paul applies such moral thinking to specific situations can be found in his responses to his Corinthian and Phrygian readers whose religious sensibility led them to focus on their participation in divine benefits made available through the divine *dynamis*. In his discussion of eating food that had been offered to idols, Paul advocates following one's individual conscience (1 Cor 8:8–9), but such *exousia* needs to be qualified by an awareness of another's condition (are they strong or weak?) and the narrative of Christ that shapes believers' lives. If those who are strong are heedless of these factors, they do wrong: "Thus, through your knowledge, the weak person is brought to destruction, *the brother for whom Christ died*. When you sin this way against your brothers and wound their consciences, you are sinning against Christ" (1 Cor 8:11–12; emphasis added).

Paul also warns those who are willing to eat at the shrines of pagan gods on the assumption that if allegiance to one lord is good, then allegiance to many lords is better. They require reminding that the exaltation of Jesus as Lord demands exclusive loyalty—all other gods are simply "so-called gods" (*legomenoi theoi*; 1 Cor 8:5), and their meals are populated by demons (10:20). When they seek more *dynamis* by participating in more cult meals, they risk incurring the wrath of the one true Lord: "You cannot drink the cup of the Lord and also the cup of demons. You cannot partake of the table of the Lord and of the table of demons. Or are we provoking the Lord to jealous anger? Are we stronger than he?" (10:21–22).

Similarly, those who treat the *kyriakon deipnon* according to the usual practices governing associations—with patrons eating first—Paul exhorts to "discern the body" (*diakrinōn to sōma*), a command that evokes both the need for communal awareness ("the body" that is the community; see 1 Cor 12:12–26 and 11:22) and "the body" that was given for them by Jesus (11:29). Paul recites the words spoken by Jesus over the bread before his arrest (11:23–25)—"this is my body that is for you"—as a narrative fragment that serves to shape a morality of mutual giving, a morality that is betrayed when some are filled and others go hungry, when "those who have nothing are shamed" (11:22).

Paul challenges those overly fascinated with the benefits of ecstatic speech to "stop being childish in your thinking." "In respect to evil," he says, "be like infants, but in your thinking be mature" (1 Cor 14:20). He wants them to exercise the spiritual gifts in the manner of adults. "When I was a child, I used to talk as a child, think as a child, reason as a child; when I became a man, I put aside childish things" (13:11)—this statement occurs at the end of Paul's encomium on *agapē*, the disposition that "does not seek its own interest" (13:5). In contrast to the "knowledge that puffs up," Paul encourages the "love that builds up" the community (8:2). It is for this reason that he prefers prophecy to tongues, for while the presence of tongues "builds up" the speaker, prophecy, using the *nous*, builds up the assembly (14:4). In short, Paul encourages the Corinthians to think in the manner he has learned from the example of Jesus (11:1), by pursuing the moral implications of their shared religious experience.

Of the Phrygian Christians in Galatia and Colossae who follow the ritual instinct of their Greco-Roman past by seeking further initiations, Paul asks to think through the implications of their baptism into Christ. Greater maturity (perfection) in Christianity results not from successive initiations but from thinking through and then enacting the moral entailments of initiation into the crucified and raised Messiah. The Gentile Galatians were baptized "into Christ," had "been clothed with Christ," and were therefore "all one in Christ"— their unity in the Holy Spirit meant that ethnic, gender, and social distinctions lose their ability to bestow status (Gal 3:27–28). Consequently, males seeking a further initiation available only to them betrayed that principle of ritual and moral liminality and reintroduced impulses toward competition and rivalry that are destructive of the community (5:15, 19–21). Paul insists that they had received the Holy Spirit (3:4; 4:6), and if they lived by that spirit, then they ought also to "walk" and "conform" themselves to that life principle (4:16, 25). The point of Christian initiation is not simply the elevation of life through divine *dynamis* but a way of life consonant with the source of that power (compare Rom 6:1–11). This way of life is marked by mutual service in love (Gal 5:13–14), and the measure of that love is provided, once more, by the example of Christ: "Bear one another's burdens, and so fulfill the pattern of the messiah [*nomos christou*]" (6:2).

Paul's response to those Colossians who, after their baptism into Christ, pursued further "perfection" or "maturity" through circumcision, asceticism, and visions—all instinctive to Religiousness A as found in Greco-Roman religion—makes the role of thinking even more explicit. Their maturity does not result from adding on but from digging deeper. Paul wants them to be filled with "recognition of [God's] will in all wisdom and spiritual understanding" (Col 1:9). To what end? That they might "walk worthily of the Lord in everything pleasing, bearing fruit in every good deed and growing in the recognition of God" (1:10). Paul connects this growth in knowledge and in moral behavior precisely with the divine *dynamis* in which they had become participants: "in all the power [*dynamis*] that empowers you according to the might [*kratos*] of his glory—toward all endurance and long-suffering with joy" (1:11).

Paul again argues morally from their religious experience of baptism, in which they were "buried together with him" and were "raised with him" through faith (Col 2:12). If then they died with Christ (2:20) and if they were raised with him (3:1), that ritual pattern should determine their moral behavior:[14] they should put to death all modes of vice and "put on" the new humanity (3:10–11), resisting all impulses that drive them to rivalry and competition and instead showing toward each other the same compassion that was shown them (3:12–13). And over all these, Paul says, they should put on *agapē*, which is the bond of perfection (*teleiotētos*, or maturity).

It is not simply that Paul urges his readers to think through the moral implications of their religious experience; it is clear that he himself regards the most profound and important manifestation of the divine *dynamis* to be the work of the Holy Spirit in the transformation of humans as moral agents. The language of transformation through the Holy Spirit occurs with some frequency in his letters. In Romans, for example, he argues that the gift of the Holy Spirit not only empowers believers to fulfill the righteous requirements of the law (8:4), to endure suffering (8:18–24), and to pray (8:26–27) but also to direct their own moral dispositions (*phronēsis*) in accord with the dispositions of the Spirit (8:4–5).

I noted above how Paul invokes the "participation in the spirit" in Philippians 2:1 when he speaks of acting within the community with the mind of Christ (2:5). Being "in Christ" (2:1), however, implies an even more profound internal transformation: Paul declares in 3:9 his desire to "be found in him" and "to know him and the power of his resurrection and the sharing of his sufferings by being conformed (*symmorphizomenos*) to his death, if somehow I may attain the resurrection from the dead" (3:10–11). In Philippians 3:20, similarly, he speaks of waiting for Jesus Christ as savior from heaven: "He will change our lowly body to conform [*symmorphon*] with his glorified body, by the power [*kata tēn energeian*) that enables him to bring all things into subjection to himself" (compare 2:11). These passages are similar to his remarkable statement in

2 Corinthians 3:17–18: "Now the Lord is the Spirit, and where the Spirit of the Lord is, there is freedom. All of us, gazing with unveiled face on the glory of the Lord, are being transformed [*metamorphoumetha*] into the same image from glory to glory, as from the Lord who is Spirit."

I conclude this brief analysis of Paul's religious sensibility by returning to Romans 12:1–2. I observed earlier that Romans 12:2 exhorts Paul's readers to be renewed in mind so that they can test what is God's will, good and pleasing and perfect. It is important to notice as well, however, that Romans 12:1 casts this moral behavior precisely in religious terms: "I urge you therefore, brothers, by the mercies of God, to offer your bodies as a living sacrifice, holy and pleasing to God, your spiritual worship." The two verses together point clearly to what I have called Religiousness B: religion as moral transformation.

JAMES AND "PURE RELIGION"

The Letter of James may well have been written to Jewish members in the first decades of the messianic movement.[15] Despite the obvious differences between Paul and James, they have more in common than at first appears—most pertinently, that they are moral teachers within the symbolic world of Torah.[16] My argument here is that they also share a religious sensibility. The resemblance is camouflaged by three factors: first, Paul is generous in speaking of his own religious experience, whereas we learn nothing whatsoever about the author of James; second, Paul's language is more Christological, constantly centering on the good news of the crucified and raised Messiah, whereas James's language is more properly theological;[17] third, Paul addresses problems in local churches that arise from specific social and religious practices of the Greco-Roman world, whereas James writes a circular letter to many communities addressing moral inconsistencies arising from the gap between the profession of faith and its practice.[18]

James shares with Paul the appreciation for human participation in divine benefits that characterizes Religiousness A. His short letter—it has only 108 verses—contains a rich set of statements concerning God (*theos*) as one whose power and presence are at work in the world. God can make "demons tremble" (2:19) as the "Lord of hosts" (5:4). God can be characterized negatively as without change or alteration (1:17), untempted by evil (1:13), and removed from human anger (1:20). Positively, God is not simply "light" but the "father of lights" (1:17) whose word of truth has "given birth" to humans as a kind of first fruits of all creatures (1:18), creating them, indeed, in his own image (3:9). James perceives God as constantly involved with humans, revealing his will in the "perfect law of liberty" (2:8–11), judging humans on the basis of his law (2:12; 4:12): "There is one lawgiver [*nomothetēs*] and judge [*kritēs*] who is able to save [*sōsai*] and destroy [*apolesai*]" (4:12).

God not only provides humans a verbal norm by which to judge them. The word of truth is also an "implanted word" that is able to save souls (James 1:21), and God has made to dwell a spirit (*pneuma*) within humans (4:5). God directs human affairs (4:15) and declares as righteous and friends those who show faith in him (2:23). God both displays and is defined by mercy and compassion (5:11). God gives the crown of life to those who love him (1:12; 2:5), shows special favor to the poor in the world (2:5), hears the cries of the oppressed (5:4), raises up those who are sick (5:15), hears the prayers of those who pray in faith (1:5–6) rather than wickedly (4:3), forgives the sins of those who confess them to each other (5:15), and stands at the gate ready to appear as judge (5:7–9).

James conceives of God as approaching humans who approach him (4:8), as raising up the lowly (4:10) and entering into friendship with humans (2:23; 4:4), but also as a God who resists those whose pride and arrogance (4:6) causes them to oppress the helpless (5:6). It is James's characterization of God as gift giver that strikes the reader most. The author makes the point three times. In 4:6, he derives from the citation of Proverbs 3:34 ("God resists the proud but gives a gift [*charis*] to the lowly") the lesson that "God gives even more gifts [*meizona de didōsin charin*]." James makes his first statement about God in 1:5, namely, that God "gives to all (*pasin*) simply (*haplōs*) and without grudging (*me oneidizontos*). Finally, there is the programmatic statement in 1:17: "Every good and perfect gift [*pasa dosis agathē kai pan dōrēma teleion*] comes down from the father of lights with whom there is neither change nor alteration." Taken together, the three statements assert that God's giving to humans is universal, abundant, without grudging, and constant.

James shows himself as a representative of Religiousness B, however, by the way in which he derives moral implications from such religious convictions and practice: his interest is far less in the benefits received from the divine *dynamis* than in the use to which they are put. Both individually and communally, he understands Christianity in terms of moral transformation. I note first the way that James, very much like Paul, uses cognitive language: he wants his readers to understand, to recognize, and not to be "empty-headed" (1:20) or "foolish" (1:26).[19] As Paul invoked the "mind of Christ" (1 Cor 2:16) as the measure for moral discernment, so does James invoke the "wisdom from above" (3:15) as the guide to one who is "wise and understanding" (3:13).

Such discernment enables his readers to see the disparities James identifies between their profession (they want to be "friends of God") and their actual practice (they are "friends of the world"; 4:4). Thus, they agree that God has blessed the poor, but they cater to the very wealthy who drag them into court (2:1–6). They claim to live by the law of loving their neighbor, but when they see their neighbors naked and starved, they stave them off with pious good wishes (2:7–13). They use their tongue to bless God but use the same tongue to curse humans created in God's image (3:1–12). They pray to God but do so wickedly because they seek to use God as a supplier of their unworthy desires (4:1–3). James declares that those considering themselves religious (*thrēskos*) but who do not control their speech have a religion that is vain or foolish (*toutou mataios hē thrēskeia*), and he proceeds to define "pure and undefiled religion [*thrēskeia*] before God" as one in which people keep themselves "unstained from the world" and "visiting orphans and widows in their affliction" (1:26–27).[20]

That James understands religion to be precisely a matter of moral practice within the faith community is shown by his final admonitions in 5:12–20, which, taken as a whole, construct a vision of solidarity within the community in contrast to the competitive and divisive behaviors he earlier condemns. What is particularly striking is the way in which he intertwines moral and religious language. Thus, he advocates simplicity in speech rather than elaborate oaths, because speech stands under God's judgment (5:12; compare 3:1; 4:12). He calls for elders to gather at the call of the weak for anointing and prayer (5:13–14). The religious act of healing, however, takes on the shape of moral correction, as members of the community also are to confess their sins to each other and pray for each other; in this process, the weak person's sins will be forgiven and members of the community will be healed (5:15–16). Finally, the correction of an erring member "saves the soul from death" (5:20) as well as "turning from error" (5:19). This section of James provides the positive ideal of Religiousness B: the point of participation in the benefits provided by the divine *dynamis* is the transformation of individuals and communities through the employment of such power in moral transformation.[21]

HEBREWS AND MORAL EDUCATION

Although I think that the Letter to the Hebrews is best understood as a form of deliberative rhetoric—urging readers to choose loyalty rather than apostasy— I appreciate why some scholars designate it as epideictic, for large portions of the composition form an encomium of the great gift God gave humans in the Messiah Jesus, who is at once fully God and fully human, the great high priest who has entered once and for all into the heavenly sanctuary where he continues to make intercession for humans.[22] The cosmic drama of the Son of God's descent into a full sharing in human mortality—including temptation, suffering, and death—and his subsequent exaltation (enthronement) at God's right hand accomplishes a range of benefits for humanity: Christ has destroyed the devil who had the power of death and freed those captive because of a fear of death (Heb 2:15); he has made purification for sins (1:3) and expiated the sins of the people (2:18); he has become the source of eternal salvation to those who obey him (5:9), obtained eternal redemption (9:12), brought many children to glory (2:10), and consecrated (2:11) and cleansed the conscience of believers (10:22); in him believers have an anchor for their souls (6:19).

In three passages, the author of Hebrews connects such affirmations concerning the benefit of Christ's work for humans to their specific experience as an assembly. In 2:3–4, he reminds his readers that their "great salvation" demanded even more attention and commitment than the message delivered through angels. The message that began with Jesus and was witnessed to by those who heard him received God's own testimony through "signs and wonders and various powerful works" (*sēmeiois te kai terasin kai poikilais dynamesin*). They also experienced various gifts of the Holy Spirit. In short, what Jesus accomplished through his death and exaltation showed itself as real in the specific and concrete benefits they received. In 6:4–5, he reminds his readers of how they were "enlightened" (*phōtisthentas*),[23] had "tasted the heavenly gift and become partakers [*metochoi*] of the Holy Spirit," had "tasted the beautiful word of God and the powers of the coming age." Finally, in 10:32–35, the author reminds readers of the earlier days "when [they] had been enlightened" (*phōtisthentes*) and had endured a variety of deprivations because of their "confidence/boldness" (*parrēsia*). As in Paul and James, such statements show a recognition and even approval of the experiences and rituals through which readers are able to participate in divine benefits.

The author of Hebrews also shares with James and Paul, however, a concern for growth in moral awareness and capacity, as well as a certain edge of impatience at his readers' reluctance to understand how religious experience has moral implications. The key passage is 5:11–6:1. Having introduced the topic of Christ as High Priest whose perfection came about because he learned obedience through the things he suffered (*emathen aph'hōn epathen ten hypokoēn*)— an expression that plays rhetorically on the axiom of Greek education, *mathein pathein* ("to learn is to suffer"), he immediately rebukes his readers for *their* incapacity for such learning: they are reluctant listeners; although they should be teachers, they need teaching; they are like children requiring milk of simple instruction rather than the solid food of advanced learning (5:11–13). He then contrasts childishness and maturity in terms of the capacity for moral reasoning.

The mature are "those who on account of habit [*dia tēn hexin*] have their moral faculties trained [*aisthētēria gegymnasmena*] to distinguish between a good thing and a bad thing" (5:14).[24]

He proposes, then, that they "move on to maturity," past the basic teaching about the Messiah and Christian ritual and doctrine (Heb 6:1–2). But in what does maturity, or "perfection" (*tēn teleiotēta*), consist? Clearly, it involves moral discernment. Most obviously, it involves the decision that believers remain loyal to their commitment of faith rather than fall away—this exhortation takes up a substantial portion of the composition and is the immediate point of 6:4–8. Is such fidelity a form of moral discernment? For this author, it is: the character trait of "faith" (*pistis*) understood as loyalty and endurance is the "good thing" that should be chosen instead of apostasy. Abraham and the other patriarchs are examples of such faithful perseverance (11:8–22), whereas Esau is the counterexample: someone who loses his patrimony because he chooses immediate gratification (12:14–17). For the author of Hebrews, the "religious" reality that is a relationship with the divine demands heroic endurance as well as exclusivity of loyalty. He understands "faith" in moral terms, as a form of "obedient hearing" that perseveres (3:1–4:13).

The moral discernment appropriate to the mature includes as well the practices that build the character of the early Christian community. They are not to neglect the assemblies out of fear of social ostracism (Heb 10:25); they are to be free of avarice and share their possessions (13:5, 16); they are to practice hospitality (13:2) and be mindful of prisoners (13:3); and they are to avoid fornication and adultery out of honor for marriage (13:4). All of this is an expression of "brotherly love" (*philadelphia*; 13:1), which involves a concern for others as well as oneself: they are to "encourage one another" (10:25) and to "rouse one another to love and good works" (10:24).

At a deeper level, though, the author of Hebrews considers growth in moral maturity to involve a form of transformation of character, specifically in imitation of Jesus. Recall that the language of "learning through suffering" occurs first with respect to Jesus as God's Son (5:8–10): even though he was a son, he learned obedience from the things he suffered. In 5:5, the author asserts that Christ "did not glorify himself" by becoming a priest but obeyed the one who appointed him. In his human condition, he cried out to the one able to save him from death and was heard because of his piety (5:7). In terms of human character, then, the priesthood of Jesus was accomplished by the disposition of faithful hearing or obedience. His obedience through death sealed the disposition that began with his entrance into the world: "Therefore, as he comes into the world, he says, 'You have not desired a sacrifice and offering. Rather, you have made for me a body. You did not take delight in holocausts and offerings for sins.' Then I said, in the scroll of the book it stands written of me, 'Behold, I am here to do your will, O God'" (10:5–9). The author suggests that the human Jesus progressively *became* God's Son in his humanity through his life of obedience. When the author chides his readers for being "reluctant listeners" and failing to move to maturity (*tēn teleitotēta*; 6:1), he deliberately connects that failure to the manner in which the Son became "mature" (*teleiōtheis*; 5:9).

That this is his understanding is shown by the author's language in the composition's rhetorical climax. He presents Jesus as the "pioneer and perfecter of faith" on whom they should "keep their eyes" (Heb 12:2). Then he immediately compares their "struggle against sin" to the discipline or education (*paideia*) of sons in Greco-Roman society. The sufferings they experience in their moral endeavor are analogous to the discipline that a father extends to the sons he loves (12:5–6). They should therefore regard their suffering as a process by which they are being transformed into a "sonship" like that of Jesus. Thus, the author states briefly, "you are enduring for the sake of an education [*eis paideian hypomenete*]; God is treating you as sons" (12:7). The same language for moral education used in 5:11–6:1 is repeated in this passage, specifically with respect to following Jesus on the path of faith. Notice how the passage concludes: "Now all instruction [*paideia*], while it is going on, seems more a matter of grief than of joy. But for those who have been fully trained [*gegymnasmenois*; compare 5:14], it yields in the end the peaceful fruit that is righteousness" (12:11).

In a manner distinctively his own, the author of Hebrews displays a religious sensibility like that of James and Paul. On the one side, he celebrates the manifestations of the divine *dynamis* in the empirical realm, all the "signs and wonders" in which his readers participate. On the other side, he seeks to push them in the direction of his own sensibility: religious commitment, for him, is a matter not merely of benefits but of moral transformation, a matter not simply of worship but of changing personal character. Faith is more than confession that Jesus is God's Son; it entails being transformed through obedience into sons like him.

OTHER FORMS OF RELIGION IN THE NEW TESTAMENT?

In this and the previous chapter, I have sketched the forms of religious sensibility that are clearly present in earliest Christianity as witnessed by the New Testament: Religiousness A (Paul's readers, the Gospels, Acts) and Religiousness B (Paul, James, Hebrews). The reader who has followed my argument to this point will appreciate, I hope, the resemblance between Religiousness A in

Christianity and my Greco-Roman example of Aelius Aristides, as well as the resemblance between Religiousness B in Christianity and my Greco-Roman example of Epictetus, and will agree that the religious sensibility in each case is substantially the same.

What about the other types of religious sensibility? There is no evidence for Religiousness D ("religion as stabilizing the world") in the New Testament. The only compositions that might be adduced in this connection are the so-called Pastoral Letters, better designated as "Letters to Paul's Delegates" (1 and 2 Timothy, Titus). Scholars who regard these letters as pseudonymous and emphasize their distance from the "authentic Paul" sometimes regard them as profoundly conservative, representing a "bourgeois piety."[25] But there is good reason to regard all three letters as coming from Christianity's first generation— with Paul as author in the broad sense of the term—and even if they come from a later period, they fall far short of the sort of "church order" they are sometimes thought to be.[26] In any case, until the church became the imperial religion under Constantine, political conditions were not such as to support a version of Christianity that was concerned with stabilizing the social order as such—in the second to third centuries, we shall see, the scope of concern was the stabilization of the *politeia* that is the church..

The question of Religiousness C ("transcending the world") is much harder. I have already noted the elements in the fourth Gospel that have been taken to represent a "Gnostic" outlook and have interpreted its dualism in quite a different manner. But the New Testament composition that most approaches a "transcending the world" sensibility is the Book of Revelation. There are undoubtedly some aspects of the writing that support that suggestion. It describes, first of all, precisely the sort of heavenly ascent and vision that are so often found in the literature of revelation. It has a decidedly negative view towards the circumambient culture: the imperial order is not positive but enslaves and persecutes God's servants and holy ones. Some of the elements most characterizing this religious sensibility, however, are lacking. There is no sense that the material order is itself a problem or that it is souls that must be liberated from the body. There is no vision of the soul's descent into materiality or its eschatological path back to the light from which it came. Revelation is, in fact, robustly positive about the divine *dynamis* at work in the empirical world. The message it contains is simply that this divine power is not obvious; it is now at work in heaven and will be shortly on earth. One must, therefore, perceive what is happening in heaven in order to grasp "what will shortly occur" on earth (Rev 1:1). Indeed, the triumph of God envisaged by the seer involves the full presence of the divine in a "new heaven and new earth" (21:1). Souls do not flee materiality and find a refuge in the realm of the spirit; instead, "God's dwelling is with the human race: he will dwell with them and they will be his people, and God himself will always be with them" (21:3). In its own odd way, Revelation can best be considered an expression of Religiousness A, for it is the saints' participation in the divine *dynamis* and their witnessing to the reality of that power in the face of rejection that imbues its entire vision.

The situation is quite different in second- and third-century Christianity, to which I turn in the next four chapters. In that period, extending roughly from the middle of the second century to the end of the third, we find the full emergence of three distinct sensibilities. We will find Religiousness A in the apocryphal Gospels and Acts. In figures like Justin Martyr and Irenaeus, we will find an even more complete embodiment of Religiousness B. And we will discover a Christian form of Religiousness C in the development of Gnosticism. As for Religiousness D, its full realization must await Constantine, but we catch glimpses of the future in the development of sacraments, hierarchy, and church orders.

12

CHRISTIANITY IN THE SECOND AND THIRD CENTURIES: PARTICIPATION IN DIVINE BENEFITS

The period of time between earliest Christianity—reflected in the writings of the New Testament—and the establishment of the once-despised cult as the religion of the empire is obviously important, for it prepared the way for a most unlikely ascendancy. It is also maddeningly elusive: much of what we would like to know is unavailable for analysis. Some things can be stated with confidence, and it is helpful to state them at once in order to provide a framework for the analysis of the ways of being Christian in this period.

HISTORICAL AND SOCIAL FRAMEWORK

Over the course of these 200 years, the sort of growth that was inferable from the New Testament writings continued. Literary (and eventually archaeological) evidence points to the existence of discrete Christian churches across the Mediterranean world: Christians were found in significant numbers in Syria, Egypt and North Africa, Asia, Greece, Dalmatia, Italy, Spain, and Gaul.[1] The process by which this growth occurred is not entirely clear. There is little real evidence for mass conversions in response to wonder-working.[2] And although some exceptional folk may have joined the movement for intellectual reasons, it is doubtful that Christianity's intellectual appeal affected many.[3] The most likely reasons for Christianity's impressive spread are childbirth—Christians did not kill their infants through exposure and could expect steady growth in numbers—and the sort of attraction of new members that occurs among associations, ancient and modern.[4]

The demographic and cultural direction of Christianity's growth, in contrast, is more than clear. The movement becomes increasingly, then defini-

172

tively, Gentile in this population and in its character. However important Jewish Christianity may have been in earlier generations, it diminishes to the point of disappearance by the mid-second century.[5] With the notable exception of Justin's *Dialogue with Trypho*, actual engagement with living Jews is replaced by literary representation of the Jews as outside the Christian religion, and a theological struggle with the interpretation of the "Old Testament."[6] Not only is the Christian movement populated by Gentiles, it unself-consciously adopts the posture of the "authentic Israel" toward Gentiles, even when its representations of "Israel" reveal an ever-greater distance from actual Judaism:[7] the battle becomes one between the complex monotheism represented by the Christians and the polytheism of the Greco-Roman world—characterized by the Christians, as I showed in Chapter 1, as a threatening realm of demonic powers.

As Christianity grew in numbers over these two centuries, so did it achieve a greater degree of organization. The New Testament writings show us scattered congregations loosely linked through networks of *koinōnia*, with only a hint (in Paul) of the church as a body encompassing various local assemblies in a larger whole. The structure of such local assemblies, furthermore, drew naturally from the social institutions that formed the starting point for the Christian group: the household and synagogue.[8] Even Paul's letters to his delegates Timothy and Titus provide only a thumbnail sketch of organization that in large measure resembles that of the synagogue and association (and these also imitated to some extent household arrangements). Most striking, such arrangements lacked any sort of religious legitimation: bishops (superintendents), deacons (helpers), and elders were not sacred offices but straightforward functions in service of the community's activities.[9] Already in the early second century there were signs of more intense communication and cooperation among local communities and the first signs of theological legitimation for assembly leadership.[10] By the end of that century, communities had uniform and theologically justified authority structures, and bishops exercised joint activity through synods. By the late third and early fourth century, Christianity had an elaborate system of internal governance, with the bishops of major cities (Alexandria, Antioch, Rome) exercising suzerainty over all the local churches in a region.[11]

Growth in numbers and organizational development led to other aspects of Christianity in the second and third centuries. Although the literary portrayal of significant Christian conversions among the noble and senatorial classes is undoubtedly exaggerated, the remarkable proliferation of literature during these years points to levels of wealth and literacy sufficient to support extensive educational and literary activities within the movement. The New Testament shows how literary Christianity was from the start, and that literary habit did not in the least diminish. Partly out of the need to stay in touch, partly out of the desire to instruct (and perhaps entertain), and partly out of a passion for clarifying Christian identity, Christians created a substantial body of literature in Latin, Syriac, and above all in Greek: letters, apocalypses, gospels, acts— these all had precedent in the New Testament. But in addition, Christians wrote a variety of liturgical and visionary texts, apologies and polemical treatises, and scriptural interpretations. It is regrettable, to be sure, that we do not have more archaeological evidence for Christian activity in this period. But we must be grateful for the garrulity of the believers and their willingness to write in such a variety of forms.

Both literary and organizational activities were generated at least in part by the increased degree of conflict within the Christian movement. The elements of diversity and even disagreement evident already in the New Testament writings emerge with greater force and seriousness over the next two centuries. The second century in particular can be seen as a period of self-definition within Christianity, when the composition of literature and the intervention of ecclesiastical leaders showed the gravity of the issues at conflict. The Quartodeciman controversy revealed divisions in liturgical practice that generated the meeting of synods and an effort by the Roman bishop to excommunicate Asian communities.[12] The Montanist movement—again emerging from Christians in Asia—challenged the adequacy of traditional teaching and teachers by its claim to a new prophecy.[13] Most of all, the congeries of teachers, schools, and writings that are more or less adequately categorized as Gnosticism stimulated the production (and a long tradition) of antiheretical literature and the massing of ecclesiastical leaders in opposition to what was perceived to be a fundamental redefinition of the movement.[14]

The most significant negative corollary of Christianity's growth and organization, however, was undoubtedly its heightened visibility and therefore its greater vulnerability to persecution. The clearer separation from Judaism meant the loss of the presumption of legal protection. The new cult was exposed to slanders concerning its practices and was liable to retaliation for its refusal to participate in the imperial cult.[15] In the first century, such harassment and persecution that Christians suffered came primarily from their fellow Jews. Over the next two centuries, persecution from fellow Gentiles grew more common. Sometimes the violence was local and limited.[16] But as the religion grew, so did the systematic efforts of the empire to suppress it.[17] The numbers of those who were killed because of their commitment to Christ can be exaggerated, but there is no question that martyrdom was a recurrently present reality for many and that social constraints were a constant factor for all who adhered to this confession.[18] During these years, being a follower of Christ meant the very real possibility of suffering a violent death like his.

In this chapter, I describe some of the evidence in second- and third-century Christianity for what I have designated Religiousness A: participation in divine benefits. This mode of religious sensibility, which places an emphasis on the immanence and availability of the divine *dynamis*, occupied a prominent position within Greco-Roman religion, was well attested in first-century Judaism, and, as I have shown, is found in the writings of the New Testament, especially in the convictions and practices of Paul's Gentile readers in Galatia and Corinth, in the four Gospels, and in the Acts of the Apostles. Before beginning this survey of the same religious type among second- and third-century Christians, I remind the reader of the limits of typology: (1) points of emphasis do not constitute exclusive or competing claims and (2) actual experience (and the literature witnessing to religious experience) often contains some small elements of other sensibilities.[19] Nevertheless, it is striking to see how relatively pure these four distinct expressions of religious sensibility appear among Christians in this period.

THE APOCRYPHAL ACTS OF APOSTLES

The New Testament Acts of the Apostles, the second volume of Luke-Acts, already displayed enough elements reminiscent of Greco-Roman novels to make an argument for its belonging to that genre at least superficially plausible, although in the end, Luke-Acts is best regarded as a form of apologetic history.[20] In the second and third centuries, Christians wrote a variety of freestanding Acts disconnected from a Gospel narrative and devoted to the adventures of the heroes first identified in the New Testament writings, especially Peter, Paul, John, Thomas, and Andrew.[21] These compositions even more closely resemble the Hellenistic novels that were written in roughly the same time frame, and they establish a mode of writing of continuing popularity within Christianity.[22]

In them, as in the picaresque novels characteristic of the age, we find the themes of frequent travel by land and sea, separation and reunification of friends and lovers, emotional infatuation, concern for social position, forces opposing the heroes and heroines, imprisonments and escape from prisons, changing clothing as disguise, a high valuation of virginity, and a fascination with animals (especially talking ones).[23] Of specific interest to me is the way in which these accounts of apostles demonstrate the characteristic features of Religiousness A.

There are elements in these compositions, to be sure, that could fit within another religious sensibility. We find in them sections of moral instruction, for example,[24] but they do not dominate and, more important, are not connected to a pedagogy of moral transformation such as we find in Religiousness B, resembling instead lists of requirements for a first conversion. Similarly, these compositions emphasize the hope for a future life as superior to present pleasure, which would align them with Religiousness C, but only occasionally do these statements approach a genuine cosmological dualism that shows contempt for material reality as such.[25] By far the dominant religious sensibility displayed in the apocryphal acts is one confident in the presence and power of the divine in the empirical world, an optimism concerning the victory of the divine *dynamis* over all visible opposition, even when it results in the martyrdom of the apostle. Each of the compositions has its distinctive interest and emphasis, which makes even more impressive the pervasive religious sensibility found in them all.

The *Acts of Thomas* (AT) is the most complete extant narrative devoted to the apostles. Written in Syriac, probably in the third century, it exemplifies the apocryphal tendency to elaborate on minor New Testament characters.[26] Thomas travels to India to bring the Gospel there, and the *Acts of Thomas* recounts his words and deeds. The narrative centers on the struggle between two kinds of power: that represented by human kings and nobles as expressed through social patterns of kinship and marriage and that represented by the apostle of Christ as expressed through extraordinary acts that threaten the domestic order—above all by drawing wives away from their husbands.[27]

The composition contains a number of substantial moral exhortations that demand not only sexual continence but the sharing of possessions and the embrace of an honest and upright life.[28] Such exhortations do not in themselves suggest a rejection of material reality but instead a relativizing of present goods in view of the eternal and better goods to be enjoyed in heaven.[29] Even the symbolism of the "Hymn of the Pearl" (or "Hymn of the Soul") found in the *Acts of Thomas* (108–112), which has been taken to represent a Gnostic outlook, can be read within its literary context as reflecting a more orthodox point of view.[30]

The narrative as a whole amply demonstrates a Religiousness A sensibility, which sees the divine *dynamis* as present and accessible in the empirical world. People have visions throughout the story,[31] and Thomas changes form in front of witnesses (AT 8) and makes prophecies that are fulfilled (6, 9). He performs exorcisms (46–47, 75–77) and a variety of miracles,[32] including a posthumous wonder worked with a secondhand relic drawn from his grave (170). He raises people from the dead.[33] Even the apostle's martyrdom is a triumph: he is buried by his followers in a royal sepulchre and appears to them the same day, declaring, "I am not here but I have gone up and received all that I was promised" (169). The king who had him killed is converted, and the Gospel is spread throughout the land (169–170).

The mood of the narrative is captured in this exchange between the king and Thomas: Misdaeus says, "Tell me who you are and by whose power you do these things," and Thomas answers, "I am a man like yourself, and do these things by the power of Jesus Christ" (AT 140). Those who heed the apostle's call and become disciples, furthermore, share in the divine benefits: "Walk rather in faith and meekness and holiness and hope, in which God rejoices, so that you may become his kinsmen, expecting from him those gifts which only a few receive" (58), and "Look upon us O Lord, because for your sake we have left our bodily consorts and our earthly fruit, in order that we may share in that true and lasting communion and bring forth true fruits, whose nature is from above, which no one can take from us, in which we abide and they abide with us" (61).[34]

The *Acts of Andrew* (AA; second–third centuries) has an extraordinarily tangled textual history,[35] but even in its shortest version bears strong resemblance to the other apocryphal acts. Once more, the narrative centers on the conflict between human power (in the imperial authorities) and divine power (at work in Christ's apostle). Andrew converts the brother (Stratocles) and then the wife (Maxilla) of the Roman proconsul Aegeates. Maxilla adopts a life of celibacy, and the enraged ruler imprisons and eventually crucifies Andrew, identified as "the man responsible for the present disruption of your household" (AA 26). The charge is not unfounded, for Andrew's exhortations focus on the contrast between earthly and heavenly goods (33, 42) and the need for believers to be "superior to the flesh, superior to the world, superior to the powers, superior to the authorities over whom you really are" (38), with the specific requirement to remaining "chaste and pure, unsullied" (40). Such language might be understood in terms of a cosmological dualism, but I think it is better understood in terms of an ethical dualism and, even more, in terms of a contest concerning the power to give life: is it derived from biological descent and human control, or does it come from the power of God and find its perfect realization in life with God? In the *Acts of Andrew*, the battle is fought in the empirical realm, and victory is achieved not by escaping the body but through bodies empowered by God.

As for Andrew, he is portrayed in familiar wonder-working terms. The apostle has a vision (AA 19), delivers a prophecy (61), and performs a spectacular exorcism (4–5). The narrative does not directly report further miracles but has Stratocles tell Aegeates of Andrew, "He performs great miracles and cures which exceed human strength, as I in part can corroborate in that I was present and saw him revive corpses" (25). Andrew himself reminds followers of "everything that happened when I was living among all of you. You saw acts performed through me which you yourselves cannot disbelieve; such signs performed that perhaps even mute nature would have cried out in acclaim" (48). Just as Maxilla is a benefactor to her servant girl (17), Andrew is a benefactor to all; Maxilla declares, "Here we are eating, while our benefactor, second to the Lord himself, is imprisoned" (27).[36]

The enraged and jealous Aegeates imprisons Andrew (*AA* 26), but the apostle's devoted followers are able to enter and leave the prison unimpeded (29–30). When the proconsul finally decides to execute Andrew, his martyrdom turns out to be the climactic episode in the battle between the imperial and the apostolic *dynamis*. In deliberate imitation of Jesus' passion narrative, Andrew is scourged (51) and led to the cross (52). He declares to Stratocles, "it is fitting for a servant of Jesus to be worthy of Jesus" (53). Unlike the Jesus of the canonical Gospels, however, Andrew greets the cross with ecstatic joy (54), smiles, and declares that "the person who belongs to Jesus and who has been recognized by him in the end cannot be punished" (55). He demonstrates the superior power of God by preaching from the cross for four days, converting many (56–59). He predicts that his death will be a form of liberation, "and after liberating myself, I will release myself from all things and become united with the one who came into being for all and exists beyond all" (61). After Andrew's triumphant death—"When he had said these things and further glorified the Lord, he handed over his spirit"—Maxilla devotes her life to the love of Christ, and her husband Aegeates commits suicide (64).

The *Acts of John* (*AJ*) is dated to the late second century; the version I discuss is edited from manuscripts reporting different sections.[37] I refrain from commenting on the section that tends to draw the most attention from scholars— namely, the dance song in 94–95—or the discussion of the Christology of the composition, except to note that the theme of changing appearance or form (metamorphoses) that we find especially in 88–93 is entirely consistent with the representations of the divine in Greco-Roman religion.[38] Similarly, the presentation of Jesus' cross as entirely a matter of light and glory (97–98) and the explicit denial that Jesus suffered on the cross—"Therefore I have suffered none of the things which they will say of me: that suffering which I showed to you and to the rest in dance, I wish it to be called a mystery" (101)—fit in a composition in which the triumph of God in the world is constantly stressed. There is no martyrdom in *AJ*; rather, the apostle, having maintained the celibacy with which he was sealed until the end, dies peacefully (113–115).

The divine *dynamis* is powerfully active in John, who experiences visions (*AJ* 18, 56) and performs healings (19–26), exorcisms (56), and resuscitations:[39] the power of the risen Lord in the apostle is displayed above all in his ability to restore life. In response to one such resuscitation, a young man declares, "God has had mercy on me, because I have seen his power" (53). The most dramatic display of John's *dynamis* is public, in the contest with the goddess Artemis at her temple in Ephesus (38–47). The worshipers of Artemis seek to kill John, but he says to them, "How many miraculous deeds did you see me perform, how many cures? And still you are hardened in the heart and cannot see clearly" (39). He challenges them, "be now converted by my God or I will die at the hands of your goddess" (40).

John prays and the altar of Artemis is split, its oblations spilled, and its priest killed at one stroke. The people of Ephesus respond, "There is only one God, that of John, only one God who has compassion for us; for you alone are God; now we have become converted, since we saw your miraculous deeds" (*AJ* 42). And they destroy the rest of the temple (44). John caps his wonders by restoring to life, at the request of the dead man's relatives, the priest of Artemis, who then also becomes a Christian (46–47).

Here, as in other passages of the *Acts of John*, the wonders of the apostle are what stimulate conversions to Christianity (see *AJ* 39, 57, 76). Gentiles who were accustomed to calling the gods their benefactors now consider John to be such because of the benefits he has brought them (27). Before his death, John declares to those who had become believers, "Brethren, fellow-servants, co-heirs, and co-partners in the kingdom of the Lord, you know the Lord, how many powers he has given you through me, how many miracles, what cures, signs, gifts, teachings, rulings, times for relaxation, services, knowledge, glories, graces, gifts, acts of faith, communion, which you have seen with your eyes, were given you by him, though they cannot be seen with these eyes and cannot be heard with these ears" (106). The religious sensibility of the *Acts of John* is summarized perfectly in the prayer of Drusiana (herself raised from the dead) before she in turn raises Fortunatus: "God of the ages, Jesus Christ, God of truth, you allowed me to see signs and wonders and granted me to partake of your name" (82).

The *Acts of Peter* (*Pet*) was probably composed in the late second century but is not extant in its entirety. The text I discuss is a composite that is drawn from disparate sources.[40] The narrative shows Paul departing Rome (1–3) and the wonder-worker Simon succeeding in drawing Christians away from their faith by his miracles (4–5); Peter is sent by God to Rome precisely to stop Simon: "I must go up to Rome to subdue the enemy and opponent of the Lord and of our

brethren" (5). With his first sermon (7), the apostle sets up the conflict that dominates the story, the contest of power between Simon and himself.

Appropriate to his mission is the depiction of Peter as a *theios anēr*: he heals,
performs exorcisms, has many visions, and raises people from the dead.[41] Peter
preaches, but he insists that "I came not only for the sake of convincing you
with words that he whom I preach is the Christ, but by reason of miraculous
deeds and powers I exhort you by faith in Jesus Christ" (*Pet* 7). Peter is told by
the steersman of the ship bringing him to Rome, "You are either a god or a
man. But as far as I can see, I think that you are a servant of God" (5). The narrative emphasizes the "signs which Peter did by the grace of Jesus Christ" (14)
and his "signs and wonders" (16, 26, 36). Immediately connected to such wonders are conversions from paganism to the Christian God (16, 26, 28, 31, 32).
Although Peter declares to the crowd, "Do not imagine that what I do, I do by
my own power; I do it in the power of my Lord Jesus Christ who is the judge of
the living and the dead" (28), the response of the Gentile population of Rome,
especially to his resuscitations, is to regard him as divine: "From that hour on
they worshipped him like a god, and the sick, whom they had at home, they
brought to his feet to be cured by him" (29).

Peter's wonder-working and winning of converts sets up the explicit contest
of power between himself and Simon Magus. Simon had won his reputation by
flying in the air (*Pet* 4), which the narrator ascribes to magic (8). He declared
himself the "Power of God" (8, 10) and worked such "miraculous deeds" (10)
that a follower erected a statue to him with the inscription, "To Simon, the
young god" (10). It appears to the people that Simon and Peter work on equal
terms; when Peter receives a prediction from a talking dog that he will have a
"hard fight with Simon the enemy of Christ," the crowd responds, "Show us
another miracle that we may believe in you as a servant of the living God, for
Simon too did many wonders in our presence, and on that account we followed
him" (12).

Simon himself makes the challenge clear: "Behold, here am I, Simon. Come
down, Peter, and I will prove that you believed in a Jewish man and the son of
a carpenter" (*Pet* 14). He sharpens the attack: "Men of Rome, is a god born? Is
he crucified? Whoever has a master is no god" (23). Peter engages Simon in a
first face-to-face contest, in which he restores to life a slave whom Simon struck
dead (25), having declared, "Now I turn to you, Simon: do one of the signs
whereby you deceived them before and I shall frustrate it through my Lord Jesus Christ" (24). The climactic contest comes when Simon seeks to recover his
earlier luster among the Romans by repeating his flying act (31) and a large
crowd gathers to see him perform his ascent: "For I ascend and will show my-

self to this people what kind of being I am" (32). Peter prays that his flight fail, and Simon falls to the earth crippled, to be stoned by some of his followers, who then join Peter. Simon commits suicide (32).

The account of Peter's martyrdom makes clear that he is a servant of God rather than a god (see *Pet* 5) while at the same time showing by his self-mastery how the power at work in him is superior to that exercised by the empire. Motivated by rage, a friend of the emperor seeks Peter's arrest because his wife, committed to chastity, no longer sleeps with him (34). In response to his followers' pleas, Peter leaves the city, but a vision of Jesus sends him back to face crucifixion in imitation of his Lord (35). When he is arrested, he declares, as did his master, that this is all God's will (36). He greets the cross gladly and requests that he be hanged upside-down (37). His self-mastery is displayed by his lengthy allegorical discourse about the significance of the cross and his way of being crucified, and he dies peacefully in prayer (38–39). After his death, he appears in a vision to his follower Marcellus (40), and the effect of his death is that Nero is afraid to persecute Christians any further (41).

The *Acts of Paul* (AP) was also probably composed in the late second century and also requires recomposition on the basis of scattered fragments.[42] The largest intact portion of the *Acts of Paul* is the *Acts of Paul and Thecla*, which circulated widely because of the separate cult devoted to the female saint.[43] The remaining portions (apart from the martyrdom) consist of a series of travels and adventures in various cities and a spurious letter of Paul to the Corinthians ("third Corinthians"). As in the canonical Acts, Paul preaches (AP 3.5–6)[44] and makes defenses (3.17), although his speeches bear little resemblance to the missionary speeches and forensic discourses in the earlier account. As in the canonical letters, Paul also writes to churches (8), although there is absolutely no similarity between his canonical letters to the Corinthians and the one that supposedly responds to a letter from the presbyters in Corinth.

Consistent with the depiction of the apostles in the other apocryphal acts, Paul is presented above all as a wonder-worker who is regarded as dangerously subversive by the protectors of the social order because his teaching on chastity—"blessed are the bodies of the virgins, for they shall be well pleasing to God and shall not lose the reward of their chastity" (AP 6)[45]—is convincing women to resist the sexual demands of their husbands. The crowd is incited to cry out, "Away with the sorcerer for he has misled all our wives" (3.15). Paul performs healings: in Myra, healing a man with dropsy and restoring sight to another (4); in Tyre, healing a dumb man (6); and in Ephesus, healing the running sore in an ear (7). He experiences visions in Myra (4) and in Ephesus (10). In Tyre, Paul performs an exorcism (6). In Ephesus, beasts flee rather than inflict harm on the apostle (7), and in Philippi, Paul restores life to a girl named Frontina (8).

It is not a shock, then, to find in Paul's sermon to the Romans a recitation of Jesus' ministry in terms of his wonder-working: "he raised the dead, healed diseases, cleansed lepers, healed the blind, made cripples whole, raised up paralytics, cleansed those possessed by demons" (AP 10). He attributes these words to Jesus: "Why are you amazed that I raise up the dead or that I make the lame walk or that I cleanse the lepers or that I raise up the sick or that I have healed the paralytic and those possessed by demons or that I have divided a little bread and satisfied many or that I have walked upon the sea, or if I have commanded the winds?" (10).

In the section of the *Acts of Paul* devoted to Thecla, the aura of wonder-worker surrounds her as well. She has visions (3.21; 3.29). The fire set to consume her does her no harm (3.22)—we are to suppose it is because of Paul's prayer for her (3.24). Neither the lioness (3.28) nor other beasts do her any harm in the arena (3.33). When she throws herself in the water in order to baptize herself, the deadly seals do not hurt her (3.34). Even when she is attached by ropes to vicious bulls who are intended to pull her to pieces, a fire burns through the ropes and she escapes unharmed (3.35). Thecla's final words to her mother express a religious sensibility not far removed from that found in Greco-Roman Religiousness A: "Theoclia my mother, can you believe that the Lord lives in heaven? For if you desire wealth the Lord will give it you through me; or if you desire your child, behold I am standing beside you" (3.43).

In the section of the *Acts of Paul* called "The Martyrdom of the Holy Apostle Paul" (with its own numbering system), the emphasis on triumph through wonder-working continues. Paul draws disciples even from the house of the emperor and restores Patroclus, the emperor's cupbearer, to life (AP 1). Patroclus announces to Nero that he now fights on the side of the king of the ages, who "destroys all kingdoms under heaven, and he alone shall remain in all eternity, and there will be no kingdom which escapes him." And others of Nero's household also declare their allegiance to "the king of the ages" (2). Nero tortures and imprisons them and orders all followers of Christ to be executed. When Paul is brought in fetters before Nero, he confronts the emperor boldly with the prediction that his kingdom also will be made subject. And upon being ordered to be beheaded, Paul prophesies that "I will rise again and appear to you, for I shall not be dead but alive to my kind, Christ Jesus, who will judge the earth" (4). Paul exemplifies philosophical calm at the moment of death, and when his head is severed, milk splashes on the tunic of the executioner (5), leading bystanders to glorify God. At the moment Nero receives the report of this wonder, Paul appears to him: "I am not dead but alive in my God" (6). Paul appears as well to his followers and to members of the emperor's household who had remained skeptical, leading them also to belief (7).

APOCRYPHAL NARRATIVE GOSPELS

Despite their compositional complexity, we have seen that the four narrative gospels of the New Testament fit best within the category of Religiousness A.[46] Just as the apocryphal acts move beyond their canonical prototype toward a more perfect expression of that sensibility, so do the extant apocryphal gospels. Unfortunately, the basis for analysis in this case is limited. Little can be said about the "Jewish-Christian Gospels," except that, according to the scant evidence we possess, they were variations of the Synoptic tradition (especially Matthew) and that the new elements they introduce are primarily in the sayings material.[47] And although the production of apocryphal gospels proved at least as popular as the composition of apocryphal acts,[48] only a handful of such compositions can confidently be dated to the period of my analysis, the second and third centuries.

Although patristic authors make mention of a *Gospel of Peter* (GP),[49] knowledge of its contents became available only with the discovery of an eighth-century manuscript in 1886–1887. Its date of composition is probably the late second century.[50] Despite the vigorous case made recently for an earlier date— and a status as an independent testimony to the passion—I agree with the scholars who see the *Gospel of Peter* as an apocryphal elaboration based on the canonical accounts.[51] Because our knowledge rests entirely on this truncated narrative, it is not possible to make judgments concerning the extent or character of the story preceding (or, for that matter, following) it. What we have is a narrative extending from a trial before Pilate to the resurrection.

Several aspects of the fragment point to a presentation of Jesus as a *theios anēr* even within the passion narrative. The narrator not only refers to Jesus consistently as "the Lord" but puts the designations "son of God" and "savior of men" in the mouths of opponents.[52] At the time of his crucifixion, Jesus "held his peace as [if] he felt no pain" (GP 10). At the moment of his death, he cries out, "My power, O power, you have forsaken me," and the narrative continues: "having said this, he was taken up" (19). The expression is sufficiently obscure to allow it to be understood as an immediate ascension. The Pharisees and Scribes refer to "these exceeding great signs" that happened at Jesus' death (28), but the ones mentioned in the narrative (earthquake, sun shining; 21–22) are less spectacular than those reported by Matthew.

The most distinctive and spectacular part of the narrative is the description of the resurrection. The guards assigned to watch the tomb see the heavens open and two men descend from heaven (GP 36) even as the stone that had been sealed with seven seals (33) starts itself to roll and move sideways, allowing the two heavenly men to enter (37). Then the soldiers see "three men come out from the sepulcher, two of them supporting the other and a cross following them and the heads of the two reaching to heaven, but that of him who was being led reached beyond the heavens" (39–40). At this moment, voices in heaven ask and answer affirmatively the question of whether the Lord had preached to those who were asleep (41). Again the heavens open and a single man descends to enter the tomb (44), the young man of Mark's Gospel who sits in the tomb and greets the women with the message "he is risen and is gone to the place from which he was sent" (56). All of these touches establish the divinity of Jesus: titles, visions, heavenly signs, and descent and ascent.

The *Protevangelium of James* (*PJ*) is the earliest extant "infancy Gospel"—that is, narratives that are devoted entirely to the birth and childhood of Jesus[53]—composed in the late second century. It extends the gospel story back to Jesus' grandparents, Joachim and Anna, and focuses on Mary, the mother of Jesus. The story is propelled by the conflict between the desire for offspring and the quest for biological purity: the virginity of Mary, which in the canonical gospel of Luke was a sign of the power of God, in the *Protoevangelium* is an absolute value to be preserved at all costs.[54] As in the apocryphal acts, devotion to God is expressed through virginity. The gospel perfectly expresses Religiousness A: the divine *dynamis* is present in the world and accessible in a variety of ways to the devout. The characters, indeed, live in a "bible world" that has little to do with actual Judaism and everything to do with the imagination: a sanctuary is made for Mary in her bedroom where the "undefiled daughters of the Hebrews" serve her (*PJ* 6.1); the three-year-old child dances on the steps of the altar in the temple (7.3); she dwells in the temple from that age forward (6.3); and when Mary reaches menarche at 12 years old, it constitutes a national crisis requiring consultation with the priests (8:1–3).

It is a world in which characters have visions and receive heavenly messengers on a regular basis (*PJ* 4.1; 4.2; 11.1–2; 14.2; 20.2). It is a world in which the child Mary walks at the age of six months (6.1) and receives food in the temple from the hand of an angel (8.2). A dove comes out of Joseph's rod and alights on his head (9.1). Zechariah is struck dumb (10.2). Before the birth of Jesus, Joseph experiences a moment of eternity, when everything on earth stands still (18.2). Jesus' birth is accompanied by a bright light around the cave, with the form of the baby emerging as the light withdraws (19.2). Salome tests Mary's postpartum virginity, and her hand is struck, but when she touches the child Jesus, she is healed (20.1–4). When Elizabeth and John are threatened, a mountain opens up to receive them, for they are protected by an angel of the Lord (22.3). Finally, when Zacharias is killed, his body disappears and all that can be found is his blood, turned to stone (24.3). Not only is the *Protevangelium of James* full of such wonders, but it shows no trace of any other religious sensibility.

The textual history of the *Infancy Gospel of Thomas* (IGT) is complex,[55] and it is not certain that the Greek version, the translation I here analyze, comes from the second or third century.[56] I include it in this discussion because it so wonderfully illustrates the tendency of the apocryphal gospels and acts toward Religiousness A. The narrator begins by stating his intention to share with Gentile readers "the mighty childhood deeds of our Lord Jesus Christ, which he did when he was born in our land" (IGT 1). The composition then moves through a series of wonders performed by Jesus from the time he was five until he was 12 years old. The composition ends with the story of Jesus teaching in the temple, taken from Luke 2:41–52.

At first blush, the narrative seems to be simply an account of Jesus as *enfant terrible*,[57] whose reckless use of his divine powers wreaks havoc on all around him. A closer reading allows us to detect a genuine shift in emphasis beginning in 8:1: the child who had formerly done mostly harm now uses his powers for good. The reader is led to appreciate the childhood of Jesus as a successful struggle to control the divine *dynamis* that at first appears to overwhelm him and to see Jesus' entrance into adulthood (at 12) as one in which that struggle between the good and evil uses of power has been resolved.

Even with this generous reading, however, the narrative's unremitting focus on the purely miraculous is extraordinary. At five years old, Jesus cleanses pooled waters with a word (IGT 2.1) and, having molded pigeons from clay, claps his hands and they fly away (2.4). A playmate who disturbs the pools of water Jesus has gathered withers at his command (3.2–3). He strikes dead another child who accidentally bumps his shoulder (4.1) and strikes blind those who complain about him (5.1). He also possesses more wisdom than his teacher (6.1–7.4). Then, all those under his curse are saved (8.2). Jesus raises a child from the dead (9), heals an injured foot (10.2), produces an unusually great harvest so that the poor can be fed (12.1–2), helps his father by making two uneven beams of wood equal in length (13.2), kills a second teacher (14.2) but then resuscitates him (15.4), heals his brother James (16.2), and restores to life a child and a workman (17.1; 18.1).

The religious outlook of the composition is communicated as well by the statements made by characters other than Jesus in response to his powerful deeds. The parents of the boy whom Jesus caused to wither ask Joseph, "what kind of child do you have, who does such things?" (*IGT* 3.3). In response to his striking people blind, witnesses respond, "Every word he speaks, whether good or evil, was a deed and became a miracle" (5.2). The teacher frustrated by Jesus' superior wisdom declares, "This child is not earth-born; he can even subdue fire. Perhaps he was begotten even before the creation of the world" (17.2). Begging Joseph to take him back home, the teacher declares, "What great thing he is, a god or an angel, I do not know what I should say" (17.4). When Jesus heals the man who had cleaved his own foot, the people worship him and declare, "Truly the spirit of God dwells in this child" (10.2). A second teacher grows annoyed with Jesus and hits him; Jesus responds by cursing the teacher, who falls in a faint on the floor. Joseph tells Mary, "Do not let him go outside the door, for all those who provoke him die" (14.3).

The final two responses to Jesus suggest his growing maturity. When Jesus raises a dead child to life, the witnesses exclaim, "Truly, this child was either a god or an angel of God, for every word of his is an accomplished deed" (*IGT* 17.2). And when he raises a workman to life—immediately before the final story of him teaching in the temple—the people are amazed and say, "This child is from heaven, for he has saved many souls from death, and is able to save them all his life long" (18.2). The *Infancy Gospel of Thomas*'s portrayal of a child-god who is able to bestow benefits or calamities at a word is an extreme case. But it clearly fits within the religious sensibility we have detected in other apocryphal narratives and with them demonstrates how religion as participation in divine benefits flourished as an expression of second- and third-century Christianity.

MONTANISM

Another manifestation of Religiousness A is the prophetic movement begun by Montanus and his female associates Priscilla and Maximilla sometime between 157 and 177 in Phrygia, which spread to Syria, Rome, and North Africa before its influence was reduced.[58] For the purposes of this study, Montanism is of interest less for its predictions of a New Jerusalem in a Phrygian town or the intense asceticism it advocated in anticipation of this eschatological event[59] than for its insistence on the contemporary experience of prophecy as a demonstration of the presence of the Holy Spirit. Maximilla is quoted as saying, "I am driven away like a wolf from the sheep. I am not a wolf. I am word and spirit and power" (*Historia Ecclesiastica* 5.16, 17).[60] The Montanist leaders claimed to continue the prophetic tradition that ran from such New Testament figures as

Agabus, Judas, Silas, and Philip's daughters,[61] to men like Ammia of Philadel-phia and Quadratus. By claiming to be spirit-filled prophets, the Montanists connected themselves experientially to one of the prime demonstrations of the divine *dynamis* in earliest Christianity. Since this movement was founded in Phrygia, where also began the Greco-Roman cult of Cybele—the Mother-Goddess whose prophets also engaged in ecstatic utterance—it is natural to link Montanism to the cultural habit of a region.[62] But this would ignore its wide-spread appeal to Christians in other areas or its valid claim to represent one of the New Testament's most important forms of witness to the presence of the living God in the world.[63] The sad state of the sources with respect to Montan-ism prevents a fuller analysis.[64] But we are certainly able to point to it as an ob-vious example of Religiousness A within the Christianity of the second and third centuries, for its claim to participate in the benefits of the divine *dynamis* is direct and emphatic.

MARTYR PIETY

I noted earlier in this chapter that persecution was increasingly a factor for Christians in the second and third centuries, and in the apocryphal acts of the apostles, I observed that the martyrdom of the apostle served as a demonstration of the divine *dynamis*, turning what seemed to be a crushing blow to the Chris-tian religion into another stage of its success among the Gentiles. It is clear that the apocryphal acts are more fiction than history. But we have enough evidence from other sources to support the proposition that in the age of persecution, a martyr piety was an important expression of Religiousness A within Christianity. We should not expect in these accounts the same sort of extravagant claims of wonder-working that we find in the acts; of more significance is the degree to which these testimonies share the same religious sensibility.

Ignatius was a bishop of Antioch who was executed sometime during the reign of Trajan (98–117). On his way to Rome, bound as a prisoner, he wrote (at least) seven letters, six to congregations in Asia Minor and Rome, and the sev-enth to Polycarp, the bishop of Smyrna. Although his letters touch on a number of concerns—resisting false teaching, recognizing the authority of bishops, maintaining unity—his own religious feeling comes through clearly. Whatever he may have been or thought before his arrest, as Ignatius faces almost certain death because of his belief, his mind and heart fasten intently on that moment when he will become, as he puts it, "a true disciple" (Ign. *Eph.* 1.2; Ign. *Rom.* 4.2) and "attain to God" (Ign. *Eph.* 12.2; Ign. *Magn.* 14.1; Ign. *Rom.* 8.3) or "attain to Jesus Christ" (Ign. *Rom.* 5.3).[65]

In Ignatius's letters, we find the distinctive shape of Religiousness A in a cult centered around the crucifixion and resurrection of Jesus. The divine *dynamis* is regarded as operative in both Jesus' death and eternal life, with the manner of his death serving as his way to God. The power in which Christians participate through the gift of the exalted one therefore draws them to the same destiny and the same reward. Ignatius declares that his spirit is "devoted to the cross" (Ign. *Eph.* 18.1), and by his death he hopes to be "worthy to show the honor of God" (Ign. *Eph.* 21.2). It is therefore of the greatest importance that the suffering and reward of Christ be real, rather than an appearance, as some false teachers claim, for Ignatius has literally staked his life on this reality: if his sufferings are only an appearance, "why am I a prisoner and why do I fight the beasts," he asks (Ign. *Tral.* 10.1). Ignatius makes the connection clear: "for this reason also we suffer, that we may be found disciples of Jesus Christ our only teacher" (Ign. *Magn.* 9.1). To embrace martyrdom, therefore, is both to bear witness to the reality of the resurrection and, at the same time, to display for others the *dynamis* that the resurrection of Jesus makes available to his followers.

In his letter to the Roman Christians, Ignatius is most explicit concerning his desire to imitate Christ—"to set to the world towards God, that I may rise to him" (Ign. *Rom.* 2.2)—for they are the ones most able either to hinder his progress or to help him on his way. He wants them to help or at least not stand in his way. Using the language of sacrifice familiar to Gentiles, he says, "Grants me nothing more than that I be poured out [*spondisthēnai*] to God, while an altar [*thysiastērion*] is still ready, that forming yourselves into a chorus [*choros*] of love, you may sing to the Father in Christ Jesus" (2.2). He asks his readers not to prevent his act of witness: "suffer me to be eaten by the beasts, through whom I can attain to God." Using a metaphor that echoes the Eucharistic ritual, he declares, "I am God's wheat, and I am ground by the teeth of the wild beasts that I may be found the pure bread of Christ" (4.1).

Indeed, he asks his readers to speed the process along: "Rather entice the wild beasts that they may become my tomb, and leave no trace of my body, that when I fall asleep I be not burdensome to any. Then I shall be truly a disciple of Jesus Christ, when the world shall not even see my body." This passage concludes with a return to the language of sacrifice: "Beseech Christ on my behalf, that I may be found a sacrifice [*thysia*] through these instruments" (Ign. *Rom.* 4.2). Ignatius sees his progress toward martyrdom as "beginning to be a disciple" (5.3) and is therefore committed to reaching the end: "suffer me to follow the example of the passion of my god" (*epitrepsate moi mimētēn einai tou pathous tou theou mou*; 6.3).

Polycarp, the bishop of Smyrna, was martyred circa 155–156. His last days and moments are recounted in a letter from the church in Smyrna to the church in Philomelium, written shortly after the events.[66] The composition nicely illustrates the truth that proximity to an event does not preclude interpretation, for this report consistently shades the story in such fashion that, as much as possible given the actual facts, Polycarp's death mimics that of Jesus. Thus, the composition opens with the assertion that all the events happened "to show us from above a martyrdom in accordance with the gospel" (*Mart. Pol.* 1.1; see also 19:1) and "that we too might become his imitators" (1.2).

Polycarp's death put an end to a persecution in which many had died, and the composition insists that Christians must "be very careful to assign the power over all to God" (*Mart. Pol.* 2.1), so that the nobility shown by those killed was due to the "grace of Christ" enabling them to despise worldly tortures, since they looked "to the good things which are preserved for those who have endured" (2.2–3). Their combat with the wild beasts (3.1) was at the same time a battle with the devil (2.4).

The depiction of Polycarp has many of the features we have seen in the apocryphal acts. He has a preliminary vision of the manner of his death (*Mart. Pol.* 5.2), and when he enters the arena to become a "partner of Christ" (*Christou koinōnos*; 6.2), he hears a voice from heaven say, "Be strong, Polycarp, and play the man" (*ischue kai andrizou*; 9.1). Polycarp astounds the proconsul with his "courage and joy" (12.1). Before he is set on fire, he recites an extensive prayer, one part of which makes explicit the theme of participation and imitation: "I bless thee, that thou hast granted me this day and hour, that I may share, among the number of the martyrs, in the cup of thy Christ, for the resurrection to everlasting life, both of soul and body in the immortality of the Holy Spirit" (14.2).

When the flame is lit and blazes up, witnesses "saw a great marvel" (*thauma*), namely, the flame surrounding the saint like a great sail, so that it seemed not as though burning flesh but "as bread that is being baked, or as gold and silver being refined in a furnace" (*Mart. Pol.* 15.2).[67] And when the executioner stabs Polycarp with a dagger, "there came out a dove, and much blood, so that the fire was quenched, and all the crowd marveled that there was such a difference between the unbelievers and the elect" (16.1). The authorities do not want to release the body "lest they leave the crucified one and begin to worship this man" (17.2), and in fact, some of the saint's associates wanted "to have fellowship with his holy flesh" (17.1). The narrator states the proper form of piety: "for him [Jesus] we worship as the Son of God, but the martyrs we love as disciples and imitators of the Lord. . . . Grant that we too may be their companions and fellow disciples" (*koinōnous kai symmathētas*; 17.3).

The accounts of the martyrdom of Justin and his companions (165 CE) and of the North African Scillitan Martyrs (180 CE) are too spare to reveal much of the piety of the martyrs, but *The Letter of the Christians in Vienne and Lyons to the Churches in Asia and Phrygia* is sufficiently developed to allow comment.[68] The persecution under Marcus Aurelius (177) is attributed to demonic powers (*Historia Ecclesiastica* 5.1.14–16; 5.1.25–27). The martyrs suffer because of their zeal for Christ (5.1.6), and their death is in imitation of Christ: Vettius "chose to lay down even his own life for the defense of the brethren, for he was and is a true disciple of Christ, and he follows the lamb wherever he goes" (5.1.10). In Sanctus, "Christ suffering in him manifested great glory, overthrowing the adversary and showing for others the example that there is nothing fearful where there is the love of the Father nor painful where there is the glory of Christ" (5.1, 23). Ponthinus was "strengthened by zeal of spirit through urgent desire of martyrdom," and in his sufferings "Christ might triumph . . . as though he was Christ himself" (5.1.29–30). Blandina, though physically weak, endured astonishing torture, for "she had put on the great and invincible athlete, Christ" (5.1.42). Thus she showed that those who "suffer for the glory of Christ have forever fellowship [*koinōnia*] with the living God" (5.1.41). There is less literary embroidery here than in the *Martyrdom of Polycarp,* but the same religious sensibility is clearly at work: the divine power is manifested through the bodies of those who bear witness to Christ.

Another important witness close to actual events is found in *The Passion of Perpetua and Felicitas.* The composition focuses on the imprisonment and death on March 7, 203, of the North African women Perpetua (noble-born) and the pregnant Felicitas (a servant), who as Catechumens were condemned under the edict of Septimus Severus forbidding conversions to Christianity (202).[69] The preface to the *Passion* makes clear that it was written to provide an example to contemporary believers to show that the divine grace was active not only among the ancients but also in present-day saints and to serve as a witness to unbelievers as well as a benefit to believers. Perpetua and Felicitas received baptism at the hands of the priest Saturus shortly after being imprisoned (1.2). The section of the narrative that is based on Perpetua's own account emphasizes the series of visions that she experiences (1.3; 2.3; 2.4; 3.2), the vision of Saturus (4.1–3), and the resistance of Perpetua to the pleas of her father (2.1–2). In the last of her visions while in prison, Perpetua sees herself becoming a man and doing battle against the devil (3.2). Perpetua is notable for her constancy and loftiness of mind, for standing up to the tribune (5.3).

The account of the actual martyrdom resembles those in the apocryphal acts, with its emphasis on the joy and bright countenance of the martyrs and their singing of psalms (*Passion* 6.1). Felicitas gave birth shortly before her execution, and the account compares the blood of her martyrdom to that of her childbirth: she washes after childbirth with a second baptism (6.1). Perpetua experiences her suffering in the Spirit and in an ecstasy (6.3); she encourages the others to stand fast in the faith and to love each other (6.3), and she guides the hand of her executioner (6.4). The bloody death of Saturus is explicitly called a second baptism (6.4). The *Passion* concludes with the same sentiment expressed in the preface: the account is meant to be exemplary, a demonstration that the new virtues may testify to the same Holy Spirit always operating, even in the present day (6.4).

A final witness to the martyr piety of the second and third centuries is Origen of Alexandria (184–253). Like Justin, Origen is one of the figures I consider in the next chapter as representing Religiousness B (religion as moral transformation). But he also sought to achieve full fellowship with Christ through martyrdom. When his father, Leonides, was executed under Septimus Severus in 202, Origen was deflected from following him by the obligation of caring for his father's family and catechetical school. Although he was not actually executed, Origen died as a result of the tortures he underwent in the persecution of Decius in 253. His *Exhortation to Martyrdom* is a protreptic discourse addressed to his friends Ambrose and Protoctetus during the persecution of Maximin Thrax in 235.[70] Typical of the great scholar, the discourse is rife with scriptural citations and allusions, but it also conveys some of the personal passion of the author for this subject. I touch on only a few of the points he makes.

Origen emphasizes first that the impression of Christ's death being a loss is wrong; it is, rather, the source of benefits (2) greater than can be imagined (13, 34, 47). With Ignatius of Antioch, Origen regards martyrdom as a means of being fully united with God (3); by leaving the body, one lives with the Lord (4). Martyrdom is an expression of the fullest love for God (6), in which the gift of oneself entirely to God (11) results in the fullness of life in return (12). Second, these benefits are not only for the one who dies: the martyr's death benefits others (30), not only through example for edification (41) but in the same way that Christ's death brought benefits to all (50). Third, Origen regards martyrdom as a contest—just as the life of faith is a contest for virtue (5)—but one that involves battling the demonic forces at work in idolatry, the idolatrous state, and the human desire for safety (18, 32, 34, 40, 45).

It is this understanding of martyrdom as a moral striving that connects it to what I have termed Religiousness B, yet the sense that this expression of the divine *dynamis* accomplishes benefits in the world here and now also makes it fit within Religiousness A. Origen states at the end of the fourth part of his exhortation, "Thus we can see what piety and the love of God, which is stronger than all other loves, can achieve against the most cruel sufferings and the severest tortures. This love of God does not tolerate the co-existence of human weakness but drives it away as an enemy alien from the whole soul. And this weakness becomes powerless in the case of one who can say, 'The Lord is my strength and my praise,' and 'I can do all things in Him who strengtheneth me, Christ Jesus, Our Lord'" (27). Paradoxically, the death that appears to the world as shameful is in fact a sharing in the triumph of Christ: "We must also sense no shame whatever at suffering what God's enemies consider to be shameful. . . . Now you appear, as it were, in triumphal procession, taking up the cross of Jesus and following him as he goes before you to appear before magistrates and kings, that by making the journey with you, he may give you a mouth of wisdom" (36).

The evidence drawn from apocryphal gospels and acts as well as from the literature concerning martyrdom suggests that in the second and third centuries, religion as participation in divine benefits flourished within Christianity. It had distinctive features, to be sure: it was not possible for Christians to participate in the regular round of "idolatrous" public worship, and their own rituals were as yet largely undeveloped. The focus for this religious sensibility therefore became the holy person or saint through whom the divine *dynamis* worked and access to whom yielded benefits for others. The supreme holy person is, to be sure, Jesus himself, and the apocryphal gospels indicate how the thaumaturgic dimension of his human existence finds expansion. Next are his apostles, whose wonder-working brought the benefits of the resurrection life to those they touched and who led the growth of the church. Finally, those who bear witness to Christ in their violent death demonstrate the working of that same resurrection power in their triumph over imperial power, demonic power, and their own human weakness.

It is not possible to make sociological deductions from forms of literature. We cannot conclude how many or what sort of Christians in the second and third centuries lived out this sort of religious sensibility. But it can be noted that apocryphal acts and gospels were written by many hands over an extended period of time and found a steady readership in many languages across many centuries, as evidenced by their complex textual histories. And it is further possible to assert that the themes that are found fictionally in the accounts of martyrdom in the apocryphal acts are found, if less spectacularly, in the sober acts of actual martyrs.

As I have done in earlier chapters, I conclude with the argument that the literature I have examined all points to the existence of a specific religious type, even while I acknowledge traces of other sensibilities. In the apocryphal acts, I noted the presence of teaching material, and in both the acts and gospels, it is possible to detect the encratism that privileges virginity. In all these texts, furthermore, the future life with God made possible through the resurrection of Jesus is much to be preferred to the benefits offered by this world. What joins these witnesses together is not simply the fact that they all emphasize the presence of the divine *dynamis* in the world and the possibility in humans sharing in the divine benefits, but the way in which the other three emphases are so little present. There is no real attention given in these writings to transformation through moral effort; rather, the divine power is displayed in signs and wonders outside the self and, in the case of martyrs, in enabling the courage to face a cruel death. The encratistic elements in these writings do not constitute a cosmic dualism that despises materiality as such; indeed, they envisage the body as well as the soul finding a future with God. Finally, and most obviously, there is nothing in these writings that serves to stabilize the social order; rather, they are wildly subversive of the social order of the Greco-Roman world and in their focus on the explosion of the divine *dynamis* operative in the world through Jesus, the apostles, and the martyrs show no particular interest in replacing that demonic *politeia* with another.

13

MORAL TRANSFORMATION IN SECOND- AND THIRD-CENTURY CHRISTIANITY

The second and third centuries, as we have seen, provide abundant testimony for the form of religious sensibility I have designated Religiousness A: in apocryphal gospels and acts, in the "new prophecy" of Montanism, and in manifestations of martyr piety. This strain of religiosity could claim to be firmly grounded in the writings of the New Testament, above all in the canonical Gospels and Acts of the Apostles, but also in those writers who, like Paul and James and the author of the Letter to the Hebrews, recognized the presence of "signs and wonders" at work in the world through the spirit of the resurrected one. In that sensibility, the experience of martyrdom—which in the eyes of outsiders seemed as futile an exercise in witnessing as was the crucifixion of Jesus—appeared as the most powerful sign and wonder of all, a way of participating in the benefits given by the power of Jesus through imitation of his triumph over suffering and death.

It was not a foregone conclusion that a religious movement so firmly based on the experience of power through the Holy Spirit, and so initially negative toward philosophy (see Rom 1:22; 1 Cor 1:20–21; Col 2:8), would display among some of its members the sort of religious sensibility that I have termed Religiousness B, which focuses not on access to divine benefits externally but rather on the way the divine *dynamis* works for the moral change in persons. In the New Testament, we saw in Paul, James, and the Letter to the Hebrews just this sort of sensibility: their religious focus is on the use of human reason in accord with the "mind of Christ" (1 Cor 2:26), the development of the virtuous life shaped by imitation of Jesus Christ, and a growing into the maturity that seeks the benefit of others more than the self. And in the second and third centuries, we find an ever more explicit "philosophical" form of Christianity develop, with a focus on moral transformation.

FIRST STEPS: CLEMENT OF ROME AND
POLYCARP OF SMYRNA

The writings attributed to Clement of Rome and Polycarp of Smyrna are all the more significant as witnesses to this way of being Christian because they are so unself-conscious in their expression of it. They do not identify themselves as philosophers or make any explicit embrace of philosophy. Their religious sensibility must be inferred from the things they choose to speak of and the things they tend to omit, the topics they emphasize and those they slight.

The *First Letter of Clement* is written from the church in Rome to the church in Corinth around 95 CE in response to the crisis created by some younger men rebelling against the authority of the established elders in the Corinthian community (37, 57).[1] In his effort to restore order to that church, Clement reveals his awareness both of being part of a second generation, following the deaths of the apostles, and of a moral authority to exhort members of another community.[2] In carrying out the task of mutual correction—manifestly a critical component in the philosophical tradition (56, 58)—Clement does not appeal to a political ideal but instead challenges and appeals to the moral character of his readers.

Two aspects of his composition immediately make us aware that Clement's missive is neither naive nor impulsive.[3] First, the letter is intensely intertextual: he makes constant use of scripture (the LXX) as well as of earlier Christian writings. His choices in this respect are instructive: he tells no stories from the Gospels about Jesus' wonders but appeals, rather, to Jesus' words of moral instruction;[4] his main concentration, indeed, is on the character of Jesus and on the manner in which he suffered. Among earlier Christian writers, Clement makes explicit use of Paul's first letter to the Corinthians and a number of allusions both to Hebrews and to James.[5] The three moral teachers I singled out as representing Religiousness B in the New Testament are also chosen by Clement to help express his own moral convictions. Second, Clement reveals an acquaintance with Greco-Roman (and Jewish) moral exhortation in the way he makes constant use of the rhetorical *topos* on envy (*peri phthonou*) as he seeks to restore harmony among his readers.[6] While such *homonoia* ("harmony") within a community has an obvious political dimension—compare the *Orations* of Dio of Prusa to Nicea and Nicomedia—and can be thought of in general as a "stabilizing of the world," the Corinthian church represents only a very small portion of "world," and the moral dimension is dominant. Indeed, much of his engagement with scripture is for the purpose of proposing negative and positive examples on the topic of envy.[7]

It is characteristic of Religiousness B to grant some recognition to the benefits that come from the divine *dynamis* outside of moral agency, and we find
such acknowledgement in 1 *Clement*. Humans are created in the image of God
(33.4), but in particular they have been favored by the work of Christ. They
have been given Christ's provision (2.1) and Christ's power (16.1). Christ's blood
was poured out for their salvation (7.4), and salvation was accomplished by
Christ the great high priest (36.1–6). The Holy Spirit has been poured out on
them abundantly (2.2). As a result, they have been called from darkness to light
(59.2) and have been given the power (or authority: *exousia*) of sovereignty (*basil-
eia*; 61.1). They have received a share in many great and glorious deeds (19.2)
and have become partakers (*metochoi*) in great and glorious promises (34.7).
Eternal life is the first but only one of the "blessed and wonderful gifts of God"
(*dōra tou theou*; 35.1), as "all glory and enlargement (*pasa doxa kai platysmos*)
were given" to them (3.1).

Distinctively characteristic of Religiousness B, however, is a concentration on
moral behavior as the true measure of religious piety. From the start of his composition, Clement speaks in the same breath of "proof of virtue" and "steadfastness of faith" as a demonstration of the Corinthians' "character" (*ēthos*; 1.2). In the
manner of Greco-Roman moralists, Clement speaks of his readers' efforts as an
"athletic contest" (*agōn*; 2.3; 7.1) to express a righteousness that consists in virtuous deeds (2.4–7; 33.1, 8). Such moral behavior articulates the "faith which is in
Christ" (22.1–8), by obeying the words with which Christ commanded certain
moral behaviors (2.1; 13.3; 46.7–8). Obedience is not mechanical but a matter of
conscience (*syneidēsis*; 34.7; 41.1) and a demonstration of love toward Christ
(49.1). This is the sort of righteousness that Paul taught in all the world (5.7).

Those caught up in a life of vice, then, must repent (1 *Clement*, 7.4–5) by
turning from foul deeds (28.1) and must gain forgiveness and seek righteousness
(48). Sanctification is a transformation of the soul (29.1) that finds expression in
deeds of holiness (30.1). Moral virtue is the "sacrifice of praise" to God (35.5–12)
just as a humble spirit is a "sacrifice of praise" (52.3): note that cultic language
is used for moral dispositions. Clement makes clear that his readers' characters
should be shaped by the character of Christ himself, above all in his manner of
suffering righteously (16.1; 17). The imitation of Christ is not simply a matter of
suffering martyrdom, although Peter and Paul stand as models of enduring in
the manner of Christ (5.1–7). Rather, the imitation of Christ is, in all circumstances, to live with the same dispositions of meekness and humility that Christ
displayed in his human character. As Clement begins to sum up his teaching
by listing the moral qualities he has tried to inculcate among his Corinthians
readers (62.2–3), he states that he has written on things that befit their religion

(*thrēskeia*), things that are "most helpful" (*ōphelimōtatōn*) for a "virtuous life" (*enareton bion*) for those who wish to guide their steps in piety (*eusebōs*) and righteousness (*dikaiōs*; 62.1). Religion and moral behavior are mutually defining.

The so-called *Second Letter of Clement* has no epistolary character and is not, in the view of most scholars, written by the same author as *1 Clement*. It is, instead, an early Christian homily from the second century, whose entire focus is the moral life of its hearers.[8] The author begins by celebrating the benefits won by "the great sufferings Jesus Christ endured for our sake" (2 *Clement*, 1.2). Before their acceptance of Christ, the author's intended audience had been ignorant worshipers of idols and their life was like death (1.5). They were in darkness. But through Christ, they have been called "son," and they have been given light (1.4); they have recovered their sight and have been saved: "He called us when we were not, and it was his will that out of nothing we should come into being" (1.6–7). They should, then, rejoice in such gifts (2.1), seeing that they were saved through mercy (3.1). But from the start as well, the author poses the question of appropriate response: "What return, then, shall we make to him, or what fruit shall we offer worthy of that which he has given us?" (1.3); and "What praise, then. Or what reward shall we give him in return for what we have received" (1.5)?

The author says explicitly that he is writing an exhortation (*enteuxis*) to stir his readers to repentance and salvation (2 *Clement*, 19.1), which means turning from unrighteousness to righteousness (*apo tēs adikias eis tēn dikaiosynēn*; 19.2; see also 13.2). Such repentance means ceasing to be a friend to this world and becoming a friend of the world to come (6.2–5) by "doing the will of Christ" (6.7) and "doing the will of the Father who called us" (10.1), which means to "follow after virtue, but [to] give up vice as the forerunner of our sins, and let us flee from ungodliness lest evil overtake us" (10.1). In words that echo Greco-Roman moral discourse, the author declares, "we are contending as athletes [*athloumen*] and are being trained [*gymnazometha*] in the contest of the living God so that we may gain the crown [*stephanōthōmen*] in that which is to come" (20.2). For this composition, the only adequate response to the gifts given by Christ is a life of virtue: "How do we confess him? By doing what he says, and not disregarding his commandments, and honoring him not only with our lips but 'with all our heart and all our mind'" (3.4). The author assures his readers, "If then we do righteousness before God we shall enter into his kingdom and shall receive his promises" (11.7). Although not written by the same author, *1 Clement* and *2 Clement* share the same way of being Christian: the gifts of God in Christ find their appropriate expression through the moral transformation of those who have received his power.

We met Polycarp of Smyrna in the previous chapter as the recipient of a letter of the martyr Ignatius of Antioch and as the subject of an encomiastic account of his martyrdom in 156. His own *Letter to the Philippians*—which he wrote to accompany a copy of Ignatius's letters requested by that church—bears only a trace of the martyr piety that suffused the letters of his episcopal colleague (see Pol. *Phil.* 1.1; 8.2) but for the most part shares the religious outlook of 1 and 2 *Clement*.[9] Polycarp, too, is a disciple of Paul, making explicit reference to the letters Paul wrote to them, "from the study of which you will be able to build yourselves up into the faith given you" (Pol. *Phil.* 3.2), and joining to a final set of moral exhortations the phrase "as Paul teaches" (11.2).[10] His composition is, in fact, a pastiche of allusions from Paul, the First Letter of Peter, and the sayings of Jesus.[11]

Polycarp spends little space on participation in benefits. He rejoices with his readers in their faith that "bears fruit unto the Lord Jesus," who suffered death for them and was raised up by God (Pol. *Phil.* 1.2–3; 2.1). They will, Polycarp says, share in his resurrection "if we do his will, and walk in his commandments, and love the things he loved," which means "refraining from all unrighteousness" (2.2). He writes, therefore, "concerning righteousness" (*peri tēs dikaiosynēs*; 3.1), and his composition stays steadily on that topic. His instructions on order in the household or household church (4.2–3; 5.3; 6.1) are not, as we have seen in Greco-Roman moralists, inconsistent with this moral focus. Polycarp rejects false teachings concerning the incarnation, the cross, and the resurrection, ascribing them to the influence of Satan (7.1) and "the foolishness of the crowd" (7.2).

He encourages his readers to keep their "pledge of righteousness" (Pol. *Phil.* 8.1) by imitating the manner of Christ's suffering—without sin, without guile— "for this is the example which he gave us in himself" (8.2). Such endurance in faith is "obeying the word of righteousness" in the manner of Ignatius and his companions and in the manner of Paul and the other apostles (9.1): all these examples ran not in vain but in "faith and righteousness" (9.2). Readers should, in their lives, "follow the example of the Lord, firm and unchangeable in faith, loving the brotherhood, affectionate to one another, joined together in the truth, forestalling one another in the gentleness of the Lord, despising no man" (10.1).

SYMBOLIC FIGURE: JUSTIN MARTYR

A new and critical stage of development in this way of being Christian occurs with Justin, whose martyrdom in 165 I mentioned in the previous chapter.[12] Justin, who taught in Rome during the reign of Antoninus Pius (138–161), deliberately and consistently casts himself as a philosopher and Christianity as a form of philosophy. His self-portrayal is displayed most fully in *The Dialogue with Trypho*.[13] Because of the manner of his dress, he is greeted as a philosopher in Ephesus by the Jewish teacher Trypho, who had fled the war in Palestine (*Dial*, 1). Justin tells Trypho that the practice of philosophy is necessary for every man (3), that it is the most honorable possession of humans, and that its business is inquiry into God (1). Using a rhetorical ploy we recognize from elsewhere (e.g., Philostratus' *Life of Apollonius*),[14] Justin describes his own philosophical quest before becoming a Christian: he tried Stoicism, Aristotelianism, and Pythagoreanism in turn, finding in each something less than satisfying. Finally, he found in Platonism the best expression of Greek philosophy, "and I expected forthwith to look upon God, for this is the end of Plato's philosophy" (2; see also *Apology*, 2.12).

An encounter with an old man, however, leads Justin to understand the truths that were unknown to Plato and others (*Dial*, 6), namely, that the soul is not by nature immortal but is so only by God's power (4–5) and that the truest knowledge is to be derived from the prophetic writings in scripture (7). He becomes a Christian: "I found this philosophy alone to be safe and profitable. Thus and for this reason I am a philosopher. Moreover I would wish that all, making a resolution similar to my own, do not keep themselves away from the words of the savior" (8). Justin's is truly the conversion from one philosophy to another. Christianity is seen as superior because of its teaching on God and because it is based not on "empty fables, or words without any foundation, but words filled with the Spirit of God, and big with power, and flourishing with grace" (9).

The remaining chapters of the *Dialogue* are devoted to establishing against Judaism a "philosophy" that can claim priority in possession of the prophets and the true teaching about God—the proper way of reading the ancient prophecies, that is, with reference to Jesus. Although prophecy is the linchpin of Justin's argument, it should be stressed that he pays only passing recognition to the signs and wonders performed by the ancient and more recent prophets, noting that "certain wonderful deeds" have also been performed by false prophets to astonish people and "glorify the spirits and demons of error" (7). It is not prophecy as a present display of the power and presence of God's spirit —that is, prophecy as a religious practice within Religiousness A—that interests Justin but the written prophecies of the past that serve as textual pointers to the claims being made by and for Jesus.

That Justin understands Christianity to be a form of philosophy is made abundantly clear in the two extant works known as his first and second apologies. In the first, he addresses the imperial court as one that has philosophers among it: "You are called philosophers and pious" (*Apology*, 1.1; 1.2). He asks of the emperor that Christians be judged in the manner that other philosophers are: many wear the garb and claim the title, but it is their works that determine whether they are true or false philosophers (1.4; 1.7). In the same way, Christians should be judged by their deeds and not merely their profession (1.8). Justin then opposes the philosophical religion of the Christians to the pagan cults. The worship of idols bears with it a false conception of God and leads to immorality among those who practice it (1.9). But God is to be served rationally and with a virtuous life: "He accepts only those who imitate the excellencies which reside in Him, temperance and justice, and philanthropy, and as many virtues as are peculiar to a God who is called by no proper name" (1.10).

Christians, he argues, are those who worship God as God deserves and desires. The persecution of Christians arises from the calumnies of demons and as pursued by the emperor almost appears to arise from "the fear lest all men become righteous and you no longer have any to punish" (*Apology*, 1.12). But Christ ("our teacher"; 1.12; 1.13) himself taught humans to be righteous and live according to the strictest norms of morality: "Brief and concise utterances fell from him, for he was no sophist, but his word was the power of God" (1.14).[15] Justin provides a series of Jesus' sayings, all of which serve to show that he was a teacher of righteousness rather than immorality (1.15–17).[16] And he declares that conversion to Christianity is fundamentally a moral conversion from wickedness to virtue; they seek to "live conformably to the good precepts of Christ, to the end that they may become partakers with us of the same joyful hope of a reward from God the ruler of all" (1.14; see also 1.28–29). The issue, then, is whether people claiming to be Christians actually live in this manner. Those who act immorally are, by this measure, not truly Christian.

If true religion is a matter of rational worship and moral life, then Justin must logically acknowledge that such philosophical religion was possible even before the teaching of Christ, and he does: "We have been taught that Christ is the first-born of God, and we have declared above that he is the Word of whom every race of men were partakers; and those who lived reasonably were Christians even though they have been thought atheists; as, among the Greeks, Socrates and Heraclitus and men like them; and among the barbarians, Abraham and Ananias and Azarias and Misael, and Elias, and many others" (*Apology*, 1.46).[17]

But this word is expressed most fully among Christians,[18] who live morally according to the words of Jesus, the Word himself, and whose worship, as Justin shows in his description of it (*Apology*, 1.61; 1.65–67), is befitting a God who desires rational worship and also shapes Christian worshipers in moral behavior: they "offer hearty prayers in common for ourselves and for the baptized person, and for all others in every place, that we may be counted worthy, now that we have learned the truth, by our works also to be found good citizens and keepers of the commandments, so that we may be saved with an everlasting salvation" (1.65).

I noted above Justin's cautious attitude toward wonder-working: both true and false prophets performed astonishing deeds (*Apology*, 1.7).[19] The same anxiety is revealed in his acknowledgement that the wonders worked by Christ could be regarded as those of a magician (1.30). He avoids this conclusion by stressing the fact that the wonders Jesus performed were not displays meant to deceive but gestures of help to those in need, and that precisely the deeds he performed had been foretold of the Christ by the ancient prophecies (1.48). But his attitude toward miracle-working in the present is clear: he tends to ascribe such thaumaturgy as the work of demons operative in rivals to the Christian message. Thus, demons sponsor the magic performed by Simon and Menander and Marcion (1.26; see also 1.56).

The apologists who were Justin's successors and contemporaries also tended, if with less emphasis, to understand Christianity in philosophical terms. In his *Address to the Greeks*, Tatian (110–172) follows the pattern of his teacher Justin, but with a much less irenic spirit.[20] He is a convert to Christianity (1) and claims firsthand knowledge of Greek religion and philosophy; he had visited many lands, studied rhetoric, and even studied the statues of the gods at Rome before he "embraced our barbarian philosophy" (35). Having had such great experience and having been driven by the desire "to discover the truth," he converted to Christianity because of the age and worth of the "barbaric writings" of scripture (29). Now being instructed in these things, he wishes to "put away my former errors and the follies of childhood" (30).

More than that, he goes on the attack in a manner far more vigorous and intense than we find in Justin. He claims that Greek culture as a whole is derivative (*Address*, 1). He attacks the philosophers of the Greek tradition explicitly and by name, concentrating on two points: the ways in which the teaching in various sects is mutually contradictory (3, 25) and the ways in which philosophers displayed vice rather than virtue in their personal behavior (2–3). Greek religion, in turn, is entirely under the influence of demons (8–9, 21–24) who seduce people by their display of power—as in healings (16–18)—and who lead people into depravity (19).

Christianity, in contrast, is characterized in terms of its sane teaching concerning God, human freedom, and future immortality for the soul that receives God's spirit (*Address*, 4–7, 11–13, 15). Because Christianity is rooted in scripture, and Moses is demonstrably prior to Greek culture (36–41), Christians can make the claim that their philosophy is older than that of the Greeks (31). Oddly, although Tatian shares Justin's notion of the *logos*, he does not recognize its presence among the righteous of the Gentiles as Justin did. Even odder, he never once mentions Jesus in his entire discourse. As for wonder-working, Tatian sees it as a feature only of demonic possession rather than an aspect of the Christian religion.

We also find no mention of Jesus' miracles in the apologetic work *To Autolycus*, by Theophilus of Antioch (ca. 168).[21] Indeed, we find again no explicit mention of Jesus. Instead, Theophilus introduces sayings with the phrase "the voice of the Gospel" (3.13; 3.14). The concentration of this apologist is entirely on teaching and behavior, the same focus we find in ancient moral philosophy. Theophilus also is a convert who is drawn to Christianity by the truth of the ancient prophecies found in scripture (1.14). In contrast to the wild inaccuracies to be found in Greek myths, the prophecies can be shown to be accurate (3.16–25). And because Christianity is in effect the realization of those scriptural prophecies, it can claim a greater antiquity and truth than anything in Greek culture (3.29).

A substantial amount of his apology is given to the dismissal of Greek religion— following the path of Justin and Tatian (see *Autolycus*, 1.9–10; 2.5–8; 3.7–8). And like Tatian, Theophilus also attacks the contradictions (3.3) and false doctrines (3.5–8) of the philosophers who make false charges against the Christians (3.4). Theophilus' positive presentation of Christianity, in turn, focuses less on doctrine than on morals, with his discussion of each moral quality drawing on scriptural support. Thus, he treats in turn God and his law (3.9), hospitality to strangers (3.10), repentance (3.11), and righteousness (3.12)—all of these receiving support exclusively from Old Testament texts. In his treatment of chastity (3.13), he draws from both Old and New Testament passages, and in discussing the demand to love enemies (3.14), Theophilus depends completely on the New Testament.

Athenagoras' *Embassy* (177) greets the co-emperors Commodus and Marcus Aurelius as "philosophers" and is closer in spirit to Justin than to Tatian, because of the way the author draws the philosophers to the side of Christians against pagan religion.[22] He begins by stating that the persecution of Christians is unjust (1–2) because the charges of atheism, cannibalism, and incest made against them are false (3). Athenagoras shows first that Christians are not atheists, because their teaching on the one God, creator of the universe, is more reasonable than (4), and superior to (7), polytheism, even when understood in terms of Father, Son, and Holy Spirit (10). This is above all because Christians maintain that God is distinct from matter while at the same time in control of creation (15–16). The Christian understanding of God is supported by the scriptures (9), whereas even the Greek poets and philosophers seek one God (5–6) in preference to the absurdities of the pagan cults (8, 14).

Athenagoras calls on these Greek poets and philosophers as allies in characterizing the pagan gods as recent and created by humans (*Embassy*, 17–19), using a form of Euhemerism to declare that the gods are simply humans elevated to a higher status (28–30). By using allegorical interpretation to save the reputation of the gods (22–23), Greek philosophers bear witness to the scandalous character of their representation in myths and their complete lack of moral character (20–21). Athenagoras repeats the charge that the healings performed at pagan shrines are the work of demons seeking to lead humans astray (26–27). Greek philosophers and poets are not entirely without blame, however, for they deny the work of divine providence in the world (25).

In response to the pagan charges of Christian immorality, Athenagoras appeals to the Gospels, drawing extensively on the words of Jesus as found in Matthew's Sermon on the Mount (*Embassy*, 11) and Luke's Sermon on the Plain (12). Jesus' teaching forbids immoral behavior and calls for the highest possible standard of love. After connecting the immorality of pagans to the immorality of their gods, Athenagoras takes pains to contrast Christian morality to pagan (34) on two specific points that respond implicitly to the charges of incest and cannibalism: Christians avoid adultery (32) and practice chastity (33), and they eschew all forms of cruelty and violence toward others (35). Finally, the teaching on the bodily resurrection serves as powerful motivation to Christian morality, for the consideration of future punishment as well as future reward stimulates Christians to please the judge of all (36). Readers of Athenagoras are once more struck by the absence of specific reference to Jesus or to the benefits he brought either through his healings or through his death and resurrection. Christianity is a set of doctrines and a way of life based on those doctrines. The realm of wonders—including healings—is the realm of demonic activity.

The question might be asked whether putting on the clothing of the philosopher was a matter, for these apologists, simply of adopting a protective coloration, rather than the expression of a mode of religiosity. Did Christians pose as philosophers in order to be better accepted in the Greco-Roman world? If we had only the second- and third-century apologetic literature, we could not answer the question definitively. It must be remembered, however, that portraying oneself—or one's movement—in philosophical terms was not necessarily a safe tactic. As we have seen, philosophers were subject to exile and even execution, especially when their doctrines were perceived by imperial powers as subversive of the state.[23] The writings of two further figures of the second and third centuries demonstrate, moreover, that thinking of Christianity in philosophical terms was more than a matter of external self-presentation and that philosophy pervaded their understanding of Christian existence from within as well.

CHRISTIANITY AS PHILOSOPHY: CLEMENT OF ALEXANDRIA

We know little about the life of Titus Flavius Clemens (ca. 150–215) apart from the fact that he was born of pagan parents, traveled widely after his conversion to Christianity, was well educated in rhetoric and philosophy, and became the student and then successor of Pantaenus, a Christian who had been a Stoic philosopher, as head of the catechetical school in Alexandria around 200.[24] His extant writings support his reputation for wide learning both in Hellenistic culture and in Jewish and Christian writings—beyond providing remarkably detailed reports concerning the Mysteries, culling philosophical and Gnostic opinions, and adducing lengthy citations from scripture, he makes explicit use of such writers as Philo of Alexandria and Clement of Rome.[25]

The architecture of Clement's three major extant works reveals something of his cultural confidence and intellectual ambition.[26] In the *Protreptikos* ("exhortation") addressed to the Gentiles, he does not defend Christianity but exhorts Greeks and Romans to join the movement and participate in its benefits. In the *Paidagogos* ("instructor/teacher"), he sketches the framework for Christian moral practice. His third volume was apparently intended to be a systematic fusion of philosophy and faith, showing how the true "Gnostic"—the Christian who had been trained morally and was capable of higher learning—might embrace the world's culture. Clement's ambition here exceeded his ability: the *Stromata* ("carpets"/"miscellanies") remains a collection of discrete discussions rather than a systematic argument. Some attention to each of these works shows why Clement represents a stage in the development of Religiousness B within Christianity beyond Justin and the other apologists.

In the *Protreptikos*, Clement addresses the Gentiles with the supreme confidence of having, in the Christian religion, the best and fullest realization of Greek philosophy. The choice of genre is itself revealing, for the protreptic discourse (*logos protreptikos*) was widely used among philosophers to encourage dedication to the life of virtue.[27] With remarkable panache, he offers a share in its benefits to those among the nations who are still in thrall to the religious rites sponsored by demons and to those whose glimpses of truth in poetry and philosophy have prepared them for a full embrace of the deepest philosophical truth. The book opens and closes with explicit calls to conversion (1 and 10–11). The chapters between cover much the same ground as we have seen in the apologists: an extensive attack on the pagan Mysteries that ascribes their power to demons and makes the point that the morals of the gods are reflected in the morals of their worshippers (2–4); a recitation of philosophers on the nature of God, recognizing the superiority of Plato in this regard, and acknowledging that some teachings among Gentiles were also inspired by God (5–6); an examination of the ways in which poets also approached some of the truth about God (7); and finally, a case made that the greatest truth—and the surest incentive to piety—is found in the prophetic scriptures (8).

The opening and closing of the book (the calls to conversion) are the most original to Clement and most helpful in locating his religious sensibility. He lists, for example, the wonders worked by "the celestial Word," as "to open the eyes of the blind and unstop the ears of the deaf, and to lead the lame or the erring to righteousness"—but what appear at first to be material healings turn out to be aspects of moral transformation. He continues, "to put a stop to corruption, to conquer death, to reconcile disobedient children to their father." Clement then states, "You have, then, God's promise, you have his love: become partakers of his grace." The reason why Christians enjoy the benefits of the best philosophy is that the Word that pervaded all things has become human: "Inasmuch as the Word was from the first, he was and is the divine source of all things; but inasmuch as he has now assumed the name Christ . . . this Word, then, the Christ, the cause of both our being at first (for he was in God) and now our well being, the very Word has now appeared as man . . . the author of all blessings to us: by whom we, being taught to live well, are sent on our way to life eternal" (*Protreptikos*, 1).

The Word who was Christ "appeared as our teacher" and "taught us to live well when he appeared as our Teacher." Using a common trope of the philosophers, Clement compares Christ the teacher to a physician who treats each moral disease appropriately. Through Christ, "God is ceaselessly exhorting us to virtue," and genuine conversion is moral transformation: "If thou desirest truly to see God, take to thyself means of purification worthy of Him, not leaves of laurel fillets interwoven with wool and purple; but wreathing thy brows with righteousness, and encircling them with the leaves of temperance, set thyself earnestly to find Christ" (*Protreptikos*, 1).

Beginning in chapter 9, Clement begins his second exhortation to conversion. He states that salvation is not possible except through faith in Jesus. And what does he mean by salvation? "Godliness, that makes a man as far as can be like God, designates God as our suitable teacher, who alone can worthily assimilate man to God." Clement understands salvation in terms of a righteous way of life: "Let us haste to salvation, to regeneration . . . and let us, by being made good, conformably follow after union, seeking after the good Monad" as instructed by "the choir-leader and teacher, the Word, reaching and resting in the same truth, and crying Abba, Father" (*Protreptikos*, 9). To have fellowship with God, it is necessary to change morally: "Let us therefore repent, and pass from ignorance to knowledge, from foolishness to wisdom, from licentiousness to self-restraint, from unrighteousness to righteousness, from godlessness to God" (10).

It is his intense focus on Jesus—so much more prominent than in earlier apologists—that makes Clement's appeal so distinctive. In this passage, he speaks of the benefits won by Jesus for humans: "For with a celerity unsurpassed and a benevolence to which we have ready access, the divine power, casting its radiance upon the earth, hath filled the universe with the seed of salvation. . . . So great a work was accomplished in so brief a space by the Lord, who though despised as to appearance, was in reality adored, the expiator of sin, the Savior, the clement, the divine Word, He that is most truly manifest deity, He that is made equal to the Lord of the universe; because He was His Son, and the Word was in God . . . assuming the character of man, and fashioning himself in flesh, he enacted the drama of human salvation" (*Protreptikos*, 10). Toward the end of his exhortation, Clement declares, "This Jesus, who is eternal, the one great High Priest of the One God and of His Father, prays for and exhorts men" (12). Still, Clement understands the salvation brought by Christ to be the power of transformation in the moral sphere. He declares, "I urge you to be saved. This Christ desires. In one word, he freely bestows life on you. And who is He? Briefly learn. The Word of truth, the Word of incorruption, that regenerates man by bringing him back to the truth—the goad that urges to salvation—He who expels destruction and pursues death—He who builds up the temple of God in men. Cleanse the temple; and pleasures and amusements abandon to the winds and the fire as a fading flower; but wisely cultivate the fruits of self-command; and present thyself to God as an offering of first-fruits, that there may be not the work alone, but also the grace of God; and both are requisite, that the friend of Christ may be rendered worthy of the kingdom, and counted worthy of the kingdom" (11).

Clement's philosophical understanding of the Christian life is obvious as well in his second composition, *Paidagogos* ("The Instructor"), which is devoted to the basic practices of those who have followed the Word's exhortation and have been baptized. Book 1 of *Paidagogos* might be called theoretical, in that it takes up the identity, nature, role, and character of the one instructing (the Word) as well as the identity and disposition of those being instructed (new Christians). Book 2 then takes up in turn all the aspects of life that must be cultivated philosophically in accordance with the Word: eating and drinking

(2.1–2), behavior at feasts (2.3–4), modes of speech (2.5–6), wealth (2.7.11–12), sleep (2.9), and sex (2.10). For each topic, Clement adduces both the teaching of scripture, the opinions of the philosophers, and the sayings of poets. By so weaving his authorities together, he creates a single culture drawn from the best in Judaism and Hellenism. In Book 3, Clement enters into even greater detail concerning the minutest aspects of Christian life in a pagan city, includ- ing issues of deportment, attendance and behavior at the public baths, personal adornment, frugality, attendance at the games, and custody of the eyes. The Book concludes with the lovely "Hymn to Christ the Savior" and the hymn "To the *Paidagogos*" (3.12). In a manner far more systematic and detailed than that of Clement of Rome and Polycarp, who wrote almost a century earlier, Clem- ent of Alexandria shapes a positive vision of how Christians might carry out their commitment to Christ in a manner that is recognizable to them and to outsiders alike as truly philosophical.

The *Stromata* is a vast compendium of religious learning directed to Chris- tians whom Clement considers to have progressed through the teaching of the Instructor to a firmly formed philosophical life.[28] Now, he turns to the shaping of a philosophical mind for those able to engage it. "But as we say that a man can be a believer without learning, so also we assert that it is impossible for a man without learning to comprehend the things that are declared in the faith" (*Stromata*, 1.6). Clement is aware of and rejects "falsely-called" Gnostics who distort the faith (3.1–18; 4. 4).[29] But he remains committed to cultivating an au- thentic Christian *gnōsis* that is philosophical in character; the perfect Christian is not one who abandons the frame of faith and the practice of virtue but one who becomes an authentic Gnostic through a deeper apprehension of faith and virtue through philosophical learning (see 4.21–23).

His comments at the start of the *Stromata* are most useful for this analysis. Clement recognizes the difficulty of sorting out what in Greek philosophy is helpful to the faith and what is not: like nuts, he says, not all of Greek philoso- phy is edible (1.1). Continuing the metaphor, he says a bit later, "The *Stromata* will contain the truth mixed up in the dogmas of philosophy, or rather covered over and hidden, as the edible part of the nut in the shell" (1.1). One thing that the Christian Gnostic must do is avoid the traditional enemy of philosophy, namely, sophistry (1.3; 1.4; 1.8): "Our much-knowing Gnostic can distinguish sophistry from philosophy, the art of decoration from gymnastics, cookery from physics, and rhetoric from dialectics, and the other sects which are according to the barbarian philosophy, from the truth itself" (1.8). Still, Clement argues that all sects of philosophy contain some element of truth (1.13). Discernment requires a sufficient knowledge of philosophy to perceive what is useful and what is not. But because Clement perceives that philosophy is "in a sense a work of divine providence," the task of discernment must be undertaken.

He argues, first, that "even if philosophy were useless, if the demonstration of its uselessness does good, it is yet useful"; likewise, it sharpens the perception of what is true when doctrines are compared (*Stromata*, 1.2). Learning what is good in philosophy can help lead one to a life of virtue (1.7) and to an appreciation of acting well over speaking well (1.10). Indeed, among the Greeks, "before the advent of the Lord, philosophy was necessary to the Greeks for righteousness; and now it becomes conducive to piety; being a kind of preparatory training to those who attain to faith through demonstration. . . . Philosophy, therefore, was a preparation, paving the way for him who is perfected in Christ" (1.5). This historical role of preparation can work also within the faith to enable the progress of the Christian: "Just as the encyclical branches of study contribute to philosophy, which is their mistress; so also philosophy itself cooperates for the acquisition of wisdom. For philosophy is the study of wisdom, and wisdom is the knowledge of things human and divine, and their causes" (1.5). More important for believers, philosophy is necessary if the scripture is fully to be understood and appreciated (1.9). And when scripture is read and fully appreciated, then 'one comes to see not only how Greek wisdom derived from the barbarian but how the wisdom of scripture is superior to that of even the greatest of Greek philosophers (1.15ff.). Clement's enthusiastic yet discriminating embrace of Greek philosophy lays the groundwork for a distinctively Christian culture, in which God's revelation and human reason are seen as mutually informing, mutually enriching.

THE CHRISTIAN PHILOSOPHER: ORIGEN OF ALEXANDRIA

We met Origen in the previous chapter through his *Exhortation to Martyrdom*, which expresses many of the convictions I have associated with Religiousness A.[30] But just as we saw in the study of Greco-Roman religion how a figure like Plutarch could include in himself elements of both Religiousness B and D, so we find in Origen the almost perfect expression of Religiousness B within Christianity. Yes, he encourages others to martyrdom, just as he himself sought it. And he celebrates the power of Christ demonstrated in such witness and the participation in the benefits to which it leads. But Origen's main interest is always in Christianity as moral transformation. It is impossible in a short discussion to do justice to one of the greatest figures in Christian intellectual history—he was at once the first great scripture scholar and first great systematic theologian as well as one of the last and greatest of apologists[31]—and my treatment of Origen necessarily focuses on the way in which he exemplifies Christianity as moral transformation, continuing and making even more pervasive the program started by Justin and brought to such an impressive stage of development by Clement.[32]

Unlike Clement and earlier apologists, Origen was born into a Christian family. His father, Leonides, was martyred under Severus in 202. Origen worked in a thoroughly pluralistic setting. He first taught in the catechetical school of Alexandria, taking over from Clement, and Alexandria's great library enabled a substantial tradition of learning in all the branches of philosophy.[33] One philosopher, known to us only as Celsus, had written, some seven years before Origen's birth, a sustained attack on Christianity.[34] The Jewish population in Alexandria was large and intellectually influential. In addition to producing the Septuagint circa 250 BCE, Alexandrian Jews had produced the prolific Philo as well as other apologetic writings.[35] Christians in Alexandria were also familiar with the heretical teachers Marcion, Valentinus, and Heracleon, who flourished some 35 years before Origen's birth.[36]

Not surprisingly, we find Origen casting Christianity as a philosophy most explicitly and emphatically in his apologetic rebuttal of the philosopher Celsus, written circa 246. The fact that a Greco-Roman philosopher of the late second century took Christianity with sufficient intellectual seriousness to devote an entire work to its defamation is itself an indication of the religion's greater visibility and its self-presentation as a form of philosophy. The issue in Origen's *Contra Celsum* is twofold: Christianity's right to claim a place within Greco-Roman culture and the legitimacy of its claim to being the authentic Israel of which scripture spoke. On one side, Origen faces a philosophical challenge in the form of a somewhat eclectic Epicureanism (*Cels*, 1.8–9). But because Celsus has cleverly made use of Jewish rebuttals of Christian claims (1.8), Origen must also face a Jewish front far more aggressive than that engaged by Justin a century earlier. And because in the eyes of pagans Christianity had become not one thing but a many-headed monster with rival claims, Origen must constantly bear in mind that the heretics also have their interpretations of scripture (5.54; 5.65), so that he must secure what he regards as the orthodox position in response to the challenge of Greek philosophy, Jewish polemic, and rival teachings within the Christian movement. *Contra Celsum* is difficult to read because of its length (eight large books), because of its apparent lack of linear argument, and perhaps also because Origen needed to keep adjusting his position while standing on shifting sands.

Origen follows the basic lines of Justin's apologetic strategy.[37] First, he argues that Christians can demonstrate the truth of their claims through the straightforward fulfillment of prophecy, with the following three refutations: (1)

Jewish claims to be the Israel that receives the promises foretold in scripture are false because historical events has made their fulfillment impossible (*Cels*, 2.8; 2.78); (2) the Gospel narratives show in great detail how the events of Jesus' life, death, and resurrection were foretold by the prophets, whereas those that speak of an earthly messianic triumph point to Jesus' second coming (1.55–56; 2.29; 4.1–2);[38] and (3) the respective destinies of the Jews and of Jesus' followers fulfill the prophecies spoken of by Jesus: the destruction of the temple and the spread of the Gospel to all nations (2.13; 4.22).

Origen argues that Christianity is the best realization of what the Greek world sought in philosophy. Like Clement, Origen is capable of drawing from the entire range of Greek literature, religion, and philosophy; unlike Clement, his knowledge of philosophy appears to be direct and in depth.[39] In seven successive chapters of *Contra Celsum*, for example, he leads the reader through close analyses of Plato's *Timaeus, Apology, Laws, Phaedrus,* and *Epistles* (6.9–17). More important, he consistently presents Christianity as a philosophical school and thereby claims a place for it in Hellenistic culture. Christians are, to be sure, morally superior to the philosophers (*Cels*, 7.47), but especially as found in Plato, Greek philosophy provides the best analogy to Christianity (3.81).

Thus, he compares what he calls the "school of Jesus" (*Cels*, 7.41) to the schools of Jews and Greeks (4.31) across a range of specific points. Jesus is like the founder of a philosophical school (1.65), not least in the way he was betrayed and suffered (2.12). Christianity has sects or parties (*haireses*), as do other philosophical schools (2.27; 5.61), which generate disputes among Christians in the way that disputes are generated among philosophical parties (6.26).[40] Christianity has stages of initiation into full membership as do Pythagorean fellowships (3.51). Like Greek philosophy, Christianity must struggle with false philosophers who profess but do not practice (4.27; 4.30) and thereby discredit the good name of the school itself. Christians, like philosophers from other schools, sometimes resist local custom on the basis of principle (5.35). The Christian traditions concerning the appearances of Jesus among his followers can be matched by those handed on in other schools (5.57). Jesus can legitimately be compared to Socrates (2.41), but the speech of Jesus in the Gospels is closer to that of Epictetus than it is to the artistically fashioned dialogues of Plato (6.2). Christian teaching is a form of healing for the passions in the manner that philosophy claims to be (3.75), and the goal of Christianity is that humans become wise (3.45).[41] It is therefore consistent that Christian philosophers follow the lead of Greek and Jewish philosophers (like Philo) and read their sacred texts "philosophically" (3.58; 3.79).[42] Perhaps most fascinating in this long list of comparisons is the way Origen uses the analogy to philosophy to counter Celsus' charge that Christians accept truths on faith without evidence: he responds that all members of philosophical schools begin with assumptions that are unproven and must start with faith (1.10).

Origen's language about philosophy places him squarely within the world of Greco-Roman moralists, the popular philosophers of the Roman Empire whose concern was not with theory but with therapy, whose passion was not for epistemology but for ethics.[43] For Christians to "seek to become wise" meant less the acquisition of knowledge than the changing of their dispositions and behavior. It meant the healing of the passions through training. Like Plutarch a century earlier, Origen saw the philosophical life in terms of a progressive transformation of the soul.[44] For Origen, the anagogical reading of scripture, in turn, had less to do with Platonic forms and more to do with moral conversion. As Plutarch sought to save the dignity of the religious myths concerning Isis and Osiris by reading them not literally but "philosophically" (*philosophikōs*), that is, interpreting their meaning to be about human transformation,[45] so did Origen read the scriptures handed down in the church "philosophically"—that is, as concerned with the transformation of the mind and the conversion of morals.

In the middle of a highly technical discussion with Dionysius on the nature of the relation between the soul and blood, for example, Origen interrupts the debate and exhorts the listeners. He quotes Romans 12:1, "I beseech you, therefore, be transformed"; and adds, "Resolve to learn that you can be transformed"; he concludes his exhortation to them with these words: "What is it I really want? To treat the matter in a way that heals the souls of my hearers."[46] This small moment perfectly captures Origen's entire motivation and goal for interpreting scripture. As a pre-Augustinian, Hellenistic moralist, Origen was optimistic concerning the human person's capacity to be reformed by knowledge. Transforming knowledge is certainly not just information, even about mystical things. Nor is it, as the Gnostics would have it, a form of self-realization. It is, rather, coming to know God through Jesus (*Cels*, 6.68) and being transformed into the mind of Christ, since Jesus is "a living pattern to men" (2.16).

The reading and study of scripture, then, is a way of advancing in such moral (spiritual) transformation into the image of Christ. When commenting on the passage in Luke's Gospel that speaks of the young man Jesus growing strong, being filled with wisdom, and having the grace of God upon him (Luke 2:40), Origen directs his listeners likewise to grow in wisdom and declares, "What is said about Jesus applies to the just. For it was not only for himself that Jesus 'progressed in wisdom and stature and grace with God and men,' but also in each of those who accept progress in 'wisdom and stature and grace,' Jesus progresses in 'wisdom and stature and grace with God and men.'"[47] In his response to Celsus, Origen emphasizes that the healings reported of Jesus in the Gospels are continuous with the healing of people's souls in the present (*Cels*, 1.67; 2.48). The good news has the power to transform lives (1.63; 8.47). Indeed, the most stunning evidence Origen can offer for the truth of Christian claims is the miracle of moral transformation in the pagan world: he points confidently to churches throughout the empire filled with people who have turned from wickedness to the teaching of Jesus and who, on that basis, live virtuous lives (1.67; 3.78; 4.4).

The authors I have surveyed in this chapter share an understanding of the divine *dynamis* as active in the transformation of human moral behavior. In various ways, they recognize the benefits God has made available in the death and resurrection of Jesus—they do not by any means deny the power that drew the attention of Religiousness A, the power manifest in miracles past and present, or the power that continued to be demonstrated in the witness of martyrdom. But their focus is on the character of the moral life that is enabled by the power of the Holy Spirit at work within human freedom.

The distinctive religious sensibility shared by these authors can also be located by means of negation: they certainly do not deny the goodness of the created order or materiality (as Religiousness C does)—they are not interested in freeing the soul from its bounds; instead, they want the soul to grow in a wisdom manifested in righteousness. Neither do they value Christianity for its ability to stabilize the world (as Religiousness D does). Although their moral universe includes appropriate behavior within the household, their gaze goes no higher; their concern is no wider. In fact, they pay little attention to a distinctive *politeia* of the Christian community. Like the Greco-Roman moralists who form their religious ancestry, they focus above all on the conversion and moral growth of the individual.

The category of philosophy did not need to be attached to such writers, for by the time of Justin, they had appropriated the designation for themselves. When we get to Clement and Origen, we find a completely natural self-understanding of the Christian religion in terms of Greco-Roman philosophy. This way of thinking about Christianity had perhaps unintended consequences. At one level, figures such as Clement and Origen continued to find moral behavior as the goal of Christian philosophy. But since good behavior depended in that world on right opinion (orthodoxy), it was natural for Clement and Origen also to include doctrine as an essential dimension of Christian philosophy, just as the apologists before them had identified the ways in which poets and philosophers occasionally "taught rightly" about the one God.

Christian Religiousness B therefore became not only the location for piety as moral endeavor but also the place where "theology"—the articulation of correct doctrine concerning God—came to be practiced. In the future, the degree of conceptual and verbal ability required to connect doctrine and morality would make Religiousness B the natural source for much of Christian intellectual life, with the accompanying tendency to think in terms of definitions and prescriptions more than in terms of the experience of power.

14

TRANSCENDING THE WORLD IN SECOND- AND THIRD-CENTURY CHRISTIANITY

In Greco-Roman religion, the first two ways of being religious celebrate the presence of the divine *dynamis* in the empirical world and differ only in emphasis—Religiousness A (as in Aelius Aristides) focuses on participation in divine benefits and Religiousness B (as in Epictetus) focuses on moral transformation. The third mode of religious sensibility seeks to transcend the empirical world, which it regards negatively as devoid of the divine *dynamis*. In Greco-Roman religion, it found mature expression in the Hermetic literature.

Religiousness C views salvation not in terms of safety and success in the present world nor in terms of the perfection of the human person as moral agent. Rather, salvation is the liberation of the human spirit from its material prison and its return to the place from which it came. Such salvation begins with a form of "self-realization" enabled by revelation from the divine realm: the spirit realizes its true identity and that its destiny is to be elsewhere—other than in the entangling grasp of matter.

I have so far shown how the first two ways of being religious are found both in the New Testament and in the literature of the second and third century. The New Testament offered scant evidence for the presence of Religiousness C in earliest Christianity. In the second half of the second century, in contrast, there is a sudden abundance of evidence pointing to a way of being Christian that conforms perfectly to the vision of the human condition, divine revelation, and flight from the world found in Greco-Roman Hermetic literature of the same period. This third type of religious sensibility arises in Christianity in connection to the movement that is broadly and problematically characterized as Gnosticism.

The subject is among the more complex and controversial in the study of ancient religions.[1] Among the many critical issues immediately facing any discussion or description of Gnosticism are (1) the relation between the outsider depictions of those considered heretics in patristic antiheretical literature and the elements found in compositions produced by movement insiders, above all but not exclusively those discovered at Nag-Hammadi;[2] (2) the origins of Gnosticism (is it pre-Christian, and does it draw mainly from Judaism or Platonism?) and its extent (does it embrace all forms of dualism?);[3] (3) the variety of expression found even within compositions everyone is willing to call Gnostic;[4] and (4) the social expressions of the sensibility: was there a "Gnostic Religion," were there distinct communities of Christian Gnostics, or were Christians with this sensibility mainly found on the margins of communities whose commitments were more exoteric?[5]

Fortunately, in asking about the presence of Religiousness C within second- and third-century Christianity, I am not required to answer or even extensively discuss such questions. My interest is not in defining a discrete movement but rather in locating a religious sensibility as it may be expressed in the activities and literature that have come to light. What is required of this analysis is simply to show the presence and shape of that sensibility among people of the second and third centuries who claimed an explicit allegiance to Christ. I am free, then, to make use of both insider and outsider sources as they converge on the points that illustrate this sensibility. I do this with more confidence because, however diverse the respective Gnostic systems are in detail, they are remarkably consistent with regard to their basic soteriology.[6] It is helpful to state at once what I understand that soteriology to be.[7]

Religiousness A and B construe the world positively: God creates all things good and directs them by his will. The cosmology of Type C, in contrast, makes a radical divide between the divine (the realm of spirit) and the empirical world (the realm of matter): matter came into existence by means of cosmic error or mischief and has no goodness in it. The anthropology of Religiousness A and B conceives of humans as drawn from the earth but bearing the divine image. Humans are free to choose: they can honor God through the right use of the world—responding to the power of God as manifested in the world or to the counterfeit and illusory power of demons who sponsor idolatry and immorality—and through righteous relations with other humans, or they can dishonor God through the misuse of freedom called idolatry and sin. The anthropology of Type C is more deterministic, with humans fixed on one of three forms: those completely defined by matter, those able to choose between matter and spirit, and those completely defined by spirit.[8]

The eschatology of Religiousness A and B is consistent with its cosmology and anthropology: the end-time means the full realization of the divine benefits already shared in this life—the resurrection of the dead and the perfection (material and moral) of the body and soul of the human person. Similarly consistent with its cosmology and anthropology, Religiousness C sees the end-time in terms of the liberation of all the sparks of light now scattered in the darkness of matter and their return to the eternal light. Only those who remove themselves from materiality are saved, for salvation is of the soul alone. By finding its true home, the soul transcends the world in which it had no part in the first place.

In Religiousness A and B, salvation comes to humans from the outside: God frees them from the alienation of sin and empowers them to a life of faith, virtue, and possibly martyrdom that would otherwise be beyond their natural capacities. In Religiousness C, salvation comes through a form of self-realization: the Gnostic comes to know what he or she is "by nature" and lives according to that realization. The only "outside" element in salvation for the Gnostic is the revelation of the true state of affairs that comes to the elect from the divine realm.

How did Type A or Type B Christians of the second and third centuries understand the figure of Christ? His role matched their construal of the divine *dynamis* and its way of operating in the empirical world. Christ was the source of the benefits in which Christians participated, with an emphasis respectively on his wonders, his teaching, or his death and resurrection. It was because of Christ that his followers could drive out demons and heal, because of Christ that they could endure suffering and death, because of Christ that they could be transformed from lives of vice to lives of virtue. Critical to all these benefits, moreover, was the conviction that Christ shared completely in the human condition, in order to empower and transform it.

The role of Christ for second- and third-century Christians of Type C was less definite. Christ is honored as a revealer of true knowledge, to be sure, but it is not always clear whether the revealer occupies a position superior to those who already also share in the divine spirit and light. In any case, those aspects of Christ most valued by Types A and B tend to be neglected or even denied by Type C. The Christ does not fully enter matter; the Christ does not truly die; the Christ does not have a bodily resurrection. And his teaching tends to be less about how to be virtuous in a crooked world than about how to keep oneself from the empirical world altogether.

IRENAEUS ON THE GNOSTICS

I will treat Irenaeus as an important figure in his own right in the next chapter. Here he provides an important outsider perspective on Type C Christians of the second century.[9] The Bishop of Lyons had predecessors and successors as a detector and critic of "heresies" or "parties" (*haireseis*) within the Christian religion, but his great work, *Detection and Overthrow of Falsely Named Gnosis* (*elenchou kai anatropēs tēs pseudōnomou gnōseōs*), written circa 180 in Greek but available to us mainly in the Latin translation commonly called *Adversus Haereses* ("Against Heresies"), is of singular importance as a comprehensive survey of the teachings he regarded as troubling in his own day and as a magisterially argued response to those teachings.[10] The degree of overlap between descriptions offered by Irenaeus and the content of some compositions deriving from Type C Christians increases our confidence in his contemporary knowledge of the figures and teachings he reports—even though his own authorial bias must be taken seriously.

When we compare the writings of Irenaeus with the firsthand compositions, we can better appreciate how his own perspective shaped his presentation.[11] In effect, Irenaeus treats the various heresies as philosophical schools: he focuses on the names of founders and their successors; he recites their doctrines—in this case taking the form of cosmogonic myths—and their ethics.[12] The approach is not unlike that of Diogenes Laertius in his *Lives of Eminent Philosophers*. Nothing approaching such a systematic display is found in the Type C compositions. Also distinctive to Irenaeus' account is the use of the sort of polemic against opponents that is common in disputes among philosophical schools in the Greco-Roman world.[13] Equally important is omission: the element that is perhaps most characteristic of the Type C compositions themselves, namely, the device of divine revelation, is totally absent from Irenaeus' account. Finally, Irenaeus considers a wider range of figures and teachings—such as Marcus, Marcion, Cerdo, and Simon—than are available for our analysis in any extant firsthand compositions.[14] I consider here only the descriptions in Irenaeus that correspond to the firsthand Type C compositions.

In Book 1 of *Adversus Haereses*, Irenaeus patiently recounts the myth of origins according to Valentinus' student Ptolemy.[15] The elaboration of eons in the Pleroma (divine fullness) serve to establish distance between the divine source and what will eventually appear as the material world and to locate the source of the visible world in passion and error (1.1.1–1.3.5).[16] Speaking of Achamoth, the offspring of Wisdom expelled from the Pleroma, Irenaeus reports, "Since she was involved with passion, and had been left outside and alone, she became subject to every aspect of manifold and diverse passion; she suffered grief, because she had not understood; fear, lest life should leave her just as light had done; uncertainty, at all of these; and everything in lack of acquaintance (*gnōsis*). . . . She—they say—accounts for the genesis of matter and essence of matter out of which this world came into being" (1.4.1–2). What came into being, however, was a mixture of elements, good and bad; some arose from her plunge into materiality, some from her essential participation in the divine, and some from her desire to return to the Pleroma: "one derived from her passion, and this was matter; another derived from her turning back, and this was the animate; another was what she brought forth, and this was the spiritual" (1.5.1).

Corresponding to this account of origins is the threefold designation of humans as consisting primarily of matter, or of soul (and therefore able to choose), or of spirit. The fates of the material and spiritual are fixed, but the psychic (those with souls) can turn either toward matter or spirit: "They postulate three species of human beings: spirituals; animates; those consisting of dust" (*Adversus Haereses*, 1.7.5). Corresponding to this threefold distinction is the difference between the visible church and the spiritual church: the first is an earthly representation of the spiritual church: "the latter, they think, is the human being that is within them, so that they have their soul from the craftsman, their bodies from dust, their fleshly elements from matter, and the spiritual human being from their mother Achamoth" (1.5.6).

The true self that alone is worth saving is not to be equated with the material shell but with the spiritual core. "Now of the three (elements) that exist, the material one, also called left, will—they say—necessarily perish, in that it is unable to receive any breath of incorruptibility. The animate one, also called right, will proceed in whatever direction it has an inclination toward, in that it is intermediate between the spiritual and the material. The spiritual has been sent so that it might be formed by being coupled to the animate and learning along with it during its time of residence in this place" (*Adversus Haereses*, 1.6.1). The end will come "when every spiritual element has been formed and perfected in acquaintance [*gnōsis*]" (1.6.1). In the meantime, the behavioral norms taught by the visible church are meant only for the psychic (animate) whose fate is yet undecided. They do not apply to the spiritual: "They hold to the doctrine that they are spiritual not by behavior, but by nature, and that they will be saved no matter what. . . . The spiritual element, which they themselves claim to be, cannot receive corruption, no matter what sorts of behavior it has to pass the time in the company of. . . . [W]hat leads one into the fullness is not behavior but the seed which was sent hither as an infant and grows to maturity in this place" (1.6.2).

Eschatology follows logically from such premises. "When all the seeds have grown to maturity," Achamoth and all the spiritual beings will be restored to their place of origin: "and the spirituals are supposed to put off their souls; become intellectual spirits; unrestrainedly and invisibly enter the fullness; and become brides of the angels that are with the savior." The psychics who have proven righteous will reside in a sort of in-between state: "the souls of the just, also, will gain repose in the place of the midpoint; for nothing animate (psychic) goes inside the fullness." And when all that deserves rescuing is rescued, then matter itself will be destroyed: "the fire that lurks within the world will flare up, catch fire, overcome all matter, be consumed along with it, and enter into definitive nonexistence" (*Adversus Haereses*, 1.7.1).

If spirit is good and eternal and matter is evil and transitory, it follows that the savior will participate in the material realm only ostensibly: "He became enveloped in a body that had animate essence but was constructed in some ineffable way so as to be visible, touchable, and capable of experiencing passion. And he did not take anything material—they say—for the material essence is not capable of receiving salvation" (*Adversus Haereses*, 1.6.1).

The heavenly savior descended into the earthly Jesus at the baptism in the form of a dove. His suffering was also only apparent: "It was not possible for him to suffer, since he was unrestrainable and invisible. Because of this, when the anointed was brought before Pilate, the spirit of the anointed that had been deposited with him was taken away. . . . What suffered, therefore, was what they consider to be the providential arrangement of events" (*Adversus Haereses*, 1.7.2). Having sketched the basic elements of this soteriology, Irenaeus displays the range of allegorical scriptural interpretation employed by the Valentinians to support their understanding of reality (1.8.1–5).[17]

Concerning the teaching of Basilides,[18] Irenaeus mentions two points of interest to my sketch of Religiousness C. First, Basilides declares that salvation is only of the soul; the body is by nature corruptible (*Adversus Haereses*, 1.24.5). This statement agrees with the one reported by Clement of Alexandria to the effect that Basilides interpreted Abraham's declaration in Genesis 23:4, "I am a stranger in the land, and a sojourner among you," to mean "that the elect are alien to the world, as if they were transcendent by nature" (*Stromata*, 4.165). Second, Basilides teaches that the Christ is an emissary from the Pleroma sent to humans to save them but was himself incapable of suffering. He "appeared on earth as a man, and he performed deeds of power. Hence he did not suffer. Rather, a certain Simon of Cyrene was forced to bear his cross for him and it was he who was ignorantly and erroneously crucified, being transformed by the other, so that he was taken for Jesus; while Jesus, for his part, assumed the form of Simon and stood by laughing at them. For because he was an incorporeal power and was the intellect of the unengendered parent, he was transformed however he willed. And thus he ascends to the one who had sent him, mocking them" (*Adversus Haereses*, 1.24.4).

Irenaeus also considers other teachers "a multitude of Gnostics [who] have sprung up, and have shown forth like mushrooms growing out of the ground" (*Adversus Haereses*, 1.29.1).[19] Among them as well we find elaborate mythic scenarios that serve to separate the all good world of spirit (the Pleroma) from the evil world of matter, while still maintaining some presence of spirit in the prison of matter. Thus, the portion of wisdom that was expelled from the Pleroma plunged into heavenly waters: "Bound, therefore, by a body composed of matter, and greatly weighed down by it, this (power) recovered it senses, and attempted to escape from the waters and ascend to its mother. But it could not do so, on account of the weight of the enveloping body. . . . When it had conceived a desire for the higher light and had received power, it put off this body in every respect and was freed from it" (1.30.3).

In this mythic account, Adam and Eve were originally nonmaterial (1.30.6), but their transgression led to their expulsion from a nonmaterial paradise into the realm of matter: "previously Adam and Eve had had nimble, shining, and as it were spiritual bodies that had been modeled at their creation; but when they came hither, these changed into darker, denser, and more sluggish ones." But the spark of light within them still enabled them to realize their true nature: "They came to a recollection of themselves, and recognized that they were naked, and that their bodies were made of matter. And they recognized that they carried death about with them. And they existed patiently, recognizing that bodies would envelop them only for a time" (*Adversus Haereses*, 1.30.9).

Among these Gnostics as well, the Christ is understood to descend into Jesus, and it was this Christ that did wonders, though he was not recognized in his true identity even by his followers. It was Jesus who was crucified while "the anointed (Christ) himself, along with wisdom (Sophia) departed for the incorruptible realm." After his death, his disciples who claimed that he had a bodily resurrection were mistaken. He was raised "in a kind of body that they call inanimate and spiritual" while his worldly parts returned to the world, but they spoke of "his animate body as if it were a worldly one" (*Adversus Haereses*, 1.30.13). The end-time happens when Jesus "receives unto himself the souls of those who have become acquainted with him, once they have left their worldly flesh. . . . This end will take place when the entire secretion of the spirit of light is gathered together and caught up into the realm of incorruptibility" (1.30.14).

Although Irenaeus is contemptuous and dismissive toward those he regards as deviant from the church's rule of faith, he conscientiously reports their views as he has come to know them. The sheer volume and variety of information he conveys as well as the energy he expends in refutation testify to the fact that a significant number of those calling themselves Christians in the second century saw themselves as spirit trapped in matter, sought in Christ the revelation of their true identity, and longed for a release from the entrapment of fleshly existence. The happy discovery of compositions written by such Christians confirms Irenaeus' report on the most essential points and makes clear that religion as transcending the world was a significant presence in second-century Christianity.

WRITINGS FROM NAG-HAMMADI

The discovery at Nag-Hammadi in 1945 of 13 codices containing 52 Coptic translations of originally Greek compositions espousing many of the views—and in some cases, bearing the same titles—identified by heresiologists expanded and complicated the study of the way of being Christian commonly called Gnostic.[20] Immediately striking was the variety of writings contained in the volumes: in addition to revelation-type compositions, we find tractates of the Hermetic literature that I earlier identified as the prime representative of Type C religion in paganism; moral discourses in the form of aphorisms, one recognizably Greco-Roman (*Sentences of Sextus*), another recognizably Christian (*Teachings of Silvanus*); an *Act of Peter* that would fit perfectly in the forms of the apocryphal *Acts of Peter* already known to us; and even a portion of Plato's *Republic*.[21] Such a mélange of compositions raises the question of the function of the collection: was the binding together of such disparate writings a matter of convenience, or was it a religious statement?

Matching the eclectic character of the collection is a diversity of outlook and expression. We nowhere find the neat lines of mythic schemata presented by Irenaeus; instead we encounter a hodgepodge of voices and viewpoints in anything but a systematic presentation. Scholars have noted ideological differences between compositions that are "Sethian" in outlook (hostility to the creator God of the Jewish scripture and little explicit Christian content) and those that are "Valentinian" (more explicitly Christian and milder in tone).[22] In terms of expression, compositions range from the wildly speculative and ecstatic (*Gospel of the Egyptians*) through the richly poetic (*Gospel of Truth*) to the soberly didactic (*Treatise on the Resurrection*). The Nag-Hammadi codices encompass a greater diversity even than that found in the New Testament collection. We cannot say whether anyone associated with these collections ever read all of them together as a collection; it is perhaps more likely that compositions were written and read individually, and the act of binding them into volumes reinforced the impression of a unified vision.

Another aspect of these writings for which heresiologists did not prepare us is the genuine religious spirit that suffuses the compositions. The polemical aims of an Irenaeus or Epiphanius (perhaps deliberately) obscured the religious sensibilities of the Gnostic Christians. Their mythic speculations therefore appeared as intellectual self-indulgence or mischief; the attack on their morals made them seem to be charlatans who deluded the gullible for their own gain. When reading the actual compositions in the Nag-Hammadi collection, however, it is difficult to deny the sense that they were written by people who were motivated by religious convictions just as authentic as those held by the Christians of Type A who produced apocryphal acts and gospels and the Christians of Type B who wrote apologies for the faith as a form of philosophy. In many of these writings, it is possible to detect the classic impulses of mysticism.[23] We find in them the longing for the absolute and eternal, driven by a sense of despair at being trapped by corruptible matter.

A particular advantage given to my analysis by the Nag-Hammadi writings is the placement of specifically and explicitly Christian compositions with other writings without any Christian element but sharing a profound cosmological dualism and search for salvation through revealed knowledge concerning the self. My argument that "ways of being Christian" are in continuity with "ways of being religious" in Greco-Roman culture is given real support by the presence, cheek by jowl, of Hermetic writings and Gnostic gospels.

In addition to such juxtapositions, the process of combination and recombination among the respective writings appears complex. It is clear, for example, that the tractate *Eugnostos the Blessed*, which has no Christian element at all, and the *Sophia of Jesus Christ* are literarily related—probably through the "Christianization" of the earlier text.[24] Quite apart from the structure of the various myths, the sheer fact of gathering such disparate compositions together suggests the desire to place Christian wisdom within the context of a larger and less particular vision of the world. While observing appropriate caution, then, we are allowed to show how the "non-Christian" and "Christian" texts manifest a deep agreement in what I have called religious sensibility. I will treat two such writings and then turn to others that are explicitly Christian in character.

The *Zostrianos* and *Allogenes* are tractates that bear no Christian stamp and are known even outside the circle of inner Christian debate.[25] *Zostrianos* recounts the spiritual ascent of the Gnostic teacher and the revelations he receives from heavenly revealers.[26] Zostrianos is able to ascend because he "had parted by means of intellect, from the corporeal darkness within [him] together with the animate chaos and desirous femininity within that chaos" (1.10). He learns by revelation that "the [kind of] person that gets saved is the one who seeks to understand and so to discover, the self and the intellect" (44.1–5). But such a search is impeded by involvement with materiality. Thus the person without enlightenment "come[s] down into the realm of generation . . . becomes speechless at the pains and infinity of material; and, although possessing immortal power, is bound in the body's advance . . . bound in strong fetters that cut by all means of evil spirits" (45.25–46.13). The one so bound needs to be saved through revelation of their true condition: "Beings are ordained to be in charge of their salvation. . . . They are incorruptible, for [they are] patterns of salvation, in which each (saved person) is stamped . . . and it is by being stamped that the person receives power from the same one of them and has that glory for a helper" (46.24–26). There are those, however, so locked in materiality that they cannot escape, "and since they have become uncomprehending of God, they shall perish" (128.10–13).

Through his heavenly ascent, multiple initiations (baptisms), and revelations of his authentic identity, Zostrianos becomes one of the emissaries who reenters the material realm in order to enlighten others. Having been empowered, "I descended to the perceptible world and I put on my ignorant material image. Although it was ignorant, I bestowed power upon it and went about preaching truth unto all. . . . I awakened a multitude that were lost" (130.4–14). The composition closes with the sermon that he preaches far and wide: "Elevate your divine element as being god. . . . Seek immutable unengenderedness. . . . Do not bathe yourselves in death, nor surrender yourselves unto ones who are inferior to you as though they were superior. Flee the madness and fetter of femininity and choose for yourselves the salvation of masculinity. . . . Save yourselves so that your soul may be saved. . . . Many fetters and chastisers are surrounding you. Flee in the short time that remains before destruction overtakes you! Behold the light! Flee the darkness! Do not let yourselves be enslaved unto destruction!" (130.19–132.4).

The tractate called *Allogenes,* or "The Foreigner," begins with an extended discourse from the female deity Youel, which Allogenes records for his son Messos (45.1–57).[27] He is to guard these revelations "in great silence and great mystery, because they are not spoken to anyone except those who are worthy, those who are able to hear" (52.20). Allogenes prays that he might receive such revelation (55.30). The second portion of the tractate describes Allogenes' mystical ascent. He prepared himself for a hundred years (57.27) and beheld the divine Barbelo, the savior:[28] "after being caught up by the eternal light out of the garment that I was wearing, and taken to a holy place, no resemblance of which could be shown forth in the world, then by great blessedness I beheld all the things that I had heard about" (56.26–38).

Allogenes is told that his blessedness resides in silence: "if you want to stand at rest, withdraw to reality and you will find it standing at rest and still, after the resemblance of what is really still and restrains all these (spiritual beings) in quietness and lack of activity" (59.18–24). If he remains in stillness, perfection can be achieved "after the pattern that resides within you," and that perfection does not become dispersed in external activities (59.37). Allogenes therefore listens, and "within me was stillness of silence. I listened to blessedness, through which I understood myself as I really am" (60.12–19). The remainder of the composition makes clear that the divine realm in itself is incomprehensible (61–68). But this by no means cancels the essential saving knowledge that has come to Allogenes: "And when I wished to stand firmly at rest, I withdrew to reality, which I found to be standing at rest and still, after an image and a re-semblance of that (image) which I was wearing. Through a manifestation of the undivided and the still, I became full of manifestation. (And) through a first manifestation of the unrecognizable, I [understood] it at the same time that I was uncomprehending of it. And from the latter I received power, having got-ten eternal strength from it" (60.24–38).

These two examples drawn from the Nag-Hammadi codices bear the clear marks of Type C religiosity in the Greco-Roman world such as we have seen also in the Hermetic literature. There is no optimism about the material world and no sense that the divine *dynamis* is active within it. Instead, salvation from the ignorance and grief associated with material existence is sought from divine revelation of the true self within elect humans that consists of spirit and the eventual liberation of that authentic self from the captivity of earthly existence. These compositions suggest that the message concerning truth is made avail-able to all through designated divine emissaries but that only some hear and re-spond appropriately. Others sink further into the mire by involving themselves in worldly distractions.

The *Apocryphon of John* illustrates the way in which an explicitly Christian framework could be placed around a revelation that had little if any Christian content.[29] The framing story resembles the legendary elaborations typical of the apocryphal acts: the apostle John is challenged by a Pharisee concerning the present location of "the man you used to follow" (1.8). Although John re-sponds that "He has returned to the place from which he came" (1.11), the query causes him consternation; he begins to pose a series of questions concerning "the savior" and his origin (1.17–26).

In the midst of his consternation, he is visited by a revealer figure, who appears in different shapes and is not explicitly named but who declares that he will reveal "what exists and what has come to be and what must come to be" (*Apocryphon of John*, 2.16). The revealer, in fact, is not Jesus but "the perfect forethought of the entirety (Pleroma)," that is, Barbelo (see 30.11). From this point forward, the composition has no specific reference to Jesus; the "anointed" (Christ) appears as a heavenly Aeon (7. 10; 7.19; 9.2) but not as an earthly figure; the first chapters of Genesis, but no writings of the New Testament, are engaged. Only the final words added to the manuscript, "Jesus is the anointed (Christ). Amen" (32.6), remind the reader of the opening section and give the composition a Christian frame.

After a lengthy exposition of the cosmic progression from unity to plurality in the realm of the Pleroma (*Apocryphon of John*, 2.26–13.15)—an exposition that resembles Irenaeus' report on the Valentinan myth of origins—the composition comes to the account of origins in Genesis 1–4 and interprets them in light of the preceding myth. Adam's material body is described as an imprisonment of the spirit: "They [the inimical rulers] brought him into the shadow of death . . . of the ignorance of darkness, and desire, and their counterfeit spirit. That is the cave of the remodeling of the body in which the brigands clothed the human being, the bond of forgetfulness. And he became a mortal human being" (21.4–13). Mortality, in turn, is perpetuated by sexual intercourse: "And to the present day sexual intercourse, which originated from the first ruler, has remained. And in the female who belonged to Adam it sowed a seed of desire. And by sexual intercourse it raised up birth in the image of the bodies. And it supplied them some of its counterfeit spirit" (24.26–32). Humans, moreover, were afflicted with forgetfulness of their higher self: "They were given the water of forgetfulness by the first ruler, so that they might not know themselves and where they had come from" (25.7–8).

In response to questions from John, the revealer makes clear that the majority of humans remain locked in matter, forgetful and ignorant, subject to all kinds of passions, locked in the prison of their bodies (27.1–10; 27.21–27; 28.21–31; 30.1–4). But there are others to whom the mysteries of salvation can be revealed, to those "who belong to the immovable race, upon whom the spirit of life will descend and dwell with power. They will attain salvation and become perfect. And they will become worthy of greatnesses . . . purified of every imperfection . . . being anxious for nothing but incorruptibility, restrained by nothing but the subsistent entity of the flesh which they wear, awaiting the time when they will be visited by those beings who take away. Such souls are worthy of eternal, incorruptible life and calling; abiding all things and enduring all things so that they might complete the contest and inherit eternal life" (25.20–26.3).

The soteriology of the *Apocryphon of John* is given full expression in the poem that concludes the revelation from Barbelo. The one who existed from the beginning as "the richness of the light" and "memory of the fullness" declares that Barbelo enters repeatedly into the darkness and chaos of materiality in order to save souls. A first time, "I traveled in the greatness of the darkness and I continued until I entered the midst of the prison" (30.17). A second time, "I entered the midst of the darkness and the interior of Hades, striving for my governance" (30.25). And then a third time, it entered the darkness, "the midst of their prison which is the prison of the body" (31.1–4). And in that form, it called to those who could hear, "O Listener, arise from heavy sleep. . . . It is I who am the forethought of the uncontaminated light. . . . Arise! Keep in mind that you are the person who has listened . . . and be wakeful (now that you have come) out of heavy sleep and out of the garment in the interior of Hades" (31.10–20). Barbelo seals those who have heard "so that from henceforth death might not have power over that person" and returns to the perfect eternal realm (31.21–37).

The Nag-Hammadi collection also contains compositions whose Christian character is unmistakable. Preeminent among them is the *Gospel of Truth*, a sermon that may derive from Valentinus himself.[30] It completely lacks the elaborate mythic structure that we have seen as characteristic in the compositions reviewed to this point. The characters in the drama are simply the Father (the unknowable God), the Word or Son who makes God known, and people in the world who are the ignorant or the knowing (Gnostic). The poetic language of the composition is thoroughly suffused with the diction of scripture, not only Genesis—which figures so prominently in other texts—but New Testament writings as well.[31] The designation "Gospel" is a misnomer if one thinks in terms of the canonical or apocryphal narratives, yet the composition begins with the "proclamation (*euangelion*) of truth" not so much in terms of recounting the deeds of Christ—although these are touched on—but in terms of the effect of the "grace that was received from the father of truth" (16.31) on humans: "the term 'proclamation' (gospel) refers to the manifestation of hope, a discovery for those who are searching for him" (17.1).

The soteriology of this explicitly, even exuberantly, Christian composition, however, fits comfortably within Religiousness C. The human condition is one of ignorance of the father, which causes agitation, fear, and error—"and error found strength and labored at her matter in emptiness . . . preparing by means of the power, in beauty, a substitute for truth" (*Gospel of Truth*, 17.17). Error dwells in a kind of fog of forgetfulness and fear that seduces people into thinking it real (17.36). It creates "disturbance and instability and indecisiveness and division" (29.1); it generates futile activity like that of "a dream in the night" (30.1).

In the *Gospel of Truth*, such forgetfulness cannot be overcome by oneself; rather, it requires revelation: "Acquaintance [*gnōsis*] from the father and the appearance of his son gave them a means to comprehend" (30.23). It was Jesus who brought this knowledge to humans: "Jesus Christ shed light upon those who were, because of forgetfulness, in darkness." His work is fundamentally that of enlightenment: "He enlightened them and gave them a way, and the way is the truth, about which he instructed them," and those who received his teaching "discovered him within them—the inconceivable uncontained, the father, who is perfect, who created the entirety" (18.18–31). The recognition of Jesus, therefore, is also a recognition of their own true self, for this is the truth Jesus conveys.

The *Gospel of Truth* pays close attention to the death of Jesus. Because Jesus revealed the truth of the father in the realm of ignorance, "error became angry at him and persecuted him. She was constrained by him and became inactive. He was nailed to a tree and became fruit of the father's acquaintance [*gnōsis*]" (18.21–26). Although Jesus was "a guide, at peace and occupied with classrooms . . . [who] came forward and uttered the word as a teacher" (19.17–19), the worldly wise opposed and despised him. "Therefore the merciful and faithful Jesus became patient and accepted the sufferings even unto taking up that book [namely, "the living book of the living; 19.34]: inasmuch as he knew that his death would mean life for many" (20.10–14). That Jesus died so others could live sounds on the surface as though it was drawn straight from the Gospels (see Mark 10:45).

The interpretation given to this death, however, is distinctive. Jesus enters into incorruptibility and eternal life in order to bring true self-knowledge to the elect: "Having entered upon the empty ways of fear, he escaped the clutches of those who had been stripped naked by forgetfulness, for he was acquaintance (*gnōsis*) and completion, and read out their contents. . . . And those who would learn, namely the living enrolled in the book of the living, learn about themselves, recovering themselves from the father and returning to him" (*Gospel of Truth*, 21.1–7). Those who are written in the book are destined for such self-realization (21.8–23) and are called by Jesus to such self-recognition: "So that whoever has acquaintance [*gnōsis*] is from above, and if called, hears, replies, and turns to the one who is calling, and goes to him. . . . Those who gain acquaintance (*gnōsis*) in this way know whence they have come and whither they will go" (22.4–13).

The process of return involves a focus on stability rather than on activity, a cultivation of the spirit rather than of matter: "It is in unity that all will gather themselves, and it is by acquaintance [*gnōsis*] that all will purify themselves out of multiplicity into unity, consuming matter within themselves as fire, and darkness by light, and death by life" (*Gospel of Truth*, 25.7–22). The human condition of error and ignorance can be compared to the breaking of jars (26.7–8), and the state of blessedness can be described in terms of rest and repose (41.3–7). Maintaining this condition demands an attention to oneself: "Focus your attention upon yourselves. Do not focus your attention upon others, that is, ones whom you have expelled. Do not return to eat what you have vomited forth. . . . Do the will of the father, for you are from him" (33.11–30).

At the end of the composition, the author praises the state of those who have recognized their true identity: "Such are they who have possessions from above, from the immeasurable greatness, straining toward the solitary and the perfect, he who is a mother to them. And they will not descend into Hades, nor do they have envy and groaning; nor is death within them. Rather, they repose in that being who gives unto himself repose, and in the vicinity of truth they are neither weary nor entangled. But it is precisely they who are the truth" (*Gospel of Truth*, 42.11–25). The *Gospel of Truth* is far more complex, subtle, and beautiful than could ever be imagined from the descriptions of Christian Gnosticism by Irenaeus. The fundamental accuracy of Irenaeus' portrayal on the central point nevertheless remains: here is a way of being Christian in which sin is ignorance and error, in which salvation is revealed through knowledge of one's own identity, and in which the role of Jesus is that of revealer and teacher.

Another Valentinian composition in the Nag-Hammadi collection is the *Treatise on the Resurrection*, which takes the form of an expository letter from a teacher to a certain Rheginus.[32] In spirit, it is close to the *Gospel of Truth* and like that composition has clear references to New Testament passages and few traces of a "larger" Gnostic myth.[33] If it did not appear in the same compilation with other more obviously Gnostic compositions, even the allusions to "repose" or "rest" in the opening lines (43.29–44.1) could be read as allusions to the New Testament Letter to the Hebrews rather than to the *Gospel of Truth*.[34] The tone of the letter is pastoral rather than speculative: the author does not approve of those who try to become learned by solving problems they cannot handle (43.25). Nevertheless, the author's understanding of the resurrection finds a natural home in the soteriological framework of the Nag-Hammadi collection.

The author reminds Rheginus that humans take on flesh when coming into the world,[35] but this "bodily envelope" is not the essential self; it is, rather, precisely what causes the essential self's alienation (*Treatise on the Resurrection*, 47.1–18). The true self is not material but spiritual. The material world is but an apparition (48.13–16; 48.26), and our life in the body is but a garment for our true self: "since we are manifestly present in this world, the world is what we wear [like a garment]" (45.28). Resurrection, then, cannot be understood in terms of the body having a future but must be understood in terms of the realization of the true self that is the spirit within humans.

Christ's resurrection is the model. He was both human and divine, "so that he might conquer death through being son of God and that through the human son might come to pass the return to the fullness [Pleroma], since from the beginning he existed as a seed of the truth from above before there came into being this cosmic structure in which lordships and divinities have become so numerous" (*Treatise on the Resurrection*, 44.27–35). Christ's resurrection, therefore, was the realization of the divine element within him and the discarding of the material frame: "I mean that laying aside the corruptible world, he exchanged it for an incorruptible eternal realm. And he raised himself up, having 'swallowed' the visible by means of the invisible and gave us the way to our immortality" (45.15–22). The resurrection of Christians, then, is a matter of being "drawn upward by him as rays are drawn by the sun, restrained by nothing. This is the resurrection of the spirit, which 'swallows' resurrection of the soul along with resurrection of the flesh" (45.28–46.1).

Resurrection is, in fact, the self-realization by the Gnostic of his or her authentic self: "But what is the meaning of resurrection? It is the uncovering at any given time of the elements that have arisen" (*Treatise on the Resurrection*, 48.3–4). The author here means the spirit of the one who has come to awareness: "The thought of those who are saved will not perish, the intellect of those who have acquaintance [*gnōsis*] with such an object will not perish" (46.23–25). The resurrection is not future but present in the experience of *gnōsis*: "It is what stands at rest; and the revealing of what truly exists. And it is what one receives in exchange for the circumstances of this world: and a migration into newness" (48.33–36). The full realization of this resurrection will happen at the death of the believers, when "the inferior element takes a loss" (47.22) and the spirit is liberated completely: "whether one who is saved will, upon taking off his body, be immediately saved, let no one doubt this" (47.35–36).

The truth of the resurrection demands concentration on what is eternal in the self rather than what is transitory: "therefore do not concentrate on particulars, O Rheginus, nor live according to the dictates of the flesh. . . . Leave the state of dispersion and bondage, and then you already have the resurrection" (*Treatise on the Resurrection*, 49.9–15). The Christian practice corresponding to such a view of the resurrection is withdrawal from involvement from the body: "Everyone should practice in many ways to gain release from this element [the body] so that one might not wander aimlessly but rather might recover one's former state of being" (49.30–34).

Finally, it is worth noting the way another thoroughly Christian composition within the Nag-Hammadi collection, the *Gospel of Thomas*, fits within the religious sensibility I have been describing.[36] It is undoubtedly the most analyzed of the compositions found in the Coptic collection for obvious reasons: its assemblage of 114 sayings from Jesus raises questions concerning its relationship to previous *agrapha*, to the canonical Gospels, to the hypothetical sayings collection Q, to the historical Jesus, and to Gnosticism.[37] Two facts make answering questions concerning its religious sensibility difficult: the lack of a narrative that might provide an interpretive framework for the sayings and the presence of other compositions in the same collection that can, if invoked, supply precisely that interpretive key.[38]

The choice of materials in the *Gospel of Thomas* is at least suggestive. There is no account of Jesus' human deeds and no story of Jesus' passion, death, and resurrection. The book consists completely in sayings, introduced with "Jesus said." The basic image of Jesus is that of teacher or revealer. The prologue introduces him as "the living Jesus." The designation can point to a postresurrection appearance or, in the framework of the *Gospel of Truth* and *Tractate on the Resurrection*, to Jesus as divine revealer at whatever point in his appearance. The revelations of Jesus, furthermore, are designated as "secret" or "obscure," indicating that they are to be understood within the context of an esoteric rather than an exoteric code. Finally, the revelatory words themselves bear the promise of life: "whoever finds the meaning of these sayings will not taste death" ([1] 32.10–12).

Self-referential statements by Jesus likewise cohere with the esoteric framework found in other Nag-Hammadi compositions. He says, "I am the light (that presides) over all. It is I who am the entirety; it is from me that the entirety has come, and to me that the entirety goes. Split a piece of wood: I am there. Lift a stone and you will find me there" (*Gospel of Thomas*, [77] 46.22–27). Jesus said, "I stood at rest in the midst of the world. And unto them I was shown forth incarnate; I found them all intoxicated. . . . When they shake off their wine then they will have a change of heart" ([28] 38.20–29). With reference to those who do have a change of heart, Jesus says, "Whoever drinks from my mouth will become like me; I, too, will become that person, and to that person obscure things will be shown forth" ([108] 50.28–29).

In a statement that resembles Matthew 11:25–27, but with a special significance to the term "repose," Jesus says, "Come to me, for my yoke is easy and my
lordship is mild, and you fill find repose for yourselves" (*Gospel of Thomas*, [90]
48.16–19). We have already seen the significance of the term "repose" for the
desired state of the Gnostic Christian. We find it again in this passage: "His
disciples said to him, 'Will the repose of the dead come to pass, and when will
the new world come?' He said to them, 'That [repose] which you are waiting for
has come, but for your part you do not recognize it" ([51] 42.7–10).

Such statements, in turn, find a context in others that point to a larger mythic
scheme: "The disciples said to Jesus, 'Tell us how our end will come to pass.'
Jesus said, 'Then have you laid bare the beginning, so that you are seeking the
end? For the end will be where the beginning is. Blessed is the person who
stands at rest in the beginning. And that person will be acquainted with the end
and will not taste death" (*Gospel of Thomas*, [18] 36.9–14). Here we see the notion of a "repose" that consists in the *gnōsis* of the true self, which makes issues
of "beginning" and "end" irrelevant: the Gnostic Christian already lives in the
end-time of the authentic resurrection.

A similar framework is demanded by this statement: "Jesus said, 'It is amazing
if it was for the spirit that flesh came into existence. And it is amazing indeed if
spirit [came into existence] for the sake of the body. But as for me, I am amazed
at how this great wealth has come to dwell in this poverty" (*Gospel of Thomas*,
[29] 38.31–34). The mythic framework is particularly obvious in this statement of
Jesus: "If they say to you, 'Where are you from?' say to them, 'It is from the light
that we have come—from the place where light, of its own accord alone, came
into existence and [stood at rest]. And it has been shown forth in their image.'
And if they say to you, 'Is it you?' say, 'we are its offspring, and we are the chosen
of the living father.' If they ask you, 'What is the sign of your father within you,'
say, 'It is movement and repose'" ([50] 41.30–42.4).

The few who are chosen by Jesus for such an esoteric existence (*Gospel of
Thomas*, [23] 38.1–2) are to bear the light within themselves ([24] 38.3–9). They
have brought diversity into unity, difference into sameness ([22] 37.20–24; [114]
51.18–24). They are like children who are naked before the onslaughts of the
material world ([21] 36.33–37.4), who are unafraid in their nakedness ([37] 39.27–-
29) and will be exalted even more than John the Baptist because of their little-
ness ([46] 41.6–10). They bear the kingdom of heaven within themselves ([3]
32.19–33.2; [70] 45.29–31) and await the revelation of what is now hidden from
the eyes of others ([5–6] 33.10–22). Until that time of full disclosure, they are to
distance themselves from involvement with the body: "Jesus said, 'Wretched is
the body that depends upon a body. And wretched is the soul that depends on

these two'" ([87] 48.4–6); he also said, "Woe to the flesh that depends upon a soul. Woe to the soul that depends on the flesh" ([112] 51.10–11).

The dualism that privileges the soul rather than the body and requires withdrawal from the body for the good of the soul extends as well to any engagement with the world. In two strikingly similar statements, Jesus says, "Whoever has become acquainted with the world has found the body, and the world is not worthy of the one who has found the body" (*Gospel of Thomas*, [80] 47.12); and "Whoever has become acquainted with the world has found a corpse, and the world is not worthy of the one who has found a corpse" ([56] 42.29). The practice of abstention from worldly engagement is explicitly commanded by Jesus: "Blessed are those who are solitary and superior, for you will find the kingdom; for since you come from it you shall return to it" ([49] 41.27–29). And again, he says, "If you do not abstain from the world, you will not find the kingdom. If you do not make the sabbath a sabbath you will not behold the father" ([27] 38.17–19). The second of these statements explicates the first: keeping the Sabbath in the framework of this gospel means maintaining the "repose" of naked, childlike identity rather than being dissipated in worldly engagement. The ideal of withdrawal is best and most briefly expressed in the saying that consists simply in the command, "Be passersby" ([42] 40.19).

The evidence brought forward in this chapter demonstrates that some Christians of the second and third centuries were perceived by others and saw themselves as a distinct "way of being Christian." In contrast to those who celebrated the benefits released by the Holy Spirit through miracles of healing and exorcism or through the miracle of moral endurance in bodily suffering—all of these forms of battle with demons—such Christians emphasized inner knowledge of their origin and destiny and withdrew from engagement with the material world. In contrast also to those who saw Christianity in terms of a philosophy that combined right doctrine and moral transformation, these Christians based themselves on secret revealed knowledge and treasured the "repose" that enabled their souls to survive the time of imprisonment in the body. They display, in short, precisely the characteristics of Religiousness C; authentic religion is not a matter of participation in divine benefits in the world or of the moral transformation of the self; it is, rather, a triumph of the essential self (the spirit) over the material world that holds it captive.

Both the strong sense of election and separateness—not to say superiority—that distinguished such Christians from the common crowd in the great church and the characterization of them as "heretical" have served to isolate and make "other" the Gnostic Christians,[39] obscuring the fact that the writers and readers of compositions such as the *Gospel of Truth* and the *Gospel of Thomas* represented, in reality, one of three "ways of being Christian" that I have identified in the second and third century. In the next chapter, I consider the fourth.

15

STABILIZING THE WORLD IN
SECOND- AND THIRD-CENTURY
CHRISTIANITY

In Greco-Roman religion, the fourth type of religiousness found expression especially among those who served as priests and ministers. On one hand, it can be seen as the supply side to Religiousness A, with which it is in closest agreement; rather than focusing on participation in the benefits given by the divine *dynamis* as made available in the round of religious practices, it focuses on making such practices available—via the keepers of the temples, the hierophants at the Mysteries, the patrons of religious associations, the sponsors of civic liturgies. They make possible and perform the sacrifices that form such a central aspect of pagan religion. On the other hand, this religious sensibility finds expression in a theoretical concern for the function of religion in society. Thus, we found in Plutarch not only a priest of the god Apollo at Delphi but a passionate defender of religion as the basis for Greek culture, against the equal threats of atheism and superstition.

It is no surprise to find Religiousness D absent from the writings of the New Testament. Earliest Christianity consisted in a loosely associated collection of local assemblies that were each sociologically marginal and powerless. The Christian message concerning the resurrection and second coming of Jesus was, in addition, threatening to any notion of a stable and enduring social order. We can note, for example, that in the New Testament, the technical language of sacrifice and priesthood, such as *prospherein dōra* ("offering gifts") and *prospherein thysia* ("offering sacrifice"), is restricted to descriptions of Jewish and Gentile practices (1 Cor 10:18; Heb 5:1; 7:27; 8:3; 9:9, 23, 26; 10:1, 5, 8, 11; 11:4) or to the death of Jesus (Rom 3:25; Heb 10:12; Eph 5:2) or is used metaphorically for Christian faith and obedience (Rom 12:1; 1 Pet 2:5; Heb 13:15–16), for effort on behalf of the community (Rom 15:16), and for a life of service to others (Phil 2:17; 4:18). The language is never applied to Christian worship.

As for concern with the stability and good order of society through religious practice, the apparent exception in the New Testament collection—the letters of Paul to his delegates Timothy and Titus—proves the point. The small amount of information that can be gleaned from them concerning leadership in the assembly is clearly both local rather than general and intimately connected to the structure of the household. Offices correspond to those found in other Hellenistic associations, including the synagogue. The concern is entirely with the moral qualities of the leaders; we learn little directly about their functions. What is most surprising is that although 1 Timothy 3:15 speaks of the household (*oikos*) as the "assembly of the living God" (*ekklēsia theou zōntos*), which could easily be taken, as it is in other Pauline letters, as a metaphorical designation of the assembly as the temple, nothing else in the letter exploits that designation. The leaders are not identified as priests; indeed, absolutely no theological legitimation is provided for local leadership in assemblies.

We would not expect the full emergence of Religiousness D in the second and third Christian centuries, for the simple reason that Christianity was still far from being the imperial religion: it was still marginal within society, still without legal property, still without official sanction as a cult, still—and increasingly—subject to persecution. Nevertheless, it is possible to trace some of the elements making up Religiousness D developing during this period. In this chapter, I begin with a return to Clement, Ignatius, and Justin, noting how they begin to use sacrificial language with respect to Christian cultic acts and ministers. I then consider some of the compositions known as "Church Orders" for insight into institutional and ritual development, before turning to a controversy involving the celebration of Easter that demanded coordinated efforts among bishops. Finally, I consider two writers of the period who can rightly be thought of in terms of Religiousness D, namely, Irenaeus of Lyons and Cyprian of Carthage.

BISHOPS AND CULT

In the second century, three writers provide important clues to three aspects of Religiousness D as it developed within Christianity: (1) the emerging role of bishops with explicit theological legitimation; (2) the liturgical role played by bishops; and (3) the use of cultic language for the assembly, the bishop, and the Eucharistic prayer of the community. I speak of "development" on these points,

because as I have suggested, the New Testament provides no theological legitimation for such leadership; the position of bishop in the New Testament appears primarily as administrative and didactic, and the Greco-Roman language
of sacrifice is not explicitly connected to the Eucharist.

I have already analyzed 1 *Clement* as exemplifying Religiousness B, and I
think that designation best fits its religious sensibility and mode of argumentation. The sheer fact that Clement writes at the end of the first century in the
name of "the church of God which sojourns in Rome" to "the church of God
which sojourns in Corinth," however, also says something about the author's
sense of church and authority. The sending and receiving of emissaries between the communities also points to a *koinōnia* that was actively practiced
(1 *Clem*, 65.1). Of special interest to the present discussion is that Clement's
concern for harmony in the Corinthian community is intimately linked to a
specific understanding of the authority vested in bishops. The apostles knew
that there would be competition for this office, so they appointed bishops and
provided for their succession (44.1–2). It is not right, therefore, to overturn those
who hold position legitimately according to that succession (44.3): "For our sin
is not small, if we eject from the episcopate *those who have blamelessly and ho-
lily offered its sacrifices*" (44.4, emphasis added).[1] Here, Clement connects the
authority of bishops to a liturgical role and describes that liturgical role in terms
of sacrifice (*prospherein ta dōra*, or offering the gifts).

In an earlier passage Clement speaks about the importance of observing the
proper order commanded by the Master (40.1-4): "He commanded us to celebrate sacrifices and services [*tas te prosphoras kai leitourgias epiteleisthai*] and
that it should not be thoughtlessly or disorderly, but at fixed times and hours . . .
so then those who offer their oblations [*poiountes tas prosphoras*] at the appointed seasons are acceptable and blessed [*euprosdektoi te kai makarioi*]."
Again, we see the technical language of sacrifice. To what extent is Clement arguing from analogy to the cult of Israel, and to what extent is he simply appropri-
ating it for Christian worship? It is difficult to say, as the following sentence
indicates: "For to the high Priest his proper ministrations are allotted, and to the
priests the proper place has been appointed, and on Levites their proper services
have been imposed. The layman [*ho laïkos*] is bound by the ordinances of the
laity" (40.5).

The next section clearly appears to be arguing from analogy to Israel, for
Clement speaks of sacrifices being offered only in Jerusalem and only by the
high priest (41.2). His overall point, then, is that there should be good order in
worship: "Let each one of us, brethren, be well pleasing to God in his own
rank, and have a good conscience, not transgressing the appointed rules of his

ministration [*tēs leitourgias autou*]" (41.1). But Clement appears to be perfectly comfortable with the inference that the bishop, as head of the community, plays a role in worship analogous to that of the high priest.

Ignatius was even bolder in asserting an authority to teach churches other than his own. Even as he made his way as a prisoner to Rome, the bishop of Antioch dispatched emissaries to communities throughout Asia Minor and sent them hortatory letters.[2] The constant theme of these letters is unity, and this unity is expressed in terms of harmony with the bishop and presbytery, while harmony is articulated through submission to the authority of the bishop and presbytery.[3] Ignatius is the first to speak of the *katholikē ekklēsia* (Ign. *Smyr.*, 8.2) in terms of assemblies so linked together, in contrast to unauthorized assemblies. As support for such submission to the authority of the bishop (and presbytery), Ignatius brings forward a variety of theological warrants. This institutional arrangement was instituted by the will of Jesus (Ign. *Eph.*, 3.2). He praises the deacon Zotion, who is "subject to the bishop as to the grace of God and to the presbytery as to the law of Jesus Christ" (Ign. *Magn.*, 2.1). The converse is someone separated "from Jesus Christ and from the bishop and the ordinances of the apostles" (Ign. *Tral.*, 7.1).

As the last statement shows, Ignatius was particularly fond of merging the institutional leadership of the assembly with the divine persons. Speaking of his fellowship with the Ephesian bishop as "not human but spiritual," he adds, "how much more do I count you blessed who are so united with him as the church is with Jesus Christ and as Jesus Christ is with the Father" (Ign. *Eph.*, 5.2).

Again, "As many as belong to God and Jesus Christ—these are with the bishop" (Ign. *Phil.*, 3.2), and "the Lord then forgives all who repent, if their repentance lead to the unity of God and the council of the bishop" (8.1). Indeed, "it is clear that we must regard the bishop as the Lord himself" (Ign. *Eph.*, 6.1), because "the bishop is a type [*typos*] of the father" (Ign. *Tral.*, 3.1), and respect shown the bishop is equivalent to respect paid to God (Ign. *Tral.*, 3.1–2). Ignatius says, "Let us then be careful not to oppose the bishop, that we may be subject to God" (Ign. *Eph.*, 5.3). He declares, "Be zealous to do all things in harmony with God, with the bishop presiding in the place of God and the presbyters in the place of the council of the Apostles, and the deacons, who are most dear to me, entrusted with the service of Jesus Christ, who was from eternity with the Father and was made manifest at the end of time. . . . Be united with the bishop and with those who preside over you as an example and lesson of immortality" (Ign. *Magn.*, 6.1–2).

In some passages, Ignatius employs specifically cultic language: "Unless a man be within the sanctuary [*entos tou thysiastēriou*, or place of sacrifice] he lacks the bread of God [*tou artou tou theou*], for if the prayer of one or two has such might, how much more has that of the bishop and of the whole church?" Here, the prayer of the community joined to that of the bishop is explicitly identified as the place of sacrifice. Ignatius says elsewhere, "He who is within the sanctuary [*entos tou thysiastēriou*] is pure, but he who is without the sanctuary is not pure; that is to say whoever does anything apart from the bishop and the presbytery and the deacons is not pure in his conscience" (Ign. *Tral.*, 7.2).

The same understanding applies to the Eucharist as well: "Be careful therefore to use one Eucharist (for there is one flesh of our Lord Jesus Christ, and one cup for union with his blood, one altar, as there is one bishop with the presbytery and the deacons my fellow servants) in order that whatever you do you may do it according to God" (Ign. *Phil.*, 4.1).

In his letter to the Smyrnaeans, Ignatius speaks of the heretics who "abstain from Eucharist and prayer, because they do not confess that the Eucharist is the flesh of our savior Jesus Christ," and declares that it is correct, in turn, not to associate with such people and that one should instead follow the truth of the Gospel and celebrate Eucharist with those who hold to it: "See that you all follow the bishop, as Jesus Christ follows the Father, and the presbytery as if it were the apostles. And reverence the deacons as the command of God. Let no one do any of the things pertaining to the church without the bishop. Let that be considered a valid Eucharist [*bebaia eucharistia*] which is celebrated by the bishop, or by one whom he appoints. Wherever the bishop appears let the congregation be present; just as wherever Jesus Christ is, there is the catholic church [*katholikē ekklēsia*]. It is not lawful [*ouk exon estin*] either to baptize or to hold an 'agape' without the bishop" (Ign. *Smyr.*, 7.1–8.2). Ignatius provides all three aspects of a developing Religiousness D: the focus on the bishop as the essential point of church unity, a thoroughgoing theological rationalization for this centrality, and identification of the bishop's role as celebrant of ritual with sacrificial overtones.

Similarly, in Justin Martyr's *First Apology*, the description of Christian worship focuses on the role of the "presider over the brethren" (*proestōti tōn adelphōn*) as the one to whom bread and wine are "offered" (*prospherein*) for his blessing (1 *Apol*, 65 and 67). That Justin is deliberate in using the technical term for sacrifice here is indicated by a passage in his *Dialogue with Trypho* that interprets Malachi 1:11—"In every place incense shall be offered unto my name and a pure offering"—with reference to the Christian cult: "He then speaks of those Gentiles, namely us, who in every place offer sacrifices [*thysiai*] to him, that is the bread of the eucharist, and also the cup of the eucharist" (*Dial*, 41).[4]

EARLY CHURCH ORDERS

The very emergence of compositions that have come to be called "church orders"[5] suggests the development of a religious sensibility focused on stabilizing the world—in this case, the world of community practice, fulfilling the Apostle's desire that all things in the assembly be done "decently and in good order" (1 Cor 14:40). Written anonymously, these orders present themselves as the "teaching" or "tradition" of the apostles, thus claiming for a once volatile movement the stabilizing influence of antiquity and apostolic authority. They occupy the position, indeed, of "holy law" for the Christian community in the second and third century, laying the foundations for what will eventually become "canon law."[6] My interest in the three compositions that can confidently be dated to the second and third century remains focused on the central authority of the bishop, his liturgical role, and the conception of Christian worship as sacrifice.

The *Didache* ("Teaching of the Twelve Apostles") is generally recognized as the earliest of church orders, though its date and history of composition is still debated.[7] Its first six chapters contain moral instruction concerning "the two ways" of life and death,[8] chapters 7–15 deal with community practice, and chapter 16 concludes with an eschatological warning. After describing the manner of baptizing (7) and praying (8), the composition turns to the Eucharistic prayer (9–10), before discussing the issue of leadership over the assembly (11–13). The main focus is on the power and problems of itinerant prophets (11–12), including their support. Of particular interest is the way the composition speaks of the support of true prophets as the support of priests: "Thou shalt take the firstfruit [*aparchē*] of the produce of the winepress and of the threshing-floor and of oxen and sheep, and shall give them as first-fruits to the prophet, for they are your high priests [*eisin hoi archiereis hymōn*]" (13.3).[9]

Immediately after this passage, the *Didache* turns to the holding of the Eucharist on the Lord's day and speaks of it as a sacrifice: "let none who has a quarrel with his fellow join in your meeting until they be reconciled, that your sacrifice not be defiled [*hina mē koinōthē hē thysia hymōn*]" (14.2). To this instruction is attached the quotation from Malachi 11:1 that was used also by Justin: "For this is that which was spoken by the Lord, 'In every place and time offer me a pure sacrifice [*prospherein moi thysias*], for I am a great king,' saith the Lord, 'and my name is wonderful among the nations'" (14.3). And immediately following this instruction is the command to make bishops and deacons worthy of the Lord, "for they also minister to you the ministry [*leitourgousi kai autoi tēn leitourgian*] of the prophets and teachers" (15.1). The *Didache*

legitimates the place of local bishops by connecting it to the charismatic authority of apostles and prophets, suggests that the bishops continue the liturgical
function of prophets, and explicitly uses sacrificial language for the Eucharist.

The *Apostolic Tradition* is an early third-century church order that is attributed to Hippolytus of Rome (ca. 170–ca. 236), although like the *Didache*, its
provenance may be Syria.[10] In it, the complete hierarchical order is found: mo-
narchical bishop, presbyterate, and diaconate, as well as other orders: readers,
virgins, widows, confessors, subdeacons, and healers. In addition to treatments
of these offices, the composition takes up baptism, the Eucharist, fasting—all
topics found in the *Didache*—as well as a variety of instructions for quotidian
aspects of life: modes of eating, lighting of lamps, times of prayer, places for
burial.[11] One has the sense, in reading the *Apostolic Tradition*, of an ever-
increasing ordering of the life of the faithful. The main focus, nevertheless, is
on the bishop, whose selection and ordination is the first topic considered (2.1–
3.6) and whose authority runs through the discussion of all other topics.

Two interrelated aspects of the bishop's increased prominence are noteworthy. The first is that here we find the bishop explicitly designated as high
priest. In the prayer for the ordination of the bishop, God is asked to gift "this
your servant, whom you have chosen for the episcopate, to feed your holy flock
and to exercise the high priesthood for you without blame, ministering night
and day." This ministry is described in specifically sacrificial terms: the bishop
is "unceasingly to propitiate your countenance and to offer to you the holy
gifts of your church" (3.4). In addition to forgiving sins and assigning lots, the
bishop is to "please you [God] in gentleness and a pure heart, offering to you a
sweet-smelling savor" (3.5). Later, in the discussion of the bishop's visiting the
sick, the composition states, "for a sick person is greatly consoled when the high
priest remembers him" (34).

The second aspect is that such sacerdotal language is emphatically absent in
discussions of the presbytery and diaconate. It is the bishop who recites the
words of the Eucharist, declaring "we offer you the bread and cup" (4.11). It is
the bishop who says the prayer over first fruits (31.1–5). But no sacrificial language appears in the discussion of ordination to the presbytery (7.1–5). And (in
the Sahidic version) a sharp line of demarcation is made between liturgical and
nonliturgical orders: "But the ordination is for the clergy for the sake of the liturgies, and the widow is appointed only for the sake of the prayer; and this belongs to everyone" (10.5). The central and sacral role of the bishop emerges
much more clearly in the *Apostolic Tradition* than in the *Didache*.

The *Didascalia Apostolorum* also comes from the third century, composed
in Greek but available today only in an early Syriac translation and Latin frag-

ments.[12] It presents itself as having been composed by a council of the apostles like that described in Acts 15 and dispatched to all the churches prior to the geographical dispersal of the apostles to the nations (24–25). More hortatory than canonical in tone, it touches on a variety of aspects of Christian life, including marriage (2–3), widows (14–15), deacons and deaconesses (16), orphans (17 and 22), contributions for the poor (18), martyrs (19), the resurrection (20), the paschal celebration (21), and heresies (23). A substantial portion of the work, however, is devoted to the bishop (4–12), and in this discussion, we find further evidence for the exaltation of this position and its identification with a sacrificial priesthood.

The first chapter devoted to the subject (4) insists that the bishop is to be a man of outstanding virtue and an example to the people. Even if not learned, he is to be so steeped in the tradition that he can instruct the people, reading and expounding the scripture. Twice in this discussion (ii.3 and ii.5), the bishop is, through scriptural allusion, identified as a priest. Chapter 4 discusses the bishop's role as judge in the church, concluding with this remarkable exhortation: "Wherefore O bishop, strive to be pure in thy works. And know thy place, that thou art set in the likeness of God almighty, and holdest the place of God almighty; and so sit in the church and teach as having authority to judge them that sin in the room of God almighty. For to you bishops it is said in the Gospel: 'That which ye shall bind on earth, shall be bound in heaven'" (ii.11). Because of this exalted status, the bishop is to listen only to God and not to laypeople: "It behoves thee not, O bishop, that being the head thou shouldst obey the tail, that is a layman, a contentious man who desires the destruction of another; but do thou regard only the word of the Lord God" (ii.13). Chapter 6 makes clear that laypeople have responsibility only for themselves, whereas the bishop bears responsibility for all, because of the office of priesthood: "As, therefore thou carriest the burden of all, be watchful; for it is written: 'The Lord said unto Moses, Thou and Aaron shall take upon you the sins of the priesthood'" (ii.17). Chapter 7 instructs laypeople to revere the bishop "as God after God almighty; for to the bishop it was said through the apostles: 'Every one that heareth you, heareth me; and every one that rejecteth you rejecteth me, and him that sent me'" (ii.19).

It is right that bishops should live from the donations made to the church, chapter 8 argues, because bishops hold the same place as priests in the Old Testament: "You also then to-day, O bishops, are priests to your people, and the levites who minister to the tabernacle of God, the holy catholic church, who stand continually before the Lord God" (ii.25). An extensive passage from Numbers 18:1–32 is quoted in support of this position: "For as you administer the office of the bishopric, so from the same office of the bishopric ought you to be nourished, as the priests and Levites and ministers who serve before God" (ii.25). The equivalence is given more development in chapter 9, which declares that the priests and Levites of the former dispensation are now the "presbyters and deacons, and the orphans and widows," and therefore ought to live on the funds donated to the church, but that the bishop occupies an even greater position: "the Levite and High Priest is the bishop. . . . He is minister of the word and mediator; but to you a teacher, and your father after God, who begot you through the water. This is your chief and your leader, and he is your mighty kind. He rules in place of the Almighty; but let him be honored by you as God, for the bishop sits for you in the place of God almighty. . . . If any man do aught without the bishop, he does it in vain, for it shall not be accounted to him as a work; for it is not fitting that any man should do aught apart from the high priest" (ii.27).

The *Didascalia* similarly justifies forbidding direct access to the bishop—laypeople must go through deacons to approach him—by invoking the analogy of the ancient temple sanctuary. In fact, justification is drawn as well from the practice of pagan temples and priesthood (ii.28). Christians are to give the bishop even more respect: "do you therefore esteem the bishop as the mouth of God" (ii.28); "Love the bishop as a father, and fear him as a king, and honour him as God" (ii.34). When the church gathers for worship, the bishop is to sit on a throne in the midst of the presbyters and removed from the laypeople (ii.57). When he says the Eucharistic prayer, it is a priestly "oblation" (ii.34; ii.36; ii.53–54).

The evidence of the early church orders confirms that provided by Clement, Ignatius, and Justin: in the second and third century, there was an increased concentration on the authority of the bishop; this position was given theological justification; and just as the Eucharist was conceived of as a sacrifice, so was the bishop's liturgical and administrative role thought of in terms of priesthood. The specific symbolism for the hierarchical language was derived from scripture. But in at least one instance (the *Didascalia*), the practices of pagan temples and priesthoods provide precedent. And, in fact, the actual arrangements of the Christian assembly resembled those of Hellenistic cultic associations more than they did the worship at the temple in Jerusalem. The "sacrifice" of the Eucharist, after all, was offered in every community and not simply in Jerusalem, and bishops who served as "priests" did so not because of tribal ancestry but because of their election by the assembly.

THE QUARTODECIMAN CONTROVERSY

In the fifth book of his *Ecclesiastical History* (*HE*), Eusebius of Caesarea describes a late second-century conflict—he characterizes it as "no small controversy"—that as much as anything else exemplifies the steady development of episcopal power within a larger Christian *politeia*. The conflict was over liturgical observance: the majority of Christians celebrated "the Savior's Passover" (*HE*, 5.23.1), that is, Easter, on the Sunday following 14th Nisan, the day of Jewish Passover; Christians in Asia Minor, however, celebrated it on the same day as the Jewish Passover, namely, 14th Nisan—thus the name "Quartodeciman" ("14th day").[13] The larger issue, however, concerned the tension between local tradition and liturgical diversity and the desire for ecclesiastical unity, especially in a period when communities were divided by heresies and threatened by persecution. Since Eusebius recounts the story in straightforward fashion and because he is our only source of information, I will simply follow his account.[14]

Eusebius begins with the position of those convinced that it was not right "to finish the fast on any day save that of the resurrection of our savior" (5.23.1), that is, Sunday. He does not elaborate theological reasons for this conviction, but he cites the various regional councils of bishops that had been held and that "expressed one and same opinion and judgment, and gave the same vote" (5.23.4): the bishops of Jerusalem and Caesarea presided over a synod of Palestinian bishops; the bishop of Rome, Victor, held a synod of his bishops; and there were further synods of bishops in Pontus, Gaul (over which Irenaeus presided), Osrhoene and the cities in that region,[15] and one convened by the bishop of Corinth, as well as "very many more" (5.23.3–4). Eusebius reports, furthermore, that the bishops in the Palestinian region, after settling their own position with respect to the custom, sent letters to every diocese communicating their decision (5.25.1). Several things emerge from this preliminary stage: first, bishops are the spokespersons for their communities; second, together with bishops of other assemblies, they make decisions that affect all assemblies; third, not all bishops are equal—some exercise regional and not merely local authority; fourth, bishops concern themselves not merely with administration and doctrine but with correctness in cultic observance; fifth, bishops maintain *koinōnia* through the exchange of letters among dioceses.

After these synods had issued their joint decision that Easter must fall on a Sunday, the bishops in Asia, led by Polycrates of Ephesus, persisted in stating that "it was necessary for them to keep the custom which had been handed down to them of old" (*HE*, 5.24.1), namely, to observe the resurrection on 14th Nisan. Polycrates also represents "many multitudes" of bishops with him when he writes a letter to Victor and the church of Rome (5.24.8). His writing specifically to Victor suggests the emerging role of Rome as the central authority among other regional centers, a natural position, given the fact that it existed in the imperial city and could claim a double apostolic foundation.[16] Polycrates makes two fundamental appeals: the Asian custom goes back to the apostle John, who "sleeps in Ephesus," and other apostolic leaders, including Philip and three of his daughters; the custom was practiced, moreover, by all of the bishops and saints of the region, including the great Polycarp of Smyrna, "both bishop and martyr," and the seven members of Polycrates' family who were bishops before him in Ephesus. All these, Polycrates avers, "kept the fourteenth day of the Passover according to the gospel, never swerving, but following according to the rule of faith" (5.24.2–7).

Three aspects of his letter demand attention. First, we learn that the bishopric can be hereditary—it has passed through eight generations of Polycrates' family—in the manner of Greco-Roman priesthoods. Second, Polycrates sees this liturgical use as consistent with the "rule of faith" (*kanona tēs pisteōs*), an important claim, because it suggests that a variety of liturgical customs can fit within the essential creed shared by all Christians: he and his fellow bishops are not heretics or sectarians but follow a different apostolic tradition than does Rome. Third, Polycrates makes an explicit appeal to the precedent set by the apostle Peter when called before the Sanhedrin in Jerusalem and told to stop preaching in the name of Jesus: "For they who have said who were greater than I, 'It is better to obey God rather than men'" (Acts 5:29).[17]

Victor of Rome immediately sent out letters announcing that all the churches in Asia and its adjacent regions were excommunicated "from the common unity" (*tēs koinēs henōseōs*) on the grounds of heresy (*heterodoxousas*; HE, 5.24.9). It was a classic case of political overreaching. A number of other bishops sent Victor letters, "sharply rebuking" him and asking him to think (*phronein*) in terms of peace and unity and love toward his "neighbor" (*plēsion*; 5.24.10). Among the letters sent to Victor was one by Irenaeus of Lyons, who agreed with Victor's position regarding Easter but disagreed with his political aggression. Eusebius says that Irenaeus exhorted Victor "suitably and at length" not "to excommunicate whole churches of God for following an ancient custom" (5.24.11) and quotes extensively from Irenaeus' letter. Irenaeus makes the point that disagreements about Easter are not recent, nor have they proven disruptive of church unity in the past: "all these lived in peace with one another and the disagreements in the fast [*diaphōnia tēs nēsteias*] confirms our agreement in the faith (*homonoia tēs pisteōs*)" (5.24.13).

His more telling point is that none of Victor's predecessors as bishop of Rome had seen fit either to impose their liturgical custom on others or refuse communion to those whose custom differed from theirs. Irenaeus recounts the specific instance when Polycarp visited Rome in the time of Anicetus (ca. 155): "although they disagreed a little about some other matters as well, they immediately made peace, having no wish for strife between them on this matter" (5.24.16). Neither Polycarp nor Anicetus was able to persuade the other of the correctness of his own observance, but "under these circumstances they communicated with each other, and in the church, Anicetus yielded the celebration of the Eucharist to Polycarp, obviously out of respect, and they parted from each other in peace, for the peace of the whole church was kept by those who observed and those who did not" (5.24.17).

The evidence I have drawn from three second-century writers, from church orders of the second and third centuries, and from Eusebius' account of the Quartodeciman controversy is insufficient to provide a full account of Christianity's internal political development in the centuries between the New Testament and Constantine. It is sufficient, however, to establish that long before Christianity achieved its position as the imperial religion, bishops had emerged as local leaders, some exercised dominance over entire regions, and some met in councils to decide disputed issues. It is also sufficient to show that episcopal power was symbolized in terms of the high priesthood of the Old Testament and that the celebration of the Eucharist by bishops was characterized in terms of sacrifice.

The synods and letters that were generated by the paschal controversy also showed how bishops were deeply involved in matters of cult and how they increasingly thought of their role in terms of the whole church (*hē ekklēsia hē katholikē*) rather than simply in terms of the local assembly. Such arrangements increasingly matched and mirrored the functions of priesthood within Greco-Roman civic cults and Hellenistic religious associations—one can think of Aelius Aristides' refusal of positions in such priestly offices at precisely the same period and in precisely the same location. Insofar as Religiousness D represents the "supply side" of Religiousness A, that is, ensuring that the practices of worship that give access to the divine *dynamis* will reliably be available, these developments within the Christian episcopacy move in the same direction.

The other dimension of Religiousness D that I have identified is found in individuals who explicitly articulate their religious ideals in terms of what I have called "stabilizing the world," who focus not on their own experience of power or on the moral transformation of themselves or others, and who certainly do not seek to flee body and community in order to save their souls, but who seek to establish genuine *eusebeia* in the public and shared practices of religion. In Greco-Roman religion, I saw Plutarch of Chaeronea as representing this way of being religious. In the second and third Christian centuries, such a sensibility is represented above all by two bishops, Irenaeus of Lyons and Cyprian of Carthage.

IRENAEUS OF LYONS

Eusebius knows Irenaeus best as an active participant in the Quartodeciman controversy. He says that "Irenaeus, who deserved his name, making an eireni-con in this way, gave exhortations of this kind for the peace of the church and served as its ambassador, for in letters he discussed the various views on the issue that had been raised, not only with Victor but with many other rulers of churches" (*HE*, 5.24.18). He makes only a brief mention of the bishop as writer.[18] But it is in his capacity as the author of *Adversus Haereses*—whose descriptions of Gnosticism and whose polemic against them we saw in Chapter 14—that we gain some sense of Irenaeus' perception of the church as a political entity that motivated both his tireless efforts to make peace among those whose differences were not a threat to the essential rule of faith and his passionate repulsion of the heretics whose myths he saw as fundamentally at odds with the truth of the Gospel. In both cases, it is critical to recognize, Irenaeus thought of "church" not in terms simply of the local assembly, or even of those assemblies over which he had direct charge, but in terms of a worldwide society bound together by clear and visible identity markers whose preservation was necessary for the society to survive.[19]

In the preface to book 1, Irenaeus identifies himself as a "resident among the Kelts . . . accustomed for the most part to use a barbarous dialect" and incapable of rhetoric or distinction in style (Pref. 3). Unlike Plutarch, then, who wrote specifically as a Greek to repulse barbarous ways—and who attacked both atheism and superstition because in different ways they led to barbarism—Irenaeus accepts Christianity as sharing in the "barbarian" wisdom of the Jews. It is part of his polemic, indeed, to suggest that some Gnostic speculations are simply reconfigurations of pagan myths (*Adversus Haereses*, 2.14). Irenaeus' defense is not of Greek culture and of the religion that supported it but of the "truth" that is found in the "oracles of God" distorted by the heretics when they claim to offer something better than "that God who created the heaven and the earth, and all things that are therein": "By means of specious and plausible words, they cunningly allure the simple-minded to inquire into their system; but they nevertheless clumsily destroy them . . . and these simple ones are unable, even in such a matter, to distinguish falsehood from truth" (Pref. 1).

Irenaeus writes to his "dear friend" (undoubtedly another bishop), then, in order to expose the falsehoods, so that his fellow bishop, in turn, "mayest explain them to all those with whom thou art connected, and exhort them to avoid such an abyss of madness and of blasphemy against Christ" (Pref. 2). His writing, in short, is a political act intended to persuade fellow teachers to align themselves with his position and to in turn persuade others. The unspoken assumption is that the "simple-minded" who are easily swayed by heresy are the unlearned laity, while those able to learn and teach soundly are those who have been assigned the role of priests and teachers within God's church. Irenaeus concludes the preface with the wish that his friend might, "according to the grace given thee by the Lord, prove an earnest and efficient minister to others, that men may no longer be drawn away by the plausible system of these heretics" (Pref. 3).

It is no accident that Irenaeus identifies the rejection of the one creator God as the central error of the Gnostics, from which all else flows, or that he devotes his entire second book to a theological argument on behalf of that one creator God (see 2.9). His theological response to the Gnostics (as he understands them, to be sure) is intellectually coherent and is necessary to at least sketch in brief, if we are to appreciate his overall strategy of Christian self-definition. If the one good God is the creator of all that is in heaven and earth, then matter is not an evil obstacle but a divine gift and the vehicle of divine power. If matter is good, in turn, then bodies are good. If bodies are good and are the arena of divine activity, then history—that is, bodies in motion through time and space—can also be the stage for divine action. From this premise, Irenaeus can argue for the full humanity of Jesus and his physical resurrection, the unity of revelation between the Old and New Testaments, and the future accomplishment of God's kingdom in the material world.[20] And if all this be granted—and Irenaeus argues that it is the plain sense of scripture[21]—then material institutions are also good and capable of bearing the divine power. Irenaeus' theology of creation and incarnation supports a vision of the church as public, historical, and thoroughly institutional. The source of truth is not the individual teacher who trades in revelation but the body of bishops who preserve the traditions of the apostles.

The diagnosis and dismissal of false teachings is, in Irenaeus' view, insufficient, for heresies are like viruses that can recur in ever changing forms. For the church to be stable in the face of the human desire for novelty and superstition, a solid framework of self-definition is required, one that is capable of responding not only to the present but to all future outbreaks of heresy among the faithful. Irenaeus' overall strategy, then, consists in establishing a tripod of Christian self-definition: the rule of faith (creed), the collection of scriptures (canon), and the teaching office of bishops (council). These correspond to the specific challenge of Gnosticism, which offered new and speculative myths, new revelatory writings, and new charismatic teachers, but they also provided a resilient framework for negotiating later internal Christian disputes.

A fascinating aspect of Irenaeus' tripod is that the three legs are not truly in-dependent but point toward each other and depend on each other from the start. Not one of them can stand alone, and the visible church cannot rest its identity simply on one in isolation from the others. Thus, the first leg of the tripod is the rule of faith, which Irenaeus introduces early in book 1: "the church, though dispersed throughout the whole world, even to the ends of the earth, has received from the apostles and their disciples this faith" (1.10.1). The faith, we see immediately, is one that is confirmed by the apostolic succes-sion and the agreement of Christians throughout the world. After Irenaeus provides a sketch of this faith—understood as a body of doctrine rather than as an existential response or as a code of ethics—in the one God and the incarnate Christ, he returns to the fact of its universal ecclesial embrace. The church as a whole carefully preserves "this preaching and this faith," in perfect harmony, "as if she possessed only one mouth": "For the churches which have been planted in Germany do not believe or hand down anything different, nor those in Gaul, nor those in the East, nor those in Egypt, nor those in Libya, nor those which have been established in the central regions of the world."[22] He adds that no "ruler of the church" (that is, bishop), "however highly gifted he may be in point of eloquence, teach[es] doctrines different from these (for no one is greater than the Master); nor, on the other hand, will he who is deficient in expression inflict injury on the tradition" (1.10.3). The point is that the tradition is greater and more central than any gift of individual insight or expression.

Similarly, although Irenaeus does not make a formal argument concerning canon as such, it is clear that there is the strongest possible relationship between the rule of faith and the writings of the Old and New Testaments. He does insist that there are, and can be, only four Gospels (3.11.1–9).[23] And his thoroughgoing use of the LXX argues implicitly that it is the source of truth about the one cre-ator God and God's activity in the world.[24] But for the other writings of the New Testament, his argument is more complex, showing how the rule of faith is not found in the Gnostic writings and claiming that Gnostic interpretations contort the public and clear sense of the writings that Christians as a whole embrace as apostolic.[25] It is entirely consistent with Irenaeus' overall perspective that he in-sists on reading Paul, for example, in terms of literary context, grammar, and syntax, for these are precisely what might be called the "institutional," structural elements of language.[26] The primacy of the traditional scriptures is secured, fi-nally, by the fact that they are the ones used by Christian teachers from the be-ginning, whereas the Gnostic texts have only recently appeared.

Irenaeus similarly places his argument from apostolic succession in book 3.3

in the context of an argument that the heretics follow neither scripture nor tradition (3.2). In contrast to the recent appearance of the heretics—"prior to Valentinus, there were no Valentinians; nor did those from Marcion exist before Marcion" (3.4.3)—the great church is able to trace its authority back to the apostles in unbroken sequence. Although Irenaeus claims that in principle the succession can be traced for all the churches, he chooses to delineate that "of the very great, the very ancient and universally known church founded and organized at Rome by the two most glorious apostles, Peter and Paul" (3.1.2). Key to his argument, to be sure, is the premise that the first bishops are successors chosen by the apostles (3.3.3) and the premise, which Irenaeus makes explicit, that if the apostles wanted to pass on secret lore they surely would have done so to "those to whom they were committing the churches themselves" (3.3.1). The fact is the opposite: all the successors of the apostles have taught the same truths that are found in the rule of faith (3.1.1–2).[27]

All of the bishops in line from the apostles, Irenaeus asserts, also read the same scripture. On this point, Irenaeus appeals to Clement of Rome, "in the third place from the apostles," and refers explicitly to his letter to the Corinthians in which he cites the tradition received from the apostles and makes use of the writings of the Old Testament (*Adversus Haereses*, 3.3.3). Similarly, Irenaeus invokes Polycarp—who knew the apostle John—as an episcopal predecessor in the battle against heresy. Just as John the disciple of the Lord fled the bath house at the entrance of the heretic Cerinthus, so did Polycarp address Marcion as the "first-born of Satan" (3.3.4).

The rule of faith and the scripture are public instruments that can be deployed publicly in a process of community definition. They are available to all, not only in the present but from the start of the Christian movement. They are secured in their existence and in their meaning by the most public instrument of all, the bishops who preserve the traditions and pass them on from generation to generation. Although Irenaeus does not take up liturgical issues in *Adversus Haereses* and does not argue for the priestly character of the bishops within their own assemblies, everything that he ascribes to these visible leaders as the stabilizers of the Christian tradition conforms perfectly to the developments I have sketched earlier in this chapter. From beginning to end, Irenaeus' argument is political in character. He does not claim that the bishops are the holiest of men or that they are the most learned, still less that they have received special revelations. He does claim that the church rests on the bishops precisely as it rests on the apostles, as the continuing bodily (institutional) presence of the incarnate God.

CYPRIAN OF CARTHAGE

Thrascius Cyprianus was born circa 200 and was trained as a rhetorician. Jerome tells us that "under the influence of the priest Caecilius, from whom he received his surname, he became a Christian, and gave all his fortune to the poor."[28] In his letter *To Donatus*, he provides a moving account of his conversion from the vanities of his pagan and professional existence. He was quickly— though not without some resistance among the presbyters—elected bishop of Carthage in 248 and was immediately forced to deal with the Decian persecution (250), which had two distinctive features: it affected the entire empire, and it required participation in pagan sacrifice from all. Many Christians submitted, and these *lapsi* ("the lapsed," that is, those who submitted to giving sacrifice or provided certifications instead) gave rise to the most serious crises of Cyprian's relatively short tenure as bishop of Carthage. When persecution was renewed under Valerian, Cyprian was martyred outside Carthage in 258.

Although he was a great admirer of Tertullian (ca. 160–225)—according to Jerome, he never let a day go by without reading "the master"[29]—Cyprian did not share Tertullian's fiery temperament or harsh sectarianism. Although two of his treatises take the form of apologies against paganism, the majority of them deal with pastoral issues.[30] He was less a scholar of scripture than a compiler of proof texts that could be used in sermons and arguments.[31] Two treatises, "On the Unity of the Church" (1) and "On the Lapsed" (3), as well as a substantial portion of his extant letters, deal with the most pressing pastoral issue he faced as a result of the Decian persecution.

His letters remind us of those reported to have been written by Irenaeus. Some are pastoral letters in the strict sense, through which he communicated to the presbytery and people of Carthage. But apart from a handful of letters that announce the ordination of individuals to various ranks and a few others that take up matters of practice, most provide direction concerning the treatment of the lapsed and other points of contention.[32] Cyprian also wrote directly to the lapsed (*Letter*, 26) as well as to confessors (those who had resisted the imperial edict; *Letters*, 15, 24, 50) and to those facing martyrdom (76, 80), similarly, confessors and martyrs, even of other communities, also wrote to him (16, 25, 43, 49, 78, 79).

The part of his correspondence that is of the greatest interest for the present study, however, concerns the letters Cyprian wrote to other churches and bishops, for these show the same sort of deliberate cultivation of *koinōnia* that we observed in the synods and letters in the Quartodeciman controversy. Thus, because some of the Carthaginian presbyters objected to his ordination as bishop, and because Cyprian withdrew when the Decian persecution began, the church in Rome wrote to inquire as to the state of affairs in the North African city (*Letter*, 2), and the Carthaginian clergy responded in defense of their bishop (3). This exchange began a long series of letters between the two churches (*Letters*, 14, 22, 28, 29, 30, 71, 73), especially between Cornelius, the bishop of Rome, and Cyprian (40, 41, 42, 44, 45, 46, 47, 48, 53, 54, 56).

The difficult problem of reconciling the lapsed—offering them repentance—persisted, especially when it was complicated by the Roman presbyter Novatian, who took a hard line against Cyprian's moderate position toward the *lapsi* and, joined by Cyprian's disgruntled presbyter Novatus, began a rigorist sectarian movement that excluded not only the lapsed but also those (like Cyprian) who were willing to receive the lapsed back into communion. Through synods over which he presided (see *Letters*, 58, 61, 71) and through letters to Rome and letters to other churches, Cyprian sought to establish the more moderate position (37, 40, 42, 51, 52, 53). Cyprian was also more moderate in his position concerning the baptism of heretics, a position that he also needed to defend, not least to the Roman bishop, Stephen (54, 57, 59, 69, 70, 71, 72, 73, 74, 81). Cyprian's constant activity over the course of 10 years demonstrates his activist conception of the bishopric and his commitment to a vision of the church that was universal rather than simply local.

Cyprian's self-understanding as a bishop and of the bishop's place in the church—precisely that enunciated by Ignatius of Antioch—is revealed in his letter of self-defense addressed to Florentius Pupianos (*Letter*, 68). He speaks of the bishop as one who "rules over the church" and says that a community lacking a bishop has no prelate, pastor, or governor; Christ does not have a representative; and God does not have a priest (*Letter*, 68.5). He claims that the martyrs from their prisons "directed letters to Cyprian the bishop, recognizing the priest of God and bearing witness to him" (68.7). He says of sectarians, "they are the church who are a people united to the priest, and the flock which adheres to its pastor. Whence you ought to know that the bishop is in the church and the church is in the bishop" (68.8). This is as strong an affirmation of the institutional character of the church as could be desired. Cyprian again identifies the bishop in terms of the priesthood: those in communion have peace with God's priests (68.8); it is God who ordains bishops as priests, and to God and his Christ, he "ceaselessly offer[s] sacrifices." And quoting an unnamed source, he concludes, "Whoso therefore does not believe Christ, who maketh the priest, shall hereafter begin to believe Him who avengeth the priest" (68.9).

Cyprian's outlook is expressed more fully in his treatise *On the Unity of the Church*, which was written in response to the schism of Novatian (described above). For Cyprian, those who lapsed from the faith in the persecution do not really threaten the church as such, because theirs was an individual fall from commitment. The great threat comes from those who challenge the very structure of the faith (*Unity*, 18). Cyprian assigns this kind of challenge to Satan: "He has invented heresies and schisms, whereby he might subvert the truth, might divide the unity. Those he cannot keep in the darkness of the old way [i.e., paganism], he circumvents and deceives by the error of a new way" (3). They are the more dangerous because, "although they do not stand firm with the Gospel of Christ and with the observation and law of Christ, they still call themselves Christians, and walking in darkness, they think that they have the light" (3).

The bond of unity in the church is a visible and explicit connection to the bishop. Christ gave authority to Peter and all the apostles as the focus of unity, and this function is passed down to the bishops: "This unity we ought firmly to hold and assert, especially those of us that are bishops who preside in the church, that we may also prove the episcopate itself to be one and undivided. . . . The episcopate is one, each part of which is held by each one for the whole. The church also is one, which is spread far and wide into a multitude by an increase of fruitfulness" (*Unity*, 5). The unity and catholicity of the church, then, are expressed, indeed embodied, in the unity and catholicity of the episcopate. The church is found in its bishops. When Cyprian asserts, then, that "He can no longer have God for his Father, who has not the church for his mother" (*Unity*, 6), he has just this sort of visible, institutional, connection in mind.

Cyprian explicitly denies that the saying of Jesus that "two or three gathered in my name" blesses any group of the faithful; if they are not in connection to their bishop, the saying is null: "He does not divide men from the church, seeing that he himself ordained and made the church" (*Unity*, 12). Cyprian again takes up the language of priesthood in this regard: "What peace, then, do the enemies of the brethren promise to themselves? What sacrifices do those who are rivals of the priests think that they celebrate?" (13). Not even martyrdom counts for anything if one is cut off from the visible church (14). Cyprian states the ideal powerfully: "God is one, and Christ is one, and his church is one, and the faith is one, and the people is joined into a substantial unity of body by the cement of concord. Unity cannot be severed; nor can one body be separated by a division of its structure, nor torn into pieces, with its entrails wrenched asunder by laceration" (23). The key phrase in this statement, though, is "separated by a division of its structure," for it is agreement with the priesthood of the bishops that constitutes, for Cyprian, the real concord of the church. He compares those who oppose the bishops with those who opposed "Moses and Aaron the priest" (18): "Does he think that he has Christ, who acts in opposition to Christ's priests, who separates himself from the company of his clergy and people? He bears arms against the church, he contends against God's appointment. An enemy of the altar, a rebel against Christ's sacrifice, for the faith faithless, for religion profane, a disobedient servant, an impious son, a hostile brother, despising the bishops, and forsaking God's priests, he dares to set up another altar, to make another prayer with unauthorized words, to profane the truth of the Lord's offering by false sacrifices" (17).

Long before it became the imperial religion, Christianity appeared institutionally as a vast network of associations that had developed a distinctive *politeia*. Its bishops were elected by the people but drew their legitimacy from a narrative of apostolic succession that fundamentally identified the visible community with its leaders. Bishops, furthermore, spoke of the church in terms of a sanctuary in which they functioned as divinely ordained priests, offering sacrifices to God through Christ. In this chapter, I have traced the visible signs of this development from Clement and Ignatius at the start of the second century to Cyprian of Carthage in the mid-third century.

The incidental language of sacrifice employed by the early writers is exploited systematically by the church orders, tentatively in the *Didache*, more confidently in the *Apostolic Tradition*, and triumphantly in the *Didascalia Apostolorum*. In Irenaeus of Lyons and Cyprian of Carthage, finally, we find bishops of important churches whose vision of Christianity is precisely that of an association centered in visible, indeed institutional, marks of identity: the rule of faith and the canon of scripture, to be sure, but above all the bishops who embody the tradition. Such bishops not only express such a vision of Christianity in their writing; what we know of their actions and letters shows that they expended great effort in bringing that vision to realization.

I have identified, in short, the same sort of religious sensibility that was detected among the priests and hierophants in Greco-Roman religion. It is a distinct "way of being Christian," not reducible to the other strains I have described. The divine *dynamis* is located in the institution, and the point of that power is to maintain and sustain the institution and thus "stabilize the world." The fascination with miracles, including the miracle of martyrdom, is not shared here. However much Cyprian values martyrdom and embraces it himself, its witness is void if not carried out in unity with the bishops. As for the "signs and wonders" that preoccupied Christianity Type A, the bishops tend to view them suspiciously as the work of demonic magic operative in heretics and schismatics, and therefore not to be encouraged among the people. We find not a trace in these compositions of Christianity as Religiousness B: this is not to say that the bishops are not interested in the moral transformation of their congregations; it is simply to observe that they seldom advert to it. Finally, as we saw in the last chapter, the bishops who were heresiologists set themselves explicitly against Christianity Type C as it emerged in second-century Gnosticism. Bishops may or may not have been mystics themselves, but their first commitment was not to personal religious experience; it was to the maintenance of the assembly and its sacrifice of the Eucharist, "decently and in good order."

16

AFTER CONSTANTINE: CHRISTIANITY
AS IMPERIAL RELIGION

Even before Constantine changed Christianity's historical situation, the religion that began as a Jewish sect based on the death and resurrection of a Jewish Messiah showed itself to have remarkable capacity for survival in the face of persecution, as well as the ability to develop religious sensibilities corresponding to those in the dominant Greco-Roman culture. As I showed in Chapter 8, Judaism itself, up to the middle of the second century when its dalliance with Hellenism effectively ended, revealed the same adaptive tendencies.

In the second and third centuries, some Christians had the same optimism about experiencing the divine power in the world as did their Greco-Roman neighbors and celebrated such power in signs and wonders that they attributed to the Holy Spirit operative because of the resurrection of Jesus. Other Christians shared the commitment of Hellenistic and Jewish philosophers to a life of moral transformation. They did not scorn the power of Jesus' name invoked in exorcisms and healings, but they regarded a life of virtue as the greatest miracle. Still other Christians fled involvement with the body and the world altogether, convinced that the divine could be found only in a transcendent realm of spirit. They cultivated secret and saving knowledge as the way to liberate the soul from its carnal prison. Finally, some Christians assumed the leadership role of bishops and, like the Greco-Roman heads of associations around them, conceived of their role in terms of priesthood, focusing their attention on the stability of the church.

Within the framework of the analysis used in this study, Christianity was a "Greco-Roman religion" virtually from the start and grew increasingly closer to the forms and expressions of religion found in the Greco-Roman environment. Rather than a foreign and forced imposition, the Greco-Roman character of

Christianity was a natural development that required no external or political assistance. As the presence and influence of living Judaism receded, moreover, Christianity's only real connection to its Jewish roots was through the reading of scripture. These sacred texts from ancient Israel were being read and interpreted, however, as Greek writings (the LXX) by people whose cultural environment, rhetorical education, and religious expectations were entirely Gentile. These four distinct types of religious sensibility—and in the second and third century they were impressively distinct in their emphasis—will emerge with Christianity itself into greater visibility when the cult of the Messiah Jesus is made the imperial religion under Constantine (272/288–337) and his successors, but they will also assume new shapes and enter into new combinations.

THE CONSTANTINIAN ERA

I use the phrase "Constantine and his successors" advisedly, because the establishment of Christianity as the imperial religion, however sudden and even unexpected, did not happen all at once or without setback.[1] Constantine's own religious motivations or intentions are of little importance.[2] Although he was baptized only shortly before his death in 337, his positive attitude toward Christianity is clear already in the declaration of religious tolerance known as the Edict of Milan (313), and his favor toward this cult that had been violently persecuted by his immediate predecessors found expression in public declarations and benefactions.[3] In 314, through the Synod of Arles, he intervened in the Donatist controversy and in 316 tried to settle it by imperial edict.[4] In 321 he declared Sunday to be a general holiday and ordered his soldiers' shields to be engraved with the sign of the cross.[5] In 325 he called and opened with an address the ecumenical council at Nicaea to settle the Arian controversy (and the still unsettled date of Easter).[6] In 330 he established the new capital in his name (Constantinople) at the ancient site of Byzantium and erected a magnificent church there in honor of the apostles.[7] Before his death, he provided the financial support for the building of the basilica of the Holy Sepulchre in Jerusalem and many other impressive basilicas in important cities.[8] He ordered and financially supported the production of 50 copies of the Bible.[9]

Such an aggressive show of imperial support on behalf of Christianity did not, however, mean that everything changed overnight. A significant portion, perhaps a majority, of the population of the empire probably remained pagan for a substantial period of time. Temples to the gods continued to exist, and worship of the gods continued to thrive. Eloquent spokespersons defended the glories of Greco-Roman religion and philosophy against the newly privileged but still barbaric Christian interloper. The philosopher Porphyry (ca. 234–305), who wrote *Against the Christians,* and Libanius of Antioch (314–394), who was a fervent admirer of the future emperor Julian, protested the closing of pagan temples.[10] They did not regard themselves as representing an obsolescent but rather a living and powerful civilization. The fact that the emperor Julian (302–363) could, in his short reign, reverse the process of Christianization and restore pagan supremacy (362–363)[11] indicates that the conditions for such restoration persisted through the fourth and into the fifth century. Augustine of Hippo became a bishop in 395, only 35 years after Julian's brief restoration, and at the end of his life, facing the invasion of the Saracens in North Africa, Augustine devoted the first part of his *City of God* to a defense of Christianity against claims by pagans that the abandonment of traditional Greco-Roman religion had brought on such disasters.[12]

The change brought about by Constantine was, nevertheless, fundamental, not least in making Christianity safe to practice publicly. It must be remembered that the imperial persecution of Christians through the time of Diocletian was increasingly purposeful and effective.[13] That Christian commitment ends logically in martyrdom is everywhere the assumption of the apocryphal Acts of the Apostles, which recount the deaths of Peter, Paul, John, Andrew, and Thomas. Of second-century figures discussed in earlier chapters, Ignatius, Polycarp, Justin, Perpetua and her companions all suffered martyrdom. Irenaeus' predecessor as bishop of Lyons was also martyred. Of third-century figures, Origen's father suffered martyrdom, and Origen himself was a confessor. Cyprian of Carthage exchanged letters with confessors and martyrs and was himself executed for the faith. While persecutions were sporadic and touched directly either those who were most visible because of their position or those who most directly confronted the imperial authority, it is clear that before the time of Constantine, the public profession of Christian faith was at least hazardous.

The Latin rhetorician Lactantius (ca. 250–ca. 325) represents in himself the pivot between the epochs. He was appointed by Diocletian to be a teacher of rhetoric at Nicomedia but lost that position when the great persecution began in 303. His great apology, *The Divine Institutes,* rehearses in seven books virtually all the arguments made by earlier apologists and may have been begun when the church was still under persecution, but the work is addressed to the emperor Constantine, "the first of the Roman princes to repudiate errors and to acknowledge the majesty of the one and only God" (1.1).[14] Lactantius clearly wants to cap the apologetic tradition in two ways. First, he wants to engage the Latin and not merely the Greek world: thus, he devotes much more attention to

Latin philosophers like Seneca and Cicero than had previous apologists, and he criticizes his Latin predecessors Tertullian and Cyprian for not having completed the job that they had undertaken.[15] Second, he does not stop at criticizing the errors and limitations of Greco-Roman religion and philosophy but constructs an impressive argument (especially in books 4–6) for a Christian culture that marries the best in the biblical and Hellenistic traditions. In another work, "Of the Manner in Which Persecutors Died," Lactantius glories in the peace that has come on the church and recounts with considerable relish the bad end that came to all the rulers who persecuted Christians, including Diocletian.[16]

Not only was the hazard of sudden and violent death removed at one stroke; Christians moved from a place of hiding to a posture of display, from a condition in which their property could be dispossessed to a condition in which property was bestowed on them, from a marginal to a central social status, from a status of mockery to one of privilege, from a situation in which the cross of Christ was the signal for danger to themselves to a situation in which the cross of Christ was emblazoned on the banners that imperial troops carried into battle.[17] History has known few such profound reversals of fortune, and it is not in the least surprising that the majority of Christians should gladly embrace their new status as the empire's favored religion. We find, in fact, that the forms of religious sensibility that leap most to sight in this new situation are the ones that most parallel the dominant expressions of religion in the earlier regimes: Religiousness A and D.

PARTICIPATION IN BENEFITS

The most visible change in Christianity's fortunes was in its forms of worship, which increasingly became *leitourgia,* a public and civic work. This was possible because public spaces became available for the open celebration of worship and prayer.[18] In the case of the great basilicas—such as that of the Holy Sepulchre in Jerusalem and the original St. Peter's in Rome—the new spaces were vast in comparison to the spaces in which worship had previously been carried out, in households or catacombs.[19] Worship naturally—even necessarily—expanded to fill such new spaces.[20]

The solemn seating of the clergy described in the *Didascalia Apostolorum*—with the bishop on his throne surrounded by the presbytery—now became more impressive when displayed in grand spaces.[21] The separate character of the clergy increasingly became marked by the wearing of distinctive garb.[22] The relatively simple Eucharistic celebration grew more complex to suit its character as the sacrifice of the new imperial religion, eventually including—in addition to the full liturgy of the word (the Mass of the Catechumens) and the liturgy of the Eucharist (the Mass of the Faithful)—processions through the impressive new spaces with the carrying of books and candles, the ringing of bells, genuflections, and the burning of incense.[23] The greater the space to fill, the longer the time the liturgy took, requiring the development of chants and litanies to accompany the solemn movement of processions.[24] Sacred sites and shrines that had once been pagan but had now been adopted by the Christians for their own use continued the sanctification of space through the worship of Christ where demons had reigned.[25]

Sacred time also expanded in at least two ways. First, Christian festivals began to replace the pagan sacred days as times of special and public worship. Constantine set the pattern with the recognition of Sunday as a general holiday. Over the next several centuries, two elaborate cycles of liturgical feasts began to emerge. One was based in the story of Christ: the earliest part of this cycle (already in the second century) was focused on Easter, with a long Lenten fast leading to the celebration of the death and resurrection during Holy Week.[26] The initiation of catechumens during the nightlong vigil preceding the feast acquired the solemnity and even the *disciplina arcana* of the Hellenistic Mysteries.[27] The seasonal cycle later expanded to include the Advent-Christmas segment, so that the entire year of worship became a liturgical reliving of the story of salvation in Christ.[28]

The other cycle was based in the cult of the saints, beginning with the martyrs and confessors.[29] Feasts dedicated to the saints celebrated the divine power at work in their lives, their deaths, and their present life with God, where they could serve as helpers to those still in the body.[30] The "sanctoral cycle" devoted to the recognition and celebration of God's work in humans therefore helped to secure the conviction concerning the "communion of saints."[31] In its full development, the veneration of the saints, involving communal "sacrifices" that commemorated their deeds, pilgrimages, prayer, and individual offerings, came to resemble the cult of the many individual gods in Greco-Roman Religiousness A, especially when devotion was further expressed through statues and paintings representing the saints. Like the many lesser gods of the Greco-Roman pantheon, so did the saints serve as protectors and patrons of those who approached them as clients.[32]

Sacred time also expanded through the development of the sacramental system that marked with a sacred character the moments of human life from birth to death.[33] The earliest and most securely grounded in New Testament precedent were baptism and the Eucharist (Lord's Supper).[34] But just as the Mysteries involved multiple initiations, so did Christianity expand its initiation process, with a second level of sacramental initiation called "confirmation."[35] Further initiation into the priesthood—which meant primarily the bishop but included by extension the presbyterate—by the third century required preliminary stages: doorkeeper, lector, exorcist, acolyte, subdeacon, and deacon.[36] There was also the sacrament of reconciliation: those who lapsed from communion either through apostasy or public sin were required to undergo a lengthy and usually public process of penance before they could be welcomed back to full participation in the Eucharist by the bishop.[37] The final ritual acts to gain the full status of sacraments were the anointing of the sick (also based in the New Testament) and marriage.[38]

The result of such liturgical expansion was that both in the cycle of each year and in the cycle of the believer's life, both space and time were sanctified. Christians after Constantine could publicly profess Christ in open assembly and publicly process through the streets singing hymns to Christ as God; they could debate Christological minutiae at the market;[39] they could find a Christian significance in many holy places, in every moment of the year, and at every stage of their lives. Simply by being part of this great and articulated communion, they participated in the divine benefits brought the world by the triumphant Christ.

Another dimension of Greco-Roman Religiousness A was the search for contact with power through media that were less structured than the formal cult, such as pilgrimages to healing shrines and prophetic oracles. As Christianity gained its public place in the Constantinian era, two loci of spontaneous power manifest themselves. The first was the cult of the martyrs that sprang up almost immediately. If the divine power was at work in the death of the saint, then some of that power might also reside in the saint's bodily remains. We find, then, the gathering of martyrs' relics, the construction of shrines to house such relics, and the popular celebration of martyrs at their graves, which could easily be confused or combined with the meals for the dead (*refrigeria*) that were celebrated at tombs by pagans.[40] If the relic of any martyr contains power, then the cross of Christ, the supreme martyr, must carry extraordinary power. Constantine's mother, Helena, initiated the quest for the cross of Christ and, when it was found, sponsored the cult devoted to the relic whose authenticity is assured by its capacity to effect healing.[41]

The second locus of spontaneous power was not the relics left by martyrs of the past but the living presence of holy men and women who practiced the "white martyrdom" of asceticism and whose bodies demonstrated the power of God to overcome the natural tendencies of the flesh and the assaults of demons.[42] As Athanasius describes him in the influential *Life of Antony*, the pioneering anchorite—the term derives from *anachōrein*, meaning "to dwell apart"—fled to the wilderness in response to the Gospel's call to radical discipleship.[43] Antony's solitary battle against demons through asceticism and prayer, however, drew multitudes to his presence, creating a "city in the desert" and forcing the saint to seek ever more remote places of solitude.[44] In many ways, Antony set a pattern: the desert fathers and mothers who sought through asceticism the sort of witness that formerly was available through martyrdom found themselves in a complex social network of communication and exchange, in which a constant feature was the search for wisdom from those regarded as holy.[45] The bodies of the saints who endured great fasting yet radiated robust good health were performances of the divine *dynamis*; the words of such saints had the power to change lives.

The declarations and *chreia* that fill the *Sayings of the Desert Fathers*, indeed, are functionally the rough equivalent of prophetic oracles in the Greco-Roman world. People traveled great distances from their cities in order to learn directly from the lips of those who triumphed over the world, the flesh, and the devil and to perhaps join their ranks.[46] Palladius' *Lausiac History* is the account of one bishop's journeys to monks scattered throughout the remote regions of the empire.[47] Its tales of ascetical accomplishment, feats of prayer, miracles, and visions are organized according to personalities, so that the focus always remains on the saint as the revelation of the divine power and as an example for imitation.[48] Palladius' account of the wealthy matron Melania, who visited various monks, was imprisoned, and became the patroness of women religious, is instructive, for it shows both how, after Constantine, Christians were found among the highest social levels of the empire and how many of them longed for a more radical form of discipleship than they saw available in their newly comfortable circumstances.[49] Palladius was the pupil of the learned archdeacon Evagrius of Pontus (345–399), whose early life in Constantinople was sophisticated and worldly, and who likewise sought salvation among the monks, first in Jerusalem and then in the Egyptian desert, where he gathered the sayings that form the basis of his ascetical works, the *Praktikos* and the *Chapters on Prayer*.[50]

The *Itinernarium Egeriae* ("Travels of Egeria") from circa 394–417 is particularly revealing of Christian Religiousness A in the late fourth century.[51] A wealthy Christian woman from Spain or Gaul, possibly a nun, travels with some companions to the Holy Land (Palestine) on a religious pilgrimage whose entire focus is on the sacred places and whose high point is the celebration of the Pasch in the city of Jerusalem during Holy Week.[52] Particularly striking is that at the biblical sites she visits are found shrines maintained by monks who lead the pilgrims in worship appropriate to the events associated with the place.[53] It is impossible not to be reminded of Pausanius' *Description of Greece*, a Greco-Roman work of the second century CE, in which a visitor from abroad visits and learns the cultural and religious lore associated with various sites in Greece.[54] Equally noteworthy is Egeria's determination to reach Tarsus of Cilicia, not because it is the home of Paul the Apostle, but because it is the site of the tomb of Thecla, the holy woman associated with Paul and the heroine of one portion of the apocryphal Acts of Paul.[55] The letter that Egeria composed for her sisters in Spain or Gaul is all the more useful because of its artlessness; it shows vividly and in detail the elements of Religiousness A as they appeared after Constantine: the search for divine power is expressed through pilgrimage because such power is associated with holy places, sacred times, and the saints. Contact with such times, places, and relics (or persons) means a participation in the divine *dynamis* resident in them.

A final but by no means insignificant expression of Christian Religiousness A after Constantine is the reading and continuing composition of apocryphal acts and gospels. The complex textual history of the compositions first written in the second and third centuries—and not included in the church's official canon—points to centuries of vigorous use in nonofficial contexts.[56] The composition of still further legendary accounts of the apostles, of Jesus and Mary, and of secondary characters like Nicodemus and Pontius Pilate shows that the same literary imagination that sought outlet in the production of romantic novels found an expression of its religious sensibility in apocryphal works that fictionally expanded the biblical universe.[57] Readers of narratives filled with signs and wonders—healings, exorcisms, resuscitations—can more easily imagine the continuity in the exercise of the divine *dynamis* displayed in the pages of this expanded Bible, and in the bodies of the saints can more quickly identify the work of driving out demons from afflicted humans with the work of driving out demons from pagan shrines and with battling demons in the solitude of prayer.

STABILIZING THE WORLD

We have seen in Greco-Roman religion that one aspect of Religiousness D is to serve as the supply side of Religiousness A: someone must staff the temples and shrines, someone must consult the oracle or interpret healing dreams, someone must prepare the sacrificial offerings, and someone must actually perform the sacrifice; above all, many people are required to support and enact the great public liturgies that on festival days expressed the religious life and piety of the *polis*.

In much the same way, Christian Religiousness D expressed itself in service to the cult that stabilized the new Christian *politeia*, which was increasingly also the *politeia* of the empire. Already in the third-century church orders, a more complex hierarchical order could be observed. Now, as Christianity moved into the larger spaces of basilicas and managed the shrines of martyrs, the same hierarchical differentiations serve the public order in a more obvious fashion.[58] In fact, the newly complex liturgies carried out in the basilicas as the Christian sacrifice required precisely complex and clearly articulated clerical offices and functions.[59]

The election of a bishop by a congregation was now an overtly political as well as religious act. The force of this observation is clear in light of schisms like the Donatist controversy, when rival bishops represented political factions dangerous to the stability of the empire.[60] Heresy could pose precisely the same threat to political order. Emperors therefore had an explicit interest in the ideological tendencies of bishops, who represented, as heads of large communities and even the faithful of an entire city—as in the case of the bishops of Rome and Antioch and Alexandria—potent political allies or opponents.[61] Because the bishop occupied such a politically significant position, the entire clerical order shared to some extent in the bishop's special status. Indeed, the sequence of grades of ordination internally appeared as a Christian version of the *cursus honorum* in the ancient Roman Republic: pursuing the sequence of ordination meant the acquisition of honor as well as obligation.[62] And, as always when religious offices also offer social advantages, power and privilege also increased the opportunities for corruption in the clergy.[63]

The practice of bishops meeting in general council, which, as we have seen, began as early as the Quartodeciman controversy in the late second century,[64] took on an even greater significance for the "stabilization of the world" in the new political order. If the bishops were unanimous in their understanding, then the church and empire could enjoy internal peace. If they were divided, strife was both religious and political. And if the bishops stood against the convictions of an emperor, it could mean political revolt of a serious kind. It was no wonder that Constantine involved himself so actively in the calling and directing of such councils as that at Arles in 314 and Nicaea in 325. According to Eusebius, Constantine thought of himself as a "bishop of external affairs" with respect to the church. It was after he forbade the worship of idols and ordered the honoring of martyrs and the observance of Christian festivals that Constantine, "On the occasion of his entertaining a company of bishops, let fall the expression, 'that he himself too was a bishop,' addressing them in my hearing in the following words: 'You are bishops whose jurisdiction is within the church:

I also am a bishop, ordained by God to oversee whatever is external to the church.' And truly his measures corresponded with his words; for he watched over his subjects with an episcopal care, and exhorted them as far as in him lay to follow a godly life."[65] The stakes were high for the Christian emperors, for if this monotheistic religion had the capability of providing the glue of society even more impressively than the polytheistic system of paganism, so could its impressive internal organization make it a threat to the political order when it fragmented through heresy or schism or, worse, when it stood unified against the will of the emperor. What was abundantly clear after Constantine was that the political importance of the bishop not only to the internal *politeia* of the church but to the *politeia* of the entire *oikoumenē* was obvious to all.

When analyzing Plutarch as a prime example of Religiousness D within Greco-Roman religion, we saw that his moral treatises (the *Moralia*) gave considerable attention to transformation among his readers, even though Plutarch's larger concern was the role of *eusebeia* in stabilizing the world. In similar fashion, many of the prominent bishops of the fourth and fifth centuries preached sermons to their congregations that made use of the moral *topoi* found among Hellenistic moralists from Aristotle forward. The pastoral sermons of Basil (330–379) and John Chrysostom (347–407) are particularly noteworthy in this respect.[66] The reason why patristic scholars consider the two centuries after Constantine to be "the golden age of patristic theology," however, is not because of such sermons.[67] It is, rather, that the bishops of the fourth and fifth centuries most resemble Plutarch—as well as their predecessor Irenaeus—in their concern for the ideological grounding for the church's institutional stability within the empire. It was with the same energy and intellectual seriousness with which Irenaeus repelled the varieties of Gnosticism that his episcopal successors applied to the rejection of subtler challenges to right belief and, therefore, to ecclesiastical unity and stability.

In a very real sense, the doctrinal disputes from Nicaea to Chalcedon can be regarded as a form of political theology. The Trinitarian and Christological controversies that dominated public theological discourse, that led up to and gained impetus from the ecumenical councils meeting under the aegis of the Christian empire in 325 and 381, had at stake the shape of the Christian *politeia* based on the rule of faith and the behavioral entailments of orthodox or heterodox belief.[68] More than that, naked political ambition and rivalry (both personal and civic) were factors throughout these controversies.[69] Like the emperor, bishop-theologians sought a *koinōnia* that embraced the entire *oikoumenē*; like the emperor, they resisted the forms of "popular religion," such as ecstatic prophecy, that could prove disruptive of the social order;[70] also like the em-

peror, they were willing to expel and exile those whose teaching did not conform to the proper understanding or practice of the faith.[71] The bishops were
unlike the emperor, however, in their willingness to sacrifice political harmony
to what they considered as "truth of the Gospel."

When caught up in the details of their lengthy arguments—the difference
between *homoousion* and *homoiousion*, for example—it is possible to lose sight
of the obvious social fact underlying the debates from every side, namely, that
the theological combatants were, for the most part, drawn from the social and
cultural elite of the new imperial order:[72] Basil, Chrysostom, Gregory of Nyssa
(335–394), and Gregory Nazianzen (329–389) all had been immersed in the
same sort of rhetorical and philosophical training as had the emperor Julian.[73]
Ambrose of Milan (338–397) had been an imperial official, indeed, governor of
Northern Italy, before his conversion to Christianity and becoming bishop of
that church. Augustine was a professor of rhetoric in Milan. Jerome (347–420)
confessed that early in his life he was more of a Ciceronian than a Christian.[74]

The rhetorical polish and philosophical acumen of the treatises and letters
themselves should remind us, to be sure, that from Justin on, Christian leaders
were increasingly drawn from the ranks of rhetoricians and public officials.[75]
The learning brought to bear on the interpretation of the Gospel story is the
learning developed within Hellenistic culture.[76] The theological arguments are
recognizably rhetorical arguments. The theological categories are undeniably
those of Greek ontology. The interpretation of texts is governed by the rules of
Greek and Latin grammar. In the theological debates carried out by bishops in
the new Christian *imperium*, the Greco-Roman religious sensibility of Plutarch
is everywhere evident.

MORAL TRANSFORMATION

Two ways of being religious in the Greco-Roman world are obviously present
in Christianity after Constantine. Religiousness A and D within Consantinian
Christianity correspond perfectly to the religious concerns for participating in
divine benefits and stabilizing the world that dominated pagan religion within
the empire before Constantine. The two other religious sensibilities exposed by
my analysis are also present but require more subtle detection. The concern for
moral transformation that is central to Religiousness B can be found to some
extent, I have suggested, in the sermons delivered by bishops to their congregations. But to find the full realization of that religious sensibility—fully realized
because expressed in a distinctive form of life—we must look at the development of Christian monasticism.

I have already mentioned the monks of the Egyptian desert when discussing Religiousness A, and for two reasons, the earliest heroes of Christian asceticism probably fit best within that category: their commitment to asceticism expressed the desire to emulate the ideal discipleship found in martyrdom, and they drew to them many people who craved contact with the power that was thought to reside in such holy men and women. Their vocation was charismatic and spontaneous rather than ordered and institutionalized. Their focus was on the individual as spiritual athlete more than on the group as a community of practice. Their style included wandering and visiting more than it did a settled existence with others in one place. The mode of expression among the desert fathers and mothers was aphoristic: their *apothegms* and *chreia* contained a wisdom based on life experience tested in the wilderness rather than on philosophical analysis of the passions or even a systematic study of scripture.[77]

Two factors worked to reshape this ascetical tradition and move it toward a Type B religious sensibility. The first is the composition of monastic rules that gave a more coherent form to the charismatic impulses of ascetics. The earliest such rule was written by Pachomius of Egypt (290–346). Between 318 and 323, this former soldier founded his first monastery, and many others followed: by the time of his death in 346, as many as 3,000 monastic communities may have been scattered throughout Egypt.[78] Pachomius' composition is not a literary masterpiece.[79] It consists mainly of discrete rules concerning various aspects of the monks' life, with special attention (in part 2) to the qualities desired in the chairman (or abbot) of the community. Pachomius' great contribution was to conceive of the monastic life not in terms of the solitary (*monos*) athlete but in terms of a common life (*koinos bios*) devoted to prayers and work.[80] His regulations for monks in common—including disciplinary measures (see part 3)—moved the ascetical life toward formal institutionalization.[81] Pachomian monks more closely resembled Greco-Roman philosophical communities, such as the Pythagoreans, and their Jewish counterparts (the Essenes), who also inhabited the desert.[82]

The worlds of monk and bishop intersected in two ways. First, a significant number of bishops were monks prior to their election to the episcopacy.[83] Second, bishops were understandably concerned about the possible excess and disorder that monks could create. Monks were therefore the frequent recipients of episcopal exhortation and instruction,[84] and bishops provided guidance through the composition of further monastic rules. Basil the Great, for example, studied the desert fathers and founded his own monastery in Cappadocia in 356. He composed *The Greater Monastic Rule* (*Patrologiae Graecae*, 31.889–

1052) and *The Lesser Rules* (*Patrologiae Graecae*, 31.1051–1306) in a catechetical style that restricts itself to basic principles, focusing particularly on what vices monks should avoid and what virtues should be pursued.[85] Augustine of Hippo also drew up a rule for nuns to help shape their observance (*Letter* 211).[86]

More elaborate were the efforts of John Cassian (360–435), a deacon and perhaps also a priest, who had spent years among the desert fathers and mothers before founding a monastery in Marseilles in 415.[87] There, in works of considerable size and even greater influence, he distilled the wisdom he had learned in the East. In his *Institutes*, he provides a rule for the behavior of coenobites but then turns to topics essential to the monastic life, namely, the battle with the passions.[88] In the *Conferences*, he places full-blown discourses on asceticism and prayer in the mouths of famous *abbas* of the desert.[89] Here we have not witty aphorisms but well-considered treatises that reveal a genuine philosophical spirit. As one reads Cassian's spokespersons dissect the passions that afflict the ascetic in his or her path to God, often with a strong element of psychological analysis, one is inevitably reminded of the analysis of vices and virtues among Greco-Roman moralists.[90]

In Cassian, then, we find the second element reshaping monasticism in the direction of religion as moral transformation, namely, the same sort of analysis of virtue and vice that were the concern of Greco-Roman moralists. It is no wonder that Cassian makes particularly vigorous use of those parts of the New Testament concerned with the same subjects.[91] Cassian decisively makes monasticism the central expression of Religiousness B in Christianity: men and women in monasteries commit themselves to a lifelong process of moral transformation.

The classic form of the monastic life in the West, however, was provided by Benedict of Nursia's *Rule for Monks* (RB), which is widely and justly recognized as a masterpiece of social legislation.[92] Written for monks taking a vow of stability (to remain in one monastery rather than wander; *RB*, 1), Benedict's *Rule* delicately balances the elements of a life dedicated to work (*labora*) and prayer (*ora*).[93] It eschews the spectacular physical asceticism of the desert: Benedictine monks are to eat, dress, and drink moderately.[94] The chief asceticism comes from life itself, when humility and obedience are cultivated under the guidance of the *Rule* and an abbot, and is tested by the daily grind of life in common.[95]

Benedict conceived of his monasteries as places for beginners rather than for adepts; he expected moral transformation to take time and much effort before the practice of virtue grew delightful. "But, as we progress in our monastic life and in faith, our hearts shall be enlarged, and we shall run with unspeakable sweetness of love in the way of God's commandments; so that, never abandoning his rule but persevering in his teaching in the monastery until death, we shall share by patience in the sufferings of Christ, that we may deserve to be partakers also of his kingdom. Amen."[96] What he aptly called his "school of the Lord's service" strongly resembled the philosophical schools of the Greco-Roman world both in form and substance. In form, monks went through stages of probation and testing (*RB*, 58); they followed a set rule and the direction of a master (1, 23); they shared possessions (33–34) and meals (41); they slept at the same time and in a shared space (22); their shared activities of work and prayer were at set times (9–18, 48); they cultivated silence and contemplation (6); they received penalties for disruptive behavior, including excommunication (23–28, 43–46); they engaged in the practices of reading and study.[97]

In substance, the point of all their activities was a certain "manner of life"— the term *conversatio morum* can be thought of as the equivalent of *anastrophē*[98]— which consisted in a constant and deliberate conversion of life. The individual reading of the monks was not systematic and scholarly but *lectio divina* ("holy reading"), carried out for personal and communal edification.[99] The communal reading in the divine office consisted of scripture, especially the Psalms, together with the hortatory writings of Ambrose, Augustine, and, above all, Gregory the Great (540–604), the most important patron of Benedictine monasticism, whose *Moralia* on the book of Job carried forward the long tradition of moral discourse based on the sacred text that extends back at least as far as Philo.[100] And among the works Benedict particularly recommended that his monks should read for their growth in the moral life were the *Institutes* and *Conferences* of John Cassian (*RB*, 73).

TRANSCENDING THE WORLD

The most radically world- and body-denying expression of Christianity flourished in the second and third centuries under the name of Gnosticism. This religious sensibility underwent the most significant changes after Constantine. In its explicit form, it moved to and beyond the margins of Christianity; in the muted form of mysticism, it found a home within the monastic life.

The Gnostic impulse was marginalized not only because of the efforts of the heresiologists but because it found an outlet in the new religious movement called Manichaeism.[101] Manes (ca. 216–276) offered a powerful version of ancient Persian dualism that could fit itself to distinct exoteric traditions such as Christianity or Buddhism.[102] The role that Christian Gnostics assigned Jesus—that of announcing the presence of divine light amid the darkness that needed to be gathered back to its source—was also assigned to Jesus (and Buddha, and Manes himself) by Manichaeism.[103] The (suitably edited) dualistic Paul who opposed flesh and spirit, God and world, was also appropriated by Manichaeism.[104]

A religion that simultaneously offered such a profoundly simple vision of the world (spirit=good and matter=evil), such a syncretistic impulse (all previous religions could be subsumed by it), and such a concrete mode of life (spirit is freed through ritual action)[105] was deeply appealing to those Christians already dualistic in temperament and alienated from the *hylic* forms of the church. Manichaeism spread rapidly, reaching Egypt before the end of the third century and reaching Rome by the beginning of the fourth. By the late fourth century, North Africa had many Manichaeans, among them the future bishop of Hippo. Augustine joined the Manichees in 373 and broke with them completely only with his baptism in 387.[106]

So deeply had Augustine been attached to Manichaeism that upon his consecration as a bishop he wrote his *Confessions* in 398–400—recounting in great detail his spiritual search that passed through Manichaeism—at least in part to reassure critics of his complete commitment to the Catholic faith.[107] A number of Augustine's early works were polemical treatises directed against the Manichees, including his attack (ca. 400) on his former teacher Faustus, whom he now regarded as a fraud (*Contra Faustum Manichaeum*).[108] Augustine's break with Manichaeism was real and sincere but perhaps not totally successful. Readers of this most brilliant of Western theologians recognize in his persistent pessimism concerning the human condition and in his distrust of human desire—especially with regard to sexuality—the lingering effect of a Manichaean dualism. Partly because of Augustine's unsurpassed influence on subsequent theology in the West, this same dualistic strain continued, evident not least in the inability of Christian theology to develop a real theology of marriage as a state of life, as distinct from an elaborate canon law concerning "the act of marriage."[109]

The Manichaean presence continued to be felt along the edges of the Christian world for centuries and found periodic expression in outbreaks of dualism among those professing Christianity but explicitly condemning the body as the impediment to the salvation of the soul. The Paulicians were a Byzantine movement whose members were persecuted in 684 and again in the ninth century. The Bogomils appeared in the Balkans and were denounced circa 972.[110] Most successful were the various groups of *Cathari* ("pure ones") in medieval Europe.[111] They were condemned in Orleans in 1022, but as the Albigensians became entrenched among the nobility of southern France, their condemnation

in 1165 and 1184 was resisted by an extended period of war between Catholic
and Albigensian forces in the twelfth and thirteenth centuries and led to the
creation of the Inquisition in 1233 as an organized effort to extirpate the virus of
Gnosticism from Christianity.[112]

A modified form of the dualistic impulse inherent in Religiousness C found
an acceptable if minor role within the ways of being Christian through its do-
mestication in monastic mysticism. Once more, the desert fathers were pivotal
in this development. It is important to note at once, however, that the ascetics
of the desert were not themselves in the least dualistic—certainly not in the
way we have seen displayed in the Orphic tradition, in the Hermetic literature,
or in Gnosticism. The ascetics of the desert affirmed the creator God who was
the father of Jesus Christ; they embraced all of scripture and had a special fond-
ness for the Psalms.[113] They regarded their flight from the world, as I have
mentioned, as a participation in a white martyrdom in imitation of Christ.[114]
Virginity and poverty were assumed and cultivated not as a rejection of God's
creation but as a mortification of "the flesh" as the seat of demonic impulses
toward idolatry and selfishness.[115] Their cultivation of prayer, although it sometimes led to visions, did not yield new revelations, and although the spiritual
athletes of the wilderness were sources of wise sayings, they were not the revealers of cosmic secrets that reached beyond the rule of faith.

In the East, Christian mysticism developed in the distinctive fashion that
has been termed *hesychastic* (from the Greek *hēsychios*, meaning silence or
quiet).[116] It had deep roots in the asceticism of the desert fathers but merged
such asceticism with a strong dose of Neoplatonism—the line runs from Origen through Gregory of Nyssa to Pseudo-Dionysius[117]—that emphasized the
apophatic approach to God as well as the kataphatic, and it wedded both approaches to the conviction that the effect of God's grace in Christ was a kind
of divinization (*theōsis*) that could be cultivated and even increased through
the span of mortal life.[118] Mystics sought a direct contact with the divine, a
contact that transcended discursive prayer, and to that end, they brought the
body and its passions under control. Celibacy, poverty, and detachment from
all earthly desires were the preliminary requisites for those who sought to transcend the world in mystical prayer.[119] But while monks sought to liberate the
soul from the entanglements of the body, their mysticism was nevertheless
shaped completely by the rule of faith.[120] The truth of the incarnation meant
that the body could never be despised as such, and among Eastern monks, the
veneration of icons as representations of the divine in human form was a beloved feature of prayer.[121]

In the West as well, mysticism thrived for a millennium within the confines of monasticism.[122] By no means were all monks mystical by inclination. As I have indicated, the form and substance of the monastic regimen in the West resembled more than anything the Religiousness B found in the Greco-Roman world in philosophical schools. But because monasteries did provide the setting for both work and prayer, and because forms of physical asceticism could be practiced there with the support of a community, those whose religious sensibility inclined toward Type C found a haven in that context.

Once more, it would be a mistake to regard the emphasis on virginity and poverty among monastic (and mendicant) mystics as evidence for an ontological dualism that regarded the body as inherently evil. Among both male and female mystics, in fact, sexual continence was connected to a mystical communion with the incarnate Christ, and poverty was construed in terms of a participation in Christ's lowly humanity.[123] Indeed, the single most consistent element in all the medieval mystics, whether monk, Beguine, or anchorite, is a concentration on the physical suffering of Christ.[124] Predominantly among female mystics of the middle ages, we also find the experience and expression of powerful visions that contain new revelations.[125] Such visions undoubtedly gave legitimacy to the leadership exercised by women in an age and church that provided them with no visible religious authority.

After Constantine, Christianity was able to express itself religiously across the entire spectrum of social and political life and in so doing revealed itself to be a Greco-Roman religion, defined, to be sure, by a commitment to one God and to the crucified and raised Messiah Jesus and shaped by the symbols of Jewish scriptures, but, in terms of religious sensibilities, displaying the full range of options found among non-Christians of their age. Indeed, during the fourth and fifth centuries, when Christianity still existed within the framework of a relatively vibrant Greco-Roman culture, its character as a Gentile religion is most clearly marked. Christians were religious in the same ways that their pagan neighbors were religious.

There is some truth, then, to the assertion of "Pagano-Papism" (see Chapter 1) that in the fourth century, Christianity took on the appearance of Greco-Roman religion. But it is only a partial truth, for Christianity had never lacked some of the characteristics of Greco-Roman religion. As I have shown, Religiousness A and Religiousness B both are well attested in the New Testament writings. Religiousness C emerges in the second century. And Religiousness D is well established already in the third century, needing only the declaration of religious tolerance for its appearance in full splendor as the new sacrificial priesthood of the empire. What really changes within Christianity in the fourth century is that the sociopolitical circumstances now allow for the full and free expression of religious sensibilities that were already present well before Constantine.

It is worth noting that as Greco-Roman influence itself contracted in the East (to become the Byzantine empire) and was overrun in the West (by barbarian invasion), and as the church adapted itself to such new circumstances, above all through the development of monasticism, the four clear forms of Greco-Roman religious expression tended to lose some of their sharp distinctions. Nevertheless, Christians continued to emphasize one of the four sensibilities. Many celebrated their participation in divine benefits and sought the divine *dynamis* in traditional public ways through attendance at Mass and making confession, through pilgrimages, relics, and prayer to their patron saints. Others committed themselves to the strenuous effort of moral transformation by taking vows and living according to the commands of a rule and abbot. Still others—fewest always in number—pursued direct experience of the divine through asceticism and prayer. And most visible of all were those bishops and other clergy who managed the institutional church as a way of stabilizing the world.

It is also worth observing that Christians of one sensibility did not necessarily understand or appreciate those of another—or even recognize the legitimacy of their way of being Christian. A classic expression of the distrust of religious experience by a monk-bishop is the letter written by Gregory of Nyssa (ca. 383) concerning the tendency of monks and hermits to travel on pilgrimage to the Holy Land—just as had Egeria at roughly this period. Gregory warns of the dangers of such enterprises (such as the loss of modesty when traveling in mixed groups), especially for those who have taken up "the higher life" and "the life according to philosophy"—that is, monks and hermits. But the fundamental problem for Gregory, who thinks in terms of moral transformation, is that seeking power in holy places is (at least for him) not real religion:

We confessed that the Christ who was manifested is Very God, much before as after our sojourn in Jerusalem. Our faith in him was not increased afterwards any more than it was diminished. Before Bethlehem we knew his being made man by means of the Virgin. Before we saw his grave we believed in His resurrection from the dead. Apart from seeing the Mount of Olives, we confessed that his ascension into heaven was real. We derived only this much of profit from our traveling thither, namely that we came to know, by being able to compare them, that our own places are far holier than those abroad.[126] Change of place does not affect any drawing nearer to God, but wherever you may be, God will come to you, if the chambers of your soul be found of such a sort that he can dwell in you. But if you keep your inner man full of wicked thoughts, even if you were on Golgotha, even if you were on the Mount of Olives, even if you stood on the memorial-rock of the resurrection, you will be as far away from receiving Christ into yourself, as one who has not even begun to confess him.[127]

EPILOGUE

The argument of this book is straightforward. I propose that the long history of Christian "attack and apology" with respect to paganism must be abandoned if any progress is to be made in understanding the relationship between Greco-Roman religion and Christianity. I find the possibility for a new and better conversation on the topic in the distinctive perspective of religious studies rather than theology. And within religious studies, I adopt a modified phenomenological approach that allows historical sources to speak as much as possible in their own terms.

A subtler appreciation for what constitutes "religious" enables in turn a more nuanced understanding of Greco-Roman religion, allowing me, for example, to view certain aspects of Hellenistic philosophy as thoroughly religious in character. My concentration, however, is not specifically on social organization, myths, doctrines, or even rituals, but on the ways in which actual human beings show themselves to be religious. The analysis of specific figures and texts as they speak in their own voice is critical to this examination. I use several interchangeable terms for the "ways of being religious," speaking of religious sensibility, religiousness, religious perspective, and even religious temperament. I distinguish these ways of being religious in terms of their distinctive ways of perceiving divine power and its function.

By far the greatest number of religious phenomena in the Greco-Roman world falls comfortably within Religiousness A: the divine power is seen to be operative in the empirical world, it is available through a variety of means, and its purpose is human participation in divine benefits. The perfect example of this religious sensibility is Aelius Aristides, whose devotion to the healing god

Asclepius organized and directed his life. A second way of being religious in the Greco-Roman world I have called Religiousness B: while not denying the divine power in the empirical world, this sensibility is interested above all in the way such power can enable moral transformation in persons. In this view, salvation is not success in external enterprises but perfection in virtue. Epictetus represents this sensibility because of the way his religious devotion is expressed totally through moral striving. Far fewer Greeks and Romans were drawn to the Orphic perspective (Religiousness C), which does not see divine power present in the empirical world but instead seeks to save the soul through escape from the material body; this religious sensibility of transcending the world finds its finest expression in the Hermetic tractate *Poimandres*. Finally, I find in Plutarch the representative of Religiousness D, which has two dimensions: on one side, it provides the religious leadership and structures for those seeking participation in benefits; on the other side, it seeks to stabilize the world by cultivating a piety that supports civilization.

My substantial analysis of Judaism between 300 BCE and 300 CE has real point within the overall argument, not only because it allowed me to test my analytic categories in a religion that seemed to others and to its own adherents as "other" in that world, but also because Judaism provides a point of comparison for nascent Christianity. Two results of the analysis are significant. First, during the time of its full engagement with Greco-Roman culture, Judaism displayed the same four modes of religious sensibility that I detected in paganism. Second, in clear contrast to Christianity, Judaism in the late second century abandoned its dalliance with Hellenistic culture and resolutely took its normative shape on the basis of its Hebrew heritage.

Earliest Christianity, in turn, reveals itself to be not only a religious movement that rapidly becomes Gentile culturally and demographically but one that increasingly reveals the same "ways of being religious" as are evident in the Greco-Roman world. Evidence from the New Testament writings supports the conclusion that in the first century, two ways of being Christian—participation in divine benefits and moral transformation—found expression. In the second and third century, all four ways of being Christian manifested themselves. Christianity as participation in divine benefits appears in apocryphal gospels and acts and in martyr piety. Christianity as moral transformation found expression in the sequence of Christian philosophers running from Clement of Rome, through Justin, to Origen. Christianity as transcending the world appeared impressively in Gnosticism. Christianity as stabilizing the world began to emerge in the priestly language used for worship and for bishops and in the political theology of controversialists like Irenaeus.

After Constantine, Christianity in the fourth and fifth centuries entered fully into its identity as a Greco-Roman religion, indeed as the imperial religion. Two results of its emancipation and imperial privilege are obvious. Christianity as participation in benefits expanded and expressed itself in the same public ways as had polytheism. And Christianity as stabilizing the world found its home in the increased political significance of bishops, councils, and orthodox teaching. In the rhetorically trained bishop-theologians of the fourth and fifth centuries, Christianity embraced and expressed its Hellenistic heritage. Christianity as moral transformation found institutional expression in monasticism, which in its mode of life and in its goals resembled the philosophical schools of the Greco-Roman world. Only Christianity as transcending the world experienced a significant eclipse. The rise of Manichaeism as a world religion (embracing the dualistic elements in Gnostic Christianity) meant that a radically dualistic outlook became heretical. A modified version of Christianity as transcending the world survived and then thrived in monastic (then mendicant) mysticism.

My analysis of Greco-Roman religion and early Christianity has a number of advantages that can be stated briefly.

1. It resists the sort of easy oversimplifications of Greco-Roman religion that reduce it to one of its elements (the Mysteries, or the Emperor Cult) while ignoring the complexity of religious practices and, even more, the multiple ways of being religious within Greco-Roman culture. My analysis not only respects that diversity but enhances it by focusing on the diverse modes of religious sensibility that the sources reveal. By using properly religious categories in my analysis of Greco-Roman sources rather than the categories of Christian theology, I have also enabled those sources to speak in their own terms rather than having to respond to alien presuppositions.

2. It avoids another common form of oversimplification by the way the relationship between paganism and early Christianity is approached. Neither paganism nor Christianity are considered as monolithic entities, and the question is not put in terms of causality or dependence. The alternatives of the arguments that "Christianity is entirely free of pagan influence" or "Christianity derives from the Mystery Cults" are shown to be false simply because they do not respect the complexity of the data. The multiple comparisons I have made among "ways of being religious" found in pagans, Jews, and Christians does respect that complexity and allows for both the similarities and the differences among the ancient religious systems to be appreciated.

3. It enables an appreciation for the diversity within earliest Christianity that goes beyond the obvious fact that the New Testament compositions responded to different circumstances in different ways, and it avoids the problematic assumption that New Testament compositions were engaged in ideological (theological) conflict—Paul against James, for example, or Matthew against Paul. By reading the New Testament in strictly religious terms—how ultimate power and its purpose are conceived—I am able to distinguish within earliest Christianity two distinct forms of religious sensibility that are there from the beginning and that are also found in the Greco-Roman culture shared by the first Gentile believers.

4. By using categories derived from Greco-Roman religion to guide my reading of both Judaism and early Christianity, this approach gives a better account of the similarities and differences between these two rival claimants to the heritage of Israel. In the period when Christianity arose, Judaism could legitimately be called a form of Greco-Roman religion because of its sustained engagement with Hellenistic culture and the ways in which its religious responses matched those of pagans. But whereas Christianity moved progressively toward the Gentile world and reached its maturity after Constantine precisely as the imperial Greco-Roman religion, Judaism turned away from its long dalliance with Hellenism and recovered its distinctive Hebrew roots.

5. By analyzing Greco-Roman religion on its own terms—or at least in terms that are not derived from Jewish or Christian theology—this approach can appreciate the religious impulses, convictions, experiences, and practices of pagans, not as weak approximations of a truth held exclusively by Jews and Christians, but instead as powerful and authentic expressions of religious truth. I do not mean doctrinal truth but, rather, true religious responses to what is perceived as ultimate. The shift in diction may be slight, from "Light to the Gentiles," which assumes among Jews and Christians a possession to be shared with the nations of the world, and "Light among Gentiles," which assumes that non-Jews and non-Christians already have a share in that possession, but the shift in perspective is huge and makes all the difference.

IMPLICATIONS OF THE STUDY

The analysis carried out on "the ways of being Christian" in Greco-Roman culture provides categories that have heuristic value for the study of other periods. Would it be possible, for example, to think of the Protestant Reformation in the sixteenth century—at least as represented by Luther and Calvin—as an effort to reduce Christianity to a single way of being religious? These classic reformers certainly rejected all the forms of Christian expression that I have identified as "participation in benefits," such as devotion to the saints, relics, and pilgrimages. At the same time, they repudiated the larger sacramental system and the priesthood that supported it, which constituted the aspect of Christianity that "stabilized the world." Finally, they had little use for mysticism or martyrdom—such as were found among the Anabaptists. At the same time, they demolished the monasticism that had been the locus for Religiousness B (moral transformation) within medieval Christianity. Their rejection of monasticism, however, was based not on a dislike for that way of being religious but on their perception that the making of religious vows and removal from ordinary life inevitably corrupted that way of being religious.

The Reformation asserted as authentically Christian precisely the way of being religious found in monasteries but extended that ideal to all Christians. It is worth noting that the apostle Paul, the preeminent representative of Religiousness B in the New Testament, is the most significant scriptural source for the Reformation's stance of *sola fide* and its understanding of faith as an obedience and trust that expressed itself in moral progress more than in ritual activity or mysticism. Closer analysis, to be sure, also reveals some of the complications inherent in the Reformation project. Calvin's *Institutes*, for example, is certainly a form of political theology. And in England, the conflicts between Anglicans and Puritans can be understood at least in part as a conflict between ways of being religious even within the Reformation, with the Anglicans asserting the continuing validity of ritual and hierarchy and the Puritans insisting on a more radical definition of Christianity in terms of the Word that leads to moral transformation. Even while acknowledging the ways in which the other modes of religiosity found a greater or lesser place within a constantly segmenting Protestantism—with denominations displaying a dizzying variety of institutional possibilities—the central religious emphasis of the Reformation remained on a moral transformation based on a Pauline version of the Gospel, at least according to the internal myth that based itself on a comparison to a post-Tridentine Catholicism that remained resolutely hierarchical, sacramental, monastic, mystical, and embarrassingly popular, all at the same time.

The four ways of being religious that emerged in the Greco-Roman context of earliest Christianity also have value for identifying and assessing differences within contemporary Christianity. Not a great deal of effort is required to discover examples of all four religious sensibilities, which cut across denominational lines and even theological positions. Christianity as participation in divine benefits flourishes in both Protestantism and Catholicism wherever there is a focus on healings or prophecy or glossolalia or pilgrimage to the presence of places made holy by saints, wherever miracle stories abound and claims to divine power and possession proliferate. Christianity as stabilizing the world is found in all those whose highest religious ambition is to be a bishop or head of a denomination, or even to administer a charity, as well as among those who labor at interfaith dialogues and ecumenical organizations. Christianity as transcending the world is found especially today in the "New Gnosticism" that appears within and outside of virtually every visible church institution, among those who think in terms of "spirituality" rather than "religion," who prefer retreats and workshops with fellow seekers to weekly worship, who regard theologies and polities as inhibitions to true Christianity, which is of the spirit rather than of the body, who consider ancient heresiologists as wicked and ancient Gnostics as good.

What about Religiousness B, the way of moral transformation? It can continue to be found within the monastic life—where that exists—and impressively in some forms of Protestantism that continue the central preoccupation with the Reformation. And across denominations, it is found in those who espouse "prophetic" Christianity and "Liberation Theology," for at heart these are concerned above all with the transformation of society and the moral improvement of humans. Not surprisingly, when one remembers the way in which universities grew out of monasteries, Religiousness B is found among academic Christians, whether they are theologians active within a church or students of religion in secular colleges and research centers. No less than the other types of Christianity do academic Christians self-select on the basis of religious temperament. It is therefore also not a surprise that academic religionists tend to define "authentic religion" in terms matching their own perceptions and commitments, that is, in terms of moral transformation within individuals and societies.

These categories also help in grasping the mutual misunderstanding and suspicion that exist among Christians of different religious sensibilities. This is not a matter of theology, morals, or even polity but of religious temperament. Christians who consider spirituality more important than religion, and the cultivation of their soul more significant than social improvement, tend to regard all material expressions of religion (especially when exclusive to one tradition) as unfortunate, underevolved, and even deeply misguided. They think popular forms of religion to be little more than superstition and consider creeds and canons and bishops as equally problematic for what they regard as authentic Christianity—one that transcends Christianity itself. At the same time, the new

Gnostics are regarded with suspicion by those who regard themselves as the protectors of community identity and have associated themselves precisely with canon, creed, and council.

Bishops, the maintainers of tradition and good order whose religious life is defined by the desire to stabilize the world, are, in turn, chronically suspicious of all forms of popular religion that may disrupt the steady round of sanctioned religious observance. They tend to look askance at glossolalia, and healings, and prophecy, except as tested by ecclesiastical inquiry. They tend to be equally resistant to claims of sainthood, unless validated through a process of ecclesiastical scrutiny. Theologians and prophetic protesters are also disturbing to the keepers of good order, who prefer catechesis to critical theology, tradition to innovation, and licensed charities to random acts of mercy. Mystics and spiritual seekers are likewise more often seen by bishops (of every variety) as irritants requiring close institutional oversight than as creative stimulants to the renewal of piety. The suspicion is reciprocated: visionaries and healers tend to regard bishops as agents of repression who prefer stale tradition to the fresh breath of the spirit. Spiritual seekers consider the keepers of the gate as blind to authentic religion, precisely because of their concern for institution.

The academic representatives of Religiousness B—pastors of liberal denominations, theologians in all denominations, and scholars of religion—have little good to say about any of the other three ways of being Christian. Popular Christianity (Religiousness A) is dismissed as superstition. Spiritual seekers are seen as narcissists whose self-involvement contributes nothing to the world. Bishops are regarded as company men whose commitment is to the preservation of the institution at any cost rather than to the cultivation of morally transformed communities. The mistrust in this case is returned from all sides as well: bishops suspect theologians and prophets of subverting the tradition; spiritual seekers think that students of religion destroy the religion of the heart with their insistence on intelligence. And those Christians who celebrate the presence of the divine in healings and tongues consider seminary professors and university professors alike as undeserving of the name of Christian because of their spirit of critical inquiry. One of the most fascinating aspects of Christianity today is the way in which these distinct religious emphases—all of which have a long and distinguished pedigree within Christianity—serve to divide Christians into mutually hostile camps.

The last way in which the categories I have used here may give rise to further study is in the analysis of non-Christian religions. I am not competent to carry out that analysis, but I suspect that the four religious sensibilities that I have found in Greco-Roman religion and in Christianity—not to mention Judaism during its Hellenistic phase—may be present in virtually all religions that have developed above the tribal or temporary level. Certainly, in the long and tense struggle in Islam between Sufism and Shari'ah, it is possible to find elements of the religious sensibilities I have described. It is even possible that the analysis that began with the ways of being religious within the Greco-Roman world may turn out to have a much more universal applicability.

A FINAL WORD

I have studiously avoided theological discourse in this study, precisely because I am convinced that, in the case of careful comparative analysis, the field of religious studies provides a more neutral and ultimately more useful form of discourse. My approach throughout has been descriptive rather than prescriptive.

But two modest theological implications for Christians do follow naturally from the analysis I have undertaken. The first concerns internal Christian ecumenism. This study suggests that the deepest divisions among Christians may not be those definable in terms of theology or polity but may be those defined by distinct ways of being religious. My analysis further suggests that there is no primitive, pristine form of Christianity that does not bear a strong resemblance to Greco-Roman religion, and that, further, the four "ways of being Christian" in the contemporary world all have some claim to legitimacy within the tradition both of Judaism and earliest Christianity. The challenge to Christians today is to embrace a catholicity of religious sensibility and expression rather than to divide on the basis of mutual suspicion of ways of being Christian that seem strange.

The second theological implication concerns Christian relations to other world religions. My analysis has shown that the age-old tradition of Christian polemic against paganism, which relegates to the realm of the demonic the religious practices of one's neighbors (distant or near, it does not matter), serves to obscure the true state of affairs both within Christianity and in other religions. In Christianity, the ways of being Christian through the ages and today are basically the same as those found in the first "world religion" engaged by Christians, the paganism of the Roman Empire. Christians are more like them than they have ever been willing to admit. Similarly, the sensibilities displayed in Greco-Roman religion, in Judaism, and in Christianity, in all likelihood correspond to those found in other world religions. They are more like Christians than Christians have ever been willing to see. Once Christians are willing to grant the element of continuity—at the level of human perception and experience—the better able Christians are to assess the ways in which they truly are different and must agree to remain different. This, it seems to me, is at least a better starting point for conversation among the religious people of the world than the one that begins in mutual ignorance and suspicion.

NOTES

1. BEYOND ATTACK AND APOLOGY

1. Tertullian, *De Praescriptione Hereticorum*, 7.
2. Oscar Wilde, *The Importance of Being Earnest* (1895), Act I.
3. L. T. Johnson, *The Writings of the New Testament: An Interpretation*, 2nd enl. ed. (Minneapolis: Fortress, 1999).
4. See, for example, Matt 23:1–39 (paralleled by Luke 11:37–52; see also John 8:44–47; 12:42–43; Rev 3:9; 2 Cor 4:3; 1 Thess 2:15–16). The debate concerning the possibility that 1 Thess 2:15–16 is an interpolation (see D. Schmidt, "I Thess 2:13–16: Linguistic Evidence for an Interpolation," *Journal of Biblical Literature* 102 [1983]: 269–279; and J. A. Weatherly, "The Authenticity of 1 Thessalonians 2:13–16: Additional Evidence," *Journal for the Study of the New Testament* 42 [1991]: 79–98) does not in the least affect the point that the passage contains early Christian polemic against unbelieving Jews.
5. See R. Ruether, *Faith and Fratricide: The Theological Roots of Anti-Semitism* (New York: Seabury, 1974); R. Eckhardt, *Jews and Christians: The Contemporary Meeting* (Bloomington: Indiana University Press, 1986); T. Linafelt, ed., *A Shadow of Glory: Reading the New Testament after the Holocaust* (New York: Routledge, 2002).
6. See L. T. Johnson, "The New Testament's Anti-Jewish Slander and the Conventions of Ancient Polemic," *Journal of Biblical Literature* 108 (1989): 419–441.
7. Among many other passages, Hos 8:1–4; 13:1–4; 14:8; Zeph 1:5–6; Mal 2:10; Jer 1:16; 2:11–13; 7:23–26; 11:1–13; 16:10–13; Ezek 20:1–8; Isa 2:7–8; 30:22; 40:18–20.
8. *Wisdom of Solomon* 14:22–28 (Revised Standard Version).
9. For discussion of the term, which could bear both positive and negative connotations, see L. T. Johnson, *The Acts of the Apostles*, ed. D. J. Harrington (Sacra Pagina 5; Collegeville, MN: Liturgical, 1992), 311–321.
10. For Paul and rhetoric, see, for example, M. M. Mitchell, *Paul and the Rhetoric of Reconciliation* (Louisville: Westminster/John Knox, 1991); and for Paul and philosophy, see A. J. Malherbe, *Paul and the Popular Philosophers* (Minneapolis: Fortress, 1989).

11. For Paul's use of witchcraft language in Galatians 3:1 and elsewhere, see J. H. Neyrey, *Paul in Other Words: A Cultural Reading of His Letters* (Louisville: Westminster/John Knox, 1990), 181–206.

12. For the social realities involved, see G. Theissen, *The Social Setting of Pauline Christianity: Essays on Corinth*, trans. J. H. Schultz (Philadelphia: Fortress, 1981); and W. A. Meeks, *The First Urban Christians: The Social World of the Apostle Paul* (New Haven, CT: Yale University Press, 1983).

13. For discussion, see A. C. Wire, *The Corinthian Women Prophets: A Reconstruction through Paul's Rhetoric* (Minneapolis: Fortress, 1990); and E. Schüssler-Fiorenza, *In Memory of Her: A Feminist Theological Reconstruction of Christian Origins* (New York: Crossroad, 1983).

14. See L. T. Johnson, "Glossolalia and the Embarrassment of Experience," in *Religious Experience in Earliest Christianity* (Minneapolis: Fortress, 1998), 105–136.

15. This theme is extensively and convincingly developed by S. Garrett, *The Demise of the Devil: Magic and the Demonic in Luke's Writings* (Minneapolis: Fortress, 1989).

16. Pagan observers of Christianity also engaged in polemic against what they perceived as a particularly noxious form of superstition; see R. L. Wilken, *The Christians as the Romans Saw Them* (New Haven, CT: Yale University Press, 1984); and especially J. G. Cook, *The Interpretation of the New Testament in Greco-Roman Paganism* (Studies and Texts in Antiquity and Christianity 3; Tübingen: JCB Mohr [Paul Siebeck], 2000).

17. In his *Address to the Greeks*, Tatian (110–172 CE) is as ruthless in the condemnation of Greek philosophy as he is of Greek religion (see 2, 19, 25, 27, 33); and Theophilus of Antioch (115–168 CE), in his *To Autolycus*, has negative comments on philosophy (III.2–3). But Theophilus also comments favorably on Greek philosophers (II.4, II.38; III.5–7) and poets (II.5–7; II.37). In his *Embassy*, Athenagoras (ca. 177 CE) cites the philosophers as agreeing with the poets' views on the gods (19). By the time of Origen (184–254 CE) and Augustine (354–430 CE), Greek philosophy, especially that of Plato, is given an honored place as part of the preparation for the gospel. From the start, furthermore, Christian apologists portrayed their own conversion in terms strongly reminiscent of conversion among philosophers (Tatian, *Address*, 29–30; Theophilus, *Autolycus*, I.14; Justin, *Discourse to the Greeks*, 1; *Dialogue with Trypho*, 3). For general lines of approach to Greek culture among the apologists, see the essays in J. Pouderon and J. Dore, eds., *Les Apologistes chrétiens et la culture grecque* (Theologie Historique 105; Paris: Beauchesne, 1998). The special consideration given the Sybil was due to the Jewish interpolations in the *Sybilline Oracles*; see J. J. Collins, "The Jewish Transformation of Sibylline Oracles," in *Seers, Sybils and Sages in Hellenistic-Roman Judaism* (Supplements to the Journal for the Study of the Old Testament 54; Leiden: Brill, 1997), 181–197. On the special status accorded the Sybil as a unique prophetic voice, see Theophilus, *Autolycus*, II.9; II.35; Clement of Alexandria, *Exhortation to the Heathen*, 2 and 4; Justin, *First Apology*, 20.

18. See, e.g., *The Letter to Diognetus*, 2; Theophilus, *Autolycus* II.1; Tertullian, *Apology*, 10; Minucius Felix, *Octavius*, 1.

19. Theophilus, *Autolycus*, I.1 (human hands); Athenagoras, *Embassy*, 18 (fabrications of poets); Tertullian, *Apology*, 13 (machinations).

20. See, e.g., Tatian, *Address*, 10; Theophilus, *Autolycus*, I.9; I.10; II.2; Athenagoras, *Embassy*, 28–30; Clement of Alexandria, *Exhortation*, 2; Tertullian, *Apology*, 10–11; Minucius Felix, *Octavius*, 21; Lactantius, *The Divine Institutes*, 1.24.

21. Tatian, *Address*, 9, 21, and 34; Athenagoras, *Embassy*, 8 and 20; Justin, *Discourse*, 1; Minucius Felix, *Octavius*, 20; Arnobius, *Against the Heathen*, I.24.

22. Origen, *Against Celsus*, VIII.24; see also VII.69.

23. Origen, *Against Celsus*, V.46; see Tatian, *Address*, 8 and 12.

24. See Tatian, *Address*, 22; Theophilus, *Autolycus*, II.8; Athenagoras, *Embassy*, 23–24; Clement of Alexandria, *Exhortation*, 3; Commodianus, *The Instructions of Commodianus*, 2–3; Augustine, *City of God*, II.24; X.26; Lactantius, *The Epitome of the Divine Institutes*, 28.

25. Augustine, *City of God*, II.29.

26. Minucius Felix, *Octavius*, 38.

27. Note the theory advanced concerning the power behind the oracles at Delphi in Plutarch, *The Obsolescence of Oracles*, 13–17 (Mor., 417A–419B).

28. *Against Celsus*, VII.69.

29. On the gods' wicked actions, see Tatian, *Address*, 8 and 9; Theophilus, *Autolycus*, I.9; II.8; Athenagoras, *Embassy*, 21; Clement of Alexandria, *Exhortation*, 2; Justin, *Discourse*, 2–3; Tertullian, *Apology*, 11; Minucius Felix, *Octavius*, 22; Arnobius, *Against the Heathen*, II.9; IV.20–37. On the effect of hearing the myths read on the emotions of the hearers, see Arnobius, *Against the Heathen*, I.17–20. On the evil deeds incited by hearing the myths, see Augustine, *City of God*, II.25.

30. See Tatian, *Address*, 22 and 33; Justin, *Discourse*, 4; Tertullian, *Apology*, 15; Augustine, *City of God*, II.26–27.

31. See Tertullian, *Apology*, 8–9; Minucius Felix, *Octavius*, 24; Arnobius, *Against the Heathen*, IV.18–23.

32. Clement of Alexandria, *Exhortation*, 4.

33. See Athenagoras, *Embassy*, 26; Minucius Felix, *Octavius*, 27.

34. Justin, *First Apology*, 54; Augustine, *City of God*, VIII.21.

35. Tatian, *Address*, 18; Justin, *First Apology*, 14; see also Lactantius, *The Divine Institutes*, 1.17–18.

36. Tertullian, *Apology*, 22–23; Origen, *Against Celsus*, VIII.61.

37. Augustine, *City of God*, XVIII.18.

38. Augustine, *City of God*, II.26.

39. Tatian, *Address*, 19; Tertullian, *Apology*, 22–23; Origen, *Against Celsus*, IV.89; IV.92.

40. See, for example, Justin, *First Apology*, 57; Tertullian, *Apology*, 27; Minucius Felix, *Octavius*, 28; Augustine, *City of God*, XXI.21.

41. The reader must be aware from the beginning that some of my positions regarding the authorship and date of New Testament compositions are not held by the majority of contemporary scholars. My ascription of 1 Timothy to Paul is not careless or accidental, but a principled decision, based on long study and disputation. I take the

position that Paul was the author of all the letters attributed to him during his lifetime but did not necessarily "write" them in the sense of individual, direct composition. Paul's "school," which many scholars think of coming into existence after his death, was active, I propose, during his ministry.

42. Justin, *First Apology*, 26, 56, and 57.

43. Cyril of Jerusalem, *Mystagogic Catachesis*, 1 and 8.

44. *First Apology*, 20, 62, and 66.

45. Origen, *Against Celsus*, I.6.

46. Minucius Felix, *Octavius*, 11.

47. Augustine, *Against Faustus the Manichaean*, 20.4.

48. On these figures, see E. Wind, *Pagan Mysteries in the Renaissance*, new and enl. ed. (New York: Barnes and Noble, 1968); and F. Copelston, *A History of Philosophy*, vol. 3: *Late Medieval and Renaissance Philosophy* (New York: Doubleday, 1963), 207–216.

49. See, e.g., M. Luther, *The Babylonian Captivity of the Church* (1520).

50. See *Historia Ecclesiae Christi* (1559–1574).

51. Cardinal Baronius, *Annales Ecclesiastici* (1588–1607).

52. Isaac Casaubon, *De Rebus Sacris et Ecclesiasticis Exercitationes* (London, 1614), especially 659–660, 684.

53. See "The Temple and the Magician," in J. Z. Smith, *Map Is Not Territory: Studies in the History of Religions* (Studies in Judaism in Late Antiquity, ed. J. Neusner, vol. 23; Leiden: E. J. Brill, 1978), 188. Smith shows the influence of Middleton (and then Charles Francois Dupuis) on the American statesmen John Adams and Thomas Jefferson in *Drudgery Divine: On the Comparison of Early Christianities and the Religions of Late Antiquity* (The Jordan Lectures in Comparative Religion 14; Chicago: University of Chicago Press, 1990), 1–35.

54. See, for example, John Toland, *Christianity Not Mysterious* (London, 1696); C. F. Dupuis, *Origine de tous les Cultes, ou Religion Universelle*, 12 vols. (Paris, 1795); Godfrey Higgins, *Anacalypsis: An Attempt to Draw Aside the Veil of the Saitic Isis; or, An Inquiry into the Origin of Languages, Nations, and Religions* (London, 1836); Thomas William Doane, *Bible Myths and Their Parallels in Other Religions* (New York: J. W. Bouton, 1882); Edwin Johnson, *Antiqua Mater: A Study in Christian Origins* (London, 1887); John Robertson, *Pagan Christs: Studies in Comparative Hierology* (London, 1911); Edward Carpenter, *Pagan and Christian Creeds* (New York: Harcourt, Brace and Howe, 1920); W. F. Vassall, *The Origin of Christianity: A Brief Study of the World's Early Beliefs and Their Influence on the Christian Church* (New York: Exposition Press, 1952).

55. It was first published in an expanded book-length form in 1858, and a third edition appeared in 1862 (Edinburgh: James Wood). A reprint from 1932 is currently available on Amazon.com.

56. W. W. Hyde, *Greek Religion and Its Survivals* (Boston: Marshall Jones, 1923), 44; see also his *Paganism to Christianity in the Roman Empire* (Philadelphia: University of Pennsylvania Press, 1946), 68–69.

57. See, for example, Thomas Chubb, *The True Gospel of Jesus Christ Vindicated* (London, 1738); this early chapter in historical Jesus research is entertainingly evoked by C. Allen, *The Human Christ*. Note that Schweitzer's classic 1906 reconstruction of the quest had as its original German title *Von Reimarus zu Wrede: Eine Geschichte der Leben-Jesu-Forschung*. Hermann Samuel Reimarus (1694–1768) borrowed from the Deist perspectives of the British. See A. Schweitzer, *The Quest of the Historical Jesus: A Critical Study of Its Progress from Reimarus to Wrede*, 1st complete ed. by J. Bowden (Minneapolis: Fortress, 2001).

58. See L. T. Johnson, *The Real Jesus: The Misguided Quest for the Historical Jesus and the Truth of the Traditional Gospels* (San Francisco: HarperSanFrancisco, 1996).

59. Two benefits of the search are clear to everyone: the intricate literary relations among the Synoptic Gospels and the character of the Gospel narratives primarily as witness accounts and interpretations of Jesus rather than as historical reports on him.

60. C. A. Lobeck, *Aglaophamus, sive de Theologiae Mysticae Graecorum Causis Libri Tres*, 2 vols. (Konigsberg: 1829). See the helpful review of literature by B. M. Metzger, "Considerations of Methodology in the Study of the Mystery Religions and Early Christianity," *Harvard Theological Review* 48 (1955): 1–20.

61. F. Loisy, *Les Mystères Païens et le Mystère Chrétien*, 2nd ed. (Paris: E. Nourry, 1930); R. Reitzestein, *Die hellenistischen Mysterienreligionen* (Leipzig: Teubner, 1910); Reitzestein, *Poimandres: Studien zur griechisch-ägyptische und frühchristliche Literatur* (Leipzig: Teubner, 1904); C. Clemen, *Primitive Christianity and Its Non-Jewish Sources*, trans. R. G. Nisbet (Edinburgh: T. & T. Clark, 1912); S. Angus, *The Mystery Religions and Christianity* (New York: Charles Scribner's Sons, 1925).

62. E. Hatch, *The Influence of Greek Ideas and Usages upon the Christian Church*, 2nd ed., ed. A. M. Fairburn (London: Williams and Norgate, 1891); on the Mysteries, see especially 283–309.

63. A. D. Nock, "Hellenistic Mysteries and Christian Sacraments," in *Early Gentile Christianity and Its Hellenistic Background* (New York: Harper and Row, 1964 [1928]), 109–145.

64. Paul's letters were challenging not least because they were the most obvious source for Mystery language and practice in early Christianity and, simultaneously, the clearest source for the "righteousness by faith" that for Protestant scholars defined authentic Christianity.

65. Loisy, *Les Mystères Païens*; S. J. Case, *Experience with the Supernatural in Early Christian Times* (New York: The Century Company, 1929), 245–263; P. Gardner, *The Religious Experience of Saint Paul* (New York: G. P. Putnam and Sons, 1911), 72–99; V. D. Macchioro, *From Orpheus to Paul: A History of Orphism* (New York: Henry Holt and Company, 1930).

66. H. A. A. Kennedy, *Saint Paul and the Mystery Religions* (London: Hodder and Stoughton, 1913); L. Cerfaux, "L'influence des 'mystères' sur les épîtres de S. Paul aux Colossiens et aux Éphésiens," in *Recueil Lucien Cerfaux: Études d'exégèse et d'histoire religieuse*, 3 vols. (Leuven: Leuven University Press, 1985), 3:279–285.

67. This geographical/cultural/temporal progression was given its first expression by W. Heitmüller, especially in "Zum Problem Paulus und Jesus," *Zeitschrift für die*

neuentestamentliche Wissenschaft 13 (1912): 320–337; was systematically developed
by W. Bousset, *Kyrios Christos: A History of the Belief in Christ from the Beginnings
of Christianity to Irenaeus*, trans. J. E. Steely (Nashville: Abingdon Press, 1970 [1926]);
and was given even greater legitimacy by R. Bultmann, *Theology of the New Testament*, 2 vols., trans. K. Grobel (London: SCM Press, 1959). I discuss the analysis further in the next chapter.

68. See *Paul and His Interpreters: A Critical History*, trans. W. Montgomery (London: A.
and C. Black, 1912); and *The Mysticism of Paul the Apostle*, trans. W. Montgomery
(London: A. and C. Black, 1931).

69. Smith, *Drudgery Divine*, 83.

70. For a discussion of the way in which Christian categories have distorted discussions
of Orphism, see R. G. Edmonds, *Plato, Aristophanes, and the "Orphic" Gold Tablets*
(Cambridge: Cambridge University Press, 2004), 29–40.

71. It is worth noting that Roman Catholic scholars have, not surprisingly, been rather
more open to a positive appreciation of the Mysteries; see H. Rahner, "The Christian
Mystery and the Pagan Mysteries," in *The Mysteries: Papers from the Eranos Year-
books*, vol. 2, ed. J. Campbell (Bollingen Series 30; Princeton, NJ: Princeton University Press, 1955), 337–401; O. Casel, *The Mystery of Christian Worship* (Westminster,
MD: Newman, 1962).

2. BEGINNING A NEW CONVERSATION

1. For Christian origins, see A. Y. Collins, ed., *Feminist Perspectives in Biblical Scholarship* (Society of Biblical Literature Centennial Publications; Chico, CA: Scholars,
1985); C. Osiek and M. Y. MacDonald, with J. Tulloch, eds., *A Woman's Place: House
Churches in Earliest Christianity* (Minneapolis: Fortress, 2006); E. Schüssler-
Fiorenza, *In Memory of Her: A Feminist Theological Reconstruction of Christian Origins* (New York: Crossroad, 1983). For the Greco-Roman world generally, see, among
many others, E. Fantham et al., *Women in the Classical World: Image and Text* (New
York: Oxford University Press, 1994); E. Cantarella, *Bisexuality in the Ancient World*,
trans. C. O'Cuilleanain (New Haven, CT: Yale University Press, 1992); A. Cameron
and A. Kuhrt, *Images of Women in Antiquity*, rev. ed. (London: Routledge, 1993);
A. Richlin, ed., *Pornography and Representation in Greece and Rome* (New York:
Oxford University Press, 1992); E. C. Keuls, *The Reign of the Phallus: Sexual Politics
in Ancient Athens* (Berkeley: University of California Press, 1985).

2. See, e.g., J. Levenson, *The Hebrew Bible, the Old Testament, and Historical Criticism:
Jews and Christians in Biblical Studies* (Louisville: Westminster/John Knox, 1993). No
one has more systematically engaged other religious traditions from the standpoint of
Judaism—and from a steadfastly religious studies perspective—than Jacob Neusner.
Among his hundreds of books, see only *Judaism and Christianity in the Age of Con-
stantine: History, Messiah, Israel, and the Initial Confrontation* (Chicago: University of
Chicago Press, 1987); Neusner et al., eds., *Ancient Israel, Judaism, and Christianity in
Contemporary Perspective* (Lanham, MD: University Press of America, 2006); J. Neusner,
E. S. Frerichs, and A.-J. Levine, eds., *Religious Writings and Religious Systems: Sys-*

temic Analysis of Holy Books in Christianity, Islam, Buddhism, Greco-Roman Religions, Ancient Israel, and Judaism (Atlanta: Scholars, 1989); Neusner et al., eds., *The Social World of Formative Christianity and Judaism: Essays in Tribute to Howard Clark Kee* (Philadelphia: Fortress, 1988); J. Neusner, E. S. Frerichs, and C. McCracken-Flesher, eds., *"To See Ourselves as Others See Us": Christians, Jews, "Others" in Late Antiquity* (Chico, CA: Scholars, 1985); Neusner, ed., *Christianity, Judaism, and Other Greco-Roman Cults: Studies for Morton Smith at Sixty* (Leiden: Brill, 1975); Neusner, ed., *Religions in Antiquity: Essays in Memory of Erwin Ramsdell Goodenough* (Leiden: Brill, 1968). For a feminist approach to formative Judaism, see A.-J. Levine, ed., *"Women Like This": New Perspectives on Jewish Women in the Greco-Roman World* (Society of Biblical Literature, Early Judaism and Its Literature 1; Atlanta: Scholars, 1991). For a thoroughly social-scientific approach, see H. Eilberg-Schartz, *The Savage in Judaism: An Anthropology of Israelite Religion and Ancient Judaism* (Bloomington: Indiana University Press, 1990).

3. For a small sampling of the rich analyses of the world's religions now regularly carried out in the context of religious studies, see G. Schopen, *Bones, Stones, and Buddhist Monks: Collected Papers on the Archaeology, Epigraphy, and Texts of Monastic Buddhism in India* (Honolulu: University of Hawaii Press, 1997); R. F. Campany, *To Live as Long as Heaven and Earth: A Translation and Study of Ge Hong's Traditions of Divine Transcendents* (Berkeley: University of California Press, 2002); H. Nakamaki, *Japanese Religions at Home and Abroad: Anthropological Perspectives* (London: RoutledgeCurzon, 2003); P. B. Courtright, *Ganesa: Lord of Obstacles, Lord of Beginnings* (New York: Oxford University Press, 1985); J. A. Berling, *The Syncretic Religion of Lin Chao-en* (New York: Columbia University Press, 1980); E. Reinders, *Borrowed Gods and Foreign Bodies: Christian Missionaries Imagine Chinese Religion* (Berkeley: University of California Press, 2004); J. B. Flueckiger, *Gender and Genre in the Folklore of Middle India* (Ithaca, NY: Cornell University Press, 1996).

4. For a sense of the distinctive culture (and distinctive tensions) in this recent academic colony, see W. H. Capps, *Religious Studies: The Making of a Discipline* (Minneapolis: Fortress, 1985); D. G. Hart, *The University Gets Religion: Religious Studies in American Higher Education* (Baltimore: Johns Hopkins University Press, 1999); T. Fitzgerald, *The Ideology of Religious Studies* (New York: Oxford University Press, 2000); M. C. Taylor, ed., *Critical Terms for Religious Studies* (Chicago: University of Chicago Press, 1998); D. Wiebe, *The Politics of Religious Studies: The Continuing Conflict with Theology within the Academy* (New York: St. Martin's Press, 1999).

5. Compare the sharply specific titles in note 4 to the grand claims implicit in such earlier works in the discipline as W. B. Kristensen, *The Meaning of Religion: Lectures in the Phenomenology of Religion*, trans. J. B. Carman (The Hague: Martinus Nijhoff, 1960); and G. Van der Leuw, *Religion in Essence and Manifestation: A Study in Phenomenology*, 2 vols. (New York: Harper and Row, 1963; 1st German ed. 1933).

6. See the carefully considered remarks by M. Jackson, "Phenomenology, Radical Empiricism, and Anthropological Critique," in *Things as They Are: New Directions in Phenomenological Anthropology*, ed. M. Jackson (Bloomington: Indiana University Press, 1996), 1–50; and my own comments on a phenomenological approach to

ancient religious phenomena in L. T. Johnson, *Religious Experience in Early Christianity: A Missing Dimension in New Testament Studies* (Minneapolis: Fortress, 1998), 39–68.

7. J. Z. Smith, *Imagining Religion from Babylon to Jonestown* (Chicago Studies in the History of Judaism; Chicago: University of Chicago Press, 1982), xiii. The categories clearly overlap, but for a sampling of studies pertinent to Christian origins, see N. K. Gottwald, ed., *The Bible and Liberation: Political and Social Hermeneutics* (Maryknoll, NY: Orbis, 1983); E. Schüssler-Fiorenza, *Bread Not Stone: The Challenge of Feminist Biblical Interpretation*, rev. ed. (Boston: Beacon, 1995); R. S. Sugitharajah, *Postcolonial Criticism and Biblical Interpretation* (Oxford: Oxford University Press, 2002).

8. See, e.g., E. A. Clark, *History, Theory, Text: Historians and the Linguistic Turn* (Cambridge, MA: Harvard University Press, 2004); and D. B. Martin and P. C. Miller, eds., *The Cultural Turn in Late Ancient Studies* (Durham, NC: Duke University Press, 2005).

9. The theoretical framework provided by Peter Berger and Thomas Luckman influences this statement; see P. L. Berger and T. Luckman, *The Social Construction of Reality: A Treatise in the Sociology of Knowledge* (Garden City, NY: Doubleday, 1967); and P. L. Berger, *The Sacred Canopy: Elements of a Sociological Theory of Religion* (Garden City, NY: Doubleday, 1967).

10. J. Wach, "The Nature of Religious Experience," in *The Comparative Study of Religions*, ed. J. M. Kitagawa (Lectures on the History of Religions, n.s. 4; New York: Columbia University Press, 1958), 27–58.

11. See especially G. Van der Leeuw, *Religion in Essence and Manifestation: A Study in Phenomenology*, 2 vols., trans. J. E. Turner (New York: Harper and Row, 1933), 1:23–42.

12. The realm of experience is, inevitably, the realm of the subjective. I emphasize in this statement "to the person having the experience" because even when ecstatic experiences are derived from self-hypnosis or drugs, the individual reports the sense of "encountering something" other than the mind's own process. We are here clearly outside the realm of the scientifically verifiable. It goes without saying that what is "perceived as ultimate" by one may not be perceived as such by another.

13. Language of "transcendence" is slippery and can easily lead to inappropriate and normative claims in a discussion that is supposed to be strictly descriptive, but if transcendence is understood functionally as "that which goes beyond" any other categories available to the one experiencing it, then "that which is perceived to be ultimate" can be called the "transcendent." It goes beyond what is simply pleasurable, beautiful, useful, or even good.

14. See R. Otto, *The Idea of the Holy: An Inquiry into the Non-Rational Factor in the Idea of the Divine and Its Relation to the Rational*, trans. J. E. Turner (New York: Harper and Row, 1963; 1st German ed. 1933), 8–11, 136; see also Wach, *The Comparative Study of Religions*, 32–35.

15. It is, in fact, a deficiency in virtually all theoretical discussions of religious experience that they tend toward individual psychology. An experience, however, can legiti-

mately be called communal, even when the specific mode of experience is inevitably personal and diverse. Thus, even though the specifics differ, it is fair to say that Elie Wiesel, Primo Levi, and Anne Frank all "experienced the Holocaust." Less dramatically, we can speak of ritual as communal experience.

16. William James observes, "It is as if there were in the human consciousness a *sense of reality, a feeling of objective presence* of what we may call '*something there,*' more deep and more general than any of the special and particular 'senses' by which the current psychology supposes existent realities to be originally revealed," in *Varieties of Religious Experience* (New York: Longmans, Green, 1902; Penguin American Library, 1982), 58 (emphasis in the original). For the participant, this intensity or sense of realness is what gives the experience its self-evident authority, one that is often not obvious to outsiders.

17. See C. Geertz, *The Interpretation of Cultures* (New York: Basic Books, 1973); W. B. Kristensen, *The Meaning of Religion: Lectures in the Phenomenology of Religion*, trans. J. B. Carman (The Hague: Martinus Nijhoff, 1960), 6–7; and my discussion of the hermeneutics of religious experience in *Faith's Freedom: A Classic Spirituality for Contemporary Christians* (Minneapolis: Fortress, 1990), 31–59.

18. M. Eliade, *Patterns in Comparative Religion* (New York World, 1963), 14; E. Durkheim, *The Elementary Forms of the Religious Life*, trans. J. W. Swain (New York: The Free Press, 1965 [1915]), 56 (division of time and space); Wach, *The Comparative Study of Religions*, 59–143 (practices).

19. I clearly adopt a position distinct from that of J. Z. Smith, for whom the organization (as in ritual) is what constitutes the sense of someplace being powerful, in *To Take Place: Toward Theory in Ritual* (Chicago Studies in the History of Judaism; Chicago: University of Chicago Press, 1987), 105.

20. See, e.g., C. J. H. Hayes, *Nationalism: A Religion* (New York: Macmillan, 1960); and R. Lloyd, *Revolutionary Religion: Christianity, Fascism, and Communism* (New York: Harper and Brothers, 1938).

21. The resemblance was noted already by Sigmund Freud; see his "Obsessive Acts and Religious Practices," in *The Standard Edition of the Complete Psychological Works of Sigmund Freud*, vol. 9, trans. and ed. J. Strachey (London: Hogarth, 1959), 9:117–127; see also E. A. Reed, *A Fall from Grace: Religion and Addiction* (PhD diss., The Union Institute, 1990).

22. See J. L. Price, ed., *From Season to Season: Sports as American Religion* (Macon, GA: Mercer University Press, 2001).

23. T. W. Harpur, "The Gift of Tongues and Interpretation," *Canadian Journal of Theology* 12 (1966): 164–171; R. H. Gundry, "Ecstatic Utterance (NEB)," *Journal of Theological Studies* n.s. 17 (1966): 306; C. Forbes, "Early Christian Inspired Speech and Hellenistic Popular Religion," *Novum Testamentum* 28 (1986): 257–270.

24. For the position that the experience comes from God and is continuous with Pentecost, see F. D. Bruner, *A Theology of the Holy Spirit: The Pentecost Experience and the New Testament Witness* (Grand Rapids, MI: Eerdmans, 1970); and W. G. MacDonald, "The Place of Tongues in Neo-Pentecostalism," in *Speaking in Tongues: A*

Guide to Research in Glossolalia, ed. W. E. Mills (Grand Rapids, MI: Eerdmans, 1986), 81–93. For the position that speaking in tongues is rooted in psychopathology, see, e.g., M. Casaubon, *A Treatise Concerning Enthusiasme as It Is an Effect of Nature: But Is Mistaken by Many for Either Divine Inspiration or Diabolical Possession*, 2nd ed. (London: Roger Daniel, 1656); J. Foster, *Natural History of Enthusiasm*, 7th ed. (London: Hodsworth and Ball, 1834).

25. In Ronald Knox's classic work, *Enthusiasm: A Chapter in the History of Religion* (New York: Oxford University Press, 1950), the phenomenon is frequently associated with features distorting of genuine Christianity (see pp. 360–366, 380, 540–559, 564); in sharp contrast, speaking in tongues is identified with the essence of Christianity in Y. A. Obiya, *The Miracle of Speaking in Tongues: Which Side Are You?* (Nigeria: Abedaya Calvary Printers, 1987), 26–37.

26. D. Christie-Murphy, *Voice from the Gods: Speaking with Tongues* (London: R. K. Paul, 1978) 248–252; I. Stevenson, *Xenoglossy: A Review and Report of a Case* (Charlottesville: University of Virginia Press, 1974). See especially L. Samarin, *Tongues of Men and Angels: The Religious Language of Pentecostalism* (New York: Macmillan, 1972).

27. See J. P. Kildahl, "Psychological Observations," in *The Charismatic Movement*, ed. M. P. Harrington (Grand Rapids, MI: Eerdmans, 1975), 124–142, and *The Psychology of Speaking in Tongues* (New York: Harper and Row, 1972), 50–53; J. T. Richardson, "Psychological Interpretations of Glossolalia: A Reexamination of Research," *Journal for the Scientific Study of Religion* 12 (1973): 199–207.

28. See F. Goodman, *Speaking in Tongues: A Cross-Cultural Study of Glossolalia* (Chicago: University of Chicago Press, 1972); H. N. Maloney and A. A. Lovekin, *Glossolalia: Behavioral Science Perspectives on Speaking in Tongues* (New York: Oxford University Press, 1985).

29. He does not mention glossolalia as such, but in *Ecstatic Religion* (Baltimore: Penguin Books, 1971), I. M. Lewis shows how claims to spirit possession serve to assert social power (see pp. 32, 101, 104–106, 110, 121).

30. M. Eliade, *Le chamanisme et les techniques archaiques de l'exstase* (Paris: Payot, 1951); L. C. May, "A Survey of Glossolalia and Related Phenomena in Non-Christian Religions," *American Anthropologist* 58 (1956): 75–96; C. G. Williams, "Ecstaticism in Hebrew Prophecy and Christian Glossolalia," *Science Religeuses* 3 (1974): 328–338; D. Aune, *Prophecy in Early Christianity and the Ancient Mediterranean World* (Grand Rapids, MI: Eerdmans, 1983); J. T. Bunn, "Glossolalia in Historical Perspective," in *Speaking in Tongues*, ed. W. G. Mills, 36–47.

31. See L. T. Johnson, "Glossolalia and the Embarrassments of Experience," in *Religious Experience in Earliest Christianity* (Minneapolis: Fortress, 1998), 105–136.

32. The literature on both discoveries is enormous, beginning with the more sensational and moving toward the more scholarly. The Dead Sea Scrolls have been used to support bizarre theories of Christian origins, as in R. H. Eisenman, *James, the Brother of Jesus: The Key to Unlocking the Secrets of Early Christianity and the Dead Sea Scrolls* (New York: Viking, 1997), and B. Thiering, *Jesus and the Riddle of the Dead Sea*

Scrolls: Unlocking the Secrets of His Life Story (San Francisco: HarperSanFrancisco, 1992); but have also provided the impetus to a richer understanding of Christianity's context in Judaism, as in M. Black, *The Scrolls and Christian Origins: Studies in the Jewish Background of the New Testament* (New York: Scribner, 1961), and J. C. Vanderkam and P. Flint, *The Meaning of the Dead Sea Scrolls: Their Significance for Understanding the Bible, Judaism, and Christianity* (San Francisco: HarperSanFrancisco, 2002). Likewise, the Nag-Hammadi writings led to sensational accounts—see J. Doresse, *The Discovery of the Nag Hammadi Texts: A Firsthand Account of the Expedition That Shook the Foundations of Christianity* (Rochester, VT: Inner Traditions, 2005)—and wide-ranging claims, as in E. Pagels, *The Gnostic Gospels* (New York: Vintage, 1989 [1979]), together with more sober assessments, as in P. Perkins, *Gnosticism and the New Testament* (Minneapolis: Fortress, 1993), and B. A. Pearson, *Early Christianity and Gnosticism in the History of Religion* (Claremont, CA: Institute for Antiquity and Christianity, 2001), as well as large collaborative scholarly examinations, as in U. Bianchi, *Le Origini dello Gnosticismo* (Leiden: E. J. Brill, 1967); B. Layton, *The Rediscovery of Gnosticism: Proceedings of the International Conference on Gnosticism at Yale, New Haven, Connecticut, March 28–31, 1978*, 2 vols. (Leiden: E. J. Brill, 1980); and C. W. Hendrick and R. Hodgson Jr., eds., *Nag Hammadi, Gnosticism, and Early Christianity* (Peabody, MA: Hendrickson, 1986).

33. See M. I. Rostovtzeff, ed., *The Excavations at Dura-Europos. Final Report; Conducted by Yale University and the French Academy of Inscriptions and Letters* (New Haven, CT: Yale University Press, 1943–1956); B. Cunliffe, ed., *Excavations in Bath, 1950–1975* (Bristol: CRAAGS, 1979).

34. E. M. Myers, E. Netzer, and C. L. Meyers, *Sepphoris* (Winona Lake, IN: Eisenbrauns, 1992); R. Talgam, *The Mosaics of the House of Dionysios at Sepphoris* (Jerusalem: Institute of Archaeology, Hebrew University of Jerusalem, 2003); L. I. Levine and E. Netzer, *Excavations at Maritime Caesarea, 1975, 1976, 1979, Final Report* (Jerusalem: Institute of Archaeology, Hebrew University of Jerusalem, 1986); A. Raban and G. Holum, eds., *Caearea Maritime: A Retrospective after Two Millennia* (Leiden: E. J. Brill, 1996); C. T. Fritsch, ed., *Studies in the History of Caesarea Maritime* (Missoula, MT: Scholars Press for the American Schools of Oriental Research, 1975).

35. G. M. A. Hanfmann and J. C. Waldbaum, *A Survey of Sardis and the Major Monuments outside the City Walls (Archaeological Exploration of Sardis, 1958)* (Cambridge, MA: Harvard University Press, 1975); F. K. Yeguel, *The Bath-Gymnasium Complex at Sardis* (Cambridge, MA: Harvard University Press, 1986); G. M. A. Hanfmann and N. Ramage, *Sculpture from Sardis: The Finds through 1975* (Cambridge, MA: Harvard University Press, 1978); G. Wiplinger, *Ephesus: 100 Years of Austrian Research*, trans. C. Luxon (Vienna: Boehlau [Oesterreichen Archaeologisches Institut], 1996); H. Koester, ed., *Ephesos: Metropolis of Asia: An Interdisciplinary Approach to Its Archaeology, Religion, and Culture* (Valley Forge, PA: Trinity International, 1975); C. K. Williams II and N. Bookidis, eds., *Corinth, the Centenary* (Princeton, NJ: American School of Classical Studies at Athens, 2003); J. Murphy-O'Connor, *St. Paul's Corinth: Text and*

Archaeology, 3rd rev. and expanded ed. (Collegeville, MN: Liturgical Press, 2002); C. C. Parslow, *Rediscovering Antiquity: Karl Weber and the Excavation of Herculaneum, Pompeii, and Stabiae* (Cambridge: Cambridge University Press, 1995); A. Wallace-Haddrill, *Houses and Society in Pompeii and Herculaneum* (Princeton, NJ: Princeton University Press, 1994); T. Kraus, *Pompeii and Herculaneum: The Living Cities of the Dead*, trans. R. E. Wolf (New York: H. N. Abrams, 1975).

36. B. P. Grenfell and A. S. Hunt, eds., *The Oxyrhynchus Papyri*, 73 vols. (London: Egypt Exploration Fund, 1898–).

37. See C. Hopkins, *The Discovery of Dura-Europas*, ed. B. Goldman (New Haven, CT: Yale University Press, 1979); M. Rostovtzeff, *Dura-Europos and Its Art* (Oxford: Clarendon Press, 1938).

38. See E. R. Goodenough, *Jewish Symbols in the Greco-Roman Period*, 13 vols. (New York: Pantheon, 1953–1968).

39. In addition to the references provided above, see A. T. Kraabel, "The Diaspora Synagogue: Archaeological and Epigraphic Evidence since Sukenik," *Aufstieg und Niedergang der römischen Welt* II.19.1 (1979): 475–510; and "Paganism and Judaism: The Sardis Evidence," in *Paganisme, Judaisme, Christianisme: Mélanges offerts à Marcel Simon*, ed. A. Benoit, M. Philonenko, and C. Vogel (Paris: Boccard, 1978), 13–33.

40. See L. Kant, "Jewish Inscriptions in Greek and Latin," *Aufstieg und Niedergang der römischen Welt*, II.20.2 (1987): 671–714.

41. See B. Brooten, *Women Leaders in the Ancient Synagogue: Inscriptional Evidence and Background Issues* (Brown Judaic Studies; Atlanta: Scholars, 1982).

42. S. Friesen, *Twice Neokoros: Ephesus, Asia, and the Cult of the Flavian Imperial Family* (Leiden: E. J. Brill, 1993).

43. See P. Harland, *Associations, Synagogues, and Congregations: Claiming a Place in Ancient Mediterranean Society* (Minneapolis: Fortress, 2003). See Brooten's demonstration in *Women Leaders*, pp. 103–137, of the lack of archaeological evidence supporting the supposed separation of women from men in the synagogue (and, by inference, of their exclusion from roles of authority), and her statement that "Ancient Jewish literature yields no hint of a strict separation of the sexes in the synagogue" (p. 138).

44. Friesen, *Twice Neokoros*, 50–112.

45. Harland, *Associations*, 89–112.

46. C. B. Welles, *Royal Correspondence in the Hellenistic Period: A Study in Greek Epigraphy* (New Haven, CT: Yale University Press, 1934); M. Wolter, *Die Pastoralbriefe als Paulustradition* (Göttingen: Vandenhoeck & Ruprecht, 1988).

47. Examples from Hellenistic Egypt are *Tebtunis Papyrus* 25 and 703; see text and discussion in A. S. Hunt and J. G. Smyly, *The Tebtunis Papyri* (London: Oxford University Press, 1933), 66–114.

48. See also Ulpian, *Duties of a Proconsul*, Book 8, in *The Digest of Justinian*, 47.11.6; Latin text edited by T. Mommsen with the aid of Paul Krueger; English translation edited by A. Watson (Philadelphia: University of Pennsylvania Press, 1985), 4:784.

49. L. T. Johnson, *The First and Second Letters to Timothy: A New Translation with Introduction and Commentary* (The Anchor Bible 35A; New York: Doubleday, 2001), 137–142.

50. As argued, for example, by M. Dibelius and H. Conzelmann, *The Pastoral Epistles*, ed. H. Koester, trans. P. Buttolph and A. Yarbro (Hermeneia; Philadelphia: Fortress Press, 1972), 5–7.

51. The effect of new discovery is greatest in the way it dislodges old certainties and opens new possibilities; everything discovered about the past has the potential to re-catalyze everything previously known (or thought to be known) about the past.

52. The translated Greek novels are available in B. P. Reardon, ed., *Collected Ancient Greek Novels* (Berkeley: University of California Press, 1989), and the Latin in F. A. Todd, *Some Ancient Novels: Leucippe and Clitophon, Daphnis and Chloe, The Satyricon, The Golden Ass* (London: Oxford University Press, 1940).

53. Walter Burkert notes, "It is the only first-person account of a mystery experience that we have," in *Ancient Mystery Cults* (Cambridge, MA: Harvard University Press, 1987), 97; and A. D. Nock calls Apuleius' account "the high-water mark of the piety which grew out of the mystery religions" in *Conversion: The Old and the New in Religion from Alexander the Great to Augustine of Hippo* (Oxford: Oxford University Press, 1933), 138.

54. H. J. Cadbury, *The Book of Acts in History* (New York: Harper and Brothers, 1955), 8.

55. R. I. Pervo, *Profit with Delight* (Philadelphia: Fortress, 1987); C. M. Thomas, *The Acts of Peter, Gospel Literature, and the Ancient Novel: Rewriting the Past* (New York: Oxford University Press, 2003).

56. See I.51; I.65–67; V.42–43; V.62–63; V.91; VI.52; VI.57; VI.66; VI.76; VII.220; VII.239; and J. D. Mikalson, *Herodotus and Religion in the Persian Wars* (Chapel Hill: University of North Carolina Press, 2003).

57. See, e.g., J. Elsner and I. Rutherford, eds., *Pilgrimage in Graeco-Roman and Early Christian Antiquity: Seeing the Gods* (Oxford: Oxford University Press, 2005); and D. Dueck, H. Lindsay, and S. Pothecary, eds., *Strabo's Cultural Geography: The Making of a Kolossourgia* (Cambridge: Cambridge University Press, 2005).

58. The *Hieroi Logoi* are found as Orations XLVII–LIII in P. Aelius Aristides, *The Complete Works*, vol. 2: *Orations XVII–LIII*, trans. C. A. Behr (Leiden: E. J. Brill, 1981).

59. See R. A. Tomlinson, *Epidauros* (Austin: University of Texas Press, 1983); T. Papadakes, *Epidauros: The Sanctuary of Asclepius*, 2nd ed. (Munich: Schnell and Steiner, 1972); H. Avalos, *Illness and Health Care in the Ancient Near East: The Role of the Temple in Greece, Mesopotamia, and Israel* (Atlanta: Scholars, 1995).

60. See J. C. Stephens, *The Religious Experience of Aelius Aristides: An Interdisciplinary Approach* (Ann Arbor, MI: University Microfilms, 1983).

61. M. C. Nussbaum, *The Therapy of Desire: Theory and Practice in Hellenistic Ethics* (Princeton, NJ: Princeton University Press, 1994); see also A. J. Malherbe, "Hellenistic Moralists and the New Testament," *Aufstieg und Niedergang der römischen Welt* II.26.1 (1992): 267–333. The religious tone of some Hellenistic philosophers was noted already in 1904 by Samuel Dill in his classic, *Roman Society from Nero to Marcus Aurelius* (New York: Meridian, 1956), where he speaks of "the philosophic theologian" (384–440). For a collection of sources, see A. A. Long, *Hellenistic Philosophy: Stoics, Epicureans, Skeptics*, 2nd ed. (Berkeley: University of California Press, 1986);

A. J. Malherbe, *Moral Exhortation: A Greco-Roman Sourcebook* (Philadelphia: West-minster, 1986).

62. Such, at any rate, is the charge laid against the Epicurean Colotes by Plutarch, in *Reply to Colotes* 17 (Mor., 1117A–B). On the origin of Pythagoras, see Iamblichus, *Life of Pythagoras*, 3–10.

63. See Philostratus, *Life of Apollonius of Tyana*, I.1; Epicurus, *Sovereign Maxims*.

64. Iamblichus, *Life of Pythagoras*, 17.72–74; 18.81; Philostratus, *Life of Apollonius of Tyana*, I.13.

65. Philostratus, *Life of Apollonius of Tyana*, I.2; VIII.7.7; *The Epistles of Heraclitus*, 4: "To Hermodorus," in *The Cynic Epistles*, ed. A. J. Malherbe (SBL Sources for Biblical Study 12; Missoula, MT: Scholars, 1977), 191–193.

66. The theme, as we shall see in a later chapter, is pervasive in Epictetus but finds its most splendid expression in his discourse on the vocation of the Cynic (*Discourse*, III.22).

67. See A. J. Malherbe, "Medical Imagery in the Pastorals," in *Texts and Testaments*, ed. W. March (San Antonio: Trinity University Press, 1980), 19–35.

68. Lucian of Samosata, *Demonax* and *Nigrinus*; see L. T. Johnson, "II Timothy and the Polemic against False Teachers: A Re-Examination," *Journal of Religious Studies* 6, no. 2 (1978): 1–26; Nock, *Conversion*, 164–186.

69. See W. Bousset, *Kyrios Christos: A History of the Belief in Christ from the Beginnings of Christianity to Irenaeus*, trans. J. E. Steely (Nashville: Abingdon Press, 1970 [1913]); R. Bultmann, *Theology of the New Testament*, 2 vols., trans. K. Grobel (New York: Charles Scribner's Sons, 1951, 1955). For a brief introduction to this influential movement, see H. Boers, "Religionsgeschichtliche Schule," in *Dictionary of Biblical Interpretation*, ed. J. H. Hayes (Nashville: Abingdon Press, 1999), 2:383–387.

70. As a consequence, the first-century Philo could be disregarded in the construction of "Normative Judaism" on the basis of the "Rabbinic Tradition," the evidence for which much postdated the first century, in the classic study by G. F. Moore, *Judaism in the First Centuries of the Christian Era*, 2 vols. (New York: Schocken, 1927).

71. The significance of the title *kyrios* is that in Paul's letters (the earliest datable Christian literature), it refers to Jesus as the exalted one who shares in God's life and power (see 1 Cor 12:1–3; Rom 10:9).

72. Bousset, *Kyrios Christos*, 31–118; Bultmann, *Theology*, 1:33–62.

73. Bousset, *Kyrios Christos*, 119–152; Bultmann, *Theology*, 1:63–184.

74. Bousset, *Kyrios Christos*, 119–120.

75. See W. Heitmueller, "Zum Problem Paulus und Jesus," *Zeitschrift für Neuentestamentliche Wissenschaft* 13 (1912): 320–337.

76. The History of Religions School was firmly committed to the methods of tradition criticism, which basically regarded narratives as repositories of earlier traditions. Proponents of this approach were unaware of the shift to narrative criticism that was being inaugurated by scholars such as H. J. Cadbury, in *The Making of Luke-Acts* (New York: Macmillan, 1927), which would lead to an appreciation of how Hellenistic the third Gospel and Acts of the Apostles actually were; see E. Plümacher, *Lukas als hellenistischer Schrifsteller* (Studien zur Umwelt des Neuen Testaments 9; Göttingen:

Vandenhoeck und Ruprecht, 1972). For the early dating of James and Hebrews, see L. T. Johnson, *The Letter of James: A New Translation with Introduction and Commentary* (The Anchor Bible 37A; New York: Doubleday, 1995), 89–123; *Brother of Jesus and Friend of God: Studies in the Letter of James* (Grand Rapids, MI: Eerdmans, 2004), 1–23; and *Hebrews: A Commentary* (The New Testament Library; Louisville: Westminster John Knox, 2006), 32–44.

77. See D. M. Hay, *Glory at the Right Hand: Psalm 110 in Early Christianity* (Society of Biblical Literature Monograph Series 18; Nashville: Abingdon, 1973).

78. Bousset brushes off this evidence in *Kyrios Christos*, 129; for a recent rereading of all the evidence, see L. W. Hurtado, *Lord Jesus Christ: Devotion to Jesus in Earliest Christianity* (Grand Rapids, MI: Eerdmans, 2003).

79. See S. Lieberman, *Greek in Jewish Palestine; Hellenism in Jewish Palestine* (New York: Jewish Theological Seminary of America, 1994 [1942]); M. Hengel, *Judaism and Hellenism: Studies in the Encounter in Palestine during the Early Hellenistic Period*, 2 vols., trans. J. Bowden (Philadelphia: Fortress, 1974). See also the important work of H. A. Fischel, *Rabbinic Literature and Greco-Roman Philosophy: A Study of Epicurea and Rhetorica in Early Midrashic Writings* (Leiden: E. J. Brill, 1973), and *Essays in Greco-Roman and Related Talmudic Literature* (New York: KTAV Publishing House, 1977); E. R. Goodenough, *Jewish Symbols in the Greco-Roman Period*, 13 vols. (New York: Pantheon, 1953–1968); as well as M. Hadas and M. Smith, *Heroes and Gods: Spiritual Biographies in Antiquity* (New York: Harper and Row, 1965).

80. According to I Maccabees 8:1–31, a treaty was made with Rome as early as the early second century BCE, but Roman presence became effective with the incursion of Pompey in 63 BCE; for the history of this period, see S. D. Cohen, *From the Maccabees to the Mishnah* (Philadelphia: Westminster, 1987).

81. On these points, see Lieberman, *Greek in Jewish Palestine* and Fischel, *Rabbinic Literature* and *Essays, passim*.

82. See the discussion in Hengel, *Judaism and Hellenism*, 1:83–106.

83. For an overview, see K. H. Jobes and M. Silva, *Invitation to the Septuagint* (Grand Rapids, MA: Baker Academic Books, 2000).

84. The fullest account is given by the *Letter of Aristeas*, in *The Old Testament Pseudepigrapha*, 2 vols., ed. J. H. Charlesworth (New York: Doubleday, 1985), 2:7–34.

85. For the difficulty of determining the numbers with any precision, see V. Tcherikover, *Hellenistic Civilization and the Jews*, trans. A. Appelbaum (New York: Atheneum, 1970), 284–295.

86. For their use of polemic, see L. T. Johnson, "The New Testament's Anti-Jewish Slander and the Conventions of Ancient Polemic," *JBL* 108 (1989): 419–441.

87. For Pseudo-Phocylides, see J. Bernays, *Über das Phokylideische Gedicht: Ein Beitrag zur hellenistischen Litteratur* (Jahresbericht des juedische-theologischen Seminars "Fraenckelschen Stiftung"; Berlin: Hertz, 1856); for Ezekiel, see C. R. Holladay, *Fragments from Hellenistic Jewish Authors II: Poets; The Epic Poets Theodotus and Philo and Ezekiel the Tragedian* (SBL Texts and Translations 30; Atlanta: Scholars, 1989), 301–529.

88. See D. A. DeSilva, *4 Maccabees* (Sheffield, U.K.: Sheffield Academic Press, 1998).

89. The strongest case is made by E. R. Goodenough, *By Light, Light: The Mystic Gospel of Hellenistic Judaism* (New Haven, CT: Yale University Press, 1935). For critical reviews of Goodenough, see A. D. Nock, *Essays on Religion and the Ancient World*, 2 vols., ed. Z. Stewart (Oxford: Clarendon Press, 1972), 2:877–894, 895–919; for a more positive appreciation, see M. Smith, "Goodenough's *Jewish Symbols* in Retrospect," *Journal of Biblical Literature* 86 (1967): 53–68. See the summary of Philo's language in Johnson, *Religious Experience*, 89–97; for the very early influence of the Mysteries on Judaism, see L. Cerfaux, "Influence des Mystères sur le Judaisme Alexandrin avant Philo," *Le Museon* 37 (1924): 29–88.

90. For a thorough analysis of Pseudo-Orpheus, see C. R. Holladay, *Fragments from Hellenistic Jewish Authors*, vol. 4: *Orphica* (SBL Texts and Translations 40; Atlanta: Scholars, 1996).

91. For an overview, see P. W. Flint and J. C. Vanderkam, eds., *The Dead Sea Scrolls after Fifty Years*, 2 vols. (Leiden: E. J. Brill, 1998).

92. See, e.g., 1QS 3.13–4.26; 6.24–7.27; 5.14–16; 8.22–26.

93. See B. Dombrowski, "*ha yachad* in 1QS and *to koinon*: An Instance of Early Greek and Jewish Synthesis," *Harvard Theological Review* 59 (1966): 293–307.

94. I take note here of a study that also focuses on the issue of power in religion and that puts Greco-Roman religion, Judaism, and Christianity into conversation, but does so in a manner very different than my own, particularly in the way these traditions are treated more or less as monolithic entities: see D. R. Edwards, *Religion and Power: Pagans, Jews, and Christians in the Greek East* (New York: Oxford University Press, 1996).

3. A PRELIMINARY PROFILE OF GRECO-ROMAN RELIGION

1. Classic studies of the Roman context include J. Carcopino, *Daily Life in Ancient Rome*, ed. H. T. Rowell, trans. E. O. Lorimer (New York: Penguin, 1985 [1940]); and S. Dill, *Roman Society from Nero to Marcus Aurelius* (New York: World Publishing Co., 1956 [1904]). More recent general treatments include M. Goodman (with J. Sherwood), *The Roman World: 44 BC–AD 180* (New York: Routledge, 1997); P. Garnsey and R. Saller, *The Roman Empire: Economy, Society, and Culture* (Berkeley: University of California Press, 1987); R. MacMullen, *Roman Social Relations: 50 B.C. to A.D. 284* (New Haven, CT: Yale University Press, 1974); F. Dupont, *Daily Life in Ancient Rome*, trans. C. Woodall (Oxford: Blackwell, 1992).

2. A select list of helpful surveys: W. Burkert, *Greek Religion*, trans. J. Raffan (Cambridge, MA: Harvard University Press, 1985); D. Feeney, *Literature and Religion at Rome: Cultures, Contexts, and Beliefs* (Cambridge: Cambridge University Press, 1998); R. MacMullen, *Paganism in the Roman Empire* (New Haven, CT: Yale University Press, 1981); L. H. Martin, *Hellenistic Religions: An Introduction* (New York: Oxford University Press, 1987); A. D. Nock, *Essays on Religion in the Ancient World*, 2 vols., ed. Z. Stewart (New York: Oxford University Press, 1972); R. M.

Ogilvie, *The Romans and Their Gods in the Age of Augustus* (New York: W. W. Norton, 1969); R. Turcan, *The Cults of the Roman Empire*, trans. A. Nevill (Cambridge, MA: Blackwell, 1996); Turcan, *The Gods of Ancient Rome: Religion in Everyday Life from Archaic to Imperial Times*, trans. A. Nevill (New York: Routledge, 2000); A. Wardman, *Religion and Statecraft among the Romans* (London: Granada, 1982).

3. Feeney, *Literature and Religion at Rome*, 22–28, points out that the interaction between Greek and Roman elements was ancient, multifaceted, and subtle. For an "evolutionary sequence" study, see, for example, G. Murray, *Five Stages of Greek Religion*, 2nd ed. (New York: Columbia University Press, 1925); for a "response to spiritual crisis" study, see H. Jonas, *The Gnostic Religion: The Message of an Alien God and the Beginnings of Christianity*, 2nd ed. (Boston: Beacon, 1963).

4. For a succinct and informed discussion of most of the topics covered in this chapter, together with extensive bibliographies for each subject, see H.-J. Klauck, *The Religious Context of Early Christianity: A Guide to Graeco-Roman Religions*, trans. B. McNeil (Minneapolis: Fortress, 2003).

5. The point is made particularly well by Ogilvie, *The Romans and Their Gods*, 8–40.

6. For the *indigitamenta*, see Turcan, *The Gods of Ancient Rome*, 2–3.

7. Plato, *Alcibiades*, 135D; *Phaedo*, 80D; *Thaetetus*, 151B; Epictetus, *Discourses*, I.1.17; III.21.12; III.22.2; 2 Macc 12:16; Acts 18:21; James 4:15.

8. Living conditions both in the country and in the city (especially in the crowded *insulae*) meant that people ate and slept in close quarters. The popularity of the public baths suggests that life with others was as much a pleasure as a necessity; see C. F. Fagan, *Bathing in Public in the Roman World* (Ann Arbor: University of Michigan Press, 1999).

9. In Sophocles' *Philoctetes*, the abandoned man's isolation from other humans is a far greater suffering than his suppurating wound. See Dupont, *Daily Life in Ancient Rome*, 10–12, 57–62.

10. Ovid's *Fasti* is a poetic commentary on the calendar in six books (covering half the year) and an important source for Roman religion.

11. For a selection of calendars recovered archaeologically (they were inscribed in public places for the guidance of the populace), see M. Beard, J. North, and S. Price, *Roman Religion, Volume 2: A Sourcebook* (Cambridge: Cambridge University Press, 1998), 60–74. The calendar for April from 6 to 9 CE has at least 10 days marked N (*nefastus*) and two days marked NP (probably indicating a half day that was inauspicious for secular activities).

12. See the essays on this topic in N. Marinatos and R. Hägg, *Greek Sanctuaries: New Approaches* (London: Routledge, 1993). A collection of primary evidence is usefully gathered by G. Stevenson, *Power and Place: Temple and Identity in the Book of Revelation* (Beihefte zur Zeitschrift für die neutestamentliche Wissenschaft 107; Berlin: Walter de Gruyter, 2001), 72–86.

13. For Athens, see W. F. Ferguson, *The Treasurers of Athena* (Cambridge, MA: Harvard University Press, 1932); for Delphi, see Herodotus, *History*, 1.14, 1.50, 1.92.

14. In ancient Greece, meat was rarely consumed apart from the communal participation in the meat of sacrifice; in Rome, meat appeared more frequently in the diet of the well-to-do and could be purchased at markets such as that in the *Forum Boarium*, where a temple of Hercules was located.

15. See Turcan, *The Gods of Ancient Rome*, 14, 58, 74.

16. See Plato, *Symposium*; Xenophon, *Symposium*; Plutarch, *Table-Talk* (Mor., 612A–748D). For a brilliant semiotic study of Greek cuisine, see J. Davidson, *Courtesans and Fish-Cakes: The Consuming Passions of Classical Athens* (New York: St. Martin's, 1998). See also P. A. Harland, *Associations, Synagogues, and Congregations: Claiming a Place in Ancient Mediterranean Society* (Minneapolis: Fortress, 2003), 55–88.

17. See R. S. Ascough, "Translocal Relationships among Voluntary Associations and Early Christianity," *Journal of Early Christian Studies* 5.2 (1997): 223–241; J. S. Kloppenborg, "Collegia and *thiasoi*: Issues in Function, Taxonomy and Membership," in *Voluntary Associations in the Graeco-Roman World*, ed. J. S. Kloppenborg and S. G. Wilson (London: Routledge, 1996), 16–30.

18. See the collected essays on the topic in M. Beard and J. North, eds., *Pagan Priests: Religion and Power in the Ancient World* (London: Duckworth, 1990); and G. J. Szemler, *The Priests of the Roman Republic: A Study of the Interactions between Priesthood and Magistracies* (Bruxelles: Latomus, 1972).

19. Breaking custom, Julius Caesar gathered several of the priestly offices to himself simultaneously and was followed in this by Augustus, who was climactically elected *pontifex maximus* in 12 BCE; for discussion, see R. Gordon, "From Republic to Principate: Priesthood, Religion, and Ideology," in Beard and North, *Pagan Priests*, 179–198.

20. See S. J. Friesen, *Twice Neokoros: Ephesus, Asia, and the Cult of the Flavian Imperial Family* (Religions in the Greco-Roman World 116; Leiden: Brill, 1993).

21. The event is reported by Livy, *History of Rome*, 29.10–14.

22. Ibid., 39.8–19

23. Plutarch, *Against Colotes*, 22 (Mor., 1119F) and 27 (Mor., 1123A).

24. Epicurus, *Sovereign Maxims* 19, 20, 21, 37, 41.

25. "Your doctrines are bad, subversive of the state, destructive of the family, not even fit for women"; see Epictetus, *Discourses*, III.7.21.

26. See E. Mary Smallwood, "Domitian's Attitude toward the Jews and Judaism," *Classical Philology* 51.1 (1956): 1–13.

27. See S. J. Friesen, "The Cult of the Roman Emperors in Ephesos: Temple Wardens, City Titles, and the Interpretation of the Revelation of John," in *Ephesos, Metropolis of Asia: An Interdisciplinary Approach to Its Archaeology, Religion, and Culture*, ed. H. Koester (Harvard Theological Studies 41; Valley Forge, PA: Trinity Press International, 1995), 229–250; Harland, *Associations, Synagogues, and Congregations*, 89–160.

28. Festivals such as the *Saturnalia* (in December) and the *Lupercalia* (in February) involved every level of society and, in the case of the *Saturnalia*, playful rituals of status reversal; see Macrobius, *Saturnalia*, 1.24 and 1.22–23.

29. Primary texts are available in R. S. Kramer, ed., *Women's Religion in the Greco-Roman World: A Sourcebook* (New York: Oxford University Press, 2004); see also her monograph, *Her Share of the Blessings: Women's Religions among Pagans, Jews, and*

Christians (New York: Oxford University Press, 1992); see also M. Parca and A. Tzaneton, *Finding Persephone: Women's Rituals in the Ancient Mediterranean* (Bloomington: Indiana University Press, 2007).

30. For helpful comments on the subject of belief, see Feeney, *Literature and Religion at Rome*, 12–46.

31. In *de Natura Deorum*, 1.2.4, Cicero states how *pietas* applies to gods and social structures alike: "Piety (*pietas*) however, like the rest of the virtues, cannot exist in mere outward show and pretence; and, with piety, reverence (*sanctitas*) and religion (*religio*) must likewise disappear. And when these are gone, life soon becomes a welter of disorder (*perturbatio*) and confusion (*confusio*); and in all probability the disappearance of piety toward the gods will entail the disappearance of loyalty (*fides*) and social union (*societas*) among men as well, and of justice herself, the queen of all the virtues." See also *de Inventione*, 2.22.65.

32. Turcan, *The Gods of Ancient Rome*, 1–13.

33. Plutarch reports the tradition that the sacrificial bull was required to shake his head to signify agreement with being sacrificed, in *The Obsolescence of Oracles*, 46C (435C). In his *Natural History*, 28.10–11, Pliny the Elder describes the care taken to fill ritual procedures exactly. Plutarch tells of sacrifices repeated up to 30 times to achieve a favorable sign from the gods (*Life of Coriolanus*, 25.7) and of a general postponing a critical battle until (after 20 unsuccessful examination of sacrificed victims) the signs were favorable with the twenty-first, encouraging him to engage the battle (*Life of Aemilius Paullus*, 17.11–12). See also Livy, *Roman History*, 8.9.1–10.

34. Aulus Gellius, *Attic Nights*, 2.28.2.

35. For a general discussion of polytheism, see R. J. Zwi Werblowsky, "Polytheism," in *Encyclopedia of Religion*, 2nd ed., ed. L. Jones (New York: Thomson Gale, 2005), 11:7315–7319.

36. For an introduction, see A. Wallace-Hadrill, ed., *Patronage in Ancient Society* (London: Routledge, 1990); and K. Lomas and T. Cornell, *Bread and Circuses: Euergetism and Municipal Patronage in Roman Italy* (London: Routledge, 2003). For inscriptional evidence, see F. W. Danker, *Benefactor: Epigraphic Study of a Graeco-Roman and New Testament Semantic Field* (St. Louis: Clayton, 1982). The practice and understanding of prayer was an area in which the Greeks and Romans genuinely differed; see M. J. Brown, *The Lord's Prayer through North African Eyes: A Window into Early Christianity* (New York: T. & T. Clark International, 2004).

37. Written in hexameters, the 15 books of the poem begin with the creation of the world and end with the deification of Julius Caesar and the start of Augustus' reign. Despite Ovid's positive view of the emperor, Augustus exiled him (for reasons unknown) in 8 CE.

38. *Metamorphoses*, 8.611–724; the story is given a Christian turn in the Acts of the Apostles 14:1–18, when Barnabas is mistaken for Zeus and Paul for Hermes by the Phrygian populace, who seek to make a sacrifice to these *theoi phainomenoi* among them. See the discussion in L. T. Johnson, *The Acts of the Apostles*, ed. D. J. Harrington (Sacra Pagina 5; Collegeville, MN: Liturgical, 1992), 245–252.

39. See, e.g., the three versions of the ascension of Romulus to the realm of the gods in Ovid, *Metamorphoses*, 14.805–851; *Fasti*, 2.481–509; and Livy, *History of Rome*, 1.16; see also the account of the apotheosis of Herakles in Diodorus Siculus, *Library of History*, 4.38.3–5 and 4.39.1–2.

40. As in Origen, *Against Celsus*, II.9–11.

41. Julius Caesar, Augustus, and Claudius were accorded posthumous divine honors; the last was the subject of Seneca's scathing satire, *Apocolocyntosis* ("The Pumpification of Claudius"). The emperor Hadrian declared his slave and lover Antinous a god when the young man died suddenly in 130 CE, thereby incurring a certain amount of ridicule; see Dio Cassius, *Roman History*, 69.11.2; Pausanius, *Description of Greece*, 8.9.7–8.

42. The complexities of the topic of syncretism are sketched by C. Colpe, in "Syncretism," trans. M. J. O'Connell, *Encyclopedia of Religion*, ed. L. Jones (New York: Thomson and Gale, 1987); and F. Graf, "Syncretism," in *Encyclopedia of Religion*, 2nd ed., ed. L. Jones (New York: Thomson and Gale, 2005), 13:8926–8938. For an example of clumsy enforcement, see 1 Macc 1:41–57 and 2 Macc 6:1–5.

43. In *Natural History*, 28.4, Pliny the Elder describes a scene of Roman priests inviting the gods of conquered peoples into communion with the Roman pantheon; see also Minucius Felix, *Octavius* 6.1–7.6.

44. In his Oration 19.6 ("A Letter to the Emperors Concerning Smyrna"), Aelius Aristides turns to Marcus Aurelius and Commodus when the city of Smyrna was destroyed by earthquake (January 177 CE): "There is no reproach in writing to you in the same fashion in which we address the gods. Indeed, for these things we pray to the gods, but you we beseech as most divine rulers."

45. See the essays in *Subject and Ruler: The Cult of the Ruling Power in Classical Antiquity*, ed. A. Small (Ann Arbor, MI: Journal of Roman Archaeology, 1996).

46. Burkert, *Greek Religion*, 88–89; see also the essays in M. Dutienne and J.-P. Vernant, *The Cuisine of Sacrifice among the Greeks*, trans. P. Wissing (Chicago: University of Chicago Press, 1989).

47. See G. Dumezil, *La Religion romaine archaique* (Paris: Puyot, 1966), 335–340.

48. See H. H. Scullard, *Festivals and Ceremonies of the Roman Republic* (Ithaca, NY: Cornell University Press, 1981).

49. Take the case of Hera's harassment of Io because of Zeus' sexual intentions toward her and the rescue of her effected by Hermes on Zeus' behalf; similarly, in Aechylus' *Eumenides*, Apollo directs Orestes to revenge the murder of his father, but the deed causes the Furies (*eumenides*) to pursue him and bring him to trial; it requires the decisive vote of Athena to free him.

50. In the *Odyssey*, VIII.266–366, we read of "the loves of Ares and Aphrodite and how they first began their affair in the house of Hephaestus," but in the *Homeric Questions*, 69, of Heraclitus and in *Compendium of Greek Theology*, 19, of Cornutus, the union of Ares and Aphrodite is interpreted as the combination of strife and love in harmony. Similarly, in *Isis and Osiris*, Plutarch warns that the Egyptian myths concerning Isis and Osiris ought not to be taken as literally true but should be interpreted "reverently and philosophically (*philosophikōs*)" (Mor., 355 B–D).

51. The same premises and the same procedures are found in Philo of Alexandria in his interpretations of Torah (as in *The Allegorical Laws*) and Origen of Alexandria in his interpretation of the Old and New Testaments (as in *Homilies on Leviticus*).

52. See the development of the theme of *pronoia* in Greco-Roman and Jewish historians in J. T. Squires, *The Plan of God in Luke-Acts* (Cambridge: Cambridge University Press, 1983).

53. In all the orations of Aelius Aristides, so filled with religious passion, there are only occasional references to moral behavior and even fewer that connect piety and morality (see *Oration*, XIV.50 and XVI.31). This is not to suggest that the worship of the gods lacked a sense of imperative; many extant inscriptions connected to places of worship prescribe both ritual and moral requirements for participation in the cult; see the selection of texts in MacMullen, *Paganism in the Roman Empire*, 12–14, 146–148; and E. Lupu, *Greek Sacred Law: A Collection of New Documents (NGSL)* (Religions in the Graeco-Roman World 152; Leiden: Brill, 2005).

54. As in Epictetus, *Discourses*, 3.17.

55. See Plutarch, *On the Delay of the Divine Vengeance* (Mor., 548B–568).

56. See W. C. Greene, *Moira: Fate, Good and Evil in Greek Thought* (New York: Harper and Row, 1963 [1944]); and Pseudo-Plutarch, *On Fate (Peri Heimarmene)* (Mor., 568B–574).

57. For a display of *Tyche* in art with interpretive essays, see S. B. Matheson, *An Obsession with Fortune: Tyche in Greek and Roman Art* (New Haven, CT: Yale University Art Gallery Bulletin, 1994).

58. For a review and discussion of the evidence, see D. E. Aune, *Prophecy in Early Christianity and the Mediterranean World* (Grand Rapids, MI: Eerdmans, 1983).

59. See Cicero, *de Divinatione*, I.1–3, I.18–19.

60. See A. Bouche-LeClerq, *Histoire de la Divination dans l'antiquité*, 4 vols. (Paris: Culture et Civilization, 1879), especially "le collège des augures," 4:262–317.

61. Burkert, *Greek Religion*, 56.

62. See Pliny, *Natural History*, 11.190; Ovid, *Metamorphoses*, XV.795.

63. In his *History*, Livy repeats many reports of portents that are interpreted as divine approval or disapproval in the midst of human affairs (e.g., I.21.8; I.45.4–7; II.42.9–11); portents also accompany extraordinary events such as the death of Julius Caesar (see also Suetonius, *Life of Caesar*, I.88) and, for that matter, the birth of Augustus (*Life of Augustus*, II.94.1–7). It becomes a literary commonplace to report portents accompanying the birth of persons who will be historically significant; see Plutarch, *Life of Alexander*, 2.3–3.9—elaborated even further by Pseudo-Callisthenes' *Alexander Romance*—and Iamblichus' *Life of Pythagoras*, 3–10; see S. I. Johnson and P. T. Struck, eds., *Mantikê: Studies in Ancient Divination* (Religions in the Graeco-Roman World 155; Leiden: Brill, 2005).

64. See Plato, *Ion*, 534A–D; *Phaedrus*, 244A; *Timaeus*, 71E–72B; and Burkert, *Greek Religion*, 109–118.

65. In Apuleius' *Metamorphoses*, VIII.27, such eunuch priests are observed: "They would throw their heads forward so their long hair fell down over their faces, then rotate them so rapidly that it wheeled about in a circle. . . . [T]hey would bite themselves

savagely, and as a climax cut their arms with the sharp knives they carried. One of them let himself go more ecstatically than the rest. Heaving deep sighs . . . as if filled with the spirit of the goddess, he pretended to go stark mad."

66. Plato, *Timaeus*, 72B; Herodotus, *History*, 8.135. Lucan (*Civil War*, 5.86–224) describes the oracles of the Delphi prophetess in more spectacular terms. As with Apuleius' description of the *Galli* belonging to Cybele, authorial perspective must be kept in mind. It is difficult to find entirely neutral, much less fully developed, witnesses in the literature.

67. There were a number of Sibyls, with the most famous being associated with Cumae in Italy. The ecstatic character of her speech is attested to by Virgil, *Aeneid*, VI.77–102 (see also Ovid, *Metamorphoses*, XIV.106–158); interpretation was the task of the *Quindecemviri Sacris Faciundis* when commanded by the Senate (Livy, *History of Rome*, 5.13.5–6). The number of members of this prestigious college was steadily increased, reaching 16. The original set of books was destroyed by the burning of the Capitol in 83 BCE, and a new collection was gathered. See H. W. Parke, *Sibyls and Sibylline Prophecy in Classical Antiquity*, ed. B. C. McGing (London: Routledge, 1988).

68. See Livy, *History of Rome*, 29.10.4–11.8; and the reconsideration of the tradition by H. Berneder, *Magna Mater Kult und Sibyllinen. Kulttransfer und annalistische Geschichtsfiktion* (Innsbrucker Beiträge zur Kulturwissenschaft 119; Innsbruck: Institut für Sprachen und Literatur der Universität Innsbruck, 2004).

69. See Tacitus, *Annals*, VI.12.

70. Plutarch, *The Obsolescence of Oracles* (Mor., 409E–438E).

71. For the centrality of the oracle in Greek history, see Herodotus, *History*, 1.51; 1.61; 1.67; 5.42–43; 5.62–63; 5.91; 6.52; 6.57; 6.66; 6.76; 6.86; 7.220; 7.239; 8.114; 8.141; and Thucydides, *History*, 2.7.55; 3.11.92; 4.13.118; 5.15.17; see also H. Bowden, *Classical Athens and the Delphic Oracle: Divination and Democracy* (Cambridge: Cambridge University Press, 2005); and (more popularly) W. J. Broad, *The Oracle: The Lost Secrets and Hidden Message of Ancient Delphi* (New York: Penguin, 2006).

72. See the account of a healing ascribed to Vespasian in Tacitus, *Histories*, 4.81. On Apollonius, see Philostratus, *Life of Apollonius of Tyana*, III.38 and 39; IV.10. For the figure of the wandering wonder worker, see L. Bieler, *Theios Aner: Das Bild des "göttlichen menschen" in Spätantike und Frühchristentum* (Darmstadt: Wissenschaftliche Buchgesellschaft, 1967 [1935–1936]); as well as the critical assessment by D. L. Tiede, *The Charismatic Figure as Miracle Worker* (Society of Biblical Literature Dissertation Series 1; Missoula, MT: Scholars, 1972).

73. See E. J. L Edelstein and L. Edelstein, *Asclepius: A Collection and Interpretation of the Testimonies*, 2 vols. (Baltimore: Johns Hopkins University Press, 1998 [1945]).

74. See W. Peek, *Inschriften aus dem Askleipieion von Epidaurus* (Berlin: Akademie-Verlag, 1969); selections in English can be found in D. R. Cartlidge and D. L. Dungan, *Documents for the Study of the Gospels* (Philadelphia: Fortress, 1980), 121–125.

75. The story is recounted by Livy, *History of Rome*, 10.47, and is rendered poetically by Ovid, *Metamorphoses*, 15.628–742; see K. Kerenyi, *Asklepios: Archetypal Image of the Physician's Existence*, trans. R. Manheim (Bollingen Series LXV.3; New York: Pantheon, 1959), 3–17.

76. In addition to the sources cited in the notes to Chapter 1, see Burkert, *Greek Religion*, 276–304; W. Burkert, *Ancient Mystery Cults* (Cambridge, MA: Harvard University Press, 1987); as well as M. W. Meyer, ed., *The Ancient Mysteries: A Sourcebook* (San Francisco: Harper and Row, 1987).

77. Burkert, *Greek Religion*, 277–278; for this conviction concerning Eleusis, see Aelius Aristides, *Oration*, I.330–341.

78. There were four distinct stages of initiation at Eleusis and seven degrees of initiation in the Mithras cult; see K. Kerenyi, *Eleusis: Archetypal Image of Mother and Daughter*, trans. R. Manheim (Bollingen Series 65; New York: Pantheon, 1967), 45–102; F. Cumont, *The Mysteries of Mithra*, trans. T. J. McCormack (Chicago: Open Court Publishing, 1910), 152–158; J. Merkelbach, *Mithras* (Königsten: Verlag Anton Hein, 1984), 86–145; for the secular advantages of initiation, see Burkert, *Ancient Mystery Cults*, 12–29.

79. See A. Motte, "Silence et Sécret dans les Mystères d'Eleusis," in *Les Rites des Initiation: Actes du Collège de Liège et de Louvain-la-Neuve, 1984*, ed. J. Ries (Louvain-la-Neuve: Centre d'Histoire des Religions, 1986), 317–334.

80. As in Clement of Alexandria, *Stromata*, 5.71–72.

81. See the collection of essays in H. P. Foley, ed., *The Homeric Hymn to Demeter: Translation, Commentary, and Interpretive Essays* (Princeton, NJ: Princeton University Press, 1994).

82. See L. J. Alderink, "The Eleusinian Mysteries in Roman Imperial Times," *Aufstieg und Niedergang der römischen Welt* II.18.2 (1984): 1259–1379.

83. Burkert, *Greek Religion*, 285.

84. L. Richardson, *A New Topographical Dictionary of Ancient Rome* (Baltimore: Johns Hopkins University Press, 1992), 211–212.

85. See R. Beck, "Mithraism since Franz Cumont," *Aufstieg und Niedergang der Römischen Welt* II.17.4 (1984): 2002–2014.

86. In *Conversion: The Old and New in Religion from Alexander the Great to Augustine of Hippo* (Lanham, MD: University Press of America, 1989 [1933]), 138, A. D. Nock calls Apuleius' account "the high-water mark of the piety that grew out of the mystery religions." Burkert, *Ancient Mystery Cults*, 97, notes that "it is the only first-person account of a mystery experience that we have."

87. *Metamorphoses*, X.38; for text, translation, and commentary, see J. G. Griffiths, *The Isis-Book (Metamorphoses Book XI)* (Leiden: E. J. Brill, 1975).

88. *Metamorphoses*, XI.5–6.

89. Ibid., XI.23–27.

90. Ibid., XI.29–30.

91. See the essays in Jas Elsner and Ian Rutherford, eds., *Pilgrimage in Graeco-Roman and Early Christian Antiquity: Seeing the Gods* (New York: Oxford University Press, 2005).

92. Apuleius of Madura claims to have undergone initiations into multiple Mysteries (*Apology*, 55), and Libanius reports that the emperor Julian "consorted with *daimones* in countless rites (*teletai*)" (cited by Nock, *Conversion*, 115).

93. For terminological and methodological discussion, see M. Meyer and P. Mirecki, eds., *Ancient Magic and Ritual Power* (Religions in Greco-Roman World 129; Leiden: Brill, 1995); D. E. Aune, "Magic and Early Christianity," *Aufstieg und Niedergang der römischen Welt* II.23.2 (1980): 1507–1557.

94. So, e.g., the first-century philosopher Apollonius of Tyana had to struggle against charges that he was a *magos* both during his life (see *Letters*, 16 and 17) and after: see Philostratus, *Life of Apollonius of Tyana*, I.2.1; V.12; Dio Cassius, *Roman History*, 77.18.4; Origen, *Against Celsus*, 6.41. Such charges could have dire consequences: for the suppression of magic, see R. MacMullen, *Enemies of the Roman Order: Treason, Unrest, and Alienation in the Empire* (Cambridge, MA: Harvard University Press, 1966), 95–127.

95. See M. Dickie, *Magic and Magicians in the Greco-Roman World* (New York: Routledge, 2001); and the essays in *Magika Hiera: Ancient Greek Magic and Religion*, ed. C. A. Faraone and D. Obbink (New York: Oxford University Press, 1991).

96. For examples, see *Arcana Mundi: Magic and the Occult in the Greek and Roman Worlds: A Collection of Ancient Texts*, translated, annotated, and introduced by G. Luck (Baltimore: Johns Hopkins University Press, 1985); and H. D. Betz, *The Great Magical Papyri in Translation, Including the Demotic Spells* (Chicago: University of Chicago Press, 1986).

97. "The boundary between it and religion is so hazy and undefinable, that it is almost impossible to tie it down and restrict it to the narrow limits of some neat turn of phrase that will hit it off and have done with it"; see J. E. Lowe, *Magic in Greek and Latin Literature* (Oxford: Basil Blackwell, 1929), 1.

98. The most important thing to note for those approaching Greco-Roman religion from the side of a developed Christianity is that all these phenomena continued to flourish well into the fourth and even fifth centuries of the "Christian Era." The restoration of "paganism" under "Julian the Apostate" (so termed by Christian martyrologies) in the late fourth century could not have been so successful were there not a substantial ground of receptivity. For this reason, and for the added one that I am not interested in causal relationships, I am free to choose as my examples of Greco-Roman religiosity figures and compositions that considerably postdate the New Testament. For the continued liveliness of "paganism," see the considered remarks of MacMullen, *Paganism in the Roman Empire*, 62–73.

99. For the positive sense, see Dio Chrysostom, *Oration*, 61.9; for the negative, see Strabo, *Geography of Greece*, 16.2.37.

100. The portrait appears in Theophrastus, *Character Types*, 16: the superstitious man reacts in fear to every phenomenon (2–9), engages in apotropaic rituals (10), consults dream interpreters and prophets and diviners (11), and seeks initiation every month (11).

101. Lucian of Samosata, *The Lover of Lies*, 13–16.

102. See Plutarch, *On Superstition*, 6–7 (Mor., 167D–168E); *Isis and Osiris*, 11 (Mor., 355D).

103. "In a trice he made them all look like children; for he was prophet, cult leader, head of synagogue, and everything, all by himself. He interpreted and explained some of their books, and even composed many, and they revered him as a god, made use of him as a lawgiver, and set him down as protector, next after that other, to be sure, whom they still worship, the man who was crucified in Palestine because he introduced this new cult into the world" (*The Passing of Peregrinus*, 11).

104. *The Passing of Peregrinus*, 42.

105. Lucian, *Alexander the False Prophet*—it is based on a real cult founder who flourished between 150 and 170 CE.

106. Epicurus, *To Menoeceus*, 123–124; 134; *Sovereign Maxims*, 1; *Fragments*, 24.58; Philodemus, *On Piety*, 18. Preeminent among philosophers condemning the immorality of religious myths was Plato, who would ban the poets from his ideal state (*Republic*, 378B–E; 398A; 595B–C).

107. See Lucian of Samosata, *Alexander the False Prophet*, 17, 25, 43, 47, 61.

108. Lucian calls Demonax "the best philosopher I know" and notes of him that he refused to offer sacrifice or be initiated at Eleusis (*Demonax*, 11), that he was critical of Proteus Peregrinus (21) as well as of a sorcerer (23), prayer to Asclepius (27), the Mysteries (34), and a soothsayer (37).

109. See the rich assortment of graffiti cited *passim* in C. A. Williams, *Roman Homosexuality: Ideologies of Masculinity in Classical Antiquity* (New York: Oxford University Press, 1999).

110. Aristophanes shows a conservative religious attitude in his criticism of Euripides' and Socrates' contemning of the Olympic gods (see *The Clouds, Thesmophoriazusae*), but he imitates Euripides by reducing the gods to characters in (sometimes bawdy) plays (see *The Birds, The Frogs*). But his plays also contain elements of genuine piety, as in the chorus of Bacchantes in *The Frogs*. In the six extant comedies of Terence, an expression of piety occurs only in *The Eunuch* (V.8). As for Plautus, his twenty extant comedies have only random religious elements: Jupiter and Mercury change form ribaldly in *Amphitryon*, the household god recites the prologue in *The Pot of Gold* (as the god Succour recites the prologue in I.3 of *The Casket*). The goddess Fortune is mentioned in passing in *Pseudolus*; and in *Curculio*, a pimp offers sacrifice in the temple of Asclepius to acquire good luck. The only mark of genuine piety occurs in *The Rope* (I.5; IV.2).

111. The main characters in Petronius' *Satyrika*, Encolpius and Giton, are thoroughly secular in outlook, regarding religious observance as a matter of low self-interest (88); they pray only for sexual success (79, 83–85) and use the language of the Mysteries for sexual orgy (16–18). For the most part, they see themselves as the playthings of Fortuna (78, 95, 96, 100, 101, 128). In contrast, Trimalchio and his guests show an ostentatious—almost superstitious—piety, covering a vulgar manner of life: Trimalchio's villa displays a plaque to the *Lares et Penates* (29), an inscription marking his membership in the "College of Augustus" (i.e., imperial cult [30]), and an ostentatious display of *dies fasti et nefasti* (30). He checks his horoscope (77) and his rooster

for *auspices* (74). His guests give voice to the conventional prayers (61, 64) and declare that the gods' anger results from lack of human piety (46)—the world is topsy-turvy as though it were *Saturnalia* (44, 69). They tell stories of witches and magic (63). Only the female character Circe expresses a genuine piety; although she eschews divination and astrology (126), she declares her conviction that "even now the gods are at work, as silent as thought" (127). For translation and notes, see Petronius, *Satyrika: A New Translation*, ed. R. B. Branham and D. Kinney (Berkeley: University of California Press, 1996). I have already mentioned Apuleius' *Metamorphoses* as a valuable source for religious practice. Other Greco-Roman novels—especially those composed in Greek—contain a wealth of religious phenomena and evince a pious, even credulous, air. In them we find revelatory dreams (Achilles Tatius, *Clitiphon and Leucippe*, I.3; II.11; IV.2; Longus, *Daphnis and Chloe*, 1.7; 2.23; Chariton of Aphrodisias, *Chaereas and Callirhoe*, IV.55; Xenophon, *The Ephesians*, 1.81; 2.89; Heliodorus, *Ethiopian Tale*, 8, 11; Pseudo-Callisthenes, *Alexander Romance*, 1.8; 1.34), festivals for a variety of gods and goddesses (*Clitophon and Leucippe*, II.2; V.2; *Daphnis and Chloe*, 2.2; *Ethiopian Tale*, 9.9–10), appearances of gods and goddesses to humans (*Ephesians*, 2.52; *Daphnis and Chloe*, 2.2; 2.5–7; 2.6–7; *Alexander Romance*, 1.33), prayer (*Clitiphon and Leucippe*, III.5; *Ephesians*, 4.114), temples of Isis (*Clitiphon and Leucippe*, V.14; *Ephesians*, 3.104), sacrifice to Dionysius (*Daphnis and Chloe*, 3.10), worship of individuals as gods or goddesses because of their beauty or power (*Clitiphon and Leucippe*, III.23; *Chaereas and Callirhoe*, I.14.1; III.2.15–17; *Ephesians*, 1.71; 1.80; 2.85; *Ethiopian Tale*, 1.2), mantic frenzy (*Clitiphon and Leucippe*, II.3; II.12; IV.9), oracles (*Ephesians*, 1.75; *Ethiopian Tale*, 2.16; 2.26; *Alexander Romance*, 1.3; 1.15; 1.47), astrology (*Alexander Romance*, 1.5), magic (*Clitiphon and Leucippe*, III.18; *Ephesians*, 1.75; *Alexander Romance*, 1.1; 1.11; 1.43), and necromancy (*Ethiopian Tale*, 6.14–15). For English translations of all these novels, see B. P. Reardon, ed., *Collected Ancient Greek Novels* (Berkeley: University of California Press, 1989).

112. The tendency to regard Epicurus as divine began with the obeisance shown him during his lifetime by Colotes (see Plutarch, *Against Colotes* (Mor., 1117 A–D) and reached full expression in Lucretius' *On the Nature of Things*; see C. J. Castner, "*De Rerum Natura* 5:101–103: Lucretius' Application of Empedoclean Language to Epicurean Doctrine," *Phoenix* 41 (1987): 40–49. In Iamblichus' *Life of Pythagoras*, the founder of the school is of divine descent at birth (3–10) and demonstrates his divinity by *thaumata* (see 36, 60–61, and 136).

The Pythagoreans took their founder's dictum, "friends hold all things in common" (see Diogenes Laertius, *Life of Pythagoras*, 8.10), and structured a community life in which all possessions were shared; see Iamblichus, *Life of Pythagoras*, 6.29–30; Porphyry, *Life of Pythagoras*, 20. In contrast, Epicurus cultivated friendship among his followers but explicitly rejected a community of possessions because it suggested a lack of trust among friends (see *Sovereign Maxims*, 14, 28; *Fragments*, 23, 34, 39, 42).

The theme of purity is restricted to the Pythagorean tradition (see Iamblichus, *Life*, 17.75; 35.257). Likewise, stages of admission are found more explicitly among the Pythagoreans (Iamblichus, *Life*, 17.72; 18.81); for expulsion, see 17.73–75.

Epicurean schools are known to have existed in Naples and Herculaneum in the first century BCE; among the compositions recovered from Herculaneum is the tractate "On Frank Criticism" (*peri parrēsias*) by the Epicurean teacher Philodemus, which is dedicated entirely to the practice of correction within the philosophical school.

113. Thus the criticism found everywhere in the literature: the false philosopher is one who professes but does not practice the life of virtue (see, e.g., Lucian, *Hermotimus*, 79; *The Dream*, 11; *Icaromenippus*, 5; *Philosophers for Sale*, 20–23; Epictetus, *Discourse*, II.1.31; II.17.26; III.5.17; Julian, *Oration*, 7.225A; 7.223C; Dio Chrysostom, *Oration*, 35.2.3.11).

   On marks of identity, see Aelius Aristides, *To Plato, in Defense of the Four*, III.663–668; Epictetus, *Discourse*, III.22.9.50); IV.8.5; Julian, *Oration*, 6.197C; 7.2223C; Dio Chrysostom, *Oration*, 35.2.3.11; Lucian, *Hermotimus*, 18–19.

   Adherents of philosophy appeared in a variety of social positions: emperor (Marcus Aurelius), court advisor (Seneca), senator (Cicero), schoolmaster (Epictetus), and wandering preacher (Dio Chrysostom). Especially in the Cynic tradition deriving from Diogenes and Antisthenes, the Socratic sense of social critic and gadfly was maintained but with a more positive nuance: the philosopher could be regarded as physician (Epictetus, *Discourse*, III.22.72–73; Dio, *Oration*, 32.10.34; Lucian, *Nigrinus*, 38; *Demonax*, 7), as general (Julian, *Oration*, 6.192C), or as "herald of the gods" (Epictetus, *Discourse*, III.22.70).

114. On turning from vice to virtue, see Lucian, *Nigrinus*, 38. In *Hermotimus*, Lucian taunts the plodding seeker after wisdom in Stoicism with the proposition that it is impossible to know which school is true unless one has tested them all, a proposition that he proceeds to show is itself impossible of fulfillment. For the motif of passing through schools until finding the right one, see Philostratus, *Life of Apollonius of Tyana*, I.7–8.

115. See the evidence collected in L. T. Johnson, "The New Testament's Anti-Jewish Slander and the Conventions of Ancient Polemic," *Journal of Biblical Literature* 108 (1989): 419–441; and "Proselytism and Witness in Earliest Christianity: A Study in Origins," in *Sharing the Book: Religious Perspectives on the Rights and Wrongs of Proselytism*, ed. J. Witte Jr. and R. C. Martin (Religion and Humans Rights 4; Maryknoll, NY: Orbis, 1999), 145–157, 376–384.

116. See Epictetus, *Discourse*, III.22.54–55. Even the mild Demonax experienced rejection (*Demonax*, 11). Philosophers were among those who experienced exile because of imperial suspicion of their subversive potential; see Philostratus, *Life of Apollonius of Tyana*, IV.35.36; VII.4; Dio Cassius, *Roman History*, 52.36.4; and MacMullen, *Enemies of the Roman Order*, 46–94.

117. For the frequent use of medical metaphors among Greco-Roman moralists, see A. J. Malherbe, *Moral Exhortation: A Greco-Roman Sourcebook* (Library of Early Christianity; Philadelphia: Westminster, 1986), *passim*; and M. C. Nussbaum, *The Therapy of Desire: Theory and Practice in Hellenistic Ethics* (Princeton, NJ: Princeton University Press, 1994).

118. See E. N. Gardiner, *Athletics in the Ancient World* (Chicago: Ares, 1980); V. C. Pfitzner, *Paul and the Agon Motif: Traditional Athletic Imagery in the Pauline Literature*

(Novum Testamentum Supp. 16; Leiden: Brill, 1967); see also Malherbe, *Moral Exhortation*, 26–27, 72, 126, 142, 159.

119. For the complexities of Orphism, see Burkert, *Greek Religion*, 290–301; L. J. Alderink, *Creation and Salvation in Ancient Orphism* (American Classical Studies 8; Chico, CA: Scholars, 1981); W. Burkert and W. Wuellner, eds., *Orphism and Bacchic Mysteries: New Evidence and Old Problems of Interpretation* (Berkeley: Center for Hermeneutical Studies in Hellenistic and Modern Culture, 1977); R. G. Edmunds, *Myths of the Underworld: Plato, Aristophanes, and the "Orphic" Golden Tablets* (Cambridge: Cambridge University Press, 2004); S. G. Cole, "Orphic Mysteries and Dionysiac Ritual," in *Greek Mysteries: The Archaeology and Ritual of Ancient Greek Secret Cults*, ed. M. B. Cosmopoulos (London: Routledge, 2003), 193–217; M. L. West, *The Orphic Poems* (Oxford: Clarendon, 1983). For the link to Pythagoreanism, see J. C. Thom, *The Pythagorean Golden Verses, with Introduction and Commentary* (Religions in the Graeco-Roman World 123; Leiden: Brill, 1995), who points to Orphic influence in *Golden Verses*, 50–51, 55–56, 67–68.

120. In the *Laws*, Plato refers to those who "abstained from flesh on the grounds that it was impious to eat it or to stain the altars of the gods with blood. It was a kind of Orphic life (*bios orphikos*) as it was called, that was led by those of our kind who were alive at that time, taking freely of all things that had no life, but abstaining from all that had life" (782C). In Plato's *Cratylus*, 400C, Socrates says, "Some say it [the body] is the tomb (*sēma*) of the soul, their notion being that the soul is buried in the present life . . . but I think it most likely that the Orphic poets gave the name, with the idea that the soul is undergoing punishment for something; they think it has the body as an enclosure to keep it safe, like a prison . . . until the penalty is paid." See also *Phaedo*, 62B; 67B–69C; *Gorgias*, 493C.

121. See MacMullen, *Paganism in the Roman Empire*, 42–48.

122. Augustus assumes the office of *Pontifex Maximus* in 12 BCE and effectively becomes the supreme authority of both religious and political life in the *oikoumenē*.

4. RELIGION AS PARTICIPATION IN DIVINE BENEFITS

1. For discussions, see G. W. Bowersock, *Greek Sophists and the Roman Empire* (Oxford: Clarendon, 1969); G. W. Bowersock, ed., *Approaches to the Second Sophistic* (University Park: University of Pennsylvania Press, 1974); T. Smitz, *Bildung und Macht: Zur sozialen und politischen Funktion der zweiten Sophistik in der griechischen Welt der Kaizerzeit* (Munich: C. H. Beck, 1997); G. A. Anderson, *The Second Sophistic: A Cultural Phenomenon in the Roman Empire* (London: Routledge, 1993); T. Whitmarsh, *The Second Sophistic* (Greece and Rome: New Surveys in the Classics 35; Oxford: Oxford University Press, 2005).

2. For the academic debates, see Whitmarsh, *The Second Sophistic*, 3–22.

3. Whitmarsh, *The Second Sophistic*, 15–19; G. R. Stanton, "Sophists and Philosophers: Problems of Classification," *American Journal of Philology* 94 (1973): 350–364.

4. The orator Demosthenes calls "Sophists" those who appeal to the crowd (*On the Crown*, 19.246; 29.13; 59.21), and Plato's *Gorgias* dismisses rhetoricians because they are more interested in persuasion and popularity than in truth; see, e.g., 453–462.

5. See Dio, *Orations*, 12.5; 22.5; 24.3; 34.3; 71.8.

6. See Whitmarsh, *The Second Sophistic*, 38–39.

7. I am using the translation from the Greek of W. C. Wright, *Philostratus, Lives of Sophists; Eunapius, Lives of Philosophers* (Loeb Classical Library; Cambridge, MA: Harvard University Press, 1921).

8. On the inscriptions, see B. Puech, *Orateurs et sophiste grecs dans les inscriptions d'époque impériale* (Paris: Librairie Philosophique J. Vrin, 2002). For Lucian, see R. B. Branham, *Unruly Eloquence: Lucian and the Comedy of Traditions* (Cambridge, MA: Harvard University Press, 1989); for Dio of Prusa, see S. C. R. Swain, ed., *Dio Chrysostom: Politics, Letters, and Philosophy* (Oxford: Oxford University Press, 2000).

9. For the Greek text of the orations of Aelius Aristides, see C. A. Behr and F. W. Lenz, *P. Aelii Aristidis Opera Quae Exstant Omnia*, vol. 1 (Leiden: Brill, 1976). I use throughout this chapter *P. Aelius Aristides: The Complete Works*, 2 vols., trans. C. A. Behr (Leiden: Brill, 1981, 1986).

10. See Behr, *Complete Works*, 1:413–426.

11. This sketch follows Behr, *Complete Works*, 1:1–4; compare A. Boulanger, *Aelius Aristide et la sophistique dans la province d'Asie au IIe siècle de notre ère* (Paris: E. de Boccard, 1968), 461–495.

12. See Behr, *Complete Works*, 1:1–4; see also C. A. Behr, *Aelius Aristides and the Sacred Tales* (Amsterdam: Adolf M. Hakkert, 1968).

13. In *Aelius Aristides and the New Testament* (Studia ad Corpus Hellenisticum Novi Testamenti; Leiden: Brill, 1980), P. W. van der Horst repeats Behr's judgments virtually verbatim. See also the opinions gathered by J. C. Stephens, *The Religious Experience of Aelius Aristides: An Interdisciplinary Approach* (PhD diss., University of California at Santa Barbara, 1982), 14–23.

14. Peter Brown notes, correctly, I think, that "the poor man has had to bear far too heavy a weight of odium psychologicum from modern scholars. He puzzles us; and it is this puzzlement which has led so many scholars into precipitate psychiatric judgment on him. We obscurely resent the fact that a degree of intimacy with the divine which would make a saint or martyr of any of us should merely serve to produce a hypochondriacal gentleman of indomitable will"; see *The Making of Late Antiquity* (Cambridge, MA: Harvard University Press, 1971), 41; quoted in Stephens, *The Religious Experience of Aelius Aristides*, 22.

15. Likewise the statement made by a contemporary of Aristides, the physician Galen (129–199) in his *Commentary on Plato's Timaeus* (quoted by Behr, *Aristides and the Sacred Tales*, 105): "I have seen many people whose body was naturally strong and whose soul was weak, inert and useless. . . . [T]hus their sicknesses have arisen from a sort of insomnia and apoplexy and enervation and sicknesses of the sort of epilepsy—and as to them, whose souls are naturally strong and whose bodies are weak I have seen only a few of them. One of them was Aristides, one of the inhabitants of Mysia.

And this one man belonged to the most prominent rank of orators. Thus it happened to him, since he was active in teaching and speaking throughout his life, that his whole body wasted away."

16. In Behr, *Complete Works*, they are listed as *Orations*, 47–52. In this section, I use the abbreviation *ST* and refer to them separately as *Sacred Tales*, 1–6, continuing to follow Behr's paragraph markers.

17. Following Behr, *Complete Works*, the following chronological assignment of material can be discerned: 144 (2.5–7; 2.50; 2.60–70); 144–145 (3.45; 4.14; 4.31–37); 145 (2.8–14; 2.45–49; 2.71–76); 145–147 (3.44; 4.14–29; 4.38–42); 146 (2.26–36; 2.51–59; 2.71–76; 3.1–6; 4.105); 147 (2.78–82; 3.7–13; 4.43–56; 4.58–62; 4.101–102); 148 (1.48–78; 3.6; 3.14–33; 4.57; 4.103–104); 149 (2.11–25; 3.37–43; 3.47–50); 152 (4.1–8; 4.95–99); 153 (4.10–13; 4.71–94); 153–154 (4.63–67); after 155 (6.1–3); 165 (2.37–45; 4.9); 166 (1.5–58 [diary]; 5.11–25); 167 (5.26–27); 170–171 (1.1–4; 1.59–60; 2.1–4; 2.81; 3.34–37; 4.30; 4.68–70; 5.38–67).

18. See L. Casson, *Travel in the Ancient World* (Baltimore: Johns Hopkins University Press, 1994).

19. See H. C. Kee, *Medicine, Miracle, and Magic in New Testament Times* (Cambridge: Cambridge University Press, 1986).

20. Excerpts from Artemidorus' *Oneirocritica* are found in G. Luck, *Arcana Mundi: Magic and the Occult in the Greek and Roman Worlds* (Baltimore: Johns Hopkins University Press, 1985), 292–298.

21. On his travels, see *ST*, 2.12–14; 2.60–61; 2.64–69; 4.2–7; 4.32–37; 5.1–10; 5.13–19. A (very) partial list of his sickness symptoms includes stomach and intestinal problems (1.4; 1.69; 2.46; 2.63; 5.1), including biliousness (2.39), indigestion (5.11) and constipation (4.9); smallpox (2.38); difficulties in breathing (2.5; 3.1; 3.16; 3.21); lesions in the throat (5.9); fever (2.44; 2.63; 3.16); perspiration (1.5); a carbuncle (1.14); a tumor (1.61–62); a catarrh (2.46); a bloody discharge (2.63); problems with his ears (2.57; 2.60) in one case causing deafness (2.68); problems in his arteries and inflammation (2.57); problems with his teeth (2.63; 4.30), his palate (1.69; 2.46), and generally with his head (1.69; 3.16).

Again, this list of his regimens is partial: he fasts completely (1.59) or abstains from meat (3.34–37); he drinks wine (3.32) or a drink containing philo (3.29) or wormwood (2.28); he purges by vomiting (1.9; 1.40; 1.50; 1.53; 1.65) or using enemas (1.59; 2.14; 2.43); he applies various saps and soaps (2.10) or medicines containing salt [on his tumor] (1.66) and smears on an egg (1.68) or mud (2.74–75); he attaches plasters (3.8; 3.1) and removes a ring (2.27); he also has phlebotomies performed on him (2.47–48; 3.10), wraps his body in wool (2.58; 5.9) and his neck with cassia (3.6), and gargles (5.9). Of special interest are the commands of the god concerning water and exposure to the elements. Aristides either abstains from bathing (1.6; 1.24; 1.26; 1.40; 1.45; 1.53; 1.54; 4.6) or bathes extravagantly in obedience to the god: in a river (2.45; 2.48); in seas and wells (1.59); and in winter weather outdoors (2.21; 2.51–53; 4.11), including in a freezing rain (2.78). He is also commanded to run unshod in winter (1.65; 2.7) and to go outside half-naked (2.80).

22. It is the grandiosity of his dreams as well as his self-satisfied sense of his great worth that make such a judgment almost unavoidable (see, e.g., 5.36–37).

23. See the discussion in Stephens, *The Religious Experience of Aelius Aristides*, 112–124.

24. Boulanger states it well when he speaks of Aristides' religious sensibility as "n'est que l'exagération de tendances communes à son époque. Sa conception de la divinité et du rôle de la providence dans le monde est tout à fait dépourvue d'originalité. Ce qu'il y a de plus personnel chez lui c'est peut-être la forme spéciale de sa vanité, dont l'exaltation affecte volontiers un caractère mystique." (Only an exaggeration of common tendencies in his age. His conception of the divine and of the role of providence in the world is entirely without originality. What is more personal to him is perhaps the special form of his vanity, whose exalted character achieves a mystical character.) In *Aelius Aristide*, 209.

25. Caution is required, to be sure, since the entirety of his work is not extant; the excerpts from his lost oration, *Against the Dancers*, found in Libanius, *Oration*, LXIV (Behr, *Complete Works*, 416–419), suggest that the theme of that oration was at least partially moral. By saying that the orator is not concerned with moral transformation, I do not suggest either that he is immoral or that there is no link between his religious sensibility and his moral character. I mean, rather, that while his extant orations suggest an extravagant and consistent celebration of "participation in benefits," we find in them hardly any specifically moral discourse, and there is no sense that he regards the divine *dynamis* itself as having as its specific task the shaping of moral character.

5. RELIGION AS MORAL TRANSFORMATION

1. The chapter called "In Search of Happiness: Philosophy and Religion," in H.-J. Klauck's *The Religious Context of Early Christianity: A Guide to Greco-Roman Religions*, trans. B. McNeil (Minneapolis: Fortress, 2003), can stand for many similar treatments. Klauck offers several justifications for a treatment of philosophy in a book on Greco-Roman religion: (1) standard handbooks include such discussions; (2) philosophy was the closest thing to psychagogy in antiquity; (3) conversion was found more in philosophy than in religion; (4) "philosophy served educated circles as a guideline for a religiously based conduct of life"; and (5) philosophy is where the existence of divinity was discussed and critiqued (332–334). Klauck's subsequent treatment is entirely devoted to the philosophers' ideas about "theological topics"—most of them chosen because they correspond to Christian preoccupations—with little or no attention paid to the way in which the practice of philosophy could be regarded as religious or to the religious sensibilities of the respective philosophers. Similarly, W. Burkert's examination of "Philosophical Religion" in *Greek Religion* consists mainly of theological ideas held by philosophers; see W. Burkert, *Greek Religion*, trans. J. Raffan (Cambridge, MA: Harvard University Press, 1985, 305–337).

2. See the discussion in Chapter 3.

3. Musonius Rufus (ca. 30–100) is little known today but was widely admired in antiquity. The emperor Julian (himself an advocate of Cynicism) mentions him in the

same breath with Socrates (*Oration*, 6.72), and Origen ranks Rufus with Heracles, Odysseus, and Socrates as "models of excellence of life" (*Against Celsus*, 3.56). Only fragments of his teaching are extant, but they make clear that Rufus (as Epictetus calls him) had a religious outlook much like that of his student; philosophy is a matter not only of theory but of practice, done in obedience to God (Frag. 16); humans are born with a natural inclination to virtue because they bear the image of God (Frag. 17); the philosopher-king who controls his passions is godlike and worthy of reverence (Frag. 8). For texts and translation, see C. E. Lutz, *Musonius Rufus: "The Roman Socrates"* (New Haven, CT: Yale University Press, 1947); for discussion, see A. C. Van Geytenbeek, *Musonius Rufus and Greek Diatribe*, trans. B. L. Hijmans (Assen: Van Gorcum, 1962).

Dio of Prusa (also called *chrysostomos*, that is, "golden mouth") was a famous member of the Second Sophistic (40–112 CE). His own sense of divine calling is found especially in the account of his "conversion" in *Orations*, 13.137 and 32.12–21. His *Oration* 12 ("Olympic Oration" or "On Man's First Conception of the Divine") is a powerful argument for the unity of divine power, taking its start in popular religious conceptions.

Marcus Aurelius (121–180 CE) was emperor from 161 to 180. He endowed four chairs of philosophy in Athens in 176. His *Meditations* in 12 books were written as a personal notebook in a vigorous *koinē* and were probably passed on privately by his family; they are first mentioned by the philosopher Themistius in 350. His personal piety is shown by his gratitude toward the gods in 1.17. In the other books, he insists that the world reveals divine reason in all its manifestations (2.1; 3.6; 4.40; 5.21; 6.9; 7.9; 8.26; 9.28; 10.6; 11.20; 12.26), and he interweaves, as does Epictetus, the sense of "following nature" and "following god" (see, e.g., 2.3; 3.6; 4.23; 5.7; 7.67; 9.1; 12.28). The king tells himself to "keep all thy thoughts on god" (6.7) and to "follow god" (7.31).

4. In his *Moral Epistle*, 41 ("On the God within Us"), Seneca the Younger (4 BCE–65 CE) provides a straightforward exposition of Stoic physics with little personal emphasis, as he does also in *Moral Epistle*, 65 ("On the First Cause"). His essay "On Consolation: To Marcia" is virtually devoid of religious language until the last paragraph, wherein he provides an odd eschatology that combines a Stoic conflagration of all things with the blessed "who have partaken of immortality" being "as seems best to god" absorbed into the new cosmos (26.4–6). *Moral Epistle*, 71 ("On the Supreme Good") does not mention God. In the essay "On the Happy Life," Seneca nods toward the propositions that virtue makes humans divine (16.1) and that the gods are rulers of the universe (20.5), but these are blips in a lengthy argument that otherwise focuses completely on following nature (*not* stated as God; 3.3) and exercising reason and self-control (8.4). Indeed, he has kind things to say about Epicurus and his teachings (13.1–2). Finally, in the lengthy essay "On Tranquility of Mind," Seneca again gives voice to the axiom that practicing virtue makes one near to being a god (2.3) but otherwise uses no religious language at all. This is the more striking in 6.1–3, which otherwise closely resembles Epictetus (*Discourses*, 3.22); but where

Epictetus refers all to God, Seneca refers nothing. The greatest point of contrast with Epictetus is found in the way language is or is not used with reference to the philosopher's own life and that of his readers. At the very least, Seneca is a "cool" medium in this respect, while Epictetus is a "hot" medium.

5. This sketch of Epictetus' life is based squarely on that provided by W. A. Oldfather, *Epictetus: The Discourses as Reported by Arrian, the Manual, and Fragments*, 2 vols. (Loeb Classical Library; Cambridge, MA: Harvard University Press, 1925), 1:vii–xxxvii. All citations from Epictetus in this chapter also draw on Oldfather's inspired (if now slightly archaic) translation. A new study of Epictetus is A. A. Long, *Epictetus: A Stoic and Socratic Guide to Life* (Oxford: Clarendon, 2002).

6. The historian Tacitus' dates are ca. 56–120; Plutarch of Chaeronea (whom I will consider in Chapter 7) lived between ca. 46 and 119. Ignatius was martyred ca. 107.

7. Celsus states, "Take Epictetus, who, when his master was twisting his leg, said smiling and unmoved, 'you will break my leg,' and when it was broken, he added, 'Did I not tell you that you would break it?'" (*Against Celsus*, 7.53); and Origen responds, "He also directs us to Epictetus, whose firmness is justly admired, although his saying when his leg was broken is not to be compared to the marvelous acts and words of Jesus which Celsus refuses to believe" (7.54).

8. For his strictness, see "On Sexual Conduct" (Frag. 12), which advocates a form of sexual morality as fully stringent as that of the first Christians; for humaneness, see "That Women too should Study Philosophy" (Frag. 3), which is notable for its insistence on gender equality with regard to mental and moral capacities.

9. The equanimity—even the impassivity—revealed by the beating incident reported by Celsus may help account for Epictetus' wry admission that to others he often appeared "as a statue" (*Discourses*, 3.9.12), even though he rejects that level of *apatheia* as an ideal: "I ought not to be unfeeling like a statue, but should maintain my relations, both natural and acquired, as a religious man, as a son, a brother, a father, a citizen" (3.2.4).

10. See the lengthy discussion of Chrysippus in Diogenes Laertius, *Lives of Eminent Philosophers*, 7.7.179–202.

11. See G. Boter, *The Encheiridion of Epictetus and Its Three Christian Adaptations: Transmission and Critical Edition* (Philosophica Antiqua 82; Leiden: Brill, 1999). For a study of the *Manual*, see K. Seddon, *Epictetus' Handbook and the Tablet of Cebes: Guides to Stoic Living* (London: Routledge, 2005).

12. See R. Bultmann, *Der Stil der paulinischen Predigt und die kynischstoische Diatribe* (Forschungen zur Religion und Literatur des Alten und Neuen Testaments; Göttingen: Vandenhoeck & Ruprecht, 1910).

13. S. K. Stowers, *The Diatribe and Paul's Letter to the Romans* (Society of Biblical Literature Dissertation Series 57; Chico, CA: Scholars, 1981).

14. A. Oltramare, *Les Origines de la diatribe romaine* (Lausanne: Payot, 1926).

15. See the discussions of A. Bonhöffer, *Epiktet und das Neue Testament* (Religionsgeschichtliche Versuche und Vorarbeiten 10; Giessen: A. Töpelmann, 1911); and D. S. Sharp, *Epictetus and the New Testament* (London: Charles H. Kelly, 1914).

16. T. Whitmarsh, *The Second Sophistic* (Oxford: Oxford University Press, 2005).

17. Oldfather, *Epictetus*, 1:xiii.

18. For general appreciations of Epictetus as a Stoic, see J. P. Herschbell, "The Stoicism of Epictetus: Twentieth Century Perspectives," *Aufstieg und Niedergang der römischen Welt* II.36.3:2 (1989): 384–440; and W. O. Stephens, *Stoic Ethics: Epictetus and Happiness as Freedom* (London: Continuum, 2007).

19. See similarly *Discourses*, 1.5.9; 2.23.21–22; 3.7.7–29; 3.24.38.

20. For a sense of Stoic doctrines, see Diogenes Laertius' extensive treatment of Zeno (the school's founder) in *Lives of Eminent Philosophers*, 7.1.1–160; and for synthetic treatments, see A. A. Long, *Hellenistic Philosophy: Stoics, Epicureans, Skeptics*, 2nd ed. (London: Duckworth, 1986); G. Reale, *A History of Ancient Philosophy*, vol. 4: *The Schools of the Imperial Age*, ed. and trans. J. R. Catan (Albany: State University of New York Press, 1990).

21. A sampling: "On Progress" (1.4); "Of Family Affection" (1.11); "Of Contentment" (1.12); "Of Steadfastness" (1.29); "On Tranquillity" (2.2); "Of Anxiety" (2.13); "On Friendship" (2.22); "Of Personal Adornment" (3.1); "Of Training" (3.12); "On Fear of Want" (3.26); "Of Freedom" (4.1); "Of Freedom from Fear" (4.7).

22. See B. L. Hijmans, *Askesis: Notes on Epictetus' Educational System* (Assen: Van Gorcum, 1959).

23. In *Lives of Eminent Philosophers*, 4.16, Diogenes Laertius recounts the story of Polemo—a notorious profligate—bursting into the school being conducted by Xenocrates, being converted, and eventually becoming head of the Academy.

24. For athletic imagery, see also *Discourses*, 1.24.1; 1.29.34; 1.29.39; 2.17.29; 2.18.27; 3.1.5; 3.4.12; 3.8.1; 3.10.6; 3.15.3; 3.21.3; 3.23.2; 4.4.30; *Encheiridion*, 29. For medical imagery, see also *Discourses*, 2.15.15; 3.10.13; 3.15.2–4.

25. An appreciative reading of Epictetus' religious sensibility is found in S. Dill, "The Philosophic Theologian," in *Roman Society from Nero to Marcus Aurelius* (New York: Meridian, 1956), 384–440.

26. Diogenes Laertius on Zeno, in *Lives*, 7.119–120.

27. "That is why we even worship those persons as gods; for we consider that what has power to confer the greatest advantage is divine" (*Discourses*, 4.1.61).

28. For references to festivals, see also *Discourses*, 2.14.24; 4.1.104; 4.1.109; 4.4.24; 4.4.46. For references to Saturnalia see also 1.29.31; 4.1.58. He twice refers to the altar of fever in Rome—a fine example of *indigitamenta* (1.19.6; 1.22.16).

29. On sacrifices, see also *Discourses*, 1.17.18–19; 1.19.25; 2.18.13; 3.21.14; 3.24.117; 4.6.32. On prayers, see also 1.29.37; 2.22.14; 3.21.14; 4.6.37; of special interest are two samples of prayer as an expression of obedience to God, in 2.16.42 and 3.24.95–98. For other passages concerning thanksgiving, see 1.16.6; 1.19.25.

30. For his usage of "by Zeus," see *Discourses*, 1.12.6; 1.17.15; 1.18.1; 2.1.7; 2.11.7; 2.12.20; 2.20.37; 3.1.29; 3.25.3; 4.5.15; for his usage of "by the gods," see 2.22.4; 3.1.36; 3.3.17; 3.19.3; 3.20.8; 4.11.25.

31. See also, e.g., *Discourses*, 1.21.1; 1.2.4; 1.6.38; 1.9.11; 1.11.1; 1.12.32; 1.13.1; 1.20.6.

32. See also, e.g., *Discourses*, 1.1.24; 1.6.10; 1.6.37; 1.12.25; 1.13.3; 1.22.15; 1.25.3; 2.22.6.

33. See also, e.g., *Discourses*, 1.2.1; 1.6.4; 1.6.14; 1.6.18; 1.6.40; 1.9.4; 1.9.24; 1.14.1.

34. See also *Discourses*, 1.25.8; 1.30.1; 3.1.44; 3.13.13; 4.1.103; *Encheiridion*, 17.

35. See also *Discourses*, 3.5.7–11; 3.8.6; 3.15.14; *Discourses* totally devoted to the theme of providence are 1.6; 1.16; and 3.17.

36. See also *Discourses*, 3.3.5; 4.5.35; 4.13.24; 4.1.103–104.

37. Epictetus states that God "has stationed by each man's side his particular *daimon*—and has committed the man to his care—and that, too, a guardian who never sleeps and is not to be beguiled. . . . God is within and your own *daimon* is within" (*Discourses*, 1.14.12–14). See also 3.1.19; 3.1.37.

38. This passage is most often analyzed with respect to the Christian, especially, Pauline, sense of vocation; see, e.g., M. D. McGehee, *Divine Appointment to Specific Social Functions in Four Greco-Roman Traditions: Paul, Epictetus, Cynics, and Qumran* (PhD diss., Brown University, 1985); and F. Watson, "Self-Sufficiency and Power: Divine and Human Agency in Epictetus and Paul," in *Divine and Human Agency in Paul and his Cultural Environment*, ed. J. M. G. Barclay and S. J. Gathercole (London: T. & T. Clark, 2006), 117–139.

39. See also *Discourses*, 3.21.19–20: "Above all the counsel of god advising him to occupy this office (of teaching philosophy), as god counseled Socrates to take the office of examining and confuting men, Diogenes the office of rebuking men in a kingly manner, and Zeno that of instructing men and laying down doctrines."

40. See also *Discourses*, 4.1.131; 4.4.34; *Encheiridion*, 53. For a discussion of the content of the hymn, see J. Thom, *Cleanthes' Hymn to Zeus: Text, Translation, and Commentary* (Tübingen: Mohr Siebeck, 2005); see also Klauck, *The Religious Context of Early Christianity*, 351–354.

6. RELIGION AS TRANSCENDING THE WORLD

1. For the full range of traditions concerning Orpheus, see W. K. C. Guthrie, *Orpheus and Greek Religion: A Study of the Orphic Movement* (Princeton, NJ: Princeton University Press, 1952), 25–68.

2. As, for example, in V. D. Macchioro, *From Orpheus to Paul: A History of Orphism* (New York: Henry Holt, 1930).

3. For an example of the former view, see Guthrie, *Orpheus and Greek Religion*. For an example of the latter, see I. M. Linforth, *The Arts of Orpheus* (Berkeley: University of California Press, 1941).

4. Every serious scholar recognizes that there is "something there" and that the "something" is difficult to discern; see the crisp and helpful discussions in W. Burkert, *Greek Religion*, trans. J. Raffan (Cambridge, MA: Harvard University Press, 1985), 290–301; L. J. Alderink, *Creation and Salvation in Ancient Orphism* (American Classical Studies 8; Chico, CA: Scholars, 1981); R. G. Edwards, *Myths of the Underworld: Plato, Aristophanes, and the "Orphic" Golden Tablets* (Cambridge: Cambridge University Press, 2004).

5. See W. Burkert and W. Wuellner, eds., *Orphism and Bacchic Mysteries: New Evidence and Old Problems of Interpretation* (Berkeley, CA: Center for Hermeneutical

Studies in Hellenistic and Modern Culture, 1977); S. G. Cole, "Orphic Mysteries and Dionysiac Ritual," in *Greek Mysteries: The Archaeology and Ritual of Ancient Greek Secret Cults*, ed. M. D. Cosmopoulos (London: Routledge, 2003), 193–217.

6. Burkert, *Greek Religion*, 161–166.

7. Most notably by the powerful thesis developed in 1872 by F. Nietzsche, *The Birth of Tragedy from the Spirit of Music*, trans. F. Golffing (New York: Doubleday Anchor, 1956). Plutarch, who was a priest of Apollo at Delphi, stresses, in contrast, the close alliance between Apollo and Dionysus, in *The E at Delphi*, 9 (Mor., 388E–389B).

8. Burkert, *Greek Religion*, 290–295.

9. Livy, *History of Rome*, 39.8–19.

10. Burkert, *Greek Religion*, 222–223.

11. Plutarch also connects Dionysus with Osiris, whose myth also included dismemberment, in *Isis and Osiris*, 35–37 (Mor., 364E–365F). For the protean aspects of Dionysus, see W. F. Otto, *Dionysus: Myth and Cult* (Bloomington: Indiana University Press, 1965).

12. Burkert, *Greek Religion*, 293–295.

13. One of the 16 gold sheets associated with Orphic beliefs contains these lines: "Who are you? Where are you from? I am a child of earth and of starry heaven, but my race is of heaven (alone)." See M. W. Meyer, ed., *The Ancient Mysteries: A Sourcebook* (San Francisco: Harper and Row, 1987), 101; on pages 102–109, Meyer also provides samples of the Orphic Hymns; fuller collections are available in Apostolos N. Athanassakis, *The Orphic Hymns: Text, Translation, and Notes* (Greco-Roman Religion Series 4; Missoula, MT: Scholars, 1977); see also M. L. West, *The Orphic Poems* (Oxford: Clarendon, 1983).

14. To assert that Pythagoras is a historical figure does not mean that determining what is historical about him is easy. What should we make, for example, of Diogenes Laertius' claim that Pythagoras was initiated into the Mysteries of Greece, Egypt, and other countries (*Lives*, 8.3)? Or that Pythagoras assigned some poems he wrote to Orpheus (8.6)? Our most complete sources are the *Lives* composed by Diogenes Laertius and Iamblichus, centuries after Pythagoras' death, and they are manifestly filled both with legendary material and later convictions; for more recent efforts, see C. J. de Vogel, *Pythagoras and Early Pythagoreanism: An Interpretation of Neglected Evidence on the Philosopher Pythagoras* (Assen: Van Gorcum, 1966); P. Gorman, *Pythagoras: A Life* (London: Routledge and K. Paul, 1979); K. S. Guthrie, *The Pythagorean Sourcebook and Library: An Anthology of Ancient Writings Which Relate to Pythagoras and Pythagorean Philosophy* (Grand Rapids, MI: Phanes, 1987).

15. For an examination of these connections, see W. Burkert, "Craft versus Sect: The Problem of Orphics and Pythagoreans," in *Jewish and Christian Self-Definition*, vol. 3: *Self-Definition in the Greco-Roman World*, ed. B. F. Meyer and E. P. Sanders (Philadelphia: Fortress, 1982), 1–22.

16. Diogenes Laertius claims that Pythagoras coined the expression (*Lives*, 8.10).

17. For these elements of common life, see Iamblichus, *Life of Pythagoras*, 6.29–30; 17.73–75; 18.81; and Porphyry, *Life of Pythagoras*, 20.

18. For sexual asceticism, see Diogenes Laertius, *Lives*, 8.9; for detachment from pleasures, see 8.18; for lustrations and vegetarianism, see 8.13; 8.33; for avoidance of animal sacrifice, see 8.22; for killing living beings, see 8.13; for simplicity of life, see 8.13.

19. Diogenes Laertius, *Lives*, 8.14; Pythagoras is said to have claimed a connection to Hermes in this fashion (8.4), and Hermes is also said to accompany souls to the uppermost region (8.31).

20. Although reason is immortal, everything material is mortal (Diogenes Laertius, *Lives*, 8.30); souls have kinship with the gods and with all other "ensouled" beings (8.27).

21. In *Republic*, 600B, Plato also makes mention of a "way of life" associated with the Pythagoreans, for which the philosopher is held in honor.

22. Translation of *Republic* by P. Shorey (Loeb Classical Library; Cambridge, MA: Harvard University Press, 1930).

23. Translation of *Cratylus* by H. N. Fowler (Loeb Classical Library; Cambridge, MA: Harvard University Press, 1926).

24. Translation of *The Laws* by R. G. Bury (Loeb Classical Library; Cambridge, MA: Harvard University Press, 1926).

25. Translation of *Phaedo* by H. N. Fowler (Loeb Classical Library; Cambridge, MA: Harvard University Press, 1914). Socrates says shortly thereafter, "Does not the purification consist in this which has been mentioned long ago in our discourse, in separating, so far as possible, the soul from the body and teaching the soul the habit of collecting and bringing itself together from all parts of the body, and living, so far as it can, both now and hereafter, alone by itself, freed from the body as from fetters?" (67C–D). And later, "True philosophers practice dying, and death is less terrible to them than to any other men. Consider it this way. They are in every way hostile to the body and they desire to have the soul apart by itself alone" (67E).

26. The most complete and best treatment of the *Hermetica* as a whole is A. Festugière's *La Révélation d'Hermès Trismégiste*, 4 vols. (Paris: J. Gabalda, 1949–1954), and his *Hermétisme et mystique païenne* (Paris: Aubier, 1967). The best critical text is that of A. D. Nock and A. J. Festugière, *Corpus Hermeticum*, 2 vols. (Paris: Société d'Edition "Les Belles Lettres," 1945); I use here—with the exception to be noted below—the text and translation of W. Scott, *Hermetica*, 4 vols. (Oxford: Clarendon, 1936). A more recent translation, with notes, is by B. P. Copenhaver, *Hermetica* (Cambridge: Cambridge University Press, 1992).

27. See Scott, *Hermetica*, 1:1–111.

28. One searches in vain for the sort of social or political incidents that are strewn in the writings of Aristides and Epictetus alike; there is nothing in these writings that grounds them in a specific period. Even references to religious practices are rare: statues of gods are mentioned (XVII; *Asclepius*, 24b); demons are associated with statues of gods (*Asclepius*, 37); and lots and divination are also mentioned (*Asclepius*, 38), as are prophetic inspiration, dreams, and healings (*Asclepius*, 23). By far the most explicit and positive notice of religious practice is found in XII.2.19, which includes among the ways in which the gods communicate with humans mantic prophecy, auspices, and haruspices. On revelation, see Festugière, *La Révélation*, 1:87; *Hermétisme*, 30.

29. See, e.g., C. J. Bleecker, "The Egyptian Background of Gnosticism," in *The Origins of Gnosticism*, ed. U. Bianchi (Leiden: Brill, 1967), 229–237; and especially Festugière, *La Révélation*, 1:68–70.

30. This position has been advanced particularly by C. H. Dodd, in *The Bible and the Greeks* (London: Hodder and Staughton, 1935) and in *The Interpretation of the Fourth Gospel* (Cambridge: Cambridge University Press, 1953).

31. The literary relationship between *Poimandres* and the second-century Shepherd of Hermas was advanced especially by R. Reitzenstein, *Poimandres; Studien zur griechisch-Ägyptischen und früchristlichen Literatur* (Leipzig: Teubner, 1904).

32. Studies that seek to harmonize the writings—such as J. Kroll, *Die Lehre des Hermes Trismegistos* (Münster: Aschendorffsche, 1928)—are therefore not useful.

33. The difficulty of categorization is revealed by the fact that two great scholars place tractates in different camps; compare Festugière, *La Révélation*, 2:ix; and the grouping of W. Bousset, cited in M. Nilsson, *Geschichte der griechischen Religion*, 2 vols. (München: C. H. Beck, 1950), 2:558.

34. In addition to the studies already listed, see E. Hänchen, "Aufbau und Theologie des Poimandres," in his collection *Gott und Mensch* (Tübingen: J. C. B. Mohr, 1965), 335–377; R. A. Segal, *The Poimandres as Myth: Scholarly Theory and Gnostic Meaning* (Religion and Reason 33; Berlin: de Gruyter, 1986); J. Büchli, *Der Poimandres: Ein paganisiertes Evangelium* (Wissenschaftliche Untersuchungen zum Neuen Testament 2.27; Tübingen: J. C. B. Mohr [Paul Siebeck], 1987); J. Holzhauser, *Der "Mythos vom Menschen" im hellenistichen Ägypten: Eine Studie zum "Poimandres" (=CH I), zu Valentin und dem gnostischen Mythos* (Beiträge zum religions-und kirchengeschichte des Altertums 33; Bodenheim: Athenäum, 1994); P. J. Södergard, *The Hermetic Piety of the Mind: A Semiotic and Cognitive Study of the Discourse of Hermes Trismegistos* (Stockholm: Almqvist & Wiksell International, 2003).

35. The understanding of Poimandres as "Shepherd of Men" is possible, although not properly a Greek word (it would be a bastard combination of *poimēn* and *anēr*). Some scholars think the term has an Egyptian origin: *pe eime n re*, or "the knowledge of Ra"; see Scott, *Hermetica* 2:16; Dodd, *Bible and the Greeks*, 99.

36. The *terminus post quem* seems to be the development of middle Platonism with Posidonius in the mid-first century CE; the *terminus ante quem* is the first known citation by Zozimus at the beginning of the fourth century. Most scholars place the *Poimandres* before the end of the second century (as in Reitzenstein, *Poimandres*, 36; Hänchen, "Aufbau," 377; and G. R. S. Mead, *Thrice-Greatest Hermes*, 2 vols. [London: Theosophical, 1906], 1:43), and Scott places it between 100 and 200 CE (*Hermetica* 2:12). The boldest effort to find a more precise date is by C. H. Dodd; in his *Bible and the Greeks*, he dates it between 130 and 140 (209), and in *Interpretation of the Fourth Gospel* he narrows it further to between 125 and 130 (12).

37. On sleep and drunkenness, see G. MacRae, "Sleep and Awakening in Gnostic Texts," in *The Origins of Gnosticism*, ed. U. Bianchi (Leiden: Brill, 1967), 504.

38. I follow the sequence found in Nock-Festugière's text. Scott, who is given to emendations, rearranges the text so that paragraphs 30–32 precede paragraphs 27–29. Scott's version makes for more drama but lacks manuscript support.

39. The hymn is lovely and includes some of the tensions we have seen in the Hermetic teaching; the most critical lines are probably "Holy is god who wills to be known and is known by them that are his own"; "holy art thou whose brightness nature has not darkened"; and the conclusion, "Accept pure offerings of speech from a soul and heart uplifted to thee, Thou of whom no words can tell, no tongue can speak, whom silence only can declare" (31).

7. RELIGION AS STABILIZING THE WORLD

1. A sense of such behind-the-scenes support activity is provided by R. MacMullen, *Paganism in the Roman Empire* (New Haven, CT: Yale University Press, 1981), 42–48.

2. See, e.g., the anonymous hymns in *The Ancient Mysteries: A Sourcebook*, ed. M. W. Meyer (San Francisco: Harper and Row, 1987), 20–30, 101–109.

3. A classic example is the way Karl Barth distinguishes Christian "faith" from "religion"; see, e.g., *Church Dogmatics*, ed. G. W. Bromiley and T. F. Torrance, trans. G. T. Thomson and H. Knight (Edinburgh: T. & T. Clark, 1956), 1:2; *The Doctrine of the Word of God*, III.17.280–361.

4. Two examples: A. C. McGiffert, *A History of Christianity in the Apostolic Age* (New York: Charles Scribner's Sons, 1897), declares that even the latter part of the New Testament showed "the subjection of the spirit to law and of the individual to the institution, and thus foreshadowed the rise of Catholicism" (672); and H. Von Campenhausen, *Ecclesiastical Authority and Spiritual Power in the Church of the First Three Centuries*, trans. J. Baker (Stanford, CA: Stanford University Press, 1969), says, "In the course of these three centuries the ideal to which Christianity had originally been committed was impaired in various ways: not only do we find rigidities of attitude, curtailment of aspiration, distortion of insight, but also in every department— an indisputable trivialization" (3).

5. "The sacrificial community is a model of Greek society," and "Thus it is for religion not just to embellish but to shape all essential forms of community"; see W. Burkert, *Greek Religion*, trans. J. Raffan (Cambridge, MA: Harvard University Press, 1985), 255.

6. "The city in turn is a sacrificial community," and "city and gods are mutually dependent on each other"; see Burkert, *Greek Religion*, 256.

7. For *leitourgein/leitourgia* as undertaking any public work out of one's own funds, see Xenophon, *Memorabilia*, 2.7.6; Aristotle, *Politics*, 1291A; *Athenian Constitution*, 29.5; as undertaking such service for the gods, see Dionysius of Halicarnassus, *Roman Antiquities*, 2.22; Aristotle, *Politics*, 1330A; Diodorus Siculus, *History*, 1.21.

8. Burkert, *Greek Religion*, 278–285.

9. Ibid., 257–258.

10. See the collection of essays in *Pagan Priests: Religion and Power in the Ancient World*, ed. M. Beard and J. North (London: Duckworth, 1990); see also H.-J. Klauck, *The Religious Context of Early Christianity: A Guide to Graeco-Roman Religions* (Minneapolis: Fortress, 2003), 30–42.

11. For a collection of primary texts pertinent to these magistracies, see N. Lewis and M. Reinhold, eds., *Roman Civilization: Selected Readings*, vol. 1: *The Republic and*

the Augustan Age, 3rd ed. (New York: Columbia University Press, 1990), 90–107. For Cicero's climb through the offices, see D. R. S. Bailey, *Cicero* (New York: Charles Scribner's Sons, 1971), 13–34.

12. Suetonius, *Lives of the Caesars*, 1.13.

13. For a helpful description of the priesthoods under the Republic, see M. Beard, "Priesthood in the Roman Republic," in *Pagan Priests*, 19–48.

14. See Dionysius of Halicarnassus, *Roman Antiquities*, 2.78.

15. Livy, *History of Rome*, 1.18.6–10; Cicero, *Laws*, 12.31.

16. Dionysius of Halicarnassus, *Roman Antiquities*, 4.72; Livy, *History of Rome*, 5.18.4–5.

17. Dionysius of Halicarnassus, *Roman Antiquities*, 2.72.4–9; Livy, *History of Rome*, 1.24.3–9; 1.32.

18. For an ancient prayer of the Arval Priests found on an inscription (*Corpus Inscriptionum Latinarum* VI.2104), see Lewis and Reinhold, *Roman Civilization*, 73.

19. See Plutarch, *Life of Romulus*, 21.3–5.

20. Beard, "Priesthood in the Roman Republic," 20–21.

21. Cicero, *Laws*, 2.8.19–2.9.22.

22. Aulus Gellius, *Attic Nights*, 10.15.1–25.

23. Dionysius of Halicarnassus, *Roman Antiquities*, 2.47.

24. Beard, "Priesthood in the Roman Republic," 21–22.

25. Klauck, *Religious Context*, 32. Caesar had narrowly escaped severe political and religious embarrassment from the scandal involving his wife, Pompeia, during the Bona Dea festival (see Plutarch, *Life of Julius Caesar*, 9.1–10.6); when he became dictator, he built a magnificent temple to Mars (Suetonius, *Life of Caesar*, 40–44). He had committed his will to the care of the Vestal Virgins, and after his death, the Senate "voted Caesar all divine and human honors at once" (Suetonius, *Life of Caesar*, 83–85).

26. See R. Gordon, "From Republic to Principate: Priesthood, Religion and Ideology," in *Pagan Priests*, 177–198.

27. "Res Gestae Divi Augusti," *Corpus Inscriptionum Latinarum*, 3.769–799; I use the translation and paragraph markings given by Lewis and Reinhold, *Roman Civilization*, 561–572.

28. See M. Beard, J. North, and S. Price, *Religions of Rome*, 2 vols. (Cambridge: Cambridge University Press, 1998), 1:186–192.

29. Indeed, as Beard, North, and Price observe, even "the traditional senatorial priesthoods retained their prestige during the early empire, and the prestige of some was actually increased by Augustus"; competition for priesthoods among the elite remained keen, but depended in greater degree on the patronage of the emperor (*Religions of Rome*, 1:191–192).

30. See the inscriptional evidence for cult priesthoods offered by Klauck, *Religious Context*, 31; R. MacMullen and E. N. Lane, eds., *Paganism and Christianity, 100–425 CE: A Sourcebook* (Minneapolis: Fortress, 1992), 29–30 (healing shrines), 34–36 (cult patrons), and 64–73 (cult associations); see in particular the inscription describing the management of the Artemis temple in Ephesus (38–41).

31. See, e.g., D. Frankfurter, *Religion in Roman Egypt: Assimilation and Resistance* (Princeton, NJ: Princeton University Press, 1998).

32. See especially the rich inscriptional evidence found in S. Friesen, *Twice Neokoros: Ephesus, Asia, and the Cult of the Flavian Imperial Family* (Religions in the Graeco-Roman World 116; Leiden: Brill 1993), and P. A. Harland, *Associations, Synagogues and Congregations: Claiming a Place in Ancient Mediterranean Society* (Minneapolis: Fortress, 2003), 115–136; see also the inscriptions for the establishing of the imperial cult in Sparta and Brittany, in MacMullen and Lane, *Paganism and Christianity*, 74–77.

33. For details of his life, see R. H. Barrow, *Plutarch and His Times* (Bloomington: Indiana University Press, 1967).

34. His father is one of the conversation partners in several of Plutarch's symposia: see, e.g., *Table-Talk*, I.2; I.3; II.8; III.7.

35. They also appear in his symposia: see, e.g., *Table-Talk*, I.2; I.3; I.8; I.9.

36. Marcus Aurelius, *Meditations*, 1.9.

37. The *Lamprias Catalogue* of Plutarch's works lists 227 separate compositions; see *Plutarch's Moralia XV: Fragments*, trans. F. H. Sandbach (Loeb Classical Library; Cambridge, MA: Harvard University Press, 1969).

38. See *Essays on Plutarch's Lives*, ed. B. Scardigli (Oxford: Clarendon, 1995); *Plutarch and the Historical Tradition*, ed. P. A. Stadter (London: Routledge, 1992); *Plutarch and His Intellectual World*, ed. J. Mossman (London: Duckworth, 1997); and C. Pelling, *Plutarch and History: Eighteen Studies* (London: Duckworth, 2002).

39. *The Education of Children* (Mor., 1–14C) (although probably spurious, it was read as Plutarch's by those nineteenth-century educators who adopted his views); *How the Young Man Should Study Poetry* (Mor., 14D–37B); *On Listening to Lectures* (Mor., 37C–48D). For influences in Shakespeare, see *Coriolanus, Antony and Cleopatra*, and *Julius Caesar*.

40. Among the compositions that reveal Plutarch's historical interests, see *The Ancient Customs of the Spartans* (Mor., 236F–240B); *Roman Questions* (Mor., 263D–291C); *Greek Questions* (Mor., 291D–304); *Sayings of Kings and Commanders* (Mor., 172B–194E); *Sayings of Romans* (Mor., 194E–208A); *Sayings of Spartans* (Mor., 208B–240B); *Sayings of Spartan Women* (Mor., 240C–242D). For his scientific curiosity, see *Natural Phenomena* (Mor., 911C–919); *Concerning the Face Which Appears in the Orb of the Moon* (Mor., 920B–945E); *On the Principle of Cold* (Mor., 945F–955C); *Whether Land or Sea Animals Are Cleverer* (Mor., 959B–985C). His *Table-Talk* in nine books (Mor., 612C–748D) continues the symposium tradition reaching back to Plato and Xenophon and ranges widely over philosophical questions.

41. See especially *On the Delay of the Divine Vengeance* (Mor., 548A–568A); *Platonic Questions* (Mor., 999C–1011E); *On the Generation of the Soul in the Timaeus* (Mor., 1012B–1030C).

42. See, e.g., *How to Tell a Flatterer from a Friend* (Mor., 48E–74E); *How a Man May Become Aware of His Progress in Virtue* (Mor., 75B–86A); *How to Profit by One's Enemies* (Mor., 86B–92); *On Moral Virtue* (Mor., 440D–452D); *On the Control of Anger* (Mor., 452F–464D); *On Tranquility of Mind* (Mor., 464E–477F). For a collection of essays relating Plutarch's moral essays to the New Testament, see H. D. Betz, ed., *Plutarch's Ethical Writings and Early Christian Literature* (Studia ad Corpus Hellenisticum Novi Testamenti; Leiden: Brill, 1978), which is much fuller in its treatment

than H. Alqvist, *Plutarch und das Neue Testament: Ein Beitrag zum Corpus Hellenisticum Novi Testamenti* (Acts Seminarii Neotestamentici Upsaliensis 15; Uppsala: Appelsberg Boktryckeri A.-B., 1946).

43. See *On the Delay of the Divine Vengeance*, 5 (Mor., 550D–E).

44. See *Should an Old Man Engage in Politics?* 4 and 17, in reference to management of the Pythian Games; and *The Oracles at Delphi*, 29, in reference to restoring the shrine.

45. For efforts to place Plutarch's religious thought in context, see H. D. Betz, ed., *Plutarch's Theological Writings and Early Christianity* (Studia ad Corpus Hellenisticum Novi Testament; Leiden: Brill, 1975), and R. Hirsch-Luipold, ed., *Gott und die Götter bei Plutarch: Götterbilder-Gottesbilder-Weltbilder* (Religionsgeschichtliche Versuche und Vorarbeiten 54; Berlin: de Gruyter, 2005).

46. I am using the translation of F. C. Babbitt, *Plutarch's Moralia* VII (Loeb Classical Library; Cambridge, MA: Harvard University Press, 1928).

47. The same element of fear is isolated in Theophrastus' sketch of the superstitious person in *Character Types*, 16 (see especially lines 2–9).

48. Plutarch connects Jewish convictions to superstition also in *On Stoic Self-Contradictions*, 38 (Mor., 1051E); that he regards Jews straightforwardly as barbarians is made clear by *Table-Talk*, IV.5: "The Jews apparently abominate pork because barbarians especially abhor skin diseases like lepra and white scale and believe that human beings are ravaged by such maladies through contagion. Now we observe that every pig is covered on the under side by lepra."

49. The translation of *Isis and Osiris*, as well as of the other Pythian compositions discussed below, is that of F. C. Babbitt, *Plutarch's Moralia* V (Loeb Classical Library; Cambridge, MA: Harvard University Press, 1936). Plutarch also dedicated *The Bravery of Women* to Clea (Mor., 242E).

50. Herodotus, *History*, II.42.

51. Oddly, the same strategy is employed with regard to the Jews. In the *Table-Talk* entitled "Who the God of the Jews Is" (IV.6), the effort is made to assimilate the Jewish god to Dionysus, through Adonis, again focusing primarily on the similarity in ritual.

52. As had Herodotus, in *History*, II.48.

53. For this and the other anti-Epicurean compositions I discuss, I use the translation of P. H. de Lacy, *Plutarch's Moralia* XIV (Loeb Classical Library; Cambridge, MA: Harvard University Press, 1967).

54. I use the translation of P. H. de Lacy and B. Einarson, *Plutarch's Moralia* VII (Loeb Classical Library; Cambridge, MA: Harvard University Press, 1959).

8. WAYS OF BEING JEWISH IN THE GRECO-ROMAN WORLD

1. For *huioi tou Israel*, see, e.g., Ex 3:9; 11:1; Lev 1:2; Num 1:2; Deut 1:3; 31:1; Josh 3:9; Judg 1:1; 1 Sam 2:28; 2 Sam 7:6; LXX Ps 76:15; 102:7; 104:6. "The Land of Judaea" (*he gē Ioudaia*) is a geographical designation (see Matt 2:1; 2:5; Luke 1:5; John 3:22; 4:9; Acts 2:14), and "the Jews" are likewise "Judeans"—i.e., "those from Judaea" (*Ioudaioi* in 2 Kings 16:6; 25:24; Neh 2:16; Isa 19:17; Jer 24:5).

2. Three indications of the turn away from Hellenism include the following: (1) in the second century CE, Jews produced three translations of Torah into Greek (by Aquila, Symmachus, Theodotion) as competitors to the Septuagint, which was co-opted by the Christians, but after that, nothing; (2) the founding compositions of classical Judaism are composed in classical Hebrew (the *Mishnah*) and Aramaic (the *Talmudim* of Babylon and the Land of Israel); (3) the *Targumim* continued the tradition of translation of the Bible into Aramaic, and the next vernacular translation (tenth century by Saadia Ben Joseph) was into Arabic.

3. Historical surveys of Judaism in this period include W. D. Davies and L. Finkelstein, eds., *Cambridge History of Judaism*, vol. 1: *The Persian Period* and vol. 2: *The Hellenistic Age* (Cambridge: Cambridge University Press, 1984 and 1989); L. L. Grabbe, *Judaism from Cyrus to Hadrian*, 2 vols. (Minneapolis: Fortress, 1992); J. H. Hayes and S. R. Mandell, *The Jewish People in Classical Antiquity: From Alexander to Bar Kochba* (Louisville: Westminster John Knox Press, 1998); and E. M. Smallwood, *The Jews under Roman Rule from Pompey to Diocletian* (Leiden: E. J. Brill, 1976).

4. See S. W. Baron, *A Social and Religious History of the Jews*, 2nd rev. and enl. ed., 8 vols. (New York: Columbia University Press, 1952–1983); J. Neusner, *A History of the Jews in Babylon*, 5 vols. (Leiden: Brill, 1965–1970).

5. For surveys on Diaspora Judaism in the West, see E. M. Smallwood, *The Jews under Roman Rule*, 220–255; J. M. G. Barclay, *Jews in the Mediterranean Diaspora: From Alexander to Trajan (323 BCE–117 CE)* (Edinburgh: T. & T. Clark, 1996); and V. Tcherikover, *Hellenistic Civilization and the Jews*, trans. J. Applebaum (New York: Athenaeum, 1970); for a collection of texts, see M. H. Williams, ed., *The Jews among Greeks and Romans: A Diasporan Sourcebook* (Baltimore: Johns Hopkins University Press, 1998).

6. See Chapter 3.

7. On Jewish associations, see P. A. Harland, *Associations, Synagogues, and Congregations: Claiming a Place in Ancient Mediterranean Society* (Minneapolis: Fortress, 2003), especially 213–238, and S. Appelbaum, "The Organization of the Jewish Communities in the Diaspora," in *Jewish People in the First Century: Historical Geography, Political History, Social, Cultural, and Religious Life and Institutions*, ed. S. Safrai and M. Stern (Compendium rerum Iudaicarum ad Novum Testamentum 1; Philadelphia: Fortress, 1974), 464–503. For inscriptional evidence, see L. H. Kant, "Jewish Inscriptions in Greek and Latin," *Aufstieg und Niedergang der römischen Welt* II.20.2 (1987): 671–713. On Jewish charity, see L. Frankel, "Charity and Charitable Institutions," in *The Jewish Encyclopedia*, ed. I. Singer (New York: Funk and Wagnalls, 1903), 3:667–670; G. F. Moore, *Judaism in the First Three Centuries of the Christian Era*, 3 vols. (1927–1930; repr., New York: Schocken Books, 1971), 2:102–179. See also G. Hamel, *Poverty and Charity in Roman Palestine, First Three Centuries C.E.* (Near Eastern Center Studies 23; Berkeley: University of California Press, 1990).

8. The Sabbath meal and Passover Seder are fundamentally domestic celebrations rather than meals shared by "the association" (*synagōgē*) as such; see B. M. Bosker, *The Origins of the Seder: The Passover Rite and Early Rabbinic Judaism* (Berkeley:

University of California Press, 1984). There is, however, some inscriptional evidence for the presence of dining areas in some synagogues (see Williams, *The Jews among Greeks and Romans*, 34–35). See L. A. Hoffman, *The Canonization of the Synagogue Service* (Notre Dame, IN: University of Notre Dame Press, 1979).

9. Leviticus 18 connects Israelite sexual conduct to the purity of the land, and when the Lord charges in Leviticus 19:2, "Be holy, for I, the Lord, your God, am holy," the command is followed immediately by the instructions to honor parents, keep the Sabbath, and avoid idols (19:3–4). The following commands in 19:5–37, furthermore, weave together ritual and moral/social dimensions of life. See H. K. Harrington, *Holiness: Rabbinic Judaism and the Greco-Roman World* (London: Routledge, 2001).

10. As noted in Chapter 1, the LXX translation of Psalm 95:5 rendered "the gods of the nations are idols" as "the gods of the nations are demons [*daimonia*]," and Wisdom of Solomon 15:27 calls the worship of idols "the reason and source and extremity of all evil."

11. As we saw earlier, Plutarch regarded the Jews' stubborn observance of the Sabbath as an example of superstition (*On Superstition*, 8). See also Horace, *Satires*, 9.67–70; Seneca, *Moral Epistles*, 95.47. Gentile understanding of the Sabbath was not always precise; Suetonius quotes the emperor Augustus to the effect that the Sabbath was a fast day (*Augustus*, 76.2).

12. For the debate over the degree and uniqueness of Israel's aniconic tradition, see T. N. D. Mettinger, *No Graven Image? Israel's Aniconism in Its Ancient Near Eastern Context* (Coniectanea Biblical OT 42; Stockholm: Almqvist and Wiskell, 1995), and T. J. Lewis, "Divine Images and Aniconism in Ancient Israel," *Journal of the American Oriental Society* 118 (1998): 36–53. Josephus describes the original (Solomonic) temple in *Antiquities*, 8.63–98, and the wonders of Herod's reconstruction in *Antiquities*, 15.380–420; 17.162; 20.219–222; *Jewish War*, 1.401. In *Against Apion*, 1.198–199, he includes a description of the temple by Hecataeus of Abdera. For the reaction of visitors from Galilee, see Mark 14:1–2; Luke 21:5; see also the description in *Letter of Aristeas*, 73–107.

13. As we saw in Plutarch, the Epicurean refusal to engage the obligations of civic piety was understood as showing themselves parasitic on society; see Apion's charge that the Jews' refusal to worship the common gods led to sedition in Josephus, *Against Apion*, 2.66–70.

14. For the payment of temple tax, see Philo, *Special Laws*, 1.76–78; Josephus, *Antiquities*, 18.311–313; Cicero, *Pro Flacco*, 28.66–69; for pilgrimage, see Philo, *Special Laws*, 1.69; Josephus, *Antiquities*, 20.49–50.

15. See, e.g., Deut 2:25; 4:6; 29:24; LXX Ps 21:27; 65:7; 85:9; Isa 66:19–20.

16. See P. Schäfer, *Judeophobia: Attitudes toward the Jews in the Ancient World* (Cambridge, MA: Harvard University Press, 1997).

17. For the literary evidence on conversion and proselytizing, see Williams, *The Jews among Greeks and Romans*, 169–172; and for debate over the extent of the phenomena, see L. H. Feldman, *Jew and Gentile in the Ancient World* (Princeton, NJ: Princeton University Press, 1993) and M. Goodman, *Mission and Conversion: Proselytizing in the Religious History of the Roman Empire* (Oxford: Clarendon, 1994).

18. For pertinent inscriptions, see Williams, *The Jews among Greeks and Romans*, 163–168; for discussion of the category in the Acts of the Apostles, see M. Wilcox, "The 'God-Fearers' in Acts—A Reconsideration," *Journal for the Study of the New Testament* 13 (1981): 102–122; and T. M. Finn, "The God-Fearers Reconsidered," *Catholic Biblical Quarterly* 47 (1985): 75–84.

19. See Tacitus, *Histories*, 5.4–5, and the charges made against the Jews by Apion in Josephus, *Against Apion*.

20. See the statements in Pliny the Elder, *Natural History*, 28.4 and Minucius Felix, *Octavius*, 6.1–7.6, as well as the premises of the pleas made by Athenagoras, *Embassy*, 1–2, and Tertullian, *Apology*, 2.1–20.

21. Tcherikover, *Hellenistic Civilization and the Jews*, 305–312; for discussion of the appropriateness of the traditional ascription of *religio licita* to Judaism in the empire, see T. Rajak, "Was There a Roman Charter for the Jews?" *Journal of Roman Studies* 74 (1984): 107–123; see also Harland, *Associations, Synagogues, and Congregations*, 220–223.

    That Rome was deeply implicated in Judaea long before taking control under Pompey in 63 BCE is shown by its alliance with the Maccabees in their revolt against Antiochus IV Epiphanes in 167 BCE (see 1 Macc 1:10; 7:2; 12:3; 15:15–24; 2 Macc 11:34).

    Because of the ever-present threat from 247 BCE to 224 CE presented by the Parthian Empire to the East, which bested the Romans in the battle of Carrhae in 53 BCE, Syria and Palestine required direct imperial control through military prefects or procurators, rather than the senatorially appointed governors in safer provinces.

22. See the passages gathered in *Greek and Latin Authors on Jews and Judaism*, 3 vols., edited with introductions, translations, and commentary by M. Stern (Jerusalem: Israel Academy of Sciences and Humanities, 1976), I:26, 148, 411–414; II:19–22, 36––41, 88–93. Dio Chrysostom testifies to the unruly character of the Alexandrian populace in *Oration*, 32; and in *Against Flaccus*, Philo speaks of the hostility of the Alexandrians toward the Jews (29) as an example of the mischief practiced by "the lazy and unoccupied mob" (33).

23. J. Z. Smith, "Fences and Neighbors: Some Contours of Early Judaism," in *Imagining Religion: From Babylon to Jonestown* (Chicago: University of Chicago Press, 1982), 1–13, 135–139.

24. The *Shema Israel* in Deut 6:4 ("Hear O Israel! The Lord is our God, the Lord alone") is followed in Deut 6:13–14 by the prohibition of idolatry: "You shall not follow other gods, such as those of the surrounding nations, lest the wrath of the Lord, your God, flare up against you and he destroy you from the face of the land; for the Lord your God, who is in your midst, is a jealous God."

25. See M. S. Smith, *The Origins of Biblical Monotheism: Israel's Polytheistic Background and the Ugaritic Texts* (New York: Oxford University Press, 2001); and J. H. Tigay, *You Shall Have No Other Gods: Israelite Religion in the Light of Hebrew Inscriptions* (Atlanta: Scholars, 1986). See the essays in L. T. Stuckenbruck and W. E. S. North, eds., *Early Jewish and Christian Monotheism* (London: T. & T. Clark, 2004).

26. See, e.g., Pss 24:1–2; 33:6–9; 47:7; 50:9–12; 65:5–8; 81:10; 95:4–6; 100:3; 102:25–27; 104:27–30; 107:9, 33–38; 111:5; 119:90; 121:2; 124:8; 136:5–9, 25; 145:15; 148:5–6.

27. See the classic contrast between the living God and dead idols in Isa 40:12–31; 44:6–-20; 46:1–13; and the attack on idolatry in Wisdom of Solomon 13:1–15:13; see also S. C. Barton, ed., *Idolatry: False Worship in the Bible, Early Judaism, and Christianity* (London: T. & T. Clark, 2007).

28. See especially Ex 19:3–8 and Deut 4:32–40.

29. On the concept of covenant, see D. R. Hillers, *Covenant: The History of a Biblical Idea* (Baltimore: Johns Hopkins University Press, 1969) and D. J. Elazar, *Covenant and Polity in Biblical Israel: Biblical Foundations and Jewish Expressions* (New Brunswick, NJ: Transaction, 1995).

30. The Prologue to Sirach (ca. 132 BCE) speaks of "the law, the prophets, and the rest of the books of our ancestors." For essays on the TaNaK, see M. J. Mulder, ed., *Mikra: Text, Translation, Reading and Interpretation of the Hebrew Bible in Ancient Judaism and Early Christianity* (Compendia rerum Iudaicarum ad Novum Testamentum 2.1; Philadelphia: Fortress, 1988).

31. Given the archaeological and literary evidence for the spread of synagogues throughout the Roman Diaspora, the statement attributed to James in Acts 15:21 appears as sober truth: "For Moses, for generations now, has had those who proclaim him in every town, as he has been read in the synagogues every Sabbath." Josephus quotes Strabo to this effect: "The Jewish people had already some into every city, and one cannot readily find any place in the world which has not received this tribe and been taken possession by it"; *Antiquities*, 14.7.

32. Throughout the five books of Moses (*Torah*), legislation deals with the Sanctuary and priests (Ex 25:1–31:18; Lev 21:1–33; 24:1–23; Num 35:1–8), the keeping of feasts (Ex 34:10–16; 35:1–3; Lev 23:1–44; Num 28:9–39; Deut 16:1–16), and sacrifices (Lev 1:1–7:38; 16:1–34; 27:1–33; Num 28:1–8). Other laws prescribe how to maintain purity in food, sex, and other contacts, which keeps the people "holy" or separate (Lev 11:1–18:30; Deut 14:1–21) in keeping with the clear mandate, "Be holy, for I, the Lord your God, am holy" (Lev 19:2). A great mass of other legislation, however, covers what might be called "social laws," regulating a wide variety of transactions (see Ex 21:1–23:19; Lev 19:1–20:27; 25:1–55; Num 35:9–36:12; Deut 14:22–15:23; 19:1–26:15).

33. Sirach already identified the Wisdom through which God created the world (24:1–7) with "the book of the Most High's Covenant, the law which Moses commanded us as an inheritance for the community of Jacob" (24:22). Later Rabbinic texts in particular stress the sapiential character of the commandments (see *m.Peah*, 1:1; *Pirke Aboth*, 3:2; 3:10; *Aboth de Rabbi Nathan*, 24).

34. The legend attached to the Greek translation of Hebrew scripture, carried out in Alexandria during the reign of Ptolemy II (285–247 BCE) by Jewish scholars from Judaea, is most extensively elaborated by *The Letter of Aristeas*. The actual texts of scripture in both the Hebrew and Greek languages exhibit considerable fluidity.

35. Josephus speaks of "the innumerable multitude of people come down from the country and even from abroad to worship God" at the great feasts (*Antiquities*, 17.214), a statement supported by Acts 2:5–11. See also the collection of texts in Williams, *The Jews among Greeks and Romans*, 67–85.

36. On this, see especially M. Hengel, *Judaism and Hellenism*, 2 vols., trans. J. Bowden (Philadelphia: Fortress, 1974); J. Goldstein, "Jewish Acceptance and Rejection of Hellenism," in *Jewish and Christian Self-Definition*, 1st U.S. ed., ed. E. P. Sanders (Philadelphia: Fortress, 1980), 2.64–87.

37. Tcherikover, *Hellenistic Civilization and the Jews*, 344–377; C. R. Holladay, "Jewish Responses to Hellenistic Culture," in *Ethnicity in Hellenistic Egypt*, ed. P. Bilde (Studies in Hellenistic Civilization 3; Aarhus: Aarhus University Press, 1992), 139–163; and "Paul and His Predecessors in the Diaspora," in *Early Christianity and Classical Culture: Comparative Studies in Honor of Abraham J. Malherbe*, ed. J. T. Fitzgerald, T. H. Olbricht, and L. M. White (Leiden: Brill, 2003), 429–460.

38. Simply at the level of diction, the Septuagint's use of *doxa* for the Hebrew *Kabod* (see Ex 16:7; 24:16), *typos* in Ex 25:39, *daimonia* in Deut 32:17 and Ps 105:37, and a phrase such as *philos isos tēs psychēs sou* in Deut 13:7, all reflect, and in turn give rise to, Hellenistic sensibilities.

39. See the comments of Aristobolos (180–145 BCE) on the Bible's way of speaking of God in terms of human limbs as signifiers for divine power: "Now these passages will find a proper explanation and will not contradict in any way what we said before. I want to urge you to accept the interpretations in their natural sense and grasp a fitting conception about God and not lapse into a mythical, popular way of thinking. For what our lawgiver Moses wishes to say, he does so at many levels, using words that appear to have other referents (I mean, to things that can be seen); yet in doing so he actually speaks about natural conditions and structures of a higher order." Translation of Aristobolos, *Fragment*, 2.1–4, in C. R. Holladay, *Fragments from Hellenistic Jewish Authors*, vol. 3: *Aristobolos* (Texts and Translations 39; Pseudepigrapha 13; Atlanta: Scholars, 1995), 137.

40. In *On the Giants*, 4, Philo declares, "So if you realize that souls and demons and angels are but different names for the same underlying object, you will cast from you that most grievous burden, the fear of demons or superstition."

41. See Philo, *On the Migration of Abraham*, 89–93; *Embassy to Gaius*, 209–212; cf. Josephus, *Against Apion*, 1.42–43.

42. See L. V. Rutgers, *The Hidden Heritage of Diaspora Judaism: Essays on Jewish Cultural Identity in the Roman World* (Leuven: Peeters, 1988), and E. P. Sanders, "Purity, Food and Offerings in the Greek-Speaking Diaspora," in *Jewish Law from Jesus to the Mishnah: Five Studies* (Philadelphia: Trinity Press International, 1990), 255–308, 359–368.

43. An early Rabbinic text is written from Jerusalem to "the residents of the exile in Babylon, and residents of the exile in Media, and of all other exiles of Israel"; see D. Pardee, *A Handbook of Ancient Hebrew Letters* (Society of Biblical Literature Sources for Biblical Study 15; Chico, CA: Scholars, 1982), 186, 199–202. Philo can speak of his readers as "sojourners on earth as in a foreign city" (*On the Cherubim*, 120; *Rewards and Punishments*, 115–118).

44. In addition to 1 and 2 Maccabees and the works of Josephus (*Antiquities of the Jews*, *Jewish War*), there is fragmentary evidence for an extensive body of historical literature

produced by Demetrius, Eupolemus, Pseudo-Eupolemus, Artapanus, Cleodemus Malchus, Aristeas, Pseudo-Hecataeus, Thallus, and Justus of Tiberias; on these, see C. R. Holladay, *Fragments from Hellenistic Jewish Authors*, vol. 1: *Historians* (Texts and Translations 20; Pseudepigrapha 10; Chico, CA: Scholars, 1983).

The outstanding examples of pleas are Josephus, *Against Apion*; and Philo's *Embassy to Gaius* and *Against Flaccus*.

Taking the form of a speech purportedly given on the anniversary of the martyrdom of Eleazar and the seven Maccabean brothers, together with their mother (reported in 2 Macc 7), 4 Maccabees is one of the most distinctive literary productions of Hellenistic Judaism, combining elements of panegyric with diatribal argument in support of the proposition that "devout reason"—in this case, exemplified by devotion to the Law of Moses—is demonstrated by command of the passions (1:1, 7).

The profoundly conservative wisdom of Ben Sira was translated from Hebrew into Greek by his grandson around 132 BCE, "for the benefit of those living abroad who wish to acquire wisdom and are disposed to live their lives according to the standards of the law" (Prologue to Sirach). Sapiential works originally written in Greek include *Wisdom of Solomon* and *The Sentences of Pseudo-Phocylides*. Elements of wisdom are found also in *Letter of Aristeas*, 4 Maccabees, and *The Testaments of the 12 Patriarchs*.

45. See, e.g., *Wisdom of Solomon* 1:6; 7:23; 12:19; *Letter of Aristeas*, 208; Josephus, *Antiquities*, 16.42; *Against Apion*, 2.291; Philo, *On the Virtues*, 51, 82, 109–118; *Decalogue*, 110; *On Abraham*, 208; *Life of Moses*, 1.198; *The Special Laws*, 4.72; Artapanus, *Fragment*, 3.

46. See the essays in J. Neusner and E. S. Frerichs, eds., *"To See Ourselves as Others See Us": Christians, Jews, and "Others" in Late Antiquity* (Chico, CA: Scholars, 1985).

47. I take up the knotty issue of Judaism and the Mysteries below, but even A. D. Nock, one of the severest critics of the position that there was an element of the Mystery in Hellenistic Judaism, admits, "undeniably, Philo used Mystery terms for hidden theological terms" (*Essays on Religion and the Ancient World*, 2 vols., ed. Z. Stewart [New York: Oxford University Press, 1972], 899). Josephus claims that Pythagoras learned wisdom from Moses (*Against Apion*, 1.164–165) and that all the Greek philosophers borrowed from Hebrew wisdom (2.281); for Judaism perceived as a philosophy by both insiders and outsiders, see Hengel, *Judaism and Hellenism*, 1.255–261.

48. In *Jewish War*, Josephus goes from being a general fighting the Romans to an advocate for the Romans against those he regards as responsible for the war—that is, the Zealots—and eventually becomes capable of stating that God was on the side of the Romans (5.369; 5.412). The fact that Philo appeals to Roman authority in *Against Flaccus* and *Embassy to Gaius* shows a basic trust in the justice of its administration.

49. On the Samaritans, see J. Bowman, *The Samaritan Problem*, trans. A. M. Johnson (Pittsburgh: Pickwick, 1975); R. J. Coggins, *Samaritans and Jews: The Origins of Samaritanism Reconsidered* (Oxford: Blackwell, 1975); and F. Dexinger, "Limits of Tolerance in Judaism: The Samaritan Example," in *Jewish and Christian Self-Definition*,

vol. 2: *Aspects of Judaism in the Greco-Roman World*, ed. E. P. Sanders (Philadelphia: Fortress, 1981), 88–114.

50. From 63 BCE on, the Hasmonean and Herodian kings served as clients of Roman patronage. In 29 BCE, Syria became an imperial province under the direct control of the emperor, and in 6 CE Judaea became a procuratorial province, with a series of more-or-less efficient military prefects, including Pontius Pilate (26–36).

 Those who returned from exile faced opposition from Samaritans (Ezra 4:1–16) and others (Neh 3:33–38) and rebuilt Jerusalem under severe duress (Neh 2:17–7:3). Part of the restoration involved separation from foreign populations (Neh 13:1–3), which entailed the dismissal of the foreign wives of many of the returnees (Neh 13: 23–29; Ezra 9:1–2; 10:16–44).

51. For the post-Exilic prophets, rebuilding the temple was the priority (Haggai 1:1–2:9; Zech 4:8–10), with the second order of business being the dismissal of the unclean among the population (Haggai 2:10–14; Zech 13:1–6; Mal 1:1–2:17). Ezra spurred on the rebuilding of the temple in the return (Ezra 3:1–13; 4:24; 5:1–17), and Nehemiah carried out needed reforms among priests (Neh 13:4–13). The purification of the temple by the Maccabees (2 Macc 10:1–8), in turn, was of such importance that it was celebrated annually as the feast of Hanukkah.

52. The vision of Ezekiel 34:1–31 was especially compelling; see J. A. Fitzmyer, *The One Who Is to Come* (Grand Rapids, MI: Eerdmans, 2007).

53. The formal promulgation of *Torah* by Ezra the Scribe (Neh 8:1–18) was part of a public profession of covenant renewal among the returned exiles (9:1–27) and the enactment of specific social legislation (9:31–40), including the public observance of the Sabbath (13:15–22) and the banning of mixed marriages (13:23–29).

54. Hellenism had made significant inroads well before Antiochus IV, with some 16 cities Hellenized and the first steps toward Jerusalem becoming a Greek *polis* taken not, as we might suspect, by Seleucids but by leading families of the city: "Let us come and make a covenant with the Gentiles round about us, for since we have separated from them many evils have come upon us" (1 Macc 1:11).

55. Josephus, *Jewish War*, 2.119–166; *Antiquities*, 18.11–25; for the beliefs and practices of all the sects, see E. P. Sanders, *Judaism: Practice and Belief, 63 BCE–66 CE* (Philadelphia: Trinity Press International, 1992).

56. The identification of those at Qumran with the Essenes is, to be sure, debated; see P. W. Flint and J. C. Vanderkam, eds., *The Dead Sea Scrolls after Fifty Years*, 2 vols. (Leiden: Brill, 1998); G. Boccaccini, *Beyond the Essene Hypothesis* (Grand Rapids, MI: Eerdmans, 1998); F. G. Martinez and J. T. Barrera, *The People of the Dead Sea Scrolls: Their Writings, Beliefs, and Practices*, trans. W. G. E. Watson (Leiden: Brill, 1995).

 The Qumran community's intensely dualistic ideology demands separation from all the "sons of the pit" (CD 6.14–7.6), with a special animus toward the "wicked priest" in Jerusalem who is accused of despoiling the possessions of the community (1QpHab 8.8–12; 11.1–6; 12.9–12).

 The hostile characterization of outsiders found in sectarian passages such as 1QS 2.4–10 and 4.9–14 are directed not at Gentiles but at those whom the War Scroll designates as "the ungodly of the covenant" (1QM 1.2), which would necessarily also involve those "men who seek smooth things," such as the Pharisees, undoubtedly regarded as overaccommodating by these separatists; see G. Vermes, *The Dead Sea Scrolls in English*, 2nd ed. (New York: Penguin, 1975).

57. The sectarians saw themselves as a "house of holiness" for the Lord, which offered spiritual sacrifices of praise and study (4QFlor 1.6; 1QS 8.6–8; 9.3–11), guided by a leadership of priests and Levites of the order of Zadok (1QS 1.11–12; 6.17–22).

    The conclusion that the Essenes were willing to fight Rome to the death is based on archaeological evidence provided by Roman coins and arrowheads of the appropriate date at the site, as well as traces of a violent fire; see J. T. Milik, *Ten Years of Discovery in the Wilderness of Judaea*, trans. J. Strugnell (Studies in Biblical Theology 26; London: SCM Press, 1959), 53–56.

58. See M. Hengel, *The Zealots*, trans. D. Smith (Edinburgh: T. & T. Clark, 1989).

59. Josephus, *Life*, 9.65; *Jewish War*, 2.118; 4.385; 5.400–402; 2.264; 5.433–444; 6.288; 5.556; 7.255–258; 7.260–262. Josephus begins as a general in charge of Galilean defenses (2.568–584) but surrenders to the Romans (3.384–398) and ends by exhorting his fellow Jews to surrender (5.361–420, 541–547), declaring his conviction with regard to the more fanatical Jewish troops, "It seemed a much lighter thing to be ruined by the Romans than by themselves" (4.2).

60. For the little that can be known about the Sadducees historically, see J. P. Meier, *A Marginal Jew: Rethinking the Historical Jesus*, vol. 3: *Companions and Competitors* (New York: Doubleday, 2001), 389–487.

61. The progression has masterfully been demonstrated by J. Neusner, *From Politics to Piety: The Emergence of Pharisaic Judaism* (Englewood Cliffs, NJ: Prentice-Hall, 1972).

62. The polemic from the side of "the pious" against those called "sinners" or "unrighteous" (such as we find in 4 Ezra 7:17–25; 1 Enoch 12:5; 15:9–10; 94:6–11; 95:4–7; 96:4—8; 98:7–16; 104:7–13; Psalms of Solomon 2:3–18; 4:1–20; 8:10–18; 14:6–10; 15:8–14) comes from a perspective that is broadly Pharisaic. J. Jeremias has argued that the Psalms of Solomon come from the bitter dispute between Pharisees and Sadducees; see *Jerusalem in the Time of Jesus*, trans. F. H. and C. H. Cave (Philadelphia: Fortress, 1969), 266.

63. On the development of Midrash, see G. Vermes, *Scripture and Tradition in Judaism*, 2nd rev. ed. (Leiden: Brill, 1973); G. Porten, "Midrash: Palestinian Jews and Hebrew Bible in the Greco-Roman Period," *Aufstieg und Niedergang der römischen Welt* II.19.2 (1979): 3–42; J. Kugel, *The Bible as It Was* (Cambridge, MA: Harvard University Press, 1997). On the Pharisees' associations dedicated to strict observance of the law, see J. Neusner, "The Fellowship (*chaburah*) in the Second Jewish Commonwealth," *Harvard Theological Review* 53 (1960): 125–142.

64. Although deficient in historical discrimination, two classic works contain a rich compendium of Rabbinic lore: G. F. Moore, *Judaism in the First Three Centuries of the Christian Era*, 2 vols. (New York: Schocken Books, 1927); and E. E. Urbach, *The Sages: Their Concepts and Beliefs*, 2 vols., trans. I. Abrahams (Jerusalem: Magnes, 1975).

65. Justly famous is the inscription discovered in Jerusalem (*Corpus Inscriptionum Judaicarum II*, No. 1404): "Theodotos, son of Vettenos, priest and *archisynagogos*, grandson of an *archisynagogos*, has built the synagogue for the reading of the law and the teaching of the commandments and the guest house and the rooms and the water facilities for a lodging for those from foreign countries who need it. His fathers and the Elders and Simonides laid the foundations." See Williams, *Jews among Greeks and Romans*, 67.

    On the synagogue, see the essays in J. Gutmann, ed., *The Synagogue: Studies in Origin, Archaeology, and Architecture* (New York: KTAV, 1975) and L. I. Levine, ed., *The Synagogue in Late Antiquity* (Philadelphia: American Schools of Oriental Research, 1987). See also S. Fine, ed., *Sacred Realm: The Emergence of the Synagogue in the Ancient World* (Oxford: Oxford University Press, 1996).

66. See L. M. White, *The Social Origins of Christian Architecture*, vol. 1: *Building God's House in the Roman World: Architectural Adaptation among Pagans, Jews, and Christians* (Harvard Theological Studies 42; Valley Forge, PA: Trinity Press International, 1990), 60–101.

67. See, e.g., Josephus, *Against Apion*, 2.175; Philo, *Against Flaccus*, 48, 116; *Embassy to Gaius*, 312. The different names used attest to a variety of functions: the synagogue can be called *synagōgē* ("gathering") or *beth ha kenesset* ("house of assembly"), emphasizing the congregation; it can be called *beth ha midrash* ("house of study"), emphasizing the reading and study of Torah; it can be called *hē proseuchē* ("place of prayer"), emphasizing worship activities. See Williams, *Jews among Greeks and Romans*, 33–37.

68. See Josephus, *Antiquities*, 17.162; 15.380–420; 20.219–222; also C. T. R. Hayward, *The Jewish Temple: A Non-Biblical Sourcebook* (New York: Routledge, 1996).

69. Josephus is the main source for the establishment of a temple at Leontopolis under Onias; see *Antiquities*, 13.65, 70; *Jewish War*, 1.33. For the modest dimensions of the shrine at Shechem, see R. J. Bull, "A Re-Examination of the Shechem Temple," *The Biblical Archaeologist* 23 (1960): 110–119.

70. The Deuteronomic reform that was initiated under Josiah (ca. 622 BCE) had the elimination of other cult sites as a key element (2 Kings 22:1–23:25); the necessity of Jerusalem being the one cult site is stated explicitly by Deuteronomy 12:1–4 and is made the principle by which various kings are assessed (1 Kings 12:25–33; 13:33; 16:29–32).

71. See the description in *Letter of Aristeas*, 83–100; J. Jeremias, *Jerusalem in the Time of Jesus: An Investigation into Economic and Social Conditions during the New Testament Period*, trans. F. H. Cave and C. H. Cave (Philadelphia: Fortress, 1969), 21–26, 126–138, 147–221.

72. See especially S. Safrai, "The Temple and the Divine Service," in *The World History of the Jewish People*, 1st series: *Ancient Times*, vol. 7: *The Herodian Period*, ed. M. Avi-Yonah (Jewish Historical Publications; New Brunswick, NJ: Rutgers University Press, 1975), 284–338.

73. The biblical legislation is found in Ex 23:14–17; Lev 23:4–22; Deut 16:1–17.

74. For the development of these ancient feasts, see R. de Vaux, *Ancient Israel*, vol. 2: *Religious Institutions* (New York: McGraw-Hill, 1965), 484–501.

75. For the crowds, see Josephus, *Antiquities*, 17.214, and Jeremias, *Jerusalem in the Time of Jesus*, 77–84; for the disruptions and riots occurring at the great pilgrimage feasts, especially Passover, see Josephus, *Antiquities*, 17.213–218; 17.254; 18.29; 18.90; 20.106; *Jewish War*, 2.40.

76. See the essays written by J. Neusner in *Formative Judaism: Religious, Historical, and Literary Studies* (Brown Judaic Studies 37; Chico, CA: Scholars, 1982); and J. Neusner and W. S. Green, eds., *Origins of Judaism: Religion, History, and Literature in Late Antiquity* (New York: Garland, 1990).

    Different dimensions of the Bar Kochba revolt are found in the essays in P. Schäfer, ed., *The Bar Kochba War Reconsidered: New Perspectives on the Second Jewish Revolt against Rome* (Tübingen: Mohr Siebeck, 2003).

77. As in *Pesikta Kahana* 60b; *bT Megillah* 31b; *Aboth de Rabbi Nathan* 4. See J. Neusner, *Rabbinic Judaism: The Documentary History of Its Formative Age* (Bethesda, MD: CDL, 1994).

78. Abraham is called *nabi'* (LXX; *prophētēs*) in Gen 20:7, and Moses is designated as prophet in Deut 18:15–18 and 34:10.

    We can distinguish three kinds of prophets in the TaNaK: those who spoke in the name of the Lord and whose writings are included among the *nebiim* (Isaiah, Jeremiah, Ezekiel, Daniel, and the 12 "Minor prophets"); those whose actions in defense of the Lord are related narratively (in particular Elijah and Elisha, but others, such as Nathan, as well); and those "false prophets" whose words led the people away from an exclusive covenant with the Lord (see Deut 18:20–22; Jer 2:26–30; 14:13–18). Note that Deut 18:9 identifies such prophets with the practices of the nations. On divination, see W. A. Beardslee, "The Casting of Lots at Qumran and in the Book of Acts," *Novum Testamentum* 4 (1960): 245–252.

79. In his brief notices, Josephus refrains from identifying as a prophet either John the Baptist (*Antiquities*, 18.116–119) or Jesus (18.63–64), although the New Testament uses the designation for both John (Matt 11:19; 14:5; Mark 11:32; Luke 1:76; 7:26–28; John 1:21) and Jesus (Luke 4:24; 7:16; 24:19; John 6:14).

80. When the beleaguered Saul could not get an answer from the Lord through the casting of lots or from the prophets, he consulted "the witch of Endor," who summons Samuel through necromancy (1 Sam 28:4–29); the odd story suggests a much larger phenomenon involving female prophets at local shrines (see Huldah the female Jerusalem prophet in 2 Kings 22:14–17), as indicated as well by the insistent repetition of warning against the consultation of mediums and soothsayers (Ex 22:17; Lev 19:26, 31; 20:6, 27; Deut 18:10–14).

81. See R. A. Horsley, *Bandits, Prophets, and Messiahs: Popular Movements in the Time of Jesus* (Minneapolis: Winston, 1985), and *Jesus and the Spiral of Violence: Popular Jewish Resistance in Roman Palestine* (San Francisco: Harper and Row, 1987).

    For Qumran, see N. A. Dahl, "Eschatology and History in Light of the Dead Sea Scrolls," in *The Future of Our Religious Past*, ed. J. M. Robinson, trans. C. E. Carlston and R. P. Scharlemann (New York: Harper and Row, 1971), 9–28; S. E. Porter and C. A. Evans, eds., *The Scrolls and the Scriptures: Qumran Fifty Years After* (Journal for the Study of the Pseudepigrapha Supplement Series 26; Sheffield: Sheffield Academic Press, 1997); for Christianity, see D. Juel, *Messianic Exegesis: Christological Interpretation of the Old Testament in Early Christianity* (Philadelphia: Fortress, 1987), and L. T. Johnson, *Septuagintal Midrash in the Speeches of Acts* (Père Marquette Lecture in Theology; Milwaukee: Marquette University Press, 2002).

82. Thus, irrespective of their chronological accuracy, passages in Acts demonstrate how the Jesus movement could be located among other "messianic" efforts (see Acts 5:33–42; 20:38).

83. The category "apocalyptic" covers a range of distinguishable entities: a genre of literature, a construction of reality, a vision of history—in every instance the term represents an abstraction drawn from a complex body of literature. Among studies, see J. J. Collins, *The Apocalyptic Imagination: An Introduction to the Jewish Matrix of Christianity*, 2nd ed. (Grand Rapids, MI: Eerdmans, 1998); C. Rowland, *The Open Heaven: A Study of Apocalyptic in Judaism and Early Christianity* (London: SPCK, 1982); and the detailed studies in D. Hellholm, ed., *Apocalypticism in the Mediterranean World and the Near East* (Tübingen: J. C. B. Mohr [Paul Siebeck], 1983).

84. Among works generally categorized as apocalyptic that can reasonably be dated within the period of this study are 1 Enoch, 2 Enoch, Apocryphon of Ezekiel, Apocalypse of Zephaniah, 4 Ezra, 2 Baruch, 3 Baruch, Apocalypse of Abraham, Apocalypse of Adam, and Apocalypse of Elijah. See the still valuable study by H. H. Rowley, *The Relevance of Apocalyptic: A Study of Jewish and Christian Apocalypses from Daniel to Revelation*, 2nd ed. (London: Lutterworth, 1961).

85. See D. S. Russell, *The Method and Message of Jewish Apocalyptic, 200 BC–100 AD* (Old Testament Library; Philadelphia: Westminster, 1964).

86. See J. J. Collins, *The Sibylline Oracles of Egyptian Judaism* (Society of Biblical Literature Dissertation Series 13; Missoula, MT: Society of Biblical Literature, 1972); R. Buitenwerf, *Book III of the Sibylline Oracles and Its Social Setting* (Studia in Veteris Testamenti Pseudepigrapha 17; Leiden: Brill, 2003).

87. The wondrous healing of Tobit, we remember, was accomplished through an angel rather than a religious ritual (*Tobit* 13:17; 11:9–15). I mention Honi and Chanina below. Josephus makes mention of healings and exorcisms (*Antiquities*, 8.45–49; *Jewish War*, 7.185). The New Testament mentions Jewish exorcists (Luke 11:19; Acts 19:13–20). The Testament of Solomon has the theme of healing through exorcism (see 1–4 and especially 18–24). Among the Qumran compositions are two extremely fragmentary texts that appear to involve the practice of exorcism (11QPsAp and 4Q560). On healing traditions, see especially J. P. Meier, *A Marginal Jew: The Historical Jesus Reconsidered*, vol. 2: *Mentor, Message, Miracles* (New York: Doubleday, 1994), 581–593. For the sparse Jewish traditions on healing generally, see J. Strange, *The Moral World of James* (PhD diss., Emory University, 2007), 253–280.

88. In Leviticus 13:1–59, those afflicted with discoloration or growths on the skin (leprosy) are to be quarantined; the role of the priest is not to heal but to confirm that healing has taken place and to guide the healed person through the rituals of integration back into the pure community (see Lev 14:1–32). These practices appear to continue into the

first century, according to the Gospel stories concerning lepers (Luke 5:12–15; 17:11–18). The same stories suggest that extreme cases of "demon possession" required the separation of the afflicted person from populated areas (see especially Mark 5:1–20).

89. A balanced view of the debate is provided by M. Smith, "Goodenough's *Jewish Symbols* in Retrospect," *Journal of Biblical Literature* 86 (1967): 53–68.

90. E. R. Goodenough, *By Light, Light: The Mystic Gospel of Hellenistic Judaism* (New Haven, CT: Yale University Press, 1963). The materials are gathered and interpreted by E. R. Goodenough, *Jewish Symbols in the Greco-Roman Period*, 13 vols. (New York: Pantheon, 1953–1968). Even before Goodenough, L. Cerfaux argued for the widespread influence of the Mysteries on Alexandrian Judaism, focusing especially on Pseudo-Orpheus; see "Influence des Mystères sur le judaisme Alexandrin avant Philo," *Le Muséon* 37 (1924): 29–88.

91. For Philo's use of Mystery symbolism, see, e.g., *On Abraham*, 122; *On Rewards and Punishments*, 121; *On the Cherubim*, 42; *Allegorical Interpretation*, 3.71; 3.100; 3.101–103; *Flight and Finding*, 85; *Sacrifices of Abel and Cain*, 53–54, 62; *On the Giants*, 53–54; *Life of Moses*, 1.158; 2.40; *On the Creation*, 71; *On the Virtues*, 178; *Posterity and Exile of Cain*, 173; *On Dreams*, 1.164; *Unchangeableness of God*, 61; *On the Contemplative Life*, 25, 28. Most striking, perhaps, is this personal statement: "I myself was initiated under Moses the God-beloved into his greater mysteries, yet when I saw the prophet Jeremiah and knew him to be not only himself enlightened but a worthy minister of the holy secrets, I was not slow to become his disciple" (*On the Cherubim*, 48).

For the extraordinarily complex redactional history of the pseudonymous work ascribed to Orpheus ("I will speak to those to whom it is permitted; shut the doors, you uninitiated, all of you alike. But you, O Museus, child of the light-bearing moon"), see C. R. Holladay, *Fragments from Hellenistic Jewish Authors*, vol. 4: *Orphica* (Texts and Translations 40; Pseudepigrapha 14; Atlanta: Scholars, 1996).

92. The Book of Proverbs and Sirach inculcate the keeping of the commandments that articulate the covenant, with special attention to social justice (see, e.g., Prov 3:27–28; 11:1; 14:31; 16:11; 17:5, 15, 23; 18:5; 19:17; 20:10; 21:3, 13, 26; 22:23; 24:15, 23–24; 25:21–22; 28:27; 29:7; 31:9, 20; Sir 3:30; 4:1, 4, 9, 22, 27; 7:3, 10; 10:7; 11:12–13; 12:3; 20; 21:5; 29:8; 31:11; 34:20–22; 35:13–14; 42:1–4). Similarly, the prophets repeatedly address the social ills that they see as a consequence of infidelity to the covenant (see, e.g., Isa 1:16–17, 23; 3:14–15; 5:7–16, 22–24; 9:17–19; 10:1–4; Jer 7:8–9; 8:11; 9:4–5; 12:11–13; 21:13–18; Hos 4:1–3; 12:8–12; Joel 4:3; Amos 2:6–7; 4:1–2; 5:12; Mic 3:9–11; 7:1–7).

93. See, e.g., Hos 14:2–10; Jer 31:31–34; Ezek 18:1–30; Joel 2:16–17; Amos 5:14–15; Jon 3:6–10.

94. Josephus, *Jewish War*, 2.119–166; *Antiquities*, 18.11–22.

95. See Hengel, *Judaism and Hellenism*, 1.243–247; 2.164–167; T. S. Beall, *Josephus' Description of the Essenes Illustrated by the Dead Sea Scrolls* (Society for New Testament Studies Monograph Series 58; Cambridge: Cambridge University Press, 1988); R. Bergmeier, *Die Essener-Berichte des Flavius Josephus, Quellenstudien zu den Essenertexten im Werk des jüdischen Historiographen* (Kampen: Kos Pharos, 1993), 79–107.

96. *On the Contemplative Life*, 13–14, 16, 18; *Hypothetica*, 11.1, 4, 11, 16; *Every Good Man Is Free*, 77, 79, 84–85.

97. See J. Neusner, *Rabbinic Traditions about the Pharisees before 70* (Leiden: Brill, 1971); A. J. Saldarini, *Pharisees, Scribes, and Sadducees in Palestinian Society: A Sociological Approach* (Wilmington, DE: M. Glazier, 1988); N. Hillel, *Proximity to Power and Jewish Sectarian Groups of the Ancient Period: A Review of the Lifestyle, Values, and Halakhah in the Pharisees, Sadducees, Essenes, and Qumran*, ed. R. Ludlam (Leiden: Brill, 2006). For the link between Sadducees and Epicureans, see J. H. Neyrey, "The Form and Background of the Polemic in 2 Peter," *Journal of Biblical Literature* 99 (1980): 407–431.

98. Apart from the loose bands of prophets attested, e.g., in 1 Sam 10:9–12 and 19:22–24, there is no trace before the Hellenistic period of intentional communities of the sort represented by the Essenes and the Pharisees; equally noteworthy, the ideal of community possessions found among the Essenes is unattested in Torah and explicitly rejected by the later Rabbinic tradition; see, e.g., *Exodus Rabbah* 31; *Leviticus Rabbah* 34; *Pirke Aboth* 5.10; *Midrash Koheleth* 1.8.

99. L. T. Johnson, "The New Testament's Anti-Jewish Slander and the Conventions of Ancient Polemic," *Journal of Biblical Literature* 108 (1989): 419–441.

100. On Qoheleth, see R. Gordis, *Koheleht: The Man and His World*, 3rd augmented ed. (New York: Schocken, 1968); J. Crenshaw, "Ecclesiastes, the Book," in *The Anchor Bible Dictionary*, ed. D. L. Freedman (New York: Doubleday, 1992), 2.271–281. On *Wisdom of Solomon*, see D. Winston, *The Wisdom of Solomon: A New Translation with Introduction and Commentary* (Anchor Bible 43; New York: Doubleday, 1964).

101. Each testament in Greek is given the subtitle of a specific virtue or vice exemplified by the respective patriarch. Thus, the *Testament of Simeon* is also *peri phthonou* ("On Envy") and the *Testament of Joseph* is also *peri sōphrosynēs* ("On Moderation"); see M. de Jonge, ed., *Testamenta XII Patriarcharum*, 2nd ed. (Leiden: Brill, 1970).

102. See D. A. de Silva, *4 Maccabees* (Guides to Apocrypha and Pseudepigrapha; Sheffield: Sheffield Academic Press, 1998).

103. It was not until the work of Jacob Bernays, *Über das Phokylidesche Gedicht: Ein Beitrag zur hellenistischen Literatur* (Jahresbericht des jüdisches-theologischen Seminars "Fränckelschen Stiftung"; Berlin: Hertz, 1856), that the composition was decisively identified as Jewish; see also P. van der Horst, *The Sentences of Pseudo-Phocylides* (Studia in Veteris Testamenti Pseudepigrapha 4; Leiden: Brill, 1978), and W. T. Wilson, *The Sentences of Pseudo-Phocylides* (Commentaries on Early Jewish Literature; Berlin: Walter de Gruyter, 2005).

104. See E. R. Goodenough, *An Introduction to Philo Judaeus* (New Haven, CT: Yale University Press, 1940); S. Sandmel, *Philo of Alexandria: An Introduction* (New York: Oxford University Press, 1979).

105. Philo is well aware of the way Gentile allegorists reinterpreted Homer in terms of moral categories (*Embassy to Gaius*, 93–113; *On the Decalogue*, 54). Like the Pythagoreans, he finds the deeper meanings of numbers (*On the Decalogue*, 20–31),

and using Platonic ideas, he can find evidence for the cosmological distinction between the material and the ideal in the two creation accounts of Genesis (*Allegorical Interpretation*, 1.31; *Questions on Genesis*, 1.4) and discover in the LXX rendering of Exodus 25:40 as *kata ton typon* the ideal heavenly temple of which the earthly is an imitation (*Questions and Answers on Exodus*, 82; *Allegorical Interpretation*, 3.102).

106. See, e.g., his comments on Gen 4:16, "And Cain went out from the face of God," which raises the issue of anthropomorphism: "Let us here raise the question whether in the books in which Moses acts as God's interpreter we ought to take his statements figuratively, since the impression made by the word in their literal sense is greatly at variance with the truth. For if the Existent has a face . . . what ground have we for rejecting the impious doctrines of Epicurus, or the atheism of the Egyptians or the mythical plots of play and poem of which the world is full?" (*On the Posterity and Exile of Cain*, 1–2). See also his interpretation of Gen 24:6–11 in *Noah's Work as a Planter*, 163–173.

107. Philo asks why in Gen 4:2 Abel is named before Cain and muses: "What, then, is the special truth [Moses] brings before us? Surely that in point of time vice is senior to virtue, but that in point of value and honor, the reverse is the case . . . for when the life of man begins, from the very cradle till the time when the age of maturity brings the great change and quenches the fiery furnace of the passions, folly, incontinence, injustice, fear, cowardice, and all the kindred maladies of the soul are his inseparable companions, and each of them is fostered and increased by nurses and tutors . . . but when the prime is past, and the throbbing fever of the passions is abated, as though the storm-winds had dropped, there begins in the man a late and hard-won calm. Virtue has lulled to rest the worst enemy of the soul, that commotion whose waves of passion follow each other in swift succession, and in that firm support of virtue he stands secure"; *On the Posterity and Exile of Cain*, translation by F. H. Colson (Loeb Classical Library; Cambridge, MA: Harvard University Press, 1927).

108. See, e.g., *On Abraham*, 275–276; *On the Migration of Abraham*, 130; in *Abraham*, Philo interprets Enos as "hope" (7–16), Enoch as "repentance" (17–26), and Noah as "repentance." His treatises on Isaac and Jacob are lost, but in his *On Joseph* he indicates that Abraham signified virtue acquired by teaching; Isaac, virtue acquired by nature; and Jacob, virtue acquired through practice (*On Joseph*, 1); see J. W. Martens, *One God, One Law: Philo of Alexandria on the Mosaic and Greco-Roman Law* (Studies in Philo of Alexandria and Mediterranean Antiquity 2; Boston: Brill, 2003).

109. In his *Life of Moses*, Philo shows the ways in which Moses perfectly fills the role of lawgiver (2.8–65), high priest (2.66–186), and prophet (2.187–291) but introduces them all with the evocation of Moses as the Philosopher-King: "The appointed leader of all these was Moses, invested with his office and kingship, not like some of those who thrust themselves into positions of power by means of arms and engines of war and strength of infantry, cavalry and navy, but on account of his goodness and nobility of conduct and the universal benevolence he never failed to show. Further, his office was bestowed on him by God, the lover of virtue and nobility, as the reward due to him" (1.148).

110. Note that Philo's treatise *On the Virtues* follows immediately on his compositions *On the Decalogue* and *On the Special Laws*. His consideration of the virtues of courage (1–50), humanity or philanthropy (51–174), repentance (175–186), and nobility (187–227), furthermore, uses the categories of Greek moral discourse to find the best expression of these virtues in the law of Moses; see P. Borgen, *Philo, John, and Paul: New Perspectives on Judaism and Early Christianity* (Brown Judaic Studies 131; Atlanta: Scholars, 1987), 17–59.

111. His treatise *On the Contemplative Life* is devoted to an admiring description of the *Therapeutae*, while the Essenes are described in *Hypothetica*, 1–11, and *Every Good Man Is Free*, 75–91; see J. E. Taylor, *Jewish Women Philosophers of First-Century Alexandria: Philo's "Therapeutae" Reconsidered* (New York: Oxford University Press, 2003).

112. The ideal human condition was thought of not in terms of freeing the soul from worldly entanglements but in terms of cultivating and caring for the earth as a garden (Gen 2:15–16). The consequence of sin was not involvement in the world but rather the distortion of the relation between the world and humans (3:14–19).

113. All the forms of personal "uncleanness" that result from contact with affliction, death, or uncontrolled flows (Lev 1–32) are capable of being "cleansed" through appropriate rituals; such uncleanness, furthermore, is fundamentally an issue of cultic preparedness for the people as such: "Moses said to the LORD, 'The people are not permitted to come up to Mount Sinai; for you yourself warned us, saying, "Set limits around the mountain and keep it holy"'" (Exod 19:23).

114. See especially J. D. Levenson, *Resurrection and the Restoration of Israel: The Ultimate Victory of the God of Life* (New Haven, CT: Yale University Press, 2006). For language about the future life, see Wisdom of Solomon 2:1–3:12. For resurrection, see Daniel 12:1–3. Belief in the resurrection of the righteous is also strongly asserted by 2 Macc 7:1–41; 4 Macc 9:8, 18:23. On apocalyptic, see D. S. Russell, *The Method and Message of Jewish Apocalyptic*, 353–390.

115. With clear autobiographical intent, Philo says that at times the mind "is seized by a sober intoxication, like those filled with Corybantic frenzy, and is inspired, possessed with a longing far other than theirs and a nobler desire. Wafted by this to the topnotch ark of things perceptible to mind, it seems to be on its way to the great King himself; but amid its longing to see him, pure and untempered rays of concentrated light stream forth like a torrent, so that by its gleams the eye of understanding is dazzled" (*On the Creation*, 71). See also his statement concerning his interpretive task: "Yet it is well for me to give thanks to God even for this, that though submerged I am not sucked down into the depths, but can also open the soul's eyes, which in my despair of comforting hope I thought had now lost their sight, and am irradiated by the light of wisdom, and am not given over to life-long darkness. So behold me daring, not only to read the sacred messages of Moses, but also in my love of knowledge to peer into each of them and unfold and reveal what is not known to the multitude" (*Special Laws*, 3.6).

Philo says the following of Moses: "He was named god and king of the whole nation, and entered, we are told, into the darkness where God was [Ex 20:21], that is, into the unseen, invisible, incorporeal and archetypal essence of existing things. Thus he beheld what is hidden from the sight of mortal nature, and, in himself and his life displayed for all to see, he has set before us, like some well-wrought picture, a piece of work beautiful and god-like, a model for all who are willing to copy it. Happy are those who imprint, or strive to imprint, that image in their souls" (*Life of Moses*, 1.158–159).

116. In Holladay's edition (*Fragments from Hellenistic Jewish Authors*, vol. 4: *Orphica*, 175–195), the critical passage is found both in Recension B and C; in the translation by M. LaFargue, "Orphica," in *The Old Testament Pseudepigrapha*, 2 vols., ed. J. H. Charlesworth (New York: Doubleday, 1983–1985), 2:795–801, it is found in the "longer version." The passage does not make clear whether it is Abraham or Moses. In Holladay's translation, the poem states that mortals do not have access to the great king, "except a certain person, a unique figure, by descent an offshoot of the Chaldean race" (B, 27–28). Lines 33–36 describe a place in the heavens and power on the earth—but does this mean God or the patriarch? See the discussion in Holladay, *Fragments*, 4:186–187.

117. See M. Himmelfarb, *Ascent to Heaven in Jewish and Christian Apocalypses* (New York: Oxford University Press, 1993). On the *Songs of Sabbath Sacrifice*, see C. A. Newsom, *Songs of Sabbath Sacrifice: A Critical Edition* (Harvard Semitic Studies 27; Atlanta: Scholars, 1985).

118. The pioneering works in this area are by G. Scholem, *Major Trends in Jewish Mysticism*, 3rd rev. ed. (New York: Schocken Books, 1954), and *Jewish Gnosticism, Merkabah Mysticism, and Talmudic Tradition* (New York: Jewish Theological Seminary of America, 1960). For such traditions in some form dating from the first century, see M. Smith, "Observations on the Hekaloth Rabbati," in *Biblical and Other Studies*, ed. A. Altmann (Cambridge, MA: Harvard University Press, 1963), 142–160.

119. Scholem, *Major Trends*, 49; M. Smith, "Observations," 154.

120. M. Smith, "Observations," 145; see also L. T. Johnson, "Gnosticism in the Rabbinic Tradition," *Resonance* 4 (1969): 5–17.

121. See J. Pakkala, *Intolerant Monolatry in the Deuteronomistic History* (Publications of the Finnish Exegetical Society 76; Göttingen: Vandenhoeck & Ruprecht, 1999).

   The distinction between the religion of ancient Israel and "biblical religion" acknowledges that the biblical compositions are as much prescriptive as they are descriptive, and that what happened religiously "on the ground" among the people of Israel was often not aligned with the perspective of the biblical authors. Not only archaeology and comparative literature but also the biblical texts themselves—above all in the space and energy spent in combating "deviance"—testify to the difference.

122. An example of such composition is the pitched battle between Elijah and the priests of Baal in the reign of Ahab (1 Kings 18:1–46), the "high places" against which the biblical texts inveigh are not only those dedicated to Canaanite gods, like Baal (2 Kings 10:18–31) but alternate locations for worshipping Yahweh, such as Bethel and Dan (see Deut 12:1–3, 29–30; 1 Kings 11:4–10; 13:33–34; 14:21–24; 15:14; 16:31–33; 22:44; 2 Kings 11:18–20; 13:16; 14:4).

123. The lesson of the Exile was that although the glory had left the temple and the land (Ezek 10:1–19), repentance was still possible without the temple (18:1–32; 33:10–20), and the word of the Lord continued to be present to the people outside the land (Ezek 33:21–22; Isa 48:1–21); indeed, the people could be purified outside the land and the temple (Ezek 36:16–38). Such convictions corresponded to the realization that the God of Israel was the creator of all the earth (Isa 40:12–31; 43:1–28) and could bring about a new creation (65:17–25; 66:22–24).

124. According to Josephus, *Antiquities*, 20.199, the high priest Annas was a Sadducee, and Josephus speaks generally of Sadducees as office-holders (*Antiquities*, 18.16–17). The Acts of the Apostles also appears to position Sadducees with the priestly class (Acts 4:1; 5:17). Josephus gives a glowing description of the priesthood in *Life*, 2; *Against Apion*, 1.188, 199, 284; 2.105, 185–196; see also *Letter of Aristeas*, 92–100.

125. The worship of the Jerusalem temple has been polluted (4QpHab 1.11–14; 5.10–14; 8.7–15; 9.9–10; 11.12). The community at Qumran is itself a holy house for Aaron (1QS 9.3–7; also 5.5–7; 8.3–9), the "temple of Israel for its sins" (4QFlor 1.1–7), which anticipates a future purified temple (11QTemple).

126. Josephus, *Jewish War*, 7.268–406. For archaeological evidence, see Y. Yadin, *Masada: Herod's Fortress and the Zealots' Last Stand* (New York: Random House, 1966).

127. See the rich inscriptional evidence gathered by L. Kant, "Jewish Inscriptions in Greek and Latin," *Aufstieg und Niedergang der römischen Welt* II.20.2 (1987): 671–713; and B. J. Brooten, *Women Leaders in the Ancient Synagogue: Inscriptional Evidence and Background Issues* (Brown Judaic Studies 36; Atlanta: Scholars, 1982).

128. See J. T. Burtchaell, *From Synagogue to Church: Public Services and Offices in the Earliest Christian Communities* (Cambridge: Cambridge University Press, 1992).

129. This theme in some ways pervades Philo's work but is perhaps most evident in *On Joseph*, of which E. R. Goodenough states, "*De Josepho* seems to me, then, to have been written from first to last with a single purpose, namely to . . . suggest that the real source for the highest political ideal of the East, the ideal of a divinely appointed and guided ruler, had had its truest presentation in Jewish literature, and highest exemplification at a time when a Jew was, in contemporary language, prefect of Egypt"; E. R. Goodenough, *The Politics of Philo Judaeus: Practice and Theory* (New Haven, CT: Yale University Press, 1938), 62.

130. In his "On the Jews," Artapanus (third–second century BCE) says of Moses: "As a grown man, he was called Mousaeus by the Greeks. This Mousaeus was the teacher of Orpheus. As a grown man he bestowed many useful benefits on mankind, for he invented boats and devices for stone construction and the Egyptians arms and the implements for drawing water and philosophy" (*Fragment*, 3).

9. THE APPEARANCE OF CHRISTIANITY IN THE GRECO-ROMAN WORLD

1. The term *Christianos* occurs only three times in the New Testament, and each use suggests its origin as an outsider designation. Acts 11:26 says that it was in the

Hellenistic city of Antioch, after the message had been addressed for the first time directly to "Greeks" (*Hellēnes*), that "the disciples were called Christians." The name identifies the movement as a cult organized around one called "the Christ"; an analogy would be the designation of members of the Unification Church as "Moonies" after its founder Reverend Moon. Similarly, Acts 26:28 has King Agrippa accuse Paul of trying to make him "play the Christian." When 1 Peter 4:16 speaks of suffering "as a Christian" (*hōs christianos*), the phrase indicates that this might be a charge put against a believer but also a name gladly embraced.

2. It is certainly possible that Jesus had contact and conflict with Pharisees (see J. P. Meier, *A Marginal Jew*, vol. 2: *Companions and Competitors* [New York: Doubleday, 2001], 289–340), but the stylized form of the controversies in the Synoptic Gospels—as in Mark 2:1–3:6—supports the view that these controversies reflect disputes between early followers of Jesus and Jewish teachers after Jesus' death; see R. Bultmann, *History of the Synoptic Tradition*, rev. ed., trans. J. Marsh (New York: Harper and Row, 1963), 11–68. The polemic against Scribes and Pharisees in Matt 23:1–36 reveals this social context most transparently; see S. Van Tilborg, *The Jewish Leaders in Matthew* (Leiden: Brill, 1972); and D. Garland, *The Intention of Matthew 23* (Leiden: Brill, 1979).

3. The classic scholarly expression of this is found in G. F. Moore, *Judaism in the First Centuries of the Christian Era*, 2 vols. (New York: Schocken, 1927), 1:1, 1:59; 1:71; 1:109. The tendency to equate Judaism and Palestinian Judaism, in turn, is continued in N. T. Wright, *The New Testament and the People of God* (Minneapolis: Fortress, 1992), e.g., 151, 248, 330–331.

4. The fragmentary literary evidence we have for Hellenistic Judaism apart from Philo is largely due to Eusebius of Caesarea's *Praeparatio Evangelica*; see C. R. Holladay, *Fragments from Hellenistic Jewish Authors*, vol. 1: *Historians* (Texts and Translations 20; Pseudepigrapha 10; Chico, CA: Scholars, 1983). Clement of Alexandria gladly made use of Philo in his own interpretation of scripture (see *Paidogogue*, 1.5; *Stromata*, 1.23–260), and Gregory of Nyssa used Philo in his *Life of Moses*, translation, introduction, and notes by E. Ferguson and A. J. Malherbe (Classics of Western Spirituality; New York: Paulist, 1978).

5. For my position on this point, in sharp contrast to that expressed by Jonathan Z. Smith (*Violent Origins: Walter Burkert, Rene Girard, and Jonathan Z. Smith on Ritual Killing and Cultural Formation*, ed. G. Hammerton-Kelly [Stanford, CA: Stanford University Press, 1987], 235), see L. T. Johnson, *Religious Experience in Earliest Christianity* (Minneapolis: Fortress, 1998), 33–37.

6. There is no definite archaeological evidence for Christianity before 180 CE; see G. Snyder, *Ante Pacem: Archaeological Evidence of Church Life before Constantine* (Macon, GA: Mercer University Press, 1985). All of the outside observers of Christians write in the very late first or second century: Josephus (37–95), Tacitus (55–117), Suetonius (75–150), Pliny the Younger (62–113), and Lucian of Samosata (120–200). As for Christian apocrypha, even those who argue that the Coptic *Gospel of Thomas* contains early sayings of Jesus recognize that its date of composition

is at the earliest mid-second century; see the discussion by Meier, *A Marginal Jew*, 1:123–139.

7. Although it is as tendentious as the works it criticizes, and although it certainly exaggerates the early dating of some New Testament compositions—above all the Gospels—J. A. T. Robinson's *Redating the New Testament* (Philadelphia: Westminster Press, 1976) remains a valuable corrective to the tendency to date much of the New Testament to the second century. It is possible for all of the compositions in the canon to have been written by 100. The most likely exception is 2 Peter; see L. T. Johnson, *Writings of the New Testament*, rev. and enl. ed. (Minneapolis: Fortress, 1999), 495–505. For the disputed date of the Pastoral Letters, see L. T. Johnson, *The First and Second Letters to Timothy* (Anchor Bible 35A; New York: Doubleday, 2001), 55–102.

8. See, e.g., such disparate exercises in *Traditionsgeschichte* as B. L. Mack, *The Lost Gospel: The Book of Q and Christian Origins* (San Francisco: HarperSanFrancisco, 1993) and G. Theissen, *The Religion of the Earliest Churches: Creating a Symbolic World*, trans. J. Bowden (Minneapolis: Fortress, 1999).

9. Again, this is in contrast to J. Z. Smith; see *Imagining Religion: From Babylon to Jonestown* (Chicago Studies in the History of Judaism; Chicago: University of Chicago Press, 1982), xii. W. Wrede's *Über Aufgabe und Methode der sogennanten neutestamentlichen Theologie* (Göttingen: Vandenhoeck & Ruprecht, 1897) was pivotal in the development of the *religionsgeschichtlich Schule*, focusing on the religious realities, rather than the theological concepts, to which the texts bear witness. Nevertheless, in Wrede's separate study of Paul, despite some attention to his "religious character" (6–30), Wrede concentrates on Paul's theology: "The religion of the apostle is theological through and through; his theology is his religion" (*Paul*, trans. E. Lummis [Boston: American Unitarian Association, 1908], 76). Similarly, O. Pfleiderer, in *Religion and Historic Faiths*, trans. D. A. Huebsch (London: T. Fisher Unwin, 1907), insists that Paul purifies the religious expressions he inherits by rendering them theologically and ethically (pp. 267–269); see also W. Bousset, *What Is Religion?* trans. F. B. Low (London: T. Fisher Unwin, 1907), 247–249. The same tendency continues in R. Bultmann's *Theology of the New Testament*, 2 vols., trans. K. Grobel (New York: Charles Scribner's Sons, 1952–55); religion is what precedes Paul, but "faith in the kerygma" is the basis of his theology.

10. In "Why the Church Rejected Gnosticism," G. MacRae states the consensus succinctly: "It is as much a dogma of scholarship as its opposite used to be: orthodoxy is not the presupposition of the church but the result of growth and development" (*Jewish and Christian Self-Definition*, vol. 1: *The Shaping of Christianity in the Second and Third Centuries*, ed. E. P. Sanders [Philadelphia: Fortress, 1980], 127).

11. See L. T. Johnson, "Koinonia: Diversity and Unity in Early Christianity," *Theology Digest* 46 (1999): 303–313.

12. In his *Ecclesiastical Authority and Spiritual Power in the Church of the First Three Centuries*, trans. J. Baker (Stanford, CA: Stanford University Press, 1969), 3, H. von Campenhausen represents a long tradition of scholarship when he states, "In the course of

these three centuries the ideal to which Christianity had originally been committed was impaired in various ways; not only do we find rigidities of attitude, curtailment of aspiration, distortion of insight, but also in every department—an indisputable trivialization."

13. For these points, see L. T. Johnson, *The Acts of the Apostles*, ed. D. J. Harrington (Sacra Pagina 5; Collegeville, MN: Liturgical, 1992), 3–11.

14. See, e.g., C. Hemer, *The Book of Acts in the Setting of Hellenistic History* (Wissenschaftliche Untersuchungen zum Neuen Testament 49; Tübingen: J. C. B. Mohr [Paul Siebeck], 1989); and M. Hengel, *Acts and the History of Earliest Christianity*, trans. J. Bowden (Philadelphia: Fortress, 1980).

15. Efforts to establish a Pauline chronology on the basis of the letters alone always end up relying on Acts, consciously or not; see R. Jewett, *A Chronology of Paul's Life* (Philadelphia: Fortress, 1979); J. Murphy-O'Connor, *Paul: A Critical Life* (Oxford: Oxford University Press, 1996).

16. In Romans (probably written from Corinth in the winter of 57), Paul declares that he had preached "from Jerusalem to Illyricum" (15:19—the latter a location not mentioned by Acts but supported by 2 Tim 4:10) and announces his intention to evangelize Spain (15:24, 28). The concentration of churches throughout Asia Minor is supported as well by the Book of Revelation 1–3 and 1 Peter 1:1.

17. Locations mentioned by Paul's letters as having at least one "assembly" (*ekklēsia*) include Rome (Rom 1:7), Corinth (1 Cor 1:2; 2 Cor 1:1), Thessalonika (1 Thess 1:1; 2 Thess 1:1), Galatia (Gal 1:2), Ephesus (Eph 1:1; 1 Tim 1:3), Philippi (Phil 1:1), Colossae (Col 1:2), Laodicaea (Col 4:16), Hierapolis (Col 4:13), and Crete (Tit 1:5).

18. With respect to persecution, the evidence in Acts (5:40; 6:12–15; 7:58; 8:1–3; 9:1–2; 12:1–3; 13:50; 14:5; 16:20–24; 17:5–7; 18:17; 22:22–29) is supported by Paul's letters (Rom 12:14; 1 Cor 4:12; 2 Cor 11:23–27; Gal 6:2; Phil 1:13–17; 1 Thess 2:14–16; 2 Thess 1:4–6; 2 Tim 4:16–17; Phlm 1) and other early writings (Heb 10:32–34; 12:4; 13:13; James 2:6; 1 Pet 3:13–17; 4:12–17; Rev 7:4–6; 12:11; 13:7).

19. If, as usually supposed (and back translation often supports), Jesus spoke in Aramaic, his words would have had to be quickly translated into Greek for transmission in the Diaspora. In terms of cultural context, the Jesus movement operated within a territory that was, however Hellenized, nevertheless predominantly Jewish; within a matter of mere years, it needed to adapt itself to a predominantly pagan environment. The movement began among a group of Jews who had followed Jesus "from the baptism of John" (Acts 1:22), but it was carried forward by those who had never known Jesus himself—see, e.g., the role of Barnabas and Silas, not to mention Paul. The adherents of the movement, furthermore, increasingly included more Gentiles than Jews. Finally, the Jesus movement was essentially rural and itinerant, but the earliest communities we know of were in cities; the transition is obvious when the imagery used by Jesus in the Synoptic Gospels is compared with that used by Paul in his letters.

20. Before the destruction of the temple in 70, a significant number of Christian leaders were violently killed. Acts tells of the stoning of Stephen (7:54–56) and of Herod's execution of James the son of Zebedee by the sword (Acts 12:2). Josephus (*Antiquities*,

20.200) confirms the execution of James the brother of the Lord in 62. The New Testament compositions foreshadow the deaths of Paul (Acts 20:25; 2 Tim 4:6–8) and Peter (John 21:18–19).

21. The accounts of relief offered to the Jerusalem church in Acts (11:29–30; 12:25) and in Paul's letters (Gal 2:10; 1 Cor 16:1–4; 2 Cor 8–9; Rom 15:25–28, 31) do not completely agree, but they confirm that the Jerusalem church was at least temporarily impoverished.

22. Luke tries to show that the Jerusalem leadership confirmed the mission to Samaria and Antioch (Acts 8:14–17; 11:22–23), but even his report on the conflict concerning the circumcision of Gentile converts (Acts 15) suggests the limits of their oversight, a lack of real power intimated also by Paul in his account of his relations with Jerusalem (Gal 2:9–12).

23. The dissemination of the new writings produced by the movement through the new technology of the codex was, in turn, of inestimable value to an ever-expanding mission.

24. I draw these claims from throughout the New Testament, although the greatest number appear in the earliest datable writings, the letters of Paul. I note that the statements do not represent a "theology" that is being argued, but rather that they belong to the category of shared religious assumptions—even if the writer needs to remind readers of this shared conviction.

25. Paul tells the socially and politically insignificant community in Corinth, "the world or life or death or the present or the future, all are yours; and you are Christ's; and Christ is God's" (1 Cor 3:22), and challenges his readers: "Do you not know that the saints will judge the world? And if the world is to be judged by us, are you incompetent to try trivial cases? Do you not know that we are to judge angels?" (1 Cor 6:2–3). The author of 1 John declares, "This is the victory that overcomes the world, our faith. Who is it that overcomes the world but he who believes that Jesus is the Son of God?" (1 John 5:4–5).

26. Paul states that the community of disciples is the place where God's purpose for the world is being disclosed: "the plan of the mystery hidden for ages in God who created all things; that through the church the manifold wisdom of God might now be made known to the principalities and powers in the heavenly places" (Eph 3:9–10).

27. On "powers and principalities," see Rom 8:38; 1 Cor 2:6–10; Eph 2:1–10; Col 1:13; 1 Pet 3:22. On "elements of the universe," see Rom 6:15–23; 2 Cor 3:6–18; Gal 3:23–4:7; Col 2:8–23.

28. Rom 8:14–15; Heb 2:14–15; 1 John 4:17–21.

29. Rom 1:16; 10:10; 1 Cor 1:18, 21; 15:2; Eph 2:5–8; Phil 1:28; Tit 3:5; James 1:21; 1 Pet 3:21; 2 Pet 3:15; Jude 3; Rev 12:10.

30. For *eleutheria*, see Rom 6:18–22; 1 Cor 9:1, 19; 2 Cor 3:17; Gal 5:1, 13; James 1:25; 1 Pet 2:1. For *parrēsia*, see Acts 2:19; 4:13, 29, 31; 2 Cor 3:12; Eph 3:12; 1 Thess 2:2; Phlm 8; Heb 4:16.

31. For peace, see Rom 5:1; 14:17; 1 Cor 7:15; 2 Cor 13:11; Eph 2:17; 4:3; Phil 4:7; Col 3:15; James 3:18. For joy, see Acts 13:52; Rom 5:3; Gal 5:22; Phil 2:2; 1 Pet 4:13; 1 John 1:4; for

joy in suffering, see 1 Thess 3:6–9; Heb 12:1–3; James 1:2; 1 Pet 4:13. For the triad of faith (*pistis*), hope (*elpis*), and love (*agapē*), see 1 Cor 13:13; 1 Thess 1:2–3; 1 Pet 1:3–9. Hope does not grieve at the death of community members (1 Thess 4:3), faith resists temptation (1 Pet 5:9), and love is not arrogant or rude (1 Cor 13:5).

32. *Exousia* is power in the sense of authority or ability (see John 1:12; 1 Cor 8:9; 9:4; 2 Cor 10:8; 13:10; 2 Thess 3:9). *Energeia* is power in the sense of making things happen or work (see 1 Cor 12:6, 11; Gal 3:5; 5:6; Eph 3:20–21; Col 1:29; 1 Thess 2:13; Phlm 6; Heb 4:12). *Dynamis* and its cognates are used most generally for power (Rom 1:16; 15:13, 19; 1 Cor 1:18; 6:14; 2 Cor 6:7; 13:4; Gal 3:5; Eph 3:20; Col 1:29; 1 Thess 1:5; 2 Thess 1:11; 2 Tim 1:7; Heb 2:4; 2 Pet 1:16. For "signs and wonders," see Acts 4:30; 5:12; 14:3; Rom 15:19; 2 Cor 12:12; Heb 2:4. For preaching the good news, see Rom 1:16; 1 Cor 1:18; 2:4; 2 Cor 4:7; 1 Thess 1:5; 2 Tim 1:8; James 1:21.

33. Rom 12:2; 1 Cor 2:16; 2 Cor 3:18; Gal 3:5; Eph 4:23; Col 3:10; 1 Pet 1:22.

34. The word "now" (*nyn*) is used with great frequency. In a single letter—Romans—Paul states that *now* God's righteousness is being revealed (3:21, 26), *now* they have been made righteous (5:9), *now* they have been reconciled with God (5:11), *now* they are freed from sin (6:22), *now* they are discharged from the law (7:6), *now* there is no condemnation for God's people (8:1), *now* the Mystery of God is being revealed (16:26). Paul says in 2 Cor 6:2, "Behold, *now* is the acceptable time, behold *now* is the day of salvation" (see also Gal 4:9; Eph 2:2; 3:5; Col 1:22, 26; 2 Tim 1:10; Heb 9:26; 1 Pet 1:12; 2:25; 3:21; 1 John 3:2) (emphases added).

35. See Rom 1:4; 16:25; 1 Cor 1:24; 5:4; 12:3; 2 Cor 1:4; 6:7; 12:9; 13:4; Eph 3:16, 20; Phil 3:10, 20–21; 2 Tim 1:7; Heb 5:7; James 4:12; 1 Pet 1:5; 2 Pet 1:16; Jude 24. For the language of *charis*, see Rom 3:24; 4:4; 5:2, 15–17; 6:1, 14; 11:5–6; 1 Cor 15:10; 2 Cor 1:12; 4:15; 8:1; Gal 1:6, 15; 5:5; Eph 2:5–7; 3:2; Col 1:6; 1 Tim 1:14; 2 Tim 2:1; Tit 2:11; 3:7; Heb 2:9; 10:29; James 4:6; 1 Pet 2:19; 3:7; 2 Pet 3:18; Jude 4.

36. See, e.g., John 20:21–23; Luke 24:47–49; Acts 2:1–4, 32–33, 38; 4:8; 10:44–47; 1 Thess 1:5; 2 Tim 1:6; 1 Cor 2:12; 12:3; Tit 3:5; Gal 4:6; 2 Cor 3:17–18; Rom 8:11; Heb 2:4; 4:12; 6:4; 1 Pet 1:12; 3:18; 4:6; 1 John 3:24; 4:13; 5:8; Jude 19, 20; Rev 2:7; 4:2; 19:10.

37. For new life, see Rom 6:4; Eph 4:24; for new covenant, see 1 Cor 11:25; 2 Cor 3:17–18; Heb 9:15; for new creation, see 2 Cor 5:17–18; Gal 5:16; for new humanity, see Eph 4:22–24; Col 3:9–10.

38. There is a fascinating agreement between insider and outsider sources on this point. The Gospels are frank in reporting the dispersal of Jesus' followers at his arrest and the need to gather them again after his resurrection (Mark 14:50–52; 16:1–8; Matt 26:56; 28:16–20; Luke 23:31–32, 49; 24:13–49; John 20:19–29). In his brief notice concerning the great fire in Rome, Tacitus (*History*, 15.44.2–8) reports that Nero fastened the blame on Christians, adding: "Christus, from whom the name had its origin, suffered the extreme penalty during the reign of Tiberius at the hands of one of our procurators, Pontius Pilate, *and a deadly superstition, thus checked for a moment, again broke out,* not only in Judaea, the first source of the evil, but also in the city" (emphasis added).

39. See the reasonable summary concerning Jesus' ministry by Meier, *A Marginal Jew*, 3:622–626.

40. In the Synoptic Gospels, Jesus begins his ministry in Galilee and is executed in Jerusalem during Passover, over a period of a year. In John, Jesus attends Passover three times, which would enable a career of at least two and a half years; see the discussion in Meier, *A Marginal Jew*, 1:372–443.

41. It is one of the secure findings of *Formsgeschichte* that Jesus' sayings were handed on by oral transmission for some 30–40 years in the form of individual units rather than as organized blocks of discourse; such "sermons" (like those in Matthew 5–7) reveal the redactional work of the evangelists. See the classic studies of Bultmann, *History of the Synoptic Tradition*; and M. Dibelius, *From Tradition to Gospel*, trans. B. Woolf (New York: Charles Scribner's Sons, 1934).

42. The designation of Jesus as charismatic by Geza Vermes in *Jesus the Jew: A Historian's Reading of the Gospels* (Philadelphia: Fortress, 1973) was followed by M. J. Borg, *Jesus, a New Vision: Spirit, Culture, and the Life of Discipleship* (San Francisco: Harper and Row, 1987). The designation is apt if understood in terms of a life responsive to inner promptings more than to external law and as engendering a powerful response (both positive and negative) among others.

43. N. A. Dahl makes an argument concerning Jesus' possible final acquiescence in the role of Messiah, based on the historicity of this *titulus*; see "The Crucified Messiah," in *Jesus the Christ: The Historical Origins of Christological Doctrine*, ed. D. H. Juel (Minneapolis: Fortress, 1991), 127–148.

    A substantial number of those thinking they are doing "histories" of Jesus ignore the character of the Gospel narratives and ascribe to him various states of messianic consciousness (see A. Schlatter, *The History of the Christ*, trans. A. J. Köstenberger [Grand Rapids, MI: Baker Books, 1997 (1923)], 125–136, 265) or intentions (see N. T. Wright, *Jesus and the Victory of God* [Minneapolis: Fortress, 1996]; and my response, "A Historiographical Response to Wright's Jesus," in *Jesus and the Restoration of Israel: A Critical Assessment of N. T. Wright's Jesus and the Victory of God*, ed. C. C. Newman [Downer's Grove, IL: Intervarsity, 1999], 206–224). Even so methodologically aware a historian as J. P. Meier is not immune; see *A Marginal Jew*, 2:298, 331, 316, 342, 349, 403, 453.

44. If one is claiming to do historical study of Christian origins, then it is a methodological imperative to begin analysis with the earliest primary (and firsthand) sources dating from 50–68 CE—including the letters of Paul and other compositions that can reasonably be assigned to the same period, such as James and Hebrews—rather than the Gospels, dating from 70–90 CE, especially since the discourse of these letters speaks of the resurrection as a present reality among believers rather than as a singular event of the past.

45. Jesus' sayings were remembered after his death, but they were selected and shaped by convictions concerning the resurrection—this fact affects every claim to locate the "authentic" words of Jesus. In any case, the transmission of his teachings did not in itself constitute his "afterlife."

46. The impression of resuscitation—the resumption of empirical existence after clinical death—is in part a consequence of the "realism" of the Gospel accounts; there is no way to express the "reality" of the resurrection narratively except through the use of physical detail. Thus, Jesus eats with his followers, speaks with them, touches them.

The most "physical" of all is Luke's account, but it is important to recognize that his empty tomb and appearance stories are part of a narrative dialectic of absence/presence that reaches its climax in the Pentecost: the ascended Jesus is now present to "all flesh" through the Holy Spirit. For this argument, see L. T. Johnson, *Living Jesus: Learning the Heart of the Gospel* (San Francisco: HarperSanFrancisco, 1999), 12–22.

47. For this argument, see Johnson, *The Writings of the New Testament*, 107–122.

48. See, e.g., Rom 1:7; 5:1; 6:23; 13:14; 14:8; 1 Cor 1:7–8; 5:4; 9:1; 15:57; 2 Cor 3:17–18; 4:5; Gal 6:14; Eph 3:11; 5:20; Phil 3:20; Col 2:6; 3:17; 1 Thess 1:3; 2:19; 5:23; 2 Thess 1:7–8; 1 Tim 1:12; 2 Tim 1:8; Phlm 5; Heb 2:3; 13:20; James 1:1; 2:1; 1 Pet 1:3; 3:15; 2 Pet 1:2, 8; 2:20; Jude 4, 17; Rev 19:16; 22:20.

49. See the summary of data in W. Foerster, *"Kyrios"* in *Theological Dictionary of the New Testament*, ed. G. Kittel, trans. G. W. Bromiley (Grand Rapids, MI: Eerdmans, 1965), 3:1041–1054.

50. See, most notably, W. Bousset, *Kyrios Christos: A History of the Belief in Christ from the Beginnings of Christianity to Irenaeus*, trans. J. E. Steely (Nashville: Abingdon, 1970), 119–152.

51. See my observations in Chapter 2.

52. For the frequent use of Ps 110 in the New Testament, see D. M. Hay, *Glory at the Right Hand: Psalm 110 in Early Christianity* (Society of Biblical Literature Monograph Series 18; Nashville: Abingdon, 1973). For the use of *kyrios* to translate Yahweh, see LXX Gen 2:4; 3:1; Ex 3:2, 3:4; 6:1; 8:22; 15:1; Ps 2:2; 9:1; 148:1; Prov 1:7; and hundreds of other passages.

53. A. F. Segal, *Two Powers in Heaven: Early Rabbinic Reports about Christianity and Gnosticism* (Boston: Brill, 2002).

54. For clearly titular uses of *Christos*, see Mark 8:29; Matt 16:16; Luke 9:20; Acts 2:36; 3:18; 8:5; 9:22; 17:3; 18:5; Rom 5:6–8; 8:9–10; 9:1–5; 1 Cor 10:4–9; 11:3; 12:12; 2 Cor 1:5; 2:15; 5:10, 17; Gal 2:17, 20; 3:13, 16; Heb 3:6; 9:28; 1 Pet 1:11; 5:10; 1 John 2:22; 5:1.

55. For discussion of the varieties of messianism, see the essays in J. H. Charlesworth, ed., *The Messiah: Developments in Earliest Judaism and Christianity* (Minneapolis: Fortress, 1992).

56. In his attack on Christianity, the philosopher Celsus puts particular stress on the manner of Jesus' death as disproving any claim that he was worthy of the designation of Son of God; Origen, *Against Celsus*, 2.21–45.

57. For efforts to analyze the growth of Christianity in sociological terms see especially R. MacMullen, *Christianizing the Roman Empire* (New Haven, CT: Yale University Press, 1984); and R. Stark, *The Rise of Christianity: A Sociologist Reconsiders History* (Princeton, NJ: Princeton University Press, 1996).

58. The relationship between the survival of intentional communities and strong boundaries is particularly well analyzed by R. M. Kantor, *Commitment and Community: Communes and Utopias in Sociological Perspective* (Cambridge, MA: Harvard University Press, 1972); and illustrated by B. D. Zablocki, *The Joyful Community: An Account of the Bruderhof, a Communal Movement Now in Its Third Generation* (Baltimore: Penguin, 1971).

59. Paul's careful argument in 1 Cor 8–10 concerning the consumption of idol food and eating at pagan shrines shows the difficulties for those who chose "not to go out of the world" (1 Cor 5:9), and it is possible that the condemnation of Jezebel in Revelation's letter to the church in Thyatira for "mislead[ing] my people to play the harlot and to eat food offered to idols" (Rev 2:20) represents a response to such Pauline practice; see C. K. Barrett, "Things Sacrificed to Idols," *New Testament Studies* 11 (1964–1965): 138–153.

     In Acts 11:3, Peter is challenged by the Jerusalem leadership not for baptizing the household of Cornelius but for "entering the homes of uncircumcised people and eating together with them," and the compromise struck by the "Jerusalem Council" clearly had the goal of allowing Jews to eat with Gentile believers, by demanding of the Gentiles a rejection of idolatry and food improperly prepared, as well as of sexual immorality (Acts 15:29). Similarly, the fight between Paul and Cephas in Antioch arose because of Cephas' "withdrawing" after he had earlier followed the practice of "eating together with the Gentiles" (*meta tōn ethnōn synesthiein*; Gal 2:12).

60. See C. Osiek and D. L. Balch, *Families in the New Testament World: Households and Household Churches* (Louisville: Westminster/John Knox, 1997).

61. In Paul's letters (written between 50 and 65 CE), he names as heads of households or household churches, Prisca and Aquila (Rom 16:4–5; 1 Cor 16:19), Gaius (Rom 16:23; 1 Cor 1:14), Stephanas (1 Cor 1:16; 16:15), and Nympha (Col 4:15); he names Chloe also as head of a household (1 Cor 1:11) and Phoebe as his patron and a deacon in the assembly at Cenchrae (Rom 16:1–2).

62. See especially G. Theissen, *The Social Setting of Pauline Christianity: Essays on Corinth*, trans. J. H. Schütz (Philadelphia: Fortress, 1982).

63. The situation of the Corinthian church is perhaps more complex than most but is nevertheless instructive. After founding the community (Acts 18:1–17; 1 Cor 1:14–17; 4:15) and leaving it, Paul visits it at least three times (1 Cor 4:19; 2 Cor 2:1; 12:13; 13:1) and asserts his authority through such visits, the sending of his personal delegates (1 Cor 4:17; 16:10–11; 2 Cor 8:16–24), and at least three letters (see 1 Cor 4:14–20; 5:3; 7:1–17; 11:13–16, 33–34; 14:26–40; 16:2; 2 Cor 10:7; 13:10). He is also aware of the claim being made on this church by other leaders traveling through it (1 Cor 1:12; 9:5; 2 Cor 2:17–3:1; 10:12–18; 11:4–6, 20–33; 12:11–13).

64. Paul's difficulty in providing guidance concerning the *charismata* in speech given by the Holy Spirit is indicated by his struggle to provide reasons for women remaining veiled while prophesying or praying in the assembly (1 Cor 11:3–16) and his lengthy discussion of the spiritual gifts in 1 Cor 12–14. His conclusion, that "everything should be done properly and in good order" (14:40), falls considerably short of an ordinance. And although "assistance and administration" (*antilēmpsis, kubernēsis*) are included among the spiritual gifts (12:28; see also "being in charge" [*prohistamenos*] in Rom 12:8), Paul does not coordinate them with the more spectacular displays.

65. Paul gives evidence for local leaders in Rom 12:7–8; 1 Cor 12:8; 16:15–18; Gal 6:6; Eph 4:11; Phil 1:1; 1 Thess 5:12–13.

66. When the evidence of Paul's undisputed letters is collated with that provided by the disputed 1 Timothy, we see that the basic form of local leadership follows the pattern of that in synagogues and Greco-Roman associations; see J. T. Burtchaell, *From Synagogue to Church: Public Services and Offices in the Earliest Christian Communities* (Cambridge: Cambridge University Press, 1992); and L. T. Johnson, *The First and Second Letters to Timothy* (Anchor Bible 35A; New York: Doubleday, 2001), 74–76.

67. Paul speaks of the Philippian church as having provided him with financial support while he was in Thessalonica and Corinth (Phil 4:15–19; 2 Cor 11:8–9). He refers to the deacon Phoebe as his patron (*prostatis*) in Cenchrae. His language of "refreshing the spirit" suggests that Stephanas, Fortunatus, and Achaicus, local householders in Corinth, were also financial supporters (1 Cor 16:15–18); Paul also mentions his hopes that Philemon, who had already "refreshed his heart," would continue to do so by returning to Paul the runaway slave Onesimus (Phlm 7–20).

     Hospitality is stated as an ideal in Heb 13:25 and 1 Pet 4:9; it is one of the desirable qualities in "supervisors" (*episkopoi*) whom we assume to be householders (1 Tim 3:2; Tit 1:8); it is requested for actual travelers (Phil 2:29; Col 4:10, Phlm 22); and it is the mechanism for a power struggle in Johannine churches (2 John 10; 3 John 5–7). Hospitality and the provision for further travel is asked in 1 Cor (16:7, 11) and is the practical point of Paul's Letter to the Romans (15:22–16:3).

     On charity, see especially Paul's discussion of care for widows in 1 Tim 5:3–16, which perfectly reflects the concerns found in synagogal systems of care (see also Acts 6:1–6).

     Paul's caustic rebuke of the Corinthians for their suing each other over *ta biōtika* ("everyday matters") in pagan courts (1 Cor 6:1–6) assumes two things: (1) like other synagogal associations, the Corinthians had mechanisms for settling local disputes concerning practice; and (2) the Corinthians were using as judges in such courts people who had no standing—thus, the appeal to outsiders by those unsatisfied with this arrangement.

68. Matt 28:19; Acts 2:38, 41; 8:12, 36; 9:18; 10:48; 16:15, 33; Rom 6:1–11; 1 Cor 1:15–16; 6:9–11; 12:13; Gal 3:27; Eph 4:5; Heb 6:1–6; 1 Pet 2:21. For the evidence, see J. Delorme, ed., *Baptism in the New Testament: A Symposium* (Baltimore: Helicon, 1964).

69. For multiple initiations at Eleusis, see L. J. Alderink, "The Eleusinian Mysteries in Roman Imperial Times," *Aufstieg und Niedergang der römischen Welt* II.17.4 (1989): 1478–1482; for Mithras, see R. Merkelbach, *Mithras* (Königstein: Verlag Anton Hain, 1984), 86–145.

70. For the pressure in the Galatian and Colossian churches to seek circumcision as a "perfecting" of the initiatory ritual of baptism, see L. T. Johnson, "Ritual Imprinting and the Politics of Perfection," in *Religious Experience in Early Christianity* (Minneapolis: Fortress, 1998), 69–103.

71. Evidence for common meals is sometimes direct (Acts 2:42, 46; [possibly 6:2]; 20:7; 27:35; 1 Cor 10:14–22; 11:17–34) and sometimes indirect (and assumed), as in Acts 10:9–16, 41; 11:3; 15:9, 20, 29; Gal 2:11–14; Rom 14:1–23; Rev 2:14, 19. For a review of the

evidence, see J. Delorme, ed., *The Eucharist in the New Testament: A Symposium*, trans. E. M. Stewart (Baltimore: Helicon, 1964).

72. The importance of meal practice is supported by the number of stories associating Jesus with a last meal with his followers (Mark 14:12–25; Matt 26:17–29; Luke 22:14–-38; John 13:2–30) his appearing to followers after his resurrection in the context of meals (Mark 16:14; Luke 24:13–35, 36–49; John 21:9–14) and his multiplication of the loaves to feed followers (Mark 6:35–44; 8:1–10; Matt 14:13–21; 15:31–39; Luke 9:10–17; John 6:1–14), which in John becomes the occasion for a Eucharistic discourse (John 6:26–59).

73. On pagan prayer, see S. Pulleyn, *Prayer in Greek Religion* (Oxford: Clarendon, 1997). For a fascinating analysis of how distinct Greek and Latin backgrounds affected the understanding of a Christian prayer, see M. J. Brown, *The Lord's Prayer through North African Eyes: A Window into Early Christianity* (New York: T. & T. Clark, 2004). On the connection between New Testament prayer and prayer in Judaism, see especially the use of the *berakah* form in Rom 1:25; 9:5; 2 Cor 1:3–7; Eph 1:3–14; 1 Pet 1:3–9. On Aramaic formulae in the New Testament, see *abba* in Gal 4:6; *maranatha* in 1 Cor 16:22; and *amēn* in 1 Cor 14:16 and very frequently elsewhere (e.g., Rom 1:25; 11:36; 15:33).

74. Pliny reports the Christians singing hymns to Christ as to God (*Letters*, 10.96.7); for the singing of hymns generally, see 1 Cor 14:26; Eph 5:19; Col 3:16; Rev 5:9; 14:3; 15:3. For hymns involving Christ, see Phil 2:6–11; Col 1:15–20; 1 Tim 3:16; 1 Pet 1:22–25; 3:18, 22; Rev 4:11; 5:9.

75. On reading, Paul tells Timothy to "attend to the prayer, reading and teaching" in the church at Ephesus in Paul's absence (1 Tim 4:13), and Paul's letters were read aloud in the assembly (2 Cor 7:8; Col 4:16; 1 Thess 5:27; 2 Thess 3:14).

On preaching, apart from the stories concerning Jesus and Paul reading and preaching in the synagogue (Luke 4:16–30; John 6:59; Acts 13:13–16) and reporting Paul preaching at the Lord's Supper (Acts 20:7–9), there is no specific evidence for preaching as part of worship, apart from the passage in 1 Tim 4:13. Here is a case where the synagogue practice was so well established that further mention may not have been necessary. Two New Testament compositions that now have the form of letters—1 Peter and Hebrews—may well have originated as sermons.

On teaching, in addition to the passages where Paul speaks of himself as a teacher (1 Cor 4:17; 1 Tim 2:7; 2 Tim 1:11), there is evidence for the office of teacher in local assemblies (Acts 13:1; 1 Cor 12:28; Rom 12:7; Gal 6:6; Eph 4:11; 1 Thess 5:12; James 3:1).

76. See D. Aune, *Prophecy in Early Christianity and the Ancient Mediterranean World* (Grand Rapids, MI: Eerdmans, 1983), 36–48; and E. Fascher, *Prophētēs: Eine sprach- und religionsgeschichtliche Untersuchung* (Geissen: A. Töpelmann, 1927). There is scattered evidence for speaking in tongues and prophecy (Mark 16:17; Acts 2:4; 10:46; 11:27; 19:6; 21:9–10; Rom 12:6; 1 Thess 5:20; 1 Tim 4:14; Rev 19:10) and for "prophets" ranked with apostles and teachers (Acts 13:1; 1 Cor 12:28; Eph 2:20; Rev 10:7), but the most important discussion is in 1 Cor 12–14, where Paul tries to sort out these gifts of the Spirit.

77. P. A. Harland, *Associations, Synagogues, and Congregations: Claiming a Place in Ancient Mediterranean Society* (Minneapolis: Fortress, 2003), 55–166.

78. Paul mentions as his personal delegates Timothy (1 Cor 4:17; 16:10–11; Phil 2:19–23; 1 Thess 3:2–6; 1 Tim 1:3), Titus (2 Cor 7:7; 8:17, 23; 12:18; Tit 1:5), Tychichus (Eph 6:21–22; Col 4:7), Ephaphroditus (Phil 2:25–30), and Phoebe (Rom 16:1–2). 3 John gives evidence of a delegate (Demetrius) sent from a leader (the Elder) to another leader in communion with him (Gaius). Gal 2:12 speaks of "the men from James" in terms of a delegation. At least some of the members of the church in Corinth sent as delegates to Paul included Chloe (1 Cor 1:11), Stephanas, Fortunatus, and Achaichus (1 Cor 16:17) and other unnamed representatives (2 Cor 8:19, 23). Acts speaks of delegates sent out by the church in Jerusalem (8:14; 11:22; 15:25, 30–33) and by the church in Antioch (11:29–30; 12:25; 13:1–3; 15:2). For the background and significance of such delegations, see M. M. Mitchell, "New Testament Envoys in the Context of Greco-Roman Diplomatic and Epistolary Conventions: The Case of Timothy and Titus," *Journal of Biblical Literature* 111 (1992): 641–662.

79. We have nine extant letters from Paul to churches (1 and 2 Corinthians, Romans, Philippians, Colossians, Ephesians, 1 and 2 Thessalonians, Galatians) but know he wrote more (see 1 Cor 5:9) and that the Corinthians wrote to him (1 Cor 7:1). The greetings in two of Paul's letters indicate a readership wider than a single assembly: "to all those through Achaia" (2 Cor 1:2) and "to the churches throughout Galatia" (Gal 1:2). Ephesians may well have been a circular letter (see Johnson, *Writings of the New Testament*, 407–413), and letters to specific churches could be exchanged (see Col 4:16). In addition, the New Testament contains two letters from the Elder (2 and 3 John); seven letters to churches in Asia from John the Seer (Rev 1–3); a letter from the Jerusalem church to believers in Antioch, Syria, and Cilicia (Acts 15:23–29); two letters from Peter—the first of them to believers in five areas of Asia Minor—and single letters from James, Jude, and the author of Hebrews.

80. Paul speaks of this collection in Gal 2:10; 1 Cor 16:1–4; 2 Cor 8–9; Rom 15:25–33: see also Acts 11:29–30; 12:25. For discussion, see D. Georgi, *Remembering the Poor: The History of Paul's Collection for Jerusalem* (Nashville: Abingdon Press, 1992); and K. F. Nickle, *The Collection: A Study in Paul's Strategy* (London: SCM Press, 1966).

81. See Tacitus, *History*, 15.44.2–8.

82. See Pliny, *Letter*, 10.96.

83. The view of the empire is entirely positive in Romans 13:1–7, 1 Tim 2:1, and 1 Peter 2:13–15. Acts is so positive toward Roman rule that an (exaggerated) case can be made that it is an apology for the empire; see P. W. Walasky, *"And So We Came to Rome": The Political Perspective of St. Luke* (Society for New Testament Studies Monograph Series 49; Cambridge: Cambridge University Press, 1973). In contrast, the Book of Revelation is entirely hostile to the empire because of the oppression of the saints (Rev 17:1–18:24); see L. L. Thompson, *The Book of Revelation: Apocalypse and Empire* (New York: Oxford University Press, 1990).

84. Although the differences should not be exaggerated, it is accurate to say that the attitudes expressed in "Johannine" literature (the Fourth Gospel, three letters of John,

and Revelation) are more sectarian—e.g., concerning "the world" and "the Jews"— than those found in the letters of Paul. The complexity of Paul's discussions in 1 Cor 5–11 is due to his insistence that the holiness of the church does not demand "going out of the world" (1 Cor 5:9–10). Thus, Paul sees Satan as a threat at the edges of the community (1 Cor 5:5; 2 Cor 11:3; 1 Thess 2:8; 1 Tim 5:15), and the first letter of John says that "the whole world is under the power of the evil one" (5:19), so that departure from the community means participating in the realm of evil (1 John 2:18–19; 3:8; 4:1–6).

It is notoriously difficult to discern any consistent eschatology, e.g., even within the undisputed Pauline letters; the differences between Revelation and other writings associated with the Johannine School lead to different conclusions concerning the appropriateness of considering it together with those other compositions; see Johnson, *Writings of the New Testament*, 579–581.

85. It is possible, for example, to make the case that Luke-Acts fits within the Greco-Roman genre of the novel, of the biography, and of the history; yet, it is also clear that, while combining elements of each of those literary types, it does so in a distinctive way; see L. T. Johnson, "Luke-Acts, Book of," in *The Anchor Bible Dictionary*, ed. D. N. Freedman (New York: Doubleday, 1992), 4:403–420.

10. NEW TESTAMENT CHRISTIANITY AS PARTICIPATION IN DIVINE BENEFITS

1. Among first-generation New Testament compositions, only James and Hebrews (and Revelation?) can with some confidence be thought of as addressed to Jewish believers. Paul's letters (50–66) are written to Gentile (Galatians, Philippians, 1 and 2 Thessalonians, Colossians, Ephesians) or possibly mixed communities (Romans, 1 and 2 Corinthians). First Peter, written at the latest circa 112 and possibly much earlier, has only Gentiles in view. The Gospels of Matthew, John, and Luke all assume the Gentile mission (Matt 20:19; John 12:20; Luke 2:32; 3:6). Acts portrays the earliest expansion as one that succeeds among Gentiles more than among Jews (Acts 13:44–47; 18:6; 28:28). The independent testimony of Acts 15 and Gal 2:1–10 of a first-generation meeting among leaders to decide the legitimacy of the Gentile mission indicates that by the year 50 it had become sufficiently important to require general and not simply local attention.

It is, in fact, extraordinarily difficult to say much historically about "Jewish Christianity," so quickly is it eclipsed by Gentile Christianity. We are reduced to drawing large conclusions from small fragments of Jewish Gospels (reported by Jerome), the legend of a migration from Jerusalem to Pella, and a difficult disentanglement of earlier materials from the fourth-century Pseudo-Clementine literature. For discussion, see G. Lüdemann, "The Successors of Pre-70 Jerusalem Christianity: A Critical Evaluation of the Pella Tradition," in *Jewish and Christian Self-Definition*, ed. E. P. Sanders (Philadelphia: Fortress, 1980), 1.161–173; R. A. Kraft, "In Search of 'Jewish Christianity' and Its 'Theology': Problems of Definition and Methodology," *Recherches de Science Religieuse* 60 (1972): 81–92; S. K. Riegel, "Jewish Christianity: Definitions and Terminology," *New Testament Studies* 24 (1978): 410–415; R. E. Brown, "Not Jewish Christianity and Gentile Christianity but Types of Jewish/Gentile Christianity," *Catholic Biblical Quarterly* 45 (1983): 74–79.

2. I remind the reader again that the line between "participation in benefits" and "magic" is often a matter of perspective. For the way in which Jesus' thaumaturgy could be read in terms of magic, see M. Smith, *Jesus the Magician* (San Francisco: Harper and Row, 1978); for a survey of the topic in the period, see D. E. Aune, "Magic in Early Christianity," *Aufstieg und Niedergang der römischen Welt* II.23.2 (1980): 1507–1557.

3. See especially W. Schmithals, *Gnosticism in Corinth*, trans. J. Steely (Nashville: Abingdon Press, 1971). On "realized eschatology," see A. C. Thiselton, "Realized Eschatology in Corinth," *New Testament Studies* 24 (1977–1978): 520–526; R. A. Horsley, "'How Can Some of You Say There Is No Resurrection of the Dead': Spiritual Elitism in Corinth," *Novum Testamentum* 20 (1978): 203–240.

4. Although Paul can speak of "among the gentiles" with reference to outsiders (1 Cor 5:1) and can say that "our fathers were all under the cloud" when referring to the Exodus (10:1), the community at Corinth undoubtedly had substantial Gentile membership. After speaking of "fornicators, idolaters, and adulterers" in 6:9–10, he adds, "as some of you used to be" (6:11). A brother who continues as an idolater needs to be shunned (5:11). Decisively, he reminds his readers in 12:2, that "when [they] were Gentiles," they were led astray by dumb idols.

5. See P. D. Gooch, *Dangerous Food: 1 Corinthians 8–10 in Its Context* (Waterloo, ON: Wilfrid Laurier University Press, 1993); and W. L. Willis, *Idol Meat in Corinth: The Pauline Argument in 1 Corinthians 8 and 10* (SBLDS 68; Chico, CA: Scholars, 1985).

6. See K. A. Munoz, *How Not to Go out of the World: First Corinthians 14:13–25 and the Social Foundations of Early Christian Expansion* (PhD diss., Emory University, 2008).

7. See G. Theissen, "Soziale Integration und sakramentales Handeln: Eine Analyze von 1 Cor XI, 17–34," *Novum Testamentum* 24 (1974): 290–317, found also in *The Social Setting of Pauline Christianity: Essays on Corinth*, ed. and trans. J. H. Schütz (Philadelphia: Fortress, 1982).

8. P. A. Harland, *Associations, Synagogues, and Congregations: Claiming a Place in Ancient Mediterranean Society* (Minneapolis: Fortress, 2003), 25–112.

9. See Plato, *Ion*, 534A–D; *Phaedrus*, 244A; *Timaeus*, 71E–72B; Plutarch, *The E at Delphi*, 387B, 391E; *Oracles at Delphi*, 397C, 399A. The language of Philo of Alexandria conforms completely: in prophecy, the divine *pneuma* "seizes" humans (*Questions on Genesis*, 4.196), "falls on" them (*Life of Moses*, 2.291), "possesses" them (*Life of Moses*, 1.175), and "fills" their mind (*Questions on Genesis*, 4:140). Philo consistently emphasizes the way the *pneuma* replaces the human mind in prophecy (*Special Laws*, 4.49; *Who Is the Heir*, 264–265; *Questions on Genesis*, 3.9; *Life of Moses*, 2.188–192). This is how God "speaks through" the prophets (*Special Laws*, 1:65). See M. J. Weaver, *Pneuma in Philo of Alexandria* (PhD diss., Notre Dame University, 1973), 115–141.

10. See Plutarch, *Obsolescence of Oracles*, and the discussion in Chapter 7.

11. For the status bestowed by ecstatic speech in communities that recognize prophecy, see I. M. Lewis, *Ecstatic Religion* (Baltimore: Penguin, 1971); for the possibility that women prophets caused dissension in the community, see E. Schüssler-Fiorenza, *In Memory of Her: A Feminist Theological Reconstruction of Christian Origins* (New York: Crossroad, 1983), 226–236; and A. C. Wire, *The Corinthian Women Prophets: A Reconstruction through Paul's Rhetoric* (Minneapolis: Fortress, 1990), 116–158.

12. Galatians 1:12; 1:17–2:10; 4:12–20; 5:2–3, 10–11; 6:17. For an extensive argument in favor of Colossians' authenticity, see G. E. Cannon, *The Use of Traditional Materials in Colossians* (Macon, GA: Mercer University Press, 1983); see also J. Murphy-O'Connor, *Paul: A Critical Life* (Oxford: Clarendon, 1996), 237–239. Even a notable proponent of the letter's pseudonymity acknowledges the possibility that it is close enough to Paul's actual career to make even the signing by Paul (Col 4:18) possible; see W. A. Meeks, *The First Urban Christians: The Social World of the Apostle Paul* (New Haven, CT: Yale University Press, 1983), 125.

13. For Paul's passion, see Gal 1:1, 6, 8, 9; 4:11; 5:7, 12; 6:17. For language concerning Torah, see 2:3, 14–19; 3:2, 10–22; 4:21–5:4; 5:11, 18; 6:12–13. For the rhetorical character, see especially J. Smit, "Galatians: A Deliberative Speech," *New Testament Studies* 35 (1989): 1–26.

14. Paul calls Epaphras "one of yourselves" (Col 4:2) and makes clear that his readers had heard the word of truth from Epaphras (1:6–7).

15. Paul's authority is assumed, not questioned (Col 1:1, 23, 25; 2:5; 4:2–4, 8–9, 18). No passage of Torah is cited in the letter, and apart from the single term "circumcision" (*peritomē*), the diction in 2:11–15 and 2:22 is extremely general: "Things written by hand as teachings" (*cheirographon tois dogmasin*) and "human instructions and teachings" (*entalmata kai didaskalias tōn anthrōpōn*).

16. The argument in Colossians intertwines the themes of baptism (1:12–13, 21–23; 2:11––15; 2:20–3:4; 3:9, 12) and of Christ (1:15–20, 27–29; 2:2–3, 6, 9; 2:14–3:1; 4:2).

17. For Galatians, see 2:8, 15–16; 3:2; 4:8–9, 21; 5:2, 4; 6:12–13; for Colossians, see 1:21, 27; 2:13; 3:11; 4:11.

18. In Galatians 4:21 and 5:2–4, the desire for circumcision seems voluntary; in 2:3 and 6:12, there is a note of coercion. Colossians is less explicit. The issue of circumcision is derived from Paul's designation of baptism as "a circumcision without hands" and the "circumcision of Christ" in 2:11, the caution against regulations dealing with handling, touching, and tasting in 2:22, and the denial of a distinction between Jew and Gentile in 3:11.

19. Of particular interest in Galatians is Paul's use of *epitelein* in 3:3, for the term has definite connections with initiation rituals; see R. S. Ascough, "The Completion of a Religious Duty: The Background of 2 Cor 8:1–15," *New Testament Studies* 42 (1996): 584–599, especially the inscriptional evidence in pages 590–594. See also *plēroma* in Gal 4:4, *plēroun* in 5:14, *telein* in 5:16, and *anaplēroun* in 6:2. In Colossians, see *teleios* in 1:28 and 4:12, *teleiotēs* in 3:14, *plēroun* in 1:9 and 2:19, *plērophoria* in 2:2, and *plērophorein* in 4:12.

20. Gal 4:17; 5:5; 6:12–13; Col 2:8, 16, 18, 23.

21. For Galatians, see, e.g., J. Tyson, "Paul's Opponents in Galatia," *Novum Testamentum* 10 (1968): 241–254; R. Jewett, "The Agitators and the Galatian Community," *New Testament Studies* 17 (1970): 198–212. For Colossians, see the several essays in F. O. Francis and W. A. Meeks, eds., *Conflict at Colossae* (Sources for Biblical Study 4; Missoula, MT: Scholars, 1975).

22. To take only the most widely known example, initiation at Eleusis involved four stages: the purification; initiation into the lesser Mysteries (at Agrae); then, initiation into the greater Mysteries (at Eleusis); then, a year later, the *epopteia* (also at Eleusis); see L. J. Alderink, "The Eleusinian Mysteries in Roman Imperial Times," *Aufstieg und Niedergang der römischen Welt* II.18.2 (1989): 1478–1482. See also the multiple initiations of Lucius, first into the cult of Isis (Apuleius, *Metamorphoses*, XI.23–25), then into the cult of Osiris (XI.27), and then still a third initiation (XI.29).

23. For status enhancement through initiation, see A. Van Gennep, *The Rites of Passage*, trans. M. B. Vizedon and G. L. Caffee (Chicago: University of Chicago Press, 1960); V. Turner, *The Ritual Process: Structure and Anti-Structure* (The Henry Lewis Morgan Lectures; Ithaca, NY: Cornell University Press, 1969); M. Milner Jr., "Status and Sacredness: Worship and Salvation as Forms of Status Transformation," *Journal for the Scientific Study of Religion* 33 (1994): 99–109.

24. For the priests of Cybele as eunuchs, see Apuleius, *Metamorphoses*, VIII.24.

25. For closer analysis, see L. T. Johnson, "Ritual Imprinting and the Politics of Perfection," in *Religious Experience in Earliest Christianity* (Minneapolis: Fortress, 1998), 69–104.

26. For the issue of the genre of the Gospels in light of Greco-Roman narratives, see J. Z. Smith, "Good News Is No News: Aretalogy and Gospels," in *Map Is Not Territory: Studies in the History of Religions* (Chicago: University of Chicago Press, 1973), 190–207; C. H. Talbert, *What Is a Gospel? The Genre of the Canonical Gospels* (Philadelphia: Fortress, 1977); R. A. Burridge, *What Are the Gospels? A Comparison with Greco-Roman Biography* (Society for New Testament Studies Monograph Series 70; Cambridge: Cambridge University Press, 1992).

27. Mark is conventionally dated circa 70, Matthew and Luke-Acts circa 85 and John circa 90. Although the distance from the events they describe is not insignificant, neither is it huge. It took some 700 years for a life of Siddhartha to be written, after all, and both Suetonius and Tacitus, when they wrote about Augustus, did so at a distance of a century.

28. See my reconstruction of the settings and processes of oral tradition (with bibliography) in L. T. Johnson, *The Writings of the New Testament: An Interpretation* (Minneapolis: Fortress, 1999), 125–153.

29. Despite fervent longing to the contrary, there are no materials in the Gospel tradition that represent a "neutral" perspective on Jesus. The resurrection is not simply an event reported at the end of the narrative; it colors the narrative from beginning to end, a point I argue in *Living Jesus: Learning the Heart of the Gospel* (San Francisco: HarperSanFrancisco, 1999).

30. For a full consideration of the literary and religious dimensions of each of the Gospels, see Johnson, *Writings of the New Testament*, 159–257, 525–557.

31. The best treatment of the infancy accounts in Matthew and Luke is provided by R. E. Brown, *Birth of the Messiah*, enl. ed. (Garden City, NY: Doubleday, 1993).

32. See C. H. Talbert, "Prophecies of Future Greatness: The Contribution of Greco-Roman Biographies to an Understanding of Luke 1:5–4:15," in *The Divine Helmsman*, ed. J. L. Crenshaw and S. Sandmel (New York: KTAV, 1980), 129–141.

33. For the following passages, I supply only the reference in Mark; the same incidents appear in Matthew and Luke.

34. Luke precedes the call of the sons of Zebedee by a miraculous catch of fishes (Luke 5:1–11); Iamblichus tells a story about Pythagoras that bears some resemblance both to Luke 5 and John 21 (*Life of Pythagoras*, 36).

35. In the context of contemporary Greco-Roman and Jewish religion, the prophecies ascribed to Jesus in the Gospels are notable in four ways: (1) the concentration of the divine spirit in a single person rather than a cult center; (2) the complete lack of technical craft accompanying his statements; (3) the sheer number of clear predictive statements; and (4) the fact that many of these statements were "fulfilled" by the time of the readers (e.g., the death of Jesus, his resurrection, the fall of the temple). All this should have had a great impact on a world in which prophecy, though deeply admired, was not experienced so vividly.

36. Although there are scattered stories attesting to the power of exorcism—see Lucian, *Lover of Lies*, 16; and Philostratus, *Life of Apollonius of Tyana*, 3.38—the number of such acts attributed to Jesus is impressive.

37. Further healings are added by Luke 7:1–10; 13:10–17; 14:1–4; 22:51. Matthew 8:5–13 and Luke 7:10 contain the additional story of the healing of a centurion's servant. On the other side, both Luke and Matthew omit the strange healing stories in Mark 7:31–-37 and 8:22–26, possibly because they too much resemble the work of a magician.

38. Luke adds the raising of the widow of Nain's son (7:11–27), a story that bears some resemblance to an account in Philostratus, *Life of Apollonius of Tyana*, 4.45.

39. The bulk of the wonders attributed to Pythagoras by Iamblichus concerns control over nature, but he is said to tame a bear that hurt people (*Life of Pythagoras*, 60) and to have turned away plagues (135). Tacitus (*History*, 4.81) cautiously relates how Vespasian "healed" a blind man and a lame man. The Talmud tells of two healings carried out through the prayers of Chanina ben Dosa (*bTBerakoth*, 34b). It must be remembered, however, that many testimonies are extant concerning the healing performed by the god Asclepius at his shrines.

40. Psalm 22:1 begins, "My God, My God, why have you forsaken me?" but includes lines of triumphant expectation: "I will utter praise in the vast assembly, I will fulfill my vows before those who fear him" (22:26); and, at the end, "And to him my soul shall live; my descendents shall serve him. Let the coming generations be told of the Lord that they may proclaim to a people yet to be born the justice he has shown" (22:30–32).

41. Woven into the bare facts of the account are details that are shaped directly and unmistakably from the words of the Psalms: Mark 15:23=Ps 69:21; Mark 15:24=Ps 22:18; Mark 15:29=Ps 22:7, 109:25; Mark 15:31=Ps 22:8; Mark 15:34=Ps 22:1; Mark 15:36=Ps 69:21.

42. Luke provides a fuller account of the same ascension in Acts 1:9–11; for discussion, see L. T. Johnson, *The Acts of the Apostles*, ed. D. J. Harrington (Sacra Pagina 5; Collegeville, MN: Liturgical, 1992), 23–32. On ascension as the confirmation of divine power, see, e.g., the accounts of the ascension of Romulus in Livy, *History of Rome*, 1.16; Ovid, *Fasti*, 2.481–509; and *Metamorphoses*, 14.805–851; and of the apotheosis of Herakles, Diodorous Siculus, *Library of History*, 4.38.3–5; 39.1–2.

43. On this theme, see especially S. R. Garrett, *The Demise of the Devil: Magic and the Demonic in Luke's Writings* (Minneapolis: Fortress, 1989).

44. On the whole range of incidents in Acts that resemble those in novels, see R. I. Pervo, *Profit with Delight: The Literary Genre of the Acts of the Apostles* (Philadelphia: Fortress, 1987). On prison escapes and Greco-Roman parallels, see J. B. Weaver, *Plots of Epiphany: Prison-Escapes in the Acts of the Apostles* (Beihefte zur Zeitschrift für die neutestamentliche Wissenschaft 131; Berlin: deGruyter, 2004).

45. The entire account has the strongest resemblance to the charming story in Ovid's *Metamorphoses*, 8.611–724, in which Zeus and Hermes are provided hospitality in Phrygia by Baucis and Philemon; see Johnson, *Acts of the Apostles*, 245–252.

46. For repentance, see Mark 1:15; 6:12; Matt 3:2; 4:17; 11:20–21; 12:41; Luke 10:13; 11:32; 13:3, 5; 15:7, 10; 16:30; 17:3; Acts 2:38; 3:19; 8:22; 17:30; 26:20. For indisputable *moral* instruction, see Matt 5:3–48; 6:19–34; 7:1–6, 12–23; 10:24–33; 18:1–18; 22:34–40; 25:14––46; Luke 6:20–49; 10:25–37; 12:13–48; 14:7–24; 16:1–18; 18:1–30; 19:11–27; 22:24–30. The amount is not insignificant, but it is dwarfed by the amount of material dedicated to showing Jesus as bringer of benefits. The striking lack of moral instruction in Acts should also be noted.

47. Peter and John, in fact, echo the words of Socrates when they declare before the Sanhedrin, "You judge whether it is righteous before God to obey you rather than to obey God" (Acts 4:19); see Plato, *Apology*, 29D: "I shall obey God rather than you, and while I have life and strength I shall never cease from the practice and teaching of philosophy." The description of the believers holding everything in common (*panta koina*), in turn, echoes the Hellenistic language about friendship (as in Aristotle, *Nicomachean Ethics*, 1168B; *Politics*, 1263A), which shapes utopian visions of the perfect philosophical community; see Plato, *Critias*, 110C–D; *Republic*, 420C–422B; 462B–464A; Iamblichus, *Life of Pythagoras*, 29–30; Porphyry, *Life of Pythagoras*, 20; Josephus, *Jewish War*, 2.122–127; Philo, *Every Good Man Is Free*, 77, 79, 84–85.

48. As I observed in the previous chapter, Acts is a partial exception to this, in that it represents the Roman order as providing a providential framework of security for the Christian movement.

49. For the designation "man from heaven," see W. A. Meeks, "The Man from Heaven in Johannine Sectarianism," *Journal of Biblical Literature* 91 (1972): 44–72.

50. The differences are enumerated in Johnson, *The Writings of the New Testament*, 528–532.

51. See, e.g., C. H. Dodd, *The Bible and the Greeks* (London: Houghton and Stodder, 1935) and *The Interpretation of the Fourth Gospel* (Cambridge: Cambridge University

Press, 1968); and the comments of R. E. Brown, *The Gospel According to John*, 2 vols. (Anchor Bible 29A–B; Garden City, NY: Doubleday, 1966), lvi–lix.

52. The approach is exemplified most notably by R. Bultmann, *The Gospel of John: A Commentary*, trans. G. Beasley-Murray, R. W. N. Hoare, and J. K. Riches (Philadelphia: Westminster, 1971 [1966]).

53. See Brown, *The Gospel according to John*, xli–xlii, lix–lxiv.

54. The limits of the approach were noted already by C. H. Kraeling, "The Fourth Gospel and Contemporary Religious Thought," *Journal of Biblical Literature* 49 (1930): 140–149; see also E. M. Yamauchi, *Pre-Christian Gnosticism: A Survey of the Proposed Evidence* (Grand Rapids, MI: Eerdmans, 1973); and the comments in Brown, *The Gospel according to John*, liii–lv.

55. See, e.g., E. H. Pagels, *The Johannine Gospel in Gnostic Exegesis: Heracleon's Commentary on John* (Nashville: Abingdon, 1973).

56. For light (*phōs*) and darkness (*skotia*), see John 1:4, 5, 7, 8, 9; 3:19, 20, 21; 5:33; 6:17; 8:12; 9:5; 11:9–10; 12:35–36, 46. For flesh (*sarx*) and spirit (*pneuma*), see John 1:13–14, 32–33; 3:5–6, 8, 34; 4:23–24; 6:51, 52, 53, 54, 55, 56, 63; 7:39; 8:15; 14:17, 26; 16:13; 17:2; 19:30; 20:22. For truth (*alētheia*) and lying (*pseustēs*), see 1:14, 17; 3:21; 4:23–24; 5:33; 6:33; 8:32, 40, 44–46, 55; 14:6, 17; 15:26; 16:7, 13; 17:17, 19; 18:37–38. For life (*zoē*) and death (*thanatos*), see 1:4; 3:15–16, 36; 4:14, 36; 5:24, 26, 29, 39–40; 6:27, 33, 35, 40, 47–48, 51, 53, 54, 63, 68; 8:12, 51–52; 10:10, 28; 11:4, 13, 25; 12:25, 33, 50; 14:6; 17:2–3; 18:32; 20:31; 21:19.

57. See Bultmann, *The Gospel of John*, 342–358, and *the Theology of the New Testament*, 2 vols., trans. K. Grobel (New York: Charles Scribner's Sons, 1951, 1955), 2:43.

58. Bultmann, *The Gospel of John*, 62–63.

59. The use of *doxa* in John (as in 1:14; 2:11; 5:41, 44; 7:18; 8:50, 54; 9:24; 11:4, 40; 12:41, 43; 17:5, 22, 24) resembles that in the LXX (as in Ex 16:7, 10; 24:16; 40:34–35; Lev 9:6; Ps 18:1; Isa 6:1, 3).

60. The Greek of LXX Exodus 34:6 is *kyrios ho theos oiktirmōn kai eleēmōn, makrothymos kai polyeleos kai alēthinos*; for the argument that John alludes to this passage, see L. J. Kuyper, "Grace and Truth: An Old Testament Description of God and Its Use in the Johannine Gospel," *Interpretation* 18 (1964): 3–19.

61. I accept the harder reading in 1:18 (*monogenēs theos*); for discussion, see Brown, *The Gospel According to John*, 1:17.

62. The statement points to something greater, not the nullification of the first by the second. The gift that comes from Jesus Christ is greater than the law but does not obliterate the fact that the law was a gift. The point is that Jesus' revelation is continuous with the way God has earlier given benefits in the empirical realm; it does not rescue humans from the empirical realm because it is devoid of divine benefits.

63. See L. Bieler, *Theios Anēr: das Bild des "göttlichen Menschen" in Spätantike und Frühchristentum* (Wien: O. Höfels, 1935).

64. Some of the *ego eimi* statements take the form of metaphors (see 6:35, 48; 8:12; 9:5; 10:5, 11; 11:25; 14:6; 15:1); others appear absolutely (4:26; 6:20; 8:28, 58; 18:5–6), and

seem to echo the *ego eimi* of God's self-identification in Torah (Exod 3:14; Isa 41:4; 43:10); see D. M. Ball, *"'I Am' in John's Gospel: Literary Function, Background, and Theological Implications* (Journal for the Study of the New Testament Supplement Series 124; Sheffield: Sheffield Academic Press, 1996).

65. Pausanius, *Description of Greece*, 6.26.1, reports a tradition concerning a miraculous supply of wine made possible by the god at the feast of Dionysus.

66. The designation is Brown's (*The Gospel According to John*, 1:cxxxviii–cxxxxix): "to those who accept him, Jesus shows his glory by returning to the Father in the 'hour' of his crucifixion, resurrection, and ascension. Fully glorified, he communicates the Spirit of life."

67. John alludes to LXX Zechariah 12:10 in 19:37: "They shall look on him whom they have pierced." The context of Zechariah suggests that John points to the outpouring of the Holy Spirit and not simply to Jesus' final breath: "I will pour out on the house of David and on the inhabitants of Jerusalem a spirit of grace and petition, and they shall look on him whom they have thrust through and shall mourn for him as one grieves over a first-born." Compare John 7:37–39: "On the last and greatest day of the feast, Jesus stood up and cried out, 'If anyone thirsts, let him come to me. Let him drink who believes in me.' As scripture has it, 'From within him rivers of living water shall flow.' Here he was referring to the Spirit, whom those that came to believe in him were to receive. There was as yet no spirit since Jesus had not yet been glorified."

11. NEW TESTAMENT CHRISTIANITY AS MORAL TRANSFORMATION

1. See especially W. A. Meeks, *The Origins of Christian Morality: The First Two Centuries* (New Haven, CT: Yale University Press, 1993).

2. Of fundamental importance for reading Paul in the context of Greco-Roman moral philosophy is the work of A. J. Malherbe, as in "Hellenistic Moralists and the New Testament," ANRW II.26.1 (1992): 267–333; and *Paul and the Popular Philosophers* (Minneapolis: Fortress, 1989).

The similarities between Epictetus and Paul have long been noted and go beyond the fact that both are in some sense slaves (by law or by self-designation), have physical disabilities (Epictetus' lameness and Paul's *astheneia* [Gal 4:13] and *skolops te sarki* [2 Cor 12:7]), and employ the dialogical teaching style of the diatribe (see R. Bultmann, *Der Stil der paulinischen Predigt und die Kynischstoische Diatribe* (Forschungen zur Religion und Literatur des Alten und Neuen Testaments; Göttingen: Vandenhoeck und Ruprecht, 1910). These similarities range across a variety of perceptions (see A. Bonhöffer, *Epiktet und das Neue Testament* [Religionsgeschichtliche Versuche und Vorarbeiten 10; Giessen: A. Töpelmann, 1911]; and D. S. Sharp, *Epictetus and the New Testament* [London: Charles H. Kelly, 1914]), including an understanding of the philosopher's role as a divine vocation; see M. D. McGehee, *Divine Appointment to Social Functions in Four Greco-Roman Traditions: Paul, Epictetus, Cynics, and Qumran* (Ann Arbor, MI: University Microfilms International, 1986).

3. The recognition of Paul as a *pneumatikos* was one of the great breakthroughs of the History of Religions school; see, e.g., H. Gunkel, *The Influence of the Holy Spirit: A View of the Apostolic Age and the Teaching of the Apostle Paul: A Biblical-Theological Study*, trans. R. A. Harrisville and P. A. Quanbeck II (Philadelphia: Fortress, 1979 [1888]), 3, 75, 77, 92; R. Reitzenstein, *Hellenistic Mystery Religions: Their Basic Ideas and Significance*, trans. J. E. Steely (Pittsburgh: Pickwick, 1978 [1926]), 426–500; O. Pfleiderer, *Christian Origins*, trans. D. A. Huebsch (New York: B. W. Huebsch, 1906), 170–171.

4. When Paul speaks of being set apart "from my mother's womb" (Gal 1:15), he alludes to the call of the prophet Jeremiah: "Before I formed you in the womb I knew you, before you were born I dedicated you, a prophet to the nations I appointed you. . . . This day I set you over nations and over kingdoms, to root up and to tear down, to destroy and to demolish, to build and to plant" (Jer 1:5–10). He refers as well to the call of the servant in Isaiah: "For now the Lord has spoken, who formed me as his servant from the womb" (Isa 49:5).

5. For the most thorough examination of 2 Cor 12:1–10, especially in the context of other Pauline religious experiences, see J. B. Wallace, *Snatched into Paradise (2 Corinthians 12:1–10): Paul's Heavenly Journey in the Context of Early Christian Experience* (PhD diss., Emory University, 2008).

6. See G. G. O'Collins, "Power Made Pefect in Weakness: II Cor 12:9–10," *Catholic Biblical Quarterly* 33 (1971): 528–537; A. E. Harvey, *Renewal through Suffering: A Study of 2 Corinthians* (Edinburgh: T. & T. Clark, 1996).

7. Paul's language of "perfection" echoes that used for the Mysteries; see Phil 1:6; 3:12; Gal 3:3; 2 Cor 8:6, 11; Rom 15:28; and R. S. Ascough, "The Completion of a Religious Duty: The Background of 2 Cor 8:1–15," *New Testament Studies* 42 (1996): 584–599.

8. See, e.g., the inscriptional evidence in R. MacMullen, *Paganism in the Roman Empire* (New Haven, CT: Yale University Press, 1981), 12–14, 146–148; and in E. Lupu, *Greek Sacred Law: A Collection of New Documents* (Religions in the Graeco-Roman World 152; Leiden: Brill, 2005).

9. Paul uses some form of "we know" (*oidamen*) with reference to shared tradition in Rom 2:2; 3:19; 5:3; 6:9; 7:14; 8:22, 28; 13:11; 1 Cor 8:1, 4; 12:2; 2 Cor 1:7; 4:14; 5:1, 6, 11, 16; Gal 2:16; 4:13; Eph 6:6, 9; Col 3:24; 4:1; 1 Thess 3:3; 4:2, 4; 5:2; 1 Tim 1:8, 9). He rebukes the lack of such awareness with the phrase "do you not know" (*ouk oidate*) in Rom 6:16; 11:2; 1 Cor 3:16; 5:6; 6:2, 3, 9, 15, 16, 19; 9:13, 24.

10. See, e.g., Paul's use of *dokimazein* ("testing") in Rom 2:18; 12:2; 14:22; 1 Cor 11:28; 2 Cor 8:8; 13:5; Gal 6:4; Eph 5:10; Phil 1:10; 1 Thess 5:21; and of *krinein/anakrinein/diakrinein* ("judging/discerning") in Rom 14:13, 23; 1 Cor 2:14, 15; 4:4; 5:12; 7:37; 10:15, 25, 27; 11:13, 29, 31; 14:24.

11. For this argument, see L. T. Johnson, "Transformation of the Mind and Moral Discernment in Paul," in *Early Christianity and Classical Culture: Studies in Honor of A. J. Malherbe*, ed. J. T. Fitzgerald, Thomas H. Olbricht, and L. White (Supplements to Novum Testamentum 110; Leiden: Brill, 2003), 215–236.

12. On this, see especially R. B. Hays, *The Faith of Jesus: The Narrative Substructure of Pauline Theology* (Society of Biblical Literature Dissertation Series 56; Chico, CA: Scholars, 1983).

13. See in particular W. S. Kurz, "Kenotic Imitation of Paul and Christ in Phil. 2 and 3," in *Discipleship in the New Testament*, ed. F. Segovia (Philadelphia: Fortress, 1985), 103–126.

14. Note the use of conditional clauses in Col 2:20 and 3:1: the prodosis is their experience, and the apodosis is the moral action.

15. See L. T. Johnson, "The Social World of James: Literary Analysis and Historical Reconstruction," in *Brother of Jesus, Friend of God: Studies in the Letter of James* (Grand Rapids, MI: Eerdmans, 2004), 101–122.

16. L. T. Johnson, *The Letter of James: A New Translation with Introduction and Commentary* (Anchor Bible 37A; New York: Doubleday, 1995), 58–65. A considerable amount of the history of critical scholarship on James has consisted in placing him in opposition to Paul, particularly on the matter of "faith and works"; for elements of this history, see Johnson, *The Letter of James*, 140–156.

17. More precisely, Paul tends to think through the implications of the death and exaltation of Jesus, whereas James, while recognizing Jesus as Lord (1:1; 2:1), tends to use Jesus' sayings in his own teaching; see L. T. Johnson and W. Wachob, "The Saying of Jesus in the Letter of James," in *Brother of Jesus, Friend of God*, 136–154.

18. For the fundamental agreement of Paul and James on the point of living out profession through *erga* ("works"/"deeds"), see Johnson, *The Letter of James*, 58–65, 236–252.

19. See, e.g., James 1:2, 3, 6, 7, 13, 16, 19, 22, 23, 24, 25, 26; 2:20; 3:1; 4:4, 5, 14, 17; 5:20.

20. James's language about "the world" (*kosmos*) expresses not a cosmological but an axiological dualism: it defines a measurement of reality that excludes God; see L. T. Johnson, "Friendship with the World and Friendship with God: A Study of Discipleship in James," in *Brother of Jesus, Friend of God*, 202–220. The phrase "visiting orphans and widows" echoes the call of the prophets to a covenantal fidelity that is expressed not alone by cultic concern but above all by moral concern; see Amos 2:6–8; 3:2; Hos 12:8–9; Mic 3:1–4; Zeph 1:9; Zech 7:8–10; Mal 3:5; Isa 3:5, 14–15; 5:7–10; Jer 22:3.

21. For the way in which religious practice is rendered as moral practice in James 5:12–20, see J. R. Strange, *The Moral World of James* (PhD diss., Emory University, 2007).

22. On Hebrews as deliberative rhetoric, see L. T. Johnson, *Hebrews: A Commentary* (The New Testament Library; Louisville: Westminster John Knox, 2006), 81–85.

    For a reading of Hebrews as epideictic rhetoric, see H. W. Attridge, *The Epistle to the Hebrews: A Commentary on the Epistle to the Hebrews* (Hermeneia; Philadelphia: Fortress, 1989), 14.

    On the Christology of Hebrews, see L. D. Hurst, "The Christology of Hebrews 1 and 2," in *The Glory of Christ in the New Testament*, ed. L. D. Hurst and N. T. Wright (New York: Clarendon, 1987), 151–164; A. Vanhoye, *Situation du Christ: Épître aux Hébreux 1 et 2* (Lectio Divina 58; Paris: Editions du Cerf, 1969).

    On Christ as the great high priest who makes intercession, see N. A. Dahl, "A New and Living Way: The Approach to God according to Hebrews 10:19–25,"

Interpretation 5 (1951): 401–412; A. Cody, O.S.B., *Heavenly Sanctuary and Liturgy in the Epistle to the Hebrews* (St. Meinrad, IN: Grail, 1960); G. W. MacRae, "Heavenly Temple and Eschatology in the Letter to the Hebrews," *Semeia* 12 (1978): 179–199.

23. The "enlightenment" here and in 10:32 in all likelihood refers to the experience of baptism (see the use of *baptisma* in 6:2 immediately preceding); see Johnson, *Hebrews*, 160–164.

24. On this, see the discussion in J. W. Thompson, *The Beginnings of Christian Philosophy: The Epistle to the Hebrews* (Catholic Biblical Quarterly Monograph Series 13; Washington, DC: Catholic Biblical Association of America, 1982).

25. The characterization is that of M. Dibelius and H. Conzelmann, *The Pastoral Epistles*, ed. H. Koester, trans. P. Buttolph and A. Yarbro (Hermeneia; Philadelphia: Fortress, 1972), 8.

26. See, e.g., H. von Campenhausen, *Ecclesiastical Authority and Spiritual Power in the Church of the First Three Centuries*, trans. J. Baker (Stanford, CA: Stanford University Press, 1969), 107–120; and more mildly, M. Y. MacDonald, *The Pauline Churches: A Socio-Historical Study of Institutionalization in the Pauline and Deutero-Pauline Writings* (Society for New Testament Studies Monograph Series; Cambridge: Cambridge University Press, 1988), 159–238. In Chapter 15, we will see how different "church orders" are from these brief circumstantial letters. On the authorship of these letters, see L. T. Johnson, *The First and Second Letters to Timothy: A New Translation with Introduction and Commentary* (Anchor Bible 35A; New York: Doubleday, 2001) 81–99.

12. CHRISTIANITY IN THE SECOND AND THIRD CENTURIES

1. For the very scanty archaeological evidence before the time of Constantine, see G. F. Snyder, *Ante Pacem: Archaeological Evidence of Church Life before Constantine*, rev. ed. (Macon, GA: Mercer University Press, 2003). For the location of Christian communities in the second and third centuries, see C. Mohrmann and F. van der Meer, *Atlas of the Early Christian World*, trans. and ed. M. F. Hedlund and H. H. Rowley (London: Nelson, 1958), 3–4.

2. The point is made emphatically and thoroughly by R. MacMullen, *Christianizing the Roman Empire* (New Haven, CT: Yale University Press, 1984).

3. For studies that place an emphasis on cognitive factors in the conversion of individuals to Christianity, see A. von Harnack, *The Mission and Expansion of Christianity in the First Three Centuries*, 2nd enl. ed., trans. and ed. J. Moffatt (New York: G. P. Putnam, 1908); and A. D. Nock, *Conversion: The Old and New in Religion from Alexander the Great to Augustine of Hippo* (Baltimore: Johns Hopkins University Press, 1998 [1933]).

4. A more sociologically nuanced view of expansion through childbirth and social networks was developed by R. Stark in *The Rise of Christianity: A Sociologist Reconsiders History* (Princeton, NJ: Princeton University Press, 1996) and found substantial

archaeological support in the research of P. Harland, *Associations, Synagogues, and Congregations: Claiming a Place in Ancient Mediterranean Society* (Minneapolis: Fortress, 2003). For a successful application of the theory to the earliest stages, see K. Munoz, *On How Not to Go out of the World* (PhD diss., Emory University, 2008).

5. See, e.g., G. Lüdemann, "The Successors of Pre-70 Jerusalem Christianity: A Critical Evaluation of the Pella Tradition," in *Jewish and Christian Self-Definition*, vol. 1., ed. E. P. Sanders (Philadelphia: Fortress, 1980), 161–173; G. Strecker, "On the Problem of Jewish Christianity," appendix 1 in W. Bauer, *Orthodoxy and Heresy in Earliest Christianity*, trans. and ed. R. Kraft and G. Krodel (Philadelphia: Fortress, 1971 [1934]), 241–285; J. Munck, "Jewish Christianity in Post-Apostolic Times," *New Testament Studies* 6 (1959–1960): 103–116.

6. Thus, the *Epistle of Barnabas* (early second century) makes a sustained argument that "the covenant is not both theirs and ours. It is ours" (4:6–7; see also 13:1), and scripture must therefore be read in light of Christ, not in the manner of the Jews, lest "we should be shipwrecked by conversion to their law" (3:6).

7. The *Protevangelium of James*, e.g., is full of "local color" that has little connection with historical realities: it refers to "The Histories of the Twelve Tribes of Israel" (1.1), a "record book of the twelve tribes of the people" (3.1), and vaguely to "the great day of the Lord" (1.2; 2.2); Mary dances on the steps of the altar in the Jerusalem temple (7.3), and a council of priests is summoned to solve the problem posed by Mary's menarche (8.2).

Justin's *Dialogue with Trypho* is an extended debate between the Christian philosopher and "a Hebrew of the circumcision [who] having escaped from the war lately carried on there [was] spending [his] days in Greece" (*Dial*, 1). The war in question is the Bar Kochba revolt (135 CE), and the location of the debate, which ranges widely over issues of belief and scriptural interpretation, is Ephesus. That the Trypho of Justin's dialogue is a fictional construction is certain, but Justin has him voice Jewish concerns with considerable plausibility; the encounter, however fictionalized, is certainly closer to reality than any subsequent contact. See T. J. Horner, *Listening to Trypho: Justin Martyr's Dialogue with Trypho Reconsidered* (Leuven: Peeters, 2001); C. D. Allert, *Revelation, Truth, Canon, and Interpretation: Studies in Justin Martyr's Dialogue with Trypho* (Supplements to Vigiliae Christianae 64; Leiden: Brill, 2002).

In his letters, Ignatius speaks of Judaism as something completely distinct from Christianity: "It is monstrous (*atopon*) to talk of Jesus Christ and to practice Judaism. For Christianity did not base its faith in Judaism, but Judaism in Christianity" (Ign. *Magn.* 10.3; see also 8.1; 9.1); and again, "if anyone interpret Judaism to you do not listen to him; for it is better to hear Christianity from the circumcised than Judaism from the uncircumcised" (Ign. *Phil.* 6.1). The *Martyrdom of Polycarp* speaks of "Gentiles and Jews" (*ethnōn kai iudaiōn*) as groups distinct from Christians (12.2) and consistently blames the Jews for pressing the state's attack on Christians (13.1; 17.2; 18.1).

8. For the household, see L. M White, *Building God's House in the Roman World: Architectural Adaptation among Pagans, Jews, and Christians* (American Schools of Oriental

Research; Baltimore: Johns Hopkins University Press, 1990); and C. Osiek and D. L. Balch, *Families in the New Testament World: Households and House Churches* (Louisville, KY: Westminster John Knox, 1997). For synagogue, see J. T. Burtchaell, *From Synagogue to Church: Public Services and Offices in the Earliest Christian Communities* (Cambridge: Cambridge University Press, 1992).

9. See the discussion in L. T. Johnson, *The First and Second Letters to Timothy: A New Translation with Introduction and Commentary* (Anchor Bible 35A; New York: Doubleday, 2001), 74–76, 217–225.

10. Already in *First Clement* (ca. 95), we find local leadership connected to the Apostles and to Christ in a line of succession (42), and in the letters of Ignatius of Antioch (ca. 110), there is an elaborate theological support for the hierarchy (see, e.g., Ign. *Rom.* 2.1; 4.1–2; 5.2; 6.1; Ign. *Magn.* 2.1; 4.1; 7.1–2; Ign. *Tral.* 2.1–3; 3.1). The statement in Ign. *Magn.* 6.1 is one among many: "be zealous to do all things in harmony with God, with the bishop presiding in the place of God and the presbyters in the place of the council of the apostles, and the deacons, who are most dear to me, entrusted with the service of Jesus Christ, who was from eternity with the Father and was made manifest at the end of time."

11. See the lists of bishops carefully noted by Eusebius in Rome, Alexandria, Antioch, and Jerusalem (*Historia Ecclesiastica* 4.1.1; 4.4.1; 4.19–20; 5.6.1–5; 5.9; 5.12; 5.22; 6.10; 6.21.1–2; 6.27; 6.29; 6.35; 7.2; 7.14; 7.28).

12. Eusebius, *Historia Ecclesiastica* 5.23–25; I will discuss this further in Chapter 15.

13. Ibid., 5.14–18.

14. I will take up this difficult and important phenomenon in Chapter 14. For preliminary discussion, see the essays in A. Marjanen, ed., *Was There a Gnostic Religion?* (Publications of the Finnish Exegetical Society 87; Göttingen: Vandenhoeck & Ruprecht, 2005).

15. These charges, some of which continue attacks made earlier on Jews, are rebutted by a remarkable series of Christian apologists in the second and third centuries: the author of *The Epistle to Diognetus*; Aristides of Athens; Justin Martyr, originally from Samaria; Tatian of Assyria; Athenagoras of Athens; Theophilus of Antioch; the North Africans Minucius Felix and Tertullian; and Origen of Alexandria. I surveyed the use of demonic language for paganism in such authors in Chapter 1, and I will return to a consideration of some of these authors when I analyze the Christian expression of Religiousness B in Chapter 13.

16. Eusebius, *Historia Ecclesiastica* 2.25.1–8 (Nero, ca. 64); 3.17–19 (Domitian, ca. 96); 3.32–33 (Trajan, 112).

17. Eusebius, *Historia Ecclesiastica* 5.1–2 (Marcus Aurelius 177); 6.1 (Septimus Severus, 193–211); 6.28 (Maximin, ca. 235); 6.39–42 (Decius, 250); 7.10 (Valerian, 257); 8.1–3 (Diocletian, 303–310).

18. See especially W. H. C. Frend, *Martyrdom and Persecution in the Early Church: A Study of a Conflict from the Maccabees to Donatus* (Oxford: Blackwell, 1965).

19. As noted before, the "magical" is always present at the edges of the "participation in divine benefits" sensibility; see H. D. Betz, *The Greek Magical Papyri in Translation*,

Including the Demotic Spells, 2nd ed. (Chicago: University of Chicago Press, 1992); and M. Meyer and R. Smith, *Ancient Christian Magic: Coptic Texts of Ritual Power* (San Francisco: HarperSanFrancisco, 1994).

20. L. T. Johnson, *The Acts of the Apostles*, ed. D. J. Harrington (Sacra Pagina 5; Collegeville, MN: Liturgical, 1992). On the relationship between the Acts of the Apostles and Greco-Roman novels, see R. I. Pervo, *Profit with Delight* (Philadelphia: Fortress, 1987).

21. My discussion of these compositions uses the edition and translation as well as the tentative dates provided by J. K. Elliott, *The Apocryphal New Testament: A Collection of Apocryphal Christian Literature in an English Translation* (Oxford: Clarendon, 1993); I leave aside the *Pseudo-Clementine Literature* not only because its tangled compositional history makes dating difficult but because it does not share in an equal degree the features I here describe. For discussion, see F. S. Jones, "The Pseudo-Clementines: A History of Research," *Second Century* 2 (1982): 1–33, 63–96.

22. The Greek novels can be found in translation in B. P. Reardon, ed., *Collected Ancient Greek Novels* (Berkeley: University of California Press, 1989); for the resemblance between such novels and the Christian *Acts*, see C. M. Thomas, *The Acts of Peter, Gospel Literature, and the Ancient Novel: Rewriting the Past* (New York: Oxford University Press, 2003).

23. For travel by land and sea, see *Acts of Andrew* (AA) 1; *Acts of John* (AJ) 18, 37, 56, 58, 62; *Acts of Paul* (AP) 1, 2, 3.1–3, 4, 6, 7, 8, 9, 10; *Acts of Peter* (Pet) 5, 6, 7; *Acts of Thomas* (AT) 3, 16, 68. For separation and reuniting of friends and lovers, see, e.g., AA 14; AP 3.40. For emotional infatuation, see AA 8, 14, 23; AP 3.7.7; AT 8, 16. For concern for social position, see, e.g., AA 1, 13, 17; AJ 18, 19, 36, 56, 73; AP 3.10; 3.13; 3.26; 3.28; 3.36; Pet 8, 17, 23, 30; AT 4, 18, 26, 62, 82. As regards forces opposing the heroes and heroines, in the novels, these would typically be parents, rulers, or brigands who separate the lovers; in the apocryphal acts, opposition tends to arise from husbands who resent the desire of wives to follow an apostle (AA 22–23, 26, 31, 36; AJ 63–65; AP 3.11–14; AT 16, 21, 89–106, 125, 138). For imprisonment and escape from prison, see AA 27, 29–30, 47; AP 3.18, 7, 11.31; AT 21, 107, 119, 143, 154, 159. For changing clothing as disguise, see, e.g., AA 28; AP 3.40. In the Hellenistic novels, virginity is prized and threatened as part of the social value of the woman; in the apocryphal acts, it is preserved or won as a sign of commitment to the message and person of the apostle; see AA 13–19, 37; AJ 63–73, 113; AP 3.7–9; Pet a, b, 34; AT 11–-13, 28, 43–44, 51–52, 126. On fascination with animals, in AJ there are bugs (60–61) and a partridge (56); in AP, there are lions (3.34, 7.16); in Pet, there are a dog (9) and fish (13); in AT, there are a serpent (30–33), a colt (39–40), and wild asses (68–70, 74, 80–81).

24. As in AA 11, 33, 40, 42, 56–58; AJ 34–36, 68; AP 3.5–6, 3.17; Pet 2.

25. Emphasis on hope for a future life in contrast to present pleasure is especially found in AT 12, 19–20, 36–37, 124, 139, and 160. Cosmological dualism is found perhaps most notably in AA 38, 61.

26. Thomas appears as an apostle only in the fourth Gospel; see also narratives devoted to figures such as Pilate, Joseph of Arimathea, Philip, Bartholomew, and Barnabas. For AT, see A. F. J. Klijn, *The Acts of Thomas: Introduction, Text, and Commentary*,

2nd rev. ed. (Supplements to Novum Testamentum 108; Leiden: Brill, 2003); M. LaFargue, *Language and Gnosis: The Opening Scenes of the Acts of Thomas* (Harvard Dissertations in Religion 18; Philadelphia: Fortress, 1985).

27. For essays on the subject, see A.-J. Levine, ed., with M. M. Robbins, *A Feminist Companion to the New Testament Apocrypha* (New York: T. & T. Clark, 2006); see also S. L. Davies, *The Revolt of the Widows: The Social World of the Apocryphal Acts* (Carbondale: Southern Illinois University Press, 1980).

28. See *AT* 12, 28, 36, 58, 79, 83–86, 88.

29. See *AT* 12, 15–16, 19–20, 36–37, 124, 139, 160.

30. See R. D. Darling, "Notes on Divesting and Vesting in the Hymn of the Pearl," in *Reading Religions in the Ancient World: Essays Presented to Robert McQueen Grant on His 90th Birthday*, ed. D. E. Aune and R. D. Young (Leiden: Brill, 2007). On the Gnostic outlook, see A. A. Bevan, ed., *The Hymn of the Soul: Contained in the Syriac Acts of Thomas* (Cambridge: Cambridge University Press, 1897). The Gnostic character of the Hymn, read on its own, is fundamental to the reconstruction of the Gnostic worldview in H. Jonas, *The Gnostic Religion* (Boston: Beacon, 1958).

31. *AT* 1, 11, 27, 29, 118, 169.

32. *AT* 20, 52, 59, 140.

33. *AT* 23, 33, 53–54, 81.

34. See also the beatitudes in *AT* 94, which link future blessing with those that are realized in the present life, as in "Blessed are the bodies of the saints, because they were deemed worthy to become temples of God, that Christ might dwell in them."

35. For a short introduction to the problems, see Elliott, *The Apocryphal New Testament*, 231–244; I am using the translation of the Acts of Andrew provided by Elliott, pp. 245–267. For more on the textual issues and possible literary interconnections, see D. R. MacDonald, *The Acts of Andrew and the Acts of Andrew and Matthias in the City of the Cannibals* (Society of Biblical Literature, Texts and Translations 33; Atlanta: Scholars, 1990), and *Christianizing Homer: The Odyssey, Plato, and the Acts of Andrew* (New York: Oxford University Press, 1994). For other issues, see the collection of essays in J. N. Bremmer, *The Apocryphal Acts of Andrew* (Leuven: Peeters, 2000).

36. The later *Epitome* of Gregory of Tours expands both the travels of the apostle and his wondrous deeds, reporting some 27 separate wonders and explicitly connecting them to the process of conversion.

37. See the discussion in Elliott, *The Apocryphal New Testament*, 303–310. The numbering in Elliott begins at 18 because the first 17 paragraphs are not considered original. Paragraph 18 brings John from Miletus to Ephesus for a lengthy stay (19–36). After a long gap, the story picks up in 87–105 with a discourse on the nature of Christ and a hymn of Christ. Then, paragraphs 37–55 report the end of John's stay in Ephesus, paragraphs 58–61 return him to Ephesus, and the text then concludes with a reconstruction of 62–86 and 106–115 reporting John's second stay in Ephesus. For further discussion of these issues, see A.-J. Festugière, *Les Actes de Jean et de Thomas: Traduction française et notes critiques* (Cahiers d'Orientalisme 6; Genève: P. Cramer,

1983); and E. Junot and J.-D. Kaestli, *Acta Johannis* (Corpus Christianorum Series Apocryphorum 1–2; Turnhout: Brepols, 1983).

38. See the helpful essays in J. N. Bremmer, ed., *The Apocryphal Acts of John* (Kampen, The Netherlands: Kok Pharos, 1995). On the dance song, see, e.g., G. Sirker-Wicklaus, *Untersuchungen zu den Johannes-Akten: untersuchungen zur Struktur, zur theologischen Tendenz und zum kirchengeschichtlichen Hintergrund der Acta Johannis* (Beiträge zur Religionscgeschichte 2; Bonn: Wehle, 1988); P. G. Schneider, *The Mystery of the Acts of John: An Interpretation of the Hymn and the Dance in Light of the Acts' Theology* (PhD diss., 2006); P. J. Lallemann, *The Acts of John: A Two-Stage Initiation into Johannine Gnosticism* (Studies on the Apocryphal Acts of the Apostles 4; Leuven: Peeters, 1998).

39. See *AJ* 22–24, 47, 52, 75, 80, 83.

40. The first two episodes (a, b) are found in distinct manuscripts. The main portion of the text (1–29) is found in the Latin Vercelli manuscript, and the martyrdom (30–40) is found in the Vercelli and a single Greek manuscript (Athos). See Elliott, *The Apocryphal New Testament*, 390–396.

41. For healings, see *Pet* a, 20, 31; for the exorcism, 11; for visions, a, 5, 6, 14, 17, 20, 21, 22, 40; for resuscitations, b, 25, 27, 28.

42. For the critical issues, see Eliott, *The Apocryphal New Testament*, 350–363; D. R. MacDonald, *The Legend and the Apostle: The Battle for Paul in Story and Canon* (Philadelphia: Fortress, 1983); and W. Rordorf, "Tradition and Composition in the *Acts of Thecla*: The State of the Question," in *The Apocryphal Acts of the Apostles*, ed. D. R. MacDonald (*Semeia* 38; Decatur, GA: Scholars, 1986), 43–52.

43. See D. R. MacDonald and A. D. Scrimgeour, "Pseudo-Chrysostom's Panegyric to Thecla: The Heroine of the *Acts of Paul* in Homily and Art," in *The Apocryphal Acts of the Apostles*, ed. D. R. MacDonald, 151–159. See also the fourth-century witness in *Egeria: Diary of a Pilgrimage*, 22–23, translated and annotated by G. E. Gingras (Ancient Christian Writers 38; New York: Newman, 1970), 86–87.

44. Paul's opening sermon to the household of Onesiphorus in Iconium ("the word of God about abstinence and the resurrection") consists of a series of 13 beatitudes that bear some resemblance to those attributed to Jesus in the Gospels of Matthew and Luke but that have their own distinctive character.

45. Likewise, the pure in heart are blessed because they shall see God, those who have kept the flesh chaste shall become a temple of God, the continent shall have God speak with them, and those who have kept aloof from the world shall be pleasing to God (*AP* 3.5). Paul is further reported as saying, "one must fear only one God and live chastely" (3.9). See E. M. Howe, "Interpretations of Paul in the Acts of Paul and Thecla," in *Pauline Studies*, ed. D. A. Hagner and M. J. Harris (Grand Rapids, MI: Eerdmans, 1980), 33–49.

46. By "compositional complexity" here I mean above all the inclusion of substantial blocks of teaching material, particularly in Matthew and Luke.

47. Within this category are the compositions we know about only from allusions in patristic writers and a handful of citations: *The Gospel According to the Hebrews, The*

Gospel of the Nazareans, and *The Gospel of the Ebionites;* of another disposition—
perhaps Gnostic—is the *Gospel of the Egyptians;* see the discussion in Elliott, *The
Apocryphal New Testament,* 3–25; and A. F. J. Klijn, "Patristic Evidence for Jewish
Christian and Aramaic Gospel Tradition," in *Text and Interpretation,* ed. E. Best and
R. McL. Wilson (Cambridge: Cambridge University Press, 1979), 169–177. Only two
narrative elements have been reported. Jerome (*de Viris Illustribus,* 3.2) says that the
Gospel according to the Hebrews relates a separate resurrection appearance to James,
and in his commentary on Matthew 12:13, Jerome states that the Gospel used by the
Nazarenes and Ebionites provides the trade of the man with the withered hand
whom Jesus heals (Elliott, *The Apocryphal New Testament,* 9, 12).

48. See the discussions of these complex developments in Elliott, *The Apocryphal New
Testament,* 84–122, 148–228.

49. It is, for example, listed by Eusebius as a composition not accepted for reading in the
churches (*Historia Ecclesiastica,* 3.3.2 and 6.12).

50. The discovery of an additional papyrus fragment (P.Oxy. 2949) accomplished two
things: it secured a date before the early third century, and its variants complicated
the question of the original text.

51. See R. E. Brown, *"The Gospel of Peter* and Canonical Gospel Authority," *New Testament Studies* 33 (1987): 321–343. For the gospel of Peter as independent testimony of
the passion, see J. D. Crossan, *Four Other Gospels* (Minneapolis: Fortress, 1985), and
The Cross that Spoke (San Francisco: HarperSanFrancisco, 1988).

52. I follow the simpler mode of citation that uses only verse numbers. For "the Lord,"
see GP 1, 3, 6, 8, 10, 18, 21, 24, 35, 50; for "Son of God," see 6, 9, 46; for "savior of
men," see 13.

53. For the later infancy gospels extending into the medieval period, see Elliott, *The
Apocryphal New Testament,* 84–122.

54. See M. F. Foskett, *A Virgin Conceived: Mary and Classical Representations of Virginity* (Bloomington: Indiana University Press, 2002).

55. See Elliott, *The Apocryphal New Testament,* 68–75.

56. Actually, I am reading Greek A, which bears the title *The Account of Thomas the Israelite Concerning the Childhood of the Lord* (Elliott, *The Apocryphal New Testament,* 75–80).

57. Elliott, *The Apocryphal New Testament,* 68.

58. See F. E. Vokes, "The Opposition to Montanism from Church and State in the
Christian Empire," in *Studia Patristica* IX, ed. F. L. Cross (Texte und Untersuchungen 103; Berlin: Akademie-Verlag, 1960), 306–315. For problems of chronology, see T.
B. Barnes, "The Chronology of Montanism," *Journal of Theological Studies* n.s. 21
(1970): 403–408; G. S. P. Freeman-Grenville, "The Date of the Outbreak of Montanism," *Journal of Ecclesiastical History* 5 (1954): 7–15.

59. The significance of the movement can be estimated from the energy used to dispel it
and the attention given it by Eusebius in *Historia Ecclesiastica,* 5.14–21.

60. See C. Trevett, *Montanism: Gender, Authority, and the New Prophecy* (Cambridge:
Cambridge University Press, 1996).

61. See Acts 12:28; 15:32; 21:9–10. These are all explicitly designated as "prophets" by the narrator.

62. Jerome claims that Montanus had been, before his conversion to Christianity, a priest of Cybele (*Letter*, 41), and a recent monograph tries to make that connection; see V.-E. Hirschmann, *Horrenda Secta: Untersuchungen zum frühchristlichen Montanismus und seinen Verbindungen zur paganen Religion Phrygians* (Historia Einzelschriften 179; Stuttgart: Franz Steiner Verlag, 2005); see also J. G. C. Anderson, "Paganism and Christianity in the Upper Tembria Valley," in *Studies in the History and Art of the Eastern Provinces of the Roman Empire* (Aberdeen: Aberdeen University Press, 1906), 193–201; W. H. C. Frend, "Montanism: A Movement of Prophecy and Regional Identity in the Early Church," *Bulletin of the John Rylands Library* 70 (1988): 25–34.

63. See D. E. Groh, "Utterance and Exegesis: Biblical Interpretation in the Montanist Crisis," in *Living Text: Essays in Honor of Ernest W. Saunders*, ed. D. E. Groh and R. Jewett (Lanham, MD: University Press of America, 1985). The most notable adherent is the great North African controversialist Tertullian (155–220), who joined the Montanists around 215 and wrote several of his severely ascetical treatises from the sect's perspective; see J. Quasten, *Patrology*, 4 vols. (Westminster, MD: Christian Classics, 1986), 2: 246–317.

64. See R. E. Heine, *The Montanist Oracles and Testimonia* (Patristic Monograph Series 14; Macon, GA: Mercer University Press, 1989); and W. Tabbernee, *Montanist Inscriptions and Testimonia: Epigraphic Sources Illustrating the History of Montanism* (Patristic Monograph Series 16; Macon, GA: Mercer University Press, 1997).

65. I use the translation of Kirsopp Lake in *The Apostolic Fathers* (Loeb Classical Library; Cambridge, MA: Harvard University Press, 1915), 1:172–277. For Ignatius, see C. C. Richardson, *The Christianity of Ignatius of Antioch* (New York: Columbia University Press, 1935); V. Corwin, *St. Ignatius and Christianity in Antioch* (New Haven, CT: Yale University Press, 1960).

66. I again use the text and translation of *The Martyrdom of St. Polycarp, Bishop of Smyrna* as found in Lake, *The Apostolic Fathers*, 2:312–343.

67. As with Ignatius's reference to being grain in the mouth of beasts, the bread metaphor might well be a reference to the Eucharist.

68. The entire letter is preserved by Eusebius, *Historia Ecclesiastica*, 5.1.1–5.2.2. For Justin and his companions, see "The Martyrdom of the Holy Martyrs, Justin, Chariton, Charites, Paeon, and Liberianus, Who Suffered at Rome," trans. M. Dods, in *The Ante-Nicene Fathers*, 10 vols., ed. A. Roberts and J. Donaldson (Peabody, MA: Hendrickson, 1994 [1885]), 1:305–306. In addition to enunciating a version of the rule of faith, Justin affirms his expectation: "I hope that, if I endure these things, I shall have his gifts"; and "Through prayer we can be saved on account of our Lord Jesus Christ, even when we have been punished, because this shall become to us salvation and confidence at the more fearful and universal judgment-seat of our Lord and Savior" (4).

For the North African Scillitan Martyrs, see H. Musurillo, *The Acts of the Christian Martyrs* (Oxford: Oxford University Press, 1972), 86–89. This account comes the closest to a transcript of the hearing, with short questions and answers; the final declaration of the seven men and five women is "today we are martyrs in heaven; thanks be to God."

69. For text and translation, see Musurillo, *The Acts of the Christian Martyrs*, 106–131; it is possible that Tertullian was the editor of the *Acts* (see Quasten, *Patrology*, 1:181–182). See also R. D. Butler, *The New Prophecy and "New Visions": Evidence of Montanism in the Passion of Perpetua and Felicitas* (Patristic Monograph Series 18; Washington, DC: Catholic University of America Press, 2006); and J. E. Salisbury, *Perpetua's Passion: The Death and Memory of a Young Roman Woman* (London: Routledge, 1997).

70. I use the translation of J. J. O'Meara, *Origen: Prayer, Exhortation to Martyrdom* (Ancient Christian Writers 19; New York: Newman, 1954).

13. MORAL TRANSFORMATION IN SECOND- AND THIRD-CENTURY CHRISTIANITY

1. I follow the translation of K. Lake, *The Apostolic Fathers*, 2 vols. (Loeb Classical Library; Cambridge, MA: Harvard University Press, 1915), 8–121; for efforts to reconstruct the social setting, see J. S. Jeffers, *Social Foundations of Early Christianity at Rome: The Congregations behind 1 Clement and the Shepherd of Hermas* (PhD diss., University of California, Irvine, 1988); and D. G. Horrell, *The Social Ethos of the Corinthians Correspondence: Interests and Ideology from 1 Corinthians to 1 Clement* (Edinburgh: T. & T. Clark, 1996).

2. He sets out to speak of noble examples of those who contended as athletes "in our generation" before reciting the "contending unto death" of Peter and Paul (5.1–7). He contrasts the upstarts in Corinth, whom he addresses, to the situation when Paul wrote, when the rivals in Corinth were at least "partisans of apostles of high reputation and of a man approved by them" (47.4). See also his sketch of apostolic succession in 43.1–5. Speaking for "the church of God which sojourns at Rome," Clement unself-consciously assumes the prerogative of correcting the Corinthian church: "our attention has been somewhat delayed in turning to the question disputed among you" (1.1). Clement not only writes to the Corinthians but sends emissaries: "we have sent faithful and prudent men. . . . [T]hey shall be witnesses between you and us" (63.3).

3. See L. Sanders, *L'Hellénisme de Saint Clément de Rome et le Paulinisme* (Louvain: Studia Hellenistica in Bibliotheca Universitatis, 1943); and C. Breytenbach and L. L. Welborn, eds., *Encounters with Hellenism: Studies on the First Letter of Clement* (Arbeiten zur Geschichte des antiken Judentums und des Urchistentums 53; Leiden: Brill, 2004).

4. He quotes "the words of the Lord Jesus" in 13.2 and 46.8 and alludes to them in 24.5.

5. In 47.1–2, Clement speaks of "the epistle of the blessed Paul the Apostle," written "to you at the beginning of his preaching," clearly referring to the content of 1 Cor 1:10 (47.3). For the use of Hebrews, see D. Hagner, *The Use of the Old and New Testaments in Clement of Rome* (Supplements to Novum Testamentum 34; Leiden: Brill, 1973), 179–237; P. Ellingworth, "Hebrews and 1 Clement: Literary Dependence or Common Tradition?" *Biblische Zeitschrift* n.s. 23 (1979): 262–269. For the use of the Letter of James, see L. T. Johnson, *The Letter of James: A New Translation with Introduction and Commentary* (Anchor Bible 37A; New York: Doubleday, 1995), 72–75.

6. On this, see L. T. Johnson, "James 3:13–4:10 and the Topos *PERI PHTHONOU*," *Novum Testamentum* 25 (1983): 327–347.

7. See, e.g., *1 Clement*, 4, 7, 9–12, 17–18, 31–32, 45–46, 51.

8. See the discussion in J. Quasten, *Patrology*, 4 vols. (Westminster, MD: Christian Classics, 1986), 1:53–58.

9. I use the translation of Lake, *The Apostolic Fathers*, 1:280–301; for the question of literary integrity, see P. N. Harrison, *Polycarp's Two Epistles to the Philippians* (Cambridge: Cambridge University Press, 1936).

10. H. von Campenhausen, *Polycarp von Smyrna und die Pastoralbriefe* (Sitzungberichte der Heidelberger Akadamie der Wissenschaften; Heidelberg: Winter, 1951), suggested that the similarities between Polycarp and the letters to Paul's delegates (1 Timothy, 2 Timothy, Titus) are to be attributed to Polycarp's authorship of them all. For the implausibility of this position, see L. T. Johnson, *The First and Second Letters to Timothy: A New Translation with Introduction and Commentary* (Anchor Bible 35A; New York: Doubleday, 2001), 298–300. See also P. Hartog, *Polycarp and the New Testament: The Occasion, Rhetoric, Theme, and Unity of the Epistle to the Philippians and Its Allusions to New Testament Literature* (Tübingen: J. C. B. Mohr, 2002).

11. For allusions to Paul, see especially 3.3–5.3; 11.2–3. For allusions to 1 Peter, see 1.3; 2.1; 7.2; 8.1; 10.1–2. For references to the teachings of Jesus, see the following: "Remember what the Lord taught when he said, 'Judge not that ye be not judged, forgive and it shall be forgiven unto you, be merciful that you may obtain mercy, with what measure ye mete, it shall be measured to you again,' and 'Blessed are the poor, and they who are persecuted for righteousness' sake, for theirs is the kingdom of heaven'" (2.3). Similarly, Polycarp tells his readers to persevere in fasting, praying to God "to lead us not into temptation, even as the Lord said, 'the spirit is willing but the flesh is weak'" (7.2).

12. For a range of studies on Justin, see W. A. Shotwell, *The Biblical Exegesis of Justin Martyr* (London: SPCK, 1965); A. J. Bellinzoni, *The Sayings of Jesus in the Writings of Justin Martyr* (Supplements to Novum Testamentum 17; Leiden: Brill, 1967); P. J. Donahue, *Jewish-Christian Controversy in the Second Century: A Study in the Dialogue of Justin Martyr* (PhD diss., Yale University, 1973); D. Trakatellis, *The Pre-Existence of Christ in the Writings of Justin Martyr* (Harvard Dissertations in Religion 6; Missoula, MT: Scholars, 1976); D. Rokeah, *Justin Martyr and the Jews* (Jewish and Christian Perspectives 5; Boston: Brill, 2002).

13. For Justin's writings, I use the translation in *The Ante-Nicene Fathers*, 10 vols., ed. A. Roberts and J. Donaldson (Peabody, MA: Hendrickson, 1994 [1885]), 1:163–302.

14. In Philostratus, *Life of Apollonius of Tyana*, the young philosopher is exposed to rhetoric and to students of Platonism, Stoicism, Aristotelianism, and Epicureanism, even though he was devoted particularly to Pythagoras (1.7).

15. For the rhetorical connection between brevity and authority, see L. T. Johnson, "Taciturnity and True Religion (James 1:26–27)," in *Greeks, Romans, and Christians: Essays in Honor of Abraham J. Malherbe*, ed. D. L. Balch, E. Ferguson, and W. A. Meeks (Minneapolis: Fortress, 1990), 329–339.

16. In his second apology, Justin argues that Jesus can be compared to Socrates, but only favorably, as one who "through his own power" found and declared the very things about God that Socrates (as reported by Plato) said were difficult to find and declare; and whereas no one followed Socrates in dying for his teaching, those believing in Christ did, "not only philosophers and scholars . . . but also artisans and people entirely uneducated, despising both glory, and fear, and death; since he is a power of the ineffable Father, and not the mere instrument of human reason" (2.10).

17. See also 2.13: "Each man spoke well in proportion to the share he had in the spermatic word [*logos spermatikos*], seeing what was related to it." For the concept, see Quasten, *Patrology*, 1:207–211.

18. See the concluding section of the second apology: "Our doctrines are not shameful, according to a sober judgment, but are indeed more lofty than all human philosophy" (2.15).

19. He is less cautious in the second apology, where he claims that "our Christian men" have exorcized by the name of Jesus numberless demoniacs throughout the world when other exorcists, using incantations and drugs, could not (2.6).

20. I use the translation of J. E. Ryland, as found in *The Ante-Nicene Fathers*, 2:65–83; on Tatian, see E. J. Hunt, *Christianity in the Second Century: The Case of Tatian* (London: Routledge, 2003).

21. I use the translation of M. Dods as found in *The Ante-Nicene Fathers*, 2:89–121; on Theophilus, see R. Rogers, *Theophilus of Antioch: The Life and Thought of a Second-Century Bishop* (Lanham, MD: Lexington, 2000).

22. I use the translation of B. P. Pratten in *The Ante-Nicene Fathers*, 2:129–148; see L. W. Barnard, *Athenagoras: A Study in Second Century Apologetic* (Theologique Historique 18; Paris: Beauchesne, 1972).

23. See R. MacMullen, *Enemies of the Roman Order: Treason, Unrest, and Alienation in the Empire* (Cambridge, MA: Harvard University Press, 1966).

24. Eusebius, *Historia Ecclesiastica*, 5.10; Quasten, *Patrology*, 2:4–36.

25. "His literary work proves that he was a man of comprehensive education extending to philosophy, poetry, archaeology, mythology, and literature. He did not, it is true, always go back to the original sources but in many instances used anthologies and florilegia" (Quasten, *Patrology*, 2.6); see also S. R. C. Lilla, *Clement of Alexandria: A*

Study in Christian Platonism and Gnosticism (Oxford Theological Monographs; London: Oxford University Press, 1971).

See the explicit use of Clement of Rome in *Stromata*, 1.8; 4.17; 6.8. He quotes Philo explicitly in 1.5; see A. van den Hoek, *Clement of Alexandria and His Use of Philo in the Stromateis: An Early Christian Reshaping of a Jewish Model* (Supplements to Vigiliae Christianae 3; Leiden: Brill, 1988).

26. See J. K. Brackett, *An Analysis of the Literary Structure and Forms in the Protrepticus and Paidogogus of Clement of Alexandria* (PhD diss., Emory University, 1986).

27. See, e.g., Epictetus, *Discourse*, 3.22; Dio Chrysostom, *Oration*, 77/78; Musonius Rufus, *Fragment*, 16; Maximus of Tyre, *Discourse*, 36. See also K. Berger, "Hellenistische Gattungen im Neuen Testament," *Aufstieg und Niedergang der römischen Welt* II.25.2 (1984): 1031–1432.

28. Clement is well aware of their unsystematic character. At the start of book 4, he states, "Let these notes of ours, as we have often said for the sake of these that consult them carelessly and unskillfully, be of varied character—and as the name itself indicates, patched together—passing constantly from one thing to another, and in the series of discussions hinting at one thing and demonstrating another. . . . The Miscellanies of notes contribute, then, to the recollection and expression of truth in the case of him who is able to investigate with reason" (4.2; see also 1.1).

29. See also Clement's rejection of the teachings of Valentinus, Marcion, and Basilides in *Stromata*, 2.8; 2.11; 3.1; 4.12, 13; 4.24; 5.1.

30. A substantial portion of book 6 of Eusebius' *Historia Ecclesiastica* is devoted to the life and works of Origen. Eusebius notes of his character, "For in his practical character were to be found to a truly marvelous degree the right actions of a most genuine philosophy (for, as the saying goes, 'as was his speech so was his manner of life' that he displayed, and 'as his manner of life, so his speech'), and it was especially for this reason that, with the cooperation of the divine power, he brought so very many to share his zeal" (6.3.7).

31. Among a rich literature on Origen, see J. Danielou, *Origen*, trans. W. Mitchell (New York: Sheed and Ward, 1951), for a consideration of all aspects of this protean figure; G. L. Prestige, "Origen: or the Claims of Religious Intelligence," in his *Fathers and Heretics* (London: SPCK, 1963), for Origen's intellectual temper; J. W. Trigg, *Origen: The Bible and Philosophy in the Third-Century Church* (Atlanta: John Knox, 1983), and K. J. Torjesen, *Hermeneutical Procedure and Theological Structure in Origen's Exegesis* (Berlin: deGruyter, 1986), for the interplay of scripture and philosophy.

32. Much of this discussion draws on my earlier study, "Origen and the Transformation of the Mind," in L. T. Johnson and W. S. Kurtz, *The Future of Catholic Biblical Scholarship: A Constructive Conversation* (Grand Rapids, MI: Eerdmans, 2002), 64–90.

33. The larger library in Alexandria had been damaged or destroyed in the Roman civil war, circa 48 BCE. The smaller library under the patronage of Serapis continued in existence until the temple (and probably with it the library) was destroyed by order of Theodosius in 391; see Socrates, *Historia Ecclesiastica*, 5.16.

34. We know this work through Origen's rebuttal, *Contra Celsum*. Origen quotes enough of Celsus' work for a substantial reconstruction; see Celsus, *On the True Doctrine: A Discourse against the Christians*, trans. R. J. Hoffmann (New York: Oxford University Press, 1987).

35. Among the writings that almost certainly come from Alexandria are *Wisdom of Solomon*; *3 Maccabees*; *4 Maccabees*; *Letter of Aristeas*; *Joseph and Aseneth*; *The Sentences of Pseudo-Phocylides*; and the works of Aristobolos, Ezekiel the Tragedian, and Pseudo-Orpheus, now available only in fragments.

36. For Origen's frequent references to "heretics" in general and by name, see Johnson, "Origen and the Transformation of the Mind," 66 n.9.

37. Part of this apologetic strategy is to vilify pagan religion as demonic; the pertinent passages from Origen are cited in Chapter 1.

38. Origen's dependence on Justin for this point is clear; see *Dialogue with Trypho*, 32–34.

39. He surely borrows from Clement, however, his perception of the role of philosophy for faith, as he states in his *Letter to Gregory Thaumaturgus*, 1: "I wish to ask you to extract from the philosophy of the Greeks what may serve as a course of study or a preparation for Christianity, and from geometry and astronomy what will serve to explain the Holy Scripture."

40. He compares the heresies within Christianity to the disputing schools both within philosophy and medicine (3.12–13).

41. Origen regularly uses the medical imagery for moral teaching that is common among Greco-Roman moralists (see *Cels*, 3.60–62; 3.74–75; 4.18).

42. Origen declares that the story of Adam can be interpreted allegorically in precisely the way that the cosmogonic myths of Hesiod are interpreted by Greek philosophers (*Cels*, 4.38), and he appeals to Plato for support (4.39).

43. See A. J. Malherbe, "Hellenistic Moralists and the New Testament," *Aufstieg und Niedergang der römischen Welt* II.26.1 (1992): 267–333.

44. See Plutarch, *Progress in Virtue* (Mor., 75A–86A).

45. Plutarch, *Isis and Osiris*, 31 (Mor., 355D).

46. *Dialogue of Origen with Heraclides and his Fellow-Bishops on the Father, the Son, and the Soul*, 13.25–15.25.

47. *Homilies on Jeremiah*, 14.10.1.

14. TRANSCENDING THE WORLD IN SECOND- AND THIRD-CENTURY CHRISTIANITY

1. For discussion of Gnosticism in its broadest aspects, see K. Rudolph, *Gnosis: The Nature and History of Gnosticism*, trans. R. McL. Wilson (San Francisco: HarperSanFrancisco, 1984); G. Filoramo, *A History of Gnosticism*, trans. A. Alcock (Cambridge: Blackwell, 1990); K. L. King, *What Is Gnosticism?* (Cambridge, MA: Belknap Press of Harvard University Press, 2003); B. A. Pearson, *Early Christianity and Gnosticism in the History of Religion* (Occasional Papers Institute for Antiquity and Christianity 42; Claremont, CA: Institute for Antiquity and Christianity, 2001). Especially for

Gnosticism's development into Manichaeism, see H.-J. Klimkeit, *Gnosis on the Silk Road: Gnostic Texts from Central Asia* (San Francisco: HarperSanFrancisco, 1993).

2. In his *First Apology*, 26 (ca. 165), Justin Martyr refers to a *syntagma* he had written against Simon, Menander, and Marcion. Irenaeus' *Adversus Haereses* (ca. 180) is acquainted with many Gnostic works but has best knowledge of Marcus and Ptolemy. Hippolytus of Rome (d. 235) wrote a *Refutation of All Heresies*. Tertullian of Carthage (ca. 200) wrote *De Praesciptione Hereticorum* and the five books of *Adversus Marcionem*. As we saw in the previous chapters, both Clement (140–215) and Origen of Alexandria (184–253) cited and rebutted Valentinus, Basilides, and Marcion. In addition, Clement collected the teachings of a Gnostic that he published as *Excerpta ex Theodoto*. Epiphanius of Salamis (315–403) represents the apogee of ancient heresy hunting, with his works *Ancoratus* and *Panarion*. Information especially about heretical tendencies in the East comes from Ephraem of Edessa (306–373) and Theodoret of Cyrus (395–466).

   Before the discovery at Nag-Hammadi, firsthand knowledge of Gnosticism could be obtained mainly from the Hermetic literature, the "Hymn of the Pearl" in the Syriac *Gospel of Thomas*, and two Coptic manuscripts from the fourth to fifth century discovered in 1778 and published in 1851: the Codex Askewianus, which contained the *Pistis Sophia*; and the Codex Brucianus, which contained the "Two Books of Jeu" and another, untitled composition. In 1896, C. Schmidt announced a further Coptic find, the Berlin Papyrus, which contained the *Gospel of Mary*, the *Apocryphon of John*, the *Sophia of Jesus Christ*, and the fragment *Act of Peter*. It was kept from full publication until shortly before the Nag-Hammadi discovery in 1945 and did not enter scholarly discussion. Some scholars also made heavy use of the Mandean literature. On these sources, see Rudolph, *Gnosis*, 25–30.

3. Under the influence especially of W. Bousset, *Hauptprobleme der Gnosis* (Forschungen zur Religion und Literatur des Alten und Neuen Testaments; Göttingen: Vandenhoeck und Ruprecht, 1907), and R. Reizenstein, *Das iranische Erlösungsmysterium: religionsgeschichtliche Untersuchungen* (Bonn: A. Marcus and E. Weber, 1921), the "history of religions school" argued for the existence of a well-formed Gnosticism prior to Christianity, complete with a myth of the "redeemed redeemer," and saw Gnosticism as an element in the development of Christianity from the time of its entry into the Greco-Roman world. See, e.g., W. Bousset, *Kyrios Christos: A History of the Belief in Christ from the Beginnings of Christianity to Irenaeus*, trans. J. E. Steely (Nashville: Abingdon, 1970); R. Bultmann, *Theology of the New Testament*, 2 vols., trans. J. E. Steely (New York: Scribner, 1951–1955); W. Schmithals, *Gnosticism in Corinth: An Investigation of the Letters to the Corinthians*, trans. J. E. Steely (Nashville: Abingdon, 1971); B. A. Pearson, *The Pneumatikos-Psychikos Terminology in 1 Corinthians: A Study in the Theology of the Opponents of Paul and Its Relation to Gnosticism* (Society of Biblical Literature Dissertations 12; Missoula, MT: Scholars, 1973). For criticism of the entire approach, see E. M. Yamauchi, *Pre-Christian Gnosticism: A Survey of the Proposed Evidences*, 2nd ed. (Grand Rapids, MI: Baker, 1973); and C. Colpe, *Die religionsgeschichtliche Schule* (Forschungen zur Religion und

Literatur des Alten und Neuen Testaments; Göttingen: Vandenhoeck und Ruprecht, 1961). On the vexed question of Gnostic origins and of terminology, see the essays in U. Bianchi, ed., *Le Origini della Gnosticismo*, Colloquio de Messina 13–18 Aprile, 1966 (Studies in the History of Religions, Supplement to *Numen* XII; Leiden: Brill, 1967).

As regards dualism, Marcion of Sinope, e.g., has a profoundly dualistic view of the world, hostility toward the Old Testament, and a Jesus who proclaims an "alien god" and advocates a strict asceticism; only a lack of cosmic mythology—and perhaps also his sectarian posture—prevents his inclusion among Gnostic teachers; see A. Harnack, *Marcion. Das Evangelium vom fremden Gott* (Texte und Untersuchungen zur Geschichte der altchristlichen Literatur; Leipzig: J. C. Hinrichs, 1924). Similarly, some scholars regard the dualistic elements in the apocryphal acts as "Gnostic"; see, e.g., J. N. Bremmer, ed., *The Apocryphal Acts of Peter: Magic, Miracles, and Gnosticism* (Studies on the Apocryphal Acts of the Apostles 3; Leuven: Peeters, 1998); and P. J. Lalleman, *The Acts of John: A Two-Stage Initiation into Johannine Gnosticism* (Studies on the Apocryphal Acts of the Apostles 4; Leuven: Peeters, 1998).

4. The discrimination between various streams in the Gnostic writings is the focus of *The Rediscovery of Gnosticism: Proceedings of the International Conference on Gnosticism at Yale, New Haven, Connecticut, March 28–31, 1978*, 2 vols., ed. B. Layton (Studies in the History of Religions; Supplements to *Numen* 41; Leiden: Brill, 1978).

5. The extreme position at one end is held by H. Jonas, *The Gnostic Religion* (Boston: Beacon Press, 1958), who argues for a coherent religion that finds expression within diverse exoteric traditions. More recently, see A. H. B. Logan, *The Gnostics: Identifying an Early Christian Cult* (London: T. & T. Clark, 2006). At the other end is M. Williams, *Rethinking "Gnosticism": An Argument for Dismantling a Dubious Category* (Princeton, NJ: Princeton University Press, 1996), who wants to abandon even the concept and in its stead speak of different interpretive strategies. Much earlier, see M. Smith, "The History of the Term Gnostikos," in *The Rediscovery of Gnosticism*, 2:796–807.

6. A soteriology, or theory of salvation, necessarily involves at least three other elements: (1) a cosmology, or understanding of the world in its origin, nature, and destiny; (2) an anthropology, or understanding of humanity in its origin, nature, and destiny; and (3) an eschatology, or theory of the end-time: what gets saved and what does not?

7. In laying out the Type C soteriology in the abstract without reference to specific texts, I recognize the danger of distorting the analysis of specific passages. Because of the complexity of the material to be analyzed, however, such a working grid has more advantages than disadvantages.

8. The lowest class of humans can be designated as "fleshly" (*sarkikoi*) or "earthly" (*choikoi*) or "material" (*hylikoi*), the last roughly equivalent to "mud-people." Such are regarded as lacking a divine spark altogether. The highest class of humans can be called "spiritual" (*pneumatikoi*) or "perfect" (*teleioi*) or "elect" (*eklektoi*): they are essentially divine but find themselves trapped in material reality. The third class of

humans is usually called *psychikoi* ("psychic" or "animate"); they have the possibility of turning in one direction or another. Reconciling freedom and determinism in the case of the psychic is not easy; see Rudolph, *Gnosis*, 78–82.

9. Neither the date of Irenaeus' birth nor the date or manner of his death is known, although his claim to have been in contact with Polycarp of Smyrna (Eusebius, *Historia Ecclesiastica*, 5.20.5–7) and his becoming bishop of Lyons circa 180 (*Historia Ecclesiastica*, 5.4.2) make the dates 140–200 plausible.

10. In book 1, Irenaeus describes the Gnostic schools, beginning with Valentinus, before turning to Simon Magus (whom he makes the source of Gnosticism) and his successors. Book 2 argues against Valentinus and Marcion on the basis of reason. Book 3 unfolds Irenaeus' framework for orthodoxy, based on the rule of faith, the canon of scripture, and the apostolic succession. In book 4, he refutes his opponents on the basis of the sayings of Jesus in the canonical Gospels. In book 5, he defends the bodily resurrection of Jesus and the righteous, developing his interpretation of scripture as a divine pedagogy on the basis of the Pauline principle of recapitulation of all things in Christ. Throughout, he vigorously engages the scriptural interpretations of the heretics and offers his own interpretation based on the grammar, syntax, and narrative logic of the texts.

11. See G. Vallee, *A Study in Anti-Gnostic Polemic: Irenaeus, Hippolytus, and Epiphanius* (Studies in Christianity and Judaism 1; Waterloo, ON: Canadian Corporation for Studies in Religion by Wilfrid University Press, 1981); and especially F. Wisse, "The Nag Hammadi Library and the Heresiologists," *Vigiliae Christianae* 25 (1971): 205–223.

12. Thus, Irenaeus begins with Valentinus and his student Ptolemy (1. Pref. 1–2; 1.11.1–4); then he treats Marcus (1.13.6–7) and his disciples (1.13.6–7) with their theories (1.14–22); next he deals with Simon Magus (1.23.1–4) and his disciples Menander (1.23.5) and with Saturninus (1.24.1–2) and Basilides (1.24.3–4). In quick succession, he treats Carpocrates (1.25), Cerinthus (1.26.1), the Ebionites (1.26.2), the Nicolaitans (1.26.3), Cerdo (1.27.1), Marcion (1.27.2–4), Tatian and the Encratites (1.28), "other Gnostics" (1.29), the Ophites and Sethians (1.30), and finally the Cainites (1.31).

13. At the level of theory, he charges them with contradictions and disagreements (*Adversus Haereses* 1.11.1), of intellectual distortions (1.9.4), of derivativeness—they are simply rehashing pagan myths (2.14.1–9)—and of deceiving themselves (1.11.1). Most memorably, he practices a form of *reductio ad absurdum* by comparing the naming of entities in the Pleroma to seeds in a melon (1.11.4). At the level of morals, he makes the usual charges of unseemly behavior (1.6.3; 1.13.3) but adds the charge of working with demons (1.13.3) and of practicing magic (1.13.4–5; 1.23.1; 1.23.4–5; 1.24.5; 1.25.3).

14. Only recently has Irenaeus' offhand reference to the Cainites' teaching on Judas, based on "a fictitious history of this kind, which they style The Gospel of Judas" (*Adversus Haereses*, 1.31.1), found unexpected confirmation in the discovery and publication (with great fanfare) of a Coptic manuscript fitting this description; see R. Kasser, M. Meyer, and G. Wurst, eds., *The Gospel of Judas: From Codex Tchacos* (Washington, DC: National Geographic, 2006).

15. For Valentinus, see A. M. McGuire, *Valentinus and the "Gnostike Hairesis": An Investigation of Valentinus's Position in the History of Gnosticism* (PhD diss., Yale University, 1983). Among the few things known about Ptolemy is that he wrote an *Epistle to Flora* that seeks to find a middle ground between those who ascribe the law of Moses entirely to God and those (like Marcion and some Sethian Gnostics) who attribute the entire law to the devil. He does this by attributing some portions to God, some to Moses, and some to the human scribes. The letter is contained in Epiphanius of Salamis' *Panarion* 33.3.1–33.7.10, and an English translation is found in B. Layton, *The Gnostic Scriptures* (Garden City, NY: Doubleday, 1987), 308–315.

16. I am using the translation provided by Layton, *Gnostic Scriptures*, 281–302.

17. See E. Pagels, *The Gnostic Paul: Gnostic Exegesis of the Pauline Letters* (Philadelphia: Fortress, 1975), and *The Johannine Gospel in Gnostic Exegesis: Heracleon's Commentary on John* (Society of Biblical Literature Monograph Series 17; Nashville: Abingdon, 1973).

18. Only fragments remain of the teaching of this philosopher who was active in Alexandria between 132 and 135. I use here the translation of Irenaeus 1.24–3.7 and the noteworthy fragments provided by Layton, *Gnostic Scriptures*, 417–443.

19. I use the translation of Irenaeus 1.30.1–1.31.1 given by Layton, *Gnostic Scriptures*, 173–181.

20. For the story of the discovery and description of contents, see Rudolph, *Gnosis*, 34–52; and especially J. M. Robinson, "Introduction," in *The Nag Hammadi Library in English*, translated by Members of the Coptic Gnostic Library Project of the Institute for Antiquity and Christianity, J. M. Robinson, Director (San Francisco: Harper and Row, 1977), 1–25.

21. The *Discourse on the Eighth and Ninth* and the section of the *Asclepius* are recognizable as Hermetic because the revealer Hermes Trismegistos is named in each (VI, 58.30; and VI, 66.25), and the *Prayer of Thanksgiving* appears in the codex between them. Throughout the rest of the chapter, all references to the Nag Hammadi writings follows the protocol of the *Nag-Hammadi Library in English* (NHLE), even when I use Layton's translation—he follows the same system. The composition is located first by its sequence in a specific codex. Thus, the *Discourse on the Eighth and Ninth* is the sixth composition in codex 6, (VI, 6) and is followed by the other two compositions (VI, 7; and VI, 8). Internal references use the section and line indications of the NHLE. Thus, the *Discourse* runs from VI 52, 1, to VI 63, 32.

   The *Sentences of Sextus* is a strongly ascetical moral instruction that is known from versions outside the Nag-Hammadi library; see F. Wisse, "The Sentences of Sextus (XII 1)," in *NHLE*, 454–459, as well as *The Sentences of Sextus*, ed. and trans. R. A. Edwards and R. A. Wild (Texts and Translations: Early Christian Literature Series 5; Chico, CA: Scholars, 1981); and H. Chadwick, *The Sentences of Sextus: A Contribution to the History of Early Christian Ethics* (Texts and Translations: Contributions to Biblical and Patristic Literature 5; Cambridge: Cambridge University Press, 1959). *The Teaching of Silvanus*, in contrast, is not known outside the Nag-Hammadi collection. Its presence there, in fact, is striking because of the thoroughly orthodox tone of the composition in all aspects. See "The Teachings of Silvanus (VII 4)," edited by F. Wisse, introduced and translated by M. L. Peel and J. Zandee, in *NHLE*, 346–361.

Given the complex compositional history of the apocryphal *Acts of Peter*, it is not surprising to find a single narrative incident appearing in isolation. See "The Act of Peter" (Bruce Codex 8502, 4), introduced and translated by J. Brashler and D. M. Parrott, in *NHLE*, 475–477. This fragment is not to be confused with another composition, *The Acts of Peter and the Twelve Apostles*, also in the collection of codices but having a distinctly Gnostic coloration. See "The Acts of Peter and the Twelve Apostles" (VI, 1)," introduced and translated by D. M. Parrott and R. McL. Wilson, in *NHLE*, 265–270. See also "Plato, Republic 588B–589B (VI 5)," introduced and translated by J. Brashler, edited by D. M. Parrott, in *NHLE*, 290–291.

22. Because Valentinian Gnosticism is more familiar, recent attention has focused on the more obscure "Sethian" writings; see A. F. J. Klijn, *Seth in Jewish, Christian, and Gnostic Literature* (Novum Testamentum Supplements 46; Leiden: Brill, 1977); see also B. Pearson, "The Figure of Seth in Gnostic Literature," and F. Wisse, "Stalking Those Elusive Sethians," in *The Rediscovery of Gnosticism*, 2:472–504, and 2:563–576.

23. Scholars have noted in particular the strong resemblances between the revelatory literature at Nag-Hammadi and Jewish Merkabah mysticism: see, e.g., G. G. Scholem, *Jewish Gnosticism, Merkabah Mysticism, and the Talmudic Tradition* (New York: Jewish Theological Seminary of New York, 1960); I. Gruenwald, *From Apocalypticism to Gnosticism: Studies in Apocalypticism, Merkavah Mysticism, and Gnosticism* (Beiträge zur Erforschung des Alten Testamens und des antiken Judentums 14; Frankfort an Main: P. Lang, 1988); and N. Deutsch, *The Gnostic Imagination: Gnosticism, Mandaeism, and Merkabah Mysticism* (Jewish Studies 13; Leiden: Brill, 1995);

24. The synoptic display of the two compositions shows how the additional elements in the *Sophia* provide a Christian framework for an earlier revelational writing; see "Eugnostos the Blessed (III, 3 and V, 1) and The Sophia of Jesus Christ (III, 4 and BG 8503, 3)," introduced and translated by D. M. Parrott, in *NHLE*, 206–228.

25. Porphyry of Tyre (223–305) was a disciple and admirer of Plotinus (205–270), the great philosopher in the Platonic tradition, and wrote a *Life of Plotinus* in which he notes (chapter 16) the philosopher's opposition to Gnostics who appealed to revelations from "Zoroaster, of Zostrianos, of Nikotheos, of the Foreigner, of Messos, and other such figures," and wrote as well a treatise called *Against the Gnostics* (which now appears as Plotinus, *Ennead*, II.9). One of Plotinus' disciples wrote a 40-chapter refutation of *The Book of Zostrianos*, says Porphyry, and Porphyry himself undertook an attack on the *Book of Zoroaster*. See Layton, *Gnostic Scriptures*, 182–184.

26. I am using the translation provided by Layton, *Gnostic Scriptures*, 125–140.

27. The name (and title) Allogenes is also rendered as "The Foreigner," as in the translation I use from Layton, *Gnostic Scriptures*, 144–148.

28. Barbelo is a major figure in Sethian myth, appearing in *Zostrianos*, 14.6; 36.14; 36.20; 37.20; 53.10; 62.21; 63.7; 83.9; 87.10; 91.19; 118.10; 119.23; 122.1; 124.11; 129.11; *Allogenes*,

51.13; 53.28; 56.27; 58.21; 59.3; 59.6; *Three Steles of Seth*, 121.21; *Melchizedek*, 5.27; 16.26; *Marsanes*, 4.11; 8.28; 43.21; *Trimorphic Protennoia*, 38.9; and *Apocryphon of John*, 4.36; 5.13; 5.19; 5.25; 5.26; 5.31.

29. I use the translation in Layton, *Gnostic Scriptures*, 28–51.

30. Speaking of the Valentinians, Irenaeus says, "they have arrived at such a pitch of audacity, as to entitle their recent writing 'the Gospel of Truth,' though it agrees in nothing with the Gospels of the Apostles, so that they really have no Gospel which is not full of blasphemies" (*Adversus Haereses*, 3.11.9). See also Layton, *Gnostic Scriptures*, 250–252, whose translation of the *Gospel of Truth* (253–264) I use.

31. See J. A. Williams, *The Interpretation of Texts and Traditions in the Gospel of Truth* (PhD diss., Yale University, 1983).

32. Translation in Layton, *Gnostic Scriptures*, 320–324.

33. There is an explicit reference to the transfiguration story (Mark 9:1–8//) in 48.6 as well as allusions to 1 Cor 15:53–54 (45.28–46.1; 48.38), 2 Cor 5:4 (45.28–46.1), and Rom 8:29 (46.25).

34. Compare the use of *katapausis* in Heb 3:11, 18; 4:1, 3, 5, 10, 11; and see O. Hofius, *Katapausis: Die Vorstellung vom endzeitlichen Ruheort im Hebräerbrief* (Wissenschaftliche Untersuchungen zum Neuen Testament 11; Tübingen: Mohr, 1970); and J. H. Wray, *Rest as a Theological Metaphor in the Epistle to the Hebrews and the Gospel of Truth; Early Christian Homiletics of Rest* (Society of Biblical Literature Dissertation Series 166; Atlanta: Scholars, 1998).

35. We recognize the strong Platonic element here, but the idea that human souls were preexistent is found also in Origen, *On First Principles*, 8.1–4, and although explicitly eschewed by Gregory of Nyssa in *On the Making of Man*, 28.1–29.11, is suggested by his language in *On Virginity*, 12.

36. I use the translation as found in Layton, *Gnostic Scriptures*, 380–399. I also employ the double numbering system, putting the number of the saying in square brackets followed by the section and line number assigned in the codices.

37. On the relationship of the *Gospel of Thomas* to the agrapha, see J. Jeremias, *The Unknown Sayings of Jesus*, trans. R. Fuller (New York: Macmillan, 1957).

The position that the *Gospel of Thomas* served, with Q, as an independent source for traditions about Jesus earlier than did the Synoptic Gospels was advanced early and vigorously by H. Koester and was taken up especially by questers for the historical Jesus, above all S. J. Patterson, *The Gospel of Thomas and Jesus* (Sonoma, CA: Polebridge, 1993); R. Funk, and J. D. Crossan, *The Historical Jesus: The Life of a Mediterranean Jewish Peasant* (San Francisco: HarperSanFrancisco, 1991). For the view that the *Gospel of Thomas* is dependent on the canonical traditions, see W. Schrage, *Das Verhältnis des Thomas-Evangeliums zur synoptischen Tradition und zu den koptischen Evangelienübersetzungen* (Zeitschrift für die neuentestamentliche Wissenschaft 29; Berlin: Töpelmann, 1964); and C. M. Tuckett, "Q and Thomas: Evidence of a Primitive 'Wisdom Gospel'? A Response to H. Koester," *Ephemeridea Theologicae Lovaninenses* 67 (1991): 346–360.

On the relationship between Q and the *Gospel of Thomas*, see, e.g., J. Kloppenburg et al. , *Q-Thomas Reader* (Sonoma, CA: Polebridge, 1990); B. Mack, *The Lost*

Gospel: The Book of Q and Christian Origins (San Francisco: HarperSanFrancisco, 1993).

For the most enthusiastic argument that the Nag Hammadi writings give access to the "real Jesus," see M. Franzmann, *Jesus in the Nag Hammadi Writings* (Edinburgh: T. & T. Clark, 1996); for the position that the Gnostic gospels are dependent on the New Testament compositions, see C. M Tuckett, *Nag Hammadi and the Gospel Tradition*, ed. J. Riches (Edinburgh: T & T. Clark, 1986).

For the position that the *Gospel of Thomas* is best understood as standing within a broader stream of Christian asceticism, see R. Valantasis, *The Gospel of Thomas* (London: Routledge, 1997).

38. L. T. Johnson, "Does a Theology of the Canonical Gospels Make Sense?" in *The Nature of New Testament Theology: Essays in Honor of Robert Morgan*, ed. C. Rowland and C. Tuckett (Oxford: Blackwell, 2006), 93–108.

39. On this, see D. Brakke, "Self-Differentiation among Christian Groups: The Gnostics and Their Opponents," in *The Cambridge History of Christianity*, vol. 1: *Origins to Constantine*, ed. M. M. Mitchell and F. M. Young (Cambridge: Cambridge University Press, 2006), 245–260.

15. STABILIZING THE WORLD IN SECOND- AND THIRD-CENTURY CHRISTIANITY

1. I use the translation of 1 *Clement* provided by K. Lake in *The Apostolic Fathers*, 2 vols. (Loeb Classical Library; Cambridge, MA: Harvard University Press, 1915), 1:8–121.

2. For emissaries to and from Ignatius and the churches of Asia, see Ign. *Phil.*, 10.2; Ign. *Eph.*, 1.2–3; 2.1; Ign. *Smyr.*, 9.3; Ign. *Poly.*, 7.1–2; 8.1.

3. Ign. *Eph.*, 4.1–2; Ign. *Magn.*, 6.1–2; Ign. *Tral.*, 2.2; Ign. *Smyr.*, 8.1 (harmony with the bishop and presbytery); Ign. *Eph.*, 2.2; 5.3; 20.2; Ign. *Magn.*, 2.1; 4.1; 8.2; Ign. *Tral.*, 2.1; 13.1; Ign. *Phil.*, 2.1; Ign. *Poly.*, 6.1 (submission to the authority of the bishop and presbytery).

4. In the preceding passage as well, Justin speaks of the Eucharist in terms of sacrifice: "'And the offering of fine flour, sirs,' I said, 'which was prescribed to be presented (*prospherein*) on behalf of those purified from leprosy,' was a type of the bread of the Eucharist, the celebration of which our Lord Jesus Christ prescribed" (*Dial*, 41).

5. For the place of these compositions in the development of the liturgy, see G. Dix, *The Shape of the Liturgy*, with additional notes by P. Marshall (New York: Seabury, 1982), especially 103–156; for their role in the development of Christian law, see L. T. Johnson, "Law in Early Christianity," in *Christianity and Law: An Introduction*, ed. J. Witte and F. S. Alexander (Cambridge: Cambridge University Press, 2008), 53–69; for their role in developing orders of clergy, see A. Faivre, "Naissance d'une hiérarchie: Les premières étapes du cursus clérical," *Theologie Historique* 40 (1977): 47–67.

6. See M. Metzger, *Les Constitutions Apostoliques: Introduction, texte critique, traduction et notes* (Sources Chrétiennes 320; Paris: Editions du Cerf, 1978).

7. The manuscript containing the composition was discovered in the Patriarchal Library of Jerusalem at Constantinople in 1875. For full discussion and an early dating (ca. 90), see J.-P. Audet, *La Didache: Instructions des Apotres* (Paris: J. Gabalda, 1958).

8. For a recent close reading of the composition, see J. H. Neyrey, *Give God the Glory: Ancient Prayer and Worship in Cultural Perspective* (Grand Rapids, MI: Eerdmans, 2007), 206–230; see also A. Milavec, *The Didache: Text, Translation, Analysis, and Commentary* (Collegeville, MN: Liturgical, 2003); and C. N. Jefford, ed., *The Didache in Context: Essays on Its Text, History, and Transmission* (Supplements to Novum Testamentum 77; Leiden: Brill, 1995).

9. I am using the translation of Lake in *The Apostolic Fathers*, 1:308–333.

10. For a full discussion, see P. F. Bradshaw, M. E. Johnson, and L. E. Phillips, *The Apostolic Tradition: A Commentary* (Hermeneia; Minneapolis: Fortress, 2002). I use their translation.

11. For example, gifts of healing (14), newcomers (15), crafts and professions (16.1–17), oil lamps at community supper (29C 1–16), supper of widows (30A 1–2), times of prayer (35.1–2), places of burial (40.1–2), sign of the cross (42.1–4), and the offering of various foods: oil (5.1–2), cheese and olives (6.1–4), and fruits (32.1–3). For an argument concerning the variety of foods used in early Christian meals, see A. McGowan, *Ascetic Eucharists: Food and Drink in Early Christian Ritual Meals* (Oxford Early Christian Studies; Oxford: Clarendon, 1999).

12. I use the translation and numbering provided by R. H. Connolly, *Didascalia Apostolorum. The Syriac Version Translated and Accompanied by the Verona Latin Fragments* (Oxford: Clarendon, 1929); see also A. Vööbus, *The Didascalia Apostolorum in Syriac* (Corpus Scriptorum Christianorum Orientalium 401–402, 407–408; Louvain: Secretariat de CorpusSCO, 1979).

13. See F. Brightman, "The Quartodeciman Question," *Journal of Theological Studies* 25 (1923–1924): 254–270; C. Dugmore, "A Note on the Quartodecimans," *Studia Patristica* 4 (1961): 411–442; C. Mohrmann, "Le Conflit Pascal au IIe Siècle—Note Philologique," *Vigiliae Christianae* 16 (1962): 154–171.

14. I use K. Lake's translation of *Historia Ecclesiastica* (*HE*), 2 vols. (Loeb Classical Library; Cambridge, MA: Harvard University Press, 1930), 1:502–513.

15. Osrhoene is the ancient designation for the area of upper Mesopotamia that includes the important ecclesial center of Edessa.

16. For the complex process by which the Roman church claimed for itself and was recognized by others as having primacy, see E. Giles, *Documents Illustrating Papal Authority, AD 96–454* (London: SPCK, 1952).

17. The declaration attributed to Peter in Acts 4:29 and 5:19 is itself an allusion to Socrates' statement before his judges, in Plato, *Apology*, 29D.

18. Eusebius, *HE*, 5.26.1, mentions letters and "published treatises" as well as a work against the Greeks, entitled *Concerning Knowledge*; the *Demonstration of the Apostolic Preaching*; and a collection of discourses: "Such is the extent of our knowledge of the works of Irenaeus."

19. See O. O'Donovan and J. L. O'Donovan, eds., *From Irenaeus to Grotius: A Source-book in Christian Political Thought, 100–1625* (Grand Rapids, MI: Eerdmans, 1999).

20. See G. Wingren, *Man and the Incarnation: A Study in the Biblical Theology of Irenaeus* (Philadelphia: Muhlenberg, 1959); and J. T. Nielsen, *Adam and Christ in the Theology of Irenaeus of Lyons: An Examination of the Function of the Adam-Christ Typology in the Adversus Haereses of Irenaeus* (Van Gorcum's Theologische Biblioteek 40; Assen: Van Gorcum, 1968).

21. Irenaeus compares the dismemberment and rearrangement of scripture by the Gnostics to the disfiguring of a beautiful mosaic of a king, in which the stones have been rearranged into the poorly executed image of a dog or fox (*Adversus Haereses*, 1.8.1).

22. The footnote to this line in *The Ante-Nicene Fathers*, 10 vols., ed. A. Roberts and J. Donaldson (Peabody, MA: Hendrickson, 1994 [1886]), 1:331, refers this characterization to the churches in Palestine.

23. Irenaeus defends the fourfold character of the Gospels—four pillars breathing out immortality on every side—on the basis of the four zones of the world and the four principal winds, but above all on the four creatures around the throne in Revelation 4:7. The fourfold Gospel, in turn, supports Irenaeus' reading of sacred history in terms of four covenants: that with Adam, that with Noah, that with Moses, and that with Christ, "which sums up all things in itself by means of the Gospel" (3.11.8).

24. Irenaeus makes vigorous use of the Pentateuch (with only a few references to Leviticus), the historical books, the Psalms, and the prophets (Isaiah, Jeremiah, Ezekiel, Daniel, Amos, Hosea, Jonah, Micah, Habakkuk, Zechariah, and Malachi). He has no references to Nahum, Zephaniah, Ruth, Judith, Chronicles, or the Books of the Maccabees.

25. The only books from the New Testament collection that Irenaeus does not quote—for quite understandable reasons (they are so tiny and situation specific)—are 3 John and Philemon. Otherwise the entire New Testament canon is robustly represented.

26. Irenaeus devotes considerable attention to the distortions of language in Gnostic interpretations (see Adversus Haereses, 1.14–18; 2.10; 2.24) and just as much attention to the proper way of reading scripture (2.25–27; 3.7–10; 3.18).

27. See G. G. Blum, *Tradition und Sukzession: Studien zum Normbegriff des Apostolischen von Paulus bis Irenaeus* (Arbeiten zur Geschichte und Theologie des Luthertums 9; Berlin: Lutherisches Verlagshaus, 1963).

28. Jerome, *De Viris Illustribus*, 67; for Cyprian's life and works, see J. Quasten, *Patrology*, 4 vols. (Westminster, MD: Christian Classics, 1986), 2:340–383.

29. Jerome, *De Viris Illustribus*, 53.

30. I follow the numbering and translation found in "Cyprian," translated by E. Wallis, in *The Ante-Nicene Fathers*, 5:263–595. Treatise 5, "To Demetrianus," defends Christians against attack, and Treatise 6, "On the Vanity of Idols," goes on the attack. For pastoral issues, see "On the Dress of Virgins" (2), "On the Lord's Prayer" (4), "On the Mortality" (7), "On Works and Alms" (8), "On Patience" (9), and "On Jealousy and Envy" (10).

31. See his "Three Books of Testimonies against the Jews" (12) and "Exhortation to Martyrdom" (11), which is a similar compilation of scriptural *topoi*.

32. On ordination, see Cyprian, *Letters*, 32, 33, 34. On matters of practice, see 7, 11, 35, 55, 65, 82. On the "lapsed," see 4, 5, 9, 10, 12, 13. On other points of contention, see 6, 8, 17, 23, 24, 27, 31, 36, 39.

16. AFTER CONSTANTINE

1. For the stages of progression, see R. L. Fox, *Pagans and Christians* (New York: Knopf, 1987); J. Pelikan, *The Excellent Empire: The Fall of Rome and the Triumph of the Church* (San Francisco: HarperSanFrancisco, 1987); R. MacMullen, *Christianizing the Roman Empire, A.D. 100–400* (New Haven, CT: Yale University Press, 1984), 86–101.

2. For a sympathetic analysis of Constantine's efforts to continue a tradition of tolerance for all religions under his regime, see H. Dorries, *Constantine and Religious Liberty*, trans. R. Bainton (New Haven, CT: Yale University Press, 1960). As early as the 340s, the Christian writer Firmicius Maternus addressed a treatise to Constantine's sons (*De Errore Profanorum Religionum*), urging the destruction of paganism by force. The full establishment of Christianity as the imperial religion takes place under Theodosius I (379–395), who refuses the Senate's desire to restore the altar of victory, forbids sacrifices to the gods, and declares Arianism to be illegal (see Socrates, *Historia Ecclesiastica*, 5.16; and Sozomen, *Historia Ecclesiastica*, 7.4, 7.17).

3. Regarding the Edict of Milan, the text of the letter from Constantine and Licinius is found in Eusebius, *Historia Ecclesiastica* (HE), 10.5.2–14. Significant elements of the declaration include the freedom of all religions to worship whatever deity the people choose (5.10.8) and the restoration of property that had been confiscated, not only to individual Christians, but to "the society as a whole" (5.10.11).

    Eusebius includes Constantine's letters ordering financial assistance to "certain ministers of the legitimate and most holy catholic religion" (*HE*, 10.6.1–5) and exempting Christian clergy from financial responsibilities to the state (10.7.1–2).

4. See Eusebius, *HE*, 10.5.18–24. The 22 canons issued by the Synod of Arles are preserved in J. D. Mansi, *Sacrorum Conciliorum Nova et Amplissima Collectio*, 31 vols. (Florence, 1759–1798), 2:463–512.

5. "He enjoined on all the subjects of the Roman empire to observe the Lord's day, as a day of rest, and also to honor the day which precedes the Sabbath" (Eusebius, *Life of Constantine*, 4.18). Even the soldiers in Constantine's army who remained pagan were required to pray as the emperor directed them on Sunday (4.19–20). On the soldiers' engraving the sign of the cross, see 4.21.

6. Eusebius says that "to God alone, the Almighty, was the healing of these differences an easy task; and Constantine appeared to be the only one on earth capable of being his minister for this good end" (*Life of Constantine*, 3.5). Eusebius reports how Constantine summons the bishops (3.6), takes his seat in the assembly of the bishops

"like some heavenly messenger of God" (3.10), and addresses the council (3.12) as well as exhorting at length the bishops about harmony at the conclusion of the council (3.17–21).

7. Eusebius, *Life of Constantine*, 4.58–60.

8. For the church of the Holy Sepulchre and other churches throughout Palestine, see Eusebius, *Life of Constantine*, 3.25–43; for churches in Constantinople in honor of the martyrs and for churches in Nicomedia and other cities, see 3.48–51; for the building of the church at Heliopolis on the site of the destroyed temple of Venus, see 3.58. Eusebius provides a fulsome account of the emperor's church building in his *Oration in Praise of the Emperor Constantine*, 9.14–19. Eusebius speaks also of Constantine's gifts of money to churches and to orphans and widows in *Life of Constantine*, 4.28. Eusebius does not mention any of Constantine's benefactions in Rome, but the Lateran Basilica is certainly his gift; see H. Brandenburg, *Ancient Churches in Rome from the Fourth to the Seventh Century* (Turnhout: Brepols, 2004), 16–54.

9. Eusebius, *Life of Constantine*, 4.36–37.

10. On the connection between Libanius and John Chrysostom, see Socrates, *Historia Ecclesiastica*, 4.3, followed by Sozomen, *Historia Ecclesiastica*, 8.2. On Libanius' admiration of the emperor Julian, see his *Autobiography* (Letter 1), 119–135, in *Libanius: Autobiography and Selected Letters*, 2 vols., trans. A. F. Norman (Loeb Classical Library; Cambridge, MA: Harvard University Press, 1992). On Libanius' protesting the closing of the temples, see especially *Oration*, 17 ("The Lament over Julian"); *Oration*, 20 ("To the Emperor Theodosius, after the Reconciliation"); and *Oration*, 30 ("To the Emperor Theodosius, for the Temples"), in *Libanius, Selected Works*, 2 vols., trans. A. F. Norman (Loeb Classical Library; Cambridge, MA: Harvard University Press, 1987).

11. The life and imperial career of the philosopher-king Julian are recounted by Socrates, *Historia Ecclesiastica*, 2.47–3.21. In 3.1, he pays grudging respect to Julian's great learning, stating that he desired to study with Libanius and, being prevented, nevertheless obtained and learned from the great rhetorician's works. Julian's *Orations* display both his extensive learning and his deep philosophical commitment.

12. The first 10 of the 24 books in *The City of God* were composed between 413 and 426. According to Augustine's *Retractions*, 2.43.2, it was after Alaric led the Visigoths in the sack of Rome in 410 that he began contemplating his response to the charges of pagans that the Christians were to blame. In *Letters*, 137 and 138, he takes up some of the specific charges made by Volosianus, proconsul of Africa. Augustine's detailed knowledge of Roman religion appears to be based substantially on a source he refers to frequently by Marcus Terentius Varro (116–27 BCE), *Antiquitates rerum humanarum et divinarum Libri XLI*.

13. Diocletian was emperor from 284 to 305. After a long period of toleration, he began (possibly at the urging of Galerius) the last great persecution by a purge of the army in 299. By an edict in Nicomedia in 303, he ordered the demolition of churches, the burning of Christian books, and the elimination of social and legal rights for Chris-

tians. In 304, sacrifice to the gods was imposed on all. Eusebius, *Historia Ecclesiastica*, 7.1–4, recounts various dimensions of imperial repression, including numerous martyrdoms throughout the empire.

14. Lactantius continues, "For when that most happy day had shone upon the world, in which the Most High God raised you to the prosperous height of power, you entered upon a dominion which was salutary and desirable for all, with an excellent beginning, when, restoring justice which had been overthrown and taken away, you expiated the most shameful deeds of others." He then affirms that God will grant the emperor "happiness, virtue, and length of days" and will hand the rule on to his descendents (*The Divine Institutes*, 1.1). A convenient translation is that of W. Fletcher in *The Ante-Nicene Fathers*, 10 vols., ed. A. Roberts and J. Donaldson (Peabody, MA: Hendrickson, 1994 [1886]), 7:9–223. The same volume contains the *Epitome of the Divine Institutes* that Lactantius composed for his brother Pentadius (7: 224–255)

15. For Seneca, see *The Divine Institutes*, 1.5; 3.15. Cicero is discussed frequently; see, e.g., 1.5; 1.15; 2.3; 3.19; 3.29. For the critique of Tertullian and Cyprian, see 5.1; 5.4.

16. For the translation of *De Mortibus Persecutorum*, see Fletcher in *Ante-Nicene Fathers*, 7:301–322. On the peace that has come to the church, Lactantius declares, "Behold, all the adversaries are destroyed, and tranquility having been re-established throughout the Roman empire, the late oppressed church arises again, and the temple of God, overthrown by the hands of the wicked, is built with more glory than before" (1). For his relish at the bad end that came to all the rulers who persecuted Christians, see *On the Manner in Which Persecutors Died*, 42.

17. Constantine "commanded that his embattled forces should be preceded in their march, not by golden images, as heretofore, but only by the standard of the cross"; Eusebius, *Life of Constantine*, 4.21.

    Although smaller communities met in households, larger Christian communities erected substantial places of worship even before Constantine; for a gathering of the data, see J. G. Davies, *The Origin and Development of Early Christian Church Architecture* (New York: Philosophical Library, 1953), 14–16.

18. At least one of the antecedent functions for the architectural form known as the basilica was to serve as courts of law, although some connect the building type to the audience chambers and throne rooms of imperial residences; see Davies, *Early Christian Church Architecture*, 19–50.

19. For the basilicas in Rome that got their start under Constantine, see R. Ross Holloway, *Constantine and Rome* (New Haven, CT: Yale University Press, 2004), 57–119; and H. Brandenburg, *Ancient Churches in Rome from the Fourth to the Seventh Century* (Bibliothèque de L'antiquité tardive 8; Turnhout: Brepols, 2004), 16–109.

20. The point is made well by G. Dix, *The Shape of the Liturgy* (New York: Seabury Press, 1982 [1945]), 303–319, and by J. Jungmann, *The Early Liturgy*, trans. F. A. Brunner (University of Notre Dame Liturgical Studies 6; Notre Dame, IN: University of Notre Dame Press, 1959), 122–174.

21. The demarcation of the hierarchy is more evident, given the structure of the basilica: the presbytery sits around the bishop, who is seated on a chair/throne on the raised bema in the rounded apse at the end of the long hall opposite the entrance. The laypeople fill the spaces that are lower and less defined by power; see Davies, *Early Christian Church Architecture*, 36–38.

22. This was a slow development. In the fourth and fifth centuries, the clothing of the bishop, e.g., was basically that of the Roman nobility rather than a distinctive cultic garb; see Dix, *Shape of the Liturgy*, 398–410.

23. The distinct elements were in the process of being joined perhaps as early as the late second century but are fully displayed as unified liturgies in the fourth and fifth centuries; see F. C. Senn, *Christian Liturgy: Catholic and Evangelical* (Minneapolis: Fortress, 1997), 73–145; Dix, *Shape of the Liturgy*, 410–436; Jungmann, The *Early Liturgy*, 122–151.

24. For the development of stational liturgies in Rome and Jerusalem, which involved lengthy processions between the churches of a city, see J. F. Baldovin, S.J., *The Urban Character of Christian Worship: The Origin, Development, and Meaning of Stational Liturgy* (Orientalia Christiana Analecta 228; Rome: Pont. Institutum Studiorum Orientalium, 1987).

25. Among the churches in Rome that displaced pagan temples are Saints Cosmas and Damian (sixth century, replacing a fourth-century temple to Romulus); Santa Maria Nova (replacing the temple of Venus and Mars); Santa Maria Sopra Minerva (a fifth-century replacement of the temple of Minerva); and, most impressively, the seventh-century dedication of Santa Maria ad Martyres in the temple called the Pantheon.

26. Dix, *Shape of the Liturgy*, 335–369; Jungmann, The *Early Liturgy*, 253–263; L. Bouyer, *Liturgical Piety* (University of Notre Dame Liturgical Studies 1; Notre Dame, IN: Notre Dame University Press, 1954), 185–199.

27. Note the unabashed language of "the mysteries" used by Cyril of Jerusalem (315–387) in the five *Mystagogic Catheceses* he devoted to the ritual of initiation for the newly baptized, and the instructions concerning the instruction of the catechumens in the mystical meaning of rites in the late fourth-century (ca. 350–380) *Apostolic Constitutions*, 7.39–44 (probably of Syrian provenance). Jungmann discusses the appropriation of this language in the fourth century in his chapter "Pagan and Christian Mysteries," in *The Early Liturgy*, 152–163. For the language of *disciplina arcana*, see Jungmann, The *Early Liturgy*, 159, and F. van der Meer, *Augustine the Bishop: The Life and Work of a Father of the Church*, trans. B. Battershaw and G. R. Lamb (London: Sheed and Ward, 1961), 354, 359, 374.

28. Bouyer, *Liturgical Piety*, 200–214; Jungmann, The *Early Liturgy*, 266–277. The late fourth-century *Apostolic Constitutions* has extensive instructions concerning Sunday (7.30), the celebration of feast days (5.13), Holy Week (5.14–20), and times of daily prayer (7.47).

29. Already in the *Martyrdom of Polycarp*, 18, the saint's devotees gather his bones as sacred relics and meet on his "birthday"—the anniversary of his martyrdom—in his honor.

30. In his *Catechetical Lecture*, 23.9, Cyril of Jerusalem speaks of the commemoration at the Eucharist of "those who have fallen asleep before us, first Patriarchs, Prophets, Apostles, Martyrs, that at their prayers and intercessions God would receive our petition."

31. Jungmann, The *Early Liturgy*, 175–187; Bouyer, *Liturgical Piety*, 215–228.

32. The "Litany of the Saints," which invokes the prayer of the holy ones, is attested in the East already in the third century and in the West from the fifth century.

33. For the historical roots of the sacraments, see B. Cooke, *Ministry to Word and Sacraments: History and Theology* (Philadelphia: Fortress, 1976).

34. See Jungmann, The *Early Liturgy*, 29–86; for discussion of scholarly inquiries into these rituals, see P. F. Bradshaw, *The Search for the Origins of Christian Worship: Sources and Methods for the Study of Early Liturgy* (New York: Oxford University Press, 1992), 131–184.

35. Dix, *Shape of the Liturgy*, 83, 260, 339; See also A. Kavanagh, *The Shape of Baptism: The Rite of Christian Intitiation* (Studies in the Reformed Rites of the Church 1; Collegeville, MN: Liturgical, 1991).

36. These offices are attested as early as 251 in a letter of the bishop of Rome Cornelius to Fabian of Antioch. According to Eusebius (*HE*, 6.43.11), the church at Rome in the mid-third century had 46 presbyters, 7 deacons, 7 subdeacons, 42 acolytes, and 52 exorcists, lectors, and doorkeepers.

37. See Jungmann, The *Early Liturgy*, 240–252. The most famous example is that recounted by Sozomen in his *Historia Ecclesiastica*, 7.25. Ambrose of Milan refused to allow Theodosius I access to his church because of his bloody deeds and "excommunicated him." Sozomen reports that "Theodosius publicly confessed his sin in the church, and during the time set apart for penance, refrained from wearing his imperial ornaments, according to the usage of mourners."

38. James 5:3–16 is the classic text supporting the anointing of the sick; see F. W. Puller, *The Anointing of the Sick in Scripture and Tradition, with Some Considerations on the Numbering of the Sacraments*, 2nd rev. ed. (London: SPCK, 1910). On marriage, see E. Schillebeeckx, *Marriage: Human Reality and Saving Mystery*, trans. N. D. Smith (New York: Sheed and Ward, 1965).

39. See the famous evocation of theological chatter among artisans and shopkeepers in Gregory Nazianzen, *First Theological Oration: Against the Eunomians*, 1–2. Regarding singing hymns in the streets, Sozomen (*HE*, 8.8) reports on the competing hymn writing of the Arians and the orthodox under John in Constantinople: "The orthodox became more distinguished, and in a short time surpassed the opposing heretics in number and processions; for they had silver crosses and lighted tapers borne before them." Such public demonstrations could also be violent. The most notorious example is the riot of the 500 monks from Nitria in defense of Cyril against the governor of Alexandria (Socrates, *HE*, 7.14).

40. Van der Meer, *Augustine the Bishop*, 498–526. See the extensive discussion of the cult of the martyrs in North Africa in the time of Augustine by van der Meer, *Augustine the Bishop*, 471–497; and P. R. L. Brown, *The Cult of the Saints: Its Rise and Function in Latin Christianity* (Chicago: University of Chicago Press, 1981). A

shrine to house a martyr's relics is known as a *martyrion*; see A. Graber, *Martyr-ium: Recherches sur le culte des reliques et l'art chrétien antique*, 2 vols. (Collège de France: Fondation Schlumberger pour les études Byzantines; Paris: Album, 1943).

41. The legend of the finding of the cross by Helena, Constantine's mother, is provided by Sozomen, *HE*, 2.1–2. In his *Life of Constantine*, 3.42–43, Eusebius mentions only her pious visit to Jerusalem to "render due reverence to the ground which the Saviour's feet had trodden" and that she had a church built on the Mount of Olives.

42. For an appreciation, see W. Harmless, S.J., *Desert Christians: An Introduction to the Literature of Early Monasticism* (New York: Oxford University Press, 2004); and P. Brown, "The Rise and Function of the Holy Man in Late Antiquity," in his *Society and the Holy in Late Antiquity* (Berkeley: University of California Press, 1982), 103–152.

43. Athanasius, *Life of Antony*, 2–4.

44. "And so, from then on, there were monasteries in the mountains and the desert was made a city by monks, who left their own people and registered themselves for the citizenship in the heavens"; *Life of Antony*, 14. I use the translation by R. C. Gregg of *Life of Antony/Athanasius* (Classics of Western Spirituality; New York: Paulist, 1980), 42–43. On the search for more remote places of solitude, see *Life of Antony*, 47–50.

45. Athanasius makes clear, indeed, that he intends his account to have an exemplary value (*Life of Antony*, 93–94). For a full treatment, see D. J. Chitty, *The Desert a City: An Introduction to the Study of Egyptian and Palestinian Monasticism under the Christian Empire* (Crestwood, NY: St. Vladimir's Seminary Press, 1999).

46. See H. Waddell, *The Desert Fathers* (Ann Arbor: University of Michigan Press, 1957 [1936]).

47. Palladius was born circa 363 and wrote his history of the monks circa 429. Its odd name comes from the fact that it is addressed to Lausus, the Royal Chamberlain. Pal-ladius tells us in the prologue that when he undertook his research, he was in "the twenty-third year of my being in the company of the brethren and of my own solitary life, my twentieth as a bishop, and the fifty-sixth year of my life as a whole." He gives an account of male and female anchorites whom he had seen or heard about "in the Egyptian desert and Libya, in the Thebaid and Syene . . . the Tabennesiotes, and those in Mesopotamia, Palestine, and Syria, and in the West, those in Rome and Campania, and points near by" (Prol., 2). See *Palladius: The Lausiac History*, trans-lated and annotated by R. T. Meyer (Ancient Christian Writers 34; New York: New-man, 1964). A similar account of the monks in Syria is provided by Theodoret of Cyrrhus (393–466) in *A History of the Monks of Syria*, translated with an introduction and notes by R. M. Price (Cistercian Studies 88; Kalamazoo, MI: Cistercian Publica-tions, 1985).

48. Thus, the opening sections deal respectively with Isidore of Alexandria (1), Doro-theus of Thebes (2), the slave girl Potmaiaena (3), Didymyus the Blind of Alexandria

(4), and the slave girl Alexandra who lived in a tomb (5). Even when the section is more general—as in "the Monks of Nitria" (7) or "the Women's Monastery" (33)—the focus remains on the works and deeds of individual ascetics.

49. *Lausiac History*, 47. Melania was a Spanish woman of wealth who was the daughter of a consul and the wife of a man of high rank. She sold her possessions for gold and traveled to the desert to visit the monks. She was imprisoned by the consul of Palestine who sought to blackmail her, but when she declared her social lineage—"I am so-and-so's daughter and so-and-so's wife. I am Christ's slave. Pray do not look upon my shabby clothes, for I could make more of myself if I would. I have made this clear to you so that you may not fall under legal charges [for imprisoning a freewoman] without knowing the reason"—she is immediately released and treated with honor (47.4). She subsequently had a monastery built for women in Jerusalem and served as a financial patron to the church (47.5–6).

50. An admiring portrait of Evagrius as the disciple of two desert monks named Macarius, together with a substantial quotation from his works, is provided by Socrates, *HE*, 4.23; for his ascetical writings, see *Evagrius Ponticus: The Praktikos and Chapters on Prayer*, translated with an introduction and notes by J. E. Bamberger, OCSO (Cistercian Studies Series 4; Kalamazoo, MI: Cistercian Publications, 1981).

51. The precise title of the fragmentary narrative is a matter of some debate; see the discussion by G. E. Gingras, *Egeria: Diary of a Pilgrimage* (Ancient Christian Writers 38; New York: Newman, 1970), 1–11.

52. *Itinerarium*, 28–40; Egeria's account is detailed and shows how much developed was the liturgy of Holy Week and how much centered in the actual places where the last days of Jesus' life were thought to have occurred.

53. Thus, when they reach the summit of Mt. Sinai and the church located there, they are greeted by a monk-priest assigned to the place and all the other monks residing there. No one lived at the very summit "for there is nothing there save the church alone and the cave where the holy man Moses was. All of the proper passage from the Book of Moses was read, the sacrifice was offered in the prescribed manner, and we received communion" (*Itinerarium*, 3). Similarly, when they reach the cave of Elijah on Mt. Horeb, "we offered a sacrifice there, and recited a very fervent prayer, and the proper passage was read from the Book of Kings. For this was always very much our custom, that whenever we should come to places that I had desired to visit, the proper passage from Scripture would be read" (*Itinerarium*, 4).

54. Thus, Pausanius' lengthy treatment of Delphi, in *Description of Greece*, 10.5–32, interweaves physical description of the site with stories associated with each aspect of the shrine.

55. Actually, her destination was Seleucia of Isauria: "Since the shrine of St. Thecla is located a three day journey from Tarsus, in Isauria, it was a great pleasure for me to go there, particularly since it was so near at hand" (*Itinerarium*, 22). The shrine of Thecla was located some 1,500 feet from the city, with a church and "countless monastic cells for men and women." Egeria follows the pattern of piety practiced at the biblical sites: "Having arrived there in the name of God, a prayer was said at the

shrine and the complete Acts of Saint Thecla was read. I then gave unceasing thanks to Christ our God, who granted to me, an unworthy woman and in no way deserving, the fulfillment of my desires in all things" (23). One could hardly ask for a purer expression of Religiousness A.

56. Thus, the *Protevangelium of James* was translated into Syriac, Ethiopic, Georgian, Sahidic, Old Church Slavonic, Armenian, and probably into Latin. The *Acts of Andrew* is attested by Greek and Coptic manuscripts, and the narrative dealing with the martyrdom is found in several Byzantine Greek versions, Latin, and Armenian. See J. K. Elliott, *The Apocryphal New Testament: A Collection of Apocryphal Christian Literature in an English Translation* (Oxford: Clarendon, 1993), 48–49, 231–235. Similar attestation is found in the case of the other compositions I discuss in Chapter 12.

57. Elliott, *Apocryphal New Testament*, 512–533, takes note of compositions dated between the fourth and sixth centuries devoted to Philip, Bartholomew, Matthew, Barnabas, Xanthippe and Polyxena, James the Greater, and James the Lesser.

The second- and third-century infancy gospels are extended and developed in compositions such as *The Gospel of Pseudo-Matthew, The Arabic Infancy Gospel, Arundel Manuscript 404*, and *The History of Joseph the Carpenter* (Elliott, *Apocryphal New Testament*, 84–122).

Stories focusing on minor characters include *The Gospel of Gamaliel* and *The Gospel of Nicodemus* (or *Acts of Pilate*). There is, in fact, an extensive collection of compositions dedicated to the figure of Pontius Pilate (see Elliott, *Apocryphal New Testament*, 164–225).

58. Eusebius (*HE*, 6.43.11) tells us that the church in Rome in the mid-third century provided resources for over 1,500 widows and persons in distress. The *Apostolic Constitutions* has extensive instructions concerning the support of widows (8.25) and the poor (4.1–10).

59. In addition to its instructions concerning the character of the bishop (2.7), the *Apostolic Constitutions* has extensive discussions of deacons and deaconesses (3.15) and instructions for the ordination of bishops (8.3–5), presbyters (8.16), deacons (8.17), deaconesses (8.19–20), subdeacons (8.21), readers (8.22), confessors (8.23), virgins (8.24), widows (8.25), and exorcists (8.26). Equally interesting, it forbids laypeople to engage in any of the activities restricted to the hierarchy (3.10).

60. See the discussion in van der Meer, *Augustine the Bishop*, 79–116.

61. To take only the extraordinary career of Athanasius, the bishop of Alexandria who was the great champion of the Nicene formula, Socrates in his *Historia Ecclesiastica* reports that Athanasius was threatened by Constantine (1.27) and then banished to Gaul by the emperor (1.35), recalled by Constantine the younger but then banished a second time (2.2), restored to his see by Constantius (2.23) but then sentenced to death by the same emperor (2.26), restored to his episcopacy by Julian (3.4) but then sentenced to death by the same emperor (3.13), and finally restored under Constans (4.13). What runs through this bizarre sequence of events is Athanasius' rabid championing of his theological position and his own bare-knuckle approach to im-

posing it, coming into conflict or agreement with the vacillating views of successive emperors.

62. See A. Faivre, "Naissance d'une hiérarchie: Les premières étapes du cursus clérical," *Theologie Historique* 40 (1977): 47–67.

63. Such problems in the clergy, though, scarcely began with Constantine. In his treatise *On the Lapsed*, 6, Cyprian of Carthage declared in the third century that in the face of persecution, "not a few bishops who ought to furnish both exhortation and example to others, despising their divine charge, became agents in secular business, forsook their throne, deserted their people, wandered about over foreign provinces, hunted the market for gainful merchandise, while brethren were starving in the church. They sought to possess money in hoards, they seized estates by crafty deceits, they increased their gains by multiplying usuries." In Rome at the same period, the deacon Nicostratus stole church revenues and refused to give up the deposits of widows and orphans (Cyprian, *Letter*, 50). See also the account Eusebius (*HE*, 7.30) gives of the charges made against Paul, the bishop of Antioch, in a letter written by the synod of bishops (ca. 269) that deposed him: "although formerly destitute and poor, and having received no wealth from his fathers, nor made anything by trade or business, he now possesses abundant wealth through his iniquities and sacrilegious acts, and through those things which he extorts from the brethren" (7.30.7). See also the charges of fraud made against Callistus of Rome by Hippolytus, *Refutation of All Heresies*, 9.6.

64. See Chapter 15.

65. Eusebius, *Life of Constantine*, 4.24.

66. See, e.g., such sermons of Basil as "Against the Rich" (*Patrologiae Graecae*, 31.278–304), "God Not the Cause of Evil" (31.329–354), "On Envy" (31.371–386), "Concerning Anger" (31.353–371), and "On Drunkenness" (31.413–464). Each could be matched by treatises on the same *topoi* by Greco-Roman moralists.

67. The designation is common, as in the two volumes in the magisterial study of patristic literature by Johannes Quasten, *Patrology* (Westminster, MD: Christian Classics, 1986): the third volume is subtitled *The Golden Age of Greek Patristic Literature* and the fourth volume is subtitled *The Golden Age of Latin Patristic Literature*.

68. Taking only the major orthodox figures among the Greeks, see Athanasius, *The Discourses against the Arians* (PG, 26.12–468) and *Apology against the Arians* (PG, 25.595–642); Cyril of Alexandria, *Treasury Concerning the Holy and Consubstantial Trinity* (PG, 75.9–565 and 75.657–1124), *Against the Blasphemies of Nestorius* (PG, 76.9–248), *On the Right Faith* (PG, 76.1133–1200), and *Twelve Anathemas against Nestorius* (PG, 76.315–385); Basil of Caesarea, *Against Eunomius* (PG, 29.497–669); Gregory of Nazianzus, *Theological Orations* (PG, 36); Gregory of Nyssa, *Against Eunomius* (PG, 45.237–1122), *Against Apollonarians* (PG, 45.1269–1278), *Against Apollonarius* (PG, 45.1123–1270), and *On the Holy Spirit against the Macedonians Who Are against the Spirit* (PG, 45.1301–1334). On the Latin side, in addition to his astonishing labors in scriptural translation and interpretation, Jerome composed *Against the Luciferians* (*Patrologiae Latine* (PL), 23.155–182), *Against Helvidius* (PL,

23.183–206), *Against Jovinian* (PL, 23.211–338), *Against John of Jerusalem* (PL, 23.355–397), *Against the Books of Rufinus* (PL, 23.397–492), *Against Vigilantius* (PL, 23.339–352), and *Against the Pelagians* (PL, 23.495–590). No one matches the polemical labors of Augustine, who composed fully 9 compositions against the Manichaeans, 21 against the Donatists, 15 against the Pelagians, 3 against Arians, and 4 against other heresies. For Augustine's perception of his antiheretical work as maintaining the healthy boundaries of the church, see van der Meer, *Augustine the Bishop*, 125–128.

69. For some of the cultural, political, and intensely personal rivalry that went into these theological debates, see W. H. C. Frend, *The Rise of Christianity* (Minneapolis: Fortress, 1984); H. C. Kee et al., *Christianity: A Social and Cultural History* (New York: Macmillan, 1991); G. L. Prestige, *Fathers and Heretics: Six Studies in Dogmatic Faith with Prologue and Epilogue* (London: SPCK, 1963).

70. In the late fourth century, the *Apostolic Constitutions*, 8.1, systematically downplays the significance of the gifts that excite Religiousness A. In the early fifth century, John Chrysostom confesses bewilderment concerning Paul's statements in 1 Corinthians 14 concerning speaking in tongues: "This whole passage is very obscure; but the obscurity is produced by our ignorance of the facts referred to and by their cessation, being such as used to occur, but no longer take place" (*Homilies on First Corinthians*, 29, 32, 35). Similarly, Augustine in the same period dismisses the significance of glossolalia as a special dispensation of the primitive church, no longer of pertinence to the church in his day (Augustine, *Homilies on First John*, 6.10; see also *On Baptism against the Donatists*, 3.18). For Augustine's nuanced approach to the miraculous generally, see van der Meer, *Augustine the Bishop*, 527–557.

71. Thus, councils were not content with refining the rule of faith (creed); in their canons, they went into considerable detail concerning the correct interpretation of the creed, together with statements of excommunication (*anathema sit*) for those holding any other interpretation. See, e.g., the selection provided by H. Denziger and A. Schönmetzer, *Enchiridion Symbolorum Definitionum et Declarationum de Rebus Fidei et Morum*, 33rd ed. (Rome: Herder, 1964), for Nicaea (53–54), Constantinople I (65–67), Ephesus (92–97), and Chalcedon (105–109), as well as the regional councils at Carthage in 418 (82–84) and Toledo in 400 (75–76).

72. See J. Pelikan, *Christianity and Classical Culture: The Metamorphosis of Natural Theology in the Christian Encounter with Hellenism* (New Haven, CT: Yale University Press, 1993).

   For the specifically theological aspects of these debates, see J. N. D. Kelly, *Early Christian Doctrine* (San Francisco: Harper and Row, 1960), 223–243; G. L. Prestige, *God in Patristic Thought* (London: SPCK, 1912); F. M. Young, *From Nicaea to Chalcedon: A Guide to the Literature and Its Background* (London: SCM Press, 1983); A. Grillmeier, *Christ in Christian Tradition: From the Apostolic Age to Chalcedon (451)*, trans. J. Bowden (Atlanta: John Knox, 1975); L. Ayres, *Nicaea and Its Legacy: An Approach to Fourth-Century Trinitarian Theology* (Oxford: Oxford University Press, 2004).

73. Despite the assertions of Socrates, *HE*, 4.26 and 6.3, little evidence supports the position that Basil, Chrysostom, and other bishops were students of the great Liban-

ius; see P. Petit, *Les Étudiants de Libanius* (Paris: Nouvelles Éditions Latines, 1957), 40–41.

74. Jerome, *Letter*, 22.30.

75. In North Africa, both Tertullian (160–225) and Cyprian (d. 258) had a rhetorical education before their conversion and brought their skills in argumentation to theology.

76. Rejecting the notion of the "hellenization of Christianity," Robert Louis Wilcken argues that "a more apt expression would be the Christianization of Hellenism, though that phrase does not capture the originality of Christian thought nor the debt owed to Jewish ways of thinking and to the Jewish Bible. Neither does it acknowledge the good and right qualities of Hellenic thinking that Christians recognized as valuable, for example, moral life understood in terms of the virtues. At the same time, one observes again and again that Christian thinking, while working within patterns of thought and conceptions rooted in Greco-Roman culture, transformed them so profoundly that in the end something quite new came into being." See *The Spirit of Early Christian Thought: Seeking the Face of God* (New Haven, CT: Yale University Press, 2003), xvi–xvii.

77. See the ancient biographical sketches of the Holy and Blessed Teacher Syncletica, the Ethiopian Moses, and Paul the Hermit, translated and annotated in *Ascetic Behavior in Greco-Roman Antiquity: A Sourcebook*, ed. V. L. Wimbush (Studies in Antiquity and Christianity; Minneapolis: Fortress, 1990); as well as the collection of source material in W. Harmless, S.J., *Desert Christians: An Introduction to the Literature of Early Monasticism* (Oxford: Oxford University Press, 2004).

78. Pachomius' life and work are briefly depicted in Sozomen, *HE*, 3.14; in Palladius, *Lausiac History*, 32; and more fully in a *Life of Pachomius*, extant, with some variations, in Greek and Coptic. For the translation of a short segment of the Coptic version dealing with the experience of a single monk (Theodore) who associated himself with Pachomius, see "Theodore's Entry into the Pachomian Movement," introduced and translated by J. E. Goehring, in *Ascetic Behavior in Greco-Roman Antiquity*, 349–356.

79. The rule was composed in Coptic, of which only fragments survive; it is extant in full only in the Latin translation by Jerome (*PL*, 23.61–99); for all the evidence, see A. Veilleux, trans., *Pachomian Koinonia: The Life, Rules, and Other Writings of Saint Pachomius and His Disciples*, 2 vols. (Cistercian Studies 45 and 46; Kalamazoo, MI: Cistercian, 1980–1981).

80. See P. H. Rousseau, *Pachomius: The Making of a Community in Fourth-Century Egypt* (Transformation of Classical Heritage 6; Berkeley: University of California Press, 1985).

81. I do not mean to suggest that coenobitism replaced other expressions of monasticism; both in the East and the West, the tradition of wandering ascetics and of anchorites (hermits) continued, most spectacularly, perhaps, in the *Stylites* (pillar-sitters) of the East, who saw Simeon Stylites (390–459) as their model, and in the West, in the fourteenth-century mystics like Julian of Norwich and Richard Rolle of Hampole, who were enclosed within the walls of churches.

82. For my discussion of these Jewish antecedents, see Chapter 8.

83. Of Greek-speaking bishops of the fourth and fifth centuries, it can be confidently asserted that 12 were monks or hermits before or during their episcopacy: Serapion of Thmuis, Cyril of Alexandria, Basil of Caesarea, Gregory of Nazianzen, Gregory of Nyssa, Amphilochius of Iconium, Epiphanius of Salamis, Diodore of Tarsus, Theodore of Mopsuestia, John Chrysostom, Milus of Ancyra, and Nestorius. Among Latin-speaking bishops, Paulinus of Nola, Augustine of Hippo, Eucherius of Lyons, Hilary of Arles, Honoratus of Arles, Salonius of Geneva, and Salvian of Marseilles had significant personal involvement with the monastic life. In his letter to Dracontius in 354 (*PG*, 25.523–534), Athanasius asserts that many monks had already in his time become bishops. It should also be remembered that the two great compilers of monastic lore (Palladius and Theodoret) were themselves bishops who had experienced the monastic life.

84. Athanasius wrote frequently to the monks of Egypt, and we have letters to monks also from Serapion, Cyril, and Nilus of Ancyra. Many more were undoubtedly written. Such episcopal oversight was not always positive: Theophilus, archbishop of Alexandria from 385 to 412, purged the monks of Nitria, especially the four "long brothers" who were enthusiastic followers of Origen.

85. The first is called in Latin *Regulae fusius tractatae*, or "Detailed Rules," and consists of 55 chapters; the second is called in Latin *Regulae brevius tractatae*, or "Short Rules," and consists of 313 short chapters. Neither version is extant in its original Greek, but emended versions have formed the basis of monastic life in the East. Quasten, *Patrology*, 3.212–213.

86. The *Regula ad servos Dei* (Letter 211) may also have been intended for the first community of men at Hippo. Augustine also composed *De Opere Monachorum Liber I* ("On the Work of Monks," *PL*, 40.547–582) for monks in Carthage, in which he stressed the need for monks to engage in manual labor; see Quasten, *Patrology*, 4.375–376.

87. On Cassian, see O. Chadwick, *John Cassian: A Study in Primitive Monasticism* (Cambridge: Cambridge University Press, 1950), and P. Rousseau, *Ascetics, Authority, and the Church in the Age of Jerome and Cassian* (Oxford: Oxford University Press, 1978).

88. He deals with the dress of monks (*Institutes of the Coenobia*, book 1), as well as assorted other rules (book 4), but spends much more time than Pachomius on the ordering of prayer in the community (books 2–3). Cassian provides extensive discussions of the spirit of gluttony (*Institutes*, book 4), fornication (6), covetousness (7), anger (8), dejection (9), accidie (10), vainglory (11), and pride (12). Note that the sequence goes from the most obvious physical temptations to the most subtle spiritual ones.

89. The *Conferences* fall into three major parts, with 24 homilies in all; each of the sermons is, in turn, divided into multiple headings. Thus, Abbot Nesteros' first conference on spiritual knowledge (book 14) considers the topic under 19 distinct headings.

90. The opening exchange between John Cassian and Abbot Moses in The First Conference of Abbot Moses is revealing. The abbot asks Cassian about the goal sought by the monk in terms that would have fit well in the mouth of Plato's Socrates (2), and he cleverly responds that "we endured all for the sake of the kingdom of heaven" (3). The Abbot pushes the disciple to think about the connection between end and means: in order to be in the kingdom of heaven, one must have purity of heart, and that requires the practice of asceticism (4).

    The psychological acuity found in Cassian's discussion of *accidie*—the affliction of "the noon-day devil" that combines boredom, restlessness, and depression (*Institutes*, 10)—is universally recognized by those who have lived the monastic life or, for that matter, experienced a "mid-life crisis."

91. Cassian uses the entire canon of scripture, but what is particularly impressive is the way he uses texts. In his discussion of *accidie* in *Institutes*, 10, e.g., he carries out a close reading of Paul's first and second letters to the Thessalonians to show how the apostle addresses the issue and recommends the practice of working with the hands as a remedy for boredom and restlessness (10.7–13).

92. The major critical issue concerning the *Rule* (ca. 530–540) is its relation to an anonymous, much longer, monastic rule called the *Regula Magistri*. I follow the judgment (and use the translation) of J. McCann that this composition is later and makes extensive use of Benedict's rule. See *The Rule of Saint Benedict*, edited and translated by J. McCann (Westminster, MD: Newman, 1952), xix–xxi; see also B. Steidle, O.S.B., *The Rule of Benedict*, with an introduction and commentary (Beuron, Germany: Beuroner Kunstverlag, 1952).

93. The phrase *ora et labora* is not found in the *Rule* but is widely understood as defining the distinctive way of Benedictine monasticism. The spirit of the phrase is seen in the use of *opus dei* ("work of God") with reference to prayer as well as to other labors (*RB*, 7) and the instruction that the cellarer should "look upon all the utensils of the monastery and its whole property as upon the sacred vessels of the altar" (31). There is actually more attention given by the *RB* to prayer (chapters 8–20, 47, 49) than to work (32, 35, 48, 57). The more impressive feature of the *Rule* is the care taken with respect to leadership (2, 3, 21, 31, 62–66) and correction of faults (23–30, 43–46). A distinct humane spirit runs through all these discussions. The constitutional genius of Benedict is shown by the way he balances the authority of the abbot (2), the council of monks (3), and the rule itself (prologue).

94. Monks are to wear the clothes worn by the locals in the area they live (*RB*, 55), their food is to be generous without leading to gluttony (39), and they are to be allowed a small amount of wine each day (40). In all these issues, Benedict sets the bar low, so that the stronger have the opportunity to do more, while the weak are not driven away.

95. The role of humility and obedience are fundamental: Benedict calls monks to "freely accept and faithfully fulfill the instructions of a loving father, that by the labor of obedience thou mayest return to him from whom thou hast strayed by the sloth of disobedience" (*RB*, prologue). See the heart of Benedictine spirituality in

RB, 4 ("The Tools of Good Works"), 5 ("Of Obedience"), 6 ("Of Silence"), and 7 ("Of Humility").

Although far more succinct than Cassian, the *Rule* reveals psychological insight into the dynamics of life together, as in its repeated warning against "murmuring"; Benedict ends his instructions concerning the distribution of goods with these words: "Above all, let not the vice of murmuring show itself in any word or sign, for any reason whatever. But if a brother be found guilty of it, let him undergo strict punishment" (34). And concerning the measure of drink, when circumstances do not allow a ration of wine, "let the monks who dwell there bless God and not murmur. Above all things do we give this admonition, that they abstain form murmuring" (40).

96. *RB*, prologue. He begins this section by stating, "therefore we must establish a school of the Lord's service."

97. Benedict did not recommend extensive reading to his monks, although *RB*, 73, recommends the thorough reading of the Old and New Testaments, the "holy catholic fathers," the wisdom of the desert fathers, and the earlier writers of monastic rules, such as Basil and Cassian. Out of such simple instructions grew the monastic culture that has aptly been called by J. LeClerq *The Love of Learning and the Desire for God: A Study of Monastic Culture* (2nd rev. ed., trans. C. Misrahi [New York: Fordham University Press, 1974]) and that ultimately provided the basis for the great universities within which humane learning was not only preserved but celebrated and advanced.

By alluding in both chapters to Acts 4:32–35, which describes the primitive community possessions in the Jerusalem church, Benedict consciously evokes the understanding of the monastery as "apostolic Christianity."

Note that degrees of excommunication involve separation from the common table, with the monk under discipline forced to eat by himself (*RB*, 24–25).

98. When received into the community after a period of probation, the monk promises obedience, stability, and *conversatio morum* (*RB*, 58). The term's precise meaning is debated since it is sometimes used as if it meant "continual conversion" (see *RB*, prologue and 1). But it can also mean "manner of life."

For the New Testament's use of *anastrophē* as "manner of life" (in the moral sense), see Gal 1:13; Eph 4:22; 1 Tim 4:12; James 3:13; 1 Pet 1:15, 18; 2:12; 3:1, 2, 16.

99. The discussion of "reading, reflecting, and praying" in the fourteenth-century anonymous mystical tractate *The Cloud of Unknowing*, 35, succinctly expresses the organic character of *lectio*.

100. Gregory the Great was a monk from 574 and was bishop of Rome (590–604). His *Dialogue*, 2, is a life of Benedict that portrays him as a prophetic figure in line with Moses and Elijah, a mystic as well as a monastic founder. Gregory put the weight of the newly powerful papal office behind the expansion of Benedictine monachism.

Gregory's *Expositio in Librum Job, sive Moralia Libri XXXV* (PL, 76.749–782) carried forward for medieval Christianity the tradition (from Philo through Origen and Nyssa) of reading scripture in a threefold manner: literal, moral, and allegorical.

101. See G. Widengren, *Mani and Manichaeism*, rev. ed., trans. C. Kessler (London: Weienfeld and Nicholson, 1955).

102. See S. N. C. Lieu, *Manichaeism in the Later Roman Empire and Medieval China: A Historical Survey* (Manchester: Manchester University Press, 1985), as well as I. Gardner and S. N. C. Lieu, *Manichaean Texts from the Roman Empire* (Cambridge: Cambridge University Press, 2004).

103. In Manichaean texts, Jesus is considered under the designations "the Luminous," "the Messiah," and "Patibilis"; see Lieu, *Manichaeism*, 161–162, as well as the texts presented by H.-J. Klimkeit in *Gnosis on the Silk Road: Gnostic Texts from Central Asia* (San Francisco: HarperSanFrancisco, 1993), 63–75.

104. See, e.g., Augustine, *Against Faustus the Manichaean*, 11.1–8.

105. On the syncretistic impulse in Manichaeism, see the studies in P. Bryder, ed., *Manichaean Studies: Proceedings of the First International Conference on Manichaeism* (Lund Studies in African and Asian Religions 1; Lund: Lund University Press, 1988), and P. Mirecki and J. Beduhn, eds., *The Light and the Darkness: Studies in Manichaeism and Its World* (Nag Hammadi and Manichaean Studies 50; Leiden: Brill, 2001).

   Jason Beduhn shows how the ritual action of eating and the "metabolism of salvation" link all forms of Manichaeism, which otherwise display considerable variety at the level of myth; see *The Manichaean Body: In Discipline and Ritual* (Baltimore: Johns Hopkins University Press, 2000).

106. See the essays in J. van Oort, O. Wermelinger, and G. Wurst, *Augustine and Manichaeism in the West: Proceedings of the Fribourg-Utrecht International Symposium of the International Association of Manichaean Studies* (Nag Hammadi and Manichaean Studies 49; Leiden: Brill, 2001).

107. Augustine, *Confessions*, 3.6–5.11.

108. *PL*, 42.207–518; see also *On the Morals of the Catholic Church and Manichaean Morals*, 2 books (*PL*, 32.1309–1378); *Concerning Two Souls* (*PL*, 42.93–112); *Against Adimantus, a Disciple of Mani* (*PL*, 42.129–172); *Debate with Felix the Manichee* (*PL*, 42.519–522); *Debate with Fortunatus the Manichee* (*PL*, 42.111–130); *On the Nature of the Good* (*PL*, 42.551–572); and *Against Secundinus the Manichee* (*PL*, 42.577–602).

109. See P. L. Reynolds, *Marriage in the Western Church: The Christianization of Marriage during the Patristic and Early Medieval Periods* (Leiden: Brill Academic Publishers, 2001).

110. See D. Obolensky, *The Bogomils: A Study in Balkan Neo-Manichaeism* (Twickenham: A. C. Hall, 1972 [1942]).

111. See M. D. Lambert, *The Cathars* (Oxford: Blackwell, 1998), and M. Barker, *The Cathars: Dualist Heretics in the High Middle Ages* (New York: Longman, 2000).

112. On the Albigensians, see H. J. Warner, *The Albigensian Heresy*, 2 vols. (New York: Russell and Russell, 1967 [1922–1928]). On the Albigensians and the organized effort to extirpate the virus of Gnosticism from Christianity, see M. D. Costen, *The Cathars and the Albigensian Crusades* (New York: St. Martin's Press, 1997), and M.

Pegg, *A Most Holy War: The Albigensian Crusade and the Battle for Christendom* (Oxford: Oxford University Press, 2008).

113. Palladius, *Lausiac History*, 55.3, reports of a woman ascetic named Silvania that "she was most erudite and fond of literature, and she turned night into day going through every writing of the ancient commentators—three million lines of Origen and two and a half million lines of Gregory, Stephen, Pierius, Basil, and other worthy men. . . . Thus it was possible for her to be liberated from 'knowledge falsely so called.'"

    For ascetics' reputation for knowing all of scripture, see *Lausiac History*, 11.4; 32.12; 37.2; 47.3; 58.1; for the special place of the Psalms, see 22.6–8; 26.3; 32.6; 43.2–3; 48.2. In Athanasius' *Letter to Marcellinus*, he instructs the deacon of the city of Alexandria in the interpretation of the Psalms, since that young man had undertaken to understand the meaning of each one (*PG*, 27.11–46). That the constant recitation of the Psalms was considered normal is shown by the offhand remark of Benedict: "For those monks show themselves very slothful in their sacred service, who in the course of a week sing less than the psalter and the customary canticles, whereas we read that our holy fathers strenuously fulfilled in a single day what I pray we lukewarm monks may perform in a whole week" (*RB*, 18).

114. See Athanasius, *Life of Antony*, 46, 79, 90.

115. It would be impossible for a Gnostic to "sin against the flesh," for the flesh was itself the source of evil; see *Lausiac History*, 11.4; 44.2; 55.2; for demonic temptation, see 16.3–5; 35.8; 38.11; 47.13; 71.1.

116. For a survey, see B. M. McGinn and J. Meyedorff, *Christian Spirituality: Origins to the Twelfth Century* (World Spirituality 16; New York: Crossroad, 1985).

117. On Origen, see his *Commentary on the Song of Songs* and his *Homilies on Numbers*; see *Origen*, translation and introduction by R. A. Greer (Classics of Western Spirituality; New York: Paulist, 1979). On Gregory of Nyssa, see above all his *Life of Moses*; see *Gregory of Nyssa, The Life of Moses*, translation, introduction, and notes by A. J. Malherbe and E. Ferguson (Classics of Western Spirituality; New York: Paulist, 1978). See *Pseudo-Dionysius: The Complete Works*, trans. C. Luibheid (Classics of Western Spirituality; New York: Paulist, 1987).

118. For the apophatic way, see Pseudo-Dionysius, *The Divine Names*, 1.1–2; 5.3–4; *The Mystical Theology*, 1–3; for divinization of the human nature through Christ as the premise to approaching God, see Pseudo-Dionysius, *Celestial Hierarchy*, 1.4–5; Gregory Palamas, *The Triads*, I.3.4–23; II.2.11–12; II.3.8–16; and J. Gross, *The Divinization of the Christian according to the Greek Fathers*, trans. P. A. Onica (Anaheim, CA: A. & C. Press, 2002).

119. See the classic display of the sequence in the 30 stages described by John Climacus, *The Ladder of Divine Ascent*: the first 26 rungs of the ladder are the stages of asceticism; only the last three stages deal explicitly with contemplation (stillness, prayer, dispassion), and the final rung is "faith, hope, love."

120. Of particular importance for ensuring the orthodox character of Eastern mysticism was the fourth-century teacher Pseudo-Macarius and the seventh-century theologian Maximus the Confessor; for the first, see *Pseudo-Macarius*, trans.

G. A. Maloney (Classics of Western Spirituality; New York: Paulist, 1992); and for the second, see *Maximus Confessor,* trans. G. A. Berthold (Classics of Western Spirituality; New York: Paulist, 1985).

121. John of Damascus, *On the Divine Images: Three Apologies against Those Who Attack the Holy Images,* trans. D. Anderson (Crestwood, NY: St. Vladimir's Seminary Press, 1980).

122. For a survey, see B. McGinn, *The Presence of God: A History of Western Christian Mysticism,* 4 vols. (New York: Crossroad, 1992–2005).

123. A select sample on sexuality as a mystical union with the incarnate Christ: Bernard of Clairvaux, *On the Song of Songs,* 55.1; 58.1–2; 68.1–3; 70.2–3; 72.2–3; 83.5–6; Hildegard of Bingen, *Scivias,* 2.1.16; 2.6; Bonaventure, *The Soul's Journey into God,* 4.5; 7.6; Catherine of Sienna, *Dialogues,* 12.98; Mechtild of Magdeberg, *The Flowing Light of the Godhead,* 1.3; 1.19; 1.23; 1.44; 2.2; 2.6; Teresa of Avila, *The Interior Castle,* 2.1.7; 7.2.1–11; *Ancrene Wisse,* 2; and everywhere in *Holy Maidenhood;* John of the Cross, *The Spiritual Canticle;* Hadewijch, *Poems in Stanzas;* and Clare of Assisi's *Four Letters to Blessed Agnes of Prague.*

Nowhere is the emphasis on poverty as participation in Christ's humility clearer than in the slender compositions of Francis of Assisi (*Letter to Brother Leo, Canticle of the Sun, The Admonitions,* and *Last Will for Clare and Her Sisters*) and of Clare of Assisi (*Four Letters to Blessed Agnes of Prague*).

124. A small sample: Bernard of Clairvaux, *On the Song of Songs,* 43.1–5; Walter Hilton, *Scale of Perfection,* 1.44; 2.2; 2.11; Richard Rolle of Hamphole, *Meditations on the Passion;* Teresa of Avila, *The Interior Castle,* 6.5.6; 6.7.1–15; 6.10.5; Bonaventure, *The Tree of Life,* 17–31; Brigitta of Sweden, *Book of Revelations,* 7.4–35; Catherine of Sienna, *Dialogues,* 4.135; Mechtild of Magdeberg, *Flowing Light of the Godhead,* 6.24; 7.18; and throughout Julian of Norwich's *Showings.*

125. Male mystics also experienced visions, but it is not characteristic of them to make such experiences central or to make them the vehicle of their teaching, such as we find in the case of Hildegard of Bingen, Catherine of Sienna, Teresa of Avila, Hadewijch, Brigitta of Sweden, and Julian of Norwich.

126. While more positive toward pilgrimages in his letter to the three women Eustathia, Ambrosia, and Basilissa (*Letter,* 17), Nyssa makes the same point concerning the corruption and immorality he witnessed in the "holy places."

127. Quasten, *Patrology,* 3.281–282, identifies this as *Letter,* 2, of the 30 added to the Nyssa collection; the translation by W. Moore and H. A. Wilson is found under the title "On Pilgrimages," in *A Select Library of the Nicene and Post-Nicene Fathers of the Christian Church,* 2nd series, 14 vols., ed. P. Schaff and H. Wace (Peabody, MA: Hendrickson, 1994 [1893]), 5:382–383.

SCRIPTURE INDEX

INDEX OF ANCIENT AUTHORS

INDEX OF MODERN AUTHORS

Smith, M. S., 329
Smith, R., 368
Smitz, T., 312
Smyly, J. G., 296
Snyder, G., 344, 365
Södergard, P. J., 322
Squires, J. T., 305
Stadter, P. A., 325
Stanton, G. R., 312
Stark, R., 350, 365
Steidle, B., 399
Stephens, J. C., 297, 313, 315
Stephens, W. O., 318
Stern, M., 329
Stevenson, G., 301
Stevenson, I., 294
Stowers, S. K., 317
Strange, J., 337, 364
Strecker, G., 365
Struck, P. T., 305
Stuckenbruck, L. T., 329
Sugitharajah, R. S., 292
Swain, S. C. R., 313
Szemler, G. J., 302

Tabbernee, W., 372
Talbert, C. H., 358, 359
Talgam, R., 295
Taylor, J. E., 341
Taylor, M. C., 291
Tcherikover, V., 299, 327, 329, 331
Theissen, G., 287, 345, 351, 356
Thiering, B., 294–295
Thiselton, A. C., 356
Thom, J. C., 312, 319
Thomas, C. M., 297, 368
Thompson, J. W., 365
Thompson, L. L., 354
Tiede, D. L., 306
Tigay, J. H., 329
Todd, F. A., 297
Tomlinson, R. A., 297
Torjesen, K. J., 376
Trakatellis, D., 374
Trevett, C., 371
Trigg, J. W., 376
Tuckett, C. M., 383, 384

Tulloch, J., 290
Turcan, R., 301, 302, 303
Turner, V., 358
Tyson, J., 358
Tzaneton, A., 303

Urbach, E. E., 334

Valantasis, R., 384
Vallee, G., 380
Van der Horst, P. W., 313, 339
Van der Leuw, G., 17, 291, 292
Van Gennep, A., 358
Van Geytenbeek, A. C., 316
Van Tilborg, S., 344
Vanderkam, J. C., 295, 300, 333
Vanhoye, A., 364
Vassall, W. F., 288
Veilleux, A., 397
Vermes, G., 334, 349
Vernant, J.-P., 304
Vokes, F. E., 371
Vööbus, A., 385

Wach, J., 17–19, 292, 293
Wachob, W., 364
Waddell, H., 392
Walasky, P. W., 354
Waldbaum, J. C., 295
Wallace, J. B., 363
Wallace-Haddrill, A., 296, 303
Wallis, E., 386
Wardman, A., 301
Warner, H. J., 401
Watson, F., 319
Weatherly, J. A., 286
Weaver, J. B., 359
Weaver, M. J., 356
Welborn, L. L., 373
Welles, C. B., 296
Werblowsky, R. J. Zwi, 303
Wermelinger, O., 401
West, M. L., 312, 320
White, L. M., 335, 366–367
Whitmarsh, T., 312, 313, 317
Widengren, G., 401
Wiebe, D., 291

SUBJECT INDEX

Abraham, 29, 114–115, 125, 126, 168, 200, 219, 336, 340, 342

Academy/university, 14, 16–17, 281

Aelius Aristides: biography, 52, 53–55, 313–314; dreams and experiences, 59–60; as an example of Religiousness A, 50–51, 63; extant orations, 52–53; illnesses, 53–55, 314; love for Asclepius, 57–58; optimism about the divine order, 57; as an orator, 51–53, 313; the *Sacred Tales*, 58–62; scant discussion of moral behavior, 63, 315; understanding of salvation, 61–62

Albigensians, 269–270, 401–402

Alexander the Great, 28, 37, 60, 99, 130, 305

Alexandria, 113, 116, 173, 204, 209, 263, 329, 338, 376, 377

Allegory: in early Christianity, 181, 203, 377, 400; among Gnostics, 219; in the Greco-Roman world, 38–39, 339–340; in Philo of Alexandria, 116–117, 124, 339–340; in Plutarch, 104–105

Allogenes, 222–224, 382, 383

Ambrose of Milan, 265, 268, 391

Amixia, 34, 113

Anchorite(s), 261

Anointing of the sick, 166, 260, 391

Anthropology: as a field of study, 16, 20; in Religiousness A, B, and C, 215–216

Anthropomorphism, 37–39, 340

Antioch, 12–13, 27, 116, 173, 263, 343–344, 347, 354

Antiochus IV Epiphanes, 113, 122, 329, 333

Antony, 261, 392

Apatheia, 102, 317

Aphrodite, 56, 304

Apocalyptic literature/writings, 122, 124, 125–126, 337

Apocryphal Acts of the Apostles: connection with Greco-Roman novels, 175, 368; after Constantine, 262; as examples of Religiousness A, 176–177, 193, 262, 276; as "Gnostic," 379; literary character of, 175; martyrdom in, 178, 181, 257; moral exhortation in, 176, 177, 181; ways of being religious in, 176

Apollo, 33, 40, 42–43, 49, 56, 57, 60, 72, 74, 81, 82, 96, 99, 100, 101, 107, 126, 234, 304, 320

Apollonius of Tyana, 25, 40, 306, 308, 311, 359, 375

Apostle(s), 150–152, 159, 239–240, 247–249, 353, 367

Apostolic succession, 236, 248–249, 252–253, 367, 373, 380

Apostolic tradition, 240, 253

Ara pacis, 94, 98

Aramaic, 27–28, 111–112, 139, 327, 346, 353

Archaeology, 21–25, 35, 81, 94, 127, 172, 174, 296, 301, 330, 334, 342, 343, 344, 365–366

Aretalogy, 62, 147

Subject Index   459

Poimandres: anthropology of, 89–90;
commission to the prophet in, 90–91;
comparison with Aelius Aristides and
Epictetus, 91–92; eschatology of, 90; as
an example of Religiousness C, 80, 91;
introduction to, 80, 88; myths of origin,
88–89. *See also* Hermetic literature
Polycarp of Smyrna: as an example of
Religiousness B, 198; Ignatius' letter to,
187; martyrdom of, 189–190
Prayer: in Christianity, 139, 258, 259, 261,
267–268, 270, 272, 353, 391, 399; in Greco-
Roman religion, 33, 45–46, 55–56, 71, 88,
139, 303, 318, 353; in Judaism, 120, 136, 139,
335, 353
Priests/priesthood: Aelius Aristides'
comments on, 35, 57; the bishop as
high priest, 240–241; as a characteristic
of Religiousness D, 95, 109, 126–127,
234, 253–254, 271–272, 276; connection
between Greco-Roman priests and
Christian bishops, 244, 255; after
Constantine, 260; Epictetus' comments
on, 71; in Greco-Roman religion, 34–35,
39–40, 48–49, 96–99, 245, 253, 255, 302,
304, 305–306, 324, 358; Jesus as the great
high priest, 166–168, 196, 206, 364–365;
in Judaism, 118, 122, 127–128, 330, 333,
334, 335, 337, 343; in the New Testament,
234–235; Plutarch as a priest, 99, 107–108,
109, 320; Plutarch's comments on, 104; in
second- and third-century Christianity,
236–237, 240–242, 251, 252–253
Prophecy: Aelius Aristides' comments
on, 56, 57, 79; as a characteristic of
Religiousness A, 50, 93, 119, 142, 157;
as a characteristic of Religiousness D,
93, 97; after Constantine, 264–265, 281;
Epictetus' comments on, 71; in Greco-
Roman religion, 39–40, 121, 145; in
Judaism, 112, 121–122, 356; in the New
Testament, 5, 132, 139, 145, 148, 149, 150,
157, 160, 162, 353; in second- and third-
century Christianity, 174, 186, 194, 199,
209–210
Protestant Reformation, 11, 278–279
Pythagoras/Pythagoreanism, 82–84

Quartodeciman controversy, 174, 242–245; as
an example of Religiousness D, 245;
summary of the controversy, 243
Qumran: discovery of, 118, 294; Essene
hypothesis, 117; as an example of
Hellenistic influence on Judaism, 30;
impact of discovery of, 21, 24

Relics, 260–261, 272, 279, 390. *See also*
Martyrdom/martyrs; Pilgrimage
Religion, defined, 17–18, 19, 64. *See also*
Greco-Roman religion; Ways of being
religious
Religion as moral transformation
(Religiousness B): in Christianity after
Constantine, 265–268; definition of,
46–47, 64–65, 158, 196, 215–216, 276; in
Greco-Roman religion, 46–47, 64–78; in
Judaism, 123–125; in the New Testament,
140–141, 158–171, 194; in second- and
third-century Christianity, 194–213,
216
Religion as participation in divine benefits
(Religiousness A): definition of, 46, 50–51,
142, 175, 215–216, 275–276; dominance in
Christianity after Constantine, 258; in
Greco-Roman religion, 42, 46, 50–63; in
Judaism, 119–123; in the New Testament,
140–141, 142–157; in second- and third-
century Christianity, 175–193, 216
Religion as stabilizing the world
(Religiousness D): definition of,
48–49, 93–95, 234, 276; dominance in
Christianity after Constantine, 258,
262–265; in Greco-Roman religion,
48–49, 93–110; in Judaism, 126–129; in
the New Testament, 170, 234–235; in
second- and third-century Christianity,
234–254
Religion as transcending the world
(Religiousness C): in Christianity after
Constantine, 268–271; definition of,
47–48, 79–80, 214–216, 276; early traces
of, 80–84; in Greco-Roman religion,
47–48, 79–92; in Judaism, 125–126; in the
New Testament, 170–171; in second- and
third-century Christianity, 214–232